SYLVANIA, LUCAS COUNTY, OHIO;

FROM FOOTPATHS TO EXPRESSWAYS AND BEYOND

VOLUME SEVEN:

Wars and Memorials, Landfills, Auto Salvage Yards, Disrupting Weather Events, Interviews and Reminiscing, Miscellaneous Subjects and Murders in Sylvania

GAYLEEN GINDY

authorHOUSE®

AuthorHouse™
1663 Liberty Drive
Bloomington, IN 47403
www.authorhouse.com
Phone: 1 (800) 839-8640

Published by AuthorHouse 07/11/2018

ISBN: 978-1-5462-5021-0 (sc)
ISBN: 978-1-5462-5020-3 (e)

Library of Congress Control Number: 2018907919

Print information available on the last page.

Any people depicted in stock imagery provided by Getty Images are models, and such images are being used for illustrative purposes only. Certain stock imagery © Getty Images.

This book is printed on acid-free paper.

TABLE OF CONTENTS

Neither a wise man nor a brave man lies down on the tracks of
history to wait for the train of the future to run over him

John Stewart

. . . .

While we are living in the present, we must celebrate life every day, knowing
that we are becoming history with every work, every action, every deed

Mattie Stepanek

. . . .

Sometimes – history needs a push.

Vladimir Lenin

. . . .

Dedicated to my family

Sam, Allan, Samantha, Audrey, Sophia and Ella
I love you!

ACKNOWLEDGEMENTS

Individuals who have helped with information in one way or another include: Sharon (Polly) Cooper, Elizabeth (Liz) Stover, Lucille Laskey, David Drake, Carolyn Micham, Melvin Micham, Gordon Deye, Alcy Downing, Richard Downing, Clark Collins, Rachel Stanton, Gerald Sobb, Leonard McMahon, Clayton Fischer, Cheryl Lavimodiere, Margie Lintner, Peggy Watts, George Eichenauer, John Plock, Jeff Ballmer, Rick Barricklow, Deb Raszka, Terry Helpman, Loren Sengstock, Tammy Martin, Tara Jacobs, Barb Taylor, Dan Hughes, Robert Oberly, Larry Wagner, Kathryn Keller, Vicki Alspach, Jennifer Howard, Sue Tuite, Lonnie Smith, Glenn Fink, John Fisher, Donald Covrett, Curtis Niles, Richard A. Campbell, Clifford Keeler, Scott Reed, Charles Tipping, Melissa Burzynski, Richard Laux, John Grayczyk, Ralph Stallsworth, Karen Keeler, Ara Smith, Hazel Smith, Robert C. Smith, Robert A. Smith, Milton Thomas Cory, Greg Roytek, Mark Weichel, Timothy Burns, Debbie Webb, Pat O'Brien, Joe Shaw. Also a big thank you to the employees at the Local History and Genealogy Department at the Toledo and Lucas County Public Library for being ever ready to drag stuff out of that backroom for me and fix the machines: James Marshall, Greg Miller, Donna Christian, Irene Martin, Mike Lara, Ann Hurley, Jill Clever and Laura Voelz. And a big thank you to R. Michael Frank, Esq., for all that you did for me during some very rough times in my life.

It is impossible to personally thank everyone that helped with information for these books, so to those that I did not specifically name, I give you thanks for your contribution.

Just so that nobody in my family can say that I did not mention them in my book I would like to mention the following names of my beloved family who have all helped me in many, many ways: Sam Gindy, Allan Gindy, Samantha Gindy, Audrey Blaisdell-Gindy, Sophia Rose Gindy, Ella Jane Gindy, Charles Sullins, Carolyn Daler-Sullins-Micham, Allan J. Gindy, Carolyn Sberna-Gindy, Melvin Micham, Sharon Dentel-Sullins, Jeff Gindy, Jill Sullins-Dallas, Mark Dallas, Pen Dallas, Marsha Rosinski-Dallas, Nick Dallas, Melissa Flores-Dallas, Luna Mae Dallas, Miles Dallas, Andrew Dallas, Bart Sullins, Julie Crayford-Sullins, Sara Sullins, Laura Sullins, Amy Sullins-Verhelst, Bob Verhelst, Bret Sullins, Charley Sullins, Jack Sullins. You are all the highlight of my life.

INTRODUCTION

This book is volume seven of my eight volume set of books that will be published about Sylvania's history. All eight volumes will be titled *Sylvania, Lucas County, Ohio; From Footpaths to Expressways and Beyond*, and each volume will have a different set of historic photos on the cover to represent the contents of that particular book. The top portion of each spine will have a letter to represent one letter in the name Sylvania. When lined up on your bookshelf the books will spell out S-Y-L-V-A-N-I-A. The volume that you are reading right now has the letter "I" on its spine.

Sylvania, Lucas County, Ohio is located in northwestern Ohio, and our north border line runs along the south border line of the Michigan state line. Monroe and Lenawee County, Michigan are our bordering neighbors to the north, and we are a suburb of Toledo, Ohio, which the township of Sylvania borders on their eastern and southeastern lines. These volumes include the history of both the city and township of Sylvania as one community, but distinguished by the words "city" or "township."

The 2010 census shows that there were 18,965 residents in the city and 29,522 residents in the township of Sylvania, for a combined population of 48,487. At this time the township continues to grow with new commercial development and new residential subdivisions, while the city of Sylvania has pretty much all been fully developed. Sylvania Township and the City of Sylvania share so many of their services that in most cases the residents don't even know which community they live in, they just know that they live in "Sylvania." A few of the services that the two communities share include fire services, rescue services, public schools, public recreation, court services, historical societies and in some cases water and sewer services. Another confusing fact is that residents of the city of Sylvania get the opportunity to vote for the three township trustees and township clerk; because the Ohio Revised Code says that the city is officially still part of its original township of Sylvania. But the township residents do not get the opportunity to vote for any of the city public officials. Police service is one service that is still operated by the two separate entities, as well as police and fire emergency dispatching services and road and street maintenance services.

To recap the volumes that have been published so far, Volume One included history of the beginning years of Sylvania, the American Indians that lived in the Northwest Territory and in the areas throughout Lucas County, before the county was established. Included was information on the locations throughout Sylvania where the Indians camped, and where their footpaths and arrowheads were found by the early settlers when they first arrived here. Volume One also includes the following other subjects: The Ohio-Michigan boundary dispute; the establishment of Lucas County; The first settlers in Sylvania; Sylvania Township and its original boundaries and annexations; the initial events; elected positions; the first land purchases; the first elections under the name of Sylvania; information from the first township minutes books; government meeting places; voting in Sylvania; a complete listing of Sylvania Township officials; how the village of Sylvania was established and later became a city; information from the first minute books of the village of Sylvania; a complete list of village/city officials; populations; merger attempts; postmasters and post offices; the Ten Mile Creek; the Ottawa River; and the establishment of a public water system in Sylvania.

Volume Two documented the early medical doctors, epidemics, diseases and illnesses, and gave biographical sketches of the early doctors in Sylvania. There is a chapter on the poor and needy, the depression years, and government work programs. Next in Volume Two is a complete history of the railroads that operated through Sylvania and on to the development of roads and how some of them got their names from the names of some of the early settlers. Sylvania was notified in 1956 of the state's intentions to build an expressway that would pass through Sylvania, and by 1958 the state started purchasing the land for the new expressway. Volume Two then ends by telling the history of some of the very early fires in Sylvania and then the early development of a volunteer fire department.

Volume Three focuses completely on the history of the Sylvania Township Fire Department, and ends with a complete listing of all those individuals who served as volunteers on the fire department, all those who served as part-paid firemen/EMTs and a separate listing of the full-time firemen/paramedics through to 2013.

Volume Four includes information regarding the sale of intoxicating liquors, the first taverns, gambling, our jails over the years and then a history of the Sylvania Township Police Department, the Village/City of Sylvania Police Division and a history of the Sylvania Municipal Court. The last chapters in volume four tell the histories of our public parks and recreational facilities in Sylvania.

Volume Five included chapters on our zoning laws and gives information on those who helped in the development and enforcement of our subdivisions, commercial areas and industrial properties. Included are discussions about our years of large growth and when the township farm lands started to boom with development. Next in volume five there were chapters on our public cemeteries and their individual histories, then a little history on undertaking, funeral parlors and funeral homes in Sylvania; and our legendary ghost stories that have been told over the years. Then volume five ended with a history of our long established and well-known businesses in Sylvania, which once operated in Sylvania, along with many that still exist here today.

Volume Six covered the history of our newspapers in Sylvania over the years, the history of our public libraries and the history of our events, festivals and annual programs. Volume Six then includes the history of our clubs, centers, camps, organizations and posts. This volume then includes a chapter on information about various "places" in Sylvania and finally ends with the history of a community within Sylvania that became known as "Silica."

This is Volume Seven of my series of history books about Sylvania, and it includes information about the wars that our residents lived through and the memorials that they built to remind our future generations of these wars. Then researched were our landfills and auto salvage yards, which up until 1999 took up a large portion of our township. Next a review of our weather related events, then miscellaneous subjects such as our bands, classic cars, our first national fast food restaurants, a frog farm in Sylvania, some of our social groups, gypsies, house moving, Mickey and Minnie Mouse, our ringing of the church bells, history the Sisters of St. Francis and their community within Sylvania, strawberry picking, the Sylvan Serenaders, telephones, Tree City U.S.A. and the mysterious Underground Railroad and Sylvania's anti-slavery meetings back before the Civil War. Finally Volume Seven ends with a list of our known murders that have occurred in Sylvania.

Volume Eight will end our series of books with the complete history of our schools and how we went from being one school system, to two separate school systems and then how we eventually merged to become one school system again in order to give our young residents the best possible education at the most economical cost to the taxpayers.

Again, it is the author's hope that these books will help to document Sylvania's history, for use by the new residents just arriving in Sylvania, and for future Sylvania residents, so that they can get "caught up." For those residents who have been in Sylvania all along, I hope that these books will help to jog your memories and give you more insight into the things that have happened before us. I hope that I have mentioned your name and/or the names of your Sylvania ancestors somewhere in these volumes.

WARS AND MEMORIALS

THE MEXICAN WAR

This war was fought between the United States and Mexico over various disagreements created over a period of two decades. This war started on 4-25-1846 and ended on 2-2-1848. The United States forces ended up invading Mexico and occupied the capital. The United States acquired from Mexico the regions of California, Nevada and Utah, most of Arizona and New Mexico, and parts of Colorado and Wyoming.

Campaigns of the Mexican War took place mainly in: Texas; New Mexico; California; Northern, Central and Eastern Mexico; and Mexico City.

In Sylvania the Sylvania Township Trustee minute book from 1844 listed those residents that were "liable to military duty in the Township of Sylvania." There were 61 names listed. This list was required by the U.S. Government, at this time, because of the threatening need for possible military action in case of a war with Mexico.

The persons liable in Sylvania Township were listed as follows in the minute book of the Sylvania Township Trustees (the Village of Sylvania did not exist yet and was still all part of Sylvania Township): John Bellman, George Rodgers, Levi W. Bradley, Ira E. Lee, Clark D. Warren, Isaac Bertholf, Ira C. Smith, William Cooper, Zurial Cook, Jr., Henry Fisher, Horace Hollister, Sherwood Snider, William Comstock, Elisha Plaistead, William Maloney, Jr., Stephen Ripley, Joseph Kimble, Hiram Parker, Isaac Lewis, Abraham Ware, Jedidiah Jessup, John L. Hendrickson, William Lee, Beebe Comstock, Alexander Fox, Almond Ellis, Stephen Porter, John Showler, William Seely, Ephraim R. Thornton, Charles Straight, Hiram A.W. Newcombe, Alonzo Parker, Ellis Parker, John Gordinier, Erastus Williams, Erastus Morse, Harris Huling, William Wiggins, Daniel B. Curtice, Elijah Durfee, Cornelius Mersereau, Foster Warren, Charles Anderson, Adolphus J. Majors, Timothy E. Minor, Frederick Lenardson, William M. Lenardson, John S. Lenardson, William Gordinier, Benjamin Joy, Lester Richardson, Horace Green, William P. Hopkins, Alfred Hopkins, James VanHorn, John VanHorn, Warren Parker, John Call, Rhial B. Vrooman, Elisha Kimble.

One company was raised in Lucas County for the Mexican War, and Daniel Chase of Manhattan (Toledo) was appointed the Captain. They left Toledo, Ohio for the field on 5-18-1847. The Toledo Guards, with Captain Willey, escorted the Company to the steamboat, and the citizens presented Captain Chase with a sword. The name of the company was Company B, 15th United State Infantry. At the end of this war Captain Chase furnished a list of deaths in his command, in a letter he wrote at Chapultepec, near the City of Mexico. He listed 34 deaths. A review of the list does not reveal any "Sylvania" names.

The outcome of this war was a United States victory. The United States had sent 78,700 soldiers and had 13,283 casualties.

THE AMERICAN CIVIL WAR

In general, the Civil War started because of differences between the free and slave states over the power of the national government to prohibit slavery in the territories that had not yet become states. Taken from *Wikipedia.org* under the subject of the "American Civil War," the following is cited: "The American Civil War was fought in the United States from 1861 to 1865. The result of a long-standing controversy over slavery, war broke out in April 1861, when Confederates attacked Fort Sumter in South Carolina, shortly after President Abraham Lincoln was inaugurated. The nationalists of the Union proclaimed loyalty to the U.S. Constitution. They faced secessionists of the Confederate States of America, who advocated for states' rights to expand slavery. Among the 34 U.S. states in February 1861, seven Southern slave states individually declared their secession from the U.S. to form the Confederate States of America, or the *South*. The Confederacy grew to include 11 slave states. The Confederacy was never diplomatically recognized by the U.S. government, nor was it recognized by any foreign country. The states that remained loyal, including the Border States where slavery was legal, were known as the *Union* or the *North*."

The event that triggered the Civil War was at Fort Sumter in Charleston, South Carolina on 4-12-1861 when they claimed this U.S. Fort as their own, and the Confederate Army on that day opened fire on the federal garrison and forced them to lower the American flag in surrender. Lincoln called out the militia and soon four more slave states seceded and joined the Confederacy. It is recorded that by the end of 1861 almost one million armed men confronted each other in war along the line stretching 1,200 miles from Virginia to Missouri.

The purpose of this chapter is not to report on all the facts and figures about the Civil War overall, but to report on how the residents in Sylvania, Ohio were affected during these war years, and report on the residents who stayed home, those that volunteered, those that came home and those that did not come home.

The following was written in the book titled *Memoirs of Lucas County and the City of Toledo – Volume 1 1910 – By Harvey Scribner – Page 186*: "When volunteers were called for by President Lincoln, in the spring of 1861, the sons of Sylvania were prompt to respond, and before the close of the war 102 citizens of the township had enlisted in the Union Army. Twenty-six died in service, two of whom—Horace Bertholf and Samuel Corbin—were in the artillery, the others were members of the various infantry regiments."

At the June 1861 session of the Lucas County Commissioners the board directed the sum of $2,000 be transferred to the Volunteer Relief Fund, to be paid to needy families of soldiers. They had previously levied a tax "for the support of the families of those that volunteered to fight for the maintenance of the Constitution and Government."

In 1861 when it was announced to our "Sylvania" residents that a war had started, Sylvania did not have their own newspaper and relied on the *Daily Toledo Blade* for their news. The following was announced in the <u>*DAILY TOLEDO BLADE* – SATURDAY EVENING, APRIL 13, 1861:</u>

THE WAR BEGUN!

Startling News from Charleston!

By our last night's telegraph report, we got the news of the commencement of hostilities at Charleston. The information then received was to the effect, that the battle was commenced by cannonading from Fort Moultrie and other points upon Sumter at 4 o'clock yesterday morning.—That the fire was moderately responded to by Maj. Anderson until 7 or 8 o'clock, when his shots were more heavy and constant.

The firing was continued throughout the day without intermission. It is said that the result of the day's contest was slight, the most material effect experienced by Sumter.

We do not learn that ANDERSON'S guns have had any serious effect upon any of the enemy's works, while it was claimed that breaches were made in his post and some of his guns disabled.

At intervals of 20 minutes firing was kept up all night on Sumter, while its guns were silent after 6 o'clock in the evening, owing, it was thought, to repairs being made by ANDERSON.—At 7 o'clock this morning he renewed his fire, but at 9 o'clock it is said that his flag was at half-mast, and a dense smoke issued from the fort.—Breeches were plainly seen in its walls. The display of his flag at half-mast might have been designed as a signal to the fleet outside.

It would seem from our afternoon's report that the government fleet took part in the bombardment today.

Allowing that the reports we get are reliable the indications are certainly not favorable for Major ANDERSON, but the reader should bear in mind that our information comes mainly from the hands of the enemy, and great allowance should be made on that account.

But whatever may be the fate of the noble hero of Sumter and his gallant little band, the cause in which he fights will not perish. They may be sacrificed, but thousands of brave men will ply to fill the gap which their loss shall create.

THE ISSUE IS MADE UP!

The blow is struck! The time when the friends of constitutional government and civil liberty must take their positions, for or against their government, has arrived! The enemies of the Union and of Freedom have at last reached the point where they warranted in opening hostilities upon the government they are bound by every consideration of loyalty and patriotism to support. The blow had long been threatened, but the hope had not entirely fled that better and wiser counsels would yet prevail, and that the civilized world would be spared the sickening spectacle of the freest and most prosperous people the earth ever bore pitted in bloody and needless war. All that forbearance and moderation on the part of the friends of order could do, has been done to avert this shocking calamity.

To say nothing of the shameless perfidy and collusion with this great tresses, which distinguished and disgraced the late Administration, the spirit of conciliation and forbearance which has marked the policy of the present Executive, has removed all excuses from the monstrous crime which is now startling the nation with its ingratitude and enormity. The history of the world furnishes not parallel, either to the madness of the offenders, or the forbearance of the Government. In any other country on the Globe, it would have been impossible for deliberate, protracted and extended armaments against the government to be carried forward openly and undisguisedly for months, as was the case in this instance. But the forbearance of the nation has been lost upon the conspirators, and has only been useful to demonstrating the moderation and prudence of the people. It is to be hoped that the good from the latter effect may offset the evils resulting from the advantage thus taken by the traitors.

The practical question now for every citizen is, What is duty! What responsibilities devolve upon you, in this emergency? We make partisan appeal. We speak not to Republicans or Democrats—natives or foreign born—but to American citizens, of all classes and divisions. The hand of the traitor is raised against your government—against all that you hold dear in civil rights and political interests. The integrity and very existence of your government is put in peril by open enemies. The Union and the Constitution which your fathers made—the legacy which their blood and suffering were for you—the greatest boon that men ever bequeathed to their posterity—long threatened, are now openly assaulted. Need we ask what you will do? There can be but one answer from an American heart, and that will be a prompt and patriotic pledge of support to the measures which the government as the chosen representative of the nation, shall devise for the vindication of its authority and the preservation of our liberties. The man who takes this position will be of the Party of Patriots—no matter what his past designation or association and he who refuses to do so, should be known as a traitor to his country and his duty. The lines will soon be drawn and we shall soon know who, if any, are so far blinded by prejudice and passion as to array themselves with the public enemy.

We are rejoiced to believe that the masses of all parties are true to their duty and guided by the best impulses of patriotism and loyalty. In our own section we have reason to look for a unity of sentiment and action which will nerve the hearts and sustain the hands of those in charge of the government, and leave no doubt as to the position of Northwestern Ohio in this crisis. Here let us suggest that immediate steps be taken by the citizens, without distinction of party, to give some expression to the public sentiment on this great question. We confidently believe such a movement would do much good in concentrating the popular feeling and encouraging our State and National authorities in the measures demanded by the exigencies of the times."

Men from Sylvania that volunteered or enlisted, in most cases, joined up with the following Regiments:

14th Infantry Regiment - Ohio Volunteer Infantry was raised almost entirely of Toledo and the men of the surrounding vicinity. Several of the men from Sylvania had joined this regiment and they left Toledo on 4-25-1861. In less than three days from the President's call for 75,000 men, this Regiment was ready for the field, and is believed to have been the first Regiment accepted by the government. Their battles were numerous and ran from June of 1861 through March of 1865, and included: Phillippi, West Virginia; Laurel Hill, West Virginia; Carrick's Ford, West Virginia; Wild Cat, Kentucky; Mill Springs, Kentucky; Shiloh, Tennessee; Corinth, Mississippi; Hoover's Gap, Tennessee; Chickamauga, Georgia; Mission Ridge, Tennessee; Ringgold, Georgia; Dalton, Georgia; Resaca, Georgia; Kennesaw County, Georgia; Utoy Creek, Georgia; Jonesboro, Georgia; and Goldsboro, North Carolina. This Regiment joined Sherman's forces at Atlanta and the Regiment participated in the "March to the Sea." According to the *Daily Toledo Blade* dated 1-3-1863: "Volunteers wanted to fill up the ranks of the old gallant 14th Ohio; no more deserving or better Regiment can be found for a lover of his country to unite his fortunes with, than this Regiment. Come forth then, to the rescue of your oppressed country, and enroll yourselves among the brave and true, and thus avoid the disgrace of a draft. My headquarters for the present are in Myers' Block, corner Monroe and Summit streets (Toledo). J.A. Chase, Captain Co. F. 14th O.V.I." According to the *Daily Toledo Blade* dated 10-1-1864 the 14th lost the biggest share of their men on 9-1-1864. At Raleigh the news of the surrender of Lee and the Rebel Army near Richmond was given. They started then for Washington, where they joined with the Grant Armies of the Union in a review before the President and his cabinet. On 6-15-1865 the 14th Ohio left Washington by rail for Parkersburg, Virginia, arriving there the 18th, then by boats to Louisville, Kentucky, camping there until 7-11-1865, and left for home, reaching Cleveland on 7-14-1865. The Regiment was paid off at Cleveland and disbanded. A large portion of the members reached Toledo on 7-21-1865, and the men from Sylvania were home by the next day. The Sylvania men who were killed while serving with the 14th included: Oscar Hendrickson; Thomas Porter; John VanOrman; John Woodmancy; John McBride; and John Oats.

18th Infantry Regiment – Ohio Volunteer Infantry – According to the list of those from Sylvania that were killed while serving in the Civil War, six of the men that were killed were listed as serving in the 18th Regiment. The 18th Infantry was organized in July of 1861 and Henry B. Carrington was appointed colonel of the regiment. The headquarters was stationed in Columbus, Ohio, and recruiting commenced on the 1st of July, 1861. Their camp was established four miles north of Columbus, known as Camp Thomas. It is recorded that nearly all the gentlemen from this regiment were from civil life and entered the military service from a variety of professions that had nothing to do with anything military. The 18th left Camp Thomas on 11-30-1861 and proceeded to Louisville, Ky., where they then reported to General Buell. On 12-16-1861 at Lebanon, Ky., Colonel Carrington turned over the command to Lieutenant-Colonel Shepherd and then he returned to Camp Thomas to complete the organization of the regiment. General Buell then assigned the 18th Infantry to the 3rd Brigade, 1st Division, Army of the Ohio, and General George H. Thomas was the division commander. For the next four years they were connected with General Thomas and they say that if you follow General Thomas' campaigns you can follow that of the 18th Regiment. After moving through parts of Louisville, they then moved through to

Nashville, Tennessee. They reached Nashville on 3-20-1862 to participate at Corinth – Savannah on the Tennessee River. During this march the officers and men suffered great hardships. The roads were knee-deep with mud and the weather was stormy. Rations were very short, shelter could not be obtained at night, and the wagon trains were delayed many days. On the 24th of April, 1862 this regiment had its first engagement with the enemy at Shiloh Creek where they drove back the enemy beyond Lick Creek and Pea Ridge, capturing some prisoners. In Corinth, Mississippi the combined Armies of the Ohio, Tennessee and Mississippi were reorganized and the 18th Infantry passed from the 1st Division, Army of the Ohio, to the 7th Division (General T.W. Sherman) of the right Wing (General Thomas) of the Army. They participated in the siege of Corinth (April 23 to May 30). After the evacuation of Corinth by the Confederates, the Union Army was reorganized and the Division to which the 18th Infantry belonged again became the 1st Division under General Thomas. The rest of their four years included more campaigns and guard duties that are just too numerous to list here.

25th Infantry Regiment - Ohio Volunteer Infantry - The first "group" of men from Sylvania to go into service in the Civil War became part of Company K of the 25th Regiment, Ohio Volunteer Infantry. The 25th was organized in June, 1861 and included recruits from various parts of the state of Ohio. The men of Lucas County became part of Company K, and they organized at Camp Chase in Toledo on 6-28-1861. When they left Toledo, they were escorted to the railroad depot on the Middlegrounds, where a large ceremony was held by the Zouave Cadets and Fire Engine Co. No. 1. Most of these men were actually just boys at ages 18 to 20 years of age. Company K was under Captain Charles W. Ferguson, and soon after they were sent to Columbus and the whole regiment was sent off to operate along the B & O Railroad in Virginia to deal with the bushwhackers. By winter time the men were without overcoats, blankets and in some cases without shoes, and they suffered severely. In early December 1861, 400 of the Regiment attacked a rebel force of 5,000 at Baldwin's Camp. Nine of their soldiers were killed and 35 were injured. Harlan Page of Sylvania was one that was wounded when his collar bone was shattered. For 18 days he lay in camp pleading, "Oh, take me home to die." His fellow comrades, some of them Sylvanians, carried Harlan Page some sixty miles to the nearest railroad. First Lieutenant Nathaniel Haughton, of Company K, telegraphed Sylvania telling them that Page was on his way home. He came home on 2-20-1862, but died exactly one week later. After the war ended, the veterans of Sylvania formed a Grand Army of the Republic (G.A.R.) post and named the post after Harlan Page – Page Post No. 471. Some of the battles fought by the 25th Regiment were: Cheat Mountain, Chance Hartsville, Rafting Creek, Monterey, Alleghany Summits, Gregory's Landing, Staatsburg, Cross Keys, Gettysburg (20 killed, 113 wounded, 50 missing), Dingle's Mill, Honey Hill, Freeman's Ford, Devereaux Neck, Swift Creek, McDowell, Greenbrier, Second Bull Run (10 killed, 78 wounded, 22 missing). Their services continued through to June of 1866, and at the end included going to Columbia, South Carolina because of the sad conditions there, caused by the liberation of the slaves. During the fall and winter of 1865 service for this regiment was extreme because of the bands of outlaws which infested the country. Several of the soldiers were wounded and one was assassinated. On 6-7-1866 the 25th Regiment left Charleston by steamer for New York and then proceeded to Columbus, Ohio, arriving 6-12-1866. From here each soldier returned to their hometowns. The list of Sylvania men that were killed while serving with this Infantry included: Matthew Davis; William Hallet, Jr.; Edwin Peck; and Harlan Page.

<u>37th Infantry Regiment</u> - Ohio Volunteer Infantry, was organized under the second call of President Lincoln when he called for 300,000 men in August of 1861. This Regiment was composed mostly of Germans, and was raised at Toledo, Cleveland and Chillicothe. It was the third German Regiment from Ohio. They were mustered into service on 10-2-1861. Their services were used through August of 1865. On 8-12-1865 they were mustered out and preceded to Cleveland, Ohio for discharge.

<u>47th Infantry Regiment</u> - Ohio Volunteer Infantry included men from all over Ohio. The men from the Lucas County area that joined this Regiment became part of Company I. They first met at Camp Clay in the Eastern suburbs of Cincinnati on 6-10-1861. Their services were used until February of 1864 and three-fourths of the men re-enlisted, making the 47th a Veteran Regiment. It entered the field in 1861 with 830 men, and at the close of the Atlanta campaign they were reduced to 120. From Washington the Regiment proceeded to Cincinnati, and then Little Rock, Arkansas where it served in the "Army of Occupation" until 8-11-1864. They left then for Camp Dennison, Ohio, where it arrived on 8-22-1864 and they were paid off and discharged after a service of 4 years, two months and 9 days. All those men from Sylvania that served with the 47th Regiment, all came home.

<u>100th Infantry Regiment</u>, Ohio Volunteer Infantry - This Regiment was organized at Toledo in July and August of 1862 and they entered service on 9-1-1862. Many of the Sylvania boys were part of this Regiment. Their important battles included: Knoxville, Tennessee; Rocky Face Dalton, Georgia; Resaca, Georgia; Cartersville, Georgia; Dallas, Georgia; Kennesaw Mountain; Chattahoochee River, Georgia; Atlanta, Georgia; Toy Creek, Georgia; Jonesboro, Georgia; Lovejoy's Station, Georgia; Etowah Creek, Georgia; Columbia, Tennessee; Spring Hill, Tennessee; Franklin, Tennessee; Nashville, Tennessee; Pursuit of Hood's Army; Town Creek; Wilmington, N.C. In its final services the 100th moved into Wilmington, North Carolina with the 23rd Corps, and actively engaged there, and then moved with Sherman's Army to Raleigh. They moved to Greensboro and then to Cleveland, Ohio, where they were mustered out on 7-1-1865, having served two years and 10 months. According to the *Daily Toledo Blade* dated 6-27-1865 "the 100th regiment arrived at Cleveland on Sunday night, 370 strong, where it was bountifully provided for by the citizens. They were escorted to the Park by the Acting Mayor and Committee." During its term of service the Regiment lost 65 men killed in battle, 142 wounded, 27 died of wounds, 108 died of disease, 325 were captured by the enemy and 85 died in Rebel prisons.

<u>111th Infantry Regiment</u> - Ohio Volunteer Infantry was another regiment that many of the Sylvania boys joined. This Regiment was raised in the counties of Lucas, Wood, Sandusky, Fulton, Williams and Defiance. It was organized in August of 1862 and they mustered into service on September 5 and 6, 1862. Their important battles included: Frankfort, Kentucky; Juff's Ferry, Tennessee; Loudon Creek, Tennessee; Campbell's Station, Tennessee; Rocky Face Ridge, Georgia; Resaca, Georgia; Kenesaw, Georgia; Dallas, Georgia; Nicojack, Georgia; Decatur, Georgia; Peachtree Creek, Georgia; Atlanta, Georgia; Lovejoy's Station, Georgia; Franklin, Tennessee; and Nashville, Tennessee. After the surrender of General Johnston, the Regiment moved to Salisbury, North Carolina and remained on garrison duty until they were sent home, reaching Cleveland, Ohio on 7-5-1865 and mustered out on the 12th of July, 1865. This Regiment entered the field with 1,050 men and received 85 recruits. Of these, 234 were discharged for disability, disease and

wounds; 200 died of disease contracted in the service; 252 were killed in battle or died of wounds; and 401 were mustered out. They reported a total of 687 casualties. The following from Sylvania that were killed while serving with the 111ᵗʰ Regiment included: Zirah Green, John Kimball, Horace Cooper, and Stauton Chappel

130ᵗʰ Infantry Regiment – Ohio Volunteer Infantry – It was originally organized as the 1ˢᵗ Ohio National Guard and included some Lucas County men. They entered service on 5-2-1864 and were mustered in on 5-13-1864 for 100 days of service under command of Colonel Charles B. Phillips. They were mustered out of service on 9-22-1864 at Toledo, Ohio. This Regiment did guard duty at Johnson's Island, and then they left for Bermuda Hundred, in the James River. Here President Lincoln spoke to them, and they were placed in the Second Brigade, Third Division, 10ᵗʰ Army Corps. On 6-22-1864 the Regiment participated in a skirmish with Rebel Pickets, losing one man wounded. On 8-11-1864 it proceeded to Fort Powhattan, where it remained until they were mustered out. On 9-7-1864 they took the transport boat Keyport, on the James River, where the boat encountered a severe storm, and barely escaped wreck. On 9-12-1864 they reached Toledo, Ohio. According to the *Daily Toledo Blade* dated 9-13-1864: "The 130ᵗʰ Regiment O.N.G. – 100 days men – arrived in this city last evening from Fort Powhatan, Virginia, and were welcomed by an immense concourse of people, with music and a national salute. So dense was the crowd that it was next to impossible to pass in a contrary direction."

182ⁿᵈ Infantry Regiment – Ohio Volunteer Infantry – the 182ⁿᵈ was not organized until August of 1864 and was mustered in for one year of service on 10-27-1864. According to the *Daily Toledo Blade* dated 8-25-1864: "We very much regret that the organization of a new regiment in this district meets with so little encouragement. Upon the assignment of a regiment to the 10ᵗʰ district special efforts have been made to send it to the field with full ranks, every one seeming to feel a personal pride in the organization." By October of 1864 a hospital for the 182ⁿᵈ Regiment O.V.I. had been established in Breed's Block, with T.J. Thompson, Acting Surgeon. On 10-10-1864 the *Daily Toledo Blade* announced that two more companies were organized at Camp Toledo for the 182ⁿᵈ Regiment O.V.I. Then the *Blade* reported on 10-19-1864 that Col. Chase and Butler had taken command of the troops at Camp Toledo and were preparing to move to Columbus. At that time there were 416 men in camp, with another 100 still absent, but expected before departing. When they did depart they reported upward of 600 men. Five Companies were organized, with Company E being the most recent to be organized (by November of 1864 they were up to Company K). On 10-28-1864 the *Columbus Dispatch* reported that the 182ⁿᵈ left for the front yesterday and that it was raised principally in the Toledo area district. Col. Lewis Butler, formerly Major in the 67ᵗʰ, and Lieut. Col. John A. Chase, formerly Captain in the 14ᵗʰ were in charge. The *Daily Toledo Blade* dated 1-16-1865 reported on the deaths in Company A of the 182ⁿᵈ O.V.I., which included four men. This Regiment was in Nashville, Tennessee from December 1864 to March of 1865, involved in the Battle of Nashville, and then did garrison at Nashville, Department of the Cumberland, until July 1865. They were mustered out of service on 7-7-1865 at Nashville and discharged at Camp Chase on 7-13-1865.

189ᵗʰ Infantry Regiment, Ohio Volunteer Infantry – This regiment was organized at Camp Chase in Columbus, Ohio, and mustered in for one year of service, as a result of the Government's call for 300,000 more men in February of 1865. Companies A through I were formed and by early

March of 1865 they were leaving Columbus for the front. Henry D. Kingsbury of Toledo was the Colonel and Norman Waite of Toledo was Major. The Captain of Company B was Miles Lathrop who had been a resident of Sylvania, but had recently moved to Toledo, and there were others in this regiment that were from Sylvania. Throughout their service a member of the regiment wrote letters to the editor of the Toledo Blade updating them on the progress of this regiment, which they printed in their newspaper. The correspondent wrote under the nickname of "Radix." This regiment arrived at Huntsville, Alabama on 3-17-1865 and then they were assigned to duty along Memphis & Charleston Railroad guarding bridges and building stockades through June of 1865. They were then assigned to post duty at Huntsville through 9-25-1865. They were mustered out of service on 9-28-1865 at Nashville, Tennessee. This regiment lost a total of 49 enlisted men during their service. One man was killed and 48 of the men died due to disease. None of the men that died were from Sylvania.

Battery H, First Regiment Ohio Light Artillery, was organized in the fall of 1861 through the efforts and influence of Harvey Kellogg, George W. Norton and others. The young men of Adams and adjoining townships (Toledo, Sylvania, Washington, Springfield) organized the company for service in the Union Army. On 9-18-1861 they went to Camp Dennison, near Cincinnati, where they were re-enforced by a squad from Marietta, Ohio, therefore, completing a Battery, which came to be Battery H, First Regiment Light Artillery. Their battle story is a long and interesting one; too long to document here. In May of 1865 this Battery marched for Washington, passing through Richmond, Bowling Green and Fredericksburg. On 6-3-1865 they turned in their guns and horses at Washington and on 6-4-1865 they took the train cars for Cleveland, Ohio, where they were given a dinner. They were mustered out and paid off on 6-14-1865. About 90 members of Battery H returned to Toledo at 12:45 p.m. on 6-15-1865 and they were met at the Railroad Depot by the Union Silver Band and a large number of Lucas County citizens. They were served dinner at the Island House, and after dinner the soldiers were escorted by the band up Summit Street in Toledo, when they returned to the Island House and then departed for their homes. The members of this Battery were given a reception and dinner on 6-21-1865 by the citizens of Adams Township and surrounding vicinity, where there were 1,200 to 1,500 persons present.

The 3rd Regiment, Ohio Volunteer Cavalry, was organized in September of 1861. Of this company which left Toledo, only 30 men returned, many of them being on detached service when they left Nashville. Their list of battles was long and full of loss. The Regiment took part in the chase after Jefferson Davis, in Wilson's command. At Selma they lost heavily in killed and wounded. Under orders from General George H. Thomas the Third Cavalry turned over its horses and arms at Macon and was then ordered to report at Nashville for muster out. Proceeding home via Louisville, the Regiment reached Camp Chase (Toledo) when it was paid off and discharged on 8-14-1865.

The above regiments covered almost all the men who volunteered or were drafted from Sylvania. There were a few Sylvania men that served in other regiments, but almost all were attached to the above regiments.

At the October 1861 session of the Lucas County Commissioners, S.A. Raymond was authorized to go to Columbus, to procure the requisite permits and information for a member of the Board of Commissioners. He was to visit the different Regiments having volunteers from Lucas County, Ohio for the purpose of securing assignments for portions of their wages, for the benefit of their families.

Samuel H. Decker was one boy from Sylvania that served during the Civil War with the Ohio 14th. He was the oldest of seven children who lived with their parents on Sylvania-Metamora Road in Sylvania Township. While serving in the Civil War he lost both of his hands in battle. According to Private Decker's disability and pension paperwork he enlisted on the 22nd day of April 1861 for three months, and he was mustered in at Camp Taylor in Cleveland, Ohio as a private with Capt. Seth B. Moe's 14th Regt. Ohio Volunteer Infantry. He was honorably discharged on 8-13-1861. Then he returned to Sylvania and on the 23rd day of August 1861 he enlisted again as a private in Co. I, 4th Regiment of the U.S. Artillery. Records show that he was enlisted by Lieut. Jones at Chicago, Ill., to serve for three years, but he was honorably discharged on 11-3-1862.

According to documents, when Samuel Decker was mustered in the second time, he was listed as 26 years of age, five feet, eight and one-half inches high, dark complexion, brown eyes, black hair and his occupation was listed as a teamster. When he was released in November of 1862, Capt. T.G. Smith wrote that he was incapable of performing the duties of a soldier because of the loss of both arms in consequence of injuries received in the service; his disability being total. His "Invalid Pension Claim Declaration" that he filled out in Lucas County on 3-9-1863, before a Probate Judge, listed "loss of both of his hands by a cannon ball discharged from one of said battery's cannons which it was his duty to sponge. The listed details of the event were reported as follows: Samuel H. Decker, hearing the report of an enemy cannon close by, supposed the report to be accompanied by the discharge of his own cannon and while in the act of sponging the last mentioned gun it discharged inflicting the disability that he received on the 8th day of October, A.D. 1862 at the battle near Perryville in the State of Kentucky by reason of which he is wholly disabled from obtaining his sustenance by manual labor. Said applicant further declares that since he was discharged he has resided in the village of Sylvania, unable to engage in any occupation for the past two months, attending school at the place last mentioned, and that he was depending in part upon the assistance of others for support."

At the 1870 census Samuel H. Decker was listed living in Sylvania at the age of 36 years old. His occupation is listed as "Door Keeper Washington D.C." His wife was Hattie Decker, listed as 28 years old, and a daughter Vina L. Decker was listed as 2 years old. Also living in the household was Jasper Otis – 12 years old, listed as a domestic servant. According to the "Health Department District of Columbia" documents, Samuel Decker died on 10-20-1903 at the age of 69 years. He was married and working as a Messenger at the House of Representatives. He had been residing in Washington DC for 36 years. He was buried in Arlington Cemetery. His widow, (second wife) Mary Frances Decker, age 48, completed a "Declaration of a Widow for Accrued Pension" which said that he had been previously married and that his first wife died in Washington D.C., on 12-29-1881. (Her name was Hattie M. Childs).

Recently (2017) I received an email from a friend, featuring a group of historical photos that he thought would be interesting to me. As I reviewed the old photos I came across this photo of a Civil War veteran and the caption read: "Civil War veteran Samuel H. Decker poses with the prosthetic arms he made for himself…somehow." I immediately realized that was Sylvania's "Samuel H. Decker." Another source said the following about Mr. Decker: "He receives a pension of $300 per year, and is a doorkeeper at the House of Representatives. He designed the prosthetics and guided his wife through building them. With the aid of this ingenious apparatus he was able to write legibly, to pick up any small objects, a pin for example, to carry packages of ordinary weight, to feed and clothe himself, and in one or two instances of disorder in the Congressional gallery has proved himself a formidable police officer." Samuel was married a second time to Mary Frances O'Callaghan in 1882 in Baltimore, Maryland. They had no children during their marriage, and Samuel lived the remainder of his life in D.C., employed as a messenger at the House of Representatives in the Capital Building, until his death at the age of 69 years in 1903 while still married to Mary F. In an 1903 General Affidavit verifying his death, so that his widow could collect her husband's pension, Samuel's two brothers, Jacob C Decker, age 66, and Lester B. Decker, age 62, both of Sylvania Township testified that they knew Samuel H. Decker from boyhood and each knew him to be married two times, with his first wife passing away in 1881, and his second marriage was to Mary Frances Decker. Samuel H. Decker was buried in Arlington National Cemetery in Washington D.C. It was reported that the "Seattle grunge band Soundgarden would later write a song paying tribute to Samuel Decker and his accomplishments, which they aptly titled "Spoonman."

Sergeant Clark N. Thorp, who grew up in Sylvania, was involved in the 1863 Battle of Chickamauga, with his unit the 19th U.S. Infantry. During this battle Thorp said that while he was retreating "amid the smoke and noise of battle" he walked straight into a Rebel line. He was captured and ended up serving a total of 19 months in Confederate prisons, and spent 11 of those months in Andersonville, the South's largest prison, located in Americus, Georgia. Sgt. Thorp wrote his memoirs of living as a prisoner in Confederate prisons, and between 1896 and 1924 he frequently recounted his stories to local church and youth groups. In one of Thorp's memoirs, he recounted an attempt that he and others made to escape the Andersonville prison. This was published in the October 2007 issue of *Civil War Times* Magazine. Thorp's memoirs were edited by George Skoch. Mr. Skoch ended his article by saying: "Thorp and his fellow soldiers were transported to Jacksonville, Fla., then on USS Constitution to "Camp Parole" in Annapolis, Md. There, they were issued rations, clothing and back pay before being sent to their respective regimental headquarters for discharge. Thorp was mustered out by the Army at Fort Wayne, Michigan, on June 22 and returned to Ohio. He found work as a railroad busman, and in 1868 married, eventually raising two sons and a daughter. Despite his Andersonville ordeal, he would live another six decades before dying in August 1927, at the age of 86, in Lakewood, Ohio."

Information gathered about Clark N. Thorp shows that he was a resident of Sylvania Township at the 1850 census, listed as nine years old, living with his parents, Peter and Phebe Thorp. At the 1860 census Clark was 18 years old and living in Toledo, serving as an apprentice carpenter, and living with David Howe, who was a master carpenter. In July of 1863 when the 10th District Civil War Draft Registration Records were taken Clark was shown as a resident of Sylvania, and serving with the 19th U.S. Infantry at that time. After the war, Mr. Thorp was married on 12-10-1868 in Huron County, Ohio to Annie McKelvey. An 1885 Cleveland, Ohio City Directory shows that he was living at 34 Cliff in Cleveland, Ohio, employed as a car builder. He died on 8-22-1927 and was buried in the Lake View Cemetery in Cleveland, Cuyahoga County, Ohio.

The following document was located among the Sylvania Area Historical Society's documents dated 2-25-1864:

"We the undersigned agree to pay the sums set opposite our respective names for the purpose of paying U.S. recruits a local bounty when credited to Sylvania Township – provided the sum raised shall clear the town from the present draft. Washington Lenardson - $50; Abraham Durfee - $20; James Richie - $10; Charles Edson - $10; R.S. Bertholf - $5; E. Kimbell - $5; Phillip Cooper - $5; I. Green - $5; Ed Bordeaux - $3; C.S. Lewis - $5; John Kroll - $5; George Gerwick - $3; Abraham Wintermute - $5; Andrew Cherry - $2; Patrick Faling - $5; William Tuttle - $5; John Connelly - $5; Henry Turner - $2; B.H. Whitney - $5; Foster Ellis - $5; J. Foreman - $2; John Cary - $10; James Andrews - $2; Jeremiah Micham - $15; Moses R. Nason - $5; N.D. Youngs - $10; H.I. & Joseph Warren - $50; Edwin Bordeaux - $5; Thomas Brimacomb - $2; J.G. Meiner - $30; Christopher Cramer - $5; Adam Schramm - $5; Edmon Cabash - $2.

At the March 1864 session of the Lucas County Commissioners it was reported that several townships had deposited in the county treasury, sums of money for payment to volunteers in the Army. The commissioners authorized the treasurer to pay out up to $3,000 in amounts of not more than $100 each to the volunteers.

At the June 1864 session of the Lucas County Commissioners, this board authorized the payment of claims to citizens of the several townships for money advanced as bounty to volunteers as follows:

Providence Township – 63 claims
Adams Township – 46 claims
Oregon – 46 claims
Manhattan – 62 claims
Swanton – 30 claims
Waterville Township – 121 claims
Sylvania Township – 116 claims
Monclova Township – 28 claims
Toledo – 1st Ward – 105 claims
Toledo – 2nd Ward – 291 claims
Toledo – 3rd Ward – 220 claims
Toledo – 4th Ward – 105 claims
Toledo – 5th Ward – 141 claims
Toledo – 6th Ward – 60 claims

These claims, in amounts, ranged from $5.00 to $280, the average being about $20.

The following letter was sent to the Sylvania Township Trustees from the Lucas County Auditor's office, James L. Smith, dated 6-9-1864: "Gentlemen, The total amount of monies advanced for the payment of bounties to volunteers from Sylvania Township, allowed by the Board of County Commissioners, at their regular session in June 1864 is one thousand and eighty-seven ($1,087) dollars.

The *Daily Toledo Blade* dated 9-24-1864 reported on the draft deficiencies in the 10ᵗʰ District, of which Sylvania was located. The 10ᵗʰ district was required to supply 707 men. Under the heading of Lucas County they needed to supply 121 men toward that 707. Of the 121 men needed from Lucas County, Sylvania was listed as needing to supply 14 men. (The 10ᵗʰ district at this time included all of Lucas County, Wood County, Fulton County, Henry County, Putnam County, Williams County, Defiance County and Paulding County, Ohio).

Then the *Daily Toledo Blade* dated 9-29-1864 listed the names of all the men that were drafted from the Tenth District and the 14 men from Sylvania that were drafted included: James M. Thompson, Ambrose Cone, Giles F. Mallett, Newell J. Bankson, Henry Hubbard, Oscar D. Moore, Dewitt Dolph, Jacob Decker, George Talbott, Charles N. Mersereau, Moses R. Nason, Jacob Vanalstine, Nicholas D. Young and Joseph Printup. The Alternates listed were: Albert C. Tucker, George A. Crandall, Jacob Church, Gilbert Cobra, William Demmin, Lewis Shay, William J. Phelps, George Helfer, Albert D. Blanchard, Luther Roberts, Alonzo Lester, David P. Baker, John Cornish and Martin Conlisk.

The *Daily Toledo Blade* of 11-1-1864 reported on a supplemental draft to fill deficiencies under the president's call for 500,000 men. The draft took place at the office of Captain Kent, Provost Marshal of the 10ᵗʰ district. The article said: "The following are the names of the fortunate persons: Sylvania Township = Deficiency 2; No. Drawn 4: A.C. Hassen, John Cory, Michael Veratt and Marshall Beach."

On 12-10-1864 the *Daily Toledo Blade* said that a meeting of the Lucas County Military Committee was held for the purpose of appointing committees in the different wards and townships of this county to correct the enrollment lists. The following gentlemen were selected to perform this work from Sylvania Township: Peleg T. Clark, W.D. Moore, Isaac Thorp, J. Warren and R.C. Thompson.

The *Daily Toledo Blade* dated 1-31-1865 reported again on the quota of men needed in the 10ᵗʰ District in each of the townships, under the last call of the President for 300,000 men. Sylvania Township was listed as needing to supply 12 men.

2-15-1865 - The following document was found among the papers preserved in the archives of the Sylvania Area Historical Society. This list came from the records of Sylvania resident A.B. West: "We the undersigned pledge ourselves to pay to Aaron B. West, Treasurer of the War Bounty Fund, the sums set opposite our respective names on or before the 15ᵗʰ day of February 1865 for the purpose of securing a sufficient number of volunteers into the U.S. service to fill our quota on the last draft ordered by the President of the U.S.: Aaron B. West $50.00; William Clampitt $50.00; James Parker $50.00; William Hogle $50.00; John Clump $50.00; John Bittner $50.00; Cyrus A. Warren $50.00; George McGlenn $50.00; James McGlenn $50.00; Rush Spaulding $50.00; Jesse Blakesley $40.00; W.D. Wells $25.00; Alden Roberts $25.00; Isaac Denman $15.00; George Dennis $10.00; Crawford Smith $50.00; John McPherson $9.00; Austin Young $30.00; David Bashaw $25.00; W.G. Lewis $5.00; Morris Cummins $40.00; Amos Thorp $25.00; David Hadley $10.00; Louis Wiseman $15.00; Christian Hobart $10.00; Daniel Roberdeaux $50.00; George P. Dolph $40.00; John Shrader $30.00; George Hagar $5.00; Martin Schrim $10.00;

Perry Segur $20.00; John Hammond $5.00; D.B. Young $28.00; Moses Trombley $25.00; Henry Beerbaum $25.00; John Gir $30.00; Christ Piper $30.00; William Shruder $30.00; J.P. Cornell $30.00; Ernest Ruwaldt $20.00; Patrick Gary $25.00; James Haskell $10.00; Warren Cooley $25.00; J. McDowell $10.00; Jasper Ferris $25.00; Harvey Gilhousen $5.00; D. Crots $20.00; David LaPoint $35.00; Philip Perry $2.00; John Richardson $30.00; Isaac Clegg $30.00; Hiram Hawley $25.00; John Gilhousen $50.00; R.E. Dein $30.00; J.H. Hobart $10.00; D.S. Dalley $35.00; William Haynes $20.00; N.E. Shattuck $40.00; Lorenzo Young $5.00; John Riel $5.00."

In May of 1865, in order to determine Sylvania's indebtedness to the Civil War veterans, the "elected" Sylvania Township Assessor canvassed the Sylvania community for names of persons who had enlisted in the Union Army. He determined that 102 soldiers and marines had served; 26 had died; 4 were disabled; there were 40 soldiers' families living in Sylvania; a total of 108 persons in those families; and 36 were in need of some sort of relief. (Sylvania Township at this time also included all of what is the city of Sylvania today, and more).

The following was written in the book titled *Memoirs of Lucas County and the City of Toledo* - Volume 1 – 1910 – By Harvey Scribner – Under the Chapter of Sylvania Township - Page 186 said: "Twenty-six died in service, two of whom—Horace Bertholf and Samuel Corbin—were in the artillery, and the others were members of various infantry regiments, to wit: William Gilpin, Oscar Hendrickson, John McBride, John Oats, Thomas Porter, John Van Orman and John Woodmansee of the Fourteenth Ohio; Uriah Cheney, Edwin Lacy, John Lane, James Lowden, James Mills and Daniel Norris of the Eighteenth Ohio; Matthew Davis, William Hallett, Harlan Page and Edwin Peck of the Twenty-fifth Ohio; Levi Palmer and Elijah Stone of the Forty-seventh Ohio; Orlando Comstock of the Sixty-seveth Ohio; Staunton Chappell, Horace Cooper, Zirah Green and John Kimball of the One Hundred and Eleventh Ohio."

There is a memorial marker in Sylvania's Veterans Memorial Field representing the Civil War casualties, but it lists only eleven names. Here are the names that were placed on that marker: "Civil War – Casualties from Sylvania, OH: Charles Brown, B. Butler, John VanOerman, George W. Holloway, Charles O. Holloway, J.V. Moore, Joseph Donovan, William Holmes, Jacob White, Ben Rhodes, Samuel Bellows."

Where this list of Sylvania's Civil War casualties came from I do not know at this time. The list of the 26 casualties in Mr. Scribner's 1910 history book came from the 1865 Sylvania Township Assessor's report that was recorded at that time and in my opinion is the accurate list of casualties for Sylvania Township. Remember at this time the village/city of Sylvania did not exist yet, and Sylvania Township encompassed the entire area.

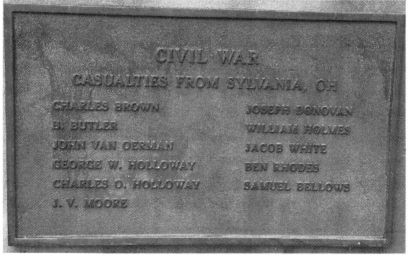

Here is the memorial marker in Sylvania's Veterans Memorial Field representing the casualties from Sylvania during the Civil War. The top portion of the marker reads: "THE GRAND ARMY OF THE REPUBLIC – IN COMMEMORATION – THE PEOPLE OF SYLVANIA COMMEMORATE THOSE SYLVANIANS WHO DIED IN SERVICE TO THE UNITED STATES IN THE CIVIL WAR – 1861 – 1865 – WE HONOR THEIR DEDICATION TO OUR COUNTRY." The bronze marker below that lists only eleven names, which was supposed to represent the casualties from Sylvania. A quick check of a few of these names finds that these men served in the Civil War, but did not die until well after the war was over. John VanOrman was a casualty, but his name is spelled wrong on the marker. For an accurate and complete list of the 26 casualties from Sylvania, which was recorded in May of 1865 by the Sylvania Township Assessor, see the previous page. (Photo taken in 2018 by Gayleen Gindy).

According to the *Daily Toledo Blade* dated 6-24-1865 General William T. Sherman visited Toledo and a very large concourse of citizens assembled at the depot to see him. It was reported that the passenger depot was filled with men, women and children. They said that after he arrived he was nearly overrun by the crowd pressing on him while he was on his way to the Island House Hotel. He spoke to the crowd from the balcony of the hotel. This was a huge event and residents of Sylvania also attended this event.

At the June 1866 session of the Lucas County Commissioners it was agreed to issue each re-enlisted veteran volunteer who received no local bounty a bond for $100.

The following are the names of the individuals who are buried or have memorials in Association Cemetery off Convent Blvd., in Sylvania, who served in the Civil War, as best can be determined: B.J. Albring, J.M. Berdell, George Bolden, John Brint, William Bryant, B. Butler, (killed in action), Samuel Butler, Charles Brown (killed in action), Benjamin Bellows, Oscar H. Bellman, C.N. Bellman, Samuel Boile, John Brimacombe, Horace Cooper, Alfred Clark, Charles Chulip, Henry Chulip, William Chulip, Orland Comstock, William Cunningham, Ambrose B. Comstock, Philip Cooper, Wesley Cooper, John Cartwright, William Cherry, Mark Cherry, Martin Cherry, R.S. Chapple, Thomas Chandler, N.E. Davis, Joseph Donovan (killed in action), Johnson Duffield, Chester Decker, Charles Edson, William Fletcher, Lucius Green, Ulysses Green, Henry Glassier, Amos Gayhart, Emiel Gayhart, Fred Hartman, Sr., Hiram Hollister, Charles Harris, Oristen Holloway, Charles Heath, Sr., William Holmes (killed in action), George W. Holloway (killed in action), Charles O. Holloway (killed in action), J.L. Harwood, Tom Hinds, A.W. Hinds, Don Hendrickson, T.B. Hank, William Hallett, Fred Jordon, Joe King, Theodore Kennedy, John Kimball, James Kirk, Jacob Kauffman, A.D. Lewis, Cornelius Mercereau, W.D. Moore, James V. Moore (killed in action), P.V. Moore, Nelson Mosier, Albert McIlrath, George Ostrander, Hiram Parker, Jr., Henry J. Parker, Alfred Pawling, Don Pease, Charles Rockenstyre, Sr., Chester Roberts, E.K. Roberts, Ben Rhodes (killed in action), William Richardson, Albert D. Randall, Louis Shay, Russell Southward, Leroy Smith, T.K. Smith, Werter Shaffer, Minor Smith, Charles Stone, Lyman Stone, Wilber Showler, Isaac Thorp, John VanOrman (killed in action), Abram Yates, William Vanalstyne, Jacob White (killed in action), James Wood, Simon Wood.

The following information was taken from gravestones in Association Cemetery regarding Civil War Veterans buried here:

William W. Richardson – First Sgt. Co. F, 128 – Ohio Infantry;
James V. Moore – Enlisted in 25th Reg. O.V.I. 9-29-1861 – died 11-30-1864 – Killed at Battle of Honey Hill (or Piney Hill) S.C. – Age 25 – "He died for his country";
William Brint – born 1-28-1840 – Co. F, 14th Ohio Volunteer Infantry;
Leroy J. Smith – died 8-6-1864 – age 24 yrs 6 months 11 days – Killed at Utah Creek, Georgia. "Rest soldier rest thy warfare is over";
Horace A. Cooper – died 1-2-1863 – Age 26 yrs. 8 months – Co. H. 111th Ohio Volunteer Infantry – Enlisted Aug. 15, 1862 Killed at the battle of Murfreesboro, Tenn. Daughter Clara age 2 died Nov. 26, 1864 (all on one stone).
Oristen Holloway- Lieut. Company H, 111 Ohio Infantry.

<u>John Brint</u> – "My Life For My Country" died 10-12-1864 – age 29 yrs. died at Nashville, Tenn. Co. F, 14th Regiment O.V.I.

<u>Nathan E. Davis</u> – Lieut. Died 11-5-1864 – Age 20 yrs. 3 months, 9 days – wounded before Richmond Oct. 13 A.D. 1864. – Company F, 39th Regiment. "Here sleeps the brave who sank to rest with all his country's honor blessed."

<u>John C. Kimball</u> – died 4-22-1864 – age 28 yrs 9 mos. – Died in hospital in Ringgold, Georgia – Private - 14th O.V.I. (Inscription eroded and not readable);

<u>George W. Holloway</u> – of 1st O. Cavalry – Died at Andersonville, Georgia Aged 21 Years; -

<u>Charles O. Holloway</u> – of 14th O. Vol. Infantry-Died at Andersonville, Ga. Aged 19 Years - Sons of T.D. & A. Holloway;

<u>William Cunningham</u> – In memory of - died 7-4-1864 – age 32 yrs 3 mos. 19 days – Bermuda Hundred, Virginia – Member of 130th Regiment Ohio National Guard (five lines eroded) ". . . He grieved to abandon his home";

<u>Jonas L. Harwood</u> – Co. H 111th Ohio Infantry;

<u>Werder H. Schaffer</u> – 1844 – 1903 – Co. K, 25th Ohio Volunteer Infantry.

<u>Albert McIlrath</u> – Co. E, 103rd - Ohio Volunteer Infantry.

<u>Martin Cherry</u> – 1836 – 1908 - Co. G, 130th Ohio Volunteer Infantry.

<u>Simon Wood</u> – 1830 – 1913 - Co. H, 111th Ohio Volunteer Infantry.

<u>Lyman B. Stone</u> – 1843 -1908 – Co. K, 25th Ohio Volunteer Infantry.

<u>C.L. Roberts</u> – Co. K. 3rd Ohio Cavalry.

<u>Albert Randall</u> – 1846 – 1918 – Cpl. Co. B, 186th Ohio Volunteer Infantry.

<u>Benjamin Albring</u> – born 11-3-1845 died 2-24-1864 – Co. F, 14th Ohio Volunteer Infantry.

<u>Ulysses Green</u> – Co. H, 111th Ohio Volunteer Infantry.

<u>William Hallett</u> – Co. A, 67th Ohio Volunteer Infantry.

<u>J.W. Cooper</u> – Co. K - 14th Ohio Volunteer Infantry.

<u>Amiel Garhart</u> – Co. G, 130th Ohio Volunteer Infantry.

<u>Samuel Boile?</u> (badly eroded name), son of B & H died 9-27-1864, age 20 year 10 months 18 days. "He has fought his last battle / And now this brave soldier is resting / His young life was given for his country / And now he sleeps in a soldier's grave."

<u>Charles Heath</u> – Son of N.B. & M – Enlisted in Co. F – 4th Michigan Volunteer Infantry 6-20-1861. Wounded 7-1-1862; Wounded 12-12-1862. Died 1863.

The following are the names of the individuals who are buried in St. Joseph's Catholic Cemetery, off Ravine Drive, in Sylvania, who served in the Civil War: John Aubry, Eli Berry, Frank Burnham, S. Colley, Daniel Donovan, Joseph Donovan, Andrew Fisher, R. Fox, William Frazier, George Frazier, B. Fisher, Charles P. Kelley, William McCloskey, Aloys Reger, Cyril Roscoe, Nicholas Willinger.

The following are the names of the individuals who are buried in Ravine Cemetery, off Ravine Drive, in Sylvania, who served in the Civil War: Amos Albring, E. Bidwell, Peter Breidling, William Bryan, James Brinnon, Henry Burnham, R.C. Burns, George Chandler, Miles Comstock, Forest Cooper, Joseph Counterman, Frank Carpenter, D.C. Dolph, Jacob Decker, Lester Decker, Joseph Dissotel, David Dolby, Mathias Elg, J.C. Fallis, Charles Fox, Thomas Gibbs, Sr., Joseph Hattersley, Silas Harvey, W. Harvey, Orville R. Hine, John Hopkins, Nicholas Huber, William Hubbard, Adrian Kidney, Percy Kiff, Samuel Kilbourne, Samuel Kimball, Miles Lathrop, Mr.

Littlefield, F.M. McDowell, M.B. Pelton, U. Petitt, George Posling, Sr., Henry Reudi, Charles Rockenstyre, Nelson Root, E.F. Sawyer, Frank Seager, Mr. Shiers, Levi Slatts, James Symmington, George VanPelt, Edwin Vesey, Henry Ward, Joe Warren, M.T. Weaver, Milton Whitney, Joseph Warren, William Webb, B. Wood.

The following gravestones in Ravine Cemetery show Civil War service:

Levi B. Slatts – born 3-8-1841 – died 3-2-1913 – Sergt Co. H – 60th Regiment O.V.I.
John VanOrman – born 5-3-1837 – died 8-5-1869 – Co. F – 14th Regiment O.V.I.
William Bryan – born 6-10-1832 – died 9-11-1895 – Company A – 124th O.V.I.
W.D. Mercereau – born 1840 – died 1920 – GAR – Company F – 140th Ohio Vol. Inf.
Samuel L. Kimball – Corpl - . Company H - 111th Ohio Infantry.
Henry E. Burnham – born 1841 – died 1926 – Company G – 101 O.V.I.
Samuel V. Bell – Company H. 31st Ohio Infantry – G.A.R.

In many cases the stones that were erected in our older cemeteries, for those killed in action, are merely memorials, due to the fact that the body of the soldier was not returned to Sylvania. Some of the stones in these cemeteries show burials at Piney Hill, N.C., Tennessee, Utah Creek, Georgia, Richmond and Bermuda Hundred, Virginia, and two brothers had died in the Andersonville Prison.

One more cemetery in Sylvania is the very large Toledo Memorial Cemetery. This cemetery was established here on the north side of Monroe Street in 1922, and I would say that most Civil War veterans had already died by 1922, but I did not inquire as to whether there were any Civil War veterans buried in this cemetery.

The Executive Documents – Printed by Order of the Senate of the United States For The Second Session of the Forty-Seventh Congress – 1882 – '83 In Five Volumes – Volume V – Part 2 – Washington Government Printing Office – 1883 – List of Pensioners On The Roll – January 1, 1883; Giving the name of each pensioner, the cause for which pensioned, the post-office address, the rate of pension per month, and the date of original allowance, As called for by Senate Resolution of December 8, 1882 – Volume III - Washington: Government Printing Office – 1883:

No. of certificate	Name of pensioner	Post-office address	Cause for which pensioned	Monthly rate	Date of original allowance
30,346	Young, James	Sylvania	Wd. R. forearm	$12.00	unknown
unknown	Sawyer, Emory F.	Sylvania	Loss r. arm	$24.00	Unknown
122,190	Bragdon, Leonard H.	Sylvania	Fracture l. patella	$4.00	Unknown
200,320	Bell, Samuel V.	Sylvania	Chr. Diarr.	$4.00	Jan. 1882

49,025	Bryan, William	Sylvania	Wd. R. thigh	$24.00	Unknown
54,004	Decker, Lester	Sylvania	Wd. l. arm	$24.00	Unknown
176,961	Wellman, Hiram	Sylvania	g.s.wd. l. cheek	$6.00	Oct. 1880
63,448	Seager, Francis M.	Sylvania	Wd. l. leg	$4.00	Unknown
17,820	Dolby, David	Sylvania	Loss sight both eyes	$72.00	Unknown
177,694	Cherry, William	Sylvania	Inj. Spine	$2.00	Oct. 1880
21,869	Cherry, Anna	Sylvania	Widow 1812	$2.00	Apr. 1879

At the 1890 census a special schedule listing the "Surviving Soldiers, Sailors, and Marines, and Widows, Etc." was prepared separate from the regular census, and although the 1890 census was destroyed by fire in 1922, these special schedules somehow survived. The following individuals were listed as still alive when this 1890 census was taken, living in Sylvania and Sylvania Township, and serving in the Civil War:

1. Wesley G. Cooper – Corporal, Company G, 130th Ohio Infantry – Enlisted 5-2-1864 – Discharged 9-22-1864 – 4 months – 20 days – P.O. Mitchaw – heart disease.
2. Martin W. Pease – Private, Company G, 6th Ohio Calvary – Enlisted 7-11-1863 – Discharged 5-1-1864 – 10 months – 7 days – P.O. Mitchaw.
3. Leonard Yates – Private, Company H, 111th Ohio Infantry – Enlsited 8-15-1862 – Discharged 6-27-1865 – 2 years – 10 months- 12 days – P.O. Sylvania – chronic diarrhea.
4. Charles W. Mersereau – Private, Company B, 128th Ohio Infantry – Enlisted 8-22-1864 – Discharged 6-9-1865 – 9 months – 17 days – P.O. Sylvania.
5. Frank Burt – Sergeant, Company A, 121st New York Infantry – Enlisted 7-23-1862 – Discharged 2-4-1863 – 6 months 11 days - P.O. Sylvania – Chronic diarrhea and rheumatism.
6. Frank Burt – Second Lieutenant, Company B, 16th New York Heavy Artillery – Enlisted 11-10-1863 Discharged – 3-1-1864 – 3 months – 20 days – P.O. Sylvania.
7. Elizabeth widow of Oristen Holloway – second Lieutenant, Company H, 111th Ohio Infantry – Enlisted 8-14-1862 Discharged 12-17-1862 – P.O. Sylvania – neuralgia of the heart.
8. George VanPelt – Private, Company G, 130th Ohio Infantry – Enlisted 5-2-1864 – Discharged – 10-22-1864 – 4 months 25 days– P.O. Sylvania.
9. Levi B. Slatts – Sergeant, Company H, 60th Ohio Infantry – Enlisted – 3-19-1864 Discharged – 7-28-1865 – P.O. Sylvania
10. Leonard H. Bragdon – Sergeant, Company H, 111th Ohio Infantry – Enlisted – 8-16-1862 Discharged – 7-7-1865 – 2 years, 10 months 22 days – P.O. Sylvania – fracture of soft patella.

11. John Brimacomb – Private, Company B, 128th Ohio Infantry – Enlisted – 8-22-1864 Discharged – 6-9-1865 – 9 months 17 days – P.O. Mitchaw.

12. Henry Ruedi – Private, Company G, 107th Ohio – Enlisted – 8-13-1862 Discharged 7-13-1865 – 2 years – 11 months – 3 days – P.O. Sylvania – gunshot wounds left arm and right arm and loss of strength.

13. Fred Hitchcock – Private, Company C, 67th Penn. Infantry – Enlisted 12-30-1861 – Discharged 12-31-1864 – 3 years.

14. Joseph H. Redman – Sergeant, Company E, 212 Penn. Infantry – Enlisted 9-1-1863 – Discharged 6-1-1865 – 1 year – 9 months – P.O. Sylvania.

15. Edward Waltz – Private, Company D, 48th Ohio Infantry – Enlisted 9-18-1862 – Discharged 11-24-1865 – 3 years – 2 months – 6 days – P.O. Sylvania.

16. Benjamin Aldrich – Private, Company L, 3rd Ohio Calvary – Enlisted 1-9-1862 Discharged 1-7-1865 – 3 years – P.O. Sylvania.

17. Smith L. Griffin – Private, Company B, 18th Michigan Eng. – Enlisted 3-7-1862 – Discharged 7-10-1865 – 3 years – 4 months – 9 days – P. O. Samaria, Monroe Co. Mich.

18. George C. Frazier – Sergeant, Company G, 81st New York Infantry – Enlisted Nov. 1862 – Discharged – 8-1-1865 – 2 years 8 months – P.O. Sylvania.

19. Ellis C. Comstock – Private, Company H, 111th Ohio Infantry – Enlisted 8-15-1862 – Discharged – 1-14-1863 – 4 months 29 days – P.O. Sylvania.

20. Samuel L. Kimbell – Corp., Company H, 111th Ohio Infantry – Enlisted 8-15-1862 – Discharged 6-27-1865 – 2 years 10 months 12 days – P.O. Sylvania - chronic diarrhea.

21. George Robinson – Private, Company B, 128th Ohio Infantry – Enlisted 8-22-1864 – Discharged 6-9-1865 – 10 months 17 days – P.O. Mitchaw.

22. Mary Thomas formerly widow of Sylvester Hoadley, Lieutenant, Company C, 111th Ohio Infantry – Enlisted 8-21-1862 – Died 10-23-1864 – 2 years 1 month 29 days – P.O. Mitchaw – Chronic diarrhea.

23. Charles A. Fox – Private, Company F, 14th Ohio Infantry – Enlisted 2-14-1864 – Discharged 7-11-1865 – 1 year 5 months 1 day – P.O. Mitchaw.

24. Amiel Garhart – Private, Company G, 130th Ohio Infantry – Enlisted - 5-2-1864 Discharged 9-22-1864 – 4 months 18 days.

25. Joseph King – Corp. – Company I, 40th Illinois Infantry – Enlisted 87-25-1861 – Discharged 2-16-1863 – 1 year 6 months 21 days.

26. Daniel Donovan – Sergeant, Company C, 1st Ohio Calvary – Enlisted 8-21-1861 – Discharged 9-13-1865 – 4 years 0 months 22 days – P.O. Sylvania.

27. Albert D. Randall – Corp. Company B, 186th Ohio Infantry – Enlisted 1-11-1865 – Discharged 9-18-1865 – 9 months 7 days - P.O. Sylvania.

28. Gordon P. Ostrander – Private – Company G, 1st Michigan Engineers – Enlisted 6-2-1864 – Discharged 9-22-1865 – P.O. Sylvania – Discharge lost.

29. Lester Decker – Private – Company 67 – Ohio Infantry – Enlisted 10-10-1861 – Discharged 7-8-1865 – P.O. Sylvania – loss of left upper arm.

30. William Bryan – Private – Company B, 124th Ohio Infantry – Enlisted 8-4-1862 – Discharged – 6-8-1865 – 2 years 10 month 4 days – P.O. Sylvania – gunshot wound in right femur.

31. Thomas B. Hank – Private – Company A, 171st Ohio Infantry – Enlisted 4-27-1864 – Discharged 8-20-1864 – 4 months 23 days – P.O. Sylvania.

32. William W. Richardson – Private – Company H, 8th Ohio Infantry – Enlisted 4-25-1861 – Discharged 7-24-1861 – 3 months 4 days and Sergeant, Company F, 128th Ohio Infantry – Enlisted 12-24-1863 Discharged 7-13-1865 – 1 year 10 months 26 days – P.O. Sylvania.

33. James E. Avery – 1st Lieutenant – Company B, 4th Michigan Infantry – Enlisted 5-16-1861 – Discharged 12-4-1862 – 1 year 6 months 18 days – P.O. Sylvania.

34. John H. Parker – Private – Company G, 130th Ohio Infantry – Enlisted 5-2-1864 – Discharged 9-22-1864 – 4 months 20 days – P.O. Sylvania.

35. Hiram W. Wellman – Sergeant, Company L, 16th Illinois Calvary – Enlisted 12-20-1862 – Discharged 8-29-1865 – 2 years 8 months – P.O. Sylvania – gunshot wound of left cheek.

36. Lyman Upham – Corp. – Company D, 4th Mass. Infantry – Enlisted 5-22-1861 – Discharged 7-22-1863 – 2 years 3 months 14 days – P.O. Sylvania.

37. Mary E. Allen – formerly widow of Oscar H. Bellman – Private – Company K, 18th Michigan Infantry – Enlisted 8-12-1862 – Discharged 6-26-1865 – 3 years 1 month 0 days – P.O. Sylvania – died of heart disease.

38. Lydia King – formerly widow of Leander H. Dean – Private – Company G, 130th Ohio Infantry – Enlisted 5-2-1864 – Discharged 9-22-1864 – 4 months 18 days – 4 months 18 days – P.O. Sylvania.

39. Alfred G. Clark – Private, Company G, 18th U.S. Infantry – Enlisted 8-2-1862 – Discharged 8-2-1865 – 3 years 0 months 0 days – P.O. Sylvania.

40. John Gahring – Private, Company K, 28th Ohio Infantry – Enlisted 2-23-1864 – 3-31-1866 – 2 years 1 month seven days – P.O. Sylvania.

41. Charles F. Hasty – Private, Company F, 14th Ohio Infantry – Enlisted March 1863 – Discharged 1865 – P.O. Richards – lost his discharge could not remember date of enlistment.

42. Charles Hibbard – P.O. Sylvania - deserter and would not answer any question about soldier record.

43. Mathias Forer – Private – Company B – 182nd Ohio Infantry – Enlisted 9-9-1863 Discharged 7-7-1864 – P.O. Sylvania – visiting family did not have his solider record.

44. George Helfer – Private, Company?, 189th Ohio Infantry – Enlisted 9-26-1864 Discharged 6-19-1865 – 1 year 3 months 7 days – P.O. Sylvania.

45. Chester H. Decker – Private, Company G. 130th Ohio Infantry – Enlisted 2-28-1865 Discharged 8-31-1865 – 4 months 25 days – P.O. Sylvania.

46. Joseph Distell – Private, Company H, 2nd N.Y. Heavy Artillery – Enlisted 10-22-1861 – Discharged 12-28-1863 – 2 years 2 months 6 days – P.O. Sylvania.

47. Frederick Hartman – Private, Company D, 195th Ohio Infantry – Enlisted 2-28-1865 Discharged 8-31-1865 – 4 months – P.O. Sylvania.

48. John W. Laimon – Sergeant – Company E, 1st Missouri Eng. Corp. – Enlisted 7-26-1861 – Discharged 9-14-1864 – 3 years 1 month 18 days – P.O. Sylvania.

49. William C. Fletcher – Sergeant – Company H, 111th Ohio Infantry – Enlisted 8-15-1862 – Discharged 6-27-1865 – 2 years 10 months 12 days – P.O. Sylvania – disability - deafness.

50. Jesse A. Fletcher – Sergeant – Company A, 9th Michigan Calvary – Enlisted 10-20-1862 Discharged 7-21-1865 – 2 years 8 months 19 days – P.O. Sylvania.

51. Harriet A. Hubbard, formerly wife of John VanOrman – Private, Company F, 14th Ohio Infantry – Enlisted 8-5-1864 – Discharged – no date listed. P.O. Sylvania – Date of death unknown.

52. Cynthia P. Potter, widow of Oliver Potter – Private, Company M, 8th Michigan Cavalry – Enlisted 6-3-1864 Discharged 12-21-1864 – 6 months 18 days – P.O. Sylvania.

53. Orville R. Hine – Private, Company E, 186 Ohio Infantry – Enlisted 2-10-1865 – Discharged 9-15-1865 – 7 months 3 days – P.O. Sylvania.

54. Thomas Gibbs – Private, Company H, 92 Ohio Infantry – Enlisted 11-18-1864 – Discharged 7-20-1865 – 8 months 2 days – P.O. Sylvania

55. James Youngs – Private, Company K, 67th Ohio Infantry – no dates listed – gunshot wound in right forearm – papers burned.

56. Mary Youngs, formerly widow of S. Chapple – Private, Company H, 111th Ohio Infantry – Enlisted 8-15-1862 Discharged – no date – date of death unknown.

57. Ambrose Comstock – Private, Company G, 130th Ohio Infantry – Enlisted 5-21-1864 – Discharged 9-22-1864 – 4 months 1 day – P.O. Sylvania.

58. James H. Burdo – Private, Company K, 25th Ohio Infantry – Enlisted 2-29-1864 – Discharged – 8-25-1865 – 1 year 6 months 18 days – P.O. Sylvania.

59. John H. Forbes – Private, Company G, 110 N.Y. Infantry – Enlisted 8-12-1862 – Discharged 3-4-1863 – 6 months 22 days – P.O. Sylvania - injury caused by bruise – side to back.

60. Romes G. Burns – Lieutenant, Company B, 8th N.Y. Heavy Artillery – Enlisted 7-28-1862 – Discharged 6-5-1865 – 2 years 5 months 23 days – P.O. Sylvania.

61. Benjamin F. Rapp – Private, Company E, 110th Ohio Infantry – Enlisted 8-21-1862 Discharged 9-4-1865 – 3 years 0 months 13 days – P.O. Sylvania.

62. William H. Hoag – Private, Company A, 18th U.S. Infantry – Enlisted 8-26-1862 Discharged 8-26-1865 – 3 years 0 months 0 days – P.O. Sylvania.

63. Oliver P. Clark – Corp., Company E, 1st Ohio Light Artillery – Enlisted 9-26-1861 Discharged 9-26-1864 – 3 years 0 months 0 days – P.O. Sylvania.

64. Samuel V. Bell – Private, Company H, 31st Ohio Infantry – Enlisted 9-10-1863 then Private, Company G, 12th Vet. R Discharged 9-14-1864 – 3 years 0 months 4 days – P.O. Sylvania.

65. Blanchard Osborn – Private, Company I, 47th Ohio Infantry – Enlisted 6-15-1861 Discharged 8-20-1864 – 3 years 2 months 5 days – P.O. Sylvania – piles and chronic dia.

66. Adelaide H. Webb widow of William J. Webb – Private, Company M, 8th Michigan Calvary – Enlisted 8-13-1864 – Discharged 5-16-1865 – 9 months days – P.O. Sylvania.

67. William Cherry – Private, Company E, 7th Ohio Infantry – Enlisted 6-3-1861 Discharged 11-19-1862 – 1 year 5 months 16 days – P.O. Sylvania.

68. Lucinda Hallett, formerly widow of Enos Partridge – Private, Company H, 111th Ohio Infantry – Enlisted 8-15-1862 Discharged – no dates listed – P.O. Sylvania.

69. William J. Smith – Private, Company A, 14th Michigan Infantry – Enlisted Feb. 1862 Discharged Nov. 1862 – 9 months – P.O. Sylvania.

70. Andrew J. Friend – Private, Company K, 152nd Indiana Infantry – Enlisted 3-8-1865 Discharged 8-30-1865 – 5 months 22 days.

71. Henry G. Glasser – Private, Company F, 37th Ohio Infantry – Enlisted 9-5-1861 Discharged 1-14-1863 – 1 year, 4 months 4 days. P.O. Sylvania.

72. Lyman B. Stone – Private – Company K, 25th Ohio Infantry – Enlisted 7-19-1861 Discharged 1-16-1864 – 3 years 5 months 16 days – P.O. Sylvania.

73. Mary C. Cartwright, formerly widow of William Hackett – No enlistment or discharge dates recorded – P.O. Sylvania – remarks – could not tell company regt. nor when W.H. enlisted.

74. John W. Cooper – Private, Company B, 14th Ohio Infantry – Enlisted 4-20-1861 Discharge 8-13-1861 – 3 months 23 days.

75. Albert McIlrath – Private, Company E, 103rd Ohio Infantry – Enlisted 8-6-1862 Discharged 6-12-1865 – 2 years 11 months 6 days – P.O. Sylvania – shock to brain and spinal cord.

76. Isaac J. Ordiway – Wagoner, Company M, 17th Michigan Infantry – Enlisted 4-18-1861 Discharged 8-7-1861 – 3 months 19 days – P.O. Auburndale – injury in left side by kick of a horse.

77. Isaac J. Ordiway – Wagoner, Company A, 17th Michigan Infantry – Enlisted 8-18-1862 Discharged 6-3-1865 – 2 years 10 months 15 days – P.O. Auburndale.

78. Daniel B. Tracy – no information – remarks – D.B.T. away from home, wife could not tell Company, Regt., enlistment date or discharge date.

79. Lydia O. Joy, formerly widow of David (unable to read name) – Private, Company A, 12th New York Cavalry – Enlisted 8-13-1862 Discharged 2-2-1864 – 1 year 5 months 25 days – Auburndale – killed in service.

80. John D. Symington – Corp., Light Battery, Steamer Autocast – no dates listed and no remarks – P.O. Auburndale.

81. Angeline Seager, widow of Frank M. Seager – Private, Company A, 14th Ohio Infantry, Enlisted 2-27-1862 – Discharged 7-11-1865 – 3 years 4 months 12 days – P. O. Sylvania – gunshot wound in left leg.

82. Jacob C. Decker – Private, Company G, 130th Ohio Infantry – Enlisted 5-2-1864 Discharged 9-22-1864 – 4 months 20 days – P.O. Sylvania.

83. Johnson Duffield – Private, Company A, 4th Michigan Infantry – Enlisted 6-20-1861 Discharged 7-6-1864 – 3 years 0 months 16 years – P.O. Sylvania.

84. Adolph Webber – no information and no dates recorded – P.O. Sylvania.

85. Catherine Smith, widow of Miner W. Smith – Corp. Company D, 4th Michigan Infantry – Enlisted 8-18-1864 Discharged 6-13-1866 – P.O. Sylvania.

86. Leonard H. Bragdon – Sergt. Company E, 17th Infantry, U.S. Veteran Reserve Corps – Enlisted 7-26-1864 Discharged 6-17-1865 – P.O. Sylvania.

87. Lyman B. Stone – Private, Company K, 75th Ohio Infantry – Enlisted 1-16-1864 Discharged 7-16-1864 – P.O. Sylvania.

88. Samuel V. Bell – Private, Company G, 12th V – Enlisted 2-18-1864 Discharged 9-14-1864 – P.O. Sylvania.

89. Lyman Upham – Corporal – Company D, 4th Mass. Infantry – Enlisted 9-17-1862 Discharged 8-25-1863.

A "Soldiers' Relief Disbursing List For Sylvania Village" that was dated 9-1-1920 said the following: "Auditor's Office, Lucas County, Ohio – To the Clerk of above named Township: The within is a list of the names of the persons in your said Township to whom relief has been awarded, and the amount payable monthly to each under the laws for the relief of honorably discharged indigent soldiers, sailors and marines of the United States, and the indigent wives, parents, widows and minor children under fifteen years of age, of such indigent or deceased soldiers sailors or marines." Signed Gabe Cooper, County Auditor.

Name: Adah Elliott – Amount per month - $8.00 - Residence – Sylvania, Ohio."

After reviewing the local newspapers through the 1930s one of the last obituary notices published for a Civil War veteran living in Sylvania was Charles C. Armstrong. The 7-9-1936 *Sylvania Sentinel* reported the following: "Civil War Veteran Dies In Home Of Son – Charles C. Armstrong Passed Away At Age of 93 Years, After Illness of Several Months – Funeral Services for Charles C. Armstrong, 93, a Civil War veteran, will be held from the Reeb Funeral Home on Saturday at 2 p.m. He was well known in Sylvania, having spent much of the time during the past ten years in the home of his son, William Addison Armstrong of North Main Street. For the past several months Mr. Armstrong has been ill at the home of another son, C.D. Armstrong, of Jutland Rd, West Toledo, where he passed away. Mr. Armstrong was born at Lockport, N.Y., on 12-1-1842, and came to Toledo with his parents at the age of 10 years, to a farm home near what was then called Manhattan. After the Civil War his parents purchased a farm on Monroe Street, and while living there Mr. Armstrong was married to Miss Frances Brainard of Ida, Michigan. For several years they lived in Wood County and then moved to the Brainard farm near where they resided until the death of Mrs. Armstrong ten years ago. At the age of 21, Mr. Armstrong enlisted in Company I of the 128th Ohio Regiment at Toledo, and after two months of training at Camp Cleveland he was assigned to guard duty at Johnson's Island, the prison camp at which Confederate officers were confined. Later he was transferred to Lima, Ohio and detailed as provost guard in that vicinity, following which he was again transferred to the island for guard duty. Surviving besides the two sons are two daughters, Mrs. Harry Carroll, of Ida, and Mrs. Otto Miller of Monroe, Michigan; eight grandchildren and five great-grandchildren. Interment will be in Memorial Park Cemetery."

GRAND ARMY OF THE REPUBLIC (G.A.R.) - PAGE POST NO. 471 & PAGE CORPS NO. 60, WOMEN'S RELIEF CORPS

In 1866 The Grand Army of the Republic (G.A.R.) was founded in Decatur, Illinois. This society was founded to strengthen fellowship among men who fought to preserve the Union, to honor those killed in the War, to provide care for their dependents, and to uphold the Constitution. It was a fraternal organization consisting of veterans who served in the American Civil War for the Northern/Federal forces. Membership was open to honorably discharged soldiers, sailors or marines of the Union armed forces who served between 4-12-1861 and 4-9-1865. In the 1870's and 1880's, the men of these G.A.R. organizations were reportedly an important political force in the north, especially in the Republican Party. The Grand Army had 409,489 members in the U.S. in 1890. It had one women member, Sarah Edmonds. She had served in the Civil War disguised as a man. The last member of the Grand Army of the Republic, Albert H. Wollson, died in 1956, and the organization was discontinued at that time.

In 1868 the National Commander-in-Chief of the G.A.R. issued a general order designating May 30th of that year "for the purpose of strewing flowers and otherwise decorating the graves of comrades who died in defense of their country during the late rebellion" adding that he hoped that a Decoration Day would continue to be observed year after year. Soon it became a legal holiday known as Decoration Day and then later better known as Memorial Day.

The G.A.R. was active in relief work, working on pension legislation for veterans and finding homes for veterans. They started the celebration of Decoration Day in the North by a general order issued by John A. Logan. The Woman's Relief Corps began as a G.A.R. women's auxiliary.

Sylvania residents who had served in the Civil War first organized a G.A.R. post in Sylvania in 1867 and according to the minutes of Sylvania Village Council dated 6-21-1867 the mayor presented a petition from Post No. 225 G.A.R. requesting to lease the council room to hold their monthly meetings. Council appointed a committee of two to make the arrangements for the use of the room. No other information is mentioned in the council minute books, and I found nothing else regarding the original G.A.R. Post in Sylvania until 1884.

Sylvania's G.A.R. Post was re-organized in 1884 under the name of Page Post No. 471 of Sylvania, and took its name from Sylvania resident Harlan Page, age 19 years, who was mortally wounded early in the Civil War while serving as a Private in Company K, 25th Regiment of the Ohio Volunteer Infantry. Harlan Page had lived in Sylvania and was the son of Jefferson and Emeline Page. Jefferson, Harlan's father, died when Harlan was young. Harlan Page was buried in the Pleasant View Cemetery in Blissfield, Michigan, beside his father, Jefferson Page, who died 2-27-1848. Harlan Page died also on February 27th, but in 1862 at the age of 19 years, 11 months, 13 days. His mother, Emeline, had remarried on 1-14-1849 to Andrew Printup, a very prominent man in Sylvania. When the 1850 census was taken in Sylvania Township, Harlan is listed living at home at the age of 7 years, with his stepfather and mother, and with his step-brothers and step-sisters, as well as his sisters Mary and Lois Page. At this census Harlan is listed as attending school. Harlan's mother and Andrew Printup were divorced shortly after the 1860 census was taken, and later Emeline B. Printup is found as a resident of Adrian, Michigan. When she died she was then buried in Pleasant View Cemetery in Blissfield, Michigan.

Here's why Sylvania's G.A.R. organization was named after Harlan Page: On 7-10-1861 Harlan Page entered service at the age of 18. He served faithfully until 12-13-1861, when in the fierce engagement at Baldwin's Camp, West Virginia, 400 Union troops, through deception by a spy, were induced to attack 5,000 Rebels, trusting to re-enforcements which owing to delay, failed to arrive. Nine of their soldiers were killed and 35 were injured. Harlan Page of Sylvania was one that was wounded when his collar bone was shattered. For 18 days he lay in camp pleading, "Oh, take me home to die." Responding to such imploring appeal, eight devoted comrades, some of them Sylvanians, carried Harlan Page some sixty miles to the nearest railroad. At Huttonsville, Harlan bade farewell to his friends and assured them that though he might never again be fit for service, he would, if able, return to cheer them by his presence. First Lieutenant, Nathaniel Haughton, of Company K telegraphed Sylvania telling them that Harlan Page was on his way home. He came home on 2-20-1862. Finally reaching home, he exclaimed "Oh how I have prayed for this hour!" His wound forbade all hope of recovery. Among his last utterances was "Oh, do not pray for my recovery; but rather, that I may rest and go home." He lived a week after and died on 2-27-1862. His commanding officer wrote the following: "Thus, in the short period of six months, had this boy exhibited the highest qualities and paid the extreme sacrifice of the true patriot and brave soldier." And another record found among the papers at the Sylvania Area Historical Society said: "The eight noble comrades of Harlan Page, by whose remarkable devotion he was enabled to reach home, and friends, were all his Company, viz: Lyman B. Stone, aged 18, wounded at Chancellorsville, 5-8-1863, and mustered out July 1864 at the expiration of his term; Werter H. Shaffer, aged 18, who served three years and was mustered out, July 1864; William Vickory, aged 21, wounded at the battle of McDowell, Virginia, 5-8-1862; James Moran, aged 22, wounded at Bull Run, August 1862, and discharged January 1863, on Surgeon's certificate of disability; James Smith; John Klinck; Michael Herbert, aged 19, killed at Chancellorsville, 5-2-1863; and Charles A. DeBolt, aged 19, wounded 5-8-1862 at McDowell, and veteranized on expiration of his term. It is due to the other members of the company here to state, that many of them offered to go with Page, if needed."

On 7-5-1884 the Grand Army of the Republic – Ex-soldiers of the Civil War of Sylvania Township met, with Captain I.P. Grover of the Forsyth Post, No. 15 present. The original officers of the re-organized Sylvania G.A.R. were:

William Bryan, Commander
O.P. Clark, Senior Vice Commander
E.F. Sawyer, Junior Vice Commander
Thomas B. Hanks, Quartermaster
M.A. Whitney, Sergeant
Malcolm Beach, Chaplin
James E. Avery – Officer of the Day
Daniel Donovan, Officer of the Guard
A.V. Comstock, Quartermaster Sergeant

According to the *Toledo Evening Bee* dated 7-14-1884 under the heading of Sylvania, Ohio it said: "At a meeting of ex-Soldiers held 6-21-1884, it was proposed to organize a Grand Army Post at Sylvania and in due time a charter was applied for and other necessary arrangements made, and accordingly on Saturday, July 5, a post of 30 members was duly organized and mustered by Capt. I.P. Grover, assisted by Col. Terry of the Forsyth Post, No. 15 of Toledo, by order of State Commander. It is expected that we will have a membership of 60 to 70 soon."

The Officers of Sylvania's G.A.R. listed in 1888 were:

William Bryan, Commander
E.F. Sawyer, Senior Vice Commander
Francis M. Segur, Junior Vice Commander
Samuel V. Bell, Adjutant
Lester B. Decker, Quartermaster
Lyman B. Upham, Surgeon
R.G. Burns, Chaplain

Thomas B. Hanks, Officer of the Day
Francis Little, Officer of the Guard
William Webb, Sergeant Major
A.D. Randall, Quartermaster Sergeant

In 1888 the following was the roster of ex-soldiers who were members of the Page Post No. 471 of Sylvania:

William Bryan, Corporal, Co. A, 124th O.V.I.
O.P. Clark, Corporal, Battery E, First O.V.L.A.
Arthur Hotchkiss, Co. K., 25th O.V.I.
Amos Gayhart, Co. G, 130th Ohio National Guard
J.W. Cooper, Corporal, Co. F, 14th O.V.I.
E.F. Sawyer, Sergeant Co. B, 18th U.S.I.
William J. Webb, Co. M, 8th Michigan U.C.
Daniel Donovan, Sergeant, Co. C 1st O.V.C.
Charles S. Bemis, Co. H. 3rd, Ohio Volunteer Calvary
M.K. Grover, Co. G. 130th Ohio National Guard
Thomas B. Hank, Co. A, 171st Ohio National Guard
A.B. Comstock – Co. G. 13th Ohio National Guard
David Dolby, Co. C, 3rd Ohio Volunteer Calvary
James E. Avery – 2nd Lieut. Co. B, 4th Michigan V.I.
A.D. Randall, Q.M. Sergt. Co. B, 186th O.V.I.
J.L. Steck, Co. A, 18th Michigan V.I.
William Cherry, Co. E, 7th O.V.I.
Francis Little Co. B, 123rd O.V.I.
Jared Ward, Co. F, 26th, Michigan V.I.
A.G. Clark, Co. G, 18th, United States Infantry
Ralf Vanhouten, Co. C, 52nd Illinois V.I.
Asa Bordeaux, Co. F, 14th O.V.I.
Malcolm Beach, Co. G, 130th Ohio National Guard
John Brimacomb – Co. B, 128th O.V.I.
Peter Brideling, Co. I, 14th O.V.I.
Lewis Ostrander, Co. F, 14th O.V.I.
Ira Beverly, Co. E, 100th O.V.I.
Eli Trombley, Co. K, 18th Michigan V.I.
D.P. Whitney, Co. A. 4th Illinois Volunteer Calvary
F.M. Seager, Co. A, 14th Ohio Volunteer Infantry
M.H. Thornton, Co. H, 29th Indiana Volunteer Infantry
Lester B. Decker, Co. F, 67th Ohio Volunteer Infantry
S.R. Thornton, Co. H, 29th Indiana Volunteer Infantry
Alfred Fay, Co. B, 2nd Michigan Volunteer Calvary
Edwin Vesey, Co. K, 24th Michigan Volunteer Calvary
Samuel V. Bell, Co. H, 31st Ohio Volunteer Calvary
C.L. Roberts, Co. K, 3rd Ohio Volunteer Calvary

O.R. Hine, Co. E, 186th Ohio Volunteer Calvary

H.M. Steck, Co. H, 15th Michigan Volunteer Calvary

Leonard H. Bragdon, Sergeant, Co. H, 111th Ohio V.I.

James Brimon, Co. E, 100th Ohio Volunteer Infantry

Casper Capaul, Co., F, 14th Ohio Volunteer Infantry

Frank Burt, 2nd Lieut. Co. A 121st N.Y. V.I.

Chester H. Decker, Co. G. 130th Ohio National Guard

Charles W. Mersereau, Co. B, 128th O.V.I.

John H. Parker, Co. G, 130th Ohio National Guard

Edwin Montgomery, Co. K, 25th Ohio Volunteer Infantry

Ebenezer Roberts, Co. K, 3rd Ohio Volunteer Calvary

A.J. Goodall, Co. H, 11th Michigan Volunteer Calvary

J.D. Disotell, Battery H, 2nd N.Y.V.H.A.

Joseph King, Corporal Co. I, 40th Illinois V.I.

Lyman Upham, Corporal, Co. D, 4th Mass V.M.

J.H. Call, Co. K, 18th Michigan V.I.

A.P. Albring, Co. K, 18th Michigan Volunteer Infantry

William Hallett, Co. A, 67th Ohio Volunteer Infantry

John Smith, Co. K, 25th Ohio Volunteer Infantry

John Baker, Co. K, 25th Ohio Volunteer Infantry

Adelbert Lewis, Co. B, 130th Ohio National Guard

George F. Chandler, Co. H. 111th Ohio Volunteer Infantry

Johnson Duffield, Sergeant, Co. A. 4th Michigan Volunteer Inf.

A.G. Washburn, Co. F, 14th Ohio Volunteer Infantry

Byron Tripp, Co. F, 14th Ohio Volunteer Infantry

James Garring, Co. K, 25th Ohio Volunteer Infantry

Henry Glaser, Co. F, 37th Ohio Volunteer Infantry

J.E. Albring, Co. D, 8th Michigan Volunteer Calvary

R.G. Burns, 1st Lt, Battery B, 8th N.Y. Art.

J.H. Burdo, Co. K, 25th Ohio Volunteer Infantry

Aloyce Reger, Co. K, 25th Ohio Volunteer Infantry

M.A. Whitney, Co. G, 130th Ohio National Guard

The Sylvania Women's Relief Corps was organized as an auxiliary of the Grand Army of the Republic, and they were chartered under the name Page Corps No. 60, Women's Relief Corp bearing the date of 10-31-1884. The goal was to aid and memorialize the Grand Army of the Republic, assist the needy Union Veterans, their families and orphans, to perpetuate the memory of those who fell in battle and to instill lessons of patriotism in the children of the land. As time went on they provided local nursing scholarships, made bandages for veterans, provided Christmas baskets for veterans and raised funds to be donated for memorials to veterans' hospitals and cemeteries. They were very active during World War I and World War II. During World War II they worked at Surgical Dressing Stations at Maplewood school in order to make dressings for the wounded helped by the Red Cross.

The *Sylvania Weekly Times* dated 9-1-1892 reported: "Hiram Wellman, Jessie Fletcher, Chester L. Roberts and a number of other Grand Army men of this city are attending the National encampment of the G.A.R.'s at Washington, D.C."

The following announcement appeared in the *Sylvania Weekly Times* in September of 1892: "ATTENTION COMRADES. Headquarters Page Post No. 471, Department of Ohio, G.A.R. Every comrade of Page Post is earnestly requested to be present at our next meeting Oct. 1, 1892, as business of great importance to the Post will be presented; do not fail to be present comrades. T.B. HANK, Post Commander."

Also in the *Sylvania Weekly Times* newspaper dated 9-1-1892 it was reported, under the column titled "Camp Fire Notes" the following article: "Wednesday evening the Grand Army of the Republic, Women's Relief Corp., S of V's and L.A.S. (Ladies Aid Society) held a camp fire and entertainment at the G.A.R. hall. The following program was rendered in a very able manner and was well received by the large number present. Opening song – "America" Recitation by Jimmy Stone; Song by Sarah Adsit; Recitation by Vern Seager; Song – "Tramp, Tramp." Following this excellent program was a debate on the subject of: "Should women be debarred from voting" Mrs. Clara Hank opened the debate for the affirmative by reading a most excellent and carefully prepared paper and one which brought forth loud applause especially from the ladies and scored many points for victory. The next was William Reger for the Negative who scored a point by stating that he thought women had ought to be satisfied as they controlled nearly everything except the voting. E.C. Edson was the next man on the affirmatives list and one would judge to hear his plea for the gentle sex, that he imagined they were all angels, never the less his points of argument were well sustained and from historical facts. Mrs. Flora Edson was next on the Negatives list and in a few well-chosen words stated that women had all they could attend to properly at home without trying to run the elections. William Bryan, the silver tongued orator and past commander of Page Post, was next on the affirmatives list and in his good natured way scored many points of victory for the women. R.G. Burns and a number of others were called upon to take part in the debate, but none of them responded. After the closing remarks of William Reger and Mrs. Hank, Chairman Hank declared the debate closed and called on Judges, Lester Stone, William Hine and C. Adsit for their verdict, which was for the affirmative, and the ladies were given three ringing cheers. After which the ladies served hot coffee and lunch. This style of entertainment is the proper movement to keep the above named orders in harmony, and it is amusing as well as entertaining."

In 1941 Mr. A.H. Randall, a life-long resident of Sylvania, and past Mayor of Sylvania, is quoted as saying: "Do you remember when the G.A.R. and the Women's Relief Corps met in the hall over what is now the Ohio Tailor store (6601 Monroe), and the camp fire held there in the back, with William Bryan commander of the G.A.R. and Julia Lathrop president of the Women's Relief Corps?"

Sylvania's G.A.R. never owned their own building, but instead rented the second floor of various buildings in the downtown Sylvania district. As mentioned, their first hall was located on the second floor of a building that was located at 6601 Monroe Street. Other buildings they rented over the years included the second floor of the building at 5645 Main Street (this hall was also known as P.H.C. Hall). (Today in 2017 this is the Hudson Gallery building); the second floor of the building at 5675 Main Street (Today in 2017 this is occupied by TK Lane's Boutique); and the second floor of the building at 5661 Main Street (Today in 2017 this is occupied by Pro Music).

At the same time that Sylvania's G.A.R. organization occupied these buildings, their women's auxiliary group, known as the Women's Relief Corps (W.R.C.), also met in the same building and usually on the same evening, but in separate rooms, or a large room divided by a large divider.

According to a story written by Kathryn Keller in 1975 that appeared in the *Sylvania Herald*, which she wrote after reading through the old minutes of the G.A.R., and the W.R.C., "One detects womanly initiatives in the G.A.R. records from time to time – i.e. – Sept. 1897 when a W.R.C. committee visited the G.A.R. to announce "They were desirous of procuring new window curtains." In 1901 there was a redecorating project. The G.A.R. made repairs to the hall and painted the woodwork, white, one coat. The W.R.C. completed the décor "by hanging paper in a manner to suit themselves" – "cost to the Post $3.10." Another part of the article said: "In the summer of 1903 the ladies needed larger quarters. A partition in the hall was to be moved as far east as possible leaving sufficient landing at the head of the stairs. A G.A.R. committee was to attend to the matter." By September nothing was done by the committee, and they were empowered to hire a carpenter. By November, still nothing done. The W.R.C. suggested that it swap rooms with the G.A.R. The boys voted that down, whereupon the partition was "rearranged" as reported on Dec. 5, 1903, with a bill from the Sylvania Lumber Co., for materials used – 42 cents. Less than a year later one of the comrades was favoring the G.A.R. with a vocal solo that caused the partition to fall down! If the truth were known, it was probably not the singer's lungs that gave the old gentlemen such a good laugh that it was entered into the minutes."

And while the G.A.R. and the W.R.C. were renting the second floor of the various buildings, they were sub-renting to other organizations. For instance, the minutes of 12-5-1897 reported that Enterprise Tent of K.O.T.M. (Knights of the Maccabees) continued their yearly lease for meetings. Then on 11-15-1902 it was noted that Enterprise Hive of L.O.T.M. (Ladies of the Maccabees) rented the G.A.R. hall for a Thanksgiving Supper. And the Woodmen of the World rented the G.A.R. hall, but it was noted that their meetings were to be so scheduled so as not to conflict with the G.A.R., W.R.C., and Maccabees meetings. Then on 1-11-1904 the Oddfellows (I.O.O.F.) rented the hall for their banquet.

In 1904 it was reported in an article in the *Sylvania Sun* newspaper dated 11-10-1904 that Steve Young and Preston Randall were in business in the building at 5661 Main Street, and it was noted that their store was located under the G.A.R. hall. So that tells us that in 1904 the G.A.R. hall was located above the business at 5661 Main Street. In Sylvania, as Memorial Day arrived, the G.A.R. and W.R.C. prepared for the day. The Veterans assembled at the G.A.R. hall, and they paraded to the cemeteries, decorated the graves of their old comrades and listened to patriotic addresses in the Grove (today the "grove" property is occupied by the Southbriar Shopping complex at Main and Convent).

One of the pages from the minutes of the WRC was dated 11-4-1911 and said: "Motion was made by Mrs. Richie Cooper, supported by Mrs. Vesey that Charlie Dolph be instructed to place a flag on the casket of every soldier in the future, whether he is a member of the G.A.R. or not. Penny collection amounted to 17 cents, members present, 21, officers present, eight. There being no further business to come before the meeting, we closed in due form with a flag salute. Surrendered in F.C. and L. by Clara Earl, Corps Secretary."

The following article appeared in the *Sylvania Sentinel* on 7-22-1915: "Thursday July 29 is the Annual Reunion of W.R.C. & G.A.R., at the home of Mrs. Eva Eldridge on the property of Charles Rockenstyre. Members are requested to be present."

In 1934 the Women's Relief Corp announced that they were celebrating their 50th year (1884) and then in 1942, according to the local newspaper, this auxiliary to the Grand Army of Republic held their 50th annual convention (1892) held at the Methodist Church with over 200 guests present. (The Methodist Church at this time was located at 5720 Main Street, now in 2017 the parking lot of Reeb Funeral Home). In 1960 they said they were celebrating 76 years of service (1884). The first president of Page Relief Corps No. 60 was Julia Lathrop. She was followed by Katy Bryan and Sophia Mercereau. Mrs. Flora Edson held that office for 32 years and the Corps placed a wreath on her grave every Memorial Day after services were held at Association Cemetery. Florence Beveridge was the Corps musician for 25 years or more.

According to an article in the *Sylvania Sentinel* dated 8-1-1935 Mr. and Mrs. Henry Brown entertained the members of the W.R.C. and their families at a picnic supper at their home on Monroe Street.

The *Sylvania Sentinel* dated 7-4-1941 reads: "Only eleven veterans of the Civil War registered for the annual encampment of the Ohio G.A.R. held in Columbus June 24-26. The age list was from 91 to 96. A camp fire held on the State House grounds was addressed by Governor Bricker. Around 1900 these annual encampments were good for an attendance of from 50,000 to 100,000."

The 10-13-1971 *Sylvania Sentinel* featured a photo on the front page. The caption reads: "Women's Relief Corp officials posed for the camera during the 79th annual district convention of the auxiliary to the Grand Army of the Republic last week in Sylvania. Shown from left are: Evelyn Gaeth, patriotic instructor; Mabel Finder, dept. treasurer; Ida Straight, dept. president; and Eloise Brown, district president. Page Corp No. 60 served as the host group for the event."

In a letter that Lulu White Lindsey wrote in the late 1970s she said that Etta Randall (maiden name Green, daughter of Dr. Horace Green) and Flora Edson used to go to the schools and present flags to the classrooms and make patriotic speeches. She said that they were W.R.C. ladies and always were in charge of decorating the soldier's graves and she and the other children would march and put wreaths over the flags on the graves.

In 1983 the *Sylvania Sentinel* newspaper featured a photo of the following women who were members of the Women's Relief Corps: Betty Fallis, Lucilla Hall, Marie Fowler, Naomi Jenkins, Mina Stillwell, Florence Turner and Frances Murr. The caption under the photo reads: "99 years and still going. The 100ᵗʰ anniversary of the founding of the Women's Relief Corps will be observed in 1984."

This Women's Relief Corp continued to meet until they were 110 years and finally disbanded in 1994 because they only had six remaining active members who ranged from 70 years to 90 years old. The six final members included: Elizabeth Gallup, Naomi Jenkins, Floris Smith, Marie Fowler, Betty Fallis and Ida Webb. The last president of the organization was Naomi Jenkins.

I have been unable to determine exactly when the Sylvania G.A.R. Post stopped meeting, but as mentioned the Women's Relief Corp continued to meet until 1994 and when they disbanded they donated all their records, original charter and other memorabilia to the Sylvania Area Historical Society. The original members of the Women's Relief Corp of Sylvania were: Julia Lathrop, Clara Hank, Helen Roberts, Louisa Decker, Elnor Clark, Margaret Glaser, Minerva Bragdon, Julia Donovan, Hattie Davis, Mahala Thorpe, Fran Forbes, Caty Bryan, Olive Thornton, Dollie Thornton, Angeline Vesey, Emeline Cherry and Louisa Bridling.

SPANISH-AMERICAN WAR

This was a brief conflict between the United States and Spain that took place between April and August 1898. This war was over the issue of the liberation of Cuba. In this war Spain relinquished sovereignty over Cuba, cedes the Philippine Islands, Puerto Rico, and Guam to the United States for the sum of $20 million.

The *Toledo Blade* dated 4-25-1898 reported "War Is Formally Declared – President Recommends Such Action By Congress – Special Message Sent To General Assembly Today – Spain First Took Action – The President today sent congress the following message, recommending a declaration of war against Spain: To the senate and house of representatives of the United States of America, I transmit to the congress, for its consideration and appropriate action, copies of correspondence recently had with the representative of Spain in the United States, with the United States minister at Madrid, and, through the latter, with the government of Spain, showing the action taken under the joint resolution approved April 20, 1898, for the recognition of the independence of the people of Cuba, demanding that the government of Spain relinquish its authority and government in the island of Cuba, and to withdraw its land and naval forces from Cuba and Cuba's waters, and directing the President of the United States to use the land and naval forces of the United States to carry these resolutions into effect."

The main battles of this war took place around Santiago de Cuba. The U.S. Army and Navy played key roles in this war. It was the Spanish-American War that led to the building of the Panama Canal.

The U.S. won this war, and this war served to further repair relations between the American North and South. The war gave both sides a common enemy for the first time since the end of the Civil War in 1865, and many friendships were formed between soldiers of northern and southern states during their tours of duty. This was an important development, since many soldiers in this war were the children of Civil War veterans on both sides.

The U.S. casualties and losses were as follows:

U.S. Army – 345 dead; 577 wounded; and 2,565 diseased.
U.S. Navy – 16 dead; and 68 wounded.

This war cost the United States $250 million. 90 percent of the lives lost in this war were from Yellow fever, typhoid fever and other infectious diseases.

The 6th Ohio Volunteer Infantry was formed in Toledo, Ohio, and is where men from Sylvania would have joined. On 4-29-1898 the unit left by rail for Columbus, Ohio, where on 5-12-1898 the unit was mustered into service. On 5-17-1898 the 6th Ohio departed for Camp George H. Thomas on the grounds of the former Civil War battlefield at Chickamauga. The camp was overcrowded, lacked in sanitation, clean water, etc. and disease spread rapidly. While at Camp Thomas the fighting of the war had ended with an armistice on 8-12-1898, however the war continued officially until the signing of the Treaty of Paris on 12-10-1898. They ended up at Camp Polland, Tennessee. The 6th then went to Charleston, South Carolina on 12-27-1898 and then boarded the Minnewaska heading for Cuba and arriving at Cienfuegos on 1-4-1899 and stayed to occupy the new lands acquired by the U.S. forces until April of 1899. They remained in Cuba and returned to the U.S. on 4-22-1899 on board the transport Sedgwick arriving at the quarantine station at Savannah, Georgia four days later. On 5-24-1899 the 6th Ohio Volunteer Infantry was mustered out of service. At the time of muster out, the unit consisted of 46 officers and 1,055 enlisted men. During their term of service the unit lost one officer and 24 enlisted men to disease. Twenty-five additional enlisted men were discharged on disability and five enlisted men deserted. These facts from "*Official History of the Ohio National Guard and Ohio Volunteers: The United States Volunteers in 1898-99, including a History of each Local Organization and each Regimental Formation from its Inception to the Present Time*" Cleveland, Ohio: The Plain Dealer Publishing Co. 1901, By Warren E. Pratt.

The headlines of the *Toledo Blade* dated 4-29-1898 read: "Toledo Soldiery Starts For Camp Bushnell – Fitting Farewell and God-Speed to the Gallant Sixteenth Regiment, Ohio National Guard – Civic and Military Organizations, Augmented by Thousands of Civilians, Cheer Them On Their First Move Toward the Uncertain Future of War's Possibilities. The thousands and thousands of persons lined up on every street gave vent to deafening cheers as the gallant boys marched along, looking neither to the right nor the left. Col. McMaken acknowledged the salutations with continuous nods of his head. The escort formed as follows: Chief Raitz with a squad of police; Mayor Jones and staff; Col. Bunker at the head of the civic societies; mail carriers; the several Grand Army organizations; Toledo colored band; Cadets Veteran corps; the two divisions of the Naval Reserves, Lieut. Commander Betts at their head; high school boys; bootblacks and newsboys' union; Uniform Rank, K of P William Tell lodge; Scott's division, No. 3 Maccabees; Toledo Musicians' Protective Association band; the famous Cherry Pickers; The Forest Post Cadets; The Toledo Light Guards; Union Veterans' Union; Maccabees, Uniform Rank, Lucas division; Col. McMaken and staff; Sixteenth Regiment band; First battalion Major

Stanbery, commanding with Cos. A, H, L, C, F and E; Second battalion, Major Parker in command, with Cos. I, K, G, D and B; The signal corps; The hospital corps; ambulance; Chief Wall with fire department; Citizens in carriages. Cannons boomed and the cheers were deafening, as the parade turned off Madison into Summit Street. Thousands of patriotic men, women and children lined the sidewalks and encroached into the street. The applause deepened into a roar as the bands started patriotic airs and company after company quickened steps to the music. Every available window in the business blocks lining Madison and Summit streets, was filled with eager faces. Eyes grew dim as the veterans of '61 marched with halting and painful steps. Cannons continued to boom, and shrill whistles from tug boats and factories added to the excitement."

By the end of June, 1898, the *Toledo Evening Bee* reported: "Toledo Again To the Front – Sends 328 More of Her Youth to Drill for War – Gone To Camp Bushnell – Naval Reserves and Battery D Get a Hearty Send-Off as they Marched to Take Train for Columbus – The Toledo Naval Reserves and Battery D, of the Ohio National Guard, have at last gone to war—and with their organizations intact and almost wholly officered as they were prior to hostilities. A cheering spectacle was presented to the patriotic people of Toledo as the train bearing 328 young men pulled out of the depot. The gallant boys left home with the God-speed of friends and parents. The marines and artillery men go to Columbus, there to be mustered into the Tenth Ohio Volunteer Infantry."

When the first American troops started returning home they were proud of the service they had given to their country and thought that their nation would be grateful to them for volunteering and winning this war. But they were wrong, and it is said that it was because they were wrong, that the stage was set for the beginning of a new kind of veteran's organization "one whose avowed purpose was that such criminal ingratitude would never again rear its head."

The following headstones are found in cemeteries in Sylvania showing service in the Spanish-American War:

- Oliver T. Hinds is listed with – 6th U.S. Cavalry, Troop G. – Ravine Cemetery.
- Ralph Calkins was from Sylvania and served. I am unable to locate his burial.
- Edwin Cline – born 10-16-1870 died 3-2-1956 – Pvt. Co. M2 Regiment Ohio Infantry Spanish-American War – buried in Association Cemetery.

In Toledo Memorial Park Cemetery the following gravestones were located:

- John Henry Asendorf, Pvt. 10th Pennsylvania Volunteer Infantry Co. C (1863-1953).
- Charles N. Comer, Private – 2nd Ohio Volunteer Infantry, Co. E (5-31-1879 died 5-6-1969).
- Rose E. Conrad, Cpl. 6th Ohio Volunteer Infantry (1877-1939).
- Eugene Johnson, Pvt. – 6th Ohio Volunteer Infantry Co. F (7-18- 1873 – 1-7-1953)
- Nelson B. King, Pvt. 10th Ohio Volunteer Infantry (4-19-1877 – 11-23-1950).
- Charles B. Scott lived in Sylvania and he is buried in Forest Cemetery in Toledo, Ohio. He served in the 10th Ohio Volunteer Infantry. Company H. Listed as an Artificer.

Other names that appeared in the Roster of the Sixth Ohio Volunteer Infantry that were residents of Sylvania, or later became residents of Sylvania:

Otto E. Beebe, Corporal, Company A
Daniel C. Moor, Company C
Harvey Decker, Corporal – Co. H
Park W. Decker, Private – Co. H
Frank Cunningham – Private – Co. L

William Koester of Sylvania usually represented the Spanish-American War Veterans at the Memorial Day observances in Sylvania. On Memorial Day in 1937 he was the Grand Marshal of the day.

The following appeared in the *Sylvania Sentinel* dated 9-8-1943: "The 37th annual reunion of the old 6th Ohio Volunteer Infantry will be held at Toledo in Memorial Hall on Wednesday, September 17, (all day). Major Arthur D. Hill asks for a large attendance as matters of utmost importance to the veterans will be under discussion. Supreme Court Judge Edward S. Mathias, a post commander-in-chief of the United Spanish War Veterans will be the speaker for the occasion."

WORLD WAR I

World War I involved more countries and caused greater destruction than any other war except World War II. The war was originally called "The Great War." The U.S. remained neutral at first, but in 1917 the U.S. joined the Allies and gave them the manpower they needed to win the war. In the fall of 1918, the Central Powers surrendered. This war eliminated emperors in Austria-Hungary, Germany and Russia and the peace treaties after this war established new nations in the defeated areas.

The following article appeared in the *Sylvania Sentinel* on 10-10-1912: "Recruits Must Prepare To Serve Seven Years – All recruits enlisting for the army after 11-1-1912, should be prepared to serve for a term of seven years, instead of three. The first four years he will be in active service. In the next three years he will be allowed to return home to pursue any calling he may desire, but he must hold himself in readiness to respond to a call to arms at any time. At the end of his three years in the reserves, he is discharged, and then is not liable to be called upon or even drafted in time of war. The new system is similar to the one in England, where each soldier, after the expiration of his term, becomes a part of the national reserve, and is at the call of the government. The Toledo district, which has been averaging about one new recruit per day, embraces quite a large territory throughout this section."

The *Sylvania Sentinel* dated 10-31-1912 reported the following: "Lucas County is losing many residents in the persons of the Greeks and Bulgarians who are leaving for their homes to enter the war, against the Turks. Nearly every day sees a party leave, and this condition holds good in all the principal cities of the country."

The *Toledo Blade* dated 4-6-1917 reported with headlines: "WILSON SIGNS PROCLAMATION; ISSUES CALL FOR VOLUNTEERS – War Resolution Formally Puts U.S. Into Conflict – President Acts Immediately Upon Passage of Act by House; Sees Peace Bring End of Armed Force." This article stated: "President Wilson today signed the resolution of congress declaring a state of war between the United States and Germany. All the naval militia and naval reserves were called to the colors with the President's signing a proclamation formally declaring a state of war between the United States and Germany. In the proclamation he called upon American citizens to give support to all measures of the government."

The 1-10-1918 *Sylvania Sentinel* published an article titled A People Aroused: "Whether or not the American people are fully aroused on all matters pertaining to the war, there can be no question as to their being wide awake to the importance of increased food production . . ."

An advertisement appeared in the *Sylvania Sentinel* on 5-30-1918: The Farmers & Merchants Bank Co. – Sylvania, Ohio – U.S.S. War Savings Stamps Will Help Win The War – There is only one way to rid your conscience of that Stamp Spectre. Buy It. If you can afford to buy one U.S. Stamp you have done all that is asked, but do it.

It was reported on 5-30-1918 that: "The latest word received from David Anderson, he was in France, on duty with the marine service." David was a Sylvania Township boy.

The following individuals were from Sylvania or Sylvania Township and served in World War I, as listed in the *Sylvania Sentinel* dated 9-12-1918 titled "The Honor Roll," and in the Ancestry. com database for "Ohio Military Men": Miss Grace Lewis, nurse, Ruth F. Felt, nurse, Harold Anderson, Dave Anderson, Carl Aiken, Harold J. Bittner, F. Blystone, Arthur Button, Seldon Brown, Earl C. Bennett, Lee Baker, Grover Brighton, Frank Burrell, Lou R. Crandall, Lewis D. Connett, Tracy G. Cook, Forest Cooper, Harry W. Cooper, Clifford D. Calkins, Audy W. Cooper, Jerome Conn, Louis F. Conrad, Earl W. Comstock, John Conrad, Ira J. Croy, Fenton P. Clark, Nace Clark, William B. Carr, Alvin Carr, Russell Cummins, George Couture, Harry Cooper, Charles Clark, Jr., Dr. Ray Comstock, Vern J. Cory, Ralph F. Cushman, Clyde J. Dean, Harley DeBruine, Pearl E. DeBruine, John Dawson, Joseph W. Diehn, Harry E. Dunbar, Percy Dings, John J. Dunbar, Charles DeLenler, Fred Dubendorfer, Welcome E. Edson, Harrison Eff, Samuel H. Eff, Carroll Fallis, Tom Fisher, Chelsea J. Friess, Harry A. French, Frank Fisher, Harvey Gillhouse, George P. Gillhouse, Earl Gibbs, George Georgeoff, Ray T. Gibbs, Grover Gildy, James Gillen, Frank W. Garry, James T. Gilliland, Max C. Griest, Earl G. Hughes, Bane Howard, Kenneth R. Howard, Wade E. Harroun (Honorably Discharged), Darrell Hawley, George I. Heath, Thomas H. Heath, Dr. Victor B. Halbert, Cyril Hittler, Tom Hartman, Hiram Hawley, Tiny Huffman, Ed. Howard, John E. Hendrickson, Waite D. Jones, John C. Jones, James A. Joyce, Howard King, Wade Harroun, John Knuth, Cyril E. Hittler, William H. Keeler, Carl H. Keller, Arby H. Kanavel, Ralph Kroll, Leland H. Knapp, William Kuhnle, Edward John Kuhnle, Clarence Knapp, Clarence King, Floyd Kilbourne, Nelson E. Kanavel, Alfred D. Kanavel, W.F. Kuhlman, Clare E. Kilbourne, Fred Kretzel, Harry S. Keating, Howard C. King, John H,. King,

Harvey J. Lewis, Oscar Lewis, Harry W. Little, Harry Lathrop, Fred J. Lochbihler, Merwyn G. Leatherman Bernard O. Maerkisch, Elbert Mallett, Thomas E. McNalley, Warren B. McGlenn, Percy Mickle, George Murphy, Lewis Murphy, O.N. Mikesell, Edgar Manley, Ross W. Markley, Vincenzo Odone, Steven Okonski, Thomas G. Overhulse, Arnold G. Paschen, Joseph J. Page, Charles Putt, Frank E. Perkins, John D. Queenan, Leo J. Reger, Lew Russell, Cleo L. Russell, Benjamin H. Repp, Archie L. Randall, Frank J. Reger, Harry Ries, Rafaela Rinaldo, Harold W. Rinear, Frank Smith, Frank Snider, Frank Smith, Holley W. Sheets, Clayton Shepard, Harry Szalkoski, Jacob Steck, Albert N. Simon, Charles Showler, Stanley Sacker, Stanley S. Stalter, Charles Shepard, Charles E. Shanks, Fred Schmitt, Rowland W. Spenker, Otto Trektie, Ashley G. Vesey, Burtis VanHaer, Ralph C. VanGlahn, Henry H. Willinger, Ralph N. Willinger, Christian Webb, Leon Webb, Walter Willinger, Earl G. Whitney, Benjamin H. Wyant, John Woodward, Fran Welsheimer, Samuel A. Watters, Earl Whitney, Nick Wilhelm, Stanley Waldie, Ralph E. West, Douglas M. Wood, Ralph W. Young, Theodore Ziehr."

The following letter was published in the *Sylvania Sentinel* on 9-12-1918 from Louis Conrad of Sylvania who was serving during World War I in the 166 Infantry Supply Co., A.E.F. in France. The letter was written to his sisters Minnie and Cora: "In France near the lines – Aug. 3, 1918. Dear sisters Minnie and Cora: Just a few lines, no time to write much, but must take the time to send a few lines to let you know that I am well, and the reason for not writing. We have been in action for the past twenty days and have had hard driving. I am well but terribly nervous from the strain of having the big guns roar from both sides day and night makes one very restless. We were in two hard fights one of them lasting six days and nights, and the other seven days and eight nights, and a previous battle lasted fifteen days. It was some fight, and we sent them over the hills on the run and they are still going with the Yanks behind them. At first they tried to break through the lines and it was up to the Yanks to stop them, which they surely did. Before they started they threw an artillery barrage the hardest ever known since the war. A few men of our company including myself were at the front lines with our mule teams as it took place. Shells were bursting around us faster than one could count them. It was our place to get supplies to the boys so we took our chance with the rest of them. It seemed that no matter which way we went to get there they would shell us on the way in and out. Do you wonder that we are nervous going through with what we have to. The Yanks are returning about two for one and the Germans sure deserve all they got. As they started over they thought they would break through land go right into some large city without stopping, but the Yanks could not be shoved to one side and let them go where they would like to. Our boys stopped them as fast as they came for many hours and then advanced making them double time over the hills, leaving a large quantity of ammunition and guns behind them. We gave them an awful surprise, and I think they are finding out more every day what the Yanks can do. The last report a few hours ago they were still retreating on the run. As it is getting near mess time for the mules I must bring this to a close. We are relieved for the present, but don't know for how long. May be sent back at any time. Give my best regards to all who ask about me and don't forget Pete Pankhurst. With love and best wishes I am ever your brother, Louis Conrad. 166 Infantry Supply Co. A.E.F. in France."

Also in the 9-12-1918 *Sylvania Sentinel* was a letter from Douglas Wood, a Sylvanian, from Camp Sherman. "Camp Sherman, Saturday, Sept. 7 – The Seventh District selects wish to thank the men who furnished the band on the day of our departure. It sure put pep and spirit in the bunch.

Everybody feeling fine and having a good time. The inspector of the barracks reported ours the cleanest and neatest he had inspected. The Captain informed us that we had the right spirit and were getting along faster than most other new men. None of us have been examined yet. We have to wait until our turn comes. About 13,000 selects have arrived in camp from Tuesday to Friday. According to reports we will be shooting at the Huns by June 1st. It will soon be over then. Seventh District – Douglas Wood."

And the following letter to the editor, again from the 9-12-1918 *Sylvania Sentinel*, discussed boys from Sylvania in a letter from J.W. Cook: It was my privilege as a representative of the T.M.C.A. to accompany the boys selected to go to Camp Sherman, Wednesday morning, September 4th from Toledo, among which were a number from Sylvania. Our train of 14 coaches took on additional numbers at Ottawa, Lima, Wapakoneta, Sidney and Troy, in all nearly 600 men. I never saw a finer lot of young men anywhere and we had a fine trip. I visited the boys in their barracks on Thursday just before noon after they had had their first morning drill. They were all feeling fine, and the Sylvania boys wanted me to send the message back home that they were all well and happy and that they did not want the folks back home to worry about them. It gives me great pleasure indeed to send the message as I sincerely feel that the folks back home have every reason to be proud of the fine boys that went out on this trip. Yours Truly, J.W. COOK."

"The Great War" or World War I, as it was later called, ended with the Allies (Belgium, British Empire, France, Greece, Italy, Portugal, Romania, Russia, Serbia, Montenegro and the United States) winning victories on all fronts in the fall of 1918 against the Central Powers (Austria-Hungary, Bulgaria, Germany, Ottoman Empire).

The headlines in the *Toledo Blade* dated 11-11-1918 reads: "Everything For Which U.S. Fought Has Been Won, Says Wilson, Telling of War End – "My Fellow Countrymen: The armistice was signed this morning. Everything for which America fought has been accomplished. It will now be our fortunate duty to assist by example, by sober, friendly council and by material aid in the establishment of just democracy throughout the world." —Woodrow Wilson." Another article in that same newspaper reads: "All Toledo Joins In Big Celebration Of World War End – Mayor Proclaims Holiday, Tens of Thousands of Workers, Children, Everbody in City's Greatest Demonstration."

According to the Official U.S. government figures, the United States had 116,516 casualties and had 234,428 wounded during World War I.

The 1-16-1919 issue of the *Sylvania Sentinel* noted several "after war" items as follows: "Help Uncle Sam find work for the returning soldiers. List your help needs with U.S. Employment Service 128 N. Huron St., Toledo" and "Every soldier returning home is permitted to retain his insurance policy on the liberal terms of the government, and it is an opportunity that will never come to them again, and the wise will not miss the opportunity."

The following article appeared also in the 1-16-1919 issue: "Representative Norman J. Gould of New York has introduced a bill to permit all non-commissioned officers and enlisted men to retain as their personal property, without cost to them, whatever clothing they may have in their possession at the time of discharge. This does the War Department one better, for the Department has recently ruled that they may retain their uniforms for four months after discharge, when those uniforms must be turned in. There is a good deal of sentiment attached by the soldier to the uniform he wore in battle. As he grows old he likes to take it from its cedar box of camphor ball wrappings, show it to the kids, or his friends, and fight his battles over again. Who has not seen the veteran of the Civil War gaze lovingly on the uniform he wore at Gettysburg, Antietam or Bull Run? An instance is recalled of an old confederate veteran who came to Richmond to attend a reunion there some years ago. He brought his old gray uniform with him and when he unpacked it to don for the parade, what was his horror to find a sizable moth hole in the shoulder of the coat. He positively refused to wear it for fear some might remark he had been shot in the back by a Yank."

The *Toledo Blade* dated 4-11-1919 reads: "Doughboys of Flanders Field March Toledo's Streets With Heroic Companies of the 37th – Tears of Joy Mingle With City's Cheer – Beneath Waving Flags, Irresistibles of the 37th Tread Again Familiary Paths of Home They Honor – Veterans of War of Five Million Dead Return to Ways of Peace – Home today came Ohio's two great hero commands, the Fighting 147th and the 112th Ammunition Train, from the War of Five Million Dead, and as they tramped the city's streets "in all their splendid youth," Toledo mingled her tears with her cheers while bravely shone the proxy Stars of Gold; and we shall think that the bright gleam of them, like a shaft upborne on memory's wing, flashed softly over land and sea to touch with light of love white crosses on far battlefields where those who could not come today are sleeping."

In March of 1919 a War Mothers Society was formed in Sylvania. Mrs. Morris, national president of the War Mothers Society, and president of the Toledo chapter, accompanied by Mrs. Mulholland, Mrs. McLain and Mrs. Webster all of Toledo, were at the Methodist Church and organized a local chapter of the War Mothers Society. The following officers were elected in Sylvania:

Mrs. Etta Randall, president;
Mrs. Jennie Hollister, first vice president;
Mrs. Sarah Comstock, second vice president;
Mrs. Clara Wood, secretary;
Mrs. B.C. Clark, treasurer.

A Soldiers' Relief Disbursing List was sent on 9-1-1920 to the Village of Sylvania from the Lucas County Auditor. This reads: "To the Clerk of the above named Township: The within is a list of the names of the persons in your Township to whom relief has been awarded, and the amount payable monthly to each under the laws for the relief of honorably discharged indigent soldiers, sailors and marines of the United States, and the indigent wives, parents, widows and minor children under fifteen years of age, of such indigent or deceased soldiers, sailors or marines: Adah Elliott - $8.00 per month, residing in Sylvania, Ohio."

On 6-16-1940 the following appeared in the *Sylvania Sentinel*: "On May 14th, 1930, just 10 years ago, Mrs. Mary Giltz, who resides with her daughter, Mrs. R.C. Niswander, sailed from New York with a contingent of other Gold Star Mothers, to visit the graves of their sons in France. At that time everything was peaceful and the numerous cemeteries were beautifully kept. Mrs. Giltz recalls the bitterness with which these mothers spoke of the Kaiser, and wonders what sorrowing mothers are thinking today of Hitler."

When the United States became involved in World War II, the United States Government required men to register. The following men who lived in Sylvania in early 1942, who had also served in World War I, had to register: Carl Aiken, Sr., Dewey Boice, Walter Winterfelt, Roy Dague, Hiram Hawley, Ralph VanGlahn, Sr., Edward G. Jacobs, Ashley Vesey, Clyde Gault, Ira Baumgartner, Harry Ries, and Lonnie Smith.

When World War I ended, Sylvania reported one loss: Joseph W. Diehn. A memorial marker in Veteran's Memorial Field does list Joseph W. Diehn on the top portion of the World War I marker. Under that there is another marker which reads: "These trees furnished by the State Highway Department. Planted November 11, 1940 to commemorate those from Lucas County, Ohio who gave their lives in the World War (1917-1918) were dedicated this date by Lucas County Council American Legion."

Joseph W. Diehn was born on 7-13-1890 and killed in action on 9-12-1918 at the age of 28 years old. His father was John Henry Diehn (1855-1925) and his mother was Sophia Dorothy Brandt-Diehn (1858-1916). He was buried in Whiteford Union Cemetery in Lambertville Monroe Co. Michigan. He enlisted in the Army on 10-2-1917, served as Private and was involved in the following battles: When he was killed he was serving with Co. A – 9th Infantry. Sylvania's American Legion Post No. 468 was named in honor of Joseph W. Diehn.

To show that Joseph W. Diehn was a resident of Sylvania Township prior to his entering World War I we did find him living in Sylvania Township, with his parents, at the 1910 census as follows:

- John Diehn – 54 years – married 28 years – farmer – owned farm – free of mortgage;
- Sofia Diehn – 51 years – wife – married 28 years – six children born – six children still living;
- Mary Diehn – daughter – 27 years – single;
- Joseph Diehn – son – 20 years – single;
- Wade Diehn – son – 17 years – single;
- Forest Diehn – son – 9 years – single.

They were also living in Sylvania Township at the 1900 census.

This is the memorial marker in Sylvania's Veterans Memorial Field representing the casualties from Sylvania during World War I. The top portion of the marker reads: "IN COMMEMORATION - THE PEOPLE OF SYLVANIA COMMEMORATE THOSE SYLVANIANS WHO DIED IN SERVICE TO THE UNITED STATES IN WORLD WAR I – 1917 – 1918." There is only one name listed as a World War I casualty and that is Joseph W. Diehn. The sign below it can be easily read without repeating it here. (Photo taken in 2018 by Gayleen Gindy).

WORLD WAR II

World War II began on 9-1-1939 when Germany Invaded Poland. Germany, with its powerful dictator, Adolf Hitler, rapidly crushed Poland, Denmark, Luxembourg, the Netherlands, Belgium, Norway, and France. By 1940, Great Britain stood alone against Hitler, and then Italy joined the war on Germany's side. The fighting soon spread to Greece and northern Africa. In June of 1941 Germany invaded the Soviet Union.

On 12-7-1941 Japan attacked the United States military bases at Pearl Harbor in Hawaii, without warning, and that brought the United States into the war on the side of The Allies. Within hours Japan struck the British colony of Hong Kong and two U.S. islands Guam and Wake Island, and then Thailand. (The other side was referred to as The Axis, and included: Germany, Albania, Bulgaria, Finland, Hungary, Italy, Japan, Romania and Thailand).

On 12-8-1941 The United States, Great Britain and Canada declared war on Japan.

The *Toledo Blade* dated 12-8-1941 reported the following: "Congress Votes For War; 1,500 Killed, 2 Warships Sunk, White House Says – Action Is Taken Against Japan – Day of Attack in Pacific Will Live in History of Infamy, F.D.R. Says. Congress today passed a resolution declaring that a state of war exists between the United States and Japan less than half an hour after President Roosevelt asked for a declaration of war because of Nippon's attacks on U.S. bases in the Pacific. The Senate vote was 82 to 0. The House vote was 388 to 1. The negative vote was cast by Congresswoman Jeannette Rankin."

1942 – Britain started saturation bombing in German cities and then the United States joined the air war. From 1943 until the end of the war bombs rained down on Germany around the clock.

7-10-1943 – Allied forces under Eisenhower landed along Sicily's south coast and for 39 days they engaged in bitter fighting with German troops.

7-25-1943 – Mussolini fell from power, after the invasion of Sicily and was imprisoned. Italy's new premier, Field Marshal Pietro Badoglio began secret peace talks with the Allies.

9-3-1943 - Italy surrendered, but Germany was determined to fight the Allies for control of Italy.

9-9-1943 – Allied forces landed at Salerno, Italy and a series of head-on assaults against well-defended German positions. By early November the Allies had almost reached Cassino, and some of the most brutal fighting of World War II occurred near Cassino.

January 1944 – Allies landed troops at Anzio, Italy, west of Cassino, but German forces kept the Allies pinned down on the beaches at Anzio for four months. Thousands of Allied soldiers died there.

May 1944 – The Allies finally broke through German defenses. Rome fell on 6-4-1944.

<u>6-6-1944</u> – D-Day – Allied infantrymen invaded the Normandy coast of northern France. Hitler's boast of German defenses being able to resist any attack along the coast was wrong.

<u>7-25-1944</u> – Allied bombers blasted a hole in the German front and the United States Third Army under Lieutenant General George S. Patton plowed through the hole, and then they rolled eastward toward Paris on 8-25-1944.

<u>August 1944</u> – Allied forces landed in southern France and moved rapidly up the Rhone River Valley, while Patton raced toward the German border and the Rhine River.

<u>9-17-1944</u> – About 20,000 paratroopers dropped behind German lines to seize bridges in the Netherlands, but bad weather and other problems hampered the operation.

<u>12-16-1944</u> – Battle of the Bulge - German troops surprised and overwhelmed the Americans in the Ardennes Forest in Belgium and Luxembourg, but within two weeks the Americans stopped the German advance near the Meuse River in Belgium.

<u>Early 1945</u> – Allies began their final assault on Germany. Hitler ordered his soldiers to fight to the death, but large numbers of German soldiers surrendered each day.

<u>4-25-1945</u> – Soviet troops surrounded Germany's capital, Berlin.

<u>4-30-1945</u> – Hitler committed suicide.

<u>5-8-1945</u> – V-E Day – Victory in Europe Day.

<u>8-6-1945</u> - An American B-29 bomber dropped the first atomic bomb on Hiroshima, Japan. On 8-9-1945, after Japanese leaders did not respond to the bombing, the U.S. dropped a larger bomb on Nagasaki, Japan.

<u>8-14-1945</u> Japan agreed to end the war.

<u>9-2-1945</u> - Japan signed the official statement of surrender and that date was declared V-J Day, or Victory over Japan Day.

The U.S. military casualties during World War II are listed at 405,399 and the number wounded listed at 671,278.

Back in the United States, in December 1940 the second selective call for military service was postponed due to the fact that they did not have adequate housing facilities and the original date was determined to be too close to Christmas. The second call was for 8,703 men from Ohio for December 2 and that this deferment did not affect the calls being sent out for additional draftees under the first federal call. Ohio had a 996-man quota in the first call.

Besides the clothes they are wearing at the time they reported, U.S. Army draftees were asked to bring one strong comfortable pair of shoes, extra suit of underclothing, three extra pairs of socks, two face and two bath towels, a comb, toothbrush, soap, toothpaste, razor and shaving soap. Trunks or boxes were not permitted in the trucks or buses which would carry the men to their headquarters.

The National Draft Headquarters set Ohio's net quota at 52,497. Gross quota was set at 94,068, but credits of 11,540 for National guardsmen and 30,031 for other enlistments were allowed. Plans were underway to have a state defense force to be known as the Ohio State Guard, completely organized around January 1st, the State Adjutant General announced. The State Guard will consist of seven battalions and supply and medical units, totaling 250 officers and 3,000 men. Under federal regulations men serving in state guards were not exempt from the draft.

The *Sylvania Sentinel* dated 6-19-1941 said that every man who had become 21 years old since 10-16-1940, and who reaches that age before midnight 7-1-1941 must register with his local selective service board July 1. Men living in Sylvania Village, Sylvania Township, Berkey Village and Richfield Township will register at the Sylvania Council Building on July 1, according to Edward G. Jacobs, member of Draft Board 22. The council building will be open until 9 p.m. on that day.

The *Sylvania Sentinel* dated 11-20-1941 printed the following headlines: "Navy Offers Splendid Opportunity To Young Men of This Community." It was reported that Harry Quinnell, the editor of the *Sylvania Sentinel*, was appointed the Navy Editor to help the Navy in giving ambitious local young men information about the opportunities the "Two Ocean" Navy was offering them for technical training and advancement as they serve their country. Mr. Quinnell had appointed four assistants to cooperate in the campaign for the Navy. They were George Corrigan of Sylvania; Fred Armitage of Berkey-Metamora Road; Clyde Gault, Central Avenue; and Vern Cory of Corey Road. These men had all served in the armed forces of the United States and could be called on for information on joining.

Washington needed men between the ages of 17 and 50, and assured that all would be given a chance by enlistment in the Navy or Naval Reserve. Secretary of Navy Knox announced: "Never in the history of the United States has there been greater opportunity for loyal young Americans to serve their country and build their futures than right now."

Harry Quinnell, Navy editor of the *Sentinel* said: "It is possible for a bright young man to increase his pay seven times during his first enlistment and he can earn as much as $125 a month. This monthly figure is actually worth much more when it is remembered that the man has few living expenses and is provided with the finest of medical and dental care. You have all your food and lodging, and also your original outfit of clothing provided by Uncle Sam free. In addition there are free sports and entertainment—even to the latest Hollywood pictures. On top of this you get free travel and adventure in colorful places—a thing few civilians can afford. When you consider the size of this country and the fact that the Navy will select only 15,000 applicants a month from many times that number throughout the United States."

In March of 1942 it was reported that over 150,000 men had enlisted in the United States Navy since the Japanese attack on Pearl Harbor, according to word received from the recruiting station in Detroit. Enlistments will continue on a volunteer basis for men between the ages of 17 and 50 years.

The *Sylvania Sentinel* dated 3-5-1942 reported the following: "Lonnie Smith of Rudyard Road, a veteran of World War No. 1 and a member of the Sylvania Post VFW is one of the younger veterans who also registered for World War No. 2."

In March of 1942 the following additional local draft numbers of the Draft Board No. 22 selectees in Sylvania were listed as follows: Lawson Lathrop 244, Harold Lucas 507, Otis Clough 316, Carl Aiken, Jr., 317, Carl Aiken, Sr. 452, W.L. Wright 777, Alvin Carr 406, Eugene Friedt 1809, R. Rader 1602, R. Hoot 1985, Fred Setzler 2046, Robert Jolley 2047, Leland Lathrop 2435, R.W. Spenker 2727, Olin Taylor 2012, C. Carroll 246, Clayton Fowler 2750, Frank Weaver 2749, Carl Davis 2753, Charles Smith 2760, Dormey Buck 2933, Wayne Armstrong 2929, Lyle O. Kirk 2951, Robert Harms 2983, Maynard Green 3196, C.J. Kahlert 2840, Milton M. Olander 3090, Charles Gruber 3279, M.E. Weaver 3274, Charles McConnell 3365, Marcus Kiefer 233, Floyd Newcomb 444.

The following appeared in the 3-26-1942 issue of the *Sylvania Sentinel*: "Richard Tracy, son of Mr. and Mrs. C.H. Tracy of Erie Street, shipped on board a tanker of the Sun Oil Company on March 9th. On Monday evening Mr. and Mrs. Tracy received a telegram from the company stating that their son is on board ship and is safe. From this they believe that the tanker on which Richard was working was one of those torpedoed during the weekend. Also in this issue of the *Sylvania Sentinel*: "SERVE IN SILENCE – If you happen to come in contact with any military information of any kind, keep it to yourself. The government is now pushing a determined "serve in silence" drive and it is being given their full cooperation of industry."

In April of 1942 it was announced that grocers, restaurant keepers and trade institutions had to start registering for their sugar rationing books at Burnham High School. This included all merchants dispensing sugar in Sylvania. The registrars for the rationing council included: William Seed, Elwood Hotchkiss, Charles Carroll, Fred V. Myers, Ronald Adams, and Roy A. Chandler. A separate application had to be completed for every person who was issued a ration book, but only one member of each family unit was required to appear at the nearest elementary school to apply for all members of the family.

On 4-2-1942 the *Sylvania Sentinel* reported: "Private Hiram Hawley, 28th Air Base Squadron, MacDill Field, Tampa, Fla., sends greetings to all his friends in "good old Sylvania" and also expresses the hope that Joseph Diehn Post, American Legion of which he is a member is doing their bit for defense." He is airplane mechanic and says he expects to be at MacDill Field for a long time."

A total of 887 men between the ages of 45 and 65 registered at the Sylvania fire engine house in April of 1942 in the fourth national military draft.

The 4-23-1942 issue of the *Sylvania Sentinel* reported: "E. Meredith Roberts, Jr. is teaching mechanical drawing for the remainder of the school year at Burnham High School, replacing

Gabor Takats who left for military service recently. Mr. Roberts had been teaching in the vocational shop for two months before assuming his new duties."

The 5-7-1942 issue of the *Sylvania Sentinel* reported the following: "High school graduates, college graduates, men who have not completed their formal education, married men—men of all walks of life between the ages of 18 and 26—may now apply for officers' training in the U.S. Army air forces under a new plan to enlist 100,000 men." Diplomas were no longer required for Army pilots. An aviation cadet was paid $75 a month from the time training started, with practically all living expenses supplied.

Another event that was occurring in Sylvania during World War II was the air raid drills. According to the 5-21-1942 *Sylvania Sentinel* Sylvania participated in a county wide air raid signal test at 9:25 p.m., on 5-15-1942. This drill revealed that the church bells at Whiteford Road were rung as scheduled, and the siren at the Medusa Cement plant blew in accordance with regulations provided. The fire siren in the village did not sound the "all clear" and investigation showed that a relay stuck in the mechanism which prevented the final blasts being blown. The siren at the France Stone Company did not blow as long as it should have because of a slight defect in that mechanism, but that too had been remedied.

At the end of May in 1942 a service flag bearing 87 stars was dedicated at Burnham High School. Each star beared the name of a youth in the armed forces of the United Nations, who at one time attended Sylvania schools. 85 of the stars represented the boys in the service and two stars represented the girls; Virginia Hanna and Betty Harroun who had enlisted as nurses. The following were listed as representing the stars: Victor Anderson, William Apple, Clayton Anstead, Lance Barbarick, Reese Beatty, Joseph Bissonnette, John Bomia, Winfield Bowman, Edwin Briggs, Bernard Brown, Pete Buyaki, John Chandler, Raymond Chandler, Arba Comstock, Robert Cook, Paul Cooper, Glenn Coutcher, Joseph Coutcher, Merle Cowell, Robert Cowell, Eugene Cruey, Allen Doerr, Harry Ducy, Ralph Duvall, Chauncey Felt, Leroy Fischer, Norman Fleig, Chelsea Friess, Beverly Futtrell, Robert Goble, Leslie Glanzman, Jack Handy, Virginia Hanna, Betty Harroun, Burdell Hansen, Clarence Haynes, Hiram Hawley, Robert Heinberger, Benton Hine, Jack Hooker, Danny Hott, Arthur Jones, Raymond Gramer, Donald Knisely, John Kruse, Herman Lang, Irwin Lang, Arthur Loomer, Edward Loomis, Arthur McKenzie, George McGlenn, Robert McGlenn, Joseph Marmar, Richard Marsh, Victor Martin, Arthur Mayer, Don Moore, John McNett, Kenneth Notestine, Charles Parker, Alfred Pemberton, Norman Portman, Henry Pucilowski, Nelson Randall, Norman Raney, Leroy Rosa, Harold Russwinkle, Arthur Shanly, Raymond Shanly, Dale Shull, Kenneth Shull, Wade Shull, Arza Smalley, Don Smith, Gale Smith, Stewart Smith, Harry Szalkowski, Dick Tracy, Raymond VanPelt, Norman VanTyle, Dale VanVorce, Tom Vineyard, Marvin Wallington, Robert Weber, Ned Welsh, Melvin Wilkinson, Matthew Wilson, Maurice Wilson, Leo Wittscheck, Robert Wood, Sherman Wonderly, Victor Warford, Milford Yeager, William Yeager, LaVerne Yeager, Arthur Yunker,

The 6-18-1942 *Sylvania Sentinel* reported: "Young men from 18 to 20 years of age will register for military service on Saturday, June 27th and on Tuesday, June 30th. The registration will be held in the hall at the Fire Engine House, and will be under the supervision of Edward G. Jacobs, member of Draft Board No. 22. All male persons born on or after 1-21-1922, and on or before 6-30-1924 are required to register."

On 7-14-1942 at 10 p.m., a trial dim-out was staged in Sylvania and Sylvania Township. Sirens and whistles were blown for five seconds on, three second off for five minutes. The all clear signal was given and was a steady whistle or siren blast for a period of two minutes. The dim-out covered a period of 20 minutes. Air raid wardens, auxiliary police, fire watchers, auxiliary firemen and regular firemen proceeded to their assigned stations upon hearing the first air raid warning signal. All firemen remained at their stations until the all clear was given, unless actual fire calls were received. The air raid wardens and auxiliary police made sure that all lights were extinguished in Sylvania village and township except manufacturing establishments and industrial plants. All theater signs, advertising and neon signs had to be extinguished. The wardens and police were required to report to Civilian Defense headquarters any person or persons refusing to cooperate with the dim-out regulations. Residents and businesses were not allowed to use their telephones unless there was an emergency. Automobiles and pedestrians were requested to proceed normally but with caution. All persons who planned to be away from home had to make sure that their lights were all extinguished before they left. Lights on bridges, parks, street traffic and warning lights were allowed to continue in operation. During the dim-out period, planes flew over to check the results.

In July of 1942 members of the Joseph W. Diehn Post American Legion, gave a royal welcome to Private First Class Hiram Hawley, when he arrived in Sylvania on furlough from camp in Florida. He had served in World War I, and had enlisted as a ground mechanic in the Army Air Corps. According to Hiram the Army was pretty much the same as it was in World War I except that he believed that the soldiers were better cared for and had more comfortable uniforms.

The flag of the Women's Relief Corps beared ten stars representing nine adopted sons of the members who were serving in the armed forces. Sergeant Dale VanVorce was the adopted son of the organization, and others represented were Norman Raney, Paul Cooper, John Chandler, Melvin Wilkinson, LaVerne Yeager, Milford Yeager, Robert Weber, Arba Comstock and Ralph Meeks.

A.H. Randall, the president of the rationing board in Sylvania, reported in July of 1942 that the new office of the board would be located in the Sylvania Savings Bank auditorium. (Today this is the Key Bank facility at 5604 Main).

In August of 1942 the *Sylvania Sentinel* newspaper started a column titled "The Mail Bag," where they published information and letters from boys and girls serving in the Armed Forces. This column continued throughout the war.

In December of 1942 Donald M. Nelson, Chairman of the War Production Board in Washington announced that war plants would be expected to stay on the job New Year's day and get out "a regular workday's production of war goods."

In that same 12-10-1942 newspaper they said: "Registration of all youths who have reached their 18th birthday begins Friday, Dec. 11. All Board 22 registrants must go to the headquarters at 1379 Sylvania Ave., West Toledo. There will be no registration in Sylvania. Those born on or before 7-1-1924, but not after Aug. 31, 1924, shall be registered on any day during the week of Dec. 11 and Dec. 17. Those born on or after Sept. 1, 1924, but not after Oct. 31, 1924, shall be registered on any day during the week of December 18-24. Those born on or after Nov. 1, 1924, but not after Dec. 31, 1924 shall be registered on any day during the period from Dec. 26 to Dec. 31. Those born on or after Jan. 1, 1925, will register on their birthday unless it falls on Sunday or a holiday. Then they will register the following day."

A Red Cross substation was established in Sylvania on 2-10-1943 with six supervisors and 21 workers. Their mission was to make dressings. Mrs. John Harroun was the supervisor of this station. A goal of 3,000 dressings per week was set for this station. They were asking for all volunteers in order to meet this quota. Mrs. Percy Dings was also a local supervisor. The National Red Cross call was for 180 million dressings by March 15.

What would you do if you were notified that your son had died of wounds received in action and then a week later you were informed that your son was not dead, but very much still alive? Here's what happened to one family in Sylvania in the early stages of WW II. Mr. Frank Smith who lived in Sylvania Township on Holt Road received a telegram first informing him that his son George V. Smith was seriously wounded in action in the Southwest Pacific area. Then the next week he received a telegram signed "Ulio, Adjutant General" informing him of the death of his son. The telegram said, "Frank Smith, Rt. NBR 1 Sylvania, Ohio, The Secretary of War desires me to express his deep regret that reports now received show that your son, Private George V. Smith, died in Southwest Pacific area." The *Sylvania Sentinel* of 2-11-1943 reported: "Pvt. Smith was born Sept. 2nd 1915 at Metamora, Ohio. He entered military service Nov. 27, 1941 and was sent overseas in April 1942. He is survived by his father, Frank Smith, Sylvania; brother, William M., Sylvania; Cpl. Paul J. of Camp Forrest, Tenn.; sisters Loretta and Gertrude Smith of Sylvania; and Mrs. Donald Allen of Ottawa Lake, Mich. His mother preceded him in death." The next week the father, Frank Smith, received another telegram dated 2-16-1943 informing him that a report had been received that his son was alive in Australia. The 3-18-1943 issue of the *Sylvania Sentinel* published a letter that George V. Smith sent to his father: ". . . Its been a long time since I have written you and I suppose you have been wondering why you have not heard from me. I promise to write more regularly from now on. I am sure you will be glad to hear that I am all right and as happy as can be expected under the circumstances. There is nothing for any of you at home to worry about, for I will be O.K. I attend Sunday Mass regularly and received Holy Communion this morning. I guess I've received just about all my Christmas packages from home. I was glad to get them, so many thanks. The meals here are good and we can buy almost anything we need at our Canteen. The only drink they serve is Coca Cola. I guess I have told you all I know of today. Hoping everyone at home is well and O.K., write soon. Son and Brother, George."

On 3-4-1943 Sylvania had a "blackout." This was in conjunction with Toledo and the entire State of Ohio. The start of the blackout was indicated by the first audible signal from the steam air raid sirens or electric sirens, as a steady blast for three minutes duration. At this point the procedure was that lights in all homes, business houses, industrial plants and all street lights would be blacked out. The traffic control lights would continue to operate. Automobiles could move at a reduced speed with their parking or dimmed lights on. Pedestrians were to proceed with caution. Then the second audible signal from the steam air raid sirens would give intermittent blasts of three minutes duration. Upon this signal all remaining lights would be blacked out except certain authorized emergency lights. Pedestrians were to take shelter, traffic except for emergency vehicles were to stop. Then finally the third audible signal would be a steady blast for three minutes duration. That would return the community to the conditions prescribed before the first signal. It was stressed that there would be NO audible all clear signal. The all clear conditions would be indicated by the turning on of all street lights and by public radio announcements. That would indicate that danger had passed and that all normal actions would be resumed.

Another goal set in March of 1943 was cigarettes to send to the men in the armed forces. In Lucas County the council of the American Legion set the goal of "one million cigarettes." To reach this goal money was being raised by the sale of tickets for a midnight stage and movie show to be held at the Paramount Theatre in Toledo on March 20th. Tickets were selling for 50 cents, and the theatre actors, films, projectionists, stage hands, musicians and theatre employees all donated their time with the permission of the unions. All money raised would go toward the purchase of cigarettes which would be distributed to the overseas stations gratis.

According to Sylvania's 1943 Burnham High School Yearbook titled "The Hourglass – 1943" Lowell Kelb was the first enlisted senior of the class of 1943. His picture is featured on a full page display which is captioned: "So near and yet so far…Our Alma Mater…He was, but he isn't… Lowell Kelb, first enlisted senior…Our service gallery…Is the woman the weaker sex?...Burnham's symphony…Hundred men and a girl."

In July of 1943 a surprise daylight air-raid drill was held in Sylvania. This was in preparation of a possible daytime enemy bombing. The exact date and time was not announced. At the steady blast of the sirens, vehicular traffic was to continue at a speed not to exceed 15 miles per hour. Pedestrians were to proceed with care and prepare to seek shelter. When the intermittent signal was sounded, traffic would halt and everyone would seek cover.

In a letter to the Toledo Chapter American Red Cross in August of 1943 Sylvania's school superintendent Ira Baumgartner informed them that the classroom in Maplewood School, which for many months, had been used by them as a Sylvania sub-station for making surgical dressings for the Armed forces had to be vacated this week in order that the school could use the classroom again. He informed the Red Cross that they were experiencing overcrowded conditions in the first grades at Maplewood School, with 102 first grade pupils in the two first grade rooms. The only room left in the building was the room being used by the Red Cross. He told them that the room had been a classroom prior to the last addition, and had been used by the Red Cross since then. They were again in need of the room as a classroom. He ended his letter by saying: "We regret this room is no longer available for use by the Red Cross and hope there will be no difficulty in finding a suitable location in Sylvania, for this good work should be carried on." The 10-28-1943 announced that the new Red Cross sub-station in Sylvania for making surgical dressings was being established in the Sylvania Community Church at 5723 Summit Street.

The 10-7-1943 issue of the *Sylvania Sentinel* reported that the Sentinel had been asked to aid in a nationwide campaign to collect 20,000,000 items of clothing for the men, women and children in Nazi-occupied Greece. Funds to purchase food and medical supplies and to finance the program of the Greek War Relief Association were being raised by Community War Chests throughout the country. The clothing was to be collected and taken to the Greek headquarters in Toledo. Nicholas Pappas was the chairman of the Greek Relief Association.

In October of 1943 H.C. Quinnell had taken over operation of the *Sylvania Sentinel* newspaper again and continued the column titled: "The Mail Bag." The following was published in the 10-7-1943 issue: "Editor's note to the men and women in the service: Since we will be editing the Sentinel for a while, Mrs. Quinnell and I wish to take this opportunity of saying "hello" to all of you. We want you to know that the folks back home think of you constantly and are trying to be as good Americans as you are. We will be glad to hear from any or all of you and wish you the best luck! H.C. Quinnell."

Another article in October of 1943 in the *Sylvania Sentinel* reported: "Recently several high government officials on the Federal Man Power Commission have stressed the fact that during 1943 more than a million women will be required for mechanical positions in War plants. They have also estimated that the total employment of women will exceed five million. Burnham High School offers courses of training in shop practice, inspection, and welding. Men and women who have training and are ready for employment will be considered first. The classes are arranged to accommodate those who may be employed in non-essential work. One machine shop class from 4 pm to 10 pm, one from 12:30 am to 6:30 am and one Saturday and Sunday PM."

In March of 1944 groups were holding tin collections to help with the war efforts. This was a collection of salvaged tin. Residents were asked to flatten the empty cans and set them at the curb on a certain date to be collected by the various groups. They were picked up by the high school kids in little red wagons and taken to a truck where they were hauled to Toledo.

The 4-27-1944 issue of the *Sylvania Sentinel* reported: "MILITARY UNIT BEING FORMED IN SYLVANIA - Major James C. Ewing, commanding officer of Headquarters and Service Company, Fourth Infantry, Ohio State Guard, announces that there are openings for one hundred men for enlistment for one year duration in the newly formed Headquarters and Service Company. Enlistees serve four nights per month unless it is the desire of the soldier to serve additional time. There will be five commissioned officers appointed who have completed their officers training and whose names appear on the eligibility list. In addition to twenty-one non-commissioned officers who will be appointed from the ranks, Major Ewing states that inasmuch as so many men from Sylvania have expressed their desire to be of service on the home front that it is his intention to offer enlistments to fifty men of this district. These men will not serve as soldiers of the regularly constituted army but of the State Guard, which is under the jurisdiction of the Fifth Service Command, United States Army. Complete uniforms are furnished and members of the organization are allotted extra gasoline for transportation. Men of Sylvania who will join this new Headquarters and Service Command are requested to communicate with Public Relations Officer A. Hiett Ward at 638 Phillips Avenue, Toledo, Lawndale 1125, nights. Call KIngswood 1501 for enlistment at their earliest convenience. On Saturday afternoon between

2:00 and 8:00 p.m. an enlistment officer will be at the Sylvania Auto Company for interviews (the Sylvania Auto Company was at 5701 Main Street). The Armory on Secor Road will be too small to accommodate the new company which will take over the Wall Street Induction Center, now being used for Selective Service induction. According to Major Ewing there has been an overflow of men desiring to join in the recent past and he encourages men interested to arrange for enlistment at once."

The following article was published in the 4-27-1944 *Sylvania Sentinel*: "Merchant Mariner Home On Furlough – Oscar Dietsch, one of the oldest men recruited in the Merchant Marines and certainly the oldest from Sylvania is home on leave after eight months in service. At sixty one years of age, Mr. Dietsch looks forty five and says he feels younger than that. His voyages have been many including a 17,000 mile trip in the short time he has been in service. He has crossed the equator twice and has been east of the International Date Line. He has brought back souvenirs from New Guinea and brought his wife a beautiful pure silk Chinese Kimono of which she is very proud. Mrs. Dietsch's greatest joy however was in her husband being able to be home on the 27th as that is the 36th anniversary of their wedding day. Mr. Dietsch's youngest son, Robert is in the Army Engineers and is in Italy. It would probably be hard to duplicate this case where the oldest in the family, the father, and the youngest are both in the service of their country. Mr. Dietsch declared that he liked the sea very much and was glad that he had gone into service. His promotion two weeks ago to 3rd Assistant Engineer proves that he has done well. Mr. Dietsch stated "the sooner everyone in this country realizes that this is everybody's war and does his part, the sooner it will be brought to victorious conclusion."

Sylvania's 1944 Burnham High School yearbook reported: "Smallest senior class…only 101… cause—large number in armed forces . . . the few left spent the year being different . . . first— broke tradition when senior pictures were taken at LaSalle's instead of Livingston's . . . had fun posing in the mirror for "Photo-reflex" camera . . . our winter formal, December 23, went over the top in popularity. . . we decorated Trilby Log Cabin with pine branches, red bows and a Christmas tree . . . danced to music of Runyan's Rhythm Jacks . . . did it again when we introduced the first issue of printed "Student Prints". . . complete with news pictures n'everything . . . honored Sylvania's history when we changed the name of yearbook to different and distinctive "Wyandotte" . . . taken from Indians who inhabited surrounding countryside "way back when" . . . committee for caps and gowns changed routine of somber black and gold to white gowns with red tassels . . . made for striking and impressive commencement ceremony . . . " Note by author: most of the male students who graduated in 1944 went on to serve in the Armed Forces.

The *Sylvania Sentinel* dated 5-4-1944 reported the following: "Mrs. Frank Harrwaldt of Berkey has received word from PFC Eugene Garreau who states that he is a prisoner somewhere in Germany. This was good news to Mrs. Harrwaldt, who raised Pvt. Garreau from a small child to manhood and feels like a real mother to him. She feared that he was dead. Pvt. Garreau was reported missing in action on Jan. 28, and no word had been heard since until Monday when Mrs. Harrwaldt received the post card through the Red Cross. The card stated that he would be able to write and receive mail at another camp to which he was being transferred." The 5-31-1945 issue of the *Sylvania Sentinel* reported that Pfc. Eugene Garreau was home after being a prisoner of the Germans in Stalig-2B. He was enjoying a 67-day furlough. Private Garreau said that the daily menu in the camp consisted of two cold boiled potatoes each and a three pound loaf of bread for 13 men, with one pound of oleomargarine for 33 men. They were marched for three days and three nights with no food at all when the Russians started bombing Stalag 2-B. The 5th Armored Division of the American Army were their liberators at the new camp."

8-10-1944 – *Sylvania Sentinel*: "Saw some of the Prisoners of War the other day at the quarry at Sylvania and Centennial Rds. They certainly didn't look as if they were missing many meals nor suffering in any other way either. In fact they looked quite content with the world and no doubt they are. If there is anything like security possible, they have it, at least for the duration. We wish we could be sure that our boys who are prisoners of the German government were receiving the same kind of treatment."

History tells us that in December of 1944 the Battle of the Bulge occurred. In this battle Germany launched its final defensive through the Ardennes region of Belgium, but they were beaten back by the allies.

This letter was published in the *Sylvania Sentinel* on 12-7-1944: "A letter from Lyle A. Waterman, S1/c, to his parents, Mr. and Mrs. C.M. Waterman, 5727 Main St., follows: Dear Mom and Dad: Just a few lines tonight to say I am fine and hope this letter finds you the same. Well, Mom, the Navy has given us permission to tell you of one of the battles we have been in. It is the Battle of Surigao Strait in the Philippines. We were in the invasion of the Leyte Island in the Philippines when we got word that the Jap navy was coming out to fight, and they sure did. But I doubt if there are any Japs living to write their people about it. It happened on Oct. 25. Sorry I can't give you time but maybe you can read the papers and find that out. It has been the largest naval battle so far in history. Our ship was given credit for helping to sink a Jap battleship and other war vessels. Boy, I tell you that is something I will never forget, seeing all the fireworks, and the next morning seeing what we had done and still in one piece. Boy, Mom, I tell you I aged 10 years that night. The battle is now over and we can sure say that our ship, along with the others, sure did our part to help bring this war to an end faster. I sure will have plenty to tell you about when I get home. I thought the sight of dead men would kind of weaken me, but there were dead men as thick as flies and all Japs. I wonder if any of the other boys from Sylvania were in that battle. Mom, when I found out we were right in the middle of the largest battle ever to take place on the seas, I turned every color in the paint shop. But we are all pretty lucky to be here talking about it. I see that Joe Hittler was in the invasion of France. I wonder how it is over there. Mom, I don't think Gordon Case took part in the naval battle. But he was in on the invasion of the Philippines. I know I had a letter from Louis and he is in Pearl Harbor. But he can have my share of that place. Mom, if you are able to get the story in the paper, let me know where. Your loving son, Lyle."

Sylvania Sentinel 12-7-1944: "Four Burnham Boys Leave For Navy – Four seniors of Burnham High School leave this week for duty in the U.S. Navy. All of them enlisted in the Navy before reaching their 18th birthday in order to pick the service of their choice instead of being drafted. One of the boys is Robert Schultz, center of the basketball team and one whose loss will be greatly felt. Two others are Joe Stykemain and Kenneth Leitner, who played regularly on the football team this past season. The fourth boy is James Fitzpatrick."

In the 1-25-1945 issue of the *Sylvania Sentinel,* Ray Corbin, editor of this newspaper wrote the following: "We have no figures on it, but we venture to say that Sylvania has been hit about as hard as any comparable community in casualties in the war. Hardly a week passes but what another name has been added to the list. Surely the good people of this community have a very real stake in the peace which will be made after victory is won. Whether they will have a voice in it is another matter. What kind of a peace do we want?"

The column in the *Sylvania Sentinel* titled "While Waiting by NIBROC" (written by Ray Corbin) writes: "We have a bit of advice for everyone today which is the cure for all troubles. Everyone seems to be strained and uneasy about everything. Our advice is to relax. What with the critical cost situation, shortage of butter, pepper, bananas, tires, gas and, in fact, just about every item you can think of, and it is easy to take a very pessimistic attitude toward the future of this country, it is no wonder that the jitters have us down. We ask, so what? Can you do anything about it? No, so just relax and the first thing we know we will be dead and then we won't know anything. Simple, is it not?"

By February of 1945 the *Sentinel* newspaper was reminding residents of the following rationing: meats and fats – Red stamps; processed foods – Blue stamps; sugar – stamp 34, tires and fuel oil.

According to records, during World War II there was a Jeep testing ground in Sylvania Township which lay between McCord Road and Holland-Sylvania Road, north of Brint Road and then south to where McCord Junior High School is now located.

According to the *Sylvania Sentinel* dated 2-22-1945: "William H. Brown, Signalman Third Class, USNR, 6920 Brint Road, Sylvania, was a crew member of the USS SC 744, which was recently lost in action off Leyte Island in the Philippines. After being badly damaged in an air attack, the 744 was kept afloat for five hours by two officers and two enlisted men who remained aboard as a damage control party. The sturdy submarine chaser succumbed to her wounds later and sank after being towed to port. In the meantime, the 744's skipper, Lieut. Donald S. Stroetzel, USNR, Geneseo, N.Y. had ordered all other surviving crew members to be evacuated to a nearby Army tug. Seven men were killed in the fatal attack. Lieut. Stroetzel has paid high tribute to Signalman Brown and his shipmates. "In maintaining battle stations and continuing to fire at attaching aircraft in the face of a strong starting attack," he said, "all hands showed excellent discipline and lived up to the highest traditions of the service." Signalman Brown is a survivor."

The following article appeared in the *Sylvania Sentinel* dated 3-22-1945: "WITH THE 101ST AIRBORNE DIVISION ON THE WESTERN FRONT – Within two days after the 101st Airborne Division pulled into Bastogne shortly after the start of the Battle of the Bulge. It was completely sealed from outside help. When the Germans demanded surrender, acting division commander Brig. Gen. Anthony C. McAuliffe answered: "Nuts." The defense was to attack continuously. At one point, the ammunition ration was 11 rounds to a gun. No planes were able to break through the low ceiling to bring support and supplies. There were too many wounded for the medics to handle. But seven days after the encirclement, the battle of the Bastogne pocket ended. A corridor has been established with our own troops. The 101st Airborne had completed another chapter in its historic march through the battles of World War II. Pvt. Thomas J.

Bayless, 6381 Monroe St., Sylvania was one of those heroes. In addition participating in the battle of Bastogne, the 506th Parachute Infantry Regiment played a major role in the success of the Normandy and Holland campaigns. It took part in the Fall of Carentan and later liberated Eindhoven, in Holland. It twice took the measure of the elite German 6th Parachute Regiment in attaining victories in France and Holland." Mr. and Mrs. J.D. Bissonnette received a card on 4-14-1945 from their son, Leo Bissonnette, dated Jan. 1, saying he was a German prisoner. On Jan. 30, the parents had received notification from the War Department that he was missing in action.

In April 1945 President Roosevelt died. He was succeeded by President Truman. On 4-28-1945 Italian partisans captured Mussolini and executed him. Two days later the German leader Adolf Hitler committed suicide in his bombproof shelter along with his mistress, Eva Braun, who he had at the last minute made his wife. On 5-2-1945 German forces surrendered in Italy to Allies. V.E. Day, or "Victory in Europe" was celebrated on 5-8-1945.

On 5-17-1945 it was announced that the Government needed and asked its citizens in the 180th week of the war against Japan to: 1. Buy your overseas service man a bond during the 7th War Loan Drive, and tell him you have done so on a V-Mail gift certificate, obtainable wherever war bonds are sold. 2. Stay on your war job until victory over Japan. If manpower needs in your industry are changing, your U.S. Employment Service Office can tell you the nearest job where you are needed. 3. Continue to buy only what you need. Reconversion has started, but America's factories cannot produce sufficient civilian goods to end the threat of inflation while Pacific war needs continue."

On 5-20-1945 a memorial service was held in the Whiteford Church of Christ for T/Sergt. Darrell Allen who was killed in action on Iwo Jima.

In June of 1945 T/Sergt Thomas addressed the Sylvania Booster Club regarding his experiences in the war. He was the nephew of Mr. and Mrs. Milton Rowe of Acres Road. Here's what a newspaper article said: "Sergt Thomas stated that he had spent nine months overseas and about one-third of that time was spent in occupied countries on foot. The first time he had to bail out was over Romania during a bombing mission at the Ploesti oil fields in August, 1944. He spent 28 days arriving back to his base in Italy, but, in retrospect, it was a lark in comparison to his second experience. This was so because it was summer and partisans of Yugoslavia took him in hand and aided his return. The crew made their escape that time and upon returning to camp expected to be treated as heroes but found that such an experience was not unusual and the crew was broken up. His second "jump" occurred over Austria on Dec. 27 when his crew had to leave their ship by parachute. The engines of the ship were not functioning properly and as a result they lost their position in the formation and were struck by flak and the number two motor caught fire and the ship rapidly lost altitude. The order came to abandon ship and he was the fourth man to jump. Of the crew's 11 men, two crashed with the plane and of the nine who jumped, Sergt. Thomas was the only man to escape capture by the Gestapo. The sergeant landed in a tree and cut himself loose as soon as possible. He then made for the mountains. He had two broken ribs and lacerations on his legs from landing in the tree. After many close calls, he finally made his way into Yugoslavia and was finally returned to his base in Italy. This time he spent 54 days in his wanderings and lost 30 pounds and suffered dysentery, bugs, exposure in blizzards, starvation and lack of sleep. It was winter instead of summer as in his first experience and as a consequence his sufferings were multiplied many times. The sergeant explained the loss of the ship by declaring that the crew was made up of men who had to bail out before from other ships and it was "just too much bad luck in one plane..." The most amazing thing about Sergt. Thomas to his listeners was his spirit and appearance. One would never suspect that this young man, 23 years old, had ever left home, least of all make his way alone through enemy country for 54 days and suffered privations that would try the soul and spirit of any man. Sergt. Thomas was sincere in stating that "he was very glad to be home in God's own country once again, and he would be satisfied to stay here for the rest of his life." Sergt. Thomas was with the 15th Air Force and was a radio operator gunner on a B-24 Liberator Bomber. He wears the Purple Heart, Good Conduct Medal, European Theater of Operations Medal, Presidential Citation, Caterpillar Club, besides wearing a pleasant smile and a soldierly bearing. He has made his home with his uncle, Milton Rowe, for the last three years and considers Sylvania his home. He has a brother, Harvey, who is in the Navy in the South Pacific."

The 6-8-1945 *Toledo Blade* featured a picture of four officers. The caption reads: "Officers of the 37th Division stand at attention as the American flag goes up once again over Bagulo. Left to right they are Brig. Gen. Charles F. Craig, Nashville, Tenn., assistant division commander; Brig. Gen. Leo M. Kreber, Columbus, O., divisional artillery commander; Col. Kenneth Cooper, 3337 Harley Rd., executive officer divisional artillery, and Major Nelson Randall, Sylvania, O., staff officer divisional artillery. General Kreber's arm is bandaged as a result of shrapnel wounds suffered several days prior to the fall of the Philippine mountain city in northern Luzon."

On 7-26-1945 the *Sylvania Sentinel* reported that Lt. Col. Victor E. Warford was home from the wars and had spent six months imprisonment as a German prisoner of war. His parents were Mr. and Mrs. Herbert Warford, 5810 Acres Road. He had been reported missing in action on 10-11-1944, just after he had been awarded the Distinguished Flying Cross and had received the promotion from Major to Lieutenant Colonel. Later he was reported a prisoner of war and he was released from Stalag 7 by the Russians on 4-29-1945. Warford had been overseas for 19 months and had not seen his daughter since she was three months old.

On 8-6-1945 after the Japanese generals refused to surrender the United States dropped an atomic bomb on the island of Hiroshima. On 8-8-1945 Russia declared war on Japan, and on 8-9-1945 the U.S. dropped an atomic bomb on the island of Nagasaki. On 8-14-1945 the Japanese unconditionally surrendered to allies ending World War II.

The 8-16-1945 issue of the *Sylvania Sentinel* reported: "The war is over and we feel very humble when we think of the many men and women who endured hardships beyond our most vivid imagination, even to the supreme sacrifice, so that people in oppressed countries might be free and that we in this country might never know the ravages of war. We pray that our leaders may be guided in dealing so wisely in the new World Wide Peace that all their efforts may not have been in vain." Another section of that same newspaper said: "It seemed that all cars headed for Toledo Tuesday evening as soon as the great news that everyone was waiting to hear was flashed over the air waves. We did too and were impressed by the lack of rowdiness in the crowd. Whole families were downtown apparently just enjoying milling around with other very happy people.

Of course there were the usual humorous incidents, but no one seemed out of control. Sylvania Main Street too had its share of happy folks who danced and sang in joyful relief."

Here's what the 8-16-1945 issue of the *Sylvania Sentinel* said: "WATCH ANNOUNCEMENT FOR V-J CELEBRATION – The Committee for a Victory Celebration in Sylvania composed of representatives from various organizations ask that we stand by for further announcement of this event. Several of the participants have been out of town this week, including Mayor Wefer, who is to preside."

The *Sylvania Sentinel* editor said this in the 8-23-1945 issue: "How much thought has been given to this problem that will soon be facing us in Sylvania? While many of our young men and women in the service have married while serving their country, many, many more will be planning on entering into that state of bliss as soon as they receive their discharge. Just where are we going to house them? Are we going to let them leave this town and go elsewhere to establish a home and rear their children? If this is not to be the case something will soon have to be done towards making suitable building sites available. Re-conversion is not our problem, but home building certainly is. Let's keep those youngsters here and build a solid community."

Sergeant Donald D. Price, son of Mrs. Nellie A. Price, Route I, Box 29, Sylvania, was with the 718th Tank Battalion on Mindanao. He was involved in the Philippine Liberation Campaign and the record of the 716th Tank Battalion was now able to be revealed. Sgt. Price reported that he was proud of their record. "Supporting the doughboys in Assault Lands on Luzon, Panay, Negros, Cebu, Jolo, Zamboanga Peninsula and on Mindanao, the tanks met and defeated the best the Japs had." Sergeant Price related: "Our tanks have fought every kind of warfare in the books. We engaged the tanks of the Nip 2nd Armored Division on the roads and on the spreading rice paddies of Luzon, we took part in the street fighting at Manila and as a part of Tank-Infantry teams we cleared the Sons of Heaven from the jungles of Mindanao. We had been continuously in Combat from the 9th of January until the termination of the Philippine Campaign, moving from operation to operation so fast that often after firing the last shot at the retreating Nips at noon, we would find ourselves loading on LST's that evening, off for another Jap held island." Sergeant Price added: "In six months of fighting our battalion killed more than 3,000 Nips. It is little wonder Infantry Divisions that operated in the Philippines regard the 716th as the 'Wolf-Pack' so highly." Sgt. Price was awarded the Bronze Star Medal for heroic action at Cebu."

The following was printed in the 9-6-1945 *Sylvania Sentinel*: "On the USS Oakland in Tokyo Bay—Eugene F. Paul, fire control man, third class, USN, Brint Rd, Sylvania, Ohio, is serving on this cruiser, which is part of the powerful Pacific fleet completing the first stages of the occupation of Japan. Under the operational control of Admiral William F. Halsey, USN."

The following items appeared in the *Sylvania Sentinel* dated 9-27-1945: "Pvt. 1/c Harold Rieger received his discharge from the army after 37 months in the service with 26 of them served in Alaska. Pvt. Rieger, his wife Ellinore and daughter Carol Jean are making their home with Mrs. Rieger's mother Mrs. Warnke on Webster Road."

"Merle E. Friess RM2/c writes to his parents Mr. and Mrs. Chelsea E. Friess from the Pacific theater and we think it is rather interesting. There are three other Friess boys in service: Corp. Chelsea E. Friess, Jr., and T/Sgt. Ellery P. Friess are both on the way home from Germany and Donald E. Friess A/S is at Sampson, N.Y."

"More than three thousand soldiers of Ohio's famed 37th (Buckeye) Division are enroute to the United States in the division's first mass return under the Army's re-adjustment program. There are many of the group who have served with the 37th since its indication in October 1940, and who will have completed five years military service by the time they are discharged."

The following were listed returning home in the 10-4-1945 *Sylvania Sentinel*: Lieutenant Betty Louise Harroun, daughter of Mr. and Mrs. John Harroun of Whiteford Road arrived home after service in England, France and Germany, Scotland and Belgium for the past two years and nine months. First Lieutenant Inez Bieber at home after serving overseas for 2 years as an Army Nurse. T/Sgt. Stanley R. Hesselbart, son of Mr. and Mrs. Clifton Hesselbart of 6768 Erie Street arrived home after spending three years and four months in service.

In November of 1945 it was reported that 14 German soldiers who were prisoners of war and kept in the camp near Blissfield, Michigan, were killed and 15 died soon after as a New York Central passenger train struck their truck at a grade crossing near Blissfield. 24 prisoners of war, an American guarding them and a civilian truck driver were in the truck and the other 11 were injured.

Also in November of 1945 the local Price and Rationing Board ended its service in the district with one of the top records. All applications for tires, food, price inquiries, and price complaints were referred to Board No. 1, 307 Superior Street. William H. Seed the chief clerk of the board called the job obnoxious. A.H. Randall was the chairman of this board during the duration. The rationing board and the clerks did all this work through a volunteer program. Some delay in processing applications from this point on was expected until they removed all the records to Toledo, but veterans and emergency cases were taken care of without delay.

In October of 1945 Mr. and Mrs. Walter C. Pattison of Route 1, Sylvania were notified by the government that their son, Pvt. Elmore W. Pattison, was liberated from Jukuoka prison camp in Japan on September 15 and was on his way home from Manila. The parents were also informed that Elmore's health was as good as could be expected. Pvt. Pattison had been a prisoner of the Japs since the surrender of Corregidor in May of 1942.

The Editor of the *Sylvania Sentinel* wrote the following in the 12-27-1945 issue of the newspaper: "We, as comparative newcomers to town, cannot help but be impressed by the greatly increased number of young men in town. The boys are coming home every day and this clears up some of the cause of the shortage of houses. Many of the returned servicemen were boys when they left, and now are husbands and fathers. This may also account for that 5 million increase in the nation's population in the last five years."

The *Sylvania Sentinel* dated 2-21-1946 said that a "Welcome Home" get together dance in honor of Sylvania servicemen and servicewomen and veterans would be held at Burnham High School on February 22. It was being sponsored by the Sylvania Alumni Association and the American Legion. Music was furnished by Stan Hesselbart and his Sylvan Serenaders.

On Memorial Day of 1948 the Sylvania community held appropriate ceremonies for a bronze memorial wall which was placed in Burnham High School on the wall as you entered the large auditorium. This memorial wall remained at this location until 2010.

In 2010 the Roll of Honor was moved to the City of Sylvania Administration Building at 6730 Monroe Street. The top of the memorial reads: Burnham High School Roll of Honor – In honor of those who answered the call of their country in World War II.

The list below are the names that appeared on the Burnham "Wall of Honor" as of May of 2010, which was moved from the old Burnham High School (6850 Monroe Street), before it was demolished, and is now located in the City of Sylvania Administration Building (6730 Monroe Street). All names with a * before the name are individuals who were marked as Casualties or Killed in Action. As I reviewed the wall and talked to various veterans it was determined that many of the names of residents that served in this war, and attended Burnham, were missing from this Burnham wall. It appears that they discontinued adding to the list at some point during the war, or had the same problem I had in the fact that yearbooks were not published during the years of 1933 thru 1940 (because of the depression years), and only the graduation class lists were available. Therefore, as the men of Sylvania entered World War II the committee could not verify whether each man had attended Burnham High School. But, a search of documents from those missing yearbook years was made and some additional documents were located among the Sylvania Area Historical Societies records. Also, Howard Pratt is listed on this "Wall of Honor" but does not have a star to indicate that he was killed in action. Harold Jasmund also needs a star to indicate that he was killed in action, and Robert O. Wood is on the Burnham wall but did not have a star. There were 27 stars on the wall out of 706 names listed, and three stars were missing, for a total of 30 Burnham High School attendee casualties on the wall. The following names appeared on the wall as of 6-30-2010:

Robert F. Adams, Carl Aiken, Jr., Alvah Alcock, Bruce Alcock, *Darrel Allen, Victor Anderson, Clayton Anstead, Robert Anstead, Robert R. Anteau, William Apple, Wayne Armstrong, Harold Asman, Robert L. Aulich, Marion Austin, Herman Bach, Julius Bach, Valentine Bach, Marshall Bacon, Clarence Baker, George Balz, C. John Bancroft, Lance H. Barbarick, Kenneth W. Barnard, Glenn Barricklow, Ralph Barricklow, Clarence Barry, John E. Barry, Ellen J. Bartell, George Bauman, R.S. Baumgartner, Leonard Beach, Robert Beach, Reese Beatty, Roy S. Becker, Bernard C. Benton, Fred Benton, Orland E. Berndt, William Bernholtz, Elmer Berry, Harold Berry, *James W. Berry, *Max Wayne Berry, Paul Bettinger, *Jess Bieber, James Billings, Jerry Bishop, Leo Bissonnette, Joe F. Bissonnette, Neil Bissonnette, Bernard Black, Charles Bleckner, Sidney Blue, Eugene Bockert, John Bomia, Eugene Bond, Allen Boprey, Winfield Bowman, James Brashear, Edwin Brattain, *Leroy Breier, Edwin Briggs, Ronald Brinning, Arthur T. Brown, *Bernard O. Brown, Donald E. Brown, Elmer Brown, Emery L. Brown, Jerome Brown, Ralph E. Brown, Walter S. Brown, William E. Brown, William H. Brown, Donald Buck, Richard Buck,

William L. Buck, Archie Buffington, James J. Bunting, Edwin W. Burnes, Robert F. Burnes, Donnabell Burton, Carl Butterfield, Howard Butterfield, Edward Butz, Richard Butz, Pete Buyaki, Leland Calkins, Ernest Campbell, Robert Carlson, Budd Carr, John Carr, Gordon Case, Melvin Case, Merlin F. Case, John Chandler, Leroy Chandler, Raymond Chandler, Stanley Chandler, John Christenson, Albert Clark, Elwood Clark, Fenton P. Clark, Melvin Clark, Roger G. Clarke, Marion Clayton, Jim A. Clegg, Richard Cline, Arba C. Comstock, Carl Comstock, Eugene Comstock, Jack Comstock, William G. Comstock, David Cook, Robert Cook, Mahlon Cooper, Paul Cooper, John F. Corrigan, Glenn Coutcher, Joseph Coutcher, Lewis Cowden, Merle Cowell, Robert Cowell, Thurlow E. Cowell, Enos J. Cowell, Jr., Thomas G. Crabtree, Glenn Crego, Lloyd Creque, Madeline D Creque, Robert Creque, Dallas Crider, Charles Crim, Eugene Cruey, Ray E. Cruey, William Cunningham, James Curry, Preston Curry, Lucy Cwiklewski, Carl J. Damico, Clark Davenport, Carl R. Davis, Richard B. Davis, Howard Day, Bryan R. J. Deer, Francis DeLano, Duane DeLauter, George Deppman, Harold Deppman, Gordon M. Deye, Roland Deye, Robert A. Dietsch, Willard D. Dixon, Carl Dorcas, Allen Dorr, Doris Double, Patrick R. Dresch, Harry C. Ducy, Rolland F. Dunn, James B. Durbin, Roger T. Durbin, Kurt A. Durst, Ray Dutton, John Duvall, Ralph Duvall, Benedict Dzienny, H. Beverly Earl, Joseph Eby, Elwood Edinger, Gerald Edinger, Kenneth Edinger, Urban Edinger, Daniel Edwards, Donald Eff, Kenneth Eggert, Joe C. Eubank, John Fallis, Wayne Farley, John Feeney, Chauncy M. Felt, Norman Felt, Sam Felt, C. Olin Fischer, Clayton F. Fischer, Leroy C. Fischer, Richard Fisher, *Robert C. Fisher, Roy D. Fitkin, James Fitzpatrick, Harold E. Flagg, Robert Flagg, Paul Fleeger, Walter H. Fleeger, Norman J. Fleig, Raymond Fleig, Sherrill Fleming, Grant Fletcher, James Follas, Jerome Follas, Joseph Follas, Junior D. Follas, Francis Foote, Morgan Ford, Robert Fowler, Robert Frankhouser, Harold French, Donald Friess, Ellery P. Friess, Merle Friess, Chelsea E. Friess, Jr., James Fuerst, Floyd Fulton, William Fulton, Lee Futrell, Harry Gaeth, Clarence Gallagher, Harold F. Gallagher, Leonard Gallagher, Friel Galliher, James Gallup, Martha Gang, Murl Gardner, Charles B. Garrett, Eugene H. Geer, Almon V. Gibbs, Forest Giffen, Donald Gillhouse, Lester Gillhouse, Jim Glanzman, Richard Glase, James W. Glase, Robert W. Goble, Kenneth Goodwin, Donald Gray, Harple Gray, Lawrence Gray, Malcolm C. Gray, Floyd Gray, Jr., Owen Griffen, Leo Grodi, LeRoy Grodi, Howard Gross, Watson Gruber, Richard Haefner, Fredrick Halbert, Harold Hall, Virginia Hanna, Burdell F. Hansen, Wilbur L. Hansen, Paul Harris, Betty Harroun, John E. Harroun, Parker Harroun, Robert Harroun, Basil M. Harroun, Jr., *Leon Harrwaldt, John Hart, Rudolph Hartkoff, Harold C. Hartman, Richard Hartman, * Lloyd R. Hartzler, Eugene Hartzog, Hiram Hawley, Clarence Haynes, Charles Hayward, Charles Heaton, William Heaton, Robert Heinberger, Stanley Hesselbart, Allen Hewitt, Harold L. Hill, Edwin Hiller, Benton Hine, Calvin Hobling, Howard Hobling, Sam Hobling, Harvey Hoddinot, Garld Holmes, Jack Hooker, Eugene Hoot, Walter Hoskins, Howard Hotchkiss, Danny Hott, *Edwin D. Howard, Kenneth Howard, Gerald Huber, Charles W. Huffman, William B. Hundley, Gordon Huss, Norman C. Huss, Charles Iffland, Allen Ihrig, Charles Ihring, Eugene Jasmund, Harold Jasmund, Raymond Jennewine, Richard Jennewine, Roy Jennewine, Eugene Jernigan, Harold Johnson, Joseph Johnson, Beryl G. Jones, *Charles William Jones, W. Allen Jones, *Arthur Jones, Jr., Harold L. Kanavel, Raymond Kanavel, Stanley Karamol, Eugene Keck, Lowell Kelb, Edward M. Keller, James Kennedy, John Kennedy, Raymond Kennedy, Robert Kern, J. Pete Kerste, Ione Kiplinger, John Kitchen, Sherman Kittle, John Kjoller, Stanley Kjoller, Carl Knavel, Dan H. Knepper, Sam J. Knepper, Donald Knisely, Ray Knisely, Edward Koch, Frank J. Koepfer, Jack Koester, William R. Koester, Rollin Koester, Daniel J. Konieczka, Melvin Konieczka, Lester

Konz, Kenneth Korth, Steve Kovach, George Kovak, George Kramer, John H. Kramer, Raymond Kramer, Donald Krieger, Earl Krieger, Medford Krieger, Sylvester Krolak, Ellis Kroll, Harley Kroll, John H. Kruse, Paul Kunz, Rose Lado, Paul Lajiness, Arnold Lancaster, Herman Lang, Irwin J. Lang, Donald Lanning, Donald L. LaPoint, Emerson L. LaPoint, Paul R. LaPoint, Kenneth Larzelere, Richard Lather, Robert Lather, Walter, Lather, Frank Laughlin, Jr., Kenneth Laux, Frederick LaVigne, Clarence Lay, Kenneth Leitner, W.G. Lenert, Harold Lewallen, Arnold Lewis, Donald Lewis, Floyd Lewis, Lester Lewis, Raymond H. Lewis, Albert Linder, Carl Linder, Otto Linder, Paul Linder, Robert Linder, Edward Lingo, Harry Lingo, Arthur Link, Floyd Lisinski, John Lisinski, Clair Little, Donald Lochbihler, Arthur E. Loomer, Edward J. Loomis, Margaret M. Loomis, Grant Lowe, Leonard Lowe, George Lucas, Dean Luse, Arthur J. Mackenzie, Ralph E. Mackenzie, Russell G. Mackenzie, Joseph Maddox, John Malloy, Archie Marmar, Joe Marmar, Alice Marsh, Arnott J. Marsh, Benjamin Marsh, Leonard Marsh, Raymond Marsh, Richard Marsh, Raymond P. Martin, Victor Martin, Claire V. Mason, Claren Maurer, Carroll Maxwell, Art Mayer, Charles McConnell, Harold McConnell, *J.E. (James E.) McCullough, Robert McDole, George V. McGlenn, Russell McGlenn, Devere H. McLees, John McNett, Eugene F. McNett, Norbert McNett, Thomas J. McNett, George McNutt, Allen Merce, Leonard Mitruk, Donald Mey, Robert Mey, Doyle Michelsen, Robert Mickens, Gerald Miller, Gilbert Miller, Harry S. Miller, Herbert C. Miller, Noble Miller, Phillip Miller, Richard Miller, *Richard W. Miller, Harry W. Mockbee, Ray Moffett, John Mohr, *Don W. Moore, Richard Moore, Richard Moore, Richard R. Moore, Robert W Moore, Gale Morningstar, *W. (Wayne) Morningstar, Howard Mull, Hascall Muntz, Robert Muntz, Mitchell Myers, Robert Napierala, Roger Napierala, Daniel Neshkoff, Daniel Neshkoff, Raymond Neshkoff, Jack B Newcomb, Duane Newton, John J. Newton, *Jack Nichols, Albert Noonan, Donald Oswalt, Robert C. Oswalt, Franklin J. Ott, Merlin J. Ott, Donald Page, L.C. Page, *Richard (H.)Palmer, Charles Parker, George H. Parsons, Robert L. Parter, Kenneth E. Paschen, Eugene Dewey Paul, Roland Pelton, Alfred E. Pemberton, Frank H. Peters, Fred Peterson, Alvin W. Phoebus, Norman Pool, Bernard H. Porter, Marinus Porter, Norma Portman, William Postlewaite, Carl Postlewaite, Thomas Powless, Howard R. Pratt, B. Edwin Price, Donald D. Price, Gordon W. Pryce, Henry S. Pucilowski, David Pugsley, Charles H. Quinnell, Bernard Raabe, Floyd L. Rader, William Ramsey, Mac Randall, Nelson H. Randall, *James S. Randall, Norman C. Raney, Leonard J. Ratz, Robert Ravely, William Ravely, Harley H. Redman, Jr., David M. Redmond, Paul Reeb, Jr., Paul Reger, Edward R. Reitz, James E. Reitz, Rolland Ries, Lester Ritenour, William Ritenour, John Ritz, Lloyd Roberts, Norman A. Roberts, Richard Roberts, *David Robinson, Jack Robinson, James Robinson, Carl Robison, Dale Robison, Kieth (as written) Robison, Vernon Root, Leroy Ross, Fred Rothfuss, H. Jean Rower, Robert A. Rower, Norman Ruff, Phil Rush, Harold Ruswinkle, Albert P. Sakel, Alvin Sanders, LeRoy Sanders, Gail G. Sanderson, Gilbert Sanderson, Hugh Sanderson, Ford Sanderson, Jr., Verlin Saunders, Gloria Schaeffer, Edwin Schieb, John Schieb, Louis Schlieman, Herbert Schofield, Robert Schultz, Arthur M. Schuster, Daniel Schuster, John Schuster John D. Schuster, George Scott, Harold Scott, Richard Scott, Lester Seiple, Robert Selent, George Semelka, John Semelka, Arthur R. Shanley, Raymond Shanley, James H. Shepard, Melvin L. Shepard, William Shepardson, James Sherk, Jack Shively, Charles Shock, William Shoemaker, Arthur J. Shull, Dale C. Shull, *Kenneth Shull, *Wade (L.) Shull, Harry D. Siefert, Richard Sloan, Arza G. Smalley, Frank Smalley, James Smalley, John E. Smalley, Arthur C Smith, Donald J. Smith, Donald W. Smith, Dwight Smith, Elwyn L. Smith, Gale Smith, George Smith, Melvin Smith, Paul C. Smith, Paul J. Smith, Stewart C. Smith, Carl Ora Snyder, Earl R. Soper,

Louis Spino, Robert Spino, *Ray Sporleder, Elwood Stacey, Elmer Stanton, Robert Steele, Marvin Stephenson, Russell Stephenson, Stanford Storer, Eugene Stough, Jack Straub, Charles Strohl, Duane Strohl, Joseph Stykemain, George Sutkaitis, Garret Swart, Arthur Sylvester, Joseph Sylvester, Harry Szalkowski, Ray Szalkowski, Anna Tabbert, Arthur Tammarine, James Tammarine, *Paul Taylor, Kenneth Tebary, Leroy Thompson, Kenneth Tittler, Donald V. Tompkins, Richard Tracy, Robert Trettin, Wallace Underwood, Ralph A. Urie, James E. Ursell, William G. Vallely, Richard VanFleet, *Ralph VanGlahn, Jr., LaVern VanHorn, LaVern VanHorn, H. VanLandingham, Gerald VanMeer, Raymond VanPelt, Norman VanTutle, Dale A. VanVorce, Arlene Vesey, Bert M. Vesey, Tom Vineyard, George Wade, Ted Wade, Harry Wagner, Dwight Wagonlander, Charles N. Waite, Richard D. Waldo, C. Elmer Walker, Marvin Wallington, William Wallington, Howard Walrod, Victor E. Warford, Lyle A. Waterman, Edward E. Watkins, William H. Watkins, Dale Webb, Harry Webb, Robert C. Weber, Wade Weber, William Weldishofer, Ned Welsh, Hobart Werner, Albert White, Harold White, Rodney E. White, Art Whitenberg, William Whitney, Larry Whittaker, Robert Whittaker, Paul I. Wilcox, Robert Wilcox, Joseph Wilcynski, Robert Wilcynski, Melvin Wilkinson, Merle E. Wilkinson, Louis E. Willard, Burton E. Williams, Jack Wilson, Leo G. Wilson, Mathew H. Wilson, Maurice H. Wilson, William H. Wilson, A. Jack Wimberly, Eleanor Wimberly, Chester Wing, Darrel Wise, Glen Wittscheck, Leo Wittscheck, John L. Wobser, Wilbert F. Wolfe, Stephen Wolinski, Victor B. Wolinski, Donald Wood, Richard Wood, Robert O. Wood, Roy V. Woodard, William Woodard, Roy Woodby, Charles Woodward, James Woodward, Zita Woodward, Donald Wright, John Wright, Robert Wright, Herman Wuwert, Ural D. Yaw, *Earl (C.) Yeager, LaVerne Yeager, Milford Yeager, William Yeager, John L. Yoey, Arthur Yunker, Harold Yunker, Charles E. Ziegler, Richard Zinkie, Clayton A. Zumbrunn, *Chester Zwayer, Clifford Zwayer.

On 8-15-2010 at 3 p.m., the Burnham High School World War II Honor Roll Memorial was re-dedicated in its new home in the City Administration Building at 6730 Monroe Street. Also dedicated was a new Commemorative plaque to honor those who served in World War II, and attended Burnham High School, but were not listed on the original wall, for unknown reasons. It was determined that the name plaques on the original wall were too fragile to remove and reset. So, to accommodate the 107 additional student names not included on the original wall, a new Memorial plaque was purchased by the Burnham Commemorative Committee and the additional names were added. Research for this new wall was completed by Gayleen Gindy and Kristina Turner by using *Sylvania Sentinel* newspapers, available Burnham High School yearbooks and class graduation photos, census records, obituary notices from the *Sylvania Sentinel* and *Toledo Blade*, cemetery records and files at the Sylvania Area Historical Society, including WW II scrapbooks, school student directories and Sylvania Schools scrapbooks binded during the depression years by WPA workers and lists of test scores for students at Burnham High School. The following additional names were added because they attended Burnham High School and served during World War II (those marked with an asterisk gave their lives for our country during World War II, bringing the total number of those killed during World War II, who attended Burnham to 36). The following are the names added to the Burnham wall:

Howard Apsey, Francis D. Basler, Ray A. Beaty, Herbert C. Berry, Wesley Berry, Franklin Bieber, Inez Bieber, Matthew E. Bieber, George A. Bond, *Kenneth F. Brodbeck, Chester Bunting, Dexter Bunting, George D. Bunting, Harold R. Bunting, Matthew J. Bunting, Carl Burton,

Dewey Burton, Kenneth Burton, William Burton, Marvin F. Carl, Richard C. Carl, Richard E. Case, Robert E. Chandler, Virginia Chandler, Carl E. Clegg, Rita Corrigan, Gerald A. Creque, Wayne O. Creque, Harold G. Cunningham, *Melvin Dauer, Frederick S. Day, James A. Dean, Mark DeBruine, William Doley, *Robert L. Fisher, Richard C. Fowler, Donald F. Friedt, Marion P. Fulton, Glenn Gesaman, Charles E. Gries, Jr., Lavern G. Gross, Jack Handy, Donald W. Hartman, Earl Hawkins, Franklin L. Heeter, Robert Hiller, Martin Hoddinot, Jr., Richard Hollister, Kenneth A. Hotchkiss, John Hott, Gordon W. Keller, Henry C. Keller, Donald H. Kennedy,*Alfred Ernest Knepper, Stanley J. Kniolek, *William Kramer, Edward D. Lajiness, Curtis Lancaster, Frank W. Markey, Jr., John Edward Mason, Robert McGlenn, Paul Mersereau, Victor Meyer, Guy V. Miller, Howard C. Miller, Norbert J. Miller, Ralph L. Miller, Gerald Morris, Delbert O. Nelson, Maynard A. Nelson, Louis L. Nevers, Paul Nevers, Curtis O. Niles, Jr., Spencer Niles, Charles E. Noonan, Gerald E. Northcott, Kenneth Notestine, Elmer Okos, Raymond S. Okos, Nicholas C. Ott, Jack H. Parsons, Cecil E. Powell, Carl Ruetz, Donald A. Ruetz, Ronald Ruetz, Walter Ruetz, Allen W. Schroeder, James S. Schwen, Robert Sloan, Grace E. Smith, Harold N. Smith, Ora Willard Snyder, Joseph P. Spino, Harold J. Tabbert, Lawrence H. Tabbert, Edwin R. Thompson, *Thaddeus Turanski, Carlton VanPelt, Robert J. Vesey, Harold F. Walker, Norman Wapshall, Thomas G. Whittaker, Myrtle I. Wiegan, Joseph E. Williams, Howard Wilson, Lavon Wilson, Sherman Wonderly.

The following teachers/faculty were working for the Sylvania School District when they entered World War II: Thaddeus S. Abell, Gerald Brandon, Donald Channey, Fern B. DeLoe, Tom L. Gillooly, John P. Hazard, Paul W. Lavin, Harold Lucas, I. William Miller, Glenn R. Morgan, Gabor Takats, and Orla A. Thomas.

Final rites were given to three returned soldiers in April of 1948. The *Sylvania Sentinel* reported: "The long journey home from the battlefield of Europe has ended for three soldiers from this area and their final interment will take place. The three who made the supreme sacrifice were Pfc. Wayne Morningstar, Pfc. Allen L. Blakeman and Cpl. Kenneth F. Brodbeck."

In 1950 Memorial Field was dedicated to the memory of 45 men who died for their country in World War II. Memorials with bronze plates and a tree were placed in Memorial Field at that time for the following 45 men: Darrell Allen, Carleton Bay, James W. Berry, Max Wayne Berry, Jess Bieber, Leroy Breier, Kenneth Brodbeck, Bernard O. Brown, Raymond Conrad, Douglas Corbin, Edward G. Carlson, Melvin Dauer, Fred Fender, Robert C. Fisher, Leon R. Harrwaldt, Lloyd Hartzler, Eddie Howard, Harold Jasmund, Arthur Jones, Jr., Charles W. Jones, Andrew Keeler, Alfred E. Knepper, William Kramer, Glen V. Mathewson, Richard Miller, Don W. Moore, Wayne Morningstar, James E. McCullough, Jack Nichols, Sylvester J. Pakulski, Richard H. Palmer, Howard Pratt, James Randall, Orin D. Reynolds, David Robinson, Kenneth Shull, Wade L. Shull, Ray Sporleder, Paul Taylor, Thaddeus H. Turanski, Ralph VanGlahn, Jr., Robert Wood, Anthony Wieczorek, Earl C. Yeager, Chester Zwayer.

Initial reports in 1949 indicated that there were 37 men from the Sylvania area that were casualties of World War II, to be honored in Memorial Field, but as plans continued there were 45 men listed. Today there is a marker in Memorial Field listing 47 men, who were casualties of World War II.

The following are the names of the Sylvania men who gave their lives for our country during World War II. These names appear either on the monument at Sylvania's Veteran's Memorial Field or the Burnham High School Honor Roll memorial which listed all those who had attended Sylvania's Burnham High School and served during World War II. Those who were killed in action appeared with a star next to their name on this honor roll.

Darrel W. Allen
Born 1921 Died 1945 – U.S. Marine Corps - Darrel is listed on the Burnham High School World War II Roll of Honor with a star indicating that he was killed in action. He is also listed on the plaque in Sylvania's Veteran's Memorial Field for World War II casualties.

At the 1940 census Darrell was living in Sylvania Township on Estess Drive, listed as 18 years old, with his parents, Everett and Vesta Allen. Mr. Allen graduated from Burnham High School in 1941. The 1941 Burnham High School yearbook, page 64, discussed the school's track team being in its second year and said: "High point man last year was Darrel Allen with a total of 59 points. Darrel was also captain of the team in 1940 and was beaten only once in the mile run in the District Meet at Bowling Green."

Darrel served in the U.S. Marine Corps, with a rank of Technical Sergeant. His date of death is listed as 3-6-1945 and his last known status is "Missing." His name is listed on the WW II monument in Honolulu, Hawaii. He was issued a U.S. Purple Heart Medal. U.S. Marine Corps Muster Rolls shows his muster date as April 1942 at the rank of assistant cook. The July 1943 muster roll shows him with the rank of chief cook. The January 1945 muster roll shows his rank as technical sergeant.

In the 9-10-1942 issue of the *Sylvania Sentinel* Darrel Allen submitted the following poem: "You can have your Navy blues, but there is another fighter, I'll introduce to you! The uniform is different, The best you've ever seen. The Germs call him the Devil Dog, but his real name is "Marine." He's trained on Paris Island, The land that God forgot. Where sand is fourteen inches deep, and the sun is scorching hot! He has set many a table, and many a dish he's dried, he's also learned to make a bed, and a broom he sure can guide! He's peeled a million onions, and twice as many spuds; He also spends his leisure time, a washing out his duds! Now, girls, please take this little tip, I'm handing out to you. Just grab yourself a good Marine, for there's nothing he can't do! And when he goes to heaven, to St. Peter he will tell, "Another Marine reporting, sir—I've served my time in Hell!"

9-21-1944 *Sylvania Sentinel*: "S-Sgt Darrel Allen, With Marines – S/Sergt. Darrell Allen, husband of Mrs. Josephine Allen, 5755 Glasgow Rd., is now on overseas duty with the Marines. The picture of his six-month old daughter, Darylene, was published in the *Sentinel* in July. Sergeant Allen is a graduate of Burnham and has not been home since June, 1943. He has been in the Marine Corps for over two years."

11-30-1944 *Sylvania Sentinel*: "Darrel Allen, U.S. Marines, was promoted Oct. 31 from S/Sergt. To Technical Sergeant. He is now stationed overseas, and is the husband of Mrs. Darrell Allen,

Glasgow Rd. He graduated from Burnham High School in 1941 and was an employee of the Medusa Cement Co. before joining the Marines in June, 1942.

1-25-1945 *Sylvania Sentinel*: "Mrs. Darrell Allen will have to celebrate her second wedding anniversary this week alone. Her husband, T/Sergt. Darrell Allen, U.S.M.C. is in the South Pacific. Mrs. Allen expects to leave shortly for her parent's home in Washington D.C."

3-29-1945 *Sylvania Sentinel*: "T-Sgt. D.W. Allen Lost on Iwo Jima – Mrs. Josephine Allen, 5755 Glasgow Rd., received the dreaded telegram from the War Department Tuesday that her husband, T-Sgt. Darrell W. Allen of the Fifth Division had been killed in action on Iwo Jima Island on March 4. Sergt. Allen graduated from Burnham High School in 1941 and had been employed by the Medusa Cement Co. as a chemist. While in school he had been an athlete of ability in high jumping and football. Surviving besides the wife are a daughter, Darylene Jo 13 months; father and mother, Mr. and Mrs. Everett Allen, 5755 Glasgow Rd.; brother, Lloyd W, Toledo; sisters Mrs. Jessie Van Pelt and Mrs. Marjie Musser, Sylvania."

Sylvania Sentinel 5-10-1945: "Memorial Service Planned for Soldier – A memorial service will be held in the Whiteford Church of Christ for T/Sergt. Darrel Allen who was killed in action on Iwo Jima Sunday, May 20. The service will be at 2:00 p.m. with the Rev. Raymond L. Wreath officiating."

The 1946 U.S. Navy's listing of next of kin, for those killed from direct enemy action, shows the following information: Ohio – Darrel W. Allen, Sgt. USMCR – wife Mrs. Darrell W. Allen, 5775 Glasgow Rd., Sylvania.

Carleton Bay
Born 1924 Died 1943 - Carleton is not listed on the Burnham High School World War II Roll of Honor. He is listed on the plaque in Sylvania's Veteran's Memorial Field for World War II casualties. He is also on the Monroe County, Michigan's list of casualties.

At the 1940 census he was 15 years old, living with his parents, Harold and Anna Bay, on Rt. 2, Ottawa Lake, Whiteford Township, Monroe County, Michigan, and listed as being in his first year of high school. At this time high school students living in Ottawa Lake, Michigan attended school at Burnham High School in Sylvania.

His military records list him as Carleton Holtz Bay. His spouse was listed as Bonnie Jean Bay. The U.S. Navy Casualties Book reports that he was killed on 2-20-1943 and was ranked as a seaman second class in the U.S. Navy Reserve. His last known status was "missing."

Sylvania Sentinel 8-6-1942: "Blue stars honoring sons and brothers of members were placed for Carlton Bay, son of Mr. and Mrs. Harold Bay of Monroe Street. . . "

The 2-25-1943 issue of the *Sylvania Sentinel* reported: "CARLTON BAY AMONG MISSING ON CAPSIZED NAVY MINESWEEP – Navy Releases Names Of Five Known Dead And Eight Missing – The Navy this week released the names of the five known dead and the eight missing crew members of a navy mine sweep which capsized in heavy seas Saturday off Coos Bay harbor. Comdr. W.R. Brust of the Coos Bay harbor navy section said continued rough waters prevented rescue workers from reaching the vessel, the YM133, to search for the missing men. The minesweeper was stranded on a sand bar 200 yards from shore. Mr. and Mrs. Harold Bay, Whiteford Road, this week were informed that their son Carlton was listed among the eight missing crew members of the minesweeper."

The 8-26-1943 issue of the *Sylvania Sentinel* printed this: "Mr. and Mrs. Howard Bay have received a telegram from the Navy Department, confirming the death of their son, Carleton Holtz Bay, who was reported missing in action when a minesweeper, of which he was a crew member, overturned in the Pacific Ocean off the coast of Washington, six months ago." Memorial services were held on 10-17-1943 in memory of Carleton Holtz Bay whose death was confirmed by the Navy Department. The service was held by the Sylvania Post, 3717 V.F.W. in P.H.C. Hall. Seaman Bay was the son of Mr. and Mrs. Harold Bay, Whiteford Road. He was a former student of Lambertville High School and was 19 years old at the time of his death, February 20, aboard a minesweeper off the Oregon coast. Before going to sea he had been at Great Lakes, Ill; Navy Pier, Chicago; and Port Townsend, Wash. He had been in service 13 months."

James Winford Berry
Born 1915 Died 1941 – U.S. Navy – James Berry was the first from Sylvania to be killed in action. James is listed on the Burnham High School World War II Roll of Honor with a star indicating that he was killed in action. He is also listed on the plaque in Sylvania's Veteran's Memorial Field for World War II casualties.

At the 1930 census he was living at home with his parents on Gower Road in Sylvania Township. He was listed as Winford Berry and was 12 years old. At the 1940 census he was 22 years old and living with his parents on Stickney Avenue in Toledo, Ohio. According to that census record James Berry's highest grade completed was the 8th grade.

The U.S. World War II Casualties Listing shows his date of death as 12-7-1941. His Rank at the time of death was fireman, second class with the U.S. Navy. He was listed as missing in action, and is listed on the Tablets of the Missing at Honolulu Memorial in Honolulu, Hawaii. He was awarded a Purple Heart.

Sylvania Sentinel 6-4-1942: "Joseph W. Diehn Post No. 468 and the American Legion Auxiliary will hold a memorial service on Monday evening in Legion Hall for James Winford Berry, who gave his life for his country at Pearl Harbor in the Japanese attack on December 7, 1942. The public is invited to attend the service which will begin at 8 o'clock. Rev. Raymond L. Wreath will speak and Glenn Morgan will sing the "Invictus.""

Sylvania Sentinel dated 2-11-1943 reads: "Mr. and Mrs. George Berry, Alger Road, are the parents of ten children, all of whom are living except James Winford, who was killed in action December 7, 1941 on the USS Arizona, when the Japs perpetrated their sneak attack on Hawaii."

7-15-1943 issue of the *Sylvania Sentinel* reported that the parents of James Berry received the Purple Heart Medal awarded to their son, Fireman second class, for military merit and wounds received in action resulting in his death 12-7-1941.

10-14-1943 *Sylvania Sentinel*: "With the enlistment of two more of their sons in the past few weeks, Mr. and Mrs. George Berry of Alger Road, now have five boys serving in the Armed forces of the United States. Another son, James Winford, lost his life at Pearl Harbor on December 7th, 1941. He was a member of the crew of the U.S.S. Arizona, and had been in the Navy one year.

The 1946 U.S. Navy listing of next of kin for those killed from direct enemy action shows the following information: Ohio – Fireman 2 c U.S.N. – parents Mr. and Mrs. George C. Berry, Box 73A Rt. 1, Sylvania.

Max Wayne Berry
Born 1911 Died 1944 – U.S. Navy - Max is listed on the Burnham High School World War II Roll of Honor with a star indicating that he was killed in action. He is also listed on the plaque in Sylvania's Veteran's Memorial Field for World War II casualties. At the 1930 census he is listed as Wayne Berry, living on Gower Road in Sylvania Township at the age of 16 years old.

His military record shows his official date of death was 4-2-1944. His name is listed on the National Memorial Cemetery of the Pacific in Honolulu, Hawaii. His service info was listed as Seaman, First Class U.S. Navy.

The 2-11-1943 *Sylvania Sentinel* reported that Mr. and Mrs. George Berry of Alger Road in Sylvania were the parents of ten children, with seven of them doing their part in the war. "Max Wayne is an armed guard at U.S.N.T. Base at Treasure Island, California."

10-14-1943 *Sylvania Sentinel*: "With the enlistment of two more of their sons in the past few weeks, Mr. and Mrs. George Berry of Alger Road, now have five boys serving in the Armed forces of the United States. Another son, James Winford, lost his life at Pearl Harbor on December 7th, 1941. He was a member of the crew of the U.S.S. Arizona, and had been in the Navy one year. The latest of their sons to enter military service is Leo Harold Berry, 28, of Sacramento, Calif., who enlisted last week, and Elmer Berry, 26, who enlisted on September 20th, and is now with the Seabees in Virginia. Other sons in the service are Max Wayne Berry, 27, in the U.S. Navy and Corp. Charles Herbert Berry, 25, who is in the Fiji Islands. They enlisted in February, 1942. Wesley Berry, 19, also in the Navy enlisted in December of 1942. In addition to their five sons, Mr. and Mrs. Berry also have a son-in-law, Roy Snyder, M.P., of Washington, D.C. in the service. He is now on furlough visiting his wife, Irene, who makes her home with her parents."

4-6-1944 *Sylvania Sentinel*: "Death of Max Berry Announced by Navy – Mr. and Mrs. George Berry, 5406 Alger Rd., for the second time during this war, were notified of the loss of a son last night. The telegram from the Navy Department merely stated that he had died while in performance of his duties and expressed the usual regrets. James Berry, another son was killed at Pearl Harbor and he was also in the Navy."

Jess John Bieber

Born 1924 Died 1944 – U.S. Navy - Jess is listed on the Burnham High School World War II Roll of Honor with a star indicating that he was killed in action. He is also listed on the plaque in Sylvania's Memorial Field for World War II casualties.

Jess John Bieber graduated from Burnham High School in Sylvania in 1943. The 1943 Sylvania Burnham High School Yearbook shows Jess Bieber as a senior. His record shows that he attended Blissfield High School his first, second and third year of high school and then attended part of his third and fourth year at Burnham in the Vocational program. Jess lived in Ottawa Lake, Monroe County, Michigan, but students from that community attended school at Sylvania's Burnham High School at that time.

Jess Bieber's date of enlistment is not found, and his official date of death is recorded as 6-20-1944. Mr. Bieber's name appears on the Honolulu, Hawaii National Memorial Cemetery of the Pacific as follows: Jess J. Bieber – Avn. Machinist's Mate 3C, USNR – Mich.

7-6-1944 *Sylvania Sentinel*: "Jess Bieber Killed in South Pacific – Mr. and Mrs. Frank Bieber of Ottawa Lake, were notified by the Navy Department on the Fourth of July that their son, Jess Bieber, A.M. 3/c, had been killed in action in the South Pacific on June 20. No details were given. Jess was the youngest of three sons and one daughter, Matthew, who is in the armed forces in the European theater of war, 2nd Lt. Inez Bieber, who is a nurse and is seeing action in Italy, and Franklin Bieber, Ottawa Lake."

8-3-1944 *Sylvania Sentinel*: "Memorial Services Held Last Sunday – Impressive memorial services were held at the Zion Lutheran Church, Ottawa Lake, last Sunday in memory of Jess John Bieber, AMM 3/c, who was killed in action on June 20 in the S. Pacific area. Jess would have been 20 years old on Aug. 19 and his death was a shock and a great loss to his family and to all those who knew him. The services were opened with the hymn "God of Our Fathers" and included the Navy Hymn, "Eternal Father Strong to Save." The Rev. Marcus Mueller gave the sermon entitled "Good Hope through Grace." Taps, by Donald Duckert concluded the service."

The 1946 U.S. Navy listing of next of kin for those killed from direct enemy action shows the following information: Michigan – Aviation Machinist's Mate Third Class U.S. Navy Reserve. Father Mr. Frank John Bieber, Ottawa Lake Michigan. His killed in action date is listed as 6-20-1944.

Leroy Daniel Breier

Born 1925 Died 1945 - Leroy is listed on the Burnham High School World War II Roll of Honor with a star indicating that he was killed in action. He is also listed on the plaque in Sylvania's Veteran's Memorial Field for World War II casualties.

At the 1940 census Leroy was living in Riga Township, Lenawee County, Michigan. He was living with his father and mother, Roy and Augusta Breier, and he was listed as 15 years old. Leroy Breier graduated from Burnham High School in 1944. The 1944 Burnham High School

Yearbook shows that Mr. Breier was a senior. His World War II Army Enlistment Record shows that he enlisted on 8-11-1944 as a Private. His date of death is recorded as 3-1-1945.

Sylvania Sentinel 3-22-1945: "Pvt. LeRoy Breier Reported Missing – Mr. and Mrs. Roy Breier, now of Archbold, but until recently of Ottawa Lake, Mich., received notice from the War Department on Monday, that their son, Pvt. LeRoy Breier, is missing in action in Germany. Pvt. Breier was home during the holidays with Leonard Harrwaldt, who has been reported killed in action, after completing their basic training at Camp Joseph Robinson and at that time became engaged to Lucille Pant, Ottawa Lake. Pvt. Breier was a graduate of Burnham High School and had entered service early last fall."

Toledo Blade 11-10-1948 – LeRoy Breier – Services for Pvt. LeRoy Breier, son of Mr. and Mrs. Roy F. Breier, Stryker, O., formerly of Ottawa Lake, Mich., will be Saturday at 3 p.m., in the Reeb Funeral Home, the Revs. Dallas Adler and Henry Ide officiating. Burial will be in Toledo Memorial Park Cemetery where Sylvania Post, VFW, assisted by the Lucas County Burial Corps, will hold a military service. Private Breier was 20 when he was killed in action in Germany 3-1-1945. He was inducted Aug. 10, 1944, and received basic training at Camp Robinson, Ark, and went overseas Jan 4, 1945. He served with the 94th Division of the Third Army. Private Breier was a graduate of Burnham High School, Sylvania. Surviving besides his parents are a sister, Mrs. Harry Meyer, Defiance, O.; brothers, Richard, Ft. Bragg, N.C.; James and John both of Stryker, and grandparents, Mr. and Mrs. Otto Lenz, Toledo."

Kenneth F. Brodbeck
Born 1919 Died 1944 – Kenneth is not listed on the Burnham High School World War II Roll of Honor. He is listed on the plaque in Sylvania's Veteran's Memorial Field for World War II casualties. He is on Monroe County, Michigan's list of casualties also. Records show that his official date of death was 11-20-1944.

At the 1940 census Kenneth was listed as 20 years old and living in Whiteford Township, Monroe County, Michigan with his mother. He was working as a truck driver and this census indicates that he only attended school through the 8th grade.

Mr. Brodbeck enlisted as a private - warrant officer on 2-26-1942. At that time he was listed as single, without dependents.

Sylvania Sentinel 6-11-1942: "Private Kenneth Brodbeck has been enjoying a furlough with relatives at Ottawa Lake. He returns to Camp Blanding, Fla., on Saturday."

Sylvania Sentinel 9-17-1942: "Here is a new address for interested friends: Pvt. Kenneth Brodbeck, 36173964, Co. C 11th Eng. 36th Inf. Div. Camp Edwards, Mass. APO 36."

Sylvania Sentinel 11-19-1942: "Kenneth Brodbeck, of Camp Edwards, Mass, is visiting friends and relatives here this week."

Sylvania Sentinel article dated 2-26-1943 reported the following: "Kenneth Brodbeck, son of Mrs. Ida Brodbeck, of Ottawa Lake, returned Thursday for military service."

Sylvania Sentinel 5-6-1943: "Pvt. Kenneth Brodbeck, 36173964, Co. C, 11th Eng. Bn. 36th Inf. Div. APO 36, c-o Postmaster New York, New York."

Sylvania Sentinel 12-28-1944: "Kenneth Brodbeck Killed in Action – Corp. Kenneth F. Brodbeck was killed in action in France. He was inducted into service on 2-26-1942, and went overseas to North Africa 4-1-1943. Corp. Brodbeck was with the 36th Division at Anzio 9-9-1943. He also entered Southern France on D-Day in 1944. He was 25 years old and was born on the farm just north of Sylvania."

Final rites were given to three returned soldiers in April 1948 "The long journey home from the battlefield of Europe has ended for three soldiers from this area and their final interment will take place – The three who made the supreme sacrifice were: Pfc. Wayne Morningstar, Pfc. Allen L. Blakeman and Corp. Kenneth F. Brodbeck."

Bernard O. Brown
Born 1922 Died 1942 – Bernard Brown was the second from Sylvania to be killed in action. Bernard is listed on the Burnham High School World War II Roll of Honor with a star to indicate that he was killed in action. He is also listed on the plaque in Sylvania's Memorial Field for World War II casualties.

At the 1940 census he was listed as living in Sylvania Township on Stewart Road, living with his father, Harry Brown. At that time Bernard was 17 years old and attending school. This census indicated that he finished three years of high school. He graduated from Burnham High School in 1940.

At this time I am unable to locate his date of enlistment and his official date of death.

Sylvania Sentinel 6-4-1942: "Mr. and Mrs. Harry C. Brown of Stewart Road received a telegram on Wednesday advising them that their son Burnard Oscar, 20, was missing in action while serving the United States Navy. When the parents last heard from him he was in service off the west coast. He enlisted a year ago. Surviving beside his parents are two sisters, Mrs. Harry Eversman of Toledo and Mrs. Paul Snook of Stewart Road."

Sylvania Sentinel 8-6-1942: "The Service Flag dedicated last Monday evening by the Ladies' Auxiliary to Post 3717, Veterans of Foreign Wars, bears a gold star in memory of Bernard Brown, son of Mr. and Mrs. Harry Brown, Stewart Road."

The 1946 U.S. Navy listing of next of kin of those killed from direct enemy action shows the following information: Ohio – Bernard O. Brown - Seaman 1c, USNR, Father - Mr. Harry Clifford Brown, Rt. 1 Box 89a, Sylvania.

Edward G. Carlson

Born 1920 Died 1944 – Edward is not listed on the Burnham High School World War II Roll of Honor. He is listed on the plaque in Sylvania's Veteran's Memorial Field for World War II casualties.

Edward's official date of enlistment is not found, his official date of death is recorded as 2-27-1944.

I was unable to locate this Carlson family in the 1940 census, but in 1942 when Edward's father, George Carl Carlson, completed his registration card for World War II he listed his address as 5762 Summit Street, Sylvania, and then put that effective 6-20-1942 he would be living at R#1 Box 40 Balfour Drive in Sylvania. He listed Mrs. Florence L. Carlson as his wife and his employer at that time was the U.S. Postal Department on Main Street in Sylvania.

Toledo Blade 2-28-1944 – "Sylvania Soldier Dies In Accident – Pvt. Edward Carlson Son of Mail Carrier – Pvt. Edward Carlson, 23, son of Mr. and Mrs. George Carlson and husband of Mrs. Betty Carlson, 5619 Balfour, Sylvania, was killed yesterday in an automobile accident in Camp Kilmer, N.J. according to word received by his parents. Details of the accident were not contained in the telegram received by this soldier's father, a rural mail carrier in Sylvania. Private Carlson's brother, Robert E. Carlson, is stationed at the Coast Guard-Marine Barracks, Naval Proving Ground, Aero, Ida. The body is being brought to the Reeb Funeral Home, Sylvania."

Raymond L. Conrad
Born 1915 Died 1944 – Raymond is not listed on the Burnham High School World War II Roll of Honor. He is listed on the plaque in Sylvania's Veteran's Memorial Field for World War II casualties.

At the 1940 census Raymond was listed living on Lawton Avenue in Toledo, Ohio. He was 24 years old and living with widowed mother, Luella Conrad. He was employed as a laborer at an electric panel company. The census also said that he had finished four years of high school.

According to a letter written in 1944 from the Headquarters 508th Parachute Infantry of the U.S. Army, by that time Sgt. Conrad was married and the letter informing his wife that he died in action in Normandy, France during the invasion of that Continent was addressed to Mrs. Henrietta A. Conrad of 443 Summer Street, Toledo, Ohio.

In a letter dated 3-13-1946 Mrs. Henrietta A. Conrad was informed that the War Department was desirous of furnishing the burial location of her husband, the late First Sergeant Raymond L. Conrad, A.S.N. 35 017 469. It was reported at this time that his remains were interred in the U.S. Military Cemetery, Blosville, France, plot F, row 6, grave 120.

World War II Army Records show that he enlisted on 3-20-1942 in Toledo, Ohio as a private. He was listed as single, without dependents and his civil occupation is listed as "unskilled occupation in production of glass and glass products."

Toledo Blade 4-22-1948 – "Raymond L. Conrad – The body of Sergt. Raymond L. Conrad, 29, paratrooper killed in action at Normandy, 7-4-1944, has been returned to Toledo for services and reburial. Sergeant Conrad was an employee of Libbey-Owens-Ford Glass Co., before entering the service. He attended Rosewood Ave. Presbyterian Church and lived at 2456 Lawton Ave. Surviving are his mother, Mrs. Lulu Conrad; sisters, Vera Conrad, Toledo, and Mrs. Ethel Flatt, Trilby, O., and brother Vernon, Bentonville, Ark. Graveside services will be tomorrow at 3 p.m. in Ravine Cemetery. The body is at the Ira Garner Funeral Home."

Douglas R. Corbin
Born 1922 Died 1945 – Douglas is not listed on the Burnham High School World War II Roll of Honor. (We know that he graduated from a high school in Deerfield, Michigan). He is listed on the plaque in Sylvania's Veteran's Memorial Field for World War II casualties. Douglas joined the service while his parents still lived in Deerfield, Mich. World War II records report Mr. Corbin's date of death as 4-26-1945. He was a private first class with the 381st Infantry 96th Division. He was awarded the Purple Heart Medal, Bronze Star Medal and other additional Army awards.

At the 1940 census Douglas Corbin was 17 years old and living with his parents in Dearborn, Wayne County, Michigan. His parents, Mr. & Mrs. Ray Corbin, moved to Sylvania after the war started. His father became the editor of *Sylvania Sentinel* newspaper during the years that Douglas was serving, including the day that his parents were notified that he was killed in action. When Douglas was on furlough he returned to his parent's home in Sylvania.

6-15-1944 *Sylvania Sentinel*: "Pvt. Douglas R. Corbin, son of Mr. and Mrs. Raymond G. Corbin, has been spending the last 10 days with his parents. He has been stationed with an infantry division in California undergoing amphibious training and returns to San Diego today. Pvt. Douglas R. Corbin, while home on furlough, had as an overnight guest, Pvt. Jefferson D. Robinson, of Perrysburg. Pvt. Robinson was a classmate of Pvt. Corbin at Bradley College in Peoria, Ill., where they were both taking civil engineering in the A.S.T.P. When the program at Bradley College was "washed up," they were both transferred to the 96th Division and are in the infantry."

1-4-1945 *Sylvania Sentinel*, written by Ray Corbin, editor of this newspaper: "We have refrained from saying anything about our son who is in the Philippines, as he said in his last letter, "Jap Hunting." Having just heard from him for the first time in too long a time, we just have to say that we are glad he is well (except for jungle rot on his feet). I did not raise my boy to be a soldier, but he is one just the same. There must be a moral in that somewhere if I could find it."

The 4-26-1945 issue of the *Sylvania Sentinel* printed a letter that Douglas R. Corbin sent to his father, Raymond G. Corbin (editor of this newspaper). It talks about the Okinawa campaign and the story written in "Time" magazine. He suggested that his father stick to the "Time magazine "for the real dope," as he said they wrote a very accurate coverage.

Notice in the *Toledo Blade* (date not listed) said: "Pfc. Douglas R. Corbin, son of Mr. and Mrs. Ray Corbin, Sylvania, was killed in action April 26 on Okinawa, the parents were told in a telegram yesterday from the War Department. His father is the editor of the *Sylvania Sentinel*. Private Corbin was attending the University of Michigan when he enlisted in the armed forces of the U.S. Army Air Corps. He entered service on 11-4-1942, was sent to Texas and was transferred to an ASTP."

5-31-1945 *Sylvania Sentinel*: "We know now how parents feel who have lost their sons in this terrible war. And we too, like other parents, had tried to steel ourselves against the possibility that we would someday receive that dreaded telegram, but how little we were prepared when it finally came. Let us all pray, but more than that let us feel, think, speak and endeavor in all ways to bring peace to the world. Only in this way can we honestly believe that "they did not die in vain." It may take generations but surely sometime in the future all peoples will come to the realization that the cost of war is too great. The war is still on and we must close ranks, even as the fighting men on Okinawa have had to do, and carry on to final victory."

Melvin W. Dauer
Born 1913 Died 1945 – U.S. Army - His name is not listed on the Burnham High School World War II Roll of Honor, but should have been. He is listed on the plaque in Sylvania's Veteran's Memorial Field for World War II casualties. He is also listed on Monroe County, Michigan's casualty list.

Melvin Dauer has a military marker in Sylvania's Toledo Memorial Park Cemetery which was requested by Margaret Dauer Elg of 4th Street, Waterville, Ohio, in April of 1949. This document shows Melvin's enlistment date was 10-29-1934 and his date of death is listed as 2-24-1945. It also shows his U.S. Regiment as: A/S Inf. 117 Inf. 30th infantry Division. USAGF.

Melvin is found in the 1928 Sylvania Burnham High School Yearbook as a Freshman. He was also found in the 1930 Sylvania Burnham High School yearbook on page 69, shown as the manager of the baseball squad and on page 36, shown as a Sophomore. In the 1931 Yearbook he was shown as a Junior. The 1932 yearbook is not available in which he would have been a Senior.

Melvin Woodrow Dauer was married in Howe, Indiana on 12-17-1938 to Francile Hariette Baer. His father is listed as Charles Jacob Dauer and mother listed as Margaret Frederika Ely Dauer. Melvin was listed as 25 years old and born in Haskins, Wood County, Ohio.

First Lieutenant Melvin W. Dauer's photo was featured in the 1943 Dayton University Yearbook as a faculty member working there as a U.S. Inf. Instructor in Military Science and Tactics.

In May of 1945 a U.S. WWII Jewish Servicemen Card was completed for Melvin W. Dauer, First Lieutenant, next of kin – Mrs. Francile H. Dauer, living at 1020 Wang Avenue, Dayton, Ohio. Branch of Service – Army.

6-7-1945 *Sylvania Sentinel*: "Memorial Service for Lt. Melvin W. Dauer – A memorial service for Lieut. Melvin W. Dauer will be held on Sunday, June 10 in the Olivet Lutheran Church, Whiteford and Alexis Roads at 2:00 p.m. The minister, Rev. Paul Getter, will be in charge and Mr. Arthur Miller, Herman Nieman and Eugene Fischer will provide the music. Lieut. Dauer was wounded last October 6 in Germany, and was hospitalized in England until Jan 4. He was sent back into action on January 23 and was with a mortar and machine gun unit as platoon commander when he made the supreme sacrifice. His death came at Julich, Germany, Feb. 24, 1945. He is survived by his widow Francele, and daughter, Janet Marie; mother, Mrs. Margaret Dauer and sister, Mrs. Roy Frank."

Melvin's wife was listed in the 1946 Dayton, Ohio Directory as: "Francile H. Dauer (widow of Melvin) clerk WF home 607 E Peach Orchard Road."

Frederick Fender
Born 1921 Died 1944 – Fred is not listed on the Burnham High School World War II Roll of Honor. He is listed on the plaque in Sylvania's Memorial Field for World War II casualties. He is also on the Monroe County, Michigan list of casualties for World War II. A check of the *Toledo Blade* obituary index revealed no obituary notice ever listed for Frederick Fender. A search for military records about Fred Fender on Ancestry.com revealed no additional information.

Robert V. Ferguson
Born 1920 Died 1944 – National Guard – He is not listed on the Burnham High School World War II Roll of Honor wall, and is not listed on the Veteran's Memorial Field World War II plaque. He has a stone in Toledo Memorial Park Cemetery in Sylvania.

His date of death is recorded as 12-25-1944. He served with the 264th Infantry Regiment 66th Division. The website known as *Find A Grave* shows the following information regarding S Sgt. Robert V. Ferguson's story: "On Christmas Eve 1944, the Belgium troopship Leopoldville, left the pier at Southampton, England with over 2,000 American soldiers assigned to the 66th Infantry Division and crossed the English Channel to France. Just 5 ½ miles from its destination, Cherbourg, the Leopoldville was torpedoed and sunk by the German submarine U-486. There were 763 American soldiers killed and the bodies of 493 were never recovered from the Channel's frigid 48 degree waters."

At the 1940 census Robert Ferguson was 19 years old and living in Milton Center, Wood County, Ohio, living with his sister and brother-in-law. Mr. Ferguson was married on 6-28-1941 to Verena J. Seiler in Fulton County, Ohio.

2-1-1945 *Sylvania Sentinel*: "Staff Sergt. Robert V. Ferguson, 24, was killed in action on Christmas Day in Belgium, according to word received from the War Department by his wife. He was the son of Mr. and Mrs. Demas Ferguson, Marsrow Dr (Sylvania Township). His wife lives with her father in Delta. Sergeant Ferguson was in the National Guard in Napoleon and was in Camp Shelby, Miss., in 1940. He was honorably discharged in February 1941, worked at the Spicer Manufacturing Co. until March, 1943, when he re-entered the Army. He arrived overseas in February, 1944, with an infantry division as a section leader of a machine gun platoon. Also surviving are a brother, Warren, in the Army and also overseas, and sisters, Fraulein, Toledo; Dorothy Kern, Minneapolis; Ruth Kreps, Milton Center; Mrs. Georgia Onlinger, New York; Mrs. Roby Nicely, Delta."

Robert C. Fisher

Born 1919 Died 1945 - Robert is listed on the Burnham High School World War II Roll of Honor with a star to indicate that he was killed in action. He is listed on the plaque in Sylvania's Veteran's Memorial Field for World War II casualties. He was not living in Sylvania or Sylvania Township at the 1930 census. I believe that Robert C. Fisher, listed on the Burnham High School World War II Roll of Honor is actually Robert L. Fisher, see below.

Robert Lafayette Fisher

Born 1919 Died 1945 – U.S. Army - Robert L. Fisher is <u>not</u> listed on the Burnham High School World War II Roll of Honor, but is probably mistakenly listed as Robert C. Fisher. He is <u>not</u> listed on the plaque in Sylvania Veteran's Memorial Field listing those killed in action. I found no newspaper articles in the *Sylvania Sentinel* listing Robert C. Fisher as a casualty, but did find Robert L. Fisher. His date of death is recorded as 4-21-1945 and he is buried in St. Joseph Cemetery in Sylvania.

At the 1920 census Robert Fisher was 11 months old and living with his parents, John and Irene Fisher, on Centennial Road in Sylvania Township. They were living with her parents, Fred and Stella Winkelfoos. By the 1930 census Robert was 11 years old and living with his grandparents, Fred and Stella Winkelfoos on Midwood Avenue in Toledo, Ohio.

Robert L. Fisher's enlistment date was 2-28-1940, and he served the rank of private first class in the 37th Division, 138th Infantry.

5-17-1945 *Sylvania Sentinel*: "Sergt. Robert L. Fisher, grandson of Fred Winkelfoos, son of John Fisher, died in a Base Hospital on Luzon Island, P.I., as the result of a serious illness. Sergt Fisher lived with his grandfather in Sylvania, and was in the Ohio State Guard at the time they were federalized. He left for overseas with the 138th Infantry Regiment of the 37th Division in April 1941."

The following article was printed in the *Toledo Blade* in 1945 (exact date unknown): Died of Illness – Pfc. Robert L. Fisher, 26, died of illness on Luzon April 21. His parents Mr. and Mrs. John R. Fisher, 1651 Pool St (Toledo), have been informed by the War Department. Private Fisher had served with the 37th Division since Feb. 8, 1940, going overseas in May 1942. Before entering the army he attended Burnham High School, Sylvania. Surviving besides his parents are stepbrothers Sgt. Bert Leo Angus, on rotation leave from the South Pacific, and Pfc. Joseph C. Angus, France and a stepsister, Mrs. Irene Slater."

Leon Richard Harrwaldt

Born 1925 Died 1945 – U.S. Army - Leon is listed on the Burnham High School World War II Roll of Honor with a star to indicate that he was killed in action. He graduated from Burnham High School in 1943. He is listed on the plaque in Sylvania's Veteran's Memorial Field for World War II casualties.

Leon's enlistment date is recorded as 8-10-1944, and his official date of death is listed as 2-5-1945. He is buried in Toledo Memorial Park in Sylvania.

At the 1940 census Leon was 14 years old and living in Riga, Lenawee, Michigan with his parents Leonard and Bertha Harrwaldt. This census says that the highest grade in school he completed was the 8th grade.

1-4-1945 *Sylvania Sentinel*: Home on First Furlough – Leon Harrwaldt, Ottawa Lake, Mich., has been home on a seven-day furlough. He has just finished his basic training at Camp Joseph P. Robinson, Ark., and reports at Fort Meade, Md., after his furlough. He is the son of Mr. and Mrs. Leonard Harrwaldt and is a graduate of Burnham High School."

3-1-1945 *Sylvania Sentinel*: "Ottawa Lake Boy Missing in Action – Pvt. Leon Harrwaldt has been missing in action in Germany since Feb. 5 according to word received by his parents, Mr. and Mrs. Leonard Harrwaldt, Ottawa Lake, Feb. 18. Leon was in an infantry division and entered service Aug. 10, 1944. He graduated from Burnham High School in June, 1943."

Sylvania Sentinel 3-22-1945: ". . . Pvt. Breier was home during the holidays, with Leonard Harrwaldt, who has been reported killed in action, after completing their basic training at Camp Joseph Robinson. . . " In July of 1945 memorial services were held for a former 1943 Burnham High School graduate. Leon Harrwaldt, son of Mr. and Mrs. Leonard Harrwaldt was inducted into the army on 8-10-1944 and went overseas early in January of 1945. He was reported to have been killed in action on 2-5-1945 in the Belgium-Luxembourg sector during the attack on Habscheid, Germany. Pvt. Leon Harrwaldt was in an infantry division."

Lloyd Ross Hartzler (Lloyd Ross Hudson-Hartzler)
Born 1922 Died 1944 – U.S. Army - Lloyd is listed on the Burnham High School World War II Roll of Honor with a star to indicate that he was killed in action. He is listed on the plaque in Sylvania's Veteran's Memorial Field for World War II casualties. Lloyd Hartzler graduated from Burnham High School in 1939.

At the 1940 census Lloyd Hartzler was listed as 18 years old and living on Sadalia Road in Sylvania Township with his step-father and mother. He was listed as employed as a clerk in a retail grocery store.

November 1944 *Toledo Blade*: "Memorial Planned For Toledo Solider – Parents Arrange For Church Service – A memorial service for their son, Pvt. Lloyd R. Hudson-Hartzler, 22, will be held by Mr. and Mrs. Wayne P. Hartzler at 2 p.m. Nov. 19 in Olivet Lutheran Church, Whiteford and Alexis Rds. The Rev. Paul R. Getter will officiate. Word of his death in action in France Aug. 27, was received by his parents Sept. 11, and a letter of confirmation reached them Sept. 13, Private Hudson-Hartzler had served with finance headquarters office of the army following induction 12-5-1942. He had been at Camp Van Dorn, Miss., Camp Bowie, Texas and at the Army and Navy General Hospital, Hot Springs, Ark., before going overseas in May, 1944. He graduated from Burnham in 1939 and for 4 years was employed at Kroger Grocery & Baking Co. Surviving besides his parents is a brother, Regis, sisters Sally Ann Hartzler, Toledo and Mrs. James R. Latham, Washington, D.C."

11-16-1944 *Sylvania Sentinel* – "Members of Joseph W. Diehn No. 468, American Legion, will participate in a memorial service to be held at Olivet Lutheran Church at 2:00 p.m. Sunday, Nov. 19, in honor of Pvt. Lloyd R. Hartzler. Pvt. Hartzler was the son of Mr. and Mrs. Wayne Hartzler, Sadalia Rd. He was reported killed in action in France on Aug. 27, 1944, and was in France on Aug 27, 1944, and was in Co. H 9th Division. Pvt. Hartzler entered the service Dec. 1, 1942, and had graduated from Burnham High School."

Edwin David Howard
Born 1924 Died 1943 – U.S. Merchant Marines - Edwin is listed on the Burnham High School World War II Roll of Honor with a star to indicate that he was killed in action. He is listed on the plaque in Sylvania's Veteran's Memorial Field for World War II casualties. He was living in the Village of Sylvania at the 1930 census with his parents, Edwin C. and Mary Howard – Edwin D. Howard was 5 years old in 1930.

At the 1940 census Edwin was 15 years old and living with his parents at 5834 Main Street in the Village of Sylvania. Edwin Howard graduated from Burnham High School in 1942. His official date of death is listed as 12-3-1943.

Toledo Blade 1-7-1944: "Sylvania Sailor Killed On First Sea Voyage – Midshipman, Edwin David Howard, Sylvania, was killed in action in the Mediterranean war zone during his first sea voyage, the Navy Department yesterday informed his parents, Mr. and Mrs. Edwin C. Howard. Edwin, who was 19, enlisted in the Merchant Marine last March and attended a school for officer candidates at Kings Point, L.I., three months. He was to have returned there for further training upon completion of the Mediterranean training cruise. He was graduated from Burnham High School, Sylvania in 1942. Edwin's father operates the Howard Gas and Oil Co., in Sylvania. Besides his parents, Edwin is survived by a brother, William K, a sister, Alice, and his grandparents, Mr. and Mrs. Edwin G. Howard, Sylvania.

Sylvania Sentinel 3-25-1944: "Mr. and Mrs. E.C. Howard have been informed by the United States Maritime Commission that a Liberty Ship will be named for their son, Edwin D. Howard, who lost his life in the service of the American Merchant Marine. The vessel is being built by the J.A. Hones Construction Company, Panama City, Fla. and will be ready for launching about the middle of February. Edwin D. Howard was born 5-25-1924, and graduated from Burnham High School in 1942. He attended Toledo University for six months taking pre-medical courses when he enlisted in the Merchant Marine and entered the Academy at King's Point, Long Island. After six months study there he went aboard a tanker ship as a cadet midshipman and cruised the Mediterranean. It was at Bari, Italy, on 12-2-1943 that his ship, along with 16 others, was caught by German planes and destroyed."

2-1-1945 *Sylvania Sentinel*: "Ship's Name Honors Edwin D. Howard – Mr. and Mrs. E.C. Howard have been informed by the United States Maritime Commission that a Liberty Ship will be named for their son, Edwin D. Howard, who lost his life in the service of the American Merchant Marines. The vessel is being built by the J.A. Jones Construction Company, Panama City, Fla., and will be ready for launching about the middle of February. The new ship will be an airplane transport for use against the Japs and the inability of the authorities to state a day for the launching will prevent the presence of the boy's parents. Edwin D. Howard was born 5-25-1924, and graduated from Burnham High School in 1942. He attended Toledo University for six months taking a pre-medical course when he enlisted in the Merchant Marine and entered the Academy at King's Point, Long Island. After six months' study there he went aboard a tanker ship as a cadet midshipman and cruised the Mediterranean. It was at Bari, Italy, on 12-2-1943 that his ship, along with 16 others, was caught by German planes and destroyed."

Harold Albert Jasmund
Born 1920 – Died 1944 – U.S. Army - Harold is listed on the Burnham High School World War II Roll of Honor, but it does not list him with a star to indicate that he was a casualty. In 2010 a star was added by the Burnham Commemorative Committee. He is listed on the plaque in Sylvania's Veteran Memorial Field for World War II casualties.

At the 1930 census Harold is 9 years old and living with his parents William and Caroline on Argonne Place in Sylvania Township. At the 1940 census Harold is listed as 19 years old and still living with his parents on Argonne Place in Sylvania Township. This census indicates that his highest grade completed was his second year of high school. At this time he was working as a laborer in the rock crushing business.

Harold's enlistment date is recorded as 8-1-1942 with the U.S. Army, and at that time he was listed as single, without dependents.

12-7-1944 *Sylvania Sentinel*: "Memorial Services for Harold Jasmund – Memorial services for Harold Jasmund, son of Mr. and Mrs. William Jasmund, R.R. 10 Box 265 W. Toledo will be held Sunday afternoon Dec. 10 at 2:30 (Ohio time) at the Olivet Lutheran Church, Whiteford Rd., the Rev. Paul Getter, pastor. Harold died in England."

Arthur Jones, Jr.
Born 1920 Died 1945 – U.S. Army Air Corps - He is listed on the Burnham High School World War II Roll of Honor with a star to indicate that he was killed in action. He is also listed on the plaque in Sylvania's Veteran's Memorial Field for World War II casualties. Arthur Jones, Jr. graduated from Burnham High School in 1941.

At the 1940 census Arthur P. Jones was living on Sylvania Avenue in Sylvania Township. He was listed as 19 years old and working as a farm hand on a truck farm. His brother Charles William Jones was also killed in action during World War II.

His official date of death is listed as 6-22-1945, and he was buried in the Long Island National Cemetery in New York.

Charles William Jones
Born 1923 Died 1945 - He is listed on the Burnham High School World War II Roll of Honor under the name of William Jones with a star to indicate that he was killed in action. He is also listed on the plaque in Sylvania's Veteran's Memorial Field for World War II casualties.

At the 1940 census William Jones was listed living on Sylvania Avenue in Sylvania Township with his father and mother Arthur and Elva Jones. He was listed as 16 years old and working as a farm hand on a truck farm in the berry picking business. He was the brother of Arthur P. Jones, who was also killed in action during World War II.

Military records list him as William C. Jones and he is documented as being enlisted on 12-26-1942, and at that time was listed as married.

4-12-1945 *Sylvania Sentinel*: "Two Sylvanians Reported Missing – Sergt. Charles W. Jones, 21, has been missing in action over Austria since March 2 the War Department has notified his parents, Mr. and Mrs. Arthur Jones. Sergt. Jones was flight engineer and waist gunner on a B124. He had won the Air Medal with two Oak Leaf clusters. A letter from his commanding officer reported Sergt. Jones missing following the collision of two planes flying in formation."

Andrew N. Keeler
Born 1916 Died 1945 - His name is not listed on the Burnham High School World War II Roll of Honor. He is also listed on the plaque in Sylvania's Veteran's Memorial Field for World War II casualties. The *Sylvania Sentinel* said he was a Toledo resident, but attended St. Joseph School in Sylvania.

The 1930 census indicates that he was 13 years old and living at home with his father and mother, Jacob and Frankie Keeler, on Dorr Street in Springfield Township, Lucas County, Ohio. The 1947 Springfield High School Yearbook listed Andrew Keeler on a list of those boys who attended Springfield School and were killed during World War II. The reason he was also listed on Sylvania's Memorial Field plaque is because he attended school in Sylvania at St. Joseph School.

Andrew's official date of death is listed as 1-12-1945 and he was a Staff Sergeant at that time with the 134th Infantry U.S.A.G.F., Ohio 35th Division. He is recorded as entering the military on 6-3-1941 as a Lucas County resident. He was buried in Calvary Cemetery in Toledo. His enlistment papers indicate that he was single, without dependents when he joined and that he had completed two years of high school.

2-1-1945 *Sylvania Sentinel*: "Former St. Joseph Student Is Killed – Staff Sergt. Andrew N. Keeler, 28, was killed in action in Belgium Jan. 12, according to word from the War Department to his parents, Mr. and Mrs. Jacob Keeler, Dorr St. Sergt. Keeler had just recently been transferred to a combat infantry division. He was inducted in June, 1941, and spent the greater part of his overseas service in England. He had attended St. Joseph's School and was graduated from Holland High School. Surviving also are brothers, Lawrence, Toledo; Herman, in the Army in England, and Bernard, in the Army in the Philippines.

Alfred Ernest. Knepper
Born 1918 Died 1943 - His name is not listed on the Burnham High School Roll of Honor. He is listed on the plaque in Sylvania's Veteran's Memorial Field for World War II casualties. He lived on Whiteford Road according to articles in the *Sylvania Sentinel* during the time that he served in World War II, with his parents.

At the 1940 census Alfred Knepper was listed as 21 years old and living on Whiteford Road in Sylvania Township with his parents, Franklin A. and Bertha B. Knepper. This census record shows that he finished his fourth year of high school and was working as a milk man for a milk company.

His enlistment documents record him as joining on 2-28-1941 with the Panama Canal Department as a Private. This shows also that he finished four years of high school and his civil occupation at this time was machinist. He is listed as single, without dependents. His official date of death was recorded as 4-17-1943 and he is buried in the North Africa American Cemetery and Memorial in Carthage, Tunis, Tunisia.

9-10-1942 issue of the *Sylvania Sentinel* reported that Alfred Knepper had left to return to service.

August 1943 *Toledo Blade*: "Notification that Pvt. Alfred E. Knepper is missing in action was received by his wife, Mrs. Jane Knepper, Sylvania, O. The message stated that Private Knepper had been missing since April 17, following the battle of Tunisia. Mrs. Knepper received a letter from her husband postmarked April 17, telling of his transfer to service transport. A graduate of DeVilbiss High School, class of 1937, he enlisted in February, 1941, and has been overseas since November, 1942. He was an employee of the Toledo Scale Co. Private Knepper is the son of Mr. and Mrs. Frank Knepper, Whiteford Rd., and brother of Goldie May Knepper same address, and Mrs. Violet Mohn, 430 14th St., Toledo."

Sylvania Sentinel 8-26-1943: "Ernest Knepper Reported Missing In Action – In a telegram received Tuesday, Mrs. Jane Knepper, Whiteford Road was informed that her husband Ernest, had been reported missing in action since April 17. Mr. and Mrs. Knepper were married two years in June. Earnest went overseas last November. He is the son of Mr. and Mrs. Frank Knepper, Whiteford Road."

The 9-2-1943 *Sylvania Sentinel* reported: "ERNEST KNEPPER REPORTED AS DEAD – The total of Sylvania deaths in World War II was raised to four this week when Mrs. Jane Knepper of Whiteford Rd. was informed Friday, Aug. 28, that her husband, Ernest Knepper, has been reported dead. Earlier in the week Mrs. Knepper had received word that Ernest was missing in action since April 17. He had been in the invasion of Tunisia. Mr. and Mrs. Knepper were married two years ago in June and resided on Whiteford Road. He is the son of Mr. and Mrs. Frank Knepper." A memorial service was held 9-20-1943 at the Olivet Lutheran Church for Alfred Earnest Knepper. It was reported that he was the son of Mr. and Mrs. Frank Knepper and the husband of Mrs. Jane Knepper. Alfred was reported killed in action in the North African campaign. Friends were invited to the memorial.

Sylvania Sentinel 4-12-1945: "Posthumous Award of Purple Heart – Pvt. Alfred (Ernest) Knepper, son of Mr. and Mrs. Frank Knepper, Whiteford Rd., has been awarded the Purple Heart medal posthumously. The certificate of award and an accolade signed by the President has been received by his mother. Pvt. Knepper was killed in action on April 17, 1943."

Stanley J. Kniolek

Born 1915 Died 1944 - He is not listed on the Burnham High School World War II Roll of Honor, and was not on the original 1950 Memorial Field list, but now (2010) he is listed on the plaque in Sylvania's Veteran's Memorial Field for World War II casualties. Stanley lived on Alexis in Sylvania Township at the 1930 census, and was 14 yrs old, living with Ted & Dorothy Norts, listed as their nephew.

At the 1940 census Stanley was listed as 4 years old, living on Alexis Road in Sylvania Township, and living with Stanley and Laura Walazek, listed as their stepson. This census record shows that he attended school through the 8th grade.

Stanley's enlistment documents report that he enlisted on 12-26-1942 as a Private in the Army. At that time he was single, without dependents. This document indicates that he finished two years of high school.

His official date of death is listed as 10-22-1944 and he was buried in Calvary Cemetery in Toledo, Ohio. When he was killed in action he was listed as a Corporal - Technician Fifth Grade. Laura Walazek completed the paperwork for him to receive a Military headstone on 9-14-1948. She was living at 4345 Alexis Road at this time.

In 1948 a reburial service was held for Corp. Stanley J. Kniolek, Sylvania, soldier killed in action at Leyte, Philippine Islands, 10-22-1944. Burial was to be at Calvary Cemetery. Corporal Kniolek, 29 at the time of his death, was the first soldier from St. Joseph's Parish killed in World War II. He had been a Sylvania resident for seven years. He had been previously wounded at the Marshall Islands, Corporal Kniolek had been awarded the Purple Heart, in addition to the Bronze Star and four battle stars. He was a medical corpsman with the 32nd Infantry, 7th Division.

Toledo Blade 9-9-1948 – "Stanley J. Kniolek, T/5, killed in action on Leyte, P.I. Oct. 22, 1944, age 29 years. Beloved son of Mr. and Mrs. Stanley Walaszek, Sylvania. O; loving brother of Stephen, Toledo. Friends may call at the Frank L. Gasiorowski Funeral Home where military services will be held Saturday at 9 a.m. and from St. Joseph's Church, Sylvania, O., at 10 a.m. Burial Calvary Cemetery. VFW Post 606 will be in charge of military services. Family will receive friends from 2 to 5 and 7 to 9:30 p.m."

William J. Kramer
Born 1919 Died 1945 - His name is not listed on the Burnham High School World War II Roll of Honor. He is listed on the plaque in Sylvania's Veteran's Memorial Field for World War II casualties.

At the 1930 census William Kramer is listed as living in Toledo at St. Anthony's Orphanage with brothers Howard and George.

At the 1940 census William Kramer is listed as 19 years old, single, and living at home with his widowed father, John Kramer, 73 years old, and four brothers (Joseph Kramer, John Howard Kramer, George Kramer and Ralph Kramer), on Spring Street in Sylvania. William was working as a laborer on street projects. This census also indicates that William completed 8 years of school.

His enlistment documents indicate that he entered service on 12-18-1942 as a Private in the Army. His official date of death is listed as 4-15-1945 and he was buried in Manila American Cemetery and Memorial in Manila, Metro Manila, National Capital Region, Philippines. His headstone inscription and interment record shows: William J. Kramer – Pfc 149 Inf. 38th Division – Ohio. Under permanent cemetery it says Ft. McKinley 7701 Block L, Row 9, Grave 31, with a cross. His father John Kramer was listed as his next of kin.

There was never an obituary notice in the *Toledo Blade* for William Kramer, and nothing mentioned in the local newspapers about his death.

Glenn V. Mathewson
Born 1923 Died 1945 - His name is not listed on the Burnham High School World War II Roll of Honor. He is listed on the plaque in Sylvania's Veteran's Memorial Field for World War II casualties. He is also listed on the Monroe County, Michigan casualties memorial.

At the 1940 census Glenn was listed as 16 years old, living with his parents, Rexford and Audrey Mathewson in Ottawa Lake, Whiteford Township, Monroe County, Michigan. This census record shows that he was attending school and had completed two years of high school so far. Also living in the household were his younger brother and three sisters. At this time residents of Ottawa Lake attended high school at Sylvania's Burnham High School. A review of the yearbooks for Burnham in 1941 when he should have graduated does not show him on the graduating class list. The 1942 book also did not show him as a graduate.

His enlistment date is recorded as 2-16-1943 in Ohio. When he was killed his rank was Corporal in the Army. The Michigan casualties of World War II listing shows that he was reported as missing on 5-22-1945 in Europe; and reported killed in action on 6-11-1945 in Europe. Documents on Ancestry.com record that "Glenn was entitled to wear three bronze battle stars on his ETO ribbon for the following battles: Battle of the Ardennes (Bulge Battle), Battle of the Rhineland, and Battle of Central Europe."

His official date of death is listed in the military records as 4-26-1945, and he has a military marker in the Whiteford Union Cemetery in Lambertville, Monroe County, Michigan with the following information: Ohio – Cpl. 11 Tank Bn – 10 Armed Division, World War II.

5-24-1945 – "Killed in Action – GLENN V. MATHEWSON – OTTAWA LAKE, Mich., May 24, Corp. Glenn V. Mathewson, 21, was killed in action April 26 in Germany; the War Department has informed his parents, Mr. and Mrs. Rexford Mathewson, Route 1, Ottawa Lake. A previous telegram on May 9 reported him missing. Corporal Mathewson had served with the Tank Battalion of the 7th Army since last September. He had been in service 26 months. Previously he worked at the Willys-Overland Motors, Inc., Toledo. Surviving besides his parents are brothers, Jack and Arlyn; sisters, Betty Mathewson and Mrs. Bonwaiva Bay, all of Ottawa Lake; and grandparents, Mr. and Mrs. T.G. Crow, Toledo."

Toledo Blade d 12-13-1948 – "Corp. Glen Vernon Mathewson, killed in Germany April 26, 1945, age 21 years. Beloved son of Mr. and Mrs. Rexford Mathewson of Ottawa Lake, Mich. Surviving besides his parents are two sisters, Mrs. Charles Ery and Betty; two brothers, Jack and Arlyn; grandparents, Mr. and Mrs. Thomas Crow. Friends may call at the Reeb Funeral Home, Sylvania, O., where services will be held Wednesday, Dec. 15, 1948 at 1 p.m. Interment Union Cemetery, the Rev. F.F. Johnson officiating."

James E. McCullough
Born 1926 Died 1945 – He is listed on the Burnham High School World War II Roll of Honor with a star to indicate that he was killed in action. He is listed on the plaque in Sylvania's Veteran's Memorial Field for World War II casualties.

At the 1940 census James McCullough is listed as 14 years old and living on Percentum Road in Sylvania Township, living with his father and mother, Edward and Hazel McCullough. He was attending school and completed the 7th grade so far.

Mr. McCullough's date of enlistment is recorded as 2-26-1944, and his date of death is listed as 6-20-1945. He was 19 years old. The inscription on his headstone reads: Ohio Pfc 5 Marines 1 Marine Division WWII. He is buried in Harman Cemetery in Gilboa, Putnam County, Ohio.

The 1946 U.S. Navy listing of next of kin for those killed from direct enemy action shows the following information: "Ohio – Pfc Edward McCullough, Rt. 2, Box 392, Percentum Road, Toledo."

The following appeared in the *Toledo Blade* dated 2-17-1949: "Services for Marine Pfc. James E. McCullough, RD 2, Percentum Road, killed in action on Okinawa 6-20-1945, will be Saturday at 1 p.m. in Reeb Funeral Home, Sylvania, the Rev. Birney Roberts, pastor of Sylvania Methodist Church officiating. Burial will be in Gilboa Ohio. The body will be in the funeral home after 5 p.m. tomorrow. Private McCullough, 19, was attached to the First Marine Division. He attended Burnham High School and was employed at Willys Overland Motors, Inc. and the Willis Floral Farm before entering service."

Richard W. Miller
Born 1925 Died 1944 – U.S. Army - He is listed on the Burnham High School World War II Roll of Honor with a star indicating that he was killed in action. He is listed on the plaque in Sylvania's Veteran's Memorial Field for World War II casualties. The 1941 Burnham High School Yearbook shows Richard Miller as a Freshman.

At the 1940 census Richard Miller was listed as 14 years old and living at home with his parents, Harold L. and Dorothy E. Miller, and 5 year old sister Lena Jane Miller, in Adams Township, Lucas County, Ohio. He is listed as attending school at that time.

His date of death is recorded as 7-6-1944 in Jellico, Campbell County, Tennessee. His mother is listed as Dorothy E. Miller living at 1823 Krieger Drive, Toledo, Ohio.

Sylvania Sentinel 7-13-1944: "Train Wreck Kills Burnham Graduate – Pvt. Richard Miller was one of those killed in the wreck of the troop train near Jelico, Tenn., last week. Pvt. Miller was the son of Mr. and Mrs. Harold Miller of Crieger Dr., Toledo. Richard graduated from Burnham High School last June. His father is Chief Electrician's Mate in the Navy, but was able to get home for the funeral, which will be at 2:30 p.m. Friday at the Boyer Funeral Home in W. Toledo."

Donald W. Moore
Born 1918 Died 1943 - He is listed on the Burnham High School World War II Roll of Honor with a star to indicate that he was killed in action. He is also listed on the plaque in Sylvania's Veteran's Memorial Field for World War II casualties.

At the 1930 census Donald was living on Alexis Road with his parents William & Grace – he is 11 years old. Donald Moore appeared in the Burnham High School yearbook as a 7ᵗʰ grader in 1932. At the 1940 census Donald Moore was listed as 21 years old and was living at home with his parents, William and Grace Moore, and two sisters and three brothers. They were living on Woods Avenue, which at that time was still part of Sylvania Township. He was listed as employed as a metal polisher. He is listed as finishing his third year of high school, but was not attending school at that time.

Donald W. Moore of Sylvania enlisted on 1-20-1942 with the Air Force, and his official date of death is reported as 8-27-1943. He was buried in Toledo Memorial Park Cemetery in Sylvania, Ohio. When he was killed in action his rank was First Lieutenant with the 8ᵗʰ Air Force.

The 9-16-1943 issue of the *Sylvania Sentinel* reported the following: "SON BORN DAY FATHER IS REPORTED MISSING IN ACTION – Lieut. and Mrs. Don W. Moore are the parents of a son, Douglas Larry, born Sept. 7ᵗʰ at Toledo Hospital. Mrs. Moore is the former Doris Troutner, daughter of Mr. and Mrs. Earl Troutner. Lieut. Moore has been serving overseas and word was received here the day his son was born, that he has been missing since Aug. 27ᵗʰ."

The *Sylvania Sentinel* dated 10-7-1943 reported the following: "A telegram was received Monday by Mr. and Mrs. William H. Moore, Flanders Road, from the War Department confirming the death of their son, Lieut. Don Moore, who had been reported as missing in action four weeks ago. Besides his parents, Lieutenant Moore is survived by his wife, the former Miss Doris Troutner, and a child born in the day he was reported as missing. Also sisters Mary Mildred and Sally, and brothers George, Paul, Robert and Ben."

Wayne A. Morningstar
Born 1926 Died 1945 – U.S. Army - He is listed on the Burnham High School World War II Roll of Honor with a star to indicate that he was killed in action. He is also listed on the plaque in Sylvania's Veteran's Memorial Field for World War II casualties.

At the 1930 census Wayne is living on Central Avenue in Sylvania Township with his parents Emery & Selome Morningstar – he is 4 years old.

At the 1940 census Wayne Morningstar was listed as 14 years old and living on Central Avenue in Sylvania Township with his parents Emery and Salome Morningstar. Wayne Morningstar graduated from Burnham High School in 1944. The 1944 Burnham High School Yearbook shows Wayne Morningstar involved with the following school activities: Hi-Y, 2,3,4; Biology Club 1; Victory Corps, 3; Camera Club, 2; Band, 1,2,3,4,; Scholarship, 1; Senior Committee, 4. (The numbers represent the year in high school that he was involved).

Mr. Morningstar's date of death is recorded as 1-7-1945 and he was buried in Toledo Memorial Park Cemetery in Sylvania.

The following appeared in the *Sylvania Sentinel* on 12-31-1943: "The address of Private Gale Morningstar is G5 G49331 Co. A, 26th Btn. 4th Blt., Aed. R.T.C. Camp Grant, Illinois."

The 5-4-1944 *Sylvania Sentinel* said that 101 Seniors would graduate from Burnham High School, with only about 91 students on stage due to many already in service. Wayne Morningstar was listed in the Army. The article said that the boys in the service would still receive their diplomas even though they were unable to be present at the exercise.

2-1-1945 *Sylvania Sentinel*: "Two Boys Reported Killed This Week – Two more Sylvania homes were made sad this week when the War Department notified the nearest of kin of the death in combat of Pfc. Wayne Morningstar and Pvt. Jack Nichols. Pfc. Morningstar was killed on Jan 7 in France and would have been 19 years of age on Jan. 24. He leaves his parents, Mr. and Mrs. Emery Morningstar, Central Ave, a brother, Corp. Gale Morningstar, who is stationed in New Jersey, and a sister, Leona, at home. He was inducted into the Army on 3-16-1944, but received credit for graduation last June in Burnham High School. . ."

The following notice appeared in the *Toledo Blade*: "Pfc. Wayne Morningstar, 19, was killed in action Jan. 7 in France according to a War Department telegram to his parents, Mr. and Mrs. E.A. Morningstar, Mail Rt. 2 W. Central Avenue. An Infantryman, Private Morningstar was inducted in March, and trained at Camp Adair, Oreg. and Fort Leonard Wood, Mo. He had been overseas three weeks. He was a graduate of Burnham High School. Also surviving are a brother Corp. Gale E., army, and sister Leona."

Final rites were given to three returned soldiers in April 1948 "The long journey home from the battlefield of Europe has ended for three soldiers from this area and their final interment will take place – The three who made the supreme sacrifice were: Pfc. Wayne Morningstar, Pfc. Allen L. Blakeman and Cap. Kenneth F. Brodbeck.

Jack Nichols
Born 1920 Died 1945 – U.S. Army - He is listed on the Burnham High School World War II Roll of Honor with a star to indicate that he was killed in action. He is also listed on the plaque in Sylvania's Veteran's Memorial Field for World War II casualties. Jack Nichols graduated from Burnham High School in 1938.

At the 1940 census Jack Nichols was listed as 19 years old and he and his wife Dorothy, 18 years old, were renting a home on Arbor Way in Sylvania Township. He was working as an attendant at a gas station.

Jack's enlistment date is recorded as 6-17-1944 and he served as a private in Company F, Michigan 333 Infantry Regiment, 84th Division. His official date of death is recorded as 1-12-1945, and he was buried in Toledo Memorial Park in Sylvania.

11-16-1944 *Sylvania Sentinel*: "Pvt. Jack Nichols has been spending a 10-day leave with his wife and family after completing his basic training at Camp Blanding, Fla.

2-1-1945 *Sylvania Sentinel*: "Two Boys Reported Killed This Week – Two more Sylvania homes were made sad this week when the War Department notified the nearest of kin of the death in combat of Pfc. Wayne Morningstar and Pvt. Jack Nichols. . . Pvt. Nicholas, 24, was killed in action in Belgium on Jan 12, according to word received by his wife, Dorothy, on Jan 30, Mrs. Nichols lives on Jolly Rd. with their two children, Jerry and Janice. He was the son of Mr. and Mrs. Norman Nichols and brother, Judson, is at home. He attended Burnham High School and had worked in Wayne, Mich., for two years prior to his induction into the Army in June, 1944."

The following appeared in an unknown 1945 newspaper: Sylvania Private Killed In Belgium – Jack Nichols Leaves Wife and 2 Children - "Pvt. Jack Nichols, 24, infantryman, of Sylvania, father of two children was killed in action in Belgium Jan. 12, according to word from the War Department to his wife, the former Dorothy Kiefer, Sylvania. Private Nichols was inducted by the army last June. A graduate of Burnham High School, he formerly was employed in Wayne, Mich. Surviving, besides his wife, are his children, Jerry and Janice; parents Mr. and Mrs. Norman Nichols, Petersburg Rd., Sylvania and brother Judson, also of Sylvania."

3-1-1945 *Sylvania Sentinel*: "Memorial Service For Jack Nichols – Memorial services will be held Sunday, March 4, at 2:30 pm in Olivet Lutheran Church, Alexis and Whiteford Rds. for Jack Nichols, who lost his life in action in Belgium, Jan 12. The Rev. Paul Getter will conduct the services. Pvt. Jack Nichols entered the Army in June, 1944, and notice came to his wife, Dorothy on Jan. 29. He left his wife and two children, Jerry and Janice, who live on Jolly RD. He was the son of Mr. and Mrs. Norman Nichols."

Sylvester J. Pakulski
Born 1926 Died 1944 - His name is not listed on the Burnham High School World War II Roll of Honor. He is listed on the plaque in Sylvania's Veteran's Memorial Field for World War II casualties. Sylvester lived in Toledo and attended school in Toledo. I am not sure how he ended up on Sylvania's Memorial, but we welcome him just the same.

At the 1940 census Sylvester was listed as 14 years old and living on East Bancroft Street in Toledo. This census shows that he had finished school through the 7th grade as of this census.

A 1941 Woodward High School, Toledo, Ohio Yearbook shows him attending school there and a 1942 Macomber Vocational High School, Toledo, Ohio shows that he was attending school there.

Mr. Pakulski's official date of death is recorded as 11-16-1944. His rank was Aviation Ordnance man Second Class with the U.S. Navy. His disposition was recorded as buried at sea by administrative decision. He is listed on the World War II monument in Honolulu, Hawaii.

The 1946 U.S. Navy listed him as killed from direct enemy action and listed his next of kin: "Mr. and Mrs. Casimar Pakulski, 922 E. Bancroft Street, Toledo."

Robert F. Palicki
Born 1921 Died 1943 – His name is not listed on the Burnham Roll of Honor, and he did not attend Burnham High School. Robert's name was not on the original 1950 list of casualties in Memorial Field, but he is listed on the plaque in Sylvania's Veteran's Memorial Field for World War II casualties now.

Robert Palicki was listed in the 1940 census as 18 years old and living on Woodland Avenue in Toledo, Ohio with his parents Robert C. and Anna Palicki, and a brother and sister. This census shows that Robert had completed 4 years of high school. Sometime after Robert was killed in action his parents purchased the home at 5245 Corey Road in Sylvania, and that's probably why he ended up on Sylvania's memorial wall.

Robert's official date of death is listed as 12-22-1943 and he died "at sea." He has a memorial in Calvary Cemetery in Toledo, Ohio. His stone reads: Lt. Robert F. Palicki – 1921 – 1943 – Gave his life in combat U.S. Army Air Force.

Toledo Blade 2-2-1949 – Services for Second Lieut. Robert F. Palicki, 22, son of Mr. and Mrs. Robert C. Palicki, 5245 Corey Rd., and formerly of 1060 Woodland Ave., will be Saturday at 9:30 a.m. in the Czolgoss Funeral Home and at 10 am. in Nativity Church. Burial in charge of Przybylski Post, American Legion, will be in Calvary Cemetery. Lieutenant Palicki was killed in action in a Liberator bomber over Germany Dec. 22, 1943. A native of Toledo, he was a graduate of Nativity School, Central Catholic High School and the University of Toledo. His sister, Elaine Ann, and brother Arthur, also survive."

Richard H. Palmer
Born 1924 Died 1945 – U.S. Army Air Corp - He is listed on the Burnham High School World War II Roll of Honor with a star to indicate that he was killed in action. He is also listed on the plaque in Sylvania's Veteran's Memorial Field for World War II casualties. Richard graduated from Burnham High School in 1943.

At the 1940 census Richard Palmer was listed as 15 years old, living on Holland-Sylvania Road, in Sylvania Township, with his parents Howard and Thelma Palmer, sister Betty, brother Robert, and his grandmother Helen Jones. Richard is listed as completing the 8th grade.

Records show that he enlisted as a Private on 7-28-1943, and was single, without dependents.

3-29-1945 *Sylvania Sentinel*: "Another Local Boy Reported Missing – Sergt. Richard Palmer, radio gunner, has been reported missing in action over the Italian front on March 10. Sergt Palmer is the son of Mr. and Mrs. Howard Palmer, Holland-Sylvania Rd. He had been stationed in Corsica. Richard graduated from Burnham High School in 1943 and was inducted in August of that year. He went overseas last December."

4-12-1945 *Sylvania Sentinel*: "Word has just been received from the 12th AAF B-25 Group in the Mediterranean theater that Richard H. Palmer, who has been reported missing in action since March 10, has been promoted from sergeant to staff sergeant."

The following notice appeared in an unidentified newspaper: "Staff Sergt R.H. Palmer has been missing in action over Italy since March 10, the War Department has told his parents, Mr. and Mrs. Howard C. Palmer, Sylvania, O. Sergeant Palmer was a radio-gunner on a B-25 on Corsica. He is a graduate of Burnham High School, and was employed by the Champion Spark Plug Co. before entering service 20 months ago. He has been overseas since December."

12-6-1945 *Sylvania Sentinel*: "Sgt. Richard Palmer Killed in Action – Mr. and Mrs. Howard Palmer, Holland-Sylvania road, were notified by telegram from the War Department on Nov. 1 of the death of their son S/Sgt Richard Palmer, in a German prison camp. A letter dated Nov. 16 from the War Department stated that Richard was being transported by the Germans to a camp in Northern Italy when he was killed in action on 3-24-1945. The inference seems to be that while being transported he either tried to escape or patriots interceded and he was killed in the resultant action. The parents were first informed last spring that their son was reported as missing as of March 10 while in action over Italy. Richard had entered service in August, 1943 after graduating from Burnham High School in June. He was twenty years old. Sgt. Palmer was a radio gunner in the Air Forces."

Howard R. Pratt
Born 1925 Died 1945 - His name is listed on the Burnham High School Roll of Honor, but does not have a star by his name to indicate that he was a casualty. In 2010 a star was added next to his name by the Burnham Commemorative Committee. Howard Pratt is listed on the plaque in Sylvania's Veteran's Memorial Field for World War II casualties.

At the 1930 census he was living at 5168 Estess, in Sylvania Township, and listed as 4 yrs old, living with his parents, Ralph C. and Marie B. Pratt, and two younger sisters. By the 1940 census he was 14 years old and living in Alexander, Athens County, Ohio, with his parents Ralph C. and Marie B. Pratt, and his four sisters and one brother. His father was employed as a common laborer on the W.P.A. at this time, and Howard is listed as attending school, in the 7th grade. Sometime after this 1940 census they must have moved back to Sylvania, because he is shown attending Sylvania's Burnham High School before entering World War II. He was featured in the 1942 Burnham High School Yearbook.

Howard's official date of death is listed as 2-19-1945. At that time he was listed as a Private First Class of the 24th U.S. Marine Corps., 4th Marine Division, and was awarded a Purple Heart Medal and Silver Star Medal. According to the U.S. Veterans' list of gravesites Howard R. Pratt was interred on 2-2-1949 in the National Memorial Cemetery of The Pacific in Honolulu, Hawaii.

The following appeared in the *Toledo Blade* on 4-9-1945: "Killed in Action – Pfc. Howard R. Pratt – Mr. and Mrs. Ralph Pratt, 2205 Locust St., Toledo, have been notified that their son, Pfc. Howard R. Pratt, a marine, was killed Feb. 19 in action on Iwo Jima. Private Pratt, who was 19, attended Burnham High School before entering the service. He had been overseas almost 27 months. The father, navy fireman first class, stationed in Little Creek, Va., entered the service 16 months ago and is at home on leave. Other than the parents, a brother, Waitman, and four sisters, Mary Belle, Edith, Ruth and Donna survive."

The 1946 U.S. Navy casualties list shows him as: Howard R. Pratt, Private First Class, USMCR – next of kin: Mr. & Mrs. Ralph Pratt, Rt. 1, Sylvania.

James S. Randall

Born 1922 Died 1944 – U.S. Army Air Corps - He is listed on the Burnham High School World War II Roll of Honor with a star to indicate that he was killed in action. He is also listed on the plaque in Sylvania's Veteran's Memorial Field for World War II casualties. James S. Randall graduated from Burnham High School in 1940.

At the 1940 census James was listed as 17 years old, living in Sylvania at 6730 Long Street, with his mother, Lora Randall, and a brother Richard who was 13 years old. James was listed as finishing his third year in high school.

The 1942 Yearbook for Ohio State University in Columbus, Ohio listed Jams S. Randall in a roll list with the class of 1944 with Phi Eta Sigma, a national honorary fraternity.

The following was reported in the 5-28-1942 *Sylvania Sentinel*: "James S. Randall, son of Mrs. Lora Randall, has recently been promoted to the rank of sergeant in Ohio State University's Reserve Officers Training Corps. These 2,500 young men paraded on Wednesday afternoon in observance of "War Activities Day" at the University."

James S. Randall's enlistment date was 1-31-1943 as a Private in Kentucky at Fort Thomas Newport. He was listed as single, without dependents, and had two years of college.

The 2-25-1943 *Sylvania Sentinel* reported the following: "The address of James S. Randall is as follows: Pvt. James S. Randall, 633rd Tech. Sch. Sq. Meteorological, Boca Raton Field, Boca Raton, Florida."

The following appeared in the *Sylvania Sentinel* on 4-8-1943: "A-C James S. Randall, 580th TSS AAF, Hotel Rantlind, Room 640, Grand Rapids, Mich."

Randall's date of death is listed as 1-2-1944 and his place of death is listed as Sacramento County, California. He was listed as a Second Lieutenant in the U.S. Army Air Forces.

Toledo Blade – date not listed: "Lieut. J.S. Randall Lost in Plane Crash – Mrs. Lora Randall received the tragic news Monday at 2:00 a.m., that her son, Lieut. James S. Randall, was one of the 13 men killed in the crash of the Flying Fortress near Sacramento, Calif., Sunday. Lieut. Randall had received his commission Nov. 29th from Kingman Field, Ariz., and was a meteorologist with the Army Air Force. He graduated from Burnham High School in May, 1940. While a senior in school, he was one of four ranked among the first ten in Lucas County in the 1940 state scholarship tests. His brother, Richard, who is a senior in Burnham High School and his mother survive. It is understood that the boy will not be brought back to Sylvania, but will be cremated in California."

1-2-1944 *Toledo Blade*: "Sylvania Flier, 12 Others Killed – Fortress Explodes Above California Field – Second Lieut. James S. Randall of Sylvania was one of the 16 men killed yesterday when a four-motored Flying Fortress exploded near McClellan Field, Sacramento, Calif., and plummeted to earth. Lieutenant Randall, who received his commission Nov. 28 at Kingman Field, Ariz., was the son of Mrs. Laura S. Randall, 6730 Long St. Sylvania. Mrs. Randall was notified at 2 a.m. today of her son's death. Lieutenant Randall, who was 21, was graduated from Burnham High School, Sylvania. He was one of four seniors ranked among the first 10 in Lucas County in the 1940 state scholarship tests. He was a meteorologist with the army air force. His mother and a brother, Richard, a student in Burnham High School, survive. An army board of inquiry today sought to ascertain from one survivor, Maj. James W. Wergen, Salinas, Calif., and hundreds of spectators why the Flying Fortress literally disintegrated and crashed in flaming wreckage. The plane, based at Kingman Field, was enroute from McChord Field, Tacoma, Wash, to Los Angeles and was not scheduled to land at McClelland Field, public relations officers said. The field had not been warned of its approach and the plane apparently crashed on the runway by pure coincidence. Hundreds of army personnel and nearby residents saw the plane come hurling out of the overcast above the field at 3,000 feet spinning and burning and scattering bits of wreckage over 15 miles. One of its engines, later found on a golf course five miles away, already had dropped off, and part of one wing and other bits of the plane fell away as the Fortress plummeted to the ground, exploding with a fear that brought thousands to the field. Witnesses saw Major Wergen parachute to the field and strike the concrete runway so hard he received four broken teeth and a possible hip fracture. Wergen did not remember getting out of the plane or pulling his parachute ripcord, officers reported after interviewing him. He could have no explanation of the crash, recalling only that the occupants were thrown together inside the fuselage as the plane seemingly went into a spin. Firemen fought flames for two hours before they were able to remove the charred bodies of the 12 dead."

Toledo Blade 1-9-1944: "Randall Memorial Rites To Be Today – Memorial services for James Randall, killed last Sunday when a B-17 Flying Fortress exploded over Sacramento, Calif., will be today at 3 p.m., in the Sylvania Community Church, with the Rev. Herbert C. Gans officiating. Surviving are his mother, Mrs. Lora Randall, and brother, Richard, Sylvania."

Orin D. Reynolds, Jr.
Born 1923 Died 1944 - His name is not listed on the Burnham High School World War II Roll of Honor, because he did not attend school at Burnham. He is listed on the plaque in Sylvania's Veteran's Memorial Field for World War II casualties. I am not sure why he is listed on Sylvania's memorial, because he never lived in Sylvania, or attended school here.

At the 1940 census Orin D. Reynolds, Jr., was listed as 15 years old and living on Dorr Street in Adams Township, Lucas County, Ohio, with his father and mother, Orin D. and Ida Reynolds. At this time he was attending school and had completed his first year of high school.

In the 1940 Woodward High School Yearbook, in Toledo, Orin Reynolds is featured as a Sophomore at that time. And then a 1941 Woodward High School newspaper called the "Tattler" reported that the Woodward Orchestra had elected officers for the year and Orin Reynolds was elected the assistant business manager. Finally, the 1942 Woodward Yearbook featured a photo of Orin "Ornie" Reynolds in the Senior section of the yearbook. The caption under his photo reads: "He's A Hard Man "Free And Easy"."

Orin's official date of enlistment is recorded as 2-26- 1943. He enlisted as a Private and was listed as completing four years of high school. His official date of death is recorded as 6-6-1944. He has a military marker in the Maplewood Cemetery in Toledo, Ohio.

Toledo Blade 6-15-1949 – "Pfc Orin D. Reynolds, Jr., beloved son of Mr. and Mrs. Orin D. Reynolds, 5044 Dorr St., Toledo (Reynolds Corners) in Normandy, France, 6-6-1944, age 19 years. Surviving besides his parents, are his brother, Sammy Glenn Reynolds at home, and his grandparents, Mr. and Mrs. Alex Rothlisberger, Holland, O. Friends may call at the Reeb Funeral Home after 5 p.m. Thursday and until Friday at 11 a.m. when removal will be made to the Epithany Lutheran Church, Reynolds and Brandon, where services will be held at 2 p.m. Interment Maplewood Cemetery. Rev. Ernest Kempfer officiating."

David Paul Robinson
Born 1925 Died 1944 – U.S. Army - He is listed on the Burnham High School World War II Roll of Honor with a star to indicate that he was killed in action. He is also listed on the plaque in Sylvania's Veteran's Memorial Field for World War II casualties.

At the 1940 census David Robinson was listed as 15 years old and living in Sylvania Township, on Chaney Road, with his parents, Elmer and Marvel Robinson and a sister Shirley. He is listed as completing school through 7th grade and was attending school at that time.

David's official enlistment date is recorded as 4-1-1943, he was listed as a Private, was single and without dependents. His official date of death is recorded as 6-19-1944.

4-29-1943 *Sylvania Sentinel*: "Pvt. David P. Robinson, Co. B 12th T. Reg. Camp Joseph T. Robinson, Ark."

8-5-1943 *Sylvania Sentinel*: "Pvt. David P. Robinson, 300th Engineer Comb. Bn., Camp White, Oregon."

8-3-1944 *Sylvania Sentinel* – Pvt. David Robinson Reported Missing – Mr. and Mrs. Elmer L. Robinson Route 11, received notice from the War Department July 24 that Pvt. David P. Robinson, their son, was reported as missing in action. It is assumed that he was in Italy. Pvt. Robinson was in the Engineers Corps. Pvt. Robinson would have been 20 years old in January, and formerly attended Burnham High School"

8-24-1944 *Sylvania Sentinel* – Pvt. David Robinson Reported Killed – Notification was received by Mr. and Mrs. Elmer Robinson, R11, that their son, Pvt. David Robinson, had been killed in action in France Aug. 5. The Robinsons had received word July 24 that their son was missing. Pvt. Robinson was in the Engineer Corps and swells the total of former Burnham students who have given their lives for the country to 15."

6-21-1945 *Sylvania Sentinel* – June 19 was a day to bring memories to Mr. and Mrs. Elmer Robinson, Rt. 11, Box 535 as it was just a year ago that their son, Pvt. David P. Robinson was killed in action. The Robinsons first received word on July 24 that their son was missing. Then on August 5th word came that he had been killed on June 19. Besides the parents he left a sister, Shirley, age 13. David was inducted into the Army 4-1-1943 and trained at Camp Joseph Robinson, Arkansas and Camp White, Oregon. He went overseas with the 300th Combat Engineers, and landed in Normandy June 14, making the supreme sacrifice just five days later. He attended Burnham High School."

Kenneth H. Shull

Born 1918 Died 1943 – U.S. Army Air Corps - He is listed on the Burnham High School World War II Roll of Honor with a star to indicate that he was killed in action. He is also listed on the plaque in Sylvania's Veteran's Memorial Field for World War II casualties. Kenneth H. Shull graduated from Burnham High School in 1936.

At the 1930 census Kenneth Shull was listed as 12 years old, living at home with his parents, Cyril and Henrietta Shull, and two brothers at 6712 Long Street in the Village of Sylvania. At the 1940 census Kenneth Shull was 22 years old and living at home with father and mother, Cyril and Henrietta Shull, and two younger brothers, Dale and Cyril. They were listed living at 5819 Acers Road, Sylvania. Kenneth was employed as a clerk at a retail grocery store and had completed four years of high school.

Kenneth H. Shull's official date of enlistment is recorded as 10-4-1941 as a Private in the Air Corps. His date of death is listed as 11-26-1943 and his burial place is listed as Carthage, Tunisia – Cemetery: North Africa. His next of kin was Laura G. Shull of 6750 Erie Street, Sylvania, and his rank was Second Lieutenant with the 322nd Fighter Control Squad.

The following information appeared in the *Sylvania Sentinel* dated 2-5-1942: "Private Kenneth Shull, of the Army Air Corps, has just completed an eight day furlough, which he spent with his parents Mr. and Mrs. Cyril Shull. Since Kenneth's enlistment he has seen much of the United States. He was first sent to a camp in Texas, then transferred to one in Bangor, Maine, and is now enroute to another in the West. Kenneth has made many flights in the huge U.S. bombers, but when he went aloft with Leonardson Griffin in a smaller plane; to his great embarrassment he became ill. Which proves, it's all in what we get used to! By the way, Kenneth has gained 30 pounds in weight, and loves his work."

Sylvania Sentinel 6-18-1942: "Private Kenneth Shull and Miss Laura Griffin, were united in marriage on Saturday evening, June 13 at the home of the bride on Erie Street. The groom is the son of Mr. and Mrs. Cyril Shull of Acres Road, and the bride is the daughter of the late Mr. and Mrs. Bayliss Griffin. The groom is on furlough awaiting appointment to the Cadet Aviation Training School."

4-29-1943 *Sylvania Sentinel*: "Kenneth H. Shull, Rt., Sylvania has been graduated from Officer's Training School, Miami Beach, Fla., and commissioned a second Lieutenant."

The following notice appeared in an unidentified newspaper, with no date: "Second Lieut. Kenneth Shull, Sylvania, is missing in action in the Mediterranean area where he was on ground duty with the air forces, the War Department has notified his wife, the former Laura Griffin. Mrs. Shull said she received the information Dec. 30 (1943), but that she has not learned whether her husband was in air action or on ground duty when he disappeared. Lieutenant Shull, 26, is a graduate of Burnham High School, Sylvania and the son of Mr. and Mrs. Cyril Shull, Sr., Acres Rd. A brother Dale, also in the Army.

January 1944 *Toledo Blade*: "Lt. Kenneth Shull Reported Missing – The War Department informed Mrs. Kenneth Shull, Dec. 30th that her husband, Lieut. Kenneth Shull, was reported missing. Lieut. Shull was in the Air Force Ground crew, and his exact location at the time of his disappearance is unknown. Mrs. Shull is the former Laura Griffin. Lieut. Shull was a graduate of Burnham High."

Wade Leroy Shull
Born 1925 Died 1943 – U.S. Army - He is listed on the Burnham High School World War II Roll of Honor with a star to indicate that he was killed in action. He is also listed on the plaque in Sylvania's Veteran's Memorial Field for World War II casualties.

At the 1940 census Wade Shull was 15 years old and living at home with his mother and step-father, Donald and Mabel DeLisle, and a brother John and sister Doris Ann. They were living on Argonne Place in Sylvania Township. He was listed as attending school and had completed the 7th grade.

Wade Shull's enlistment date is recorded as 10-16-1941 (16 years old) serving with D Company, First Raider Battalion, First Marine Raider Regiment. His official date of death is listed as 7-23-1943 with a rank of Private First Class. Wade has a headstone in Toledo Memorial Park Cemetery in Sylvania.

The *Sylvania Sentinel* of 2-4-1943 reads: "Word has been received by Mr. and Mrs. Deo Shull that their grandson, Pfc. Wade Shull, who is with the Marine Corps, has landed safely and his address now is Pfc. Wade L. Shull, Unit No. 975, U.S.M.C. c-o Postmaster, San Francisco, California.

The following was printed in the *Sylvania Sentinel* on 7-29-1943: "Word was received as the Sentinel goes to press of the death of Wade Shull, 18, in the South Pacific area. Wade was the grandson of Mr. and Mrs. Deo Shull, Sylvania with whom he made his home, before entering the service. He was sent overseas December 6, 1942. A telegram from the War Department stated that Wade had died July 23. No mention was made of the cause of death. Mrs. Shull had received a letter from Wade last week, saying that he was fine. The letter had been written on the 30th of June."

July 1943 *Toledo Blade*: "Toledo Marine Dies Of Wounds – Pfc. Wade L. Shull Pacific Casualty – A message from the Navy Department has shattered the hope of a Toledo mother that her son, reported missing in action in the Solomons, still lived. When Mrs. Mabel DeLyle of 1408 Walnut St. was informed weeks ago that her son, Pfc. Wade L. Shull, 18, of the marines, was missing, she told only relatives and close friends. She kept the news from the public while she cherished the hope he was alive. Then came the telegram the other day that shifted the marine's name from the missing in action list to the killed in action. It told of his dying of wounds received July 23 during the heavy fighting in the South Pacific on those last days of July when so many from Toledo were killed. For a time Mrs. DeLyle thought her son was en route home on a hospital ship. Shull was born near Sylvania but had lived several years in Toledo. He was a student at Macomber Vocational High School when he enlisted in the marines Oct. 29, 1941. He trained at Parris Island, S.C. and Quantico, Va., and sailed from San Diego, Calif., in November, 1942. He reached New Caledonia on Christmas Day. Surviving besides his mother, are his father, Dilgert L. Shull, 734 Noble St. Toledo; brother, John Shull, and a sister, Doris Ann Shull."

Raymond Sporleder
Born 1922 Died 1943 – U.S. Army - He is listed on the Burnham High School Roll of Honor with a star representing that he was killed in action. He is also listed on the plaque in Sylvania's Veteran's Memorial Field for World War II casualties.

Raymond Sporleder never appeared to live in Sylvania or attend school in Sylvania. The 1940 census lists him as 18 years old and living at home with his brother and sister-in-law, Dennis and Edith Sporleder in Center Township, Jennings County, Indiana. Also living in the household was Raymond's father, Roy L. Sporleder, listed as widowed. It appears that his only tie to Sylvania was the fact that his grandparents, Mr. and Mrs. George Sporleder lived in Sylvania. Is there a chance that he lived with his grandparents here in Sylvania for a time, and attended Burnham High School while living here?

At the 1930 census George and Carrie Sporleder, Raymond's grandparents, were living on Whiteford Road in Sylvania Township with their son John Sporleder – 21 years old. At the 1940 census Raymond's grandparents, George W. and Carrie Sporleder were living on Brint Road in Sylvania Township. George is listed as being born in Indiana.

Raymond's official date of death is recorded as 8-11-1943 and he is recorded as having a headstone in Vernon Cemetery in Vernon Township, Jennings County, Indiana. The headstone reads: Raymond D. Sporleder - Indiana – Pfc 30th Infantry – World War II – Born 4-18-1922 – Died 8-11-1943.

Raymond's mother's name was Pearl Eberwein, she married Roy Sporleder in 1914 in Zenas, Indiana. She died in 1924 when Raymond was only two years old. Raymond's widowed father, Roy Sporleder, died on 12-30-1943, shortly after his son was killed in action. He died while living in North Vernon, Jennings County, Indiana. Roy's father is listed as George W. Sporleder who lived in Sylvania, Ohio.

The following appeared in the *Sylvania Sentinel* on 9-6-1943: "RAYMOND SPORLEDER KILLED IN ACTION – Word has been received by Mr. and Mrs. George Sporleder that their grandson, Raymond Sporleder was killed in action August 11 in the last letter that he sent it was just after the Tunisian campaign. He was permitted to tell he had been in the latter part of the campaign under General Montgomery of the British Eighth Army. He told of being in French Morocco and Algiers, of seeing German and Italian boys being taken prisoners, some being very young but in good spirits. He also told of swimming in the Mediterranean Sea."

Paul W. Taylor

Born 1920 Died 1943 – U.S. Army - He is listed on the Burnham High School World War II Roll of Honor with a star to indicate that he was killed in action. He is also listed on the plaque in Sylvania's Veteran's Memorial Field for World War II casualties. Paul W. Taylor graduated from Burnham High school in 1938.

At the 1940 census Paul Taylor was living in Sylvania Township, on McCord Road, list as 20 years old. He was living with his father and three sisters. His father is listed as widowed and working as an engineer maintenance man at a restaurant. Paul was listed as a new employee, but it did not list his type of employment and graduated from high school.

Paul's official date of enlistment is recorded as 11-27-1941 and at that time he was listed as single, without dependents. His official date of death is listed as 12-28-1943.

Toledo Blade – January 1944: "Toledo Serviceman Dies In Hospital Overseas – Staff Sergt. Paul W. Taylor, 23, McCord Rd., who had been overseas with a coast artillery unit since last September, died Dec. 28 in an army hospital in Ireland, according to word received by his wife, Mrs. Florence Taylor, Pontiac, Mich. The cause of death was not disclosed. However, members of the family previously had received a letter from Sergeant Taylor saying he was hospitalized Nov. 17 for a head injury. Sergeant Taylor was head of an anti-aircraft gun crew, his family said. The message from the War Department arrived New Year's Eve and said a letter with details of the case would follow. It has not yet arrived. Sergeant Taylor was graduated from Burnham High School, Sylvania, in 1938 and was employed in the DeVilbiss Manufacturing Co. He entered the service in 1941, and while attending a technical training school in Pontiac, Mich., was married to a Pontiac girl. Surviving beside his wife and parents are sisters Mrs. Ruth Kovach, Mrs. Betty Jane Haas, Miss Martha Taylor, all of Toledo, and Miss Rosann Taylor of Port Clinton, O."

Thadeus Henry Turanski

Born 1921 Died 1944 – U.S. Army Air Corps - His name is not listed on the Burnham Veteran's Memorial Field for World War II casualties.

At the 1940 census Thadeus Turanski was listed as 19 years old and living at home on Central Avenue in Sylvania Township with his mother Anna Mieszkalski, a brother William – 28 years; and two lodgers. His mother was listed as a widow, working as the proprietor of a night club. William was working as the bartender and Thadeus was working as the waiter at that night club. This census says that Thadeus had completed four years of high school, but I am unable to determine where he had graduated from.

Thadeus H. Turanski's official date of enlistment is recorded as 8-26-1942, and his date of death is listed as 6-29-1944. He served with the 319th Fighter Squad. He has a government headstone in Toledo Memorial Park Cemetery in Sylvania, Lucas County, Ohio.

Toledo Blade 6-29-1949 – "Thaddeus Turanski – The body of Second Lieut. Thaddeus H. Turanski, son of Mrs. Anna T. Mieszkalski, West Central Ave., Sylvania has been returned from Italy for reburial. Lieutenant Turanski was killed 6-29-1944, while flying a P-51 near Foggia, Italy. He was a member of the 319th Fighter Squadron. In Toledo, he was a member of the Civilian Air Reserve before joining the Air Force in 1942. He received his pilot's wings at Williams Field, Chandler, Ariz. He was graduated from Longfellow School and Alliance College, Cambridge Springs Pa., and he attended the University of Toledo. He was a member of Group 520, Polish National Alliance. Also surviving are a son, Richard, and brothers, William, Sylvania, and Arthur, Detroit. Roman (Buddy) Frankowski Post, VFW, will be in charge of military services at 8 a.m. Saturday in the Steve Gasiorowski Mortuary. An honor guard will be posted from 7 to 9 p.m., Friday. Burial will be in Toledo Memorial Park Cemetery."

A brother, William A. Turanski, for many years owned property at 6655 W. Central Avenue, in Sylvania Township (southeast corner of Central and McCord). He also operated the Greenwood Village Nite Club on Central Avenue in the 1940s. On 7-10-1946 the property at 6635 W. Central Avenue was acquired by the Veterans of Foreign Wars and was named the Turanski/VanGlahn Post No. 7372 in honor of Thaddeus Turanski and Ralph VanGlahn, Jr., who were both killed while serving in World War II.

Ralph C. VanGlahn, Jr.
Born 1923 Died 1943 – U.S. Navy Gunner - He is listed on the Burnham High School World War II Roll of Honor with a star to indicate that he was killed in action. He is also listed on the plaque in Sylvania's Veteran's Memorial Field for World War II casualties.

At the 1940 census Ralph VanGlahn was living on Central Avenue in Sylvania Township with his father and two sisters. Ralph was 16 years old and attending school, completing his second year of high school. His father's employment was listed as constable for the village of Sylvania and he was listed as widowed.

Mr. VanGlahn graduated from Burnham High School in 1941. His official date of date is recorded as 9-7-1943 and he is listed as missing in action or buried at sea.

The following was printed in the 12-31-1942 *Sylvania Sentinel*: "Word that Ralph VanGlahn, Jr., graduate of Burnham in 1941, and now serving in the Naval Air Corps has been promoted to 3rd Class Petty Officer upon graduation from the Aviation Service School on Dec. 24, has been received. His present address is: Ralph VanGlahn, Jr., 4-G-13-W-12, Barracks 12, Aviation Service Schools, U.S. Naval Air Station, Jacksonville, Florida. He has been in the service for 5 months."

3-18-1943 *Sylvania Sentinel* listed the following address: "Ralph VanGlahn, Jr., A.O.M. 3-c. Bar E, Dorm 19, Treasure Island, San Francisco, Calif."

3-25-1943 *Sylvania Sentinel* reported the following address change: "Ralph VanGlahn, Jr., A.O.M., 3-c Hdq. Sqr. 8, Fleet Air Wing 8, c-o Fleet Post office, San Francisco, California."

9-23-1943 *Sylvania Sentinel* reported: "Mr. and Mrs. Ralph VanGlahn, Talmadge Rd., were informed by the Navy Department last Thursday that their son, Petty Officer Ralph VanGlahn, Jr., an aerial gunner, has been listed as missing in action in the South Pacific. The message said the plane of which the son was a crew member, failed to return from a mission. Mr. VanGlahn said they had received a letter from Ralph, dated Aug. 30, in which he told them he didn't have much time to write because he wanted to get his guns cleaned in preparation for another mission. He would never allow anyone else to care for his guns, Mr. VanGlahn said. Ralph, who is 20, was graduated from Burnham High School in 1941 and enlisted in July, 1942. He went overseas last April after training at Great Lakes, Ill; Jacksonville, Fla., Almeda and Hollywood, Calif. At Hollywood he was the only one of the group of 100 to attain a perfect score as a marksman. He played football while at Burnham and took part in other school activities."

1-24-1944 *Toledo Blade*: "Natives Explain Seaman's Death – VanGlahn, 9 Others Killed Near Gilberts – Information told by natives of the Gilbert Islands after the Allied invasion helped explain today the disappearance of a navy torpedo bomber and the death of Petty Officer Ralph VanGlahn, Jr., 20, Talmadge Rd., Sylvania Township. Mr. VanGlahn, a former Sylvania High School football player, previously had been reported missing in action since Sept. 17, said his parents, Mr. and Mrs. Ralph VanGlahn, Sr. This week the father received a letter from E.R. Saunders, commanding officer of Mr. VanGlahn's flight squadron. Saunders said the Toledo youth a top turret gunner, and nine other crew members of a navy bomber were believed to have lost their lives in a crash near the Gilbert Islands. Natives recovered the body of the plane's radioman; they told Americans who invaded the islands. All crew members are thought to have died instantly. Mr. VanGlahn is the first of 274 men of St. Paul's Lutheran Church congregation now in service to be killed in the war, the Rev. S.C. Michelfelder, pastor, said. While in training in Hollywood, Calif., Mr. VanGlahn was the only man of 100 in his outfit to make a perfect score as a marksman. He is survived by his father, a justice of the peace in Sylvania; his mother, an employee in the personal tax office in Lucas County Court House, and sisters, Mrs. Norbert Dominique, Mrs. Harry Miller and Jane VanGlahn, all of Sylvania. Memorial services will be held in connection with the regular church services at 10:45 a.m. Sunday in St. Paul's Church. Private services will be at 10:30 a.m. in the church chapel, Mrs. Michelfelder announced today."

1-27-1944 *Sylvania Sentinel*: "Natives Confirm VanGlahn's Death – Information told by natives of the Gilbert Islands after the Allied Invasion helped explain today the disappearance of a Navy torpedo bomber and the death of Petty Officer Ralph VanGlahn, Jr. 20, Talmadge Rd., Sylvania township. VanGlahn, a former Burnham high school football player, previously had been reported missing in action since Sept. 17. This week the parents, Mr. and Mrs. Ralph VanGlahn, Sr., received a letter from E.R. Saunders commanding officer of VanGlahn's flight squadron. Saunders said the Sylvania youth a top turret gunner, and nine other crew members of a Navy bomber were believed to have lost their lives in a crash near the Gilbert Islands. Natives recovered the body of the plane's radioman; they told Americans who invaded the islands. All crew members are thought to have died instantly. While in training in Hollywood, Calif., VanGlahn was the only man of 100 in his outfit to make a perfect score as a marksman. He is survived by his father, justice of the peace, his mother, an employee in the personal tax office in Lucas County court house, and sisters, Mrs. Norbert Dominique, Mrs. Harry Miller and Jane VanGlahn, all of Sylvania."

February 1944 *Toledo Blade*: "Citation Posthumously Awarded Sylvania Flier – Mr. and Mrs. Ralph VanGlahn, Sr., 3151 Talmadge Rd., Sylvania Township, today received a citation and Air Medal from James V. Forrestal, secretary of the navy, posthumously awarded their son, Petty Officer Ralph VanGlahn, Jr., killed in action Sept. 17 in Gilbert Islands. Petty Officer VanGlahn was a top turret gunner on a Navy torpedo bomber, which was lost in a crash in the Gilberts while on a bombing mission. He was the first to be killed in the war of 274 men of St. Paul's Lutheran Church now in service."

The 1946 U.S. Navy listing of next of kin for those killed from direct enemy action shows the following information: Ohio – Aviation Ordnance man 3rd c, USNR – Father Mr. Ralph VanGlahn, Sr., Rt. 2, Box 24, Toledo (Talmadge Rd. – Sylvania Township). Ralph VanGlahn graduated from Burnham High School in 1941.

On 7-10-1946 the property at 6635 W. Central Avenue, in Sylvania Township, was acquired by the Veterans of Foreign Wars and was named the Turanski/VanGlahn Post No. 7372 in honor of Thaddeus Turanski and Ralph VanGlahn, Jr., who were both killed while serving in World War II. This post sold this property in 1984 and by 1985 the structure on this parcel was demolished to make way for a new office building.

Anthony Wieczorek
Born 1909 – Died 1944 - His name is not listed on the Burnham High School World War II Roll of Honor. He is listed on the plaque in Sylvania's Veteran's Memorial Field for World War II casualties.

At the 1940 census Anthony Wieczorek, Jr. was listed as 30 years old and living on Moffat Drive at Central Avenue in Sylvania Township. He was living at home with his parents, Anthony and Mary Wieczorek, and four younger brothers and three younger sisters. Anthony, Jr., is listed as completing school through the sixth grade. His employment at this time is listed as bartender at a café.

According to Anthony Wieczorek, Sr.'s World War II registration card that he completed in 1942 he listed his place of residence as Moffat Avenue near Central Avenue in Sylvania Township. His employment was listed as self- truck farming in Sylvania Township.

Anthony's enlistment date is recorded as 6-6-1941 as a Private, listed as single, without dependents. His official date of death is recorded as 6-17-1944 and his death place France. He has a memorial marker in Calvary Cemetery in Toledo, Ohio. Records show that he served with the 38th Infantry Regiment Second Infantry Division.

Toledo Blade 2-7-1948 – "Wieczorek Rites Set For Monday – Overseas Soldier Will Be Reburied – Services for Pfc. Anthony Wieczorek, 35, killed in Normandy 6-17-1944, and whose body has been returned to Toledo for reburial will be Monday at 8:15 a.m., at the Urbanski Mortuary and at 9 a.m., at the Church of the Little Flower. Burial will be in Calvary Cemetery. Pfc. Wieczorek was the son of Mr. and Mrs. Anthony Wieczorek, Box 156, R.D. 2, Toledo. Before entering the service 6-6-1941, he was employed by the Bingham Stamping Co. The body arrived yesterday. Surviving besides his parents are Mrs. Sophie Grandowicz, Mrs. Verna Jankowski and Mrs. Mary Teaberry, and brothers, Wallace, John and Edward Wieczorek, all of Toledo."

Robert O. Wood

Born 1920 Died 1943 – He is listed on the Burnham High School World War II Roll of Honor, but there is not a star to indicate that he was killed in action. In 2010 a star was added by the Burnham Commemorative Committee. He is listed on the plaque in Sylvania's Veteran's Memorial Field for World War II casualties. Robert Wood graduated from Burnham High School in 1938.

At the 1940 census Robert Wood was 19 years old and living at 6712 Erie Street in the Village of Sylvania. He was living with his father and mother, Douglas and Helen Wood, a sister Ruth and two brothers, Donald and Richard. This census record shows that Robert had completed four years of high school. He was working as a clerk at a retail grocery store.

Robert's date of enlistment is recorded as 1-20-1942 as an aviation cadet with the Air Corps, and his official date of death is listed as 12-20-1943. At that time he was a second lieutenant in the U.S. Army Air Forces and a member of the 392nd Bomber Squadron, 30th Bomber Group, Heavy. He was awarded the Distinguished Flying Cross, Air Medal and Purple Heart. He is listed on the Tablets of the Missing at Honolulu Memorial in Hawaii, and he was listed as missing in action or buried at sea.

The *Sylvania Sentinel* dated 2-5-1942 reported: "Robert Wood, son of Mr. and Mrs. Douglas Wood, has enlisted in the Army Air Corps Cadets, and is stationed at Williams Field, in Chandler, Arizona."

Sylvania Sentinel dated 4-8-1943: "Among the six young bombardier students from Ohio graduating this week from Victorville Army School after a vigorous 26-week course winding up with combat bombing missions over the Mojave Desert is Robert Orson Wood, son of Mrs. Helen Wood, 5714 Phillips ave., Sylvania. He was commissioned second lieutenant and given bombardier wings.

7-29-1943 issue of the *Sylvania Sentinel* said: "Lt. Robert O. Wood, 38th Bomb Sqdn., March Field, Riverside, Calif."

December 1943 *Toledo Blade*: "Sylvania Flier Missing In Action – Lieut. Robert O. Wood, 23, Sylvania, has been missing in action since Dec. 20 in the Central Pacific war theater where he was serving as a bombardier, the War Department has informed his mother, Mrs. Helen Wood. Lieutenant Wood enlisted in the army air forces Jan. 19, 1942 and trained at Victorville, Calif. He was graduated from Burnham High School, Sylvania, in 1938. A brother Donald is with an army unit overseas, presumably in England. Another brother, Richard, and a sister, Mrs. Ruth Green, are in Sylvania."

12-30-1943 *Sylvania Sentinel* – "Lt. Robert Wood, Bombardier, Missing – Mrs. Helen Wood received a telegram from the War Department that her son, Lt. Robert Wood, bombardier, has been reported missing since December 21. He was in action in the Central Pacific at the time. Lt. Wood entered the Army Air Force as a cadet Jan. 19, 1942, and graduated from Victorville, Calif. Lt. Wood, or Bob as he is known by his friends, graduated from Burnham High School in 1938. He played in the band and orchestra all during his high school. He has a brother in service, Donald, who is also overseas."

Sylvania Sentinel 3-22-1945: "Posthumous Award To Lt. Robert Wood – The D.F.C. and Air Medal were awarded posthumously to Lieut. Robert O. Wood and T/Sergt James H. Crisp last Friday, March 16, in the home of Mrs. Helen Wood, Capt. Andrews, Baer Field, Ind., made the awards to the mother of the young lieutenant, Mrs. Helen Wood, and to the wife of the sergeant, Mrs. James H. Crisp. Mrs. Crisp and her son, Jimmy, came to Sylvania from her home in Prestonburg, Ky., for the award. T/Sergt. Crisp was a radio gunner in the crew of the B-24 Liberator bomber of which Lieut. Wood was pilot and they both were reported missing in action in the Marshalls Dec. 21, 1943. On Jan. 21, 1944 the War Department notified the mother and wife that they were presumed to be dead."

<u>Earl Clyde Yeager</u>
Born 1917 Died 1944 - U.S. Army Air Corps - He is listed on the Burnham High School World War II Roll of Honor plaque, with a star indicating that he was killed in action. He is also listed on the plaque in Sylvania's Veteran's Memorial Field for World War II casualties. Earl C. Yeager graduated from Burnham High School in 1935.

At the 1940 census Earl Yeager was 23 years old and living with his parents, Henry and Josephine Yeager, at 5109 Allen Street in Sylvania. Also living in the household at that time was a brother Milford, brother LaVern, sister Donelda and sister Nina. Earl was employed as a plumber's helper and he had completed four years of high school.

Earl Yeager married Roselyn Harroun on 3-19-1941. Earl C. Yeager's official enlistment date is recorded as 12-28-1942, and his official date of death is listed as 4-25-1944. He served with the Army and his rank was recorded as technician fifth grade. He has a military marker in Association Cemetery in Sylvania which reads: "Earl C. Yeager – Ohio – TEC5 1905 Engr. Avn. Bn. World War II – March 14, 1917   April 25 1944."

The following article appeared in the *Toledo Blade*: "Three of Yeager Family Now in Armed Forces – Three sons of Mr. and Mrs. Henry Yeager, Sylvania, O are in the armed forces. Pfc. Milford Yeager, an engineer, is overseas; Pfc. LaVern S. Yeager, in the infantry, is in California, and Corp. Earl C. Yeager is in the air forces overseas. Earl recently spent a furlough with his parents and his wife, Roselynn."

April 1944 *Toledo Blade*: "Vehicle Accident Kills Earl Yeager In Burma – A telegram from the War Department Sunday notified Mrs. Roselyn Yeager of the death of her husband, T-5 Earl Yeager, as the result of an accident in a vehicle in Burma on April 23. Earl had been in the service since

January 1943. He was well known in Sylvania and had worked for the village prior to entering the Army. Surviving him besides the widow are two sons, Thomas age 2 ½ year and Carl 15 months."

Chester W. Zwayer
Born 1927 Died 1945 - He is listed on the Burnham High School World War II Roll of Honor, with a star to indicate that he was killed in action. He is also listed on the plaque in Sylvania's Veteran's Memorial Field for World War II casualties. (Although this plaque lists him as born in 1925 and died in 1944).

At the 1940 census Chester William Zwayer was listed as 13 years old, and was living at home with his parents, L. Ernest and Mary E. Zwayer, in Glendale, Los Angeles, California. This census indicates that in 1935 the family lived in Bryan, Williams County, Ohio. The father was working as a building contractor.

According to the World War II registration card that was completed by Chester Zwayer's father in 1942 he is listed as Levi Ernest Zwayer, living at 2224 Vaness Drive, Holland, Ohio, 52 years old. (This is outside of the limits of Sylvania Township, but residents could still attend high school in Sylvania).

Chester W. Zwayer graduated from Burnham High School in 1944. The index of the 1944 Yearbook shows the activities that Chester Zwayer was involved in while attending high school (the number represents the year of high school he was involved) as follows: Football, 3; Intramurals, 2; Vocational Club, 3; Burbank, California, 1. This tells us that Chester attended his Freshman year in Burbank, California and then attended his last three years of high school at Sylvania's Burnham High School.

Chester has a military marker in the Restland Memorial Park in Nashville, Howard County, Arkansas, which is where his family moved after Chester entered World War II. His marker reads: "In Memory of Chester William Zwayer – S1 – U.S. Navy – Jan 3 1927 – Dec. 17, 1945.

---------End of those killed in action during World War II-----------

Today, in 2018, the marker representing the casualties of World War II in Sylvania's Veteran's Memorial Field lists 47 men killed in action. In most cases the men listed on this marker either lived in Sylvania (village or township), attended school in Sylvania or had a close relative that lived here. Back in the 1940s students living in the communities surrounding Sylvania (Ottawa Lake, Michigan; Riga Township, Michigan; Adams Township, Ohio; etc.) could attend our high school, because their community did not have a high school at that time. Arrangements were made for each community to pay the Sylvania school treasury a set fee per student to attend our high school, therefore if you attended school in Sylvania your name was eligible to be included on our list.

The memorial marker in Sylvania's Veterans Memorial Field representing the casualties from Sylvania during World War II is shown above. It was this war that claimed the most of our residents. On this marker we list 47 casualties. The top of this memorial reads: "IN COMMEMORATION – THE PEOPLE OF SYLVANIA COMMEMORATE THOSE SYLVANIANS WHO DIED IN SERVICE TO THE UNITED STATED IN WORLD WAR II – 1941 – 1945." For a complete list and description of each of these men, along with the details of their deaths, read the earlier pages. (Photo taken in 2018 by Gayleen Gindy).

The original Burnham High School Roll of Honor was cast in bronze in 1948, and hung on the wall in front of the auditorium of Burnham High School, which used to be located at 6850 Monroe Street in Sylvania. In 2009 when school officials were making arrangements to demolish the old Burnham High School, at that time the large bronze marker was moved to the Sylvania Administration Building located at 6730 Monroe Street.

In June of 1984 the Ohio National Guard began searching for U.S. Army veterans who participated in the Philippine Islands Campaign in World War II during the period 12-7-1941 through 5-10-1942. Four Army National Guard units participated in the campaign, including the 192nd Tank Battalion which was made up of soldiers from Ohio, Illinois, Kentucky and Wisconsin. The Secretary of the Army had recently approved the Bronze Star award for U.S. Army veterans who fought to save the Philippines. This campaign was regarded as one of the most difficult ever fought by the U.S. Army. Major General Raymond Galloway adjutant general of Ohio said "Any Ohio Army veteran <u>living or dead</u> who participated in the Philippines Island Campaign is eligible for the award."

Finally, in 1985, a Sylvania Township resident, Alexander A. Drabik, was honored for his contributions to World War II. Mr. Drabik's name is mentioned in every book written about World War II, and included in "American Heroes From Hammermills Paper Company." Mr. Drabik attended a dedication of a plaque on the remaining towers of the Remagen Bridge. At this dedication Mr. Drabik posed for a picture with the first German prisoner that he took as he fought his way across the bridge 40 years earlier. On 3-7-1945 Sergeant Alexander A. Drabik led 10 riflemen across the Ludendorff Bridge at Remagen, fighting every step of the way. He was credited with shortening the war and saving as many as 50,000 allied lives. He was awarded the Distinguished Service Cross for his courage. He was also issued the Purple Heart medal and the Good Conduct Award. On 3-7-1985, 40 years after the event, the Ninth U.S. Armored Division was honored in Luxembourg and Remagen. The "Reconciliation at Remagen" focused on the struggle for the Ludendorff Bridge. German forces had tried to destroy the bridge and prevent the American troops from crossing it, but Drabik and his men got across and took prisoners as they went. The victory shattered German morale. A bronze memorial plaque was mounted on the remaining bridge towers at Remagen on 3-7-1985. It was the first memorial or monument to U.S. military war dead to be approved for installation in former enemy territory. Double honors were given to the 9th U.S. Armored Division. A memorial monument, almost 10 feet tall, was unveiled at Medernach, Luxembourg on 3-3-1985. The four faces on the monument have bronze plaques telling of the deeds and accomplishments of the 9th Armored Division and its three combat commanders.

In 2011 an Ohio Historical Society marker was dedicated in front of Alexander Drabik's home where he was born at 9336 Wolfinger Road, located in Sylvania Township. According to records Alexander Drabik was a Sergeant in the United States Army, enlisting in October of 1942. Sergeant Drabik was the first Allied soldier in Nazi Germany east of the Rhine River during World War II. According to the *Sylvania Herald* dated 9-22-2010: "The Drabik Family History Group is pleased to announce the submission of an application in late September 2010 to the Ohio Historical Society for a marker to honor Alexander Drabik. Sergeant Drabik was the first Allied soldier in Nazi Germany east of the Rhine River during World War II. Alexander Albert Drabik was born to polish immigrants, John Drabik and Frances Lewandowski Drabik from Szymbroze, Hohensalze, Germany, on Dec. 28, 1910 in a log cabin at present-day 9336 Wolfinger Road in Sylvania Township, OH. The youngest son of 14 children, he attended Dorr Street Elementary School in Springfield Township.

An ordinary man who worked as a meat cutter, he enlisted in the United States Army in October, 1942. Fighting in the Battle of the Bulge, he was wounded on Dec. 17, 1944, in Breitfeld, Belgium, and he received the Purple Heart on 1-23-1945, Sergeant Drabik led 10 soldiers from Company A of the 27th Armored Infantry Battalion of the 9th Armored Division across the Ludendorff railroad bridge in Remagen, Germany to the east side of the Rhine River. Realizing that the bridge was ready for demolition, he and his men ran through heavy machine fire, small arms and direct 20mm gun fire. Artillery shells and two explosions complicated the crossing, but Drabik and the soldiers continued across the bridge. He cleared the bridge towers of snipers and demolition crews. Despite machine gun fire and shell fire, he eradicated snipers and gun crews positioned along the Rhine bank and cliffs.

Sergeant Alexander Drabik was awarded the Distinguished Service Cross on 3-27-1945, for "extraordinary heroism in action against the enemy" and "unflinching valor." His actions and leadership are significant for he contributed to the installation of the first bridgehead across the Rhine River, shortened the war and saved 50,000 lives. Alexander Drabik was the first soldier of an invading army to cross the Rhine River since the days of Julius Caesar and the Roman Republic. The family dedication of the Ohio Historical Society marker is tentatively scheduled for Sunday, 5-8-2011, VE Day. Family, friends and the public will be welcome to attend the ceremony and reception. The Drabik Family History Group is an informal association of the descendants of John Drabik and Frances Lewandowski Drabik and Valentine Drabik and Eva Dybalski Drabik. Founded in 2008, its purpose is to share genealogical information and to remember its most famous relative. For information on contributions to the Drabik OHS Marker Fund, contact Jacqueline Konwinski." (For additional information see Wolfinger Road).

WORLD WAR II VICTORY BOARD

Communities all over the United States were erecting "victory boards" once World War II started. As men and women from the village of Sylvania and Sylvania Township were being called to duty Earl Orewiler of Orewiler's Barber (5687 Main Street) shop started keeping track of the names of these men and women at his barber shop. As time went on the list was getting longer and longer and it was decided that an official victory board should be erected. These victory boards were erected in order to publicly keep track of the men and women who were serving their country in the armed forces during World War II, and keep track of those who lost their lives. Sylvania's Archie J. Collins volunteered to paint the names on the victory board, and faithfully continued this as the names were provided to him. Here's how it got started in Sylvania:

In August of 1942 Earl Orewiler, local resident who operated a barber shop in downtown Sylvania, started keeping track of the men in the Sylvania district serving in the military service. He had this list on display in the window of his barber shop. By the middle of August 1942 he listed 168 names. This started the "honor roll" list in Sylvania.

Then according to an article in the *Sylvania Sentinel* on 10-15-1942 the Sylvania Booster Club organized a committee to look into constructing a "Victory Board" or "Honor Roll" in Sylvania. A businessman by the name of Fred Myers had voluntarily offered the use of his used car sales lot on the east side of Main Street in downtown Sylvania (5678 Main Street). By November of 1942 the Booster Club announced that construction would begin on the erection of this victory board. The original board was 27 feet in length and 15 feet in height and consisted of eleven panels with removable name plates, which would give room for over 500 names. By the end of the war two more panels had to be added to each side.

The 11-12-1942 issue of the *Sylvania Sentinel* said that this week the Victory Board would be erected on the lot donated for this purpose by Fred Myers, on Main Street.

The *Sylvania Sentinel* of 11-19-1942 reported: "The Sylvania Victory Board Committee is asking that all names of Sylvania village and township men and women who have enlisted in the armed forces be sent to Fred Myers, chairman, so that they may be placed on the Board. Everyone should cooperate in this, so that no one, who is eligible to have their name on the board, will be forgotten. The names of the drafted men are available."

The 12-31-1942 issue of the *Sylvania Sentinel* reported that more names are being added to the Victory Board and said that if you had a name to be added the committee in charge of securing the names for the board wanted to remind folks who have sons in service, that the present board, planned by the Boosters Club, was intended for the names of those from Sylvania village and township only. The committee was also instructed to include only those who are actually in uniform and are receiving pay from the government. If Reserves have been included, it had been a mistake. Names were to be sent to the Chairman of the Committee or left at Orewiler's Barber Shop.

The 2-18-1943 *Sylvania Sentinel* again gave the criteria for those men and women who would be added to the Victory Board: "To Place a Name on the Board: 1. The person must be a resident of Sylvania village of township at the time he enters the service; 2. He must be in uniform and receiving pay from Uncle Sam. (The names of Reserves are not to be on the board at the present time); 3. Place the name on a postal card, with LOCAL address and branch of service and mail to Rev. John Dickhaut, Sylvania, Ohio."

Archie Collins, who was in charge of painting the names on the Victory Board said that there were about 650 names of servicemen now on the board as of 11-15-1943, and that he had an additional 100 names for which there was no room.

On 12-15-1943 the *Sylvania Sentinel* reported that the Booster Club needed more funds for the erection and upkeep of the Victory Board. The board was entirely inadequate in size to hold all the names of the Sylvania boys in service. They needed to erect panels on each end to carry the additional names.

5-1-1944 – The American Legion and Veterans of Foreign Wars were present at the village council meeting and requested that the village officials approve a donation of $50 to the Memorial Day Committee. They reported that the Victory Board would be dedicated on Memorial Day and recommended that Main Street be closed during the program. Council agreed to the request.

The 5-4-1944 issue of the *Sylvania Sentinel* reported: "The Booster Club members have asked the Memorial Day committee to conduct dedication ceremonies for the Victory Board on Memorial Day. The dedication will be part of the day's program and with the great number of names on the board, all of which represent some boy or girl from this township in service, a large crowd of spectators is expected to be present. With changes in the board underway and with hopes that it will be fully completed by the date set, Sylvania can well be proud of the memorial to its sons and daughters in service."

The top photo shows Sylvania's "Victory Board" that was constructed in order to list all residents of Sylvania and Sylvania Township who had entered World War II. All the communities throughout the United States were keeping them during this war. Our victory board was located at 5684 Main Street, on property were in 2018 the Edward Jones offices are located. The bottom photo shows what the board looked like just after the war ended, after the two side panels had to be added for additional names. (Photos belong to the Sylvania Area Historical Society).

The following article appeared in the *Sylvania Sentinel* dated 8-30-1945: "The shiftless manner in which the grounds in front of the Honor Roll are kept must be depressing to the returning veterans as it is to many townspeople. Several different merchants have mentioned it to us and asked who is responsible for its upkeep. Well, we will ask too, who is responsible? We can't use that old gag "there's a war on," but good gosh neither should we use the other. The war's over."

In 1946, after the war, Mr. Myers requested that he be given the use of his property back and requested that the board be moved to a permanent location or dismantled. It was agreed that the victory board would be dismantled and the names cast in bronze for a permanent record. (This was never completed). At this time the community was raising funds to build Mickey Smith, a Sylvania war hero who had lost both of his legs in battle, a home. After the home was built, and it came time to build a garage for the home, the people of Sylvania decided that the wood from the Victory Board would be used in the construction of the garage and the landscaping would also be used at the Mickey Smith Home. The Mickey Smith home was built at 5927 Garden Park Drive and still stands today in 2018. See page 103 of the book titled *Images of America – Sylvania* by Gaye E. Gindy and Trini L. Wenninger published by Arcadia Publishing – 2006 for a picture of Sylvania's Victory Board.

In January of 1947 Arch J. Collins died. His obituary notice in the *Sylvania Sentinel* said that he would be remembered for his fine work on the Victory Board during the war.

In February of 1947 Clayton Fischer, Adjutant of the Joseph Diehn Post, American Legion, appeared before Sylvania Village Council to suggest that something be done towards proper disposal of the Victory Board. Mr. Fischer reported that the national program of the American Legion called for fitting ceremonies in conjunction with removal of Honor Rolls or Victory Boards all over the country, and that many communities were permitting their Victory Boards to become an eyesore through neglect. The Joseph Diehn Post did not want this to continue to happen in Sylvania and therefore offered its service in anyway desired by the village council. It was agreed that council would call a meeting of the various organizations of the community and decide on the disposal of the Victory Board. The meeting was called for 3-5-1947 in the Legion Hall.

The following appeared in the *Sylvania Sentinel*: "It is nearly time that the Honor Roll on Main Street be moved, as the owner of the lot on which it is erected has other uses for the space. Since the board is not of a permanent nature and was never intended to be such, it might be well for someone to give some thought as to what to do about it. Perhaps a bronze plaque with the names of those who died in service or, if the cost would not be prohibitive, the names of all just as they now appear on the board. We would like to have some opinions sent in to the Sentinel regarding this matter. Have you any ideas? Please send them in."

Sylvania Sentinel dated 3-13-1947: "Tentative plans were adopted for the removal of the Victory Board at a meeting of representatives of the American Legion, Veterans of Foreign Wars, and the village council on March 5. One suggested plan, which will probably be adopted, was that the names of all the men and women on the Honor Roll be inscribed on a parchment which would be leather bound and enclosed in a glass case, copies of which would be given to the Sylvania Public Library, the American Legion, the Veterans of Foreign wars, and possibly one copy to the council building. It was thought that in this way could the record best be made permanent, and be on display in a suitable form for posterity. It was expected that the Victory Board itself will be removed on Decoration Day with suitable ceremony which will officially close that chapter in the history of Sylvania's part in the recent war. It is planned to give the lumber in the structure to the Mickey Smith Fund for use in a proposed garage."

3-17-1947 – Council reported that at a meeting of the civic organizations they called for the removal of the Victory Board. Two members of the American Legion, two members of Veterans of Foreign Wars and two members of village council were to arrange for the removal and appropriate program.

The 4-10-1947 issue of the *Sylvania Sentinel* reported: "Several comments have been heard about the appearance of the Victory Board. The high winds raised havoc with one end and it is to be hoped that nothing will interfere with the plans of the Legion post to remove the board by Memorial Day."

The 5-15-1947 *Sylvania Sentinel* said: "Memorial Day Committee – A brief ceremony will take place at the Victory Board which will note the official removal of the board from the Main Street property and the final disposition of the honored names of the men and women in service from Sylvania."

And then the 5-29-1947 *Sylvania Sentinel* said: "The parade will halt at the Victory Board and Mayor Wefer will announce to the public the removal of the Victory Board, assisted by the Commanders of the American Legion and V.F.W. A wreath will be placed at the base of the flag pole."

On Memorial Day of 1947 Mayor Wefer announced that all the names on the Victory Board would be reproduced on parchment and kept for posterity. Where is this list today? – The list from the Victory Board had hundreds more veterans listed than the list from the Burnham Roll of Honor. A thorough search of the Sylvania Area Historical Society collections, the Toledo-Lucas County Public Library and the Sylvania Public Library revealed no list, no bronze plaque and no record other than a couple photos.

The 6-19-1947 *Sylvania Sentinel* reported: "We think the American Legion is to be complimented for removing the Victory Board in such fine manner. The lumber was given to the Mickey Smith committee for use in building a garage, and the trees were also given to Sylvania's own hero for beautifying his yard."

Anyone knowing about the list from Sylvania's old World War II Victory Board is asked to come forward. Can it be that no one ever copied down the names from this memorial before it was dismantled? We do have the list that was published in the *Sylvania Sentinel* on 11-30-1942, but this list only included about one-fourth of the names that ended up on the memorial.

On Memorial Day of 1950 a military air formation emphasized the solemn ceremony dedicating the Sylvania Memorial Field and the World War II Memorial. Today we call this Veteran's Memorial Field.

STEWARD "MICKEY" SMITH – SYLVANIA'S WORLD WAR II HERO

The home at 5927 Garden Park Drive in Sylvania is truly one of Sylvania's World War II memorials, and should be dedicated as one. Steward "Mickey" Smith was born in August of 1919. His parents died when he was a young boy, leaving him an orphan. He was taken in by Mr. and Mrs. Andrew Sheldon of Argonne Place in Sylvania Township. Some say that Mickey for a period of time also lived in the home that was located at 6606 Erie Street, right on the northwest corner of Main and Erie (burnt to the ground in December of 2009). He graduated from Burnham High School in 1939. On 3-18-1941 he entered the Army and trained in Texas. In February of 1943, during an approved leave, he married Edith Moore who was from Boston, Mass. Mickey was sent overseas in May of 1943. He landed in Africa in July of 1943, where he took part in the invasion of Africa. At the end of 1943, or early 1944, Mickey and Edith had a daughter and named her Carol.

On September of 1943 Sgt Smith became involved in the invasion of Sicily, in the battle of Salerno, and by November the battle of Cassino. It is said that some of the most brutal fighting of World War II occurred in Cassino. In January of 1944, Sgt. Smith's unit landed in Anzio under the command of General Mark Clark of the Fifth Army. In May of 1944, they finally broke through German defenses. Sgt. Smith was then transferred to General Patton's 7th Army just in time to take part in the invasion of France. He was in the Headquarters Division in the Intelligence Department. His duty was to take prisoners and get information as to the positions of the enemy. On 9-29-1944 Mickey was injured while involved in the invasion of France and lost both of his legs.

Sgt. Smith was brought back to the United States to a hospital in Atlantic City, New Jersey. His wife and daughter moved to Atlantic City to be near him. Besides the Purple Heart Medal, Sgt. Smith was awarded the Combat Infantryman's Badge and the Bronze Star, which was awarded to him for meritorious achievements performed while in enemy territory.

In September of 1945, the Sylvania Ladies Auxiliary of the Joseph W. Diehn Post No. 468 American Legion laid the ground work for a benefit fund for Mickey Smith with a donation of $50. The Auxiliary enlisted the help of the Sentinel Publishing Company to get the word out. Soon donations were being made to the fund by Sylvania residents to help alleviate some of the material sufferings of Mickey. It was reported that as soon as Mickey was well enough he, his wife, and daughter planned to make Sylvania their home.

After just one week, $222 had been collected. By October plans were afoot for a huge benefit show at the high school auditorium for the disabled hero and the *Sylvania Sentinel* reported on 10-4-1945 that the "Mickey Smith Funds Now Totals $895." Residents of Sylvania were canvassing the neighborhoods collecting funds and collections were being accepted at the Sylvania Savings Bank, Lentz & Stern Drug Store, Red & White Store and Wagonlander's Store. The *Sentinel* listed all those making donations in their newspaper each week and as the lists grew longer, and the funds grew bigger, there was talk of building a home for Sgt. Smith and his family.

The front page of the 10-18-1945 issue of the *Sylvania Sentinel* featured a picture of Sergeant Smith with his wife and daughter on the famous boardwalk in Atlantic City where the England General Hospital was located, where he was convalescing. He had sent a letter of appreciation and said that it was always his dream to own his own home. So, it was officially decided that the funds collected would purchase a lot in Sylvania and a home would be constructed on that lot.

For months, benefits were held to raise more funds. The Burnham Athletic Association held a football game to raise money, the Student Council of Burnham High School conducted a fundraising campaign in school, the Hillview PTA held a Harvest Festival and many more fundraisers were held. Various companies began making offers to help with the construction of the home, and a party was held at the Sylvania fire hall to raise money too. All through November and December of 1945 funds continued to increase through individual donations and fundraisers. The whole Sylvania community was involved in this project and by December 20th the Sentinel reported a total of $4,937.34 collected. This was a lot of money in 1945!

On 1-22-1946 a parcel of land was purchased at 5927 Garden Park Drive and the deed was recorded in the name of Steward and Edith Smith. The plans for the proposed home received Mickey's approval, and the architect, Mr. Dewitt Grow, completed the final plans and specifications, and soon after, initial materials were purchased.

In the meantime, the 2-14-1946 issue of the *Sylvania Sentinel* reported that Sgt. Smith was in the M. England Hospital, formerly Haddon Hall, and the hospital was expected to be closed to servicemen as a hospital on 3-1-1946. Sgt. Smith was making progress. He had new plastic artificial limbs which were lighter weight and made walking easier. He was shown in this issue of the *Sylvania Sentinel* walking with a cane. Mickey was to be discharged from the Army in March of 1946.

The 3-28-1946 *Sentinel* reported that the shortage of building supplies was making it difficult, but it was hoped that ground would soon be broken for the erection of the hero's home. Mickey, Edith and his daughter were staying with his brother Ralph Smith on Plainview Drive in Sylvania Township by this time. In May of 1946 ground was broken for the "Mickey Smith Home" under the direction of Ray Chappalear, contractor and Sylvania resident. James Cowell laid out the lines for the house and drove the stakes. Sylvania village workmen started digging the excavation for the foundation and concrete blocks were laid the weekend of May 18th. Walter Dankert, a mason, volunteered his time to do the block laying free of charge. William Burch, cement contractor, poured the footings, free of charge, and the materials for the construction of the house were on order. A plea for volunteers was made in the *Sylvania Sentinel* on May 23rd to lay the concrete blocks and that weekend they were rained out, with a yard full of volunteers willing and able to help. It was agreed they would all meet Thursday night, after work, to do the concrete work. On Wednesday 7-25-1946 carpenters started work on the frame of the home, under the volunteer direction of Wayne Roberts, contractor and Sylvania resident. Also helping Mr. Roberts was Fred Ellsworth, Burnham High School faculty, and Ira Baumgartner, Superintendent of Sylvania schools.

On August 1st, the *Sentinel* reported that the house was completed except for the roof. The committee extended an invitation to all men who could give a day or two to help in the building of the home. Mr. Wayne Roberts was supervising the job, and received the help of many hands to expedite the work. Mr. Roberts said, "just bring a hammer and good will, all other materials will be provided". The Lucas County Insurance Board offered to give Mickey a three year fire and extended coverage insurance policy and also a builder's risk policy to cover the property while it was under construction; Elmer Cline, Sylvania resident, plumber, and volunteer fireman did the plumbing; Kent Eley, Sylvania resident, and electrician, did the electrical work; heating was being installed by the Fry Heating Engineers; and Ed Plum, Sylvania resident, built the fireplace and chimney.

By 8-22-1946 it was reported that Congress passed a bill to provide each amputee veteran of the war with an automobile. By September 22, the house had been standing waiting for rock lath, or plaster board and all replies were the same, "there was none in this area, but a train car was expected at anytime". Nails had been a most elusive article also. The *Sentinel* said, "Just think of it, the greatest national income in history, the largest number of employed persons in history, the most money in the banks, but we can't build a home". It was also said that inside doors were absolutely impossible to obtain at this time. Their only wish was for Mickey to spend Christmas in his new home, but this did not happen.

Finally, on 1-19-1947, this home was open for public inspection. So many people had donated their spare time and their hard earned money to build this home, that they were invited to view the home in its completion. The *Sentinel* reported that 2,000 people came to view the new home, and William Burkett, owner of Landscape Nursery offered to landscape the property. Many household gifts were brought by visiting residents to the Smiths during this open house. The Mickey Smith committee reported that $800 was needed to pay off all expenses, to guarantee the home was free and clear to Mickey. This money was soon donated. Mickey, Edith and Carol moved into the home on 1-20-1947.

This is a photo of the "Mickey Smith" home that the Sylvania community built for their World War II amputee veteran at 5927 Garden Park Drive. This photo was taken shortly after the house was completed. The Smith family moved into the home in January of 1947. Property deed records show that ownership of the property was granted to Steward C. & Edith Smith on 1-22-1946, and they sold it on 7-15-1954 to Elmer N. & Mildred M. Hogg. Remember the garage was built using the salvaged wood from the old World War II "Victory Board" after it was dismantled. (Photo belongs to the Sylvania Area Historical Society).

Remember the World War II Victory Board that was constructed on the property at 5684 Main Street (on the property just south of J & G Pizza)? This victory board was a large; three section wood board, listing all the residents of Sylvania who served in the war. After the war, in May of 1947, this Victory Board was dismantled. The wood from this World War II Memorial was used to build Mickey Smith a garage and the evergreen trees and bushes that once surrounded this memorial were moved to the property of Mickey Smith on Garden Park Drive.

This property and home on Garden Park are truly a World War II Memorial, representing Sylvania and its generous people in their effort to help a fellow veteran and Sylvanian.

According to the 9-4-1951 minutes of Sylvania Village Council, Stewart C. Smith of 5927 Garden Park Drive was granted a building permit to enlarge the kitchen and add a screened porch at an estimated cost of $2,000. Council approved this request.

The *Sylvania Sentinel* dated 3-22-1956 reported the following about Mickey Smith: "Bob Burge has taught many young men to fly since he first began pushing a bi-plane around the heavens back in 1932—"But," commented the owner of Centennial Terrace, "I never saw anything like this fellow I visited in Sarasota last month." Burge said he flew his Tri-Pacer to Florida for a ten week vacation in January and immediately looked up a friend who moved there from Sylvania last year. Their conversation gravitated to flying. Burge's friend confessed a longing to fly. "Although he had never been up, he always thought he would have made a good pilot." Burge told me at the Firemen's Banquet the other night. "Well," continued Burge, "We went to the airport along with two of his friends—a Tri Pacer seats four—and as soon as we were aloft I let him take the controls." "I never saw anything like it," muttered Burge over and over. He flew the thing like a veteran." "After flying around for a while," continued Burge, "I told him to take her in." "And," he confided incredulously, "He landed the thing. That boy could solo with less than two hours of instruction. I never saw anything like it—a natural that's all—just a natural." Who was the fellow? It was Mickey Smith, Sylvania's legless veteran—the hero who lost both legs to his hips in World War II. Mickey is building a house in Sarasota and has been working as a dental laboratory technician there. One of the companions on Mickey's debut as a pilot was Dean Miller of Blissfield and another friend a paraplegic, whose name Bob doesn't recall. During his ten week stay Burge also visited George Smith, another transplanted Sylvanian who runs a drive-in theater there, and Bob Tallman, brother of our local Doctor 'C.A.'"

Mickey died young in an auto accident, and it is said that Mickey's widow and child moved back to her hometown in Massachusetts. The "Mickey Smith" home was sold to Elmer Hogg in July of 1954.

WORLD WAR II ENDS – TEENAGERS ARE URGED TO RETURN TO BURNHAM HIGH SCHOOL

In the fall of 1945, as World War II was coming to an end, and the boys and girls were returning from service, they were being urged to return to Burnham High School and obtain their diplomas.

But not only were these boys and girls being urged to do this, so were the teenagers who stopped attending school so that they could work in the war plants at home. It was reported in the *Sylvania Sentinel* that during the war 401 boys and girls between the ages of 14 and 17 years old had stopped attending school and were working. 96 of these were full time and had dropped out of school entirely. 305 were employed in part-time jobs, and some attending school only part of the time. These numbers were recorded up to 7-1-1945. The superintendent of schools said: "Now that the war is over, many of the jobs previously held by teenage boys and girls will be filled by older people. It is then imperative that every effort be made to encourage these children to return to school and complete their education. The responsibility and obligation is even greater when youth must prepare for post war services and the duties of citizenship. Lack of high school education limits your opportunities and possibilities. Amazing new developments have been taking place during the war in science, mechanics, transportation, industry, government and world organization. Learn about these developments in high school so you will be a more able worker."

The superintendent went on to say: "Post war standards will be higher. Many employers, during the war, didn't expect you to have high school education. After war, the breaks will go to boys and girls who are high school graduates. Even a few hours of school a day are better than no school at all. If you must work, try to do it on a school-and-work schedule. Ask your school principal to help you work out such a schedule. Money is a cause of much that happened in this world and dropping out of school is no exception. Young people quit because they want to earn money to buy better clothes, attend movies, or help keep up a car. The family may be in financial difficulties, and the children may be urged to leave by parents who hope they will contribute something to the family support. If you are one of those who are thinking of quitting school, ask yourself this question, suppose that I quit and then can't find work. Then what? Then what often means a long period of tramping from one employment office to another or idle loafing on street corners or at home. It may also mean a handicap in future years, for today employers tend to prefer high school graduates."

KOREAN WAR

The Korean War started on 6-25-1950 when troops from Communist-ruled North Korea invaded South Korea. Sixteen United Nation countries sent troops to help the South Koreans and 41 countries sent military equipment or food and other supplies. The United States sent 90 percent of the troops, military equipment and supplies; not including South Korea.

The Korean War ended on 7-27-1953 when the United Nations and North Korea signed an armistice agreement. It is said that the Korean War was one of the bloodiest wars in history.

At their greatest strength, the South Korean and United Nations forces totaled almost 1,110,000 soldiers. About 590,000 were South Korean, and about 480,000 were Americans. On 7-1-1950 part of the U.S. Army 24th Infantry Division flew from Japan to Pusan at the southern tip of Korea. On 7-5-1950 American troops first fought the North Koreans at Osan.

In the end the United States military casualties were reported as follows:

Dead = 54,246
Wounded = 103,284
Prisoners or missing = 5,178

A memorial in Memorial Field in Sylvania lists two casualties: Don J. Doremus and William C. Kroll.

There is one more casualty of the Korean War that was from Sylvania, Ohio, and that was Walter G. Archambo. He attended Burnham High School (this high school went from 7th grade to 12th grade) in 1946, 1947 and 1948 and his picture appears in these yearbooks; he would have graduated in 1950. He did not appear in the 1949 or 1950 yearbooks. He became a casualty of the Korean War on 9-15-1950.

The following information is recorded in the records of the "U.S. Military Personnel who Died from Hostile Action" in the Korean War 1950 to 1957 – Records of the Office of the Secretary of Defense, Record Group 330, regarding the three men that were from Sylvania, Ohio:

PFC WALTER G. ARCHAMBO – 7th Cavalry Regiment – I Co., First Cavalry Division – Army – Hostile, Died (KIA) – Date of Loss: 9-15-1950 – Service #RA15284388, Lucas County, Ohio – Location of Loss – Taegu Area – Year of Birth 1931 – Comments: Private First Class Archambo was a member of Company I, 3rd Battalion, 7th Cavalry Regiment, First Cavalry Division. He was killed in action while fighting the enemy in South Korea on 9-15-1950.

The following obituary notice appeared in the *Toledo Blade* on 6-7-1951: "Walter G. Archambo – Pfc. age 19, of 2244 Vaness Dr., Toledo. Killed in action in Taegu, Korea, Sept. 15, 1950. He attended Burnham High School, Sylvania, then worked for the Seven Up Bottling Co. before enlisting in the army in August, 1949. Surviving are his father, Murland L.; stepmother, Evelyn; mother, Mrs. Lelia Mae Jordon, Point Place; twin sister, Mrs. Wilma Butz, Toledo; brother, Murland A., at home., and grandmother, Mrs. Ada Foote, Point Place. Friends may call at the Reeb Funeral Home, Sylvania, after 7 p.m. Thursday evening. Military services will be conducted at 3 p.m. Saturday, 6-9-1951, by the Turanski-VanGlahn VFW Post No. 7372. Interment Toledo Memorial Park."

PVT. DON JUAN DOREMUS – 5th Marine Regiment – H CO 3 B N – First Marine Division – Marines – Hostile, Died KIA – Date of Loss 3-29-1953 – Service #1227327 – Sylvania, Ohio Location of Loss: Western Outposts – Nevada Cities (South Korea) – Born 5-29-1931 – Comments: Private Doremus was a member of Company H, 3rd Battalion, 5th Marines, 1st Marine Division. He was killed in action while fighting the enemy in Korea on 3-26-1953. His remains were not recovered. Don J. Doremus was from Sylvania and his military records actually list his hometown as Sylvania, Ohio.

At the 1940 census Don J. Doremus was listed as 9 years old and living at home with his parents, William and Pricilla Doremus, and his brothers and sisters on Meade Road in Sylvania Township. According to this census Don Doremus had completed school through the first grade.

There was no listing in the *Toledo Blade* obituary index at the Toledo-Lucas County Public Library for Don Doremus. His name is listed in the National Memorial Cemetery of the Pacific in Honolulu, Hawaii. His remains were not recovered.

PVT WILLIAM CHARLES KROLL – 65th Infantry Regiment – 3rd Infantry Division – Army – Hostile, Died (KIA) – Date of Loss: 7-17-1953 – Service #: US52168737 – hometown Toledo, Ohio – Location of Loss: Kumsong – Born: 5-27-1932 – Comments: Private Kroll was a member of the 65th Infantry Regiment, 3rd Infantry Division. He was serving as a volunteer for the evacuation of the wounded on 7-17-1953, when his vehicle struck an enemy land mine.

William Charles Kroll – although U.S. Military, Korean War Casualty Files show that his hometown was Toledo, Ohio, he does appear as an 8th grader in the 1947 Burnham Wyandotte Yearbook, and he does appear as a Freshman in the 1948 Burnham Wyandotte Yearbook. He again appears in the 1949 Burnham Wyandotte Yearbook, now as a sophomore. He is in the 1950 Burnham Wyandotte Yearbook as a Junior. Records show that he graduated from Burnham in 1951.

At the 1940 census William C. Kroll was listed as 8 years old and living on Sylvania Avenue in Sylvania Township with his parents, Edwin and Claire Kroll and a brother and sister.

He became a casualty of the Korean War on 7-17-1953. *Toledo Blade* 10-3-1953 – "Pvt. William C. Kroll – Services will be in the Reeb Mortuary, Sylvania, 2 p.m. Tuesday for Pvt. William C. Kroll, killed in action in Korea on July 17. Private Kroll, 21, was the son of Mr. and Mrs. Edwin C. Kroll, Dorr St., RD 1, Holland. He was with the army medical corps; he was killed when a land mine exploded. Born in Toledo, Private Kroll was graduated from Burnham High School in Sylvania in 1951 where he played guard on the football team. He was a carpenter apprentice for A. Bentley & Sons Co., before entering service Sept. 25, 1952. Also surviving are brothers, James, Sylvania, Thomas and David, Holland; sisters Mrs. Robert Billau, Toledo, and Shirley and Linda, Holland, and grandparents, Mrs. Emma Kroll, Sylvania, and William Schofield, Sr., Sylvania. The body will be in the mortuary tomorrow afternoon. The Rev. Robert E. Behrens, pastor of First Congregational Church, Sylvania will conduct services. Burial will be in Toledo Memorial Park Cemetery."

The following information appeared in the *Sylvania Sentinel* on 2-8-1951: "Robert L. Hentges, electrician's mate, third class, USN, son of Mr. and Mrs. Herman Hentges of 5523 McLain Dr. Sylvania, is serving aboard the aircraft carrier USSS Leyte in Korean waters. The Leyte entered combat October 8 after a record-breaking voyage from Beirut, Lebanon, via the Panama Canal. The 18,513 nautical mile journey—three quarters of the way around the world—was completed in less than 35 days. Only hours after she entered the Korean area, the Leyte launched the first of more than 3,000 aerial sorties against the enemy. She has since sent her planes over enemy-held territory from Wonsan to the Ualu River Boundary between Korea and Manchuria."

Under the column of "Men In The Service" in the *Sylvania Sentinel* dated 4-5-1951 the following appears: "Louis F. Smith, airman recruit, USN, son of Mr. and Mrs. John W. Smith, 6723 Long St., is receiving his first military instruction at the Naval Training Center, Great Lakes, Ill., under the Navy's recruit training program. Pvt. Eugene C. Holt, son of Mr. and Mrs. Ivan W. Holt, 5825 Highland Drive, has been assigned to Sheppard AFB, Tex. for technical training in the Air Force aircraft and engine mechanic career field. He completed his indoctrination training at Sampson on March 29."

4-12-1951 *Sylvania Sentinel* – Men In Service:
"Private Rolland McCormick, 15444845, Flight 1134, 3740 B.M.T.G. Sheppard A.F.B., Wichita Falls, Texas.

Private Richard Micham, 15444846, Flight 1134, 3740 B.M.T.G., Sheppard A.F.B., Wichita Falls, Texas.

Howard N. Punches, seaman recruit, USN, son of Mr. and Mrs. H.A. Punches of Route 1, Box 9, musician during his 12-week Naval Indoctrination period at the Naval Training Center, Great Lakes, Ill., and is using his musical talents with the Recruiting Training Command Band. The recruit band marches at all recruit reviews held at the training center, and also, makes occasional trips to nearby communities to participate in civic events requiring a musical aggregation."

Jack Watkins, of Reeb Funeral Home in Sylvania, was drafted by the Army and assigned to the 2nd Reconnaissance Company of the 2nd Infantry Division. His unit was responsible for patrolling North Korean lines at night. They were to scout their positions and attempt to capture soldiers for interrogation. While on one of these patrols Jack and eight other men were ambushed by North Korean and Chinese soldiers. Four in the crew were wounded. Jack managed to carry one of the wounded soldiers to safety and helped with the evacuation of another. He was awarded the Bronze Star for valor and received the Presidential Unit Citation, Korean Occupation Medal and Good Conduct medal."

The *Sylvania Sentinel-Herald* reported the following on 9-23-1952: "BRONZE STAR HOLDER RETURNS TO SYLVANIA – Corporal Jack Watkins, who ate last Christmas dinner somewhere in Korea, returned to Sylvania last Friday after 10 months of combat duty—returned with a purple heart and a bronze star for heroic action under enemy fire. The lanky, happy-go-lucky soldier who knows almost everyone the length and breadth of the town will terminate a 21 month tour of duty after the expiration of a 30 day leave. Jack's indoctrination under fire began the day after Christmas. While plodding along the rocky terrain of Korea in 20 below zero weather, he was knocked unconscious by the concussion of enemy mortar fire and was hit with fragments. It was after his release from the hospital that he earned the bronze star. The war department phrases of a General Order put it this way, "On 30 Aug. 52 in the face of intense enemy fire, Corporal Jack Watkins carried one seriously wounded man to safety and then, disregarding personal safety returned to direct the evacuation of another. His prompt and unhesitating action saved one man from possible capture by the enemy and definitely aided the chances of recovery of the other. Corporal Watkin's heroic action and devotion to duty reflected great credit upon himself and are in keeping with the highest tradition of a military service." Jack was a medical aid man for a company and was on advanced patrol with five other GI's. About 15 men of the company were following. Jack and his five companions were plodding along in a crouch next to a stone fence. Suddenly an ambush of about 50 Chinese Reds opened fire. Five men fell. Jack dove into a ditch. When firing ceased he raised his head above the embankment and saw the Chinese preparing to take two seriously wounded soldiers as captives. Jack opened fire with an M-1 until they retreated and he was able to pull one man to safety. Under covering fire the other soldier was also removed to safety. The Lieutenant in charge of the platoon, though wounded, observed Watkin's action and recommended him for the citation. Jack was hit on the hand during the encounter—but the injury was minor. Friends were sorry that he shaved off a fabulous red, handle-bar mustache. "It had to go," commented Jack. He plans to enter Toledo University after his discharge. "I'm sure glad to be home," said Jack. And the town's glad to have him too. "He is the son of Mr. and Mrs. John Watkins, 5730 North Main."

Jack Watkins did go on to attend the University of Toledo and then Cincinnati College of Mortuary Science and returned to work at Reeb Funeral Home. He became partner and general manager in this business and still works there today in 2011. He served on Sylvania City Council, was a very active volunteer member of the Sylvania Township Fire Department for 25 years and served the city as safety director for a period of time.

Thank you Jack for your service, as well as all veterans of the Korean War.

Sylvania Sentinel-Herald 1-8-1953: "Lt. Paul Wilcox Missing in Korea – Lt. Paul Wilcox, Burnham graduate and former Sylvanian, but who resided in Cleveland until his recall to service in the Air Force, is reported missing in North Korea. Mrs. Wilcox, the former Judy Minogue, received word New Year's Day in Cleveland of her husband's plane being shot down behind the enemy lines. Radar-Navigator on a B-29, Lt. Wilcox's plane was returning from a bombing mission when an enemy fighter plane attacked and disabled it. This was his tenth mission. . ." After the war ended Lieut. Paul Wilcox was released by the Reds and Freedom Village in Korea, after being a prisoner of war since January of 1953. Lt. Wilcox was a sports director for station WGAR in Cleveland at the time of his recall to active service, after serving as a flier in World War II.

According to the Sylvania *Sentinel-Herald* dated 2-10-1955 Corporal Russell E. Knoblauch of 5137 Allen Street was awarded a Certificate of Achievement for his part in "Operation Glory," the exchange of war dead between the United Nations Command and the Communists during 1954. He was a member of Company "A" of the famed 772d Military Police Battalion in Korea and took part in an operation unique in military history. The article reported that never before had two opposing forces exchanged deceased personnel buried in each other's territory during an armed truce. "Under the provisions of the Military Armistice Agreement, the body exchange took place in the demilitarized zone near the 38th parallel. It began on 9-1-1954 and lasted for 60 days. UN forces returned some 14,000 Chinese and North Korean bodies, and received some 4,000 United Nations Command remains from the Communists."

There is a memorial marker in Sylvania's Veteran's Memorial Field representing the Korean War and on that marker it lists two lost from Sylvania: "William C. Kroll – Don J. Doremus." Pfc Walter G. Archambo is not listed on this marker.

VIETNAM WAR

In an effort to briefly explain what was going on during the Vietnam War, I found the following information on-line at Wikepedia.com. The war started in 1957 and ended in 1975. Vietnam was a small country in Southeast Asia that was divided into Communist-ruled North Vietnam and non-Communist South Vietnam. North Vietnam rebels, along with trained South Vietnam rebels tried to take over South Vietnam. The U.S. and the South Vietnam army attempted to stop this but they could not. North Vietnam wanted to unite into a single Communist nation. The United States had adopted a policy of helping any nation threatened by Communists. China and the Soviet Union gave Northern Vietnam war materials, but did not send troops.

From 1957 to 1965 the war consisted of a struggle between the South Vietnamese army and communist-trained South Vietnamese rebels known as the Viet Cong. From 1965 to 1969 North Vietnam and the United States did most of the fighting, while being helped by Australia, New Zealand, the Philippines, South Korea and Thailand. The United States had 60,000 troops in Vietnam in mid-1965, but by 1969 that increased to over 543,000.

By 1969 it seemed that the war would never end. It was in 1969 that the United States started slowly withdrawing their troops.

The *Sentinel* newspaper throughout the war published a section known as "In the Armed Forces" and would report on the various residents of Sylvania that were entering, serving or receiving training for the war. A few of the names that appeared in this column included:

- 11-10-1966: Pvt. Robert L. Smith, son of Mr. and Mrs. Lloyd Smith of Stewart Road, a 1965 graduate of Sylvania High School had completed 14 weeks of automotive repair training in Maryland. He then left for Heidelberg, Germany with the 517th Division – Heavy Equipment.
- 11-10-1966: Army Sergeant Anthony J. Licata, Jr. 18, son of Mr. and Mrs. Anthony J. Licata, 5130 Arbor Way, participated in the defense of Camp Radcliff at An Khe, home of the 1st Air Cavalry Division's base camp in Vietnam. He was providing security along the barrier line, known to the troops as the "green line," a 22-kilometer long defense encirclement around the division base camp and its famous "golf course," the world's largest and busiest heliport. He was a team leader in Company C., 2nd Battalion of the division's 5th Cavalry.
- 2-2-1967: Francis J. Raymond, 22, son of Mrs. Margaret A. Bergstrom, Sylvania Avenue, Sylvania, was commissioned an Army Second Lieutenant after graduating from the Infantry Officer Candidate School.
- 2-2-1967: Seaman Recruit William J. Johnson, 18, USN, son of Mr. and Mrs. William J. Johnson of Central Avenue., Sylvania, graduated from Navy basic training at the Naval Training Center at Great Lakes, Illinois. In the first weeks of naval service he studied military subjects and lived and worked under conditions similar to those he will encounter on his first ship or at his first shore station.

- 2-2-1967: Seaman Recruit David E. Friess, 19, son of Mr. and Mrs. Chelsea E. Friess, of 5016 Trellis Way, Sylvania, completed his two weeks of annual active duty for training at the Naval Training Center, Great Lakes. Ill.
- 2-16-1967: Airman William C. Millard, son of Mr. and Mrs. William C. Millard of 5737 Dennison Drive was selected for technical training at Ft. Lee, Virginia, as a U.S. Air Force food service specialist. He had just completed basic training at Lackland, AFB, Texas. He was a graduate of Sylvania High School.
- Marine Private Gerald T. Dryer, son of Mr. and Mrs. Eugene A. Dryer of 5222 Arbor Way, Sylvania, had graduated from eight weeks of recruit training at the Marine Corps Recruit Depot. The training emphasized on rigid physical conditioning and survival techniques, both at sea and ashore, to develop self-confidence and endurance.

At the end of the war, in January of 1973, arrangements were made for a cease-fire and the last of the American ground troops left Vietnam by March. The peace talks broke down, and fighting started up again, but U.S. troops did not return. The war finally ended when South Vietnam surrendered on 4-30-1975 and Saigon fell to the communist forces of North Vietnam.

The Department of Defense reported a total of 47,072 American casualties, and South Vietnam lost more than 1 million. The war left most of Vietnam in shambles.

At the end of the Vietnam War there were 2,583 unaccounted for American prisoners, missing in action or killed in action/body not recovered. As of 10-1-1998, 2,079 Americans are still missing and unaccounted for, over 90% of whom were lost in Vietnam or in areas of Laos and Cambodia where Vietnamese forces operated during the war. Of the 2,079 Americans still missing and unaccounted for, 468 were at sea/over water losses. Official intelligence indicates that Americans known to have been alive in captivity in Vietnam, Laos and Cambodia were not returned at the end of the war. U.S. Government does not rule out the possibility that American POWS could still be held.

The following article was published in the 3-31-1966 issue of *The Sentinel*: "Mr. and Mrs. Harry H. Turner, Jr., of 3309 Warner Drive, have received a telegram stating their son, PFC Lawrence A. Turner of the U.S. Marine Corps, was injured on March 13 in the vicinity of the Chulai area. He received wounds in the face, chest, and both arms while engaged in action against hostile forces. The telegram stated that his condition was good and he was treated at his battalion first aid station and returned to duty. PFC Turner is with the Seventh Division of the U.S. Marine Corps."

The *Sylvania Sentinel* published a column in their newspaper titled "Service News." A few of the names listed under this column as serving in the war from Sylvania included:

Airman Gary L. Shufelt, son of Mr. and Mrs. Claude E. Shufelt of 5834 Elden Drive. He was a Sylvania High School graduate.

Airman Edwin M. Shock – son of Mr. and Mrs. Charles A. Shock of 4819 Woodland Lane. He was a 1967 graduate of Sylvania High School.

L/Cpl. Gerald T. Dryer, son of Mr. and Mrs. Eugene Dryer, Arbor Way, stationed at Quang Tri.

A/1C William Dryer, son of Mr. and Mrs. Eugene Dryer, Arbor Way, stationed at Langley Air Force Base in Virginia.

Kenneth D. Beadle, son of Mr. and Mrs. William E. Beadle of 6868 Sylvania Avenue, on duty in Phu Cat AB, Vietnam. An aircraft maintenance superintendent. A 1948 graduate of Burnham High School.

David J. Baranski, son of Mr. and Mrs. Joseph F. Baranski of 4739 N. Crestridge was promoted to airman first class in the U.S. Air Force. He was a dental specialist and graduate of Sylvania High School.

James E. Pickett, son of Mr. and Mrs. Russell E. Pickett of 5152 S. Main Street was commissioned a second lieutenant in the U.S. Air Force. He was a 1962 graduate of Sylvania High School.

Staff Sergeant Gary R. Harrison, son of Mr. and Mrs. Cecil Harrison of 5030 Argonne Place, Sylvania, a member of a unit that earned the U.S. Air Force Outstanding Unit Award. A carpenter in the 21st Composite Wing at Elmendorf AFB, Alaska.

Michael D. LeRoy, son of Mrs. Alice A. Ousky of 6929 Blossman Road, was commissioned as second lieutenant in the U.S. Air Force upon graduation from Officer Training School. He was a 1960 graduate of Burnham High School.

Sergeant Albert F. Takacs, Jr., son of Mr. and Mrs. Albert F. Takacs, Sr., of 5023 Trellis Way, a member of the unit that earned U.S. Air Force Outstanding Unit award. He was a supply inventory specialist in the 21st Composite Wing at Elmendorf AFB, Alaska. He was a graduate of Sylvania High School.

Sergeant Zelda J. Hesser, daughter of Mr. and Mrs. Howard P. Hesser, 6036 Blossman Road, has arrived for duty at Chaimite AFB, Ill. Sergeant Hesser, was a transportation specialist, and was assigned to a unit of the Air Training Command. She had previously served at Misawa AB, Japan. She was a 1970 graduate of Sylvania High School.

In 1969 Airman Charles R. Wilson, son of Mr. and Mrs. Leo G. Wilson of 6125 Glasgow Road had completed basic training at Lackland AFB, Tex. He was assigned to Chanute AFB, Ill., for training in aircraft maintenance. He attended Sylvania High School.

8-20-1969 – Mr. and Mrs. Harry Helpman, Glasgow Road, have returned from a visit to their daughter and her husband, Mr. and Mrs. Bill Ehrsam. Flying over on 7-23-1969, they visited at Bill's home base, Augsburg, Germany and also in Austria.

The following men from Sylvania, Ohio were listed among the U.S. casualties, and are listed on the Vietnam War Memorial in Sylvania's Memorial Field:

<u>Albert Franklin Baird –</u> SP/5 – Army – Date of Birth 10-17-1933 - Date of casualty – 3-1-1966. The following was printed in the 3-10-1966 issue of the *Sylvania Sentinel*: "Baird Killed in Viet Nam – Albert Baird, 32, was killed near Qui Nhon, a seaport supply center on the Viet Nam coast. The initial telegram stated that he had been killed in action by a gunshot wound in the throat, but a second telegram to his wife, Mrs. Nancy Baird, Langham Drive, Sylvania stated that an investigation had revealed that the fatal gunshot wound was accidental. Specialist Albert Baird, who had served in the U.S. Army for 11 years as a diesel mechanic with the 253rd. Transportation Detachment had been in South Vietnam since last May. He was born in Erie, Michigan, and graduated from Monroe High School in Monroe, Michigan, serving four years in the Navy before he became an army career man. He is survived by his wife, Nancy, (the former Nancy Jean Diller) his children, Sandra, 11; Michael, 9; Kathleen, 6; and Albert Scott, 3. His father, Donald Fredrick, Ontario St., Toledo; his mother Mrs. Pearl Baird, Temperance, Mich., brothers, Reece of Erie, and Neville Jr. of Temperance, and sisters: Mrs. Elizabeth Mills, Temperance; Mrs. Thelma Cousino, Erie; Mrs. Regina Foster, Monroe, and Mrs. Freda Rowland's of Britton, Michigan. Services will be held Thursday at H.H. Birkenkamp Mortuary in Trilby."

According to the *Toledo Blade* dated 3-2-1966: " . . . Mrs. Baird said that the army's initial telegraph, which she received while conducting a Brownie meeting at Hillview School, said that her husband was killed in action by a gunshot wound in the throat. However, a second telegraph received last night from Maj. Gen. J.C. Lambert said that investigation revealed that the gunshot wound was accidental. Specialist Baird, a Diesel mechanic with the 253rd Transportation Detachment, had been in South Vietnam since last May. "It was a terrible shock," Mrs. Baird said, "My husband wrote that he was the man behind the lines, and that I shouldn't worry because he was not in any real danger."

<u>Andrew Thomas Brassfield</u> – SSgt. – Army – Date of Birth 2-4-1937 – Date of casualty – 4-6-1970. *Toledo Blade* 6-24-1970 – "Area Serviceman Killed In Action – Sylvania Twp. GI 16-Year Veteran – A U.S. Army Green Beret, Staff Sgt. Thomas Andrew Brassfield, 33, of Sylvania Township, listed as missing for nearly three months, has been reported killed in action in Vietnam. Sergeant Brassfield, a 16-year army veteran on his second tour of duty in Vietnam, had been listed as missing since April 6. His parents, Mr. and Mrs. Flynn Brassfield, of 6123 Stewart Rd., were told by army reserve officials at the University of Toledo that he was presumed killed during an enemy attack on a reconnaissance patrol he was leading in enemy territory. The body has not been recovered and the change of status from missing to dead came from findings of a military review board, an officer said. Sergeant Brassfield left Burnham High School in the 11th grade in 1954 to enlist in the army. He finished school in service. Before going to Vietnam, where he joined the Special Forces, he served in Germany and Okinawa. He was a member of the Fifth Special Forces Group. Also surviving are his sons, Ronald and Michael, and daughters, Angela and Annette, all of Columbus, Ga.; sisters, Mrs. Marie Bush, of Holland, and Mrs. Helen Collins, of St. Louis; brother, Robert of Sylvania; foster sisters, Mrs. Myrtle North, and Mrs. Ruby Kirby, both of St. Louis, Mrs. Marlene Morris, of Detroit, and Pamela Townsend, of Sylvania, and foster brothers, Samuel Carter of Chicago; William Carter, of St. Louis, and Charles Wilkins, of Union City, Tenn."

<u>Frank Ochoa Florez</u> – PFC – Army – Date of Birth 6-23-1945 - Date of casualty 10-27-1965. *Toledo Blade* 10-29-1965 – "Sylvania Twp. Soldier Killed – Frank Florez, Jr. Slain In Vietnam – A paratrooper from Sylvania Township has been killed in action in Vietnam, the Defense Department reported. Pfc. Frank Florez, Jr. 20, of 5236 Calvin Ave., Sylvania, was listed among the casualties released yesterday. Mr. Florez was born in Waterville, O., and moved to Sylvania in 1949. He played baseball in the Little League and was a member of the football and wrestling teams at Sylvania High School. He was a member of St. Joseph's Church. Mr. Florez worked for a restaurant for eight months before enlisting in the army a year ago. He was trained as a paratrooper at Fort Knox. Ky. and went to Vietnam 7-14-1965, as a member of the 327th Airborne Regiment. Surviving are his mother, Mrs. Lupe Florez; father, Frank, Sr., of Toledo; sister Mrs. Caroline Faz, Adrian, Mich; Mrs. Lupe Lizcano, Toledo, and Theresa Ann, and brother, Michael Anthony, both at home and grandparents, Mr. and Mrs. Pedro Florez, San Antonio, Tex. The body will be in Reeb Mortuary."

<u>Chris Walter Frankhauser</u> – Cpl. – Army – Date of Birth 10-24-1946 – Date of casualty – 5-9-1968. *Toledo Blade* 7-19-1968: "Sylvania GI Dies in Vietnam – Chris Frankhauser Is Combat Victim – Army Cpl. Chris Frankhauser, 21, son of Mr. and Mrs. Robert Frankhauser, of 5946 Rudyard Rd., Sylvania, died of wounds received in Vietnam combat, the Defense Department reported Thursday. Corporal Frankhauser was stationed at Quang Tri, and was reported missing in action May 9. He had been transferred there following service at Khe Sanh. He was an expediter for Scholz Homes, Inc., before entering the service in July, 1967. He had been in Vietnam since January. Also surviving are brothers, Victor and John, both at home, and William and Robert, of Toledo, and grandparents, Mrs. Ruth Schaedler and Mr. and Mrs. Chris Frankhauser, all of Sylvania."

<u>Dennis Herron,</u> Pfc – Army – Date of Birth 6-24-1949 - Date of casualty 5-31-1968. *Toledo Blade* 6-4-1968: "Sylvania Youth Dies in Vietnam – Wounds Are Fatal to Dennis Herron – A Sylvania youth died in Vietnam last week, a year from the day he enlisted in the army. Pfc. Dennis Herron, 18, son of Mr. and Mrs. Max Herron, of 5604 McLain Dr., died Friday of wounds, his family was informed. No details were given other than he was injured by enemy action. Private Herron enlisted 5-31-1967, took basic training at Fort Jackson, S.C., and later was stationed at Fort McClellan, Ala., before going to Vietnam last November. He received a Bronze Star medal and Purple Heart after he was injured in action in December, but returned to duty after two weeks of treatment. He attended Sylvania High School and was a member of Olivet Lutheran Church. Also surviving are his brother Michael, and sister, Mrs. Sharon Cornell, both of Sylvania, and grandmother, Mrs. Nancy Young, of Toledo. The body will be returned to the Reeb Mortuary, Sylvania, for services."

<u>Steven Michael Ingle</u> – Pfc – Army – Date of Birth 1-7-1951 - Date of casualty 6-4-1971. *Toledo Blade* 6-5-1971 – "Pvt. Steven M. Ingle – Beloved son of Mr. and Mrs. Edwin Ingle, of 5750 Flanders Rd., Sylvania, Friday, age 20 years. Surviving besides his parents are sisters Mrs. Sandra Presnell and Miss Brenda Ingle, both of Sylvania; brothers, Larry and Gary, both of Toledo; and Lee Ingle of Sylvania; grandparents, Mr. and Mrs. Cornelius Baker, Streator, Ill., and grandfather, Carl W. Ingle, Napoleon, O. Friends may call at the Reeb Funeral Home, Sylvania after 2 p.m. Sunday, where services will be held Tuesday at 1 p.m. Rev. Elwood L. Rose of First

United Methodist Church, Sylvania, officiating. Interment Toledo Memorial Park." According to military records Mr. Ingle was killed in a "non-battle" private auto accident, not related to enemy attack. The auto accident occurred in Fulton County, Ohio and Mr. Ingle was driving. According to U.S. Army Personnel and Dependent Casualties records his tour start date was 5-5-1971; his date of death was 6-4-1971; and his report date was 6-22-1971. His military class was shown as "Enlisted Personnel" and his Personnel Category was listed as "AWOL Army."

Harry Frank LaLonde, Jr. – SP/4 – Army – Date of Birth – 1-27-1947 - Date casualty 9-16-1969. *Toledo Blade* 9-24-1969 – "Sylvania Soldier Killed In Action – Commanding Tank On Combat Mission – Spec. 4 Harry F. LaLonde, Jr., 22 of 2650 Elmwood Road, Sylvania, was killed in action in Vietnam last Tuesday, according to an army department telegram received by his parents. The telegram stated that Corporal LaLonde was commanding a scout tank on combat operation when the tank encountered Viet Cong troops. Specialist LaLonde had just been promoted to tank commander. In the last letter received by his parents, dated Sept. 12, he stated that he was hospitalized with malaria but expected to be released from the hospital within a few days. He had been in Vietnam 10-1/2 months. He entered service 4-1-1968. Born in Toledo, Corporal LaLonde was a graduate of Sylvania High School and attended the University of Toledo Community and Technical College one year. He was employed by the United Parcel Co. and Challenge and Cook Co. of Bryan before entering the service. Surviving are his parents, Mr. and Mrs. Harry F. LaLonde, Sr.; brothers, Steven, of Toledo, and Alan, at home; sister, Mrs. Janice Strong, of Chicago, and grandmother, Mrs. Caroline Demote, of Sylvania. The body will be in the Neville Mortuary for services."

Raymond Sharp Loftus III – Cpl. – Army – Date of Birth 11-12-1947 – Date of casualty 7-3-1968. *Toledo Blade* 7-6-1968 – "Sylvania GI Dies In Vietnam – Shrapnel Fatal To R.S. Loftus, III – Pfc. Raymond S. Loftus, III, 20, a 1966 graduate of Sylvania High School was killed Wednesday during combat duty in South Vietnam. In a message from the defense department, his parents, Mr. and Mrs. Raymond S. Loftus, Jr., 3625 Victory Ave., Toledo were told that their son died of severe shrapnel wounds during an engagement with the enemy. A resident of Sylvania most of his life, Private Loftus enlisted in the army shortly after graduation. He was a member of St. Joseph's Church, in Sylvania. He was the grandson of Raymond S. Loftus, Sr. Toledo Community Chest and Boy Scout executive and veteran secretary-treasurer of the Toledo Rotary Club, who died Nov. 7, 1964. Also surviving are his sisters, Mrs. Linda Moy, of Toledo, and Mrs. Patricia Connors, of Lambertville, Mich.; brothers, Chris, Bruce, and Timmy, all at home; grandmothers, Mrs. Irene McMahon, of Malone, N.Y., and Mrs. Blanche Loftus, of Toledo. The body will be returned to the Reeb Mortuary in Sylvania."

Dale Arden Palm – Pfc – Army – Date of Birth – 7-30-1947 - Date of casualty 9-12-1968. *Toledo Blade* 9-23-1968 – "Services for Pfc Dale A. Palm, 21, son of Mrs. Nellie Palm, of 2252 St. Charles Road., Sylvania Township, killed Sept. 12 in Vietnam by direct enemy fire, will be Thursday at 1 p.m. in the Reeb Mortuary, Sylvania." *Toledo Blade* 9-24-1968 – "Pfc. Dale A. Palm – beloved son of Mrs. Nellie Palm, of 2252 St. Charles Rd., Toledo (Sylvania Twp), Sept. 12, age 21 years. Surviving besides his mother are sister, Joyce Palm, and brother, Kenneth Palm, both at home; Gilbert Palm, of Toledo. Friends may call at the Reeb Funeral Home, Sylvania, after 7 p.m. Tuesday, where services will be held Thursday at 1 p.m. Interment Toledo Memorial

Park." The U.S., Vietnam War Military Casualties reported the following for Dale Arden Palm: 21 years old, home city Toledo, Ohio. Death date 9-12-1968 in South Vietnam. Tour Start date 4-21-1968, Department of the Army, Selective Service, Private First Class – A Co. Regiment 28th Infantry, First Battalion.

Carl Harmon Peters, Jr. – Sgt. – Army – Date of Birth – 3-13-1947 - Date of casualty 3-23-1969. *Toledo Blade* 3-27-1969: "Sylvania Man Vietnam Victim – Hit by Rocket on Mercy Mission – A Sylvania man, Sgt. Carl H. Peters, Jr., 22 died Sunday of wounds suffered in Vietnam Thanksgiving Day, the Defense Department said Wednesday. Sergeant Peters, son of Mr. and Mrs. Carl Peters, of 5809 Wakefield Dr., died in Walter Reed Army Hospital, Washington, D.C. He was wounded by a rocket when he went to aid a squad member injured by another rocket, according to the Defense Department. The action occurred during an enemy assault northwest of Saigon. Sergeant Peters was a squad leader in the 25th Infantry Division and had been in the Army since February, 1967. He went to Vietnam in February, 1968. A native of Teaneck, N.J., he was a graduate of Eaton, O., High School, and had lived in Sylvania three years. He also studied dramatics for two years at Northwestern University. Also surviving are a sister, Anne, of Cincinnati; a brother James, at home; grandmothers, Mrs. W.B. Peters, of Appalachia, Va., and Mrs. B.G. Montgomery, of South Hill, Va. Services were at Fort Myers, Va., with burial in Arlington National Cemetery." The U.S., Vietnam War Military Casualties report shows that the casualty occurred in South Vietnam and that his pay grade was Sergeant in A Company, 27th Infantry Regiment, Second Battalion. His service occupation was light weapons infantry. Details of his injuries included the fact that Peters was wounded in the Republic of Vietnam on Thanksgiving Day which resulted in the removal of his left leg below the knee. He was transferred to Washington several weeks later for additional treatment. He contacted malaria and melloidosis, and was listed in critical condition several weeks before his death.

Ronald Lee Rusek – Cpl. Army – Date of Birth – 12-26-1947 - Date of casualty 7-28-1968. *Toledo Blade* 8-5-1968 – "Ronald Rusek – Services for Pfc. Ronald L. Rusek, 20, of 3121 Fairbanks Ave., Sylvania, who was killed July 28 in Vietnam, will be Wednesday at 1 p.m. in the Reeb Mortuary, Sylvania, with burial in Ottawa Hills Memorial Park. Private Rusek, a lifelong area resident, graduated in 1967 from Sylvania High School and worked as a truck loader for the Allen V. Smith Co. before entering the army last November. Surviving are his parents, Mrs. and Mrs. Peter Rusek; sister Laura Lean; brothers, Peter F. Jr., and George M.; grandmother, Mrs. Stella Rusek; grandmother and step-grandfather, Mrs. and Mrs. William H. Carpenter, and grandfather, Peter Putnam, all of Toledo." Records show that Corporal Peters was killed in South Vietnam by an explosive device while serving in the Army. He was listed as a ground casualty and his body was recovered.

Billy Robert Wohlgamuth – Pfc. – Marine Corp – Date of Birth 3-11-1947 – Date of casualty 10-26-1967. *Toledo Blade* 11-1-1967: "Sylvania Youth Killed in War – Marine In Vietnam About Six Weeks – A Sylvania marine, who arrived in Vietnam about six weeks ago, was killed Thursday. Pfc. Billy R. Wohlgamuth, 20, son of Mr. and Mrs. Wilbur Wohlgamuth, of 4921 Barton Pl., Sylvania, was killed by enemy rifle fire in Quang Tri Province while in the defensive position with his unit, Company E, Second Battalion, Fourth Marine regiment. Private Wohlgamuth had been employed at Lake Park Nursing Home, Sylvania, and had attended Sylvania High School before enlisting in April. Also surviving are his brothers, Richard, Roger and Gary, and a sister, Joyce, all at home, and grandparents, Wilbur D. Wohlgamuth of Sylvania, and William Weber and Mrs. Ora Weber, both of Toledo."

Nabil Mahood Youssef – PFC – Army – Date of Birth 9-13-1946 - Date of casualty 5-26-1967. *Toledo Blade* 6-1-1967: "Toledo Soldier Dies in Combat – Whitmer High Grad Was Copter Gunner – Army Pfc. Nabil M. Youssef, 20, of 4101 Harvest Lane, who had been in Vietnam since Jan. 8, was killed in action Friday. He was a helicopter machine gunner. Born in Norfolk, Va., Private Youssef lived in Toledo two years. He was a graduate of Whitmer High School and attended the University of Toledo for a semester before his induction into the army last September. Before coming to Toledo he attended high school for two years in Amman, Jordan, where his sister, Mrs. Nahida Salah lives. His brother, Eddie Youssef, of Sylvania, said Nadil was planning to study business administration at TU after his release from the army. Also surviving are his father M. Youssef, of Chicago, and another brother, Joseph, of Toledo. Services will be Friday at 2 p.m., in the Islamic Center of Toledo, with burial in Ottawa Hills Memorial Park. The body is in the Ansberg-West Mortuary."

One burial in Sylvania's Association Cemetery is Thomas D. Barbarick – born 10-31-1952 – died 8-12-1973 – Ohio A.B.U.S. Air Force - Vietnam. Thomas' death did not occur while serving in Vietnam, instead his death was a result of drag racing. *Toledo Blade* 8-13-1973: "Thomas D. Barbarick of 2648 North Crissey Rd., died of head and neck injuries after the car he was driving turned over several times in the 5500 block of Nebraska Ave. . . . The two drivers bet $20 when they arranged the race in a restaurant at Nebraska and Reynolds Road. Then the cars headed west on Nebraska and reached speeds estimated at between 100 and 110 mph. The car young Barbarick was driving jumped the curb and rolled over several times before it came to a rest 166 feet from where it left the roadway…Mr. Barbarick was a veteran of the Vietnam War and was a member of the Sylvania Baptist Church. Surviving are his parents, Mr. and Mrs. Lance Barbarick, Sr., sister, Mrs. Lela Abbott, and brothers, Lance, Jr., and Timothy . . ."

Another burial in Sylvania's Association Cemetery is Scott P. Russell – born 7-5-1941 – died 6-3-1972 – Adj. I VP 44 USN Flight Engineer. *Toledo Blade* 6-6-1972: "Area Man Dies In Navy Crash – Plane Struck Cliff In Gibraltar Straits – Scott Paul Russell, 29, petty officer first class and son of Mr. and Mrs. John A. Russell, of 5430 Silvertown Dr., Sylvania, was 1 of 14 men killed Saturday when a navy anti-submarine patrol plane crashed on the Moroccan side of the Straits of Gibraltar. A spokesman for Brunswick Naval Air Station, Brunswick, Me., said today that 12 of the men on board, including Mr. Russell were attached to a patrol squadron permanently based at Brunswick. The spokesman said that the four engine Orion plane had been airborne about an hour on routine patrol when it crashed into a cliff due south of Algeciras, Spain. The accident is under investigation, he said. The plane had taken off from Rota Naval Air Station, Spain. Mr. Russell's parents received a telegraph Sunday reporting that their son was missing following the crash and a letter Monday confirming that he was dead, although his body had not been recovered. Mr. Russell joined the navy in 1960, his mother, Mrs. Wilda Russell, said. He previously had served at Patuxent River Naval Air Station, Lexington Park, Md. She said he had been in Spain only for a couple of weeks. When Mr. Russell was home in April, the family held an early celebration of his 30th birthday, which would have been July 5, he attended the former Burnham High School in Sylvania. Also surviving are his daughters, Becky and Rayna; grandmother, Mrs. Grace Martin; brother, John T., and sisters, Mrs. Marlee Small, Mrs. Bette Jo Miley, and Mrs. Bridget Eck."

Robert Paul Phillips – SSgt – Army – Date of Birth 7-31-1949 - Date of casualty 6-23-1970 (still missing in action). Robert Paul Phillips lived in Sylvania when he entered the service of the U.S. Army. The following information is known:

NAME: ROBERT PAUL PHILLIPS
RANK/BRANCH: E2/ US ARMY
UNIT: 595th Signal Company, 36th Signal Battalion, 2nd Signal Group, 1st Signal Brigade
DATE OF BIRTH: 7-31-1949
DATE OF LOSS: 6-23-1970
COUNTRY OF LOSS: SOUTH VIETNAM
STATUS: PRISONER OF WAR (IN 1973)
HOME CITY OF RECORD: SYLVANIA, OHIO

On 6-23-1970 Robert P. Phillips and two other members of the 595th Signal Company departed the town of Lai Khe in South Vietnam to drive to Phuoc Vinh. They never arrived at their intended destination and were declared missing.

In September of 1970 a Viet Cong was captured and said he was part of the ambush of the three men and he claimed that one of the men (Pederson) had been killed and buried near the location of the incident. War officials reported that enemy POWs claimed that two of the individuals were captured alive during the ambush of their vehicle and that the two were initially taken to the Sub-Region 5 Headquarters and then taken from South Vietnam in the direction of Cambodia. Other reports alleged they were in a prison and attempted to escape, resulting in one being killed and the other successfully escaping.

In 1973, 591 American prisoners were returned home. Robert P. Phillips and the two other members: James M. Rozo and Joe P. Pederson were not among them.

Rozo, Phillips and Pederson were all listed as POW at the end of Operation Homecoming. They were later declared dead/body not recovered.

In October of 1985, Rozo's parents were informed that their son escaped prison in 1973 and was not recaptured. His whereabouts are unknown.

The Joint Casualty Resolution Center field investigators in Vietnam have located witnesses to the imprisonment of the three Americans. Two were in captivity when they reportedly attempted to escape from a jungle prison and were killed by mines around the prison.

The Secretary of the Army approved Presumptive Findings of death for the three men: Pederson on 9-1-1978, Phillips on 2-13-1979, and Rozo on 5-18-1979.

ROBERT PAUL PHILLIPS, (7-31-1949 - 2-13-1979) YOUR HOMETOWN OF SYLVANIA, OHIO HONORS YOUR MEMORY AND THE MEMORY OF EVERY OTHER SOLDIER, MARINE, SAILOR AND AIRMAN WHO SERVED IN VIETNAM.

The Blade of Toledo reported on 4-30-1975 the following: "South Vietnam Government Surrenders; Viet Cong, Hanoi Forces Occupy Capital – After nearly two decades of involvement and the loss of 56,000 American lives, the United States pulled out of South Vietnam Tuesday and heard a call from President Ford to avoid recriminations about the past."

There is a memorial marker representing the Vietnam War in Sylvania's Veterans Memorial Field which lists the following casualties from Sylvania: "Albert Franklin Baird; Andrew Thomas Brassfield; Frank Ochoa Florez; Christopher Walter Frankhauser; Dennis Herron; Harry Frank LaLonde, Jr.; Raymond Sharp Loftus III; Dale Arden Palm; Carl Harmon Peters, Jr.; Robert Paul Phillips; Ronald Lee Rusek; Billy Robert Wohlgamuth; and Nabil Mahood Youssef."

The last war that is represented on a memorial marker in Sylvania's Veterans Memorial Field is the Vietnam War. The top of this marker reads: "IN COMMEMORATION – THIS MEMORIAL IS ERECTED IN MEMORY OF THE MEN AND WOMEN FROM THE SYLVANIA AREA WHO DIED IN SERVICE TO THE UNITED STATES OF AMERICA DURING THE VIETNAM WAR – 1964 – 1975 – WE ARE PROUD TO HONOR THEIR DEDICATION TO OUR COUNTRY." There are 13 names listed as casualties of the Vietnam War from Sylvania on the bottom part of this memorial. (Photo taken in 2018 by Gayleen Gindy).

PERSIAN GULF WAR

(Operation Desert Storm) – 1990 to 1991 – This war was between Iraq and a coalition of 39 countries. Iraq invaded Kuwait on 8-2-1990. The United Nations Security Council officially declared an end to this war on 4-11-1991.

The Blade of Toledo dated 1-17-1991 reported the following: "Storm in the desert – Warplanes pound Iraq continuously – The United States and its allies pounded Iraq with two waves of air strikes in a furious bid to drive Saddam Hussein's armies from Kuwait and break his military might. In Baghdad, radio stations broadcast recitations from the Koran, the Moslem book of Holy Scripture and several hours after allied planes launched their attack, an announcer said "War started today. We will teach America and its allies a lesson."

The total deaths reported in this war were 1,972. The total U.S. battle deaths is 147. U.S. Wounded = 467. A search of the list of those killed in battle did not reveal any of the men or women to have listed their hometown as Sylvania, Ohio.

All history after the Persian Gulf War I will leave for the next historian to write, as it has become far too complicated for me.

MEMORIAL DAY IN SYLVANIA

Memorial Day was officially proclaimed on 5-5-1868 by General John Logan, National Commander of the Grand Army of the Republic, and was first observed on 5-30-1868 when flowers were placed on the graves of Union and Confederate soldiers at Arlington National Cemetery. The first state to officially recognize the holiday was New York in 1873. By 1890 it was recognized by all of the northern states. The general order he proclaimed said that Decoration Day was set aside "for the purpose of strewing flowers and otherwise decorating the graves of comrades who died in defense of their country during the late rebellion." With the added note that Decoration Day would continue to be observed year after year. The South refused to acknowledge the day, honoring their dead on separate days until after World War I.

Memorial Day is geared toward the memory of those who died in battle while Veterans Day is meant to honor the living vets. Decoration Day or Memorial Day has always been an important day in Sylvania from the first in 1868. Ambrose Comstock of Sylvania, who had served during the Civil War as a Private in the 130th Regiment Co. G Ohio Volunteer Infantry under General Grant, was in charge of the Memorial Day parade each year and actually led the parade in Sylvania with his drum, until he passed away in 1910. Ambrose Comstock took part in numerous skirmishes along the Shenandoah Valley, the James River, around Petersburg and Richmond. Many of the men who had returned to Sylvania after serving in the war were disabled. For instance, William Fletcher had lost his hearing; William Bryan was crippled when a bullet tore off his heel; Hiram Wellman had a bullet imbedded in his head that he lived with the rest of his life; among others.

The *Toledo Blade* dated 5-31-1871 featured the following article: "Decoration Day In Sylvania – Sylvania has a Post of the Grand Army of the Republic in good working order, and under its excellent management the ceremonies of Decoration day work conducted in a most becoming and successful manner. At about eleven o'clock a procession was formed at the village, consisting of the members of the Grand Army, in their new uniform of blue blouse, white belt and neat military cap the Cooper's Union, and the Good Templars both in the regalia of their respective orders, the children of the Methodist and Congregational Sunday Schools, and citizens generally. Led by martial music the procession marched to the cemetery. In an adjoining grove a large assemblage gathered for appropriate speeches. Rev. Mr. Kalb of the M.E. Church, presided, commencing the exercise by reading selections of scripture and offering prayer. The singers composing the choirs of the two churches united in singing in most excellent style several appropriate pieces. After a short address on the significance of Memorial Day, by Rev. R. McCone, the procession formed and passed through the cemeteries, garlanding every soldier's grave. The ladies of Sylvania had bestowed thought and skill on their floral offerings, but the feeling of affectionate memory which animated many hearts gave a higher meaning to the beautiful ceremonial"

The *Sylvania Weekly Times* dated 5-29-1891 reported the following line-up for the Decoration Day event to be held Saturday 5-30-1891: "Parade will form at 10 o'clock AM (Sharp) on Division Street. Right in front of G.A.R. hall line extending North in the following order: Martial music; band; Page Post and Ex. Soldiers; Franklin camp; and other societies; citizens on foot; citizens in carriages; G.A.R. Vets in Barouche. The Line of March was listed as follows: First to Ravine Cemetery; Exercises; Prayer by Chaplin Bellman; Decoration of Graves; Music by Band; Decoration of graves in St. Joseph cemetery by committee on decoration; Line reform and march to Association cemetery; Exercises; Prayer by the Rev. John Poucher; Decoration of graves; Martial music; Music by the Band; Line reform S. of V, on the right and march to the G.A.R. hall; service at the hall; vocal music; Prayer by the Rev. C.N. Bellman; vocal music."

Ambrose Comstock was also a member of the Grand Army of the Republic (G.A.R.), and each year the G.A.R. and W.R.C. (Women's Relief Corp.) would all prepare for the events of the annual Memorial Day celebration in Sylvania. Veterans assembled at the G.A.R. hall located on the southwest corner of Main and Monroe before they paraded to the local cemeteries, where they would decorate the graves of their old comrades and listen to patriotic addresses in the depot grove, located where Southbriar shopping complex is today.

After Ambrose Comstock died in 1910 then Henry Burnham and Dana Chandler seemed to take charge of the Memorial Day parade and events. Needless to say, when plans were made to establish a Boy Scout Troop in Sylvania, Henry Burnham called an organizational meeting at the Congregational Church on Summit Street in 1917. Dana Chandler and his two sons attended and Mr. Chandler was appointed the "scoutmaster," while Henry Burnham became the first "drillmaster" of the first Boy Scout troop in Sylvania. And so it was that Mr. Chandler and Mr. Burnham included the Boy Scouts in making the necessary plans for the Memorial Day parade each year, and they were taught to properly march in the parade.

Glenn Chandler was a Sylvania resident most of his life and was the son of Scoutmaster Dana Chandler. He was interviewed by Kathryn M. Keller, Sylvania Historian, in 1975, and he said that the Boy Scout troop had six buglers. Wayne Armstrong was the head bugler. There were snare drums and Glenn Chandler himself beat the base drum. One Memorial Day Glenn Chandler delivered Lincoln's Gettysburg Address after his grandfather, Thomas Giles Chandler, who was a Civil War veteran, coached him for the event. He said that in preparation for the Memorial Day march to each of the local cemeteries, the Boy Scouts met at Henry Burnham's home, which was located at the corner of Maplewood and School Drive. His home was surrounded by cedar trees and lilac bushes. The boys carefully clipped lilac blossoms and sprigs of cedar and made small bouquets to be laid beside the flags on the soldiers' graves. The oratory after decorating the graves took place at Depot Grove, which was located on the southwest corner of Convent and Main Street where the Southbriar shopping center is located today in 2017. He said that there was a grandstand at that location where the necessary speakers stood to talk, and residents would sit comfortably on the shaded grass for the hour or more of speeches

The Memorial Day of 1921 was reported to be the "best in the history of Sylvania" according to the *Sylvania Sentinel* dated 6-2-1921. The parade started at Dr. Halbert's corner at Erie and Main, and heading the parade were the Boy Scouts, followed by the Girl Scouts, then the Grand Army of the Republic (G.A.R.), and then the band, Legion Firing Squad, World War Veterans, Woman's Relief Corps, school children and last of all the citizens in their automobiles. They all marched south on Main Street until the parade came to a halt at the bridge of the Ten Mile Creek, when the waters were strewn with flowers in honor of those who died in service. Then they marched to Ravine Cemetery and assembled in the west part of the cemetery. "Logan's general orders were read by Mr. Burnham followed by Lincoln's Gettysburg Address by Glenn Chandler." Then they marched to Association Cemetery where more ceremonies were held. Each of the individuals in formation was presented, courtesy of the Joseph W. Diehn American Legion post of Sylvania, a red Flanders Memorial Poppy. These poppies grew over northern France circling the shell holes and bordered the graves of the American dead; therefore it was adopted as the National Legion Flower. The artificial poppies were made in France and the money went to orphaned children of northern France.

Memorial Day in 1927 reported very few G.A.R. left in their ranks. At promptly 9:30 the parade moved down Main Street to the Ten Mile creek where the W.R.C. strewed flowers on the water in memory of the sailor dead. From there the parade moved to the Legion Field on Ravine Drive, where there was a crowd of about 1,200. Here Fred Crandall gave two readings, "The Spires of Oxford" and "In Flanders Fields." Then Rev. Stowell and Ed Jacobs read the Legion ritual. Boy Scouts decorated the graves of the soldiers in Ravine Cemetery. The Legion firing squad fired a salute and the bugler blew "taps," then they moved on to Association Cemetery where additional services were held. At Depot Grove the Community Church quartet sang and Rev. George M. Wilson gave a short talk. The Women's Relief Corp (W.R.C.) held their ritual service and their quartet sang a song. After that the procession moved back to town where a luncheon was served in the W.R.C. hall.

This was our Memorial Day parade in 1930 heading east on Ravine Drive toward St. Joseph Cemetery and then Ravine Cemetery. After that they marched across the street to Legion Field, which was a ten-acre parcel of land off Ravine Drive that the local American Legion group owned from 1924 until 1940. (Photo owned by Sylvania Area Historical Society).

These same events occurred at the Memorial Day celebrations in 1931, except this time they started promptly at 10 a.m., in Burnham Park where the various organizations assembled to pay homage to the patriotic dead. At the conclusion of the services in the park, the organizations formed a parade and marched to the Ten Mile Creek, where the W.R.C. held short services on the bridge in honor of the sailor dead. Little Jane Paschen dropped flowers on the waters of the creek honoring the heroes of the sea. The parade then moved to Ravine Cemetery for grave decorating, gun fires by the Legion and buglers played "Taps." Then on to Association Cemetery for more services while the Boy Scouts again decorated the graves. Then the parade marched back to town where the members of the American Legion drove to Memorial Park Cemetery and conducted short services at the Soldiers' Monument. Boy Scouts placed a wreath at the foot of the monument. At twelve noon an aerial bomb was fired and the Boy Scouts raised all flags in the town from half-mast to full mast.

6-6-1932 - According to the minutes of the Sylvania Township Volunteer Fire Department "Chief Williams expressed his satisfaction with the fine showing the fire company made in the local Memorial Day parade. As this was the first public appearance of the lads in their new uniforms, and in any parade, the chief wanted his sentiments known."

The Memorial Service in Sylvania in 1939 was held with a parade that formed on Maplewood Avenue at Burnham Park. Moving down Maplewood to Main Street to Convent Blvd., to Association Cemetery. Marchers will then ride in the busses of the Sylvania Board of Education from Association Cemetery to St. Joseph's and Ravine cemeteries, then to Memorial Park Cemetery. At the conclusion of the services at Memorial Park the Boy Scout troops will be in charge of raising flags on Main Street to full mast. It is urged that all merchants display the American flag on Main Street, placing the flags at half-mast in the morning.

During World War II Memorial Day Services became very important to the citizens of Sylvania. The following was reported on 5-21-1942: "In cooperation with the Memorial Day Committee the Religious Work Committee of the Sylvania Association of Churches is planning a memorial service to be held on Sunday afternoon, May 31 at 2:30 in Burnham auditorium. Ministers of Sylvania have been asked to cooperate in this religious service to which all patriotic organizations have been invited." The roll of honored dead was read by Rev. Pohly. The Memorial Day exercises in Sylvania began at Burnham Park at 9:15 a.m., and the program opened with the hymn "America" played by Burnham High School Band. Rev. A.L. Anderson gave the invocation and the Boy Scout Troops placed a wreath on the Burnham Memorial and conducted a flag ceremony. The parade formed on Maplewood Avenue and headed to Main Street. It went south on Main Street, pausing at the bridge where services in honor of the sailor dead were conducted. Vern Cory, Commander of the American Legion and William C. Miller, Commander of the Veterans of Foreign Wars placed flowers on the waters of the creek, the firing squad saluted the dead and taps was sounded. The parade then continued to Association Cemetery where their ritual at the mound was held, the band played "Nearer My God to Thee." The flag ceremony was conducted and the firing squad saluted the dead and taps was sounded. The marchers were then transported in buses to St. Joseph's and Ravine Cemeteries on Ravine Drive where they were addressed and the VFW ritual was read, and finally a wreath was placed upon the grave of Henry E. Burnham. At each cemetery the Boy Scout troops decorated the graves of all soldiers, sailors and members of the Women's Relief Corps. The parade then continued in buses to Memorial Park Cemetery where the main services of the day were held at the Soldiers and Sailors monument.

The 1943 Memorial Day services started at Memorial Park Cemetery at the Soldiers and Sailors monument. The Sylvania Post V.F.W. was in charge of the program at the cemetery. Church services were conducted by the Sylvania Association of Churches, and were held in the Burnham Auditorium beginning at 1:30 p.m. immediately after the services the parade formed in the Burnham High School drive and marched to the cemetery, where there were speakers and other events. All service men and women, Civilian Defense, Firemen and all school children were invited to participate in the parade. It was announced that due to a ruling of the Ohio Transportation Department buses from the school would no longer be available and a complete change in the procedure from other years was arranged. Trucks were provided to transport members of the Burnham Band at the conclusion of the program in Memorial Park Cemetery, to Ravine Cemetery and St. Joseph's and then Association Cemetery where the Women's Relief Corps were in charge. Services were held at the mound and wreaths were placed on the graves of the honored dead. All the Sylvania area Boy Scout troops were present to assist, due to the fact that many were not able to participate because they were employed in defense plants, and they were required to put in a full day's work.

Memorial Day in 1945 was celebrated with a parade led by the Burnham High School band, a parade made up of veteran's organizations, their Auxiliaries, the W.R.C., Boy and Girl Scouts and school children who visited four cemeteries in Sylvania. They started at Burnham Park and stopped at the Victory Board at 5678 Main Street to lay a wreath in honor of those who died in service of the present war. Stopping again on the bridge on S. Main St., to drop flowers on the water in honor of the sailors dead and stopping at Association, Ravine and St Joseph's cemeteries. The parade ended at Memorial Field where the main program was held.

In 1950 the Memorial Day celebration was spent dedicating Sylvania's new Memorial Field on May 30th. 45 men of Sylvania who lost their lives in world conflicts were marked with bronze markers and maple trees, one for each of the 45 war dead. Nelson Randall was the general chairman of the arrangements, and at 10:45, a formation of fighter planes of the Ohio Air National Guard from Mansfield, Ohio, flew overhead and made several passes over the field. The color guard then raised the flag and lowered it to half-mast. Four men from the various troops were chosen to place wreaths on the Markers along the avenue of trees while the chairman read off the names of the boys in whose honor the field was dedicated.

In 1964 the Memorial Day services and parade were held on Saturday morning. Religious services were held first at Memorial Field with speakers Rev. J. Harold Hopkins and Rev. Martin Shaner. The parade then formed at Memorial Field and moved south on Garden Park to Erie Street, to Main Street; south on Main Street, halting on the Ten Mile Creek Bridge where flowers were placed upon the water in honor of the Sailor Dead, then to Convent Boulevard; west on Convent to Association Cemetery and into that cemetery where services were conducted at the mound with the Women's Relief Corps in charge. Those taking part in this parade included veteran groups and their auxiliaries. The Twirlerettes from Temperance, Mich., Explorer Scouts, Boy Scouts, Girl Scouts, Brownies, Campfire Girls, 4-H Club groups and other youth units. Services were then held at St. Joseph and Ravine Cemeteries and finally at Toledo Memorial Park Cemetery. Judge Conners was the main speaker on the program at Toledo Memorial Park Cemetery.

The 5-28-1969 *Toledo Blade* announced "As they have for more than 30 years, Sylvania area veterans groups will conduct a parade and services at various cemeteries. This year they are stressing participation of youth groups, such as Boy and Girl Scout troops, "to convey the meaning of the holiday to the youngsters," a spokesman said. The activities will begin with a service a Memorial Field, north of Erie Street in Sylvania, starting at 9:15 a.m. The parade, featuring the Sylvania and Whiteford high school bands, will travel down Erie to Main Street, south to Monroe Street, to Ten-Mile Creek, where naval veterans will be memorialized with a wreath on the water. From there, the parade will continue to Toledo Memorial Park for a 10 a.m., service conducted by American Legion posts and the Marine Corps League to honor the 3,600 veterans buried there. Sylvania Councilman George Fletcher will speak. Participants will then board school buses for services at Ravine and St. Joseph's Cemeteries, conducted by VFW posts, and then to Sylvania Township Cemetery on Convent Boulevard for services conducted by the Women's Relief Corps. The Marine Corps League will conduct an additional service in Toledo Memorial Park at the grave of Louis Diamond, for whom the league's local detachment is named."

In August of 1974 a birthday party was held for Clyde Gault of Sylvania for his 89th birthday. According to the 8-21-1974 *Sylvania Sentinel* Mr. Gault had been the grand marshal during the annual Memorial Day Parade for almost 50 years.

The Memorial Day celebrations in 1977 were held on May 30 with a parade as in former years. Units assembled at the Crescent of Memorial Trees north of the ball diamonds in Memorial Field. The parade traveled south on Garden Park Drive to Erie Street, east on Erie Street to Main Street; south on Main to Ravine Drive; east on Ravine to Ravine Cemetery where tribute was made at the grave of Henry E. Burnham. The parade then headed back Ravine Drive to Main Street; south on Main to Convent Blvd; west on Convent to Association Cemetery, where the ritual of the Women's' Relief Corp concluded the public services for the day. School buses were available at Association Cemetery to shuttle the marchers back to Memorial Field.

According to the minutes of the Sylvania Township Trustees they donated $100 to the Sylvania Memorial Day Committee each year starting in the 1960s and through the 1990s for the purchase of flags and programs for the annual event. Throughout the years that he worked as the village/city Clayton Fischer was put in charge of the parade and service. He was a World War II veteran, worked full-time at the City of Sylvania, and was involved with the local VFW Post. The City of Sylvania also donated $100 to this committee. This practice was continued for many years.

In early May of 1978 Clayton Fischer invited area residents to take part in the annual Memorial Day Parade scheduled for Monday, 5-29-1978. Mr. Fischer coordinated the parade with the cooperation of the Women's Relief Corps, Joseph W. Diehn Post, American Legion and Auxiliary, Veterans of Foreign Wars 3717 and Veterans of Foreign Wars 7372 and Auxiliaries.

Morning rains forced the cancellation of the Memorial Day parade in 1979.

In 1980 the Memorial Day parade in Sylvania formed at Memorial Field, where services were held at 9 a.m. and then services were held at the Ten Mile Creek bridge on Main Street, and then at Ravine and St. Joseph cemeteries, and then on to Association Cemetery on Convent Blvd. An article in the *Sylvania Sentinel* dated 5-21-1980 invited Cub Scouts and youth groups who were interested in marching in the Monday, May 26, Memorial Day parade. They were urged to contact Clayton Fischer, at the City of Sylvania, if they were interested. The article said that Mr. Fischer had been associated with the Memorial Day activities since 1946. The names of veterans and auxiliary members who had passed away during the past year were to be turned into Mr. Fischer. Parade participants were to assemble at Memorial Field at 9 a.m. after which a brief service will be held at 9:15. The parade would then stop at the Ten Mile Creek Bridge, via Garden Park and Erie. A wreath was to be deposited upon the water in remembrance of those who were lost at sea. Brief services followed at Ravine and St. Joseph cemeteries after which the participants returned to Main Street and proceeded to Association Cemetery on Convent Blvd. where the Women's Relief Corps conducted a service. At the end of the program school buses transported the children back to Memorial Field.

By 1983 it was reported that Clayton Fischer had served as the organizer of the Memorial Day observance for many years. He served as secretary-treasurer of the Memorial Day committee for almost 50 years. It was reported that not only did he arrange the annual parade and memorial services at the various cemeteries, he personally placed American flags at some 250 graves of veterans or auxiliary members at St. Joseph's and Ravine cemeteries and also on the 50 memorial trees in Memorial Field. He also saw to it that flags were distributed to veteran organizations to decorate some 300 other graves in Association Cemetery.

In December of 1983 Mayor James E. Seney formed an ad hoc committee to foster community interest for the acquisition and installation of a bronze, life-size statue of a serviceman to be placed in Memorial Field. The following were appointed to the committee: James Cole, general chairman; Jack Watkins, honorary chairman; Dale Reinbolt, treasurer; and Art Landseadel, coordinator; Deane Allen; Leonard Biel; Joseph Boyle; Art Cole; George Eichenauer; Joseph Eisler; Clayton Fischer; Robert Garrison; Brad Heaps; Robert Hinkle; Dr. Gordon R. Hoffman; Sharon Lange; Sister Mary Ann; Sister Augustine; James Maxwell; William McCann; Rev. George A. Schmit; Carole Seney; George Seney; Rev. Sanord Souers; Barbara States, Dale Stoll, Glen Taylor; Norman Thal, Jr.; Lucy Travis; James Walker; David Zaski; and Sue Christmyer.

According to the *Sylvania Herald* dated 1-25-1984 a kick-off rally for the Sylvania War Memorial Fund had been called "a good beginning" by the Committee Chairman James Cole. The kick-off event was held on 1-18-1984 in the Cardinal Room of Churchill's in Starlite Plaza, and garnered some $8,000 in donations, pledges and goods and services needed for the project. The mayor had appointed a "Mayor's Ad Hoc Committee" to help raise $25,000 in order to purchase and erect a life-sized bronze statue of a soldier in full battle dress in the Memorial Grove at Sylvania's Memorial Field. Jack Watkins was named Sylvania's most honored Korean War veteran and honorary chairman. During the rally, Major General Walter A. Churchill (U.S.M.C. retired) presented a $1,000 check for the memorial. A pledge of $1,000 was also received from the staff and administrators of Sylvania City Schools. Lighting, electrical materials and labor for the installation of the memorial were received from Joe Eisler of The Lighting Center and Fred Noffen, Sr., and Fred Noffen, Jr., of Imperial Electric and Alarms. All the concrete work, including labor, materials and transportation were pledged by R.L. Mohr Company, Robert E. Hall Concrete, Inc., Peter Simon Company, Inc., and Richard Stansley of Sylvester Trucking Company. Those who donated to the memorial were promised that they would have their names listed and placed in a time capsule in the statue's base.

Mayor James Seney when forming the committee to arrange for funds appointed John Watkins the honorary chairman, James Cole, President of Sylvania Area Chamber of Commerce, was chairman of the fundraising drive and parade. A goal of $25,000 was set early in 1984 to pay for the statue, flag poles, flags, pedestal, lighting & Etc."

On Memorial Day – 5-28-1984 the statue in Memorial Field was dedicated. The following information was documented: "The statue in Sylvania's Memorial Field is a replica of a statue located in Huntington, West Virginia. The artist, Thomas Emery of California used as his model, United States Marine Corps Corporal Timothy Schulte, Camp Pendleton, California. Mr. Emery and his family were in Sylvania for the parade and dedication of the statue in Memorial Field on Memorial Day, 5-28-1984. (In 1991 this statue was moved to the front lawn of the Sylvania Administration Building at 6730 Monroe Street).

Also at the Memorial Day celebrations in 1984 Brian Johnson, a fourth grade student of St. Joseph Elementary School, had won the contest for designing the City of Sylvania's flag. He received a certificate from Mayor James E. Seney and on Memorial Day of 1984 was the first official viewing of the completed flag.

The 1985 Memorial Day celebration was observed on 5-27-1985 with the traditional parade. The Mayor announced that this year's activities would be dedicated to those soldiers who died in battle. Special invitations were sent for veterans of all wars to march in the parade. The Memorial Day committee was asking every veteran to help commemorate the day and memory of fallen comrades by taking part in the parade and ceremonies.

The 2004 Memorial Day parade started at Lourdes College and moved to Veteran Memorial Field. Rain drizzled during the festivities, but the skies cleared by afternoon.

The 2005 Memorial Day services were held at Toledo Memorial Park Cemetery, but the parade started at Lourdes College and ended at Veterans Memorial Field. An F-16 flyover and the release of 50 doves were part of the ceremony at Memorial Field.

The 2006 services started at Toledo Memorial Park Cemetery at 9 a.m., and the parade followed at 10 a.m. from Main Street to Erie Street and on to Veterans Memorial Field.

In 2010 the Mayor of Sylvania, Craig Stough, announced that the parade and services were sponsored by the local veteran's organizations and assisted by the City of Sylvania and Sylvania Recreation. The Northview and Southview High School bands were part of the parade and ceremonies too. The ceremonies started at 9 a.m. with a memorial ceremony at Toledo Memorial Park near the 85 foot Veterans Memorial Monument. He reported that over 10,000 veterans were laid to rest in the cemetery, and that an American Flag was posted on the grave of each one, which created a sea of flags. Then at 10:00 a.m. the parade started from Lourdes College and heads north on Main Street, through downtown Sylvania, and then continued on to Veterans Memorial Field, where a service followed at the north end of the Veterans Memorial Field. The parade included both high school bands, local veterans, military, scout and civic groups and local political dignitaries. At 11 a.m., a 30-minute Memorial Day service honoring America's Veterans was held, with Mayor Stough serving as master of ceremonies. The ceremony featured a fly-over by an Ohio Air National Guard unit.

For many years now the Sylvania Memorial Day Parade has been ending its serve in Veteran's Memorial Field off Woodrow Drive.

It was noted that five large bronze monuments were in place in Memorial Field describing five American wars and listing the Sylvania area residents who gave up their lives in those conflicts.

The five markers in Memorial Field list the casualties of five different wars. Represented on each of the five markers are the Civil War, World War I, World War II, the Korean War and the Vietnam War.

One more note: I will leave the additional wars that the United States became involved in after the Persian Gulf War for the next historian to write about. But, I do want to mention one more Sylvania veteran who was severely wounded in Iraq.

Matthew Drake, a 2001 Sylvania Northview High School graduate, wrestler and bodybuilder, was working as a certified personal trainer before entering the service of his country. His sacrifices were beyond the call of duty. He was serving in the Army as a Special Operations solider, when on 10-15-2004 he was driving a three-ton military vehicle in Qaim, Iraq, and a suicide bomber slammed into his Army vehicle. Two of his military colleagues and their Iraqi interpreter were killed while Matthew Drake was the only one to survive. Matthew suffered massive injuries that included brain and skull trauma, a fractured spinal vertebra, two broken clavicles, a fractured upper right arm, mandible fractures, first through third-degree burns, and glass and shrapnel in his head, face, neck and throat. Medical experts did not expect Army Special 4 Matthew Drake to live, but he did.

He was in a comma for three months and doctors were uncertain if he would ever walk, talk or be able to take care of himself in any way.

By July of 2005 organizers were planning a "Matthew's Independence Day" fund-raising party. The goal was to help raise money for the many needs that Matthew and his family were facing. Organizers wanted to be able to construct an 800 square foot addition to the Sylvania family home so that he could live independently when he recovered from his injuries.

Sean Savage, a Sylvania resident, spearheaded the fund raising effort, after his son Drew heard about Matthew Drake's war injuries and told his dad. Mr. Savage started the campaign and called it Matthew's Independence Day Campaign. The estimated cost was $100,000 and as of the 4th of July, 2005, more than $40,000 had been raised, with donors in 14 states contributing through a website, as well as many local residents.

Members of the Army Ohio National Guard 323rd Military Police Company held a car wash and raised $4,000. Then a private Ann Arbor facility specializing in treatment of brain and spinal-cord injuries donated the cost of his treatment at that facility, estimated at $1,200 a day for three months.

Specialist Drake's short-term memory was affected, and he did not remember anything about the bombing, although he did have his long-term memory and remembered most everything that happened before the bombing.

The money was raised, the addition was added, and Matthew continued to improve over time, with numerous setbacks along the way. The Army classified him as 100% disabled and retired Matthew from active duty, but Matthew's therapy continued.

On 4-18-2005 Matthew "stood" in uniform and received three medals: a Purple Heart, Army Commendation Medal, and War on Terrorist Medal. The medals were presented to Matthew by General Douglas Brown.

Thank you Matthew for your service and contributions to our national security. We know that your sacrifices were huge, and your hometown of Sylvania, Ohio will always remember the sacrifices that you made. May God Bless You and Look Over You Always!

The Memorial Day of 2014 started at 9 a.m. with a memorial ceremony at Toledo Memorial Park near the 85 foot high Veterans Memorial Monument. At this cemetery there were over 12,000 veterans laid to rest and an American flag was posted on each of those graves, creating "a sea of flags." After that the Memorial Day Parade assembled at St. Joseph Church and headed north on Main Street at 10:15, through the downtown and continued on to Veterans Memorial Field off of Woodrow Drive.

MEMORIAL FIELD

The first mention of a "Memorial Field" was on 10-15-1945 when the minutes of Sylvania Village Council said that Ira Baumgartner, Superintendent of schools, attended the village council meeting and presented a post war plan for a living memorial and a community project. He reported that the present athletic field was to be abandoned, and that the school board was planning the purchase of 20 acres of land known as Peak field, to be used as an athletic field, swimming pool, tennis courts, stadium and bus garage. It was to be owned by the school board and the cost would be about $90,000, not including the property. (This was Memorial Field).

Lucas County real estate records show that on 4-22-1920 Fred O. Peak had purchased Lot 4, Lot 7 and Lot 8 of the 1859 Assessors Plat. On 10-1-1945 after Fred Peak died the property was willed to Belle Peak. On 8-13-1946 the Sylvania Exempted Village School District purchased the property, which then became Memorial Field.

On 7-7-1949 is was announced that the property known as the "Peak property" was purchased and would become "Memorial Field" and a recreation center was planned for the property, to include a living memorial for each of our 37 young men who gave their lives for their country in World War II, with the planting of a live tree and bronze plaque in memory of each of them. On 5-30-1950 a dedication was held for Memorial Field with a 21-gun salute honoring our war heroes. On 7-29-1949 a benefit dance was held at Centennial Terrace to raise funds to purchase a fence to enclose Memorial Field.

The 8-4-1949 *Sylvania Sentinel* reported: "A meeting has been called for Friday night at Burnham High School of the general committee appointed to raise funds for the purchase and erection of the new fence for the enclosing of Memorial Field. Mr. George Wilson, chairman, urged that all members be present with a report on sale of tickets to the benefit dance last Friday night. In order for the fence to be erected in time for the first football game, it will be necessary for the contract to be signed with Douglas Fence Company which submitted the lowest bid, $7,993. No report is available as to the sale of tickets as of this time, but a large number of Sylvanians were on the dance floor dancing to the music of Clyde Trask at Centennial Terrance Friday night."

From August 1949 through December 1949 funds were raised by the Sylvania Memorial Fund Committee. The goal was set at $11,200, and by December 1st $10,366.88 had been donated. The committee consisted of: George Wilson, chairman; Walter Hoshal, Jr., vice chairman; Ben Schlatter, finance chairman; Verna Buck, secretary; Ed Brighton, Elmer Robinson, Don Holliday, Clarence Meinen, Roberta Keller, Rev. W. Haupt, Rev. Edward Johnson and Ray Corbin. The Captains were: Special solicitations - Paul Zeitner, Joseph Bissonnette, Harold James, Robert Adams, Robert Wilcox; Ticket sales – Ed Brighton, Leota Bremforder, and Clarence Meinen.

A four-page flyer was distributed throughout the community that announced: "Sylvania's World War No. II Memorial Drive – September 13 to October 17" (1949). The flyer encouraged residents of Sylvania to "Give – To Build Youth! – To Honor Men!" The third page of this flyer said: "Pictured above is the proposed Memorial Field as it will appear when it is finally completed. The field is located on 20 acres of land in the north end of Sylvania, known as the Peak property. The acreage extends west of Main St. to the old Counter farm and from Woodrow and Garden Park Drives on the south, north almost to the state line. The field has been graded and tiled to provide for proper drainage and the football playing field is in shape for play this fall with lights and bleachers installed. A sentimental aspect of the field will be trees planted along graveled paths commemorating those boys of the village and township who gave their lives in World War II. Bronze plaques will be placed at the foot of each tree with the names of the deceased veterans inscribed thereon."

By December 1949 many of the original plans for Memorial Field had been abandoned. Now the plans were for: a football field, fencing the entire property, bronze plaques for 37 deceased veterans during World War II, trees for each veteran, miscellaneous park equipment, including picnic tables, small metal fire places, badminton, volley ball, horseshoe courts and football score board.

Initial reports in 1949 indicated that there were 37 men from the Sylvania area that were casualties of World War II, to be honored in Memorial Field, but as plans continued there were 45 men listed. Today there is a marker in Memorial Field listing 47 men, who were casualties of World War II.

5-1-1950 – The minutes of Sylvania Village Council said: Because of additional expenses of the Sylvania Memorial Day Committee in dedicating Memorial Field this year, our contribution to this Committee for 1950 will be increased to $100 for this purpose this year; and the Clerk be authorized to amend the appropriation ordinance for 1950 by transferring $100 from street cleaning in the service fund to a Memorial Day appropriation.

The 5-12-1950 *Sylvania Sentinel* reported: "With plans being completed for the dedication program at Sylvania Memorial Field on Decoration Day, this village should have the largest congregation of people within its borders seen here in many a day. The trees planted as a memorial to each deceased veteran of World War II are all in place and leafing out. The stones with the names of the veteran inscribed in bronze are all ready for placing on foundations and the memorial road between the trees is stoned ready for the big day. Nelson Randall, who is in charge of the dedication ceremonies, has provided some outstanding features for the parade preceding the program which will have General Cooper as the speaker. Sylvania can be very proud of its efforts in providing such a field as a permanent memorial to its sons who gave their all for their country in time of war. As a bereaved father, this writer can gladly add his congratulations to the committee which undertook the gathering of funds necessary to bring the Memorial Field to as successful fruition. We believe that the boys themselves would be glad to know (and maybe they do) that, in their names, the people of Sylvania Township have decided that the coming generations would have a proper place for recreation, and in a small way at least, make for a better world that they died to preserve and provide."

In 1950 Memorial Field was dedicated to the memory of 45 men who died for their country in World War II. Memorials with bronze plates and a tree were placed in Memorial Field at that time for the following 45 men: Darrell Allen, Carleton Bay, James W. Berry, Max Wayne Berry, Jess Bieber, Leroy Breier, Kenneth Brodbeck, Bernard O. Brown, Raymond Conrad, Douglas Corbin, Edward G. Carlson, Melvin Dauer, Fred Fender, Robert C. Fisher, Leon R. Harrwaldt, Lloyd Hartzler, Eddie Howard, Harold Jasmund, Arthur Jones, Jr., Charles W. Jones, Andrew Keeler, Alfred E. Knepper, William Kramer, Glen V. Mathewson, Richard Miller, Don W. Moore, Wayne Morningstar, James E. McCullough, Jack Nichols, Sylvester J. Pakulski, Richard H. Palmer, Howard Pratt, James Randall, Orin D. Reynolds, David Robinson, Kenneth Shull, Wade L. Shull, Ray Sporleder, Paul Taylor, Thaddeus H. Turanski, Ralph VanGlahn, Jr., Robert Wood, Anthony Wieczorek, Earl C. Yeager, Chester Zwayer.

This photo is marked on the back as May 30, 1950 – Sylvania Memorial Day - which makes it the dedication program for Sylvania's Veterans Memorial Field. At this event Memorial Field was dedicated to the memory of 45 Sylvania men who were killed while serving during World War II. Newspapers the next day reported that 4,000 people attended this ceremony. (Photo owned by Sylvania Area Historical Society).

On 6-1-1950 the *Sylvania Sentinel* reported that 4,000 people attended the dedication ceremony of Memorial Field which included a 21-gun salute honoring 45 war heroes and the formation of fighter planes of the Ohio Air National Guard from Mansfield, Ohio flew overhead. Detachments from the Ohio National Guard, Company A, 148th Infantry; Headquarters Battery, 140th Field Artillery Battalion; detachment of U.S. Naval Reserve; detachment, U.S. Marine Corps Reserve; members of veterans posts of the village and township, drawn up in parade formation for the ceremony.

In July of 1952 the *Sentinel-Herald* reported that in 1950 Memorial Field was dedicated with a crowd of nearly 4,000 people attending the dedication, and after addresses were made planes of the 140th Artillery Battalion dropped flowers on the markers at the foot of 45 silver maples which had been planted and lined the "Avenue of Trees." By the summer of 1951, nearly all the trees were dead and had to be replaced. By the end of the summer of 1951 more trees were dead. And by June of 1952 only 25 trees were still struggling for life. In July of 1952 nearly all the trees were dead again and needed to be replaced. The old Memorial Field fund still had $1,600 which they earmarked for a score board and replacing 18 dead maples along the Avenue of Trees. They reported that the biggest problem was the fact that the only water available on the property was a small water fountain, and you couldn't even fit a small bucket in the fountain in order to water the trees. But, there was hope, because a new school employee, David Huffman, had been assigned as custodian of the field for the summer, and was paid from the operating budget of the school system. The school track coach, Louis Whitman, expressed concern about the oval running track at Memorial Field because the old one in the rear of Burnham High School was going to be eliminated to allow the expansion of Maplewood school. The control board was also looking into the construction of toilet facilities at Memorial Field. There was talk of placing a half mill levy on the ballot, but many doubted that the voters would approve a levy, and the only hope for the continued development of Memorial Field was a rodeo that was being planned as a fund raiser by the Chamber of Commerce.

The 7-3-1952 *Sentinel-Herald* reported: "On the advice of an attorney member of the Memorial Field Board, already working members of the group were "rechristened" by a new resolution of the School Board last Monday night. The Board reappointed the seven member panel after Harold James found the minutes of two years ago to be "vague." Although the new resolution retains the seven original members of the board it makes their responsibility one of advisement. Any final action will result from the school board. Orlo Thomas, Burnham Athletic Director and a member of the Memorial Field Board took the second step in awakening the Memorial Field Movement by submitting a set of rules for use and operation of the field. The rules formulated by Coach Thomas, require a permit issued by the school superintendent. The permit will make the holder responsible for any damage caused by a visiting group or attending spectators. With the two resolutions tucked away in the minutes in legal fashion, attorney Harold James opened a discussion with the comment, "and now the $64 question is—where do we get some money to run the field?"

On 5-14-1953 Ira Baumgartner, Superintendent of Schools, completed an application for building permit with the Village of Sylvania to build a "comfort station" in Memorial Field. This "comfort station" was to have 5 stools and 1 urinal. The builder was listed as Bernard Webb of Brint Road in Sylvania. The size of the building was listed as 20 x 40 feet and 12 feet high. The exterior walls were to be built of steel. The estimated cost was listed as $5,000. This permit was approved by council.

In 1954 the group known as the Villagers took charge of the annual Sylvania Fourth of July celebrations held at Memorial Field. They repeated the program for many more years after. In 1955 Maplewood's kindergarten building was constructed in Memorial Field.

On 4-15-1956 the Village of Sylvania and Diehn Post 468 were host to 96 American Legion post units in the First District of the Ohio American Legion. Post Commander Dale Bruns announced that the event would be the biggest and finest parade since Sylvania's centennial. Nearly 40 marching units were invited to compete for trophies. The parade formed at Memorial Field and proceeded to Erie to Phillips to Maplewood to Main to Monroe Streets, and then the parade ended with exhibitions on Main Street, with a reviewing stand at the Chandler Hardware parking lot.

The 7-19-1956 *Sentinel-Herald* newspaper announced that Ben Schlatter tendered his resignation as Chairman of the Memorial Field Committee because he was tired of begging for funds to give the park some semblance of respectability. He said that he was convinced that the 20 acre plot of school property could not be operated successfully on a volunteer basis. He said that they had no funds left to carry on, people were continually crabbing about conditions, and they didn't have the funds to do anything about it. He said that in 1955 the school board had budgeted $1,650 for the care and operation of the field, and they spent $1,200 of that amount very carefully. Mr. Schlatter also said that local residents generally agreed that the field is a mess, with piles of railroad ties, old iron and a set of decaying bleachers. The weeds were knee deep in uncut grass and the picnic area was a shambles, while the seats of the kiddie swings were hidden in the shade of waving weeds. The local vets had cleaned up the Veteran's Memorial portion of the field so that it would look presentable for Memorial Day, but they were infuriated when they found debris littering the row of stone markers honoring Sylvania's dead.

A memorial in Memorial Field lists two Sylvania casualties for the Korean War: Don J. Doremus and William C. Kroll.

The Fourth of July in Sylvania in 1959 was a little different. The Sylvania Township Recreation Association was sponsoring a "Family Fun Day" celebration in Sylvania at Memorial Field.

In July of 1960 the Villagers organization sponsored train and pony rides, and the annual Family Fun Day celebration on the 4th of July at Memorial Field.

In July of 1961 the Sylvania Township Park Board held their budget hearing for the year 1962 and it was noted in an article in the *Sylvania Sentinel Herald* that they adopted a resolution calling to operate Memorial Field in Sylvania during 1962 and underwrite a recreation program. The board submitted this to the Sylvania Board of Education who owned the field and they set aside $5,500 for the program.

In 1964 the fireworks display was sponsored by the Sylvania Recreation Department, and the display was held at Memorial Field, where All-Star baseball games were featured in the afternoon between the various leagues, including Pee-Wees, Midgets, Knot Holes and girl's leagues. Jim Glase was the recreation director.

In 1964 the Memorial Day services and parade were held on Saturday morning. Religious services were held first at Memorial Field with speakers Rev. J. Harold Hopkins and Rev. Martin Shaner. The parade then formed and moved south on Garden Park to Erie Street,

The famous Cole 3-ring Wild Animal Circus appeared under canvas in Memorial Field for two days in June of 1964.

In January of 1966 the Recreation Committee of Sylvania City Council, volunteer firemen, Exchange Club members and other Sylvania residents constructed an ice skating rink in Memorial Field.

4-21-1966 - Mr. Ed Smith and Mr. Andrew Mortemore were present at this Sylvania Township trustee meeting and presented plans for the development of Memorial Field and requested aid in the project. The trustees questioned the legality of township monies being spent on school board property. The clerk was asked to obtain an opinion from Harry Frieberg, Lucas County Prosecutor.

5-25-1966 - A meeting was called for the purpose of entering into a lease agreement with the Sylvania City School District for Memorial Field. It was agreed that lessor (the Sylvania School Board) hereby leases to the lessee (Sylvania Township Trustees) the acreage located on the northerly section of the City of Sylvania known as Memorial Field, excluding that portion occupied by the Kindergarten building, for recreational activities and facilities, at a cost of $1.00.

In May of 1967 Jim Glase was again hired by the Sylvania Township Recreation Association as the recreation director. By June of 1967 the board agreed to continue to call themselves STRA, or Sylvania Township Recreation Association, and the summer program was kicked off at Memorial Field.

5-1-1969 - The Sylvania Township Trustees were to join in with the City of Sylvania and the Sylvania City School District in repairing the roadway through Memorial Field. Each agency would share the cost for the joint venture. Mr. Elmer Robinson would be in charge of the operation and the clerk would attend to billing the costs.

James Seney and Robert Garrison, co-chairman of the Sylvania Community Recreation Committee appeared before the Sylvania Board of Education on 1-25-1971 and requested a cooperative agreement which would allow the Association to use Memorial Field for year-round recreational activities. The board said they would consider the request and announce their decision in the near future.

In 1971 the City of Sylvania's Recreation Department sponsored the 4th of July fireworks display at Memorial Field on Sunday, July 4th. They reported that the fireworks display would be the biggest and best show ever held in Sylvania. Gates opened at 7:00 p.m. Admission was 25 cents per child, and preschoolers were admitted free. Profits would be used for recreation programs.

In September of 1971 the second annual Sylvania Jaycee "Bean Festival" was held in Memorial Field.

In June of 1972, 432 residents of Sylvania signed a petition and presented it to Sylvania's city council protesting delays in completing repairs and improvements at Memorial Field. The complaint was that 1,100 young people on 60 baseball and softball teams would only have the use of five fields at Stranahan and Highland schools.

In 1972 the Villagers started the first phase of an elaborate master plan of plantings at the Memorial Field recreation complex. Evergreens, flowering trees, shade trees and shrubs were planted.

It was in the summer of 1974 that Sylvania City Council approved the expenditure of building a recreation building in Memorial Field. By August of 1974 they approved an additional $4,2181.98 to go toward completion of the building.

By the spring of 1977 surrounding residents were complaining about noise and crime at Memorial Field. Sylvania City Council requested that a letter be sent to the Sylvania chief of police requesting strict enforcement of past legislation which prohibits ball playing at Memorial Field on Sunday and after certain hours in the evening. Council took this action to alleviate complaints from bordering residents who said that ball teams, many of them from outside the city, were playing late games and were getting loud and rowdy.

Sylvania City Council, upon the recommendation of Mayor James Seney, voted in August of 1978 to do away with the men's softball diamond at Memorial Field. Mayor Seney noted that "the diamond has outlived its usefulness and that all equipment is to be removed and placed where needed." It was also recommended that no other facility be built there because of the closeness to a residential area.

In 1983 Mayor James E. Seney appointed an Ad Hoc Committee for the War Memorial Fund to raise funds for a life-sized bronze statue of a soldier to be placed in Memorial Grove of Memorial Field honoring all of the war dead of the Sylvania area. The committee was headed by a general chairman who was James L. Cole, an honorary chairman who was Jack Watkins, a treasurer who was Dale Reinbolt and a coordinator who was Art Landseadel. Other members of the committee included: Coordinating Secretary Carole Seney, Deane Allen, Leonard Biel, Joseph Boyle, Art Cole, Sue Christmyer, George Eichenauer, Joseph Eisler, Clayton Fischer, Robert Garrison, Brad Heaps, Robert Hinkle, Gordon Hoffman, Sharon Lange, Sister Mary Ann, William McCann, Msgr. Jerome E. Schmit, George Seney, Barbara States, Dale Stoll, Glen Taylor, Norman Thal, Jr., Lucy Travis, Jamie Walker and David Zaski. These individuals were given the job of determining a suitable memorial and its location.

According to the *Sylvania Herald* dated 1-25-1984 a kick-off rally for the Sylvania War Memorial Fund had been called "a good beginning" by the Committee Chairman James Cole. The kick-off event was held on 1-18-1984 in the Cardinal Room of Churchill's in Starlite Plaza, and garnered some $8,000 in donations, pledges and goods and services needed for the project. The mayor had appointed a "Mayor's Ad Hoc Committee" to help raise $25,000 in order to purchase and erect a life-sized bronze statue of a soldier in full battle dress in the Memorial Grove at Sylvania's Memorial Field. Jack Watkins was named Sylvania's most honored Korean War veteran and honorary chairman.

On Memorial Day – 5-28-1984 the statue in Memorial Field was dedicated. The following information was documented: "The statue in Sylvania's Memorial Field is a replica of a statue located in Huntington, West Virginia. The artist, Thomas Emery of California used as his model, United States Marine Corps Corporal Timothy Schulte, Camp Pendleton, California. Mr. Emery and his family were in Sylvania for the parade and dedication of the statue in Memorial Field on Memorial Day, 5-28-1984.

The July 4th, 1985 events in Sylvania included a day of festivities sponsored by the Sylvania Community Services Center. Activities began with a costume contest and a decorated-bike parade beginning at 9:45 a.m., in Burnham Park, and then bikes paraded to Memorial Field where awards were presented at 10:30 a.m. At Memorial Field the Sylvania Area Recreation Coalition sponsored league baseball and softball games until 4 p.m.

In December of 1987 members of the Sylvania Township Fire Department gathered in Memorial Field to plant a blue spruce tree in honor of their fallen chief, Joseph Wallace. Those present at the tree planting were: Dave Shock, Mike Ramm, Ron Slaughterbeck, Phil Kauffman, Kevin Mills, Fire Chief David Drake, Kenneth Howell, Ray Segur, Jim Comstock, Jeff Young, Jeff Kline, Mark Ball, Bill Whitman, Joe Draime, Jim Ball, Tom Curdes, Tom Hassen, Bill Hendricks, Jeff Nowak, Dale Gottfried and Al Jerram.

It was sometime after 1988 that Memorial Field became Veterans Memorial Field. I don't know if this was an official act or if the name was just used one time and it stuck.

By early November 1988 the Sylvania Area Joint Recreation District had completed the following at Veterans Memorial Field: reconditioned existing four ball diamonds, improve the drains and adding stone to the concourse, relocating the existing play equipment, fixing the existing tennis and basketball courts and placing 20 picnic tables, grills and additional trash barrels throughout the park.

In 1991, after the City of Sylvania had established a new administration building at 6730 Monroe Street, the soldier statue that was in Memorial Field was moved to the front of the administration building and placed on a new base. A new bronze plaque was installed at that time along with two other bronze plaques. It was sometime after that the tank was moved to Memorial Field.

Today, the five markers in Memorial Field list the casualties of five different wars. Represented on each of the five markers are the Civil War, World War I, World War II, the Korean War and the Vietnam War. Here are the listed casualties for each of these wars (These lists are different than the initial listing when Memorial Field was first established):

Civil War casualties – 1861 - 1865

Charles Brown, B. Butler, John VanOrman, George W. Holloway, J.V. Moore, Joseph Donovan, William Holmes, Jacob White, Ben Rhodes, Samuel Bellows.

World War I – 1914 – 1918

Joseph W. Diehn

World War II – 1939 - 1945

Darrell Allen, Carlton H. Bay, James W. Berry, Max Wayne Berry, Jess Bieber, Leroy Breier, Kenneth Brodbeck, Bernard O. Brown, Edward Carlson, Raymond Conrad, Douglas Corbin, Melvin Dauer, Fred Fender, Robert C. Fisher, Leon R. Harrwaldt, Lloyd Hartzler, Edwin D. Howard, Harold Jasmund, Arthur P. Jones, Jr., Charles W. Jones, Andrew Keeler, Alfred E. Knepper, Stanley J. Kniolek (not on original list), William Kramer, Glen V. Mathewson, James E. McCullough, Richard Miller, Don W. Moore, Wayne Morningstar, Jack Nichols, Sylvester J. Pakulski, Robert F. Palicki (not on original list), Richard Palmer, Howard Pratt, James S. Randall, Orin D. Reynolds, David Robinson, Kenneth Shull, Wade L. Shull, Ray Sporleder, Paul Taylor, Thaddeus Turanski, Ralph VanGlahn, Anthony Wieczorek, Robert Wood, Earl Yeager, Chester Zwayer

Korean War – 1950-1953

William C. Kroll, Don J. Doremus

Vietnam War – 1957 - 1975

Albert Franklin Baird, Andrew Thomas Brassfield, Frank Ochoa Florez, Christopher Walter, Dennis Herron, Harry Frank LaLonde, Raymond Sharp Loftus, III, Dale Arden Palm, Carl Harmon Peters, Jr., Robert Paul Phillips, Ronald Lee Rusek, Billy Robert Wohlgamuth, Nabil Mahood Youssef.

LANDFILLS / DUMPS / AUTO SALVAGE YARDS

LANDFILLS / DUMPS

The first time that the village officials made plans for a community dump was in 1945. Before that refuse was either buried on your private property or burned. According to the minutes of Sylvania Village Council dated 4-2-1945, they were making plans to use an old pond in Sylvania's south side, by the New York Central Railroad property, as a dump for village use. The minutes said that they planned to contact the N.Y.C.R.R. for a proposition to use the pond as a place for the village to dump ashes, cans, etc., but no garbage. Neighbors on Allen Street, Spring Street and Railroad Street objected to this proposal. Then village council offered to extend sanitary sewers to their area in return. All were in favor of the plan, except for one. The pond on this property, which is shown on our 1875 map and 1900 map, is gone today; filled in by several years of dumping ashes and rubbish here.

9-17-1945 – The minutes of village council reported that Solicitor Dague had not received any further word from the New York Central Railroad Co. in regard to "the dumping of rubbish" on their grounds.

10-15-1945 – Village council received word from the New York Central Railroad Company approving the use of their property along the tracks for use as a community dump. By the 4-1-1946 meeting of council it was reported that a number of unfavorable reports on the use and condition of the dump on the N.Y.C.R.R. grounds were brought to the attention of council. The clerk was to prepare an ordinance to regulate the use of the dump and that a nominal charge would be made. On 4-15-1946 council agreed to hire a watchman for the dump and pay him $3 per day, with the dump being open on Wednesdays and Saturdays only.

According to the minutes of Sylvania village council dated 8-5-1946 it reads: "Earl Smith was present and reported that Walter Avery was dumping paper and other inflammable material in the dump. The clerk was instructed to write Mr. Avery and inform him of the conditions named in the lease with New York Central Railroad."

In the meantime, in Sylvania Township, the first mention of a public dump in the township was on 7-2-1947, when the Sylvania Township Trustees met and passed a resolution to install the necessary tile in the ravine owned by Elmer Little on Monroe Street so that it could be used as a public dump by residents of Sylvania Township only. On 11-22-1911 Elmer Little had acquired the 8.43 acres on the north side of Monroe Street where the Bentbrook Addition subdivision is located today (Bentbrook Road, Burgess Road and Lynnhaven Drive). Elmer E. Little lived at 5588 Monroe Street, according to the 1957 Suburban Directory, and his home was at the corner of Monroe and Silvertown. It was on the part of his property to the west of his home that Mr. Little allowed the dumping.

In 1947 Charles Kellogg was employed by the township trustees as a caretaker of the newly created Sylvania Township dump. The dump was open for business two days a week from 12 to 8 p.m., and beginning in 1948 the Sylvania Township Trustees were paying Elmer Little as a "dump watchman" through 1953. After that there is no mention of continued use of Elmer Little's property for dumping. That may be because a county dump was established in the township in 1953 on King Road.

Back in the Village of Sylvania, on 4-19-1948, the Sylvania Village Council minutes stated: "A complaint concerning the village dump was made by the resident near it. The mayor was authorized to place an employee at the dump to have control over refuse which was placed in the dump."

7-20-1950 – The minutes of Sylvania Village Council shows a payment to Floyd Heilman for grading at the dump - $35. By March of 1951 Floyd Heilman was still being paid for grading at the dump.

In 1953 the Lucas County Commissioners purchased property at 3535 King Road. This property was on the west side of King Road, south of Sylvania Avenue. This was a dump that residents of Lucas County, and garbage collection companies used to dump all types of garbage from this point in time.

The following classified ad appeared in the 1-13-1955 *Sentinel Herald* newspaper, and every other week for over a year: "SYLVANIA CARRY ALL. We collect Garbage, Rubbish, Ashes, Commercial and Residential. L.A. Waterman LU2-2691, 5723 Main." This individual was more than likely hauling the items they collected to the county dump on King Road at this time. He just provided the service of hauling it there.

5-4-1964 - At a public meeting the trustees declared the week of 5-21-1964 as spring clean-up week in the township. Junk and rubbish could be hauled to the dump, by the residents, at no charge, and the trustees would pay the landfill fees. The resident just had to prove that he was a township resident and he could take whatever he wanted to get rid of to the dump free of charge.

9-21-1967 - The trustee minutes indicate that an unlimited garbage pick-up was being offered in Sylvania Township on 10-25-1967. This was accomplished by the township road workers and they used the King Road landfill to dispose of this garbage. This service was provided by the township until the King Road Landfill closed.

After the King Road landfill closed up the residents of Sylvania no longer had a convenient place to take their garbage and unwanted junk. (Details of the closing of the King Road landfill are discussed in more detail in this volume).

In 1975, for the first time, the Sylvania Township Trustees opened bids from garbage collection companies to offer what they called an "unlimited pickup." Two bids were received; one from Benton Village Sanitation Service at $9.00 per compacted cubic yard and one from Fondessy Enterprises, Inc. for $9.85 per compacted cubic yard. The trustees accepted the bid from Benton Village and after this first pickup was complete, on 11-6-1975 the trustees paid them $10,053 for this unlimited pick-up.

10-16-1975 - The trustees requested that the Lucas County prosecutor take action against the City of Toledo to prohibit the dumping of sludge from the city's water reclamation division within Sylvania Township.

LANDFILLS - KING ROAD

Here are the details of the King Road landfill, which was located in Sylvania Township off King Road, and had a street address of 3535 King Road. The entrance was located on the west side of King Road, south of Sylvania Avenue and north of where Covert Road comes out to King Road.

In reviewing the records of the Lucas County auditor the following property was purchased on the following dates: 104.37 acres – 3535 King Road – purchased by The Board of County Commissioners of Lucas County on 12-31-1953 from George E. Moor of 2010 Adams Street in Toledo, Ohio. The landfill property ran along the north and south line of the old Toledo, Angola & Western Railroad tracks.

In January of 1954 the Lucas County Sanitary Engineer, Raymond Hall, reported on the county garbage control projects to members of the Lucas County Trustee and Clerks Association. Mr. Hall explained that he preferred to call the proposed dump sites "sanitary landfills," and said that the county commissioners were establishing landfills on Jackman Road near the Michigan line, one in Sylvania on King Road and one in East Toledo. He explained that these landfills would be used by 10 licensed haulers in the county to deposit their garbage. Although he said that the county did not intend to regulate garbage collection rates, the licensed haulers were going to be charged 15 cents per customer for using the sites, which would cover the cost of operation plus a yearly payment on the land so that in 10 years, when the sites were no longer useable they could become parks at little cost to the taxpayers. Mr. Hall explained that the method employed was a ten ton bulldozer that trampled the material to a firm mass and then covered the area three times a day. He said that 10,500 homes in the county were served by independent haulers.

A neighbor of the King Road site, who had purchased property here before the landfill was established, said that in 1954 the county started tearing down the woods next to his house and shortly after opened the King Road landfill. He said that the serenity of watching deer in the woods was replaced by the nonstop roar of dump trucks and bulldozers, day, after day, after day.

In about 1965 the Park Forest Development Company was established. The Lucas County Commissioners hired this company to run their King Road landfill for them, but later it was determined that they got the bid for the job, without even bidding. And that they kept all the profits from running the landfill, with not one dime being paid to the county commissioners as owners of the land. Names mentioned as being involved with this company included a member of one of America's leading Mafia families, Joseph Barbara, Jr., and legendary Toledo gangster Leonard "Chalky Red" Yaranowsky. In his early years he was said to have been a member of the Licavoli gang, who had been charged with conspiracy to commit murder in 1935. Two years after the Park Forest Company took over the landfill, Mr. Barbara was arrested on extortion and rape charges in Michigan, and he sold the rest of his shares in the company to partner Yaranowsky. Some of the people that were hired by this company to operate the landfill included: Harry Leonard (a/k/a Leonard Yaranowski), Orval Bevel, Bob Freeman, Ken Freeman, Mr. Cooper and Richard Wilcox.

According to the minutes of the Sylvania Township Trustees dated 5-6-1965 - Alexander E. Lind of 7551 Deanville was present at the trustee meeting and requested that the trustees help clean up his neighborhood. He reported that neighbors on Deanville Road were storing reclaimed materials from the dump in their yards.

In April of 1967 the Lucas County Commissioners were talking about the possibility of using the King Road landfill property for the construction of a county incinerator. This was one of two sites that the county was considering for a $5 million incinerator plant. The Sylvania Township residents immediately began forming a committee to oppose any action aimed at putting this incinerator on King Road. Officials of the city of Sylvania also objected to the plan. After everything was said and done the King Road site was not chosen for the incinerator.

On 5-8-1967 the Lucas County Commissioners approved and signed a five-year contract with the Park Forest Company to operate the King Road landfill, with the option of continuing the contract for another five years, if approved by the commissioners at that time. This original contract called for no fees to be collected by the county from the company, even though the firm ended up grossing an income estimated at up to $50,000 per month.

In the minute book of the Sylvania Township Trustees dated 9-21-1967 it was noted that a discussion was held regarding the possible lease of the county land located on King Road, for recreational purposes. But then after the meeting in October of 1967, by a vote 2 to 1, a motion to continue negotiations with the Lucas County Commissioners on the proposed lease arrangement was defeated. Sylvania Township trustee Fred Bostleman wanted to continue the negotiations and pursue the land for a possible recreation site, while Trustees James Weldishofer and Earl Box stopped the effort. Mr. Box made his feeling known by calling the proposed recreation site a "big white elephant" and questioned the location of the site for use by children. Trustee Chairman

James Weldishofer also objected to the site on the basis of an expected high vandalism rate and the use of a dump for recreation no matter how well reclaimed. Mr. Bostleman felt that they needed to look to the future when the land will be more valuable. He said "this is no way to take care of a dump in Sylvania Township." And also said: "we should improve the land instead of just letting the dump stay there and continue to be a sore spot. How will we ever get rid of the dump if we don't take this chance to improve the land and turn it into a recreation area?" Mr. Weldishofer suggested that the county develop the property for the benefit of all the residents of Lucas County.

10-13-1967 - The trustees authorized the clerk to prepare an offer to purchase the parcel of land known as the King Road Land Reclamation site from the Lucas County Commissioners containing about 10.6 acres for $11,500.00 subject to the lease with the Park Forest Development Co.

10-19-1967 - The records indicate that the county commissioners turned down the offer to purchase the King Road property but will continue to negotiate a lease agreement.

In February of 1969 the Sylvania Township Trustees were discussing the problem of increased dumping of refuse in the township, because the city dumps were all closed, and the only dump in Lucas County was the King Road dump. The problem was that when residents arrived to the King Road landfill and found it closed then they were dumping their garbage in the ditches and streets nearby.

On 2-6-1969 the following was noted in the trustee minute book: "Dumping on streets in Sylvania Township has been a growing concern for all departments. The trustees agreed to write to the Lucas County Commissioners to request that the landfill on King Road be kept open from 7:30 a.m., until 6:00 p.m., instead of the present 4:00 p.m., to eliminate dumping along the streets." (It was noted that the dump was being run by Park Forest Development Co).

According to the *Toledo Blade* dated 4-24-1969 a meeting was held between the Lucas County Commissioners (Sol Wittenberg, William Gernheuser and James Holzemer); the Toledo city manager, Mr. Gross; Orville Bevel, Jr., president of Park Forest; and Prosecutor Harry Friberg. At this meeting the city of Toledo officials offered to operate the county-owned King Road landfill. It was noted that Park Forest Development Inc., was running the landfill under a five-year contract. The article said that Mr. Gross and Mr. Gernheuser argued at this meeting, and that Mr. Gernheuser objected to the city of Toledo taking over the dump, and he told Mr. Gross that the city (Toledo) did not have a landfill at Dura, but a "dirty, germ-ridden, rat-infested dump." Mr. Gernheuser also told Mr. Gross that residents of the southwestern part of Lucas County, including township trustees, went on record opposing the city taking over the operation. Commissioner Wittenberg questioned Mr. Bevel as to whether his company had any Detroit interests involved in the King Road landfill and Mr. Bevel said that there were absolutely no Detroit interests, but then refused to reveal the stockholders or others involved in the Park Forest business. At the request of the commissioners, Prosecutor Friberg was looking into the legality of the contract with Park Forest and whether the county could get out of the contract.

Also, according to this article, a resolution dated 5-8-1967 between the commissioners at that time (Guy Neeper, William Gernheuser and Sol Wittenberg) was passed giving the firm a five year contract.

6-26-1969 - The trustees met and discussed a copy of a letter received from W.J. Butts regarding possible contamination of well water because of the King Road landfill. It was agreed that the letter would be sent to the Board of Health and County Commissioners.

The *Toledo Blade* dated 8-13-1969 said: "Park Forest Development, Inc. will be asked to meet with the county commissioners next week to discuss a possible renegotiation of the King Road landfill contract. Sol J. Wittenberg, president of the board of commissioners, said a letter asking for a meeting will be sent to Orville Bevel, Jr., Park Forest president. Renegotiation has been suggested because it had been discovered that Park Forest is grossing thousands of dollars monthly while paying the county nothing for the use of its land. . . . Commissioner James Holzemer and Mr. Wittenberg have said they intend to demand that Mr. Bevel reveal the names of persons involved in the Park Forest corporation or there will be no contract between the firm and the county. Commissioner William Gernheuser said he too, would like to know the identity of those involved in the corporation, but does not think that the county can declare the contract void if Mr. Bevel refuses to divulge the information. The firm presently has a five-year contract with the county. Park Forest is an extension of a Detroit refuse hauling operation headed by two men with police records."

In September of 1969 it was agreed that a service fee of $24,000 per year, or 5 percent of the gross revenue from the King Road landfill would be paid to the county by the landfill operators, Park Forest Development, Inc. The president of Park Forest, Orville Bevel, Jr., agreed to the fee in a letter that he sent to the county commissioners. The letter made no mention of the request by Commissioner James M. Holzemer for a list of the stockholders of Park Forest.

The 10-29-1969 *Toledo Blade* reported the following: "Harry Leonard, on record as the sole stockholder of Park Forest Development, Inc., has told *The Blade* that he earlier had bought out partner Joseph Barbara, Jr.'s interest in the King Road landfill. The $50,000 purchase, agreed upon Jan 10, was completed in March; about two years after county commissioners signed a five-year contract with Park Forest to operate the county's 104-acre landfill. The premium is to be paid to Barbara over a five-year period, beginning 1-10-1970, Mr. Leonard said. The sale came some three months after Barbara had been indicted on charges of extortion and rape." " . . . Barbara and the Vitales were identified as key underworld figures in Detroit in U.S. Senate committee testimony in 1963. Mr. Leonard, 64, of 7933 Secor Rd., Lambertville, Mich., said he had been acquainted with relatives of Barbara, and went into the landfill business here with him "as a favor." Meanwhile, Orville Bevel, Jr., listed as president and a board member of Park Forest, had worked for Barbara in Michigan and was later hired to operate the King Road site, according to Mr. Leonard. Though the landfill is operated on county-owned land, Mr. Leonard said he has had to invest $150,000 to $180,000 to get the King Road site established as a landfill. . . .He would gladly turn the landfill back to the county for reasonable compensation for the firm's investment, Mr. Leonard stated. Melvin Nusbaum, attorney for the firm and its former secretary-treasurer, said that only a small number of the 250 authorized shares in the corporation has been sold. The company does not expect to sell any more of the shares unless the business grows much larger, he said. . . .”

It was reported at the end of October, 1969 that Mr. Leonard said that there was no connection between Park Forest Development Co., here and Park Forest Development Co., of Michigan. According to him the name of the local firm came from Mr. Bevel. Also reported was the fact that on 2-24-1969 Park Forest of Michigan was incorporated by Nicholas Micelli, Barbara's brother-in-law, of Mr. Clemens, Mich., and Paul Vitale and Anthony Corrado, both of Grosse Pointe Park, Mich. He said that Mr. Micelli was on the King Road scene when Park Forest first took it over. The *Toledo Blade* said that Mr. Leonard, who was known as “Chalky Red,” pleaded guilty to an extortion charge in 1934, reduced from a charge of conspiracy to murder in connection with four gangland slayings during the prohibition area. In an interview Mr. Leonard denied that he was ever a member of the Yonnie Licavoli gang.

By early 1970 it was reported that Harry Leonard was still the sole stockholder of Park Forest Development, Inc., the operator of the King Road landfill. It was said that the city of Toledo paid $60,000 a year to dump 25 percent of its refuse in the King Road landfill. At the end of January 1970 Park Forest Development, Inc., was cited by the county health sanitarian for violation of state health regulations at the King Road landfill. The health department said that the private company was not covering refuse with an impervious material to protect against contamination of underground water. Other violations noted included failure to cover refuse daily, inadequate amounts of cover material being used and papers blowing loose around the landfill. Mr. Cooper, operator of the landfill business, which was owned by Harry Leonard, explained that cold weather had prevented his equipment operators from covering the refuse daily. Health officials were told that King Road was accepting an estimated 1,000 to 1,500 cubic yards of refuse per day.

A 1-31-1970 *Toledo Blade* article said: “Mr. Leonard was listed as the only stockholder of Park Forest Development, Inc., which operates the county's 104-acre landfill, in a report demanded by county commissioners disclosing the firm's ownership. Mr. Leonard, also known as Chalky Red, told the *Blade* in October that he bought out Joseph Barbara, Jr., of Detroit, as a partner for $50,000. About three months after Barbara was indicted on charges of extortion and rape. Barbara was identified as a key underworld figure in Detroit in U.S. Senate committee testimony in 1963.”

The following article appeared in the *Toledo Blade* on 2-9-1970: “County To Cancel Pact For King Road Landfill – Officials Hope To Buy Equipment Now Used By Private Operating Firm – County commissioners today voted unanimously to terminate their contract with Park Forest Development, Inc., private operators of a county-owned King Road landfill. In a letter written by Commissioner Gernheuser to Harry Leonard, owner of the firm, the commissioners said the action is no reflection on what “we consider the best landfill operation in the state.” “We believe it to be in the best interest of everyone for the county to assume operation,” commissioners stated in the letter. Park Forest was cited last week by the county health sanitarian for violation of state health regulations at the landfill. The county's purchase offer will be based on appraisals of the equipment and other improvements at the site, commissioners said. No financing arrangement by the county has been decided upon. Mr. Gernheuser noted that to take over the operation immediately, the county will have to purchase at fair market value the heavy equipment, buildings, scale and other improvements on the 104-acre site. Raymond Hall, county sanitary engineer, will make arrangements for immediate takeover of the operation, Mr. Gernheuser said. The letter was signed by Commissioners William Gernheuser, Sol Wittenberg and James Holzemer. City Manager Gross, when informed of the county takeover, said the city of Toledo is interested in discussing again using the King Road landfill. City trucks were prohibited by Park Forest from dumping at the county site last August because Toledo was $8,000 in arrears on a contract with the firm. City officials said they could not contact the landfill manager to formulate a contract. Subsequently, the city began dumping at other sites, a move that significantly cut revenue at King Road. The *Blade* revealed in April that Park Forest was an extension of Detroit hauling operations controlled by Joseph Barbara, Jr., 32, of Fraser, Mich., and his father-in-law Peter Vitale, 54, of Mount Clemens, Mich. Barbara currently is serving a 7 to 20 year sentence for extortion and a charge of rape is pending against him. The commissioners had signed the contract with Park Forest to operate the landfill in May, 1967. They said that the land would be graded, seeded and reclaimed for ball diamonds and a recreational area. Nothing will be paid to Park Forest for the 45 acres of land that they have reclaimed, Mr. Wittenberg said."

According to the minutes of the Sylvania Township Trustees, in 1971, after receiving complaints from nearby residents, they agreed to request that the Lucas County Commissioners place dumpsters at the entrance of the landfill on King Road, so that when they are closed people will not dump in other areas.

In April of 1971 the Sylvania township road superintendent, Emery Meyers, reported that 93 loads of trash had been picked up during their unlimited trash pick-up in the township and delivered to the King Road dump. On 4-22-1971 the road superintendent reported that they were 85% completed in the western portion of the township and had picked up 93 truckloads of junk, consisting of 427 yards, and it cost them $213.50 to dump it at the King Road landfill.

By December of 1971 a report claimed alleged leachate pollution of surrounding wells from the Lucas County landfill on King Road. The Sylvania Township Trustees received a report regarding samples of well water from private homes in the immediate vicinity of the landfill and sent them to the State Department of Health for analysis.

The minutes of the Sylvania Township Zoning Commission dated 12-13-1971 read: "In the presence of Mr. Slotterbeck and attorney, Norman Bischoff, Mr. Rhoades reported that a leakage is coming down the railroad track and can be traced to the King Road landfill. Samples have been made of water in this area. It is recommended that Medusa not start digging until results from the tests are made. Reports should be available from the State by the end of January 1972. Mr. Slotterbeck asked if Medusa could excavate just to remove shrubs and trees. Mr. Sharpless said there should be no digging and added that samples for the tests were taken today. Mr. Rhoades, zoning inspector, indicated this was a serious problem and township needs to know what can be done, it is a chemical condition which needs to be corrected. Mr. Rhoades also said that Medusa understood sand and gravel extraction was a permitted use since they had a copy of the old code for zoning. The new code indicates it is a conditional use; this is why Mr. Slotterbeck did not come in for a permit to extract sand and gravel. Mrs. Sharpless asked if Medusa planned to level property. Mr. Slotterbeck was not aware of the knoll referred to and agreed to level area. Mr. James Billings and Harold Thebeau, Silica Road residents were present and expressed their concern for extraction, flooding and general circumstances."

12-7-1972 – The Sylvania Township trustees approved taking all necessary steps to prohibit the expanded use of the sanitary landfill on King Road, including turning the matter over to the township solicitor for legal advice.

In May of 1973 the King Road landfill, which county commissioners had been saying would be closed in early June, was going to remain open until at least July 1 because the commissioners had not yet found another sanitary landfill site.

On 6-29-1973 it was reported that the landfill would remain open another 45 to 60 days because the county commissioners still had not found another sanitary landfill site.

On 9-6-1973 the Sylvania Township road superintendent told the Sylvania Township Trustees that there could be no unlimited trash pick-up in the township because the King Road landfill was not available to dispose of the trash. Prior to this, each year in the spring, (beginning in 1967) the township offered a once a year trash pick-up where the township road crews would pick up an unlimited amount of trash from each resident in the township. This work was accomplished by the employees of the Sylvania Township Road Department, and the refuse was taken to this King Road landfill which was located off King Road south of Sylvania Avenue.

The 9-12-1973 issue of the *Toledo Blade* said: "Closing of the King Road landfill to commercial haulers by the county commissioners threatens garbage and refuse collection service to more than 6,500 homes and businesses in western Lucas County, haulers said Tuesday. "We've got no place to dump as of today." Ernest Meyer of Shaffer Road near Swanton, said. "With no place to put the stuff, it's hard to say just how we'll be able to pick it up." James Piasecki, of 1417 Albon Rd., Holland, said. County commissioners closed the landfill to commercial haulers; effective Sept. 1, in what they said was a move to keep the landfill open to county residents for another eight months. They said they are looking for another landfill site. . . ."

In October of 1975, for the first time, the Sylvania Township Trustees opened bids for a private company to provide the annual unlimited pick-up of refuse due to the fact that they no longer had access to a landfill. At this time they also changed the pick-up from a spring pick-up to a fall pick-up. By the end of the pick-up in November of 1975 the trustees paid Benton's Village Sanitation Service $10,053 for the unlimited pick-up.

A *Toledo Blade* article dated 12-24-1975 reported that Gary E. Rumpf, who had been laid off by the county commissioners on 11-2-1974, as part of the phasing out of the King Road landfill, where he worked, was ordered reinstated under a court order by Common Pleas Judge Francis Pietrykowski. The judge ordered the action pending a court appeal by the commissioners, who were challenging the 9-24-1975 ruling of the State Personnel Board of Review who ordered the reinstatement.

In March of 1976 Harold Mowery, township road superintendent, was asking the Sylvania Township Trustees what the road crews should do about disposal of dead animals and roadside refuse, leaves, etc., with the closing of the King Road landfill. The trustees suggested that the Board of Health be contacted about the animal situation, and temporary use of the Hageman Road dump, in Toledo, be used until a permanent site can be located. Mr. Mowery noted that an abandoned quarry was considered, but access to it had been denied, and it was against the law to bury the animals found along the roadways.

Even after the landfill closed the county continued to use the property as a trash transfer station until the early 1990s. It was reported that after the landfill closed, trees and plant life began to re-emerge, slowly transforming the old site into a park-like setting. Then a pit was dug to provide dirt to cover up the trash, and the pit was filling with water.

In September of 1984 the Lucas County officials opened bids for building a waterline to the King Road area. It was reported that the county was paying for the 11,000 foot long line to serve the area because some wells had become contaminated by seepage from the former King Road landfill which had closed nearly eight years ago. The county officials also justified the expense for the line, at their expense, to help business expansion in the area. The 10-inch diameter line would be installed along King Road between Central and Sylvania avenues and extend to Trotter, Covert and Deanville roads. Although the line was being built at the county's expense, the tap-in fees were still the responsibility of the property owners.

In November of 1987 the Lucas County Sanitary Engineers and the Lucas County Commissioners hired the Midwest Environmental Consulting, Inc., of 3539 Glendale Avenue, Toledo Ohio to do an Environmental Assessment of the King Road Landfill. Their report preface said: "As environmental issues have reached the forefront of people's minds over the past several years, many questions and concerns developed regarding the environmental condition of old landfills and dumps. Lucas County's King Road landfill is no exception to that trend. In fact, it is evident that local residents and governmental agencies have been concerned with the King Road Landfill, even before its closure in 1976. It is the intent of this report to eliminate, lessen or factualize those concerns. To determine if environmental problems exist at the King Road Landfill, it was decided to initially conduct a thorough review of all available information and correlate that information with applicable standards. Collectively, available information indicates a potential for environmental problems existing at the King Road Landfill. Concerns regarding the landfill's environmental condition are justified. However, insufficient data makes it impossible to quantify the threat to the environment. Available information indicates the primary actions which lead to degradation of the ground and surface waters included the fact that the landfill was improperly sited according to today's standards. The geological characteristics, shallow ground water supply, local usage of ground water, and ground/surface water inter-relationship indicates the landfill should not have been constructed in this area. Available records indicate that the county commissioners purchased the land on 12-31-1953 from Mr. George E. Moor. The land reportedly was not used previously for residential, agricultural, commercial or industrial purposes. The entire 104 acre area was covered with heavy woods and brush prior to its use as a landfill. Beginning in January, 1954, waste was disposed at the facility under direction of the Lucas County Sanitary Engineer. The facility was operated as a dump by Lucas County until 5-8-1967. Park Forrest

Development, Inc. was then contracted to operate the King Road Landfill for a period of five years. The five year contract was terminated on 3-15-1970 after which Lucas County resumed responsibilities for operation of the facility. After prohibiting use of the landfill by commercial haulers on 8-21-1973, the landfill's operation gradually lessoned. During 1976, Lucas County officially ceased operation of the King Road Landfill. Since 1976, very few modifications of the facility have been undertaken. A transfer station has been operated on the portion of the landfill near the Main gate along King Road since 5-23-1980. Also, since 7-31-1978, the Flying Tigers R.C. Model Club, Inc. have used approximately three acres near the landfill's center for model aircraft recreation."

As the report from Midwest Environmental Consulting, Inc., continued they said: "In January 1954, the Lucas County Sanitary Engineer began operations at the King Road Landfill. On 1-29-1954, the Lucas County Health Commissioner had inspected the facility and found it to be a "very desirable site." No engineered plans or operational permits were obtained or required. A bulldozer was used to clear trees and brush, excavate soil, compact the waste, and apply soil cover. This operation initiated near the gate (which still exists) along King Road at the railroad embankment. The excavation/disposal operation progressed in a westerly-southwesterly direction. Reportedly, the King Road Landfill began as a "well-kept model landfill" and gradually diminished to an open dump by late 1966. The Board of Lucas County Commissioners attempted to improve the operational quality of the landfill on 5-8-1967 by contracting Park Forrest Development, Inc., to take over daily operations. Under Park Forrest Development, Inc., the operations were improved, but concerns regarding the type and quantity of wastes, and alleged connections between the company owners and organized crime, forced the Board of Lucas County Commissioners to terminate the contract. On 5-16-1970, the Lucas County Sanitary Engineer regained responsibility of the landfill's operation. During Park Forrest Development, Inc.'s operation, the majority of remaining unused land was cleared and excavated. Also, a railroad crossing was constructed to gain access to the 25 acre parcel north of the railroad tracks. This permitted excavation of soil for operational uses at the landfill. After 3-16-1970, the Lucas County Sanitary Engineer was again responsible for operation. A considerable number of private haulers, commercial haulers and municipalities continued to dispose waste at the landfill. Throughout the operating life of the King Road Landfill, the waste occasionally caught fire. The fires were contained on-site with assistance from local fire departments. The perimeter drainage ditches are functional, but stagnate waters are present at various locations. Debris, man-made paths, and erosional affects have created dams which impede the flow of surface waters. Based on visual observations, water quality within the draining ditches is questionable. Surface waters are the outlet point and in some stagnet areas are somewhat odorous and have rust-like color characteristics.

The Midwest Environmental Consulting report concluded: that "Aesthetically, the King Road Landfill is very displeasing. The combination of loose rubbish, debris, eroded cover, sporadic vegetation, stagnet water, etc., create a poor image of the area. Many questions relative to the subsurface condition are imposed simply because of what's on the surface. Phase I – 1.) The county should install waterlines for the area surrounding the landfill and require all property owners (residential, commercial and industrial) to tie into the waterlines. This action is justified from realization of the potential contamination problem in the area. 2.) Fill in the few low areas on the top of the landfill where water is ponded. This will prevent excessive surface water infiltration into the landfill. 3) Clean up debris (junk) that has been illegally dumped at the landfill since it has been closed. This dumping mainly occurs on Silica Road near the former Toledo Angola and Western Railroad right-of-way, and the west end of Covert Road. To keep the exterior of the landfill clean, scheduled shocking and services will be required. 4) No dumping signs with the appropriate county law and fine should be posted around the perimeter of the landfill. 5) A one time clean up of the total surface of the landfill should be accomplished. There are such items as old tires and other large debris that have worked their way up the cover material. This task might be accomplished by county welfare labor with county supervision and equipment."

In 1988 the Lucas County Commissioners discovered that the water runoff from the old King Road landfill was carrying contaminants into the Ten Mile Creek. In 1989 the Ohio Attorney General Anthony Celebrezze, Jr., filed a lawsuit to force Lucas County to seal the dump in accordance with requirements set by the Ohio EPA.

A 7-29-1991 article in the *Toledo Blade* said: "Lucas County residents who have been dumping trash at the county's three refuse transfer stations will have to find an alternative method of disposal when the sites are permanently closed on Wednesday. With operating funds running out, county commissioners have voted to close the trash drop-off sites located in Sylvania, Swanton and Jerusalem township. The three sites were opened about 15 years ago when the county closed its King Road landfill in Sylvania Township, said Larry Gamble, county sanitary engineer. The stations, which provide a service for township residents without trash collection, are intended to combat illegal dumping in rural areas."

In 1992 the Lucas County Commissioners entered into a consent agreement with the Ohio Environmental Protection Agency to remediate the King Road landfill property. It had been determined that hazardous materials had been buried there during the time that the county operated it as a dump. By the end 1992 the county had spent more than $2 million to comply with the agreement. They had installed a security fence, monitoring equipment and set up a remedial investigation, and an investigation to determine the source of hazardous waste that may have been dumped in the landfill was starting also. The county commissioners hired David Weinbrecht, a former Toledo police detective, for $2,500 to identify companies that dumped waste at the 104-acre site at 3535 King Road back in the days of operation. Anthony Pizza, Lucas County Prosecutor, said that the county would ask the companies to provide financial assistant for the costly study that the Ohio EPA was demanding. The county was also taking depositions from former King Road dump employees. It was reported that the landfill opened in 1953 and they stopped accepting waste in 1976, and that since then the landfill had been leaking pollutants into the Ten Mile Creek, which flowed into the Ottawa River.

In 1993 the county commissioners routed water runoff from the old landfill to its wastewater treatment plant. A line and pumping station were constructed to link the site between King and Silica roads with an existing line at McCord, and the leachate was transferred to the Maumee River Wastewater Treatment Plant. It was said that if the sewer line could be used as an economic generator, encouraging new businesses to locate along Central between McCord and Centennial Road, it would be about the only good thing that was ever generated by this landfill.

According to an article in the *Toledo Blade* on 3-18-1993 the residents on King Road were reporting that their well water was tasting bad and kept getting worse in the last five years. The Ohio Environmental Protection Agency had ordered last year that the county install a fence and post the warning signs until it determined whether any hazardous waste had contaminated the soil, streams and ground water. The county would also spend another $1 million to build a sewer system to remove polluted liquid called leachate that was leaking from the dump. The EPA had collected water samples on Sept. 10 from seven residential wells within a half-mile of the landfill. EPA records indicated that seven compounds were found in one well, but the agency was evaluating the results. So far metals such as lead, copper and nickel were not showing up and they said that was a good sign.

On 10-19-1993 the Lucas County Commissioners purchased a 12.2 acre site at 3575 Silica Road which backed up to the old King Road landfill. The King Road entrance to the landfill had been closed off and they were using the Silica Road property to gain access to their 104-acre site for their remediation project. This property was also fenced in to keep citizens off that property.

In 1998 the Lucas County prosecutor's office reached an agreement in the U.S. Bankruptcy Court to get about $360,000 from U.S. Reduction for one company's share of the clean-up of the former King Road landfill. The Ohio Environmental Protection Agency had ordered the county commissioners to remediate the 104-acre site, because it was contaminated from industrial and waste dumping over the years that it was in use. The head of the prosecutor's civil litigation section, Steven Papadimos, reported that so far no legal action had been taken against any of the local firms that helped contribute to the contaminated site. The county moved against the U.S. Reduction because one of the firms had filed bankruptcy and the county wanted to make sure they were able to recover something to help toward the clean-up. The county had also located four former employees who worked at the King Road landfill in the 1960s, who testified that one company regularly dumped aluminum dust that contained hazardous elements. The company's creditors, and the court, approved the payment of $362,500 to the county.

Efforts were being made to determine all the materials that may have been dumped at this landfill, through about 60 businesses and agencies that had been identified as having used the dump site. They were trying to determine what percentage each played of the total cost they would have to pay for the clean-up. The county had obtained estimates to remove the toxins from the dump and the highest estimate was $14.6 million.

By January of 1999 the Lucas County Commissioners filed a lawsuit against 59 companies and governmental agencies in an effort to try to recover the costs to clean-up the property. The lawsuit contended that the defendants contributed to the contaminated condition of the site by disposing of, or arranging for the disposal of waste materials. Some of the companies and agencies that were listed in the lawsuit were: Sylvania Township, Allied Chemical Corp., Dana Corp., DeVilbiss, Doehler-Jarvis, Dura Automotive Systems, General Mills, General Motors Corp., Grimes Aerospace, Libbey Glass, R.H. Oberly Co., Inc., Ohio Bell Telephone Company, Rudolph/Libbe, Inc., Owens-Illinois Inc., Acklin Stamping Co., Teledyne Inc. Toledo Blade Co., Toledo Edison, Waste Management of Ohio, University of Toledo, Ohio Department of Transportation, the cities of Toledo, Sylvania and Maumee.

On 1-12-1999 the *Toledo Blade* featured an article by Michael D. Sallah, Blade National Affairs Writer, who reported that the Lucas County Commissioners' lawsuit was seeking additional funds to help clean up the King Road landfill site at 3535 King Road. The article started out by saying: "Joseph Barbara, Jr. was a member of one of America's leading Mafia families, a 200 pound strongman whose rap sheet for extortion, rape, and conspiracy was legendary. His family hosted the first known meeting of Mafia leaders across the nation—a gathering that became the most famous in the annuals of American crime. But the large, round New York native with the booming voice had ties to the Lucas County's underworld—literally. For years, he ran one of the Toledo area's largest waste sites, the King Road landfill in Sylvania Township. And now, decades later, questions are being raised about the role that he played there—and what was dumped there. The secrets of the old landfill and the people who controlled the lucrative waste business are emerging as part of a lawsuit filed by Lucas County Commissioners in federal court in Toledo . . ."

The article also said: ". . . For three years, the firm that ran the dump on behalf of the county was headed by Barbara and legendary Toledo gangster Leonard "Chalky Red" Yaranowsky. And records from that period, as well as how much money was taken in for dumping fees—are nonexistent county officials acknowledged . . ."

The 1-12-1999 *Toledo Blade* article continued and reported: ". . . Not until the real ownership of the company was revealed in a series of *Blade* stories three years later did citizens begin asking questions about the deal. Two years after Barbara's company took over the landfill, he was arrested on extortion and rape charges in Michigan. Because of his problems, he sold the rest of his shares in the company to his partner, Yaranowsky, for $50,000, reports stated. The two men were at the waste site numerous times in the late 1960s, directing traffic and ordering workers. The landfill was one of the busiest in northwest Ohio at the time, taking in between $30,000 and $52,000 a month, county officials estimated at the time . . ."

". . . The three county commissioners at the time, William Gernheuser, Guy Neeper, and Sol Wittenberg, have since died. Also deceased is the county prosecutor who reviewed the contract, Harry Friberg. The commissioners voted 2-1 to let the new company take over the dump, with Mr. Neeper dissenting. He complained at the time that commissioners should have let other companies bid for the job . . ."

Also mentioned the firm, Park Forest Development, was awarded the contract to manage the landfill for the county, but that no bids were ever accepted, they were just given the job and the county at that time did not require that they pay any of the collected fees back to the county. And then the company went out of business in 1971.

By the middle of January of 1999 it was again reported that the landfill was never lined with an impermeable barrier or capped. Over time the pollution got so bad that the private wells were ruined, and the water smelled so bad that surrounding residents could not drink it. The city of Toledo had extended the waterlines to the area, which was paid for by the county, so that the residents who had contaminated wells could hook up to the water. And the county told area residents that there would be a "no well zone" surrounding the old site. They found that high levels of pollutants, the most serious being cancer-causing arsenic was embedded in the soil. In

January of 2001 the *Toledo Blade* dated 1-12-2001 said: "King landfill cap could cost county up to $15 M – It's probably still at least another year away from happening, but Lucas County could end up spending $10 million to $15 million to cap the King Road landfill in Sylvania Township. The county also appears to be proceeding with plans to declare its first "no-well zone" in the immediate area around the dump, which would forbid a dozen or more homes and businesses from drilling private water wells. The action appears necessary because of the presence of numerous chemicals, including cancer-causing arsenic, officials said. . . "

In August of 2004 the *Toledo Blade* was reporting that the Lucas County Commissioners were waiting to hear from the Ohio Environmental Protection Agency about whether their proposal would be accepted to turn part of the former landfill into a park that would include an extension of the University Parks Trail. This article reported that the county had been working with the EPA since it was discovered in 1988, that the water runoff was carrying contaminants into the Ten Mile Creek. One part of an article in the *Toledo Blade* dated 8-15-2004, written by Dale Emch, *Blade* Staff Writer said: ". . .Lance Keiffer, an assistant Lucas County prosecutor working on the project, said the possibility that plants are cleansing the area around the landfill creates an alternative to placing a synthetic cap over the trash and just growing grass. "We want to return at least a portion of this back to a positive use for the people of the county," Mr. Keiffer said while looking over the pond that's part of the site. . . ."

On 7-13-2010 the Lucas County Commissioners purchased an additional 21.48 acres of property at 3750 Silica Road, which connected to their original 104-acre parcel on the north side. This had been the property of the Pioneer Gun Club.

In September of 2012 the State of Ohio Environmental Protection Agency – Division of Environmental Response and Revitalization, submitted a "Decision Document for the Remediation of the King Road Landfill". This document said that the selected remedy chosen from the December 2010 Preferred Plan was possible as a result of the exemption issued by the Director of Ohio EPA on 4-16-2009 from the current construction standards for a solid waste cap. The exemption allowed for an alternative cap. The Plan included a groundwater monitoring system, the collection of hazardous gases which form within the site, an operation & maintenance program, an environmental covenant to limit use of the site, supplemental cover and an evapotranspirative cover, control of the site to eliminate public contact with dangerous areas, permitted beneficial reuse, and the establishment of an administrative "No Well Zone" in conjunction with ensuring that all local receptors are linked to the municipal water supply. All existing measures to control leachate discharge from the site must be retained.

This September 2012 report continued by saying: "The remedy will require the installation of additional soil cover in areas previously identified as having exposed waste or less than 24 inches of soil above the waste. The remedial design for the cover must be approved by Ohio EPA and the cover must pass a post-construction inspection by Ohio EPA. Operation and maintenance of the cover must be provided for 30 years, at a minimum, through the development of an Operation and Maintenance (O&M) Plan, to be approved by Ohio EPA." This document goes on for 58 pages.

AUTO SALVAGE YARDS IN SYLVANIA

Up until about the year 1999 Sylvania Township had quite a few auto salvage yards within the boundaries of its township, each having hundreds, if not thousands of old, wrecked, or junked vehicles stored on their property. These salvage yards, in their peak, can be seen in the various aerial views of Sylvania over the years, especially the 1963 aerial view. The earliest mention of an auto salvage yard was the one located on the west side of Holland-Sylvania Road operated by Gradon Hall. The salvage yards in Sylvania seem to have arrived as follows:

- Gradon Hall Auto Parts – 4300 – 4400 Holland-Sylvania – west side of street - started in later 1930s.
- Central Auto Parts – 6007 W. Central Avenue – started about 1947.
- Monroe Auto Parts / Alexis Auto Parts – 5318-5320 Alexis Road – started about 1948.
- Diller's Auto Parts – 4440 Holland-Sylvania Road - started in 1954.
- Diller's Auto Parts – 7550 Sylvania Avenue – north side – started in 1958.
- Diller's Auto Parts – 7551 Sylvania Avenue - south side - started in 1960.
- Alexis Auto Parts – 8061 Sylvania Avenue – south side – started in 1978.
- A-J's Auto Parts – 7635 Sylvania Avenue – south side – started in 1979.
- King Road Auto Parts – 3845 King Road – west side – started in 1980.

AUTO SALVAGE YARD – GRADON HALL AUTO PARTS

According to the 7-20-1939 *Sylvania Sentinel* Gradon Hall was operating an auto salvage yard on Holland-Sylvania Road as early 1939. The article reported that Otto Herzig was employed at Gradon Hall Auto Parts on Holland-Sylvania Road, two miles south of downtown Sylvania, and was attempting to turn into the drive of the Hall property when he was struck in the rear. Another indication that Mr. Hall was operating an auto salvage yard in Sylvania Township was the minutes of the Sylvania Township Volunteer Fire Department which reported that in 1940 Gradon Hall Auto Parts had donated a windshield for the fire pumper.

Real estate records show that Gradon and Millie Hall purchased the following parcels along the west side of Holland-Sylvania Road in the 1930s and through to the 1950s. This is where they lived and operated an auto salvage yard:

Parcel No. 1 – 4421 Holland-Sylvania Road – Assessor No. 30-012-033 purchased on 7-22-1935 by Margaret S. Hall and transferred into the name of Millie I. Hall on 8-12-1936, then sold on 3-18-1952 to M.J. Francill. In 1972 Clarence S. & Patrica Hackney purchased this parcel. This parcel had a large commercial structure on it, which looked like the size of a four car garage, but without bay doors. They used the address 4403 Holland-Sylvania Road as their commercial address.

Parcel No. 2 – 4407 Holland-Sylvania Road – Assessor No. 30-012-032 purchased on 7-22-1935 by Millie I. Hall. Sold on 5-27-1952 to E.H. Stevens and in 1972 sold to Clarence S. and Patricia Hackney. A 1948 Directory shows that Gradon Hall was living on this parcel. This parcel had a one-story home on it with a wing on the north side.

Parcel No. 3 – 4405 Holland-Sylvania Road – Assessor No. 30-012-031 purchased on 11-29-48 by Gradon and Millie Hall. On 3-18-1952 sold to M.J. Francill and in 1990 sold to Sam Hackney. The record shows no structure at the time that the Halls owned this parcel.

Parcel No. 4 – 4403 Holland-Sylvania Road – Assessor No. 30-012-111 purchased on 11-29-48 by Gradon and Millie Hall. On 3-18-1952 sold to M.J. Francill. There was no structure on this parcel when the Halls owned it. A structure was built here by 1965 after Betty Grill purchased the parcel.

Parcel No. 5 – 4401 Holland-Sylvania Road – Assessor No. 30-012-090 purchased on 8-22-1935 by Millie I. Hall, transferred into Gradon and Millie Hall's names on 11-29-1949, and on 9-15-1955 sold to Frank Snider. This was shown as a vacant lot during this time.

NOTE: There was a parcel listed as 4323 Holland-Sylvania Road – Assessor No. 30-012-067 that the Halls did not own here, and a 1948 Directory listed Frank Snider living here. There was a small one-story home on this parcel with a one-car detached garage on the south side rear of the house.

Parcel No. 6 – 4321 Holland-Sylvania Road – Assessor No. 30-012-030 purchased by Gradon Hall on 5-11-1939, and sold on 3-15-1952 to M.J. Francill.

Parcel No. 7 – 4315 Holland-Sylvania Road – Assessor No. 30-012-029 purchased by Gradon & Millie I. Hall on 7-9-1937 and sold to M.J. Francill on 3-18-1952. This property was purchased in 1968 by Sophie Rapp and she had a house moved to this address that once sat on the northeast corner of Holland-Sylvania Road and Sylvania Avenue.

Parcel No. 8 – 4305 Holland-Sylvania Road – Assessor No. 30-012-112 purchased by Gradon Frank and Millie I. Hall on 7-9-1937 and sold on 3-18-1952 to M.J. Francill. There was no structure shown on this property at this time, but in 1964 Roy E. and Dorothy J. Brashear purchased this parcel and a home was constructed here.

So, the earliest piece of property here in the 4300 to 4400 Block of Holland-Sylvania that was purchased by Gradon or Millie Hall was in 1935.

Gradon Hall was born in 1909 and at the 1910 census he was one year old and living at home with his father and mother, Clyde F. and Pearl S. Hall, with siblings Harold R. Hall – 6 years; Lola B. Hall – 5 years; Evelyn Hall – 3 years. They were living on Ayers Avenue in the 7th Ward of Toledo, Ohio.

At the 1920 census Gradon Hall was living with his parents and was listed as 10 years old. They were living in Washington Township, Lucas County, on Southern Blvd. His parents were listed as Clyde Hall – 38 years and Pearl Hall – 34 years. His father was working as a contractor in cement work. He and six other siblings were living in the household.

A 1927 Toledo City Directory listed him living at 717 Page Street in Toledo, Ohio. He was listed as a mechanic.

At the 1930 census he was living on King Road in Sylvania Township with his father, Clyde Hall – 50 years old, and five siblings (Irwin Hall – 18 years; Geraldine – 16 years; Clyde, Jr. – 14 year; Frances – 10 years; Ernest – 8 years). Gradon was listed as 21 years old, single, and working as a laborer at the Medusa Cement Plant. His father, and brother Irwin, were also listed as working at the Medusa Cement Plant.

By 1931 Gradon Hall was married to Millie Whelchel in Grant County, Indiana, and on 4-6-1932 they had their first child while living in Marion, Grant County, Indiana; a daughter they named Dorothy Martell Hall. Her birth certificate shows that at that time Gradon's occupation was listed as a laborer.

By the 1940 census Gradon and Millie Hall were listed living on Holland-Sylvania Road in Sylvania Township and he was 31 years old. His occupation was listed as "junk yard – own business." His wife Millie was 26 years old, and living at home was a daughter, Martell D. Hall – 8 years old; a son Marvin Hall – 5 years old; a daughter Marjorie Hall – 5 years old; a son Kenneth C. Hall – 4 years old; and a daughter Judith C Hall – 9 months old.

By 1952 Gradon and Millie Hall sold all their property here along Holland-Sylvania Road, except the parcel at 4401 Holland-Sylvania, which wasn't sold out of their names until 1955.

Gradon Frank Hall died in 1967 in Delta, Fulton County, Ohio and was buried in Sylvania's Ravine Cemetery. He was 58 years old when he died. His wife Millie died in 2008, at the age of 94 years, while living in Carthage, Panola County, Texas. She was also buried in Ravine Cemetery here in Sylvania, next to her husband.

Gradon Hall's obituary notice appeared in the *Toledo Blade* on 10-18-1967 and said that he died at his home at RD 1, Box 88 A in Delta, Ohio. This obituary said that he was a cement contractor and surviving were his wife Millie; daughters, Mrs. Dorothy Roberts, of Reading, Mich.; Mrs. Margery Paradysz, of San Diego, Calif.; Mrs. June Rushlow, Mrs. Vonetta Jaeger, both of Toledo; sons, Marvin F., of Saramento, Calif.; Kenneth E., of Delta; mother, Mrs. Pearl Mills; sisters, Leola Hall, Mrs. Frances McCartney, Mrs. Ernestine Bloomfield; brothers, Harold R., Irving B., Clyde B., all of Toledo, half-brother, Mark O. Mills, of Tyler, Mich., and 13 grandchildren.

So, it appears that Gradon Hall operated his auto salvage yard here on Holland-Sylvania Road from about 1937 until 1952.

AUTO SALVAGE YARD – CENTRAL AUTO PARTS – 6007 W. CENTRAL AVENUE

Central Auto Parts was located on the south side of Central Avenue, just west of where Holland-Sylvania Road intersects. The address that they used was 6007 W. Central Avenue. There were three parcels here on the south side of Central Avenue, totaling four acres, which were owned by Ida Linver, the wife of Joseph J. Linver, who operated Central Auto Parts here. They seemed to have purchased here as early as 1947.

A 1947-1948 Lucas County Farm Directory listed the following for Joseph Linver: "Joseph Linver (Betty), Washington Twp., #2617 Drummond, Toledo, Phone La-8706 Toledo, (O), Part owner, Wabash Scrap Material Co.; Michael 3, Preston 10 months."

The 1947-1948 Lucas County Farm Directory listing for the south side of Central Avenue, between Holland-Sylvania Road and Marsrow Road shows the following starting at Holland-Sylvania Road and heading west:

SERVICE STATION – (C.S. Schmidt Sohio)
Frankies Shoe Shop
Gilbert DeCort – Box #94-B
Vacant House
GARAGE – (White Star, U.S. 20) Box #198)

This tells us that the Central Auto Parts business had not yet operated here on Central Avenue yet. It was in 1947 that the Linver family purchased property here along Central Avenue.

The parcels that were owned by the Linver family along the south side of Central Avenue, west of Holland-Sylvania Road included:

PARCEL NO. 1 – 2.11 acre parcel – Parcel No. 78-39517 – Assessor No. 30-14-044 – Address known as 5957 W. Central Avenue – in 2017 had a 1.926 acreage balance for this parcel.

10-10-1947 – Ida Linver – 2608 Fulton St. Toledo, Ohio;
9-26-1968 – Mikro Realty Inc., Fostoria Ohio
12-20-1976 – Robert McLoughlin – 60 Chafin Ridge, Columbus, Ohio
1-19-1988 – Robert J. & Elsa B. McLoughlin, - 20803 123rd Dr. Sun City, AR
6-1-2000 – Friendly Ice Cream Corporation, a MA Corp.
6-1-2000 – 6055 West Central Avenue Limited an OH Limited
1-23-2003 – 5957 West Central Avenue Limited, an OH LTD Liability Co.

PARCEL NO. 2 - .89 acre parcel – Parcel No. 78-39511 – Assessor No. 30-14-045 – Address: 6001 W. Central Avenue - 1985 Yark purchased multiple parcels to include 78-39524 and 78-39771 – In 2013 gave up .07 acres for r/w leaving .82 acres – there was a one-story block commercial building on this parcel

10-10-1947 – Ida Linver – 2608 Fulton Street, Toledo, Ohio

2-8-1985 – Charles W. Linver – 3010 W. Central #207, Toledo, Ohio

2-27-1985 – Yark Oldsmobile Inc. an OH Corp. – 6019 W. Central

4-1-2014 – Yark Automotive Group Inc. an Oh Corp.

PARCEL NO. 3 – 1 acre parcel – Parcel No. 78-39524 – Assessor No. 30-14-021 – Address: 6007 W. Central – shows no building as of 1963 – In 2014 gave up .075 acres for R/W leaving .925 acres. This parcel had the Central Auto Parts commercial building on it, which faced Central Avenue

5-27-1937 – Raymond F. Gilmore

10-31-1955 – Ida Linver – 2834 Drummond Road, Toledo, Ohio

2-8-1985 – Charles W. Linver – 3010 W. Central Apt. #207, Toledo, Ohio

2-22-1985 – Yark Oldsmobile Inc. – shows multiple parcel sale see 78-39511 also.

4-1-2014 – Yark Automotive Group Inc. an Oh Corp.

The first available Polk Suburban Directory that listed the addresses and businesses in Sylvania was in 1957 and that directory listed them as follows: "6007 W. Central – Central Auto Parts – auto parts."

On 8-4-1961 Paul A. Dyer, of 3019 Sequoia Road, was issued a zoning permit to build a 60 x 60 foot extension to an existing building on the property at 6007 W. Central Avenue. The building extension was to be one-story, frame and block, and to be used for auto parts sales.

The 1962-1963 Sylvania Directory provided a list of the Automotive Parts businesses in Sylvania, where five businesses were listed. One of those listed was Central Auto Parts at 6007 W. Central Avenue – TU2-3357.

A 1963 aerial view of that corner shows a large parcel on the south side of Central Avenue, west of Holland-Sylvania Road, loaded with vehicles.

A 1969 Sylvania Business and Professional Directory listed the following under businesses: "Central Auto Parts – Automobile Parts – Supplies – New – 6007 W. Central Ave. Toledo 43615 – 841-3364 – Charles Linver, Manager."

The 1971 Sylvania Business Directory listed the following under the heading of Automobile – Parts and Supplies: "Central Auto Parts – 6007 W. Central – 882-2095."

On 2-22-1972 Central Auto Parts requested zoning approval for a new free-standing billboard sign, to be 10 x 25 feet. This request was approved on that same date.

Joseph Linver, the original owner of the Central Auto Parts business, died in January of 1973. His obituary notice appeared in the *Toledo Blade* on 1-20-1973 as follows: "Joseph J. Linver, 74, of 2834 Drummond Rd., died Friday in Toledo Hospital. He founded Central Auto Parts, 35 years ago and was the company president before retiring 7 years ago. He was former treasurer of Meadowbrook Synagogue. Surviving are his wife Ida; son, Charles; daughter, Mrs. Elaine

Silverblatt; sister, Mrs. Ida Gellman; Brothers, Harry, Sol, Louis, Michael, and Samuel Linver. Services will be at 3:30 p.m. Sunday in Zimmerman-Wick Mortuary. The family requests any tributes be in the form of contributions to the Woodley Road Synagogue."

The 1976 Sylvania Area Business and Professions Directory listed the following under Automobile and Supplies: "Central Auto Parts – 6007 W. Central, Toledo 43615 – Charles Linver, Owner 1947 (E) – 841-3364."

The 1978 Sylvania Business and Professional Directory listed the following under Automobile – Parts & Supplies: Central Auto Parts – 6007 W. Central – 841-3364."

According to Lucas County real estate records on 2-8-1985 Ida Linver transferred .89 acres of her property to her son Charles W Linver and then he sold that on 2-27-1985 to Yark Oldsmobile. She also transferred the 1 acre parcel known at 6007 W. Central Avenue, where their block building use located, to her son on 2-8-1985 and he sold it to Yark Oldsmobile on 2-22-1985.

On 4-5-1985 Yark Oldsmobile, Inc. requested a zoning change for the property located at the rear of 6007 and 6009 W. Central Avenue from R-A Residential to C-2 Commercial. Donald J. Yark, Jr. wrote: "If the foregoing zoning change is granted, applicant intends to use the subject property in connection with the applicant's automobile dealership operated on the property abutting the subject property to the west." On 9-19-1985 the Sylvania Township Trustees approved the zoning change request with the condition that the site grading and drainage plan be approved by Lucas County Engineer, as well as landscaping and screening plan be submitted and approved by the Sylvania Township Zoning Commission prior to issuance of building permit or zoning certificate. The property consisted of 3.43 acres and the present use was listed as a vacant fenced lot. (This was the property that Central Auto Parts stored all their salvaged autos for their auto parts business). It was noted that the property that fronted on Central Avenue was already zoned commercially and being used for auto parts sales, and changing this back property to the R-A zoning would make it consistent with its front property, and the surrounding property on the west, east and north. (At this time the Central Auto Parts building was still shown on the front portion of the property and Yark was purchasing and changing the zoning on the rear 3.43 acres). Yark Oldsmobile had already located their dealership to the west, at 6019 W. Central Avenue, by this time, and they reported that they would be using this additional property for parking vehicles, etc., consistent with their existing dealership to the west.

On 5-7-1985 the property owner, listed as Central Auto Parts, requested zoning approval to install a temporary 5 x 5 foot double faced electric sign on their property listed as 6007 W. Central Avenue.

In June of 1985 Jim Yark Olds/AMC requested zoning approval to make alterations to the exterior and interior of the existing 60 x 100 foot building that was used by Central Auto Parts at 6007 W. Central Avenue. Yark would be using the building for their sales and service facility.

The property owner of this property where Central Auto Parts was from 1947 until 1985 was Ida S. Linver. She died in 1998 and her obituary notice reads: "Ida S. Linver, of Pelham Rd., Toledo, died Saturday, September 19, 1998 in the Hospice of Northwest Ohio, Perrysburg, at the age of 92. The widow of Joseph J. Linver, she was the bookkeeper until 1985 for the former Central Auto Parts, a company owned and operated by her late husband and later operated by her son, Charles W. Linver. In her earlier years she had also been employed as an office worker for the former LaSalle and Koch Department Store in downtown Toledo. She was a member of Congregation Etz Chayim and its Sisterhood, and the Friendship Club at Pelham Manor. Surviving are her son, Charles W. (Alice) Linver; grandchildren, Jay (Eva) Linver, Lori Linver, Lynne (Gary) Hager of Beaverton, OR, and Tina Sliverblatt; grant-grandchildren, Emily and Haley; as well as nieces and nephews.

AUTO SALVAGE YARD – MONROE AUTO PARTS/ALEXIS AUTO PARTS – 5318 ALEXIS ROAD

The next auto salvage yard to be established in Sylvania Township was first known as Monroe Auto Parts, but was located on Alexis Road (It may have been on Monroe Street first, but I have not been able to verify that at this time).

According to the 12-1-1949 issue of the *Sylvania Sentinel* the Monroe Auto Parts was located at 5318 Alexis Road at that time. Today in 2017 this would be the property where the Dave White Chevrolet Collision Center is located at 5328 Alexis, and our Sylvania Post office property is at the rear of this parcel. The street named Post Office Way was cut through this property in 1997 after the Dave White subdivision was platted. According to documents the street was built by the U.S. Postal Service.

According to the obituary notice of Louis Shiff, who died in 1992 at the age of 91 years old, he was the co-founder of the Alexis Auto Parts. His son, Myer Shiff, who went by Mike Shiff, was the other co-founder.

Here I will give a little background on the Shiff family, who operated the Alexis Auto Parts here on Alexis from about 1948 until 1978. In 1922 before Louis came to Sylvania the Fostoria Directory listed Louis Shiff living at 523 N. Poplar, and shows his occupation as a junk dealer. In that same directory his brother, Myer Shiff, was listed as the proprietor of the Fostoria Iron & Metal Co. and living at 417 W. North.

At the 1930 census Louis Shiff was still living in Fostoria, Ohio. He was listed as 27 years old, and wife Eva was listed as 31 years old. Their children living at home were listed as Sylvia – 8 years old; Carl – 5 years old; and Myer – 2 years old. Louis' occupation was listed as "dealer – junk." This census shows that both he and his wife arrived in the United States from Russia in 1921.

The 1932 Fostoria, Ohio Directory listed Louis Shiff living in Fostoria and listed as the proprietor of Shiff's Auto Wrecking Co., living at 441 Union Court, and then it listed Shiff's Auto Wrecking Co., Louis Shiff, proprietor, with an address of Rear 440 S. Wood. Louis' brother, Myer Shiff was listed as the proprietor of the Fostoria Iron & Metal Co., and living at 654 N. Poplar.

At the 1940 census Louis Shiff was still living in Fostoria, Ohio. He was listed as 39 years old and born in Russia. He was listed as a laborer at a junk yard. Also living in the household was his wife Eva – 40 years old; daughter Sylvia – 18 years old; son Carl – 14 years old; and son Myer – 11 years old.

Sometime after the 1940 census Louis Shiff and his family moved to Lucas County, and opened up the Monroe Auto Parts in Sylvania Township on Alexis Road. They later changed the name to the Alexis Auto Parts.

On the Ancestry.com website there is a photo of a Myer Shiff in the Napoleon High School Yearbook dated 1945 and a Myer Shiff is pictured in the 1946 Bowling Green University Yearbook.

The property at 5318/5320 Alexis Road is where the Alexis Auto Parts business was located. This parcel consisted of 8 acres by that time and county real estate records show the following information, and the following owners of this parcel over the years as follows:

PARCEL NO. 1 – 5318 a/k/a 5320 Alexis Road – Assessor No. 30-009-013 then changed to 30-009-046 – After annexed to the city the Assessor No. became 45-167-006. The original Parcel No. was 78-13414 when in Township, then changed to 82-09407 when annexed to the City – Legal Description as of 1915: Range 6, Town 9 Section 11, NE 1/4, West ½, S.L. Fuller Subdivision No. 2, **except the East 45.4 foot front by 74.8 foot rear:**

- Unknown date - E.A. Lenderson
- 1897 – George Calkins - NE ¼ of W1/2 of Section 11 – Sub Lot No. 2
- 11-10-1899 – Hannah Felt - NE ¼ of W1/2 of Section 11 – Sub Lot No. 2
- 1-2-1915 Hannah & Samuel H. Felt sold the East 45.4 foot front by 74.8 foot rear, which was a narrow pie-shaped parcel on the west side of the 10 acre parcel, leaving 8 acres, to Close Realty Company to be added to the Fruitland Subdivision.
- 5-21-1928 – Samuel H. Felt - 8 acres in Sub Lot No. 2
- 5-21-1928 – The Ohio Savings Bank & Trust Co., Trustee – 8 acres
- 7-7-1934 – Harry, Frank R. and Chauncey Felt, Myrtle F. Lake, Ruth F. Randall – 8 acres
- 11-22-1948 – Chauncey M. Felt, Jr. – 8 acres
- 6-27-1969 – Ethelyn M. Crego – 8 acres
- 9-1-1978 – Dave White Chevrolet, Inc. an Ohio Corp. – 8 acres (the legal description at this time still includes the "exception" of the East 45.4 ft front by 74.8 ft. rear.

The 1947-1948 Lucas County Farm Directory listed a vacant house at 5318 Alexis Road, then known as State Route No. 568. Real estate records indicate that there was a large two-story house on this property, and a large barn behind the house. Records indicate that originally this property was assigned an assessor number of 30-009-013, which was then later changed to 30-009-046.

In 1948 the eight acre parcel transferred into Chauncey M. Felt, Jr's name, after being in the names of all of Samuel Felt's children since 1934. 1948 was probably about the time that the auto salvage yard was started here. The 1947-1948 Lucas County Farm Directory listed C.M. Felt (Lolella) living on the south side of Alexis Road and listed as follows: "RFD #1 Sylvania,

Sylvania Twp., Route #568, (O), Odd Jobs. Living at home was James 27, Hanna 26, Samuel 29. In 1948 when Chauncey M. Felt, Jr. acquired this property his mailing address was listed as 1314 Shenandoah Road, Toledo.

As mentioned, the auto salvage yard was already in business here in 1949 at 5318 Alexis Road, because of the article in the *Sylvania Sentinel*. While Louis (father) and Myer "Mike" (son) Shiff ran their auto salvage yard here they rented the property from Chauncey M. Felt, Jr., probably starting in 1948, and then in 1969 they rented the use of the property from Ethelyn M. Crego, widow of Elmer Crego, through 1978.

The 1958, 1959, 1960, 1961, 1962, 1963, 1964, 1965, 1966, 1967 and 1968 Polk Suburban Directories listed the following at the address of 5318 Alexis Road: Sandy Trail Kennels; Alexis Auto Parts; Bud S. Clark, with each having a separate phone number listed.

Records show that on 6-8-1959, Myer Shiff, of Alexis Auto Parts, 5318 Alexis, completed an "Application for Zoning Approval" requesting permission to build a 25 x 25 foot frame and stone building to be used as an office and parts building. This application shows that his parcel is 150 feet by 520 feet.

On 5-31-1961 Elmer Crego of 5395 Monroe Street completed an "Application for Zoning Approval" requesting permission to construct a 22 x 30 foot wood frame building to be used as an office at 5318 Alexis Road. (Elmer Crego was renting a portion of this property from the Felt family members at this time. He was a well-known auto dealer in Sylvania Township, operating his business at 5401 Monroe Street at the corner of Vineyard).

The 12-9-1965 *Toledo Blade* featured a small advertisement in the classified ad section which reads: ALEXIS AUTO PARTS – 5318 Alexis – 882-7168.

The 1968 Wyandotte Sylvania High School Yearbook featured an advertisement in the back of the yearbook which reads: "882-7168 – Louis & Mike Shiff – Parts for All Cars – Priced to Please – ALEXIS AUTO PARTS – Free Nationwide "Hot Line" Phone Parts Locator Service – 5318 Alexis Road – Sylvania, Ohio 43560."

In 1969 Ethelyn Crego purchased the 8 acre parcel where Louis and Mike Shiff had been operating their auto salvage yard since before 1949. Ethelyn's husband was Elmer Crego. In 1957 Elmer & Ethelyn Crego had purchased the home at 5216 Alexis, just a little to the east of the salvage yard property. Elmer Crego died in 1966, and in 1969 his widow purchased the property here, while the Shiffs continued to rent the property from her until 1978. According to the transfer card, when Ethelyn Crego purchased the 8 acre parcel in 1969 her mailing address was listed as 4841 Vineyard Road in Sylvania Township. When Mrs. Crego purchased this parcel in 1969 there was still a large two-story home, with a large barn to the rear of the house, on the property, a 26 x 30 wood frame building and a 25 x 25 foot frame and stone building.

The 1969 Sylvania Business and Professional Directory listed: Alexis Auto Parts – 5318 Alexis Road, Sylvania 43560 – 882-7168 (D) Terry Schuette, Mgr. Mike Shiff, Owner – Automotive Parts - Used.

The 1969, 1970, 1971, 1972, 1973, 1974, 1975, 1976, 1977 Polk Suburban Directory listed the following at 5318 Alexis Road: Alexis Auto Parts; and Bud S. Clark. Records for Bud S. Clark indicate that he was living here in the home on this property and died in 1977. His obituary notice said" "Bud S. Clark, 71, of 5318 Alexis Rd., Sylvania, died Sunday in St. Charles Hospital. Mr. Clark was a mechanic six years for A & E Rental Center Co. Prior to that he was a mechanic 29 years for the former Crego Motor Sales. Surviving are his wife, Dorothy, and daughter, Mrs. Marcia Obliske."

The 1971 Sylvania Business Directory listed the following under the heading of Automobile – Parts and Supplies: "Alexis Auto Parts – 5318 Alexis – 882-7168."

In August of 1971 Myer Shiff, brother of Louis Shiff, and uncle of Myer "Mike" Shiff, died while living in Fostoria, Ohio. His obituary notice appeared in the *Toledo Blade* on 8-11-1971 as follows: "MYER SHIFF – Founded Fostoria Scrap Metal Firm – Myer Shiff, 77, a prominent Fostoria businessman and former Toledo resident, died Tuesday in Fostoria City Hospital. Mr. Shiff, a native of Russia, was founder and chairman of the board of the Fostoria Iron & Metal Co., a scrap metal reclamation firm. He immigrated to the United States in 1913 and moved to Toledo in 1917, where he purchased a horse and wagon and entered the scrap metal business. Nine years later he moved to Fostoria and founded the metal processing operation there. He was a director of the Seneca Radio Corp., and a past president of the Seneca County Heart Association. Surviving are his wife, Mary, daughters, Mrs. Yetta Wernick and Mrs. Carolyn Markhoff; sons Harry and Jay, brother Louis of Sylvania, and a step brother Jacob Stein, of Toledo." (His brother Louis named his son Myer Shiff after him).

The 1973 Wyandotte Sylvania High School Yearbook featured the following advertisement in the back of the yearbook: "882-7168 – Louis and Mike Shiff – Parts for All Cars – Priced to Please – ALEXIS AUTO PARTS – Free Nationwide "Hot Line" Phone Parts Locator Service – 5318 Alexis Road – Sylvania, Ohio."

The 1976 Sylvania Area Business and Professions Directory listed the following under Automobile Parts and Supplies – Uses: "Alexis Auto Parts – 5318 Alexis, Sylvania 43560 – Mike Shiff, Owner 1951 (D)

The 1978 Suburban Directory still listed Alexis Auto Parts and Bud S. Clark (Bud's widow may have still been living here) at 5318 Alexis Road, and then by the 1979 Suburban Directory 5318 Alexis Road was listed as vacant through 1983.

This 8-acre parcel had been vacated as an auto salvage yard in 1978 and then the auto salvage yard was moved to the western part of Sylvania Township at that time by the Shiffs.

On 9-1-1978 Dave White Chevrolet Inc., an Ohio Corp., of 5880 Monroe Street, purchased the 8 acre parcel from Ethelyn M. Crego. In 1979 Hugh D. White submitted a petition to the City of Sylvania asking that they annex this property, but now the parcel was listed as having 9.97 acres, instead of the 8 acres. The property was officially annexed from Sylvania Township to the City of Sylvania on 7-21-1980. This property remained vacant from 1980 until 1995 when the Dave White Collision Center was built on the front lot known as 5328 Alexis Road.

While in the preliminary stages of the property's re-development, in November 1995 plans were submitted by Dave White for an auto-body shop at 5328 Alexis Road, on a portion of the subject property. These preliminary plans show that he had originally sectioned off a 5.8 acre parcel for his lot. The "architectural site plan" did not show details of the remainder of the property. Dave White's Collision Center was constructed in 1995.

By 1997 the U.S. Postal Service became interested in purchasing enough acreage to build a new Sylvania Post Office on the rear portion of this property, with plans for a road leading to their property. In May of 1997 the Sylvania Municipal Planning Commission gave final plat approval for the Dave White Subdivision. The minutes stated that "The U.S. Post Office can't buy the property until the plat is recorded and they can't commit to doing the project until they buy the property. The post office will build the road and extend the sewers."

On 7-22-1997 the Amended Plat of the Dave White Subdivision was recorded with the Lucas County Recorder and included five lots on a 9.97 acre parcel.

The 1997 plat established five lots in the Dave White Subdivision as follows:

- Lot No. 1 – 3.329 acres – Parcel No. 82-93365 – Assessor No. 45-167-006
- Lot No. 2 – 1.53 acres – Parcel No. 82-93366 – Assessor No. 45-167-007
- Lot No. 3 - 2.782 acres – Parcel No. 82-93367 – Assessor No. 45-167-008
- Lot No. 4 - .632 acres – Parcel No. 82-93368 – Assessor No. 45-167-009
- Lot A - .017 acres – Parcel No. 82-93369 – Assessor No. 45-167-010

This adds up to 8.29 acres, leaving 1.68 acres for the road to be known as Post Office Way.

I would like to note here that the property went from an 8 acre parcel when Dave White Chevrolet purchased it in 1978, to a 9.97 acre parcel in 1979 when Hugh D. White filed a petition to annex the property from the township to the City of Sylvania. It was probably surveyed and they found the additional acreage in the end. So I wondered why for over 50 years the parcel was listed as just 8 acres, and in digging back further the following was found:

In 1915 Samuel H. and Hannah Felt sold a pie-shaped piece of their then 10 acres to Close Realty Company, leaving 8 acres. Then on 12-7-1915 Close Realty Company added that 2 acre pie-shaped parcel to the rear properties of the Fruitland Farms Subdivision, which the Close Realty Company had established to the west of this property. The legal description of the 2 acre parcel they sold in 1915 was listed as: The NE ¼ of Section 11 in S.L. Fullers Subdivision, the West ½ of Lot 2, the East 45.4 foot front by 74.8 foot rear running the full span of the length of the property. A separate transfer card was never made on this new pie-shaped parcel that was established, so that leads me to believe that Close Realty either purchased the narrow parcel to straighten up the rear lots of their subdivision, or to give them a buffer between their new Fruitland subdivision and the 8 acre parcel. There were no zoning laws in effect at this time. The 1933 ditch map for Section 11 does show the long narrow parcel, separate from the 8 acres, and is the only map I have seen that shows this parcel.

All transfer cards from 1915 through 1978 show the legal description for this 8 acre site as follows: Range 6, Town 9 Section 11, NE 1/4, West ½, S.L. Fuller Subdivision No. 2, **except the East 45.4 foot front by 74.8 foot rear.** The first document I came across that gave that excepted property back to Mr. White was the 1979 annexation map.

Apparently, by 1997, this pie-shaped piece of property was added back to this property, restoring it back to the original 10 acre parcel, or now 9.97 acres, as noted on the annexation documents and the plat approval documents. The extra 1.97 acres comes from that 1915 transfer that the Felts made with the Close Realty Company.

AUTO SALVAGE YARD – ALEXIS AUTO PARTS – 8061 SYLVANIA AVENUE

In 1978 the Alexis Auto Parts business, and auto salvage yard, was moved from 5318 Alexis Road to 8061 Sylvania Avenue by the owners, Louis and Myer "Mike" Shiff. This time, instead of renting the property, they purchased the property that was the old Rauh fertilizer plant property. This new property that Alexis Auto Parts was moving to originally had a very large factory on it where they manufactured lime fertilizers and agricultural lime products. (for additional information on this factory see Volume Five - the chapter on Silica).

The property at 8061 Sylvania Avenue was the second parcel that Mr. Shiff used for his auto salvage business that was started in about 1948 at 5318 Alexis Road. Here are the details of the past and current owners of this second property.

<u>PARCEL NO. 2 – 8061 Sylvania Avenue</u> originally had 10.10 acres and was assigned Assessor No. 30-022-038, but was later reduced down to 9.69 acres. The owners over the years were:

4-28-1904 – James J. Robinson
Unknown date – Willard D. Robinson
3-20-1912 – Lee K. Forsythe
5-8-1913 – Ohio Standard Chemical Co.
1-11-1916 – J.L. Stadler & H Rendering Fertilizer Co.
6-1-1927 – The Stadler Products Company
8-29-1932 – E. Rauh & Sons Fertilizer Co.
12-10-1962 – International Minerals & Chemical Corp.
2-5-1970 – R.H. Oberly Co. Inc. an Ohio Corp.
6-14-1977 – Linda H. Shiff

In 1913 the Ohio Standard Chemical Co. constructed a large fertilizer plant on the ten acre parcel and they manufactured fertilizers here until 1967. In 1970 after the Robert H. Oberly Company purchased the property and factory, he was immediately ordered by the Sylvania Township Trustees to demolish the structure because of complaints of problems on the property. By June of 1970 the fire chief ordered the building to be repaired and all dangerous conditions remedied. By April of 1971 Mr. Oberly requested a permit for warehousing on the property, but township officials ordered that the plant be demolished and debris removed from the property. Township officials received quotes to have the building demolished and carried away, with the lowest quote being $31,000.

But, instead Mr. Oberly asked that he be permitted to allow Surface Combustion to use the building to manufacture equipment used in the disposal of combustion liquid waste. The plant was described at this time as 70-foot high in places, largely wooden structure. By 1972 Mr. Oberly had fenced the entire property, and had finally agreed to tear down the old factory building within the year. It appears that by 1973 the old fertilizer plant was gone. Mr. Oberly continued to own the property until he sold it in 1977 to Linda Shiff, the wife of Myer "Mike" Shiff who requested that he be permitted to use the property as an auto salvage yard.

On 4-21-1977 the Sylvania Township Trustees accepted the recommendation of the Sylvania Township Zoning Commission to approve the request of Mike Shiff to use property located at 8061 Sylvania Avenue as an auto and metal salvage operation. They set the condition that no body hulks shall be stored in front of the rear line of the present office building. It was at this time that the auto parts junk yard was moved from Alexis Road to Sylvania Avenue. The property was transferred from R.H. Oberly Co. Inc. to Linda H. Shiff on 6-14-1977. The total acreage at this time was 10.10 acres.

At the April 1977 zoning meeting Mr. Shiff said he would have a small used car lot along Sylvania Avenue, customer parking near the office building and storage of 500-600 car bodies behind the office. The property was fenced with a 7-8 foot chain link fence and evergreens would be placed along the front line. Mr. Oberly, former owner of the property was to have the property cleaned up within six months. The Board of Zoning Appeals had placed restrictions upon the use; that there would be no shredding, baling or scrap processing done on the site.

The following advertisement appeared in the classified section of the *Toledo Blade* on 9-17-1980: "ALEXIS AUTO PARTS – MOTORS – TRANSMISSIONS – ELECTRICAL AND BODY PARTS – RADIATORS REPAIRED – INSTALLATION AVAILABLE – 882-7168 – 8061 Sylvania near Centennial Rd."

Telephone Directories from 1980 through 2002 show Mike Shiff living at 5316 Fox Run in Sylvania Township. A search of that address shows that Myer and Linda H. Shiff purchased the property in 1973, and the house was constructed on that property in 1973. They owned the property until Linda Sustin Shiff sold it in 2017. Before living here they are found purchasing the home at 4719 Imperial Drive in Toledo in 1965 and they owned that home until they sold it in 1974.

Louis Shiff, father of Myer Shiff, died in June of 1992 and his obituary appeared in the *Toledo Blade* on 6-7-1992 as follows: "Mr. Louis Shiff, age 91 years, formerly of Nantucket Dr., died Friday in his residence at the Darlington House. Widower of Eva Shiff, he was co-founder of the Alexis Auto Parts, a member of Congregation Etz Chayim and its Men's Club. Surviving are his son, Mike Shiff; daughter, Sylvia Turner; 5 grandchildren and 2 great-grandchildren. Graveside services will be held Tuesday at 1 p.m. in Beth Shalom Cemetery, Oregon, OH. Following services friends will be received at the Mike Shiff residence, Fox Run. Tributes referred to the Darlington House, Congregation Etz Chayim or donor's choice. Arrangements by Robert H. Wick Funeral Home, 2426 N. Reynolds Rd;"

On 4-26-2011 the property at 8061 Sylvania Avenue was sold by Linda Sustin Shiff, Trustee, to Rockstar Transportation Inc., using the mailing address of 3793 Silica Road, Sylvania, Ohio. By early 2012 the Alexis Auto Parts property at 8061 Sylvania Avenue was completely cleared of the junk autos and the property was being cleaned up. In 2013 they sold the property for $300,000 to State Route Properties LLC an Ohio Limited. In 2017 the property is occupied by A & J Landscape Center.

AUTO SALVAGE YARD – DILLER'S – HOLLAND-SYLVANIA ROAD

Oliver "Spud" Diller was the next to open up an auto salvage yard in Sylvania Township. About the time that Gradon Hall quit his auto salvage yard across the street, Mr. Diller opened one at 4440 Holland-Sylvania Road in 1954. Sylvania Township zoning records indicate that at that time there were no zoning regulations in place for this portion of the township that would have prohibited this type of business.

According to Lucas County real estate records, on 8-24-1954 Oliver & Lorene Diller purchased the 9.72 acre site on the east side of Holland-Sylvania Road. This location became known as Diller's Auto Parts or later Spud's Auto Parts. As of 1955 the Lucas County records were showing that there was a small structure on the 9.72 acre parcel.

Here's the list of owners of the 9.72 acre parcel according to Lucas County Real Estate records – Assessor No. 30-012-016 – Parcel No. 78-21097 – Originally known as 4430 Holland-Sylvania Road:

8-2-1906 – Emma Henes 47.35 acres
9-2-1916 – Melissa Memminger – 10 acres
8-24-1954 – Oliver & Lorene Diller – 9.72 acres
9-14-1962 – Lorene Diller
2-7-2003 – Yvonne A. Diller, Trustee, et. al
2-7-2003 – Investco Holdings LLC
9-26-2007 – Sylvania Chelsea Place LLC an Ohio Limited
10-1-2015 – Chelsea Garden Apartments LLC a Delaware

In 1956 Oliver Diller purchased the home at 4450 Holland-Sylvania Road, to the north of the salvage yard, which had 6.65 acres, and he and wife Lorene lived here until 1972. The home and rear yard were then fenced off and the back property was used for auto salvage storage also. There was a small house in the front south corner of this parcel, which contained .26 acres. This was split off back in 1947 before the Dillers purchased the two properties here.

Here's the list of owners of this 6.65 acre parcel – Assessor No. 30-012-015 – Parcel No. 78-21071 – There was an old red brick house on this parcel. The address was originally known as 4450 Holland-Sylvania Road:

Unknown Date - Olive Dilley
3-3-1919 – Alsinda Dilley Bartlett
3-7-1919 – Seldon A. Dilley
2-13-1931 – Fernando Woodruff
8-4-1942 – Eliza H. Woodruff
6-28-1945 – Frank Boice & Mabel Boice
6-28-1945 – Millard H. and Hermine E. Badman

NOTE: In 1947 Mr. and Mrs. Badman split off .26 acres fronting on Holland-Sylvania Road, and sold to Harold D. and Betty B. Hall – This parcel had a small home on it using the address of 4444 Holland-Sylvania Road built in 1948. In 1951 they sold to Edwin & Jacqueline Biler who owned the home until 2001.

9-20-1956 – Oliver Diller
9-14-1962 – Lorene Diller
2-7-2003 – Yvonne A. Diller, et. al, Trustees
2-7-2003 – Investco Holdings LLC
9-26-2007 – Sylvania Chelsea Place LLC an Ohio Limited
10-1-2015 – Chelsea Garden Apartments LLC a Delaware

At this point I will give some information on Oliver Diller, the man who started this auto salvage yard here at 4440 Holland-Sylvania Avenue.

In 1934 Oliver Diller, age 17 years, is recorded as marrying Margaret Cooper in Lucas County, Ohio. His father is listed as Chancey Diller and mother listed as Cathryn Kolb.

In 1936 Oliver and Margaret had a son, naming him Robert Wayne Diller. Then two years later they had another son, and named him Lawrence Oliver Diller.

At the 1940 census Oliver and Margaret Diller were living on Rudyard Road in Sylvania Township. This census record shows that he owned his home valued at $300. He attended school through the fourth grade. He was employed as a laborer in sewer work.

Sometime after this census Oliver and Margaret had a daughter and named her Cleo. Margaret and Oliver were divorced before 1947. The date of divorce cannot be determined at this time.

On 2-20-1946 Oliver Diller purchased the home at 5849 Vail Avenue in Washington Township, Lucas County, Ohio, along with two other parcels on Vail Avenue.

I am not sure this is accurate, but Ancestry.com shows Oliver Diller marrying a Mary Jane Lewallen on 12-14-1947, and again his parents are listed as Chancey Diller and Catherine Kolb.

Records then show that on 8-9-1948 Oliver Diller married Viola Wills, both of 5849 Vail Avenue, Toledo Ohio. His parents were listed as Chancey Diller and Catherine Kolb. This document indicates that he was married twice before. Viola Wills' parents were listed as J.W. Pemberton and Ida Akins. She had been married to William Wills. Sometime before 1954 Oliver Diller was divorced from Viola.

According to the 1947-1948-1949 Lucas County Farm Directory Oliver Diller was listed living in RFD #8 Toledo, Washington Township, 5849 Vail Avenue, at this time. He is listed as a Machine Operator at the Chevrolet Co., His children listed at that time were: Robert 12, Larry 9, Cleo 5.

In April of 1952 Oliver Diller is recorded as marrying Lorene Myles in Monroe County, Michigan. His father is listed as Kenneth Diller and mother as Katherine Kolb. His birth place is listed as Rockwood, Ohio. Oliver and Lorene had children but I am unable to verify names and dates at this time.

Military records show that Oliver Diller's son Robert Diller enlisted in the service of the United States on 5-1-1953. He is recorded as serving until 4-30-1956.

It was at this point in 1954 that Oliver and Lorene Diller purchased the 9.72 acres on Holland-Sylvania Road in Sylvania Township and started his auto salvage yard business. Then two years later, in 1956, they purchased the 6 acre parcel and moved into the home to the north of the 9.72 acre parcel.

After Oliver Diller started the auto salvage yard here, surrounding property owners objected to this type of business. The 9-30-1954 *Sylvania Sentinel* said: "Elmer Robinson, Chairman of the Sylvania Board of Trustees, is planning a series of informal meetings among residents of the township east of McCord Road in response to residents' request for zoning in that area, he said. The recent installation of an old auto graveyard on Holland-Sylvania Road inspired the most recent agitation for a zoning program, he added. Property owners in other parts of the township have also voted interest in getting a zoning program on the ballot next May, he said . . ."

By 1956 a zoning resolution had been approved in the township, and according to the 3-28-1957 *Sentinel-Herald*, Mr. Robert Diller, owner of Diller's Auto Parts, 4440 Holland-Sylvania Rd. was served notice of non-conforming use of property and he appeared before the zoning commission to answer to the charges of operating a junk yard on the site which was zoned residential. The area was unzoned when Mr. Diller moved into the area. Mr. Diller was informed that the present zoning permitted uses of buildings and lands which were lawful at the time zoning went into effect, however, any new uses or additions, such as the new sign on the property must conform to the regulations. According to the minutes of the meeting, Mr. Diller became indignant over the board's demands. Mr. Diller was instructed to file a request for zoning change to bring his property into conforming use. Records show that this was not accomplished.

In 1958 Oliver Diller started two more auto salvage yards in Sylvania Township in the 7500 Block of Sylvania Avenue; one on the north side of the street and one on the south side of the street. His two sons, Robert W. and Larry O. Diller, appear to be managing those two yards while Oliver continued to operate the one here on Holland-Sylvania Road.

On 12-22-1958 Oliver Diller of 4450 Holland-Sylvania Road purchased the first of his properties on Sylvania Avenue, west of King Road. This was a 5 acre parcel at 7550 Sylvania Avenue, on the north side of Sylvania Avenue, west of King Road. In 1961 he transferred this parcel into the name of Larry Oliver Diller (his son).This parcel had a one-story home on it.

Next, on 3-11-1960 Robert W. Diller purchased a 10 acre parcel on the south side of Sylvania Avenue from Elson Pemberton. In 1963 this parcel was transferred into Oliver Diller's name.

On 4-11-1960 Oliver Diller purchased a 20.96 acre parcel on the north side of Sylvania Avenue. This property transferred back and forth between Oliver and his wife Lorene until in 1979 it transferred to Larry Oliver Diller.

A 1962 - 1963 Sylvania Telephone Directory listed Bob's Auto Parts at 7550 Sylvania Avenue and Diller Auto Parts at 4440 Holland-Sylvania Road under the heading of Automotive Parts. That same directory on a separate page listed the following under the name of Diller:

- Diller Auto Parts, Salvage auto parts – 4440 Holland-Sylvania – 882-2095.
- Diller, Larry O., Bob's Auto Parts, self-employed (Barbara) Robie 2, Vickie 1, Sandra 1 month –TU2-6156.
- Diller, Oliver, self-employed (Lorene) Marcia 4, Walter 3, Michael 1 month. – 4450 Holland-Sylvania Road – 882-2095.

On 2-4-1963 a zoning permit was issued to Oliver Diller at 4440 Holland-Sylvania Road to move an office building from the rear of the property to the front of the property, along the north side of the 9 acre parcel, along Holland-Sylvania Road.

In 1963 Oliver Diller purchased additional property at 5849 Vail Avenue in Toledo. At this time his home address was listed as 4440 Holland-Sylvania Road. He sold this property on Vail Avenue in 1965.

Then in 1964 Oliver & Larry Oliver Diller (father and son) purchased an additional 77.16 acres on the north side of Sylvania Avenue, to the west of the 20 acre parcel that Oliver had purchased in 1958. On 4-5-1971 the 77.16 acres transferred to Larry Oliver Diller. This property had a large old farmhouse and large barn on it, with other small out-buildings on it. The historical society has photos of the property just before it was all demolished. The transfer card shows the original address as 7550 Sylvania and then changed the address to 7810 Sylvania Avenue. It appears that Larry Diller and his family lived in this home on this 77 acre parcel for many years.

In 1965 Robert W. and Yvonne A. Diller purchased a home at 3014 Gradwohl Road in Sylvania Township.

In 1965 Larry Oliver Diller and his step-mother Lorene Diller purchased a 10 acre parcel at 7731 Sylvania Avenue, on the south side of Sylvania Avenue. This property transferred in 1971 to Lorene Diller, then in 1976 it transferred to Oliver Diller and in 1980 this property transferred to Larry Oliver and Barbara Ann Diller.

In July of 1968 Mrs. Lorene Diller was issued a zoning permit to install a swimming pool in the fenced in area of the home at 4450 Holland-Sylvania Road. Records indicate that Oliver and his wife Lorene were living in this home at this time, just to the north of their auto salvage yard.

The following advertisement appeared in the *Toledo Blade* classified section in 1969: "AT SPUD'S AUTO PARTS – Open 7 days. Two locations to serve you, Angola-Crissey Rd., 865-5755 and Old Diller Auto Parts, 4440 Holland-Sylvania Rd. Managed and owned by Spud's 882-2095. This is not a sale. Year round prices. Alternators $4 - $10, batteries $15, exchange doors $10 and up, third members $8 and up, motors $25 and up, radiators $20 and up. This is an example of our everyday prices. 40 acres of cars!"

A 1971 *Sylvania Business Directory* listed the following under the heading of "Automobile – Parts & Supplies": Diller's Auto Parts – 7550 Sylvania – 882-2095. There was no listing for the auto parts business on Holland-Sylvania in this directory.

On 3-13-1972 Oliver and Lorene Diller purchased the home at 3440 Herr Road in Sylvania Township. They owned this home until 1990. When they purchased the home they were listed living at Rt 2 Box 378, Swanton, Ohio. The transfer card shows that in 1979 the property tax invoices where being sent to 866 Cumberland, South Venice, Florida. At this time Oliver and Lorene Diller continued to own the home at 4450 Holland-Sylvania Road, to the north of their auto salvage yard also.

On 6-26-1978 the Sylvania Township Zoning Inspector inspected the property known as 4440 and 4450 Holland-Sylvania Road and documented the following: "Recent activity found some vehicles being towed to the property. The gates were open and signs erected indicating that the yard was open for business – said property having lost its non-conforming status, (because the business had not operated here for a period of time) and would constitute an illegal operation. A notice of zoning violation was prepared this date along with an inspector's recommendation for correction, said documents mailed with a certificate of mailing and copies of same placed in file."

After a court proceeding at the Sylvania Municipal Court it was determined that Mr. Diller's property here was still considered non-conforming and allowed because he was grandfathered. In a letter from the Lucas County Prosecutor dated 8-29-1978 the Sylvania Township Zoning Inspector, Lloyd Rhoades, was told to not pursue the zoning violation because they could not prove that the auto salvage yard had not operated in two years, and in fact Oliver Diller could prove that he had been operating as a salvage yard continually since he opened in the 1950s.

On 11-11-1984 a fire call was made to Diller Auto Parts at 4440 Holland-Sylvania Road. According to the Sylvania Township Fire Department report they were called to the scene of a fire at 10:44 p.m. and when they arrived a structure was on fire and appeared to be arson. Captain Ralph Stallsworth wrote the following under remarks: "Buildings NW door was ajar upon arrival of the first engine company. Pop machine inside building had door pryed open and a police report was made." After returning to the station at 1:26 a.m. they were again called back to the building at 5:45 a.m. and dumped an additional 3,000 gallons of water on the debris in the building.

On 11-8-1985 Robert W. Diller of 3014 Gradwohl Road completed an application for appeal through the Sylvania Township Board of Zoning Appeals, for the property at 4430 Holland-Sylvania Road, asking permission to repair a concrete block building listed as 26 x 30 feet and located on their property. On the bottom of the application the zoning inspector, Richard J. Downing, wrote the following on 11-8-1985: "According to Lucas County Building Inspection, subject building is more than 60 percent destroyed by fire, therefore, per section 1000.4 page 48 of the Sylvania Township Zoning Resolution, the building is not rebuildable." Mr. Diller was appealing that decision and at the public meeting held on 12-16-1985 a letter was read from the inspector of the Lucas County Building Regulations Department stating that he made an inspection of the fire damage to the garage and found that the block walls and steel supports were damaged. Mr. Diller had his attorney present who convinced the board that the building was not 60 percent damaged and in the end the board granted the permit to re-build the building on the property.

On 2-1-1990 Oliver Diller died. He was the father of Robert and Larry Diller. Oliver was the first "Diller" family member to start an auto salvage yard in Sylvania Township on Holland-Sylvania Road. His obituary notice appeared in the *Toledo Blade* dated 2-2-1990 as follows: "Oliver (Spud) Diller, 75, of Herr Rd., Sylvania, passed away February 1 in Riverside Hospital. He was the owner and operator of Diller's and Bob's Auto Parts for 40 years. He retired in 1978. He was a Navy Veteran of WW II. He is survived by his wife, Lorene; daughters, Mrs. Cleo Kopec. Mrs. Marcia York; sons, Robert, Larry, Wayne, Michael Diller; sister, Ms. Ruby Diller; 25 grandchildren, 35 great-grandchildren. Services will be Monday at 11 a.m. in the Reeb Funeral Home, 5712 N. Main St., Sylvania, OH where visitation will begin after 7 p.m. Saturday. The family requests tributes to the donor's choice or to the American Heart Association."

Robert "Spud" Diller died on 5-8-1997. Mark Zaborney, *Blade* Staff Writer wrote the following in the *Toledo Blade* on 5-9-1997: "Robert "Spud" Diller, the owner of used auto parts businesses for more than 40 years who was known for his private acts of charity, died of a heart attack yesterday in his Sylvania home. He was 61. Mr. Diller, who had diabetes, underwent kidney dialysis three days a week at the St. Vincent Mercy Medical Center dialysis center, Westgate. Yet he still ran Spud's Auto Parts, Crissey and Angola roads, and Diller's Auto Parts, on Holland-Sylvania Road.

On 5-22-1998 a mound of approximately 5,000 tires caught fire at Spud's Auto Parts here on Holland-Sylvania Road which sent a thick cloud of smoke billowing into the air that could be seen as far as Bowling Green, Ohio. The flames from the fire shot 60 feet into the air, and firefighters found a pile of tires that was 20 feet high and 125 feet wide.

In 1999 Diller family members began selling all their property on the north and south side of Sylvania Avenue, where Oliver's sons Robert and Larry had been operating auto salvage yards here since 1958.

In July of 2000 Robert and Lorene Diller, and their attorney Jerome Parker, attended the Sylvania Township Zoning Commission meeting requesting a zoning change from A-4 Rural Residential to R-5 Multi-family for the rear 12.955 acres at 4440 N. Holland-Sylvania Road, and from A-4 Rural Residential to C-2 Highway and General Commercial for the front 3.579 acres at 4440 and 4444 N. Holland-Sylvania Road owned by both Mr. and Mrs. Diller and Jacqueline L. Biler. It was announced at this meeting that Mr. and Mrs. Diller were under contract with Plaza Properties and their President and Chief Operating Officer Mr. Harlan Ruben, a long-time development company that develops up-scale apartments. It was pointed out at this meeting that it had been one of the goals of the "Future Land Use Plan" to eliminate the junk yards in the township. The Sylvania Township Zoning Commission recommended that the zoning change be approved, and then the Sylvania Township Trustees approved the zoning change shortly after, and the property was cleared of the junk vehicles.

So, it appears that the auto salvage business existed here on Holland-Sylvania Road, by the Diller family, until 2000 and was officially transferred and sold to Investco Holdings as of 2-7-2003.

The *Toledo Blade* – Robin Erb, Blade Staff Writer, reported on 8-31-2000: "A mainstay salvage yard along Holland-Sylvania Road will become a gated community and office park by 2002, a developer promises.

"We're talking very high end, first-class apartments," said Harlan Ruben, vice-president of Columbus-based Plaza Properties. Among the features of the 160, stone-motif, one or two-bedroom apartments will be vaulted ceilings, skylights, balconies, patios, fireplaces, and options for individual security systems, he said. Rent most likely will start at $650 monthly for a one-bedroom unit, Mr. Ruben said. An office and retail complex at the front portion of the 3-1/2 acre site will fit into the stone village motif, he said. Details still must be finalized.

The site, about a half-mile north of Sylvania Avenue, is adjacent to the 19-parcel office park, Renaissance Place, being developed by Mercurio Developers, Inc. To the north of the property is Camp Miakonda. . . ." "Meanwhile, the change means a scaling back of a decades-old, family-owned business. Spud's Auto Salvage business had been opened in the 1950s by Oliver Diller and for years was run by his son, Robert "Spud" Diller, and his children. But the founder died years ago. His son died in 1997. Despite a good business, the family has decided to consolidate its operations to its site at Spud's Auto Parts, Crissey and Angola roads. "I hate closing it up," Mr. Diller's widow, Yvonne said. Two sons, a daughter, and a son-in-law now run the businesses, she said. "But it got so busy, and they really need to have a life of their own."

On 1-28-2006 Spud R. Diller died at the age of 48 while living in Swanton, Ohio. His obituary notice appeared in the *Toledo Blade* on 1-30-2006. He was the son of Robert W. and Yvonne A. Diller. His brothers and sisters included: Robert Diller Jr., Kathy Diller-Strub, Wendy Diller-Valdez, Sue Diller-Valdez, Bonnie Diller-Strait, Teresa Diller-Bergquist, Larry Diller and Shawn

Diller. According to the *The Blade* of Toledo dated 1-29-2006 – Vehicle falls, kills the owner of salvage shop" – "The owner of a well-known auto salvage business was killed yesterday when a car fell on him while he was working underneath it, Lucas County Sheriff's Office said. Spud R. Diller, 48, owner of Auggie's Auto Parts, 641 South Crissey Rd, Spencer Township, was removing an axle from a Ford Probe with the front end hoisted up by tow truck when it fell on him just before 5 p.m., sheriff's Detective Mark Woodruff said. Mr. Diller was pronounced dead at the scene at 5:10 p.m., said Steve Kahle, a Lucas County coroner's office investigator. The tow line appeared to have slipped from where it was hooked onto the car, causing it to fall onto Mr. Diller, who was sitting on the ground underneath. The line was not broken, Detective Woodruff said. Mr. Diller of 4292 Fulton County Rd 1-2, Swanton, worked in the car salvage business with his family for years. His grandfather, Oliver Diller, started Spud's Auto Salvage in the 1950s. It later was operated by Spud's father, Robert "Spud" Diller, until his death in 1997. Mr. Diller and his siblings took over and consolidated Spud's Auto Parts and Diller's Auto Parts. The Sylvania Township site, 4440 Holland-Sylvania Rd., closed in 2000."

Today in 2010 the property is occupied by the Chelsea Place apartment complex, using an address of 4430 Holland-Sylvania Road.

AUTO SALVAGE YARD – DILLER'S – NORTH SIDE OF SYLVANIA AVENUE

Another of Diller's Auto Parts was located at 7550 Sylvania Avenue, on the north side of Sylvania Avenue, a little west of King Road, in Sylvania Township. (For a complete history of the Diller family see the history written about their Holland-Sylvania Auto Salvage Yard). In looking over the real estate records, Oliver Diller first purchased five acres of land on the north side of the street, at 7520 Sylvania Avenue, on 12-22-1958. This property had a small one-story home on it.

Then on 4-11-1960 Oliver M. Diller purchased a little over 20 acres to the west of the five acres and started an auto salvage yard here. This property transferred back and forth between Oliver M. Diller and his wife Lorene Diller over the years until on 2-9-1979 the property was transferred to the name of Larry Oliver Diller.

Then on 4-30-1964 Oliver & Larry Oliver Diller (father and son) purchased an additional 77.16 acres on the north side of Sylvania Avenue, to the west of the 20 acre parcel that Oliver had purchased in 1958. On 4-5-1971 the 77.16 acres transferred to Larry Oliver Diller. This property had a large old farmhouse and large barn on it, with other small out-buildings on it. The transfer card shows the original address at 7550 Sylvania and then the address changed to 7810 Sylvania Avenue. It appears that Larry Diller and his family lived in this home on this 77 acre parcel for many years.

Here are the three parcels on the north side of Sylvania Avenue that were purchased by the Diller family, showing the owners over the years:

PARCEL NO. 1 – Parcel No. 78-24824 – Assessor No. 30-021-017 – 5.09 acres – original street address – 7520 Sylvania Avenue – Small one-story home:

1865 - Emeline A. Wadsworth
5-28-1868 – Daniel F. Cook
12-24-1906 - Williams, et al. heirs of D.F. Cook, deceased
12-24-1906 - George M. Deer, et al.
12-21-1908 – Katherine Marsh
12-22-1958 – Oliver Diller
3-14-1961 – Larry Oliver Diller
4-16-1999 – A.R.E.A. Title Agency, Inc.

PARCEL NO. 2 – Parcel No. 78-34844 – Assessor No. 30-021-018 – 20.76 acres – original street address – 7636 Sylvania Avenue - no structure shown on this parcel:

1865 - Emmeline A. Wadsworth
5-28-1868 – Daniel F. Cook
11-19-1906 – H.S.M. Sewell
3-12-1907 – Cook Land Company
8-7-1914 – Maurice Marsh
3-9-1960 – Thomas Marsh, et al
3-9-1960 – Elson Pemberton, et al
4-11-1960 – Oliver M. Diller
9-14-1962 – Lorene Diller, et al
2-10-1962 – Oliver M. Diller, et al
2-17-1967 – Oliver M. Diller
9-22-1976 – Lorene Diller
2-9-1979 – Larry Oliver Diller
4-16-1999 - A.R.E.A. Title Agency, Inc., Trustee
4-10-2003 – Sylvan King Investors Ltd.

PARCEL NO. 3 – Parcel No. 78-24921 – Assessor No. 30-021-019 – 77.16 acres – original address 7816 Sylvania Avenue - Large two-story farm house with large barn:

1860 - Fitch Dewey and wife
1863 – Mark Marsh
1888 - John E. Marsh, Heir of Mark Marsh
1-24-1901 – George M. Marsh
9-7-1943 – Robert L. & Verlie H. Williams
4-9-1951 – Kenneth & Bernice Wistinghausen
4-30-1964 – Oliver Diller and Larry Oliver Diller
4-6-1971 – Larry Oliver Diller
4-16-1999 – A.R.E.A. Title Agency, Inc., Trustee
At this point this 77.16 acre parcel was split up and made part of several different plats.

So Oliver, Robert and Larry Diller operated Diller's Auto Parts here, possibly first on the 5 acre parcel starting in 1958, then added the 20 acre parcel in 1960, and then added the 77 acres in 1964. Property was added on the south side of Sylvania Avenue for additional auto salvage yard space. (See the separate history for the properties purchased by the Dillers on the south side of Sylvania Avenue).

A local newspaper reported in July of 1964 that a Toledo man was arrested for assault with intent to kill Larry Diller of 7550 Sylvania Avenue. Mr. Diller reported to police that he had just returned from checking Diller's Auto Parts next door and he saw a person standing by a car about 15 ft. from his house. The suspect started walking backwards to the rear of the lot and Mr. Diller called for him to stop, and when the man didn't, Mr. Diller fired a bullet into the air. The intruder turned and ran towards the woods located north of the junk yard, with Mr. Diller in pursuit. He caught the suspect and on the way back a fight ensued. The suspect started beating Mr. Diller on the head and then attempted to strangle him. Mr. Diller played 'dead' and the suspect reached for the gun then Mr. Diller hit him, then the suspect beat him up again and again. Mr. Diller was bleeding badly about the head when police arrived. The suspect was later found by officials on King Road in a ditch filled with tall weeds, arrested and taken to the Lucas County jail.

The 10-2-1969 issue of the *Sylvania Herald* newspaper (not to be confused with the *Sylvania Sentinel* newspaper which was also being published at this time) featured a picture of a man nailing up fencing along the property line of Diller's. The article said that the fencing did little to hide the piles and heaps of car bodies stacked up on the property. The caption reads: "Does Diller's Fence Conceal "Junk" – Diller's Auto Parts located on Sylvania Avenue near King has been the subject of much controversy in Sylvania Township because of the unsightly appearance of its grounds. The Lucas County Sheriff's Office issued an order for fencing to be installed on the grounds. Progress is underway and completion is expected in eight days according to Edward Elliott, a Diller employee. Will fencing be sufficient?"

The 1969 Sylvania Business and Professional Directory listed the following: "Bob's Auto Parts – 7550 Sylvania Avenue – Sylvania 43560 – 882-8357 – Bob Diller, Mgr. – Auto Parts and Supplies Used and Rebuilt."

According to a 11-6-1969 article in *The Sylvania Tribune* "Sylvania Township junk yards, including Diller's Auto Parts located on Sylvania Avenue near King were the target of the Lucas County Board of Commissioners during their regular meeting last Thursday. Sol Wittenburg, president of the board of commissioners, emphasized that the junk yards were a real eyesore and that he would like to find a means to get rid of them. A public nuisance law was suggested to tackle the problem. The above photo was taken October 1 when new fencing was being erected at Dillers by order of the Lucas County Sheriff's Department."

The 1971 Sylvania Business Directory listed the following under the heading of Automobile – Parts and Supplies – "Diller's Auto Parts – 7550 Sylvania Avenue – 882-2095."

In 1976 a zoning permit for a conditional use was granted to the Dillers for constructing a storage building for automobile parts at 7550 Sylvania Avenue. The building was a frame one-story building that was 54 feet x 184 feet. The application signed by Larry Diller on 8-26-1976 listed the name of the applicant as Larry Diller of Bob's Auto Parts, 7550 Sylvania Avenue. The existing use was shown as "auto and metal salvage operations" on M-3 Heavy Industrial zoned property. The application was approved with the following conditions: "Erect building 184 ft. x 54 ft. provided fences included at all points between and from building to building according to state code. Off-street parking to be fenced and parking area to be used by customers and not for parking junk cars. Gate could be used between buildings." The drawing for the proposed building was showing a 36 x 40 foot existing building on the property and the new 54 foot by 184 foot Morton building.

The following advertisement appeared in the *Toledo Blade* classified section on 9-17-1980: "BOB'S AUTO PARTS – Parts for old and late model cars, motors, transmissions, rear ends, drive shafts, alternators, starters, brake rotors. We buy junk batteries HIGHEST PRICES PAID FOR JUNK CARS. 7550 Sylvania Ave., Sylvania. 885-2526, 882-7179, 882-8357. Open 6 days 8-6 p.m. Sun 9-5. Buying Gold, Silver, Rings, etc."

According to a 1982 map, Larry Diller owned 97.86 acres of land on the north side of Sylvania Avenue where he and his brother, Robert Diller, operated his auto salvage yard.

On 2-1-1990 Oliver Diller died. He was the father of Robert and Larry Diller. Oliver was the first Diller to start an auto salvage yard in Sylvania Township on Holland-Sylvania Road. His obituary notice appeared in the *Toledo Blade* dated 2-2-1990 as follows: "Oliver (Spud) Diller, 75, of Herr Rd., Sylvania, passed away February 1 in Riverside Hospital. He was the owner and operator of Diller's and Bob's Auto Parts for 40 years. He retired in 1978. He was a Navy Veteran of WW II. He is survived by his wife, Lorene; daughters, Mrs. Cleo Kopec. Mrs. Marcia York; sons, Robert, Larry, Wayne, Michael Diller; sister, Ms. Ruby Diller; 25 grandchildren, 35 great-grandchildren. Service will be Monday at 11 a.m. in the Reeb Funeral Home, 5712 N. Main St., Sylvania, OH where visitation will begin after 7 p.m. Saturday. The family requests tributes to the donor's choice or to the American Heart Association."

The first Polk Suburban Directory that was published, which listed addresses on Sylvania Avenue west of King Road, was the 1997 directory. That directory listed the following at 7550 Sylvania Avenue: "BOB'S AUTO PARTS – motor vehicle parts used – 882-8357 – Larry O. Diller.

Robert "Spud" Diller died on 5-8-1997. Mark Zaborney, *Blade* Staff Writer wrote the following in the *Toledo Blade* on 5-9-1997: "Robert "Spud" Diller, the owner of used auto parts businesses for more than 40 years who was known for his private acts of charity, died of a heart attack yesterday in his Sylvania home. He was 61. Mr. Diller, who had diabetes, underwent kidney dialysis three days a week at the St. Vincent Mercy Medical Center dialysis center, Westgate. Yet he still ran Spud's Auto Parts, Crissey and Angola roads, and Diller's Auto Parts, on Holland-Sylvania Road. He sold used autos as well as used parts. "He went to all the auctions and bought cars," his son, Robert, Jr., said. "He had control of everything. He was the man." He never thought of resting, his daughter, Kathy Strub, said. "He said he's not a whole person without working," she said. His father, the late Oliver Diller, was in the auto parts business—and was nicknamed "Spud." "People just automatically started calling my father 'Spud,'" his daughter said. "My dad and grandpa resembled each other quite a bit." After service in the Marine Corps, Mr. Diller opened his first business at Crissey and Dorr Street. He bought his first used cars on credit from Toledo auto dealerships. About a dozen people worked for him most recently. His sons will run the businesses, son Robert, Jr., said. Mr. Diller, through the business, learned about the hardships of others and he went out of his way to help. When parents couldn't afford toys at Christmas, he would deliver gifts—but only after the children were asleep so they would think the toys were coming from Santa Claus. He'd deliver turkeys at Thanksgiving to families.

He took in young people whose parents had thrown them out of the house "and raised them," his son said. "They worked for him, but he always made sure they got good grades and graduated," he said. "My dad loved everybody. He was a very good man, but don't take his kindness as a weakness. He was a powerful man; he was a bull when he was younger. My dad loved doing anything for anybody, but he wanted people to do better for their lives. Don't just take handouts." Mr. Diller grew up in the neighborhood known as Trilby, near Alexis and Secor roads, and attended Whitmer High School. He was a frequent visitor to Raceway Park, where he once owned a horse. Poker games with friends could last until 6 a.m., but he had to give them up the past year because of his health, his son said.

Still, "his family came first," his daughter said. Robert, Jr. added: "He was good to every one of them."

Surviving are his wife, Yvonne; sons, Spud, Robert, Jr., Larry, and Shawn; daughters, Kathy Strub, Wendy Valdez, Susan Valdez, Bonnie Diller and Teresa Bergquist; brothers, Larry and Wayne; sisters, Cleo Kopec and Marcia Eissa; stepmother, Lorene; 33 grandchildren, and four great-grandchildren. Services will be at 11 a.m., Monday in the Maison-Dardenne Mortuary, Maumee, where the body will be after 6 p.m. tomorrow. The family requests tributes to the American Diabetes Association."

The 1998-1999 Suburban Directory listed the following on the north side of Sylvania Avenue from King Road west to where Silica intersects across the street:

- 7510 Sylvania – Nicholas L. Meisner, Remodeling-Drywall
- 7514 Sylvania – Builders Choice – single family construction
- 7518 Sylvania – Inspirational Book Distributor – book stores
- 7550 Sylvania – Bobs Auto Parts – motor vehicle parts – used – Larry O Diller and Barbara A. Diller.
- 7816 Sylvania – Dorothy Rising
- 7842 Sylvania – Clifford Keeler

In 1999 Sylvania Township officials were given the opportunity to rezone 160 acres at Sylvania Avenue and King Road for a large commercial development to consist of residential and commercial businesses. It was reported that it would eliminate the three auto salvage yards that had been operated at that intersection for more than 40 years by the Diller family. The plans called for a Kroger superstore at the southwest corner of the intersection along with up to 100,000 square feet of other commercial outlets. And the property on the north side of Sylvania Avenue was to include more than 300 housing units of both single-family and apartments, and some additional commercial and office uses east of that. Although trustees listened to more than three hours of opposition to the project from heavy industrial property owners to the west of this property, who said that locating residential properties next to heavy industry was not compatible, the trustees still approved the zoning change. The trustees said that even though the Sylvania Township land use plan recommended that the property be saved for industrial use, they were just happy to see all the junk yards cleaned up.

At the 7-21-1999 Sylvania Township Zoning Commission meeting Mr. Bob Gersten, representing the Sylvan King Investors, stated that most of the salvage yards would be cleared by the end of the year 1999 and the auto salvage yard on the north would be completely cleared by 12-31-2000.

An article in the 9-9-1999 *Toledo Blade* reported: "The ambitious Sylvan King Investors project is moving forward with demolition plans that will allow for a shopping center, housing, and light industrial complex to replace three auto salvage yards at Sylvania Avenue and King Road. A detailed site plan is expected to go to the Lucas County Plan Commission in two weeks. Bob Gersten, one of the lead developers, said several old and mostly abandoned houses in the area known as Deanville at the southwest corner of Sylvania and King will soon be razed. A shopping center, with a 65,000 square-foot Kroger grocery store, will occupy the corner. Mr. Gersten expects the Kroger project to be well under way by late next month. More than 300 single-family homes and apartment units will be northwest of the corner, as will an assisted-living center. "When we were first approached about this project, we figured that it would be next to impossible to clean up that land and make it economically feasible, but as we looked into it, we found that all the junk cars are stored 'dry,' that is all the fluids are drained out in just one or two areas," Mr. Gersten said. "There are a couple of rather small areas that need some clean-up, but it's nowhere near as much as we would have guessed." The cars are not expected to leave the salvage yards in any recognizable condition. They will be crushed and trucked to the scrap recycling plants. Dealing with the tires might be more of a problem; Mr. Gersten estimates the developers will have 700,000 tires to dispose of. He estimated the cleanup would cost $2 million."

According to a 4-12-2000 article in the *Toledo Blade* – Neighbors Section: "If you think the corner of Sylvania Avenue and King Road looks different now, wait a year. Workers have already torn down several old homes and moved hundreds of rusting automobiles from an area southwest of the intersection to make way for a new Kroger Super Store and related retail development. The activity is the first visual indication of the 164-acre single family, multiple-family and commercial/retail development planned for the area by Sylvan King Investors. The plot is located on both sides of Sylvania Avenue, west of King Road. The land previously housed two large automobile salvage yards containing an estimated 35,000 car bodies and in excess of 750,000 used tires. A few older homes, most unoccupied were also on the site . . ."

AUTO SALVAGE YARD – DILLER'S – SOUTH SIDE OF SYLVANIA AVENUE

The third of Diller's auto salvage yards that was located in Sylvania Township was on the south side of Sylvania Avenue, across the street from Diller's Auto Parts.

It was Oliver Diller who first started the auto parts business in Sylvania Township on Holland-Sylvania Road in 1954. It was sons Robert Wayne and Larry Oliver who branched off and continued to run auto parts businesses in Sylvania Township.

The first property that was purchased by a Diller family member on the south side of Sylvania Avenue, between King and Centennial, was on 4-11-1960 when Robert W. Diller of 4450 Holland-Sylvania Road, purchased a ten acre parcel known as 7563 Sylvania Avenue, located on the south side of Sylvania Avenue. There was a large two-story farm house with Chandler Block front porch, located on this property. From the photo it looks like there was a good sized barn behind the house, and a small garage to the east side of the house.

The second piece of property that was purchased on the south side of Sylvania Avenue was on 3-19-1965 when Lawrence Oliver and Lorene Diller (son of Oliver Diller and his step-mother) purchased 10 acres of land, known as 7731 Sylvania Avenue, from Louis C. and Doris G. Steusloff. This property was transferred into Lawrence Oliver & Lorene Diller's names on 2-19-1965 (both listed living at 4450 Holland-Sylvania Road) then transferred into just Lorene Diller's name in 1971, (she living at County Road 3, Swanton, Ohio at that time), then transferred to Oliver Diller's name in 1976 (living at 3440 Herr Road, Sylvania) and then in 1980 transferred into Larry O. and Barbara Ann Diller's name, listed living at 7810 Sylvania Avenue. There was a two-story up-right house on this property, with one-story wing on the property when it was purchased.

The Diller family members purchased the following parcels located on the south side of Sylvania Avenue, which they used for auto salvage storage. This lists the owners of the property before, during and after the Dillers purchased the properties:

PARCEL NO 1 – Parcel No. 78-30251 – Assessor No. 30-022-018 - 10 acres – Address was known as 7635 Sylvania Avenue. This parcel had a large two-story farmhouse, barn and garage on it:

11-18-1913 – Maurice Marsh
3-9-1960 – Thomas Marsh, et al
3-9-1960 – Elson Pemberton et al
4-11-1960 – Robert W. Diller
6-25-1963 – Oliver Diller
2-16-1979 – Sold 1.096 acres to Jack Lenavitt, et al (parcel with house)
7-20-1982 – Sold 1.096 acres to Arnold W. & Georgia Jean Stansley (house)
7-20-1982 – Sold 8.904 acres to Arnold W. & Georgia Jean Stansley
4-20-1990 – Sold 8.904 acres to The John Bond Company

8-25-2000 – A.R.E.A. Title Agency Inc. Trustee

<u>PARCEL NO. 2</u> – Parcel No. 78-30337 – Assessor No. 30-022-016 – 10 acres – Address was known as 7731 Sylvania Avenue – This parcel had a two-story up-right with a one-story wing farmhouse on it:

8-29-1941 – Louis C. & Doris G. Steusloff
3-19-1965 – Lawrence Oliver Diller and Lorene Diller
4-6-1971 – Lorene Diller
9-22-1976 – Oliver M. Diller
8-18-1980 – Larry Oliver and Barbara Ann Diller
4-16-1999 – A.R.E.A. Title Agency, Inc., Trustee

On 4-12-1965 Robert W. and Yvonne A. Diller purchased the home at 3014 Gradwohl Road in Sylvania Township. They owned this home until he died in 1990 and she sold the house in 2000.

Starting in 1972 Larry and Barbara Diller started buying up the lots along Sylvania Avenue that had been platted in the 1940s into the Deanville subdivision. These lots that I checked were the ones that lined along Sylvania Avenue, starting at the corner of King Road and running west. The first two lots they purchased were on 5-17-1972. County real estate records show Larry Oliver and Barbara Ann Diller of 7550 Sylvania Avenue purchasing Lot No. 10 and 11 of the Deanville subdivision, with the addresses of 7559 and 7557 Sylvania Avenue, from Iva Gailes. At this time a one-story home took up both lots.

In 1973 Robert W. and Yvonne Diller purchased a 10 acre parcel at Crissey Road and Angola Road in Springfield Township, Lucas County, Ohio. On this property they operated another of the "Diller Auto Salvage Yards." They owned this property until 2003. The Dillers may have purchased other properties throughout Lucas County, but my focus was on Sylvania Township only.

On 4-13-1976 Larry and Barbara Diller of 7550 Sylvania Avenue purchased Lot No. 7 in the Deanville subdivision having an address of 7637 Sylvania Avenue, from Charles B. Garrett, and a few months later, on 7-23-1976 Anna Oliver sold Lot No. 6 in the Deanville subdivision, having an address of 7531 Sylvania Avenue, to Larry O. and Barbara Diller. Lot No. 6 had a small one-story home on it, and Lot No. 7 had a brick 1-1/2 story home on it that looks like it may have been a commercial building at one time.

On 6-10-1981 Larry Oliver and Barbara Ann Diller purchased the property known as Lot No. 4 in the Deanville subdivision having an address of 7521 Sylvania Avenue, from James Fudge. This lot had small a one-story home on it that looks like an addition was added on the east side using spare wood pieces.

On 8-27-1986 Larry O. and Barbara A. Diller of 7810 Sylvania Avenue purchased Lot No. 8 and Lot No. 9 in the Deanville subdivision, having an address of 7541 and 7547 Sylvania Avenue from Lige Thompson. Lot No. 8 had a small one-story red-brick home on it, and Lot No 9 also had a very small home on it that was sided with asphalt material made to look like bricks.

On 9-2-1987 Larry O. and Barbara A. Diller purchased the property known as Lot No. 3 in the Deanville subdivision having an address of 7513 Sylvania Avenue, from Sarah Kizer. On that same date Larry O. and Barbara Ann Diller of 7810 Sylvania Avenue also purchased Lot No. 5 in the Deanville subdivision having an address of 7627 Sylvania Avenue, from Sarah Kizer. Lot No. 3 had a small one-story home on it with a front porch that was enclosed, and Lot No. 5 was shown as vacant.

So, by 1987 Larry Oliver and Barbara Ann Diller owned Lots 3 through 11 in the Deanville subdivision, all facing the street on the south side of Sylvania Avenue, starting two lots west of King Road. The first two lots (Lots No. 1 and 2) located directly on the southwest corner of Sylvania and King Road had been owned by Solomon & Artenca Carter, then purchased in 1972 by the Gallaghers and then in 1983 sold to Richard Guyton. There is a small one-story home on Lot No. 2 with a one-car garage just to the east of the home, located right at the corner of Sylvania Avenue and King Road.

The first Polk Suburban Directory that was published, which listed addresses on Sylvania Avenue west of King Road, was the 1997 directory. That directory listed only one "auto parts" business west of King, on the south side of the street, and that was "A-J'S AUTO PARTS – scrap waste motor vehicles."

The 1998-1999 Suburban Directory listed the following on the south side of Sylvania Avenue from King Road west to where Silica intersects across the street:

- 7505 Sylvania – Richard Guyton
- 7509 Sylvania – Iola M. Rising
- 7547 Sylvania – Robbie L. Servis
- 7551 Sylvania – James K McGuire and Kimberly C. McGuire
- 7553 Sylvania – A-Js Auto Parts – scrap motor vehicles
- 7651 Sylvania – Jack Booher
- 7755 Sylvania – Innovative Handling & Metal Fab.
- 7811 Sylvania – Kevin J. Anderson
- 7831 Sylvania – William Carroll

In 1999 Sylvania Township officials were given the opportunity to rezone 160 acres at Sylvania Avenue and King Road for a large commercial development to consist of residential and commercial businesses. It was reported that it would eliminate the three auto salvage yards that had been operated at that intersection for more than 40 years by the Diller family. The plans called for a Kroger superstore at the southwest corner of the intersection along with up to 100,000 square feet of other commercial outlets. And the property on the north side of Sylvania Avenue was to include more than 300 housing units of both single-family and apartments, and some additional commercial and office uses east of that. Although trustees listened to more than three hours of opposition to the project from heavy industrial property owners to the west of this property, who said that locating residential properties next to heavy industry was not compatible, the trustees still approved the zoning change. The trustees said that even though the Sylvania Township land use plan recommended that the property be saved for industrial use, they were just happy to see all the junk yards cleaned up.

At the 7-21-1999 Sylvania Township Zoning Commission meeting Mr. Bob Gersten, representing the Sylvan King Investors, stated that most of the salvage yards would be cleared by the end of the year 1999 and the auto salvage yard on the north would be completely cleared by 12-31-2000.

An article in the 9-9-1999 *Toledo Blade* reported that several old and mostly abandoned houses in the area known as Deanville on the southwest corner of King and Sylvania were to be razed soon and a shopping center with 65,000 square feet would be underway soon. This article said that the two auto salvage yards on the south side of Sylvania Avenue, west of King Road, would also be cleared as part of the Kroger development that could contain as much as 100,000 square feet of commercial space in addition to the supermarket.

According to a 4-12-2000 article in the *Toledo Blade* – Neighbors Section: "If you think the corner of Sylvania Avenue and King Road looks different now, wait a year. Workers have already torn down several old homes and moved hundreds of rusting automobiles from an area southwest of the intersection to make way for a new Kroger Super Store and related retail development. The activity is the first visual indication of the 164-acre single family, multiple-family and commercial/retail development planned for the area by Sylvan King Investors. The plot is located on both sides of Sylvania Avenue, west of King Road. The land previously housed two large automobile salvage yards containing an estimated 35,000 car bodies and in excess of 750,000 used tires. A few older homes, most unoccupied were also on the site . . ."

AUTO SALVAGE YARD – A-J'S AUTO PARTS – 7553 SYLVANIA AVENUE

A-J's Auto Parts was located on the south side of Sylvania, just east of where the Diller's operated another one of their auto salvage yards. The parcel was originally a ten acre site with a large two-story catalog home on it, with a large barn to the rear. The original address listed was 7553 Sylvania, then it was changed to 7635 Sylvania Avenue. Here's the information on the parcel where A-J's Auto Parts was established:

PARCEL 1 – PARCEL NO. 78-30251 – ASSESSOR NO, 30-022-018 – 10 ACRES – IN 1990 PARCEL SPLIT – 8.904 ACRES BECAME PARCEL NO. 78-30254 AND ASSESSOR NO: 30-022-086 WHILE THE REMAINING 1.096 ACRE PARCEL KEPT THE ORIGINAL PARCEL NO. AND ASSESSOR NO. AND HAD THE LARGE CATALOG HOME ON IT. HERE'S THE OWNERS OVER THE YEARS:

11-19-1913 – Maurice Marsh
3-9-1960 – Thomas Marsh, et al.
3-9-1960 – Elson Pemberton, et al.

4-11-1960 – Robert W. Diller

6-25-1963 – Oliver Diller

2-16-1979 – Jack M. Lenavitt et al.

7-20-1982 – Arnold W. & Georgia Jean Stansley – 10 acres

3-20-1990 – John Bond Company – 8.904 acres

8-7-1996 – Linn Gorney

3-6-2000 – A.R.E.A. Title Agency Inc.

A May 1975 aerial view of the south side of Sylvania Avenue, west of King, shows two separate auto salvage yards. The first one was on this 10 acre site, and the second one is west of that and was the Diller property. This aerial view shows that an auto salvage yard had already been started on this property while Oliver Diller still owned it. In 1979 Oliver Diller sold this 10 acre parcel to Jack M. Lenavitt, who was the brother-in-law of Arnold Stansley. Then in 1982 Arnold W. & Georgia Jean Stansley purchased the property and owned it until 1990 when they sold to John Bond Company, and split the parcel at that time, separating the house from the back property.

It appears that Arnold Stansley and Jack Lenavitt started operating A-J's Auto Parts in 1979 and A-J probably stood for Arnold and Jack.

While Oliver Diller still owned the back 8 acres, Mr. Stansley requested permission from the Sylvania Township Zoning Appeals Board for a conditional use permit to operate an auto salvage yard on the property known as 7635 Sylvania Avenue, and he was requesting a permit for sand extraction to level to the grade of the road.

So, on 10-22-1979 Arnold W. Stansley was to appear before the Sylvania Township Zoning Appeals Board so they could hear his request to use his property for the storage of salvaged automobiles for resale. A notice of the public hearing was sent to the owner of the property at that time, Oliver Diller. Mr. Diller returned the notice and wrote on the document that "Arnold Stansley has my permission to put in storage and auto salvage and resale – I have moved to Florida and can't be there. Signed – Mr. Oliver Diller."

On 10-16-1979 Mr. Jack M. Lenavitt, Attorney at Law, and Arnold W. Stansley informed the Sylvania Township Zoning Inspector that the public notice that was mailed to the applicant and adjoining property owners was inaccurate and inconsistent with what their zoning application requested. They said that "because of the change which we deem inappropriate and done for political reasons meant to embarrass Richard Stansley, and his campaign, we withdraw our application for sand extraction."

Mr. Lenavitt and Mr. Stansley re-applied to the zoning office of Sylvania Township for a conditional use for the property and the application was submitted to the Lucas County Plan Commission for a recommendation. On 7-25-1980 the Toledo-Lucas County Plan Commission reviewed the request by Arnold W. Stansley and Jack M. Lenavitt and recommended that the Appeals Board approve the conditional use request for the 10 acre parcel. It was noted that the parcel had a single-family home on it, and they approved the request subject to the following conditions: 1) In the event that the Ohio Department of Natural Resources exemption requirements are not complied with, a surface mining permit from the ODNR Bureau of Reclamation shall be required; 2) A solid opaque fence shall be provided along the eastern boundary of the property; 3) A site grading plan shall be submitted to the Lucas County Engineer for review and approval. Regarding the land it was commented that the land was composed of various and sundry sand hills which were well above grade and would prove unsightly if vehicles were placed upon them.

On 8-25-1980 the Sylvania Township Zoning Appeals Board heard the request from Arnold W. Stansley and Jack M. Lenavitt requesting sand extraction to level the property to the grade of the road, to make the land suitable for a salvage yard. At that meeting the appeals board approved the conditional use permit.

In the fall of 1987 the Sylvania Township Zoning Inspector issued a notice of zoning violation to the Stansleys regarding the removal of dirt from the property. At that time they assured the zoning inspector that no more materials would be removed from the property and they would slope the hills and refill the property where necessary to the grade of Sylvania Avenue.

The 1997 Polk Suburban Directory was the first directory to list addresses on Sylvania Avenue, west of King Road. This directory listed the following: 7553 Sylvania - A-J's Auto Parts – scrap waste motor vehicles – 885-4699.

According to Sylvania Township zoning records, in August of 1994, Mr. Arnold Stansley requested that the Sylvania Township Zoning Commission allow the temporary storage of vehicles in an M-3 Heavy Industrial Zoning District as a conditional use. Then in June of 1994 Arnold Stansley withdrew his request to use the property at 7557 Sylvania as a salvage yard, and requested to be able to temporarily store cars involved in accidents awaiting insurance adjustment.

In the meantime, the request had already been forwarded to the plan commission, and in October of 1994 the Toledo-Lucas County Plan Commission returned their recommendation regarding Mr. Stansley's request. They recommended that disabled/inoperable vehicle storage be added to the M-1 and M-3 Industrial classifications as a conditional use requiring board approval. Mr. Stansley had withdrawn his request by this time and therefore did not request board approval.

The 1998-1999 Suburban Directory shows that A-Js Auto Parts at 7553 Sylvania Avenue was the only auto salvage yard on the south side of Sylvania Avenue at that time. Listed as: 7553 Sylvania – A-JS Auto Parts – scrap motor vehicles.

By the 2000 Suburban Directory A-J's was no longer listed on Sylvania Avenue and in fact there was no listing for 7553 Sylvania Avenue at all. There was a listing for 7551 Sylvania Avenue where James K. and Kimberly C. McGuire were listed living.

AUTO SALVAGE YARD – KING ROAD AUTO PARTS (K.R.A.P.) – 3845 KING ROAD

This auto salvage yard was located on the west side of King Road, south of Sylvania Avenue. This operation involved one parcel which was a 20 acre parcel that was just south of where the Deanville subdivision used to be located. There was a large two-story farmhouse on this property, along with a barn and several other small farm structures up until about the year 2000.

The 20 acre parcel where this auto salvage yard was established was known as parcel No. 78-30187 – Assessor No. 30-022-002, and had an address of 3845 King Road. The Lucas County Real Estate records for this property show the following individuals owned the property over the years:

6-23-1865 – Daniel F. Cook
11-19-1906 – Edward W. Heath
11-12-1913 – Edith A. Dean
1921 – Ashley and Clara E. Marsh
4-6-1927 – Clara E. Marsh
4-6-1977 – Sylvania Savings Bank, Trustee
9-26-1980 – Ronald J. Gorney, Trustee
6-28-1983 – The Port Lawrence Title & Trust Co.
11-22-1996 – Joseph P. Sheehy, Trustee
8-9-1999 – DD & D Investment Inc.
9-10-1999 – A.R.E.A. Title Agency, Inc., Trustee

The first to own the property with the home on it was Ashley and Clara (Huber) Marsh. They were married in 1918 in Lucas County, Ohio. They both were born and grew up in Sylvania Township and lived in the Sylvania Avenue and King Road area. Ashley Marsh is listed as a farmer in the 1920 and 1930 census records, and then by the 1940 census he was listed as working as a locomotive fireman at the quarry, working on a W.P.A. project. At the 1940 census Ashley was 45 years old and Clara was 38 years old. Living at home were their children: Richard – 21 years old; Raymond – 18 years old; Edith – 16 years old; Clara – 13 years old.

From 1921 until 1977 this property was used for farming purposes. In 1977 the bank became trustee of the 20 acres that Ashley and Clara Marsh owned, maybe because they still had a mortgage on the property. Ashley Marsh died in 1979 and the bank sold the property in 1980. Clara Marsh died in 1984 and her obituary notice said that she was 82 years old and had formerly lived on King Road. She had been living for 13 years in the Briarfield Nursing Home in Sylvania and was the widow of Ashley Marsh. That means that she had been living in the nursing home since 1971.

In 1980 Ronald J. Gorney purchased this 20 acre parcel from the bank, with plans to use it for an auto salvage business. In reviewing the records of the Sylvania Township Zoning office the earliest record for commercial use of this property, after the Marsh family moved out, was in April of

1979, when Ron J. Gorney of 2330 Broadway Street in Toledo, Ohio requested a conditional use permit to allow an auto and metal salvage operation in the 3800 block of King Road, on a 20 acre parcel in the NE ¼ of the NE ¼ in Section 20. According to Mr. Gorney's letter of intent he said that he intended to operate an auto metal salvage yard on the 20 acre parcel, which he intended to purchase from the Sylvania Savings Bank. He said that he would accumulate automobiles that are classified as worn out, wrecked, or parts thereof are to be dismantled, with salvage of usable parts and resale of new and used auto parts. He also said that he currently owned and operated an auto and metal salvage business in Toledo and that he was well experienced with all phases of this type of enterprise.

The request by Mr. Gorney was denied by the Sylvania Township Zoning Appeals Board and then he appealed their decision through the Lucas County Court of Appeals. On 5-18-1981 the zoning appeals board was forced to grant the request to operate the auto salvage yard here by order of the L.C. Court of Appeals.

A review of various Lucas County records shows that Ronald J. Gorney's name appears on the property deed record for property in Toledo at the corner of Broadway and the Wabash Railway. This record shows that he purchased this property on 10-8-1974, transferred it to Mark S. Gorney on 12-24-1986, and then Mark Gorney sold that property in 2008 to Pheasant Run Development LLC. According to records on *Ancestry.com* Ronald J. Gorney had the following addresses over the years: 1981 – 812 Lorain, Toledo, Ohio; 1984 – 2330 Broadway, Toledo, Ohio; 1987 – 2330 Broadway; 1995 – 9425 Creekside, Toledo, Ohio.

In 1960 Suzanne L. Gorney is shown purchasing a home at 1141 Metcalf Road in Toledo. The current home on this property is shown as being constructed by 1961. Divorce records show that Ronald J. Gorney married Suzanne L. in 1954 and they were divorced in 1970. They had two minor children at that time: Ronald J. Gorney, Jr. and Mark S. Gorney. Property deed records for this home at 1141 Metcalf shows that in 2004 Suzanne L. Gorney-Pack transferred this home into the names of Ronald J. Gorney, Jr. and Mark S. Gorney, with Suzanne L. Gorney-Pack reserving a life-lease on the property.

More details on Ronald J. Gorney, Sr., from *Ancestry.com* included another marriage record in 1979 to Alice Jane Sharrai in Florida, and then a divorce in 1996 from Alice. Those records indicate that they had been married for 17 years.

In 1998 Ron Gorney purchased property in Toledo from the forfeited land properties at Waterworks Drive at Broadway Avenue. The legal description says: River tract 10 & 11 R/W strip South from canal to Wabash RR R/W. This property still remains in Ron Gorney's name as Trustee. His mailing address was listed as 5133 Telegraph Road, Toledo, Ohio. The property record for 5133 Telegraph Road lists the owner as D.D. & D. Investments and the older transfers show that this building was originally owned by Glass Bowl Lanes Inc. and sat on 4.79 acres.

Regarding the property here in Sylvania Township at 3845 King Road, complaints started coming in as of March of 1983 because of many violations: no proper fencing, a mobile home stored on the property in front of the fencing and abandoned vehicles in the parking lot. Mr. Gorney was notified by the zoning inspector, and apparently attempted to clean the operation up at that time, but it appeared to be an on-going problem.

The next zoning request on file at the Sylvania Township Zoning Office for this property was requested by Ron Gorney on 3-30-1987 for U-Pull-It Auto Parts at 3845 King Road, and the installation of a double faced wood pole sign. He also requested to make renovations to the two-story dwelling at this time.

It appears that Ron's son Mark Gorney took over this King Road business in 1990 because another zoning permit on file at the Sylvania Township Zoning office shows that on 6-22-1990, Mark S. Gorney of K.R.A.P. (King Road Auto Parts) requested a zoning permit. On this permit he wanted to renovate the current home on the property by changing windows, making three offices, a storage area, counter and display area, lounge area, guard room, second floor rear deck and stairs on the outside, with a bathroom and kitchen to be used for the auto salvage yard business.

Mark Gorney had married Linn Butler in 1987 and she died in 2006 at the age of 46 years old. Her obituary notice said that she lived in Sylvania and: "She married Mark Gorney and together they owned and operated a salvage business." She is shown survived by her husband, Mark; mother, Edwina; children, Christopher Butler, Jennifer Piasecki and Daniel Gorney.

In July of 1991 the Sylvania Township Zoning Inspector filed a complaint because of the condition of the fence. Some repairs were made at this time, but the fencing along King Road consisted of poles with rusty metal corrugated looking material, which was spray-painted with white paint, and arrows, with the words "parking" running all across the front of the property. Remember?

In July of 1996 the zoning inspector for Sylvania Township issued a zoning complaint to Ms. Linn Gorney of 3845 King Road stating that a semi-trailer without wheels was located in the front yard of the property. Wrecked vehicles were parked in front yard outside of the fence in violation of zoning laws. Charges were filed in court and Linn Gorney appeared in court on 12-5-1996, with agreements to move all vehicles behind the fencing.

Between 1997 and 1999 the zoning office dealt with many complaints regarding signs installed with no permits issued and vehicles again parked outside of the fencing.

By March of 1999 the Sylvania Township Zoning Inspector cited the King Road Auto Parts owners with not having the salvage yard properly screened with a minimum 8 foot fence; signs at the establishment that were not approved by zoning; and all the vehicles along King Road were in plain sight of the public and had to be screened. In October of 1999 the zoning inspector visited the property and took photos. He reported that the entire parking lot was filled with wrecked vehicles and said: "It is difficult to believe that a business that is aware it is going to court because of this violation would blatantly continue to violate the zoning resolution."

All through 1999 this auto salvage business had special events where they would post signs all over the fencing along the road that read: "$25.00 per person – All you can carry – used auto parts." At this event customers were parked all along King Road and complaints were made to the police department because of the mess that it created.

A major fire occurred in the residential home that had been converted over to offices. The fire was suspected to be arson related and was posted by the fire department at that time. The property was found to be loaded with hundreds of old tires, old vehicle parts and hundreds of dismantled old vehicles.

In the later part of 1999 the property was sold to A.R.E.A. Title Agency, Inc., Trustee, and the property was cleaned up at that time. In 2006 this property was annexed from Sylvania Township to the City of Sylvania and today in 2018 this 20 acre parcel is part of a road known as Sylvan Lakes Blvd., which extended from Sylvania Avenue and wraps around the back of the Kroger store and ends up running through to this property and out to King Road.

The top left photo shows the Ashley and Clara (Huber) Marsh home at 3845 King Road in about 1940, while they still owned the 20 acre parcel. The top right photo shows the home in 1999 after the fire. The bottom left shows another side of the house after the fire. The bottom right photo shows what the back portion of this 20 acre parcel looked like at the time of the fire. (Photos taken by Gayleen Gindy).

WEATHER EVENTS

While researching Sylvania's history I came across references that referred to the various extreme weather conditions that occurred over the years, which would have been witnessed by the residents of Sylvania. It has been suggested that Northwest Ohio is located at the eastern tip of "tornado alley." According to one reference, just before midnight on 3-4-1880 a tornado did considerable damage to downtown Toledo and East Toledo, and caused considerable wind damage in the entire Lucas County, Ohio. The Palm Sunday tornado of 1920 actually did hit Sylvania and is discussed further in this book. On 3-19-1948 we had the highest winds ever measured, up to that point, with gusts of 87 miles per hour. On 4-11-1965 a tornado hit in Toledo and 15 were killed and 208 injured.

Regarding research of changes in our weather since we first arrived in the Toledo region the following was discussed in the book titled: *The Changing Toledo Region* – A Naturalist's Point of View by Harold Mayfield – Reprinted 1967: "The most profound change that has occurred in the Toledo region since the coming of civilized man is the drop in water table. It has come about as a result of man-made drainage and laying the land bare by removal of the tree cover. These steps, essential as they were to the opening of this land to agriculture, had far-reaching consequences little dreamed of by the people who toll them. As seen by the naturalist, the draining and clearing of the land has given a western character to the landscape; that is, it has replaced the wet forest and wet prairie with dry fields superficially like the plains of the Southwest. Even the climate may have been altered somewhat by civilization. Under the dense canopy of the continuous forest, with surface water everywhere, the humidity was surely higher and the summer temperatures on sunshiny days were lower than on the dry fields and sunbaked pavements of today. Extremes of temperatures both upward and downward, were probably moderated."

In this chapter I have included the various weather related incidents in Sylvania that have come to my attention during my research in writing this series of books. This may not be a complete list, and is only a list of the weather related incidents that have come to my attention.

THE DROUGHT OF 1838

Northwest Ohio suffered a terrible dry spell in the summer and fall of 1838. It did not rain from Monroe, Michigan to Norwalk, Ohio from July 3rd to October 15th. During this period of time animals, driven by thirst, boldly entered the newly settled downtown area of Sylvania in search of water. Wild animals are said to have collected on the banks of the Ottawa River and approaching the town.

As the summer dragged on the smaller rivers and creeks completely dried up and mature trees died from lack of water.

NOAH C. SCOTT – WEATHER REPORTER

Mr. Scott lived in Sylvania Township from 1872 until he died in 1899. During part of this time Mr. Scott served as a government weather reporter for the township, making monthly reports to the Weather Bureau in Washington D.C. In 1870 the government got involved in keeping records of the weather in various areas of the United States when a joint Congressional resolution required that the Secretary of War start taking meteorological observations at the military stations in the states and territories. They also required that they give notice on the northern Great Lakes and seacoast by telegraph of the approach and force of storms. It was said that this Weather Bureau started keeping track of the weather in this area in 1884.

In 1890 an Act was passed actually creating a Weather Bureau within the Department of Agriculture, and in 1891 this Weather Bureau became responsible for carrying out experiments, and issuing flood warnings to the public. In 1887 Major General Adolphus Greely took over as director of the Weather Bureau and served until 1891. From 1891 until 1895 Professor Mark W. Harrington was the director, and from 1895 until 1913 Professor Willis Luther Moore was named the chief of the Weather Bureau. It was in 1895 that the first daily weather map was published by the Weather Bureau.

The exact dates that Mr. Scott did this work are not known for sure, but according to the biography published in 1895 in the book titled: *Portrait and Biographical Record of City of Toledo and Lucas and Wood Counties, Ohio* Chicago – Chapman Publishing Company – 1895, about Mr. Scott, he was doing this work at that time. This biographical sketch of Noah C. Scott said, in part: "He is Government Weather Reporter for his township, making monthly reports to the Bureau at Washington." Mr. Scott died in 1899. It is not known when Mr. Scott started this work for the Bureau.

The 1895 sketch about Noah C. Scott also said: "Our subject remained with his father until 21 years old, when he left home, and, going to sea, was engaged in the whaling service for five years, cruising in the Indian Ocean. On again becoming a permanent resident of *terra firma*." Family records report that he was paid on a commission basis according to the barrels of oil rendered from the blubber of the whales.

This sketch about Mr. Scott also said: "While on the sea Mr. Scott was enabled to save quite a sum of money, and thus was able to make a good start when ready to invest his earnings. After locating in this county he began running a sawmill, which he operated for two years, then traded it for a farm in Williams County. In 1872 he became a resident of Lucas County, where he purchased 80 acres of land, on which he has resided ever since."

Sylvania records show that in 1875 Noah Scott was involved with the First Methodist Church in Sylvania and was actually serving on the building committee of this church in 1875 when the brick parsonage was constructed on North Main Street. Mr. Scott was also an active member of the Sylvania Masonic Lodge and the Republican Party. He was elected as a School Director in his school district and was a Township Road Supervisor also while living in Sylvania.

Noah had married Helen Britton and they had five children together. In 1873 when they came to Sylvania Township they brought their five children here to live. At the 1880 census Noah and Helen were listed living in Sylvania Township as follows:

Noah C. Scott – 51 years – occupation - farmer;
Helen M. Scott – wife – 41 years old – keeping house;
Lottie E. Scott - daughter - 21 years – occupation – teacher;
Leander W. Scott – son - 19 years – no occupation listed;
Inez Scott – daughter - 17 years - student;
Charlie B. Scott – son - 12 years - student;
Cornelia B. Scott –daughter - 8 years old - student.

According to the 1895 biography their daughter Lottie married Hiram Palen and lived in Fountain City, Indiana; Mary Inez was the wife of Harry Johanning and lived in Toledo; their son Leander was an agent for the Lake Shore Railroad in Detroit, Michigan; and the other son Charles B. was still living at home. It does not mention the whereabouts of their youngest child Cornelia Scott who was born in 1872.

The 1890 census is not available and by the 1900 census Noah had passed away and Helen is found living on Sylvania-Metamora Road in Sylvania Township. She was 61 years old and listed as a widow owning the farm free of mortgage. Her son Charles was living with her as a single man at the age of 36 years old, listed as a farm laborer.

At the 1910 census Helen was 71 years old and living with her was a couple by the name of Elmer and Viola Ducatt, who were operating the 80 acre farm. Helen sold the farm to Fred O. Peak (her son-in-law) on 3-25-1912 and died shortly after in 1912.

This story of Noah C. Scott of Sylvania Township serving for the government as a weather reporter was very interesting to me, and I am sure he reported on many of our weather issues and

I would love to see his records, but I have not been able to locate those as of this date. It is not known who from this area took over the job of reporting the weather after he was gone.

THE UNUSUAL SNOWSTORM OF MAY 21-22, 1883

Spring had already arrived in Sylvania and the yearly crops and flowers were going strong when a snowstorm hit Northwestern Ohio. On the afternoon of 5-21-1883, snow began to fall, and by suppertime the ground was covered with four or five inches of snow. The following entry was made in the diary of a Sylvania person: "This is one of the strangest sights I ever witnessed in all my life. Fruit trees of all kinds in full bloom, wheat knee high, clover nearly the same height, peas and potatoes all up, lilac bushes nearly in full bloom; indeed everything is clothed in green, but covered with a mantle of snow. On the morning of May 22nd we found the ground covered with some 6 or 7 inches; wheat and clover flat on the ground, much field corn was up, and some fields had already been cultivated. That fall we had a hard frost on Sept. 6th."

The following was found written in the *Toledo Blade*. The date of the article is unknown: A sleigh ride in May: I remember very well the snowstorm on 5-21-1883," writes Charles R. Ford of Riga, Michigan. "I was a lad at home on my father's farm at that time and our six acres of corn was high enough to cultivate when the snow fell. I hitched up a horse and sleigh, drove a mile and a half to my girl's house, took her to the home of my uncle, L.R. Ford for dinner and made the round trip over the snow. I am 89 years old and writing without glasses." Mr. Ford resides in a house built in 1892. . . Mrs. C.J. Brower, of Sparta, Wisc. formerly of Pemberville, also remembers the snow of May, 1883."

According to the *Sylvania Sentinel* dated 7-8-1965: "On 5-19-1883 during a historic spring snow storm Reuben W. Borough, the author of the new book, 'Jubilant Crusader' was born over his father's harness shop. Ansted and Borough Proprietors, on Main Street, in Sylvania. His father's skill in harness making was well known in the area for the next 25 years." According to page 117 of Reuben W. Borough's autobiography titled "Jubilant Crusader," he was born on 5-19-1883 in Sylvania, Ohio, the son of Jonas M. and Phoebe M. Borough. The family moved to Samaria, Michigan, when he was a child and then to Marshall, Michigan, where he graduated from high school. His father established a buggy company in Marshall, Michigan called Borough and Blood Buggy Company.

Apparently Mrs. Borough continued to visit Sylvania because a 6-30-1893 issue of the *Sylvania Weekly Times* said: "Mrs. J.M. Borough and daughter of Samaria, Mich., was in this city visiting Mrs. M.E. Vesey this week."

THE WEATHER BUREAU STARTS KEEPING TRACK OF SNOWFALLS

The Weather Bureau started keeping track of heavy snowfalls beginning in 1884, so this snowstorm was the first heavy one recorded in their records. The Toledo area, including Sylvania, received 9.8 inches by the time the snow was done. After that, the next heavy fall was 8.1 inches on 3-21-1888, and then on December 2 and 3rd, 1893, 9.6 inches.

TORNADO HITS NW OHIO – SYLVANIA HIT HARDEST – SEPT. 1887

According to the local newspaper on 9-7-1887 a destructive tornado struck the Northwestern Ohio Insane asylum, located just beyond the Toledo city limits. Buildings were unroofed, chimneys blown down and fences obliterated.

The tornado first struck the tri-state fairgrounds, and then went to the southeast in a track about 100 yards wide and reaching the insane asylum badly injuring the slate roofs of various buildings. The tornado, which was accompanied by hail and lightning, crossed the old line of the Lake Shore railroad between Adrian and Clayton, and proceeded in a southerly direction, crossed the Air Line road. The Air Line junction freight-cars were blown from the track, barns unroofed and much other damage was done.

It was reported that Sylvania, Ohio, received the most disastrous effect of this storm.

THE GREAT SNOWSTORM OF 2-12-1894

This was a serious snowstorm which not only hit Sylvania, but the surrounding communities, including Toledo. Reports said that this was not only bad because of the amount of snow that fell (8 inches) but also because of the high winds that drifted the snow. But they also say that this snowfall was not as deep as the snowfall of February 1900.

THE TREMENDOUS SNOW FALL OF FEBRUARY 1900

According to the *Toledo Blade* dated 2-28-1900, Toledo and the surrounding suburbs were enjoying the heaviest snow storm ever recorded in the annals of the local weather bureau; although they admitted that the weather bureau records of snow fall only went back to 1884. On 2-28-1900 it started snowing at 12:20 a.m., and by 7:00 in the morning, less than 7 hours later, over seven inches had fallen. Then from that time until noon, four more inches had fallen and more fell throughout the day. This snowfall was a shock to the residents because although there was snow forecasted, there was nothing to indicate that the snow would be as heavy as it was.

By noon of 3-1-1900 the snow had finally stopped and 22 inches of snow had fallen, with a possibility of more flurries that night. All streets, railroad routes and community traction routes were impassible and an emergency was called. The entire Sylvania community was crippled by this snowstorm and they were not equipped to clear this amount of snow from the streets.

According to the minutes of Sylvania Village Council and Sylvania Township Trustees, many men were hired to help clear the roads. Some businesses with trucks were employed to haul snow from the streets. Snow was piled up in areas to a height of from six to ten feet. Merchants, coal men, grocers and butchers found it impossible to deliver their goods and business in most lines were practically suspended for a period of a week until everyone could get dug out from this storm. The local newspaper reported that there were very few people out on the streets and school was let out early the first day it hit, and on the second day a few of the students arrived for school, but they were sent home, with a compliment from the principal for the fortitude in braving the snow and gave them the remainder of the day to reach their homes again, on foot, of course. Also at the high school in Sylvania, on Main Street, a force of men were hired to remove the heavy snow from the roof top so that the weight of the snow would not cause damage.

Andrew Reger, Sylvania's local shoe shop owner, reported that once the residents were able to start getting out of their homes and get around that he did a thriving business on "over shoes" and "rubber boots."

Railroad service through Sylvania stopped, which also meant that mail service was also stopped, but according to the reports the mail carriers still delivered what mail they already had, which they said these carriers suffered severely in the blinding blizzard snowstorm.

The *Toledo Blade* on 3-1-1900 reported the following story about one of their reporters: "What's on today? Asked the mathematical report of the city editor this morning. "Take your shovel," was the reply, "and go out and shovel all the snow that has fallen in Toledo, into the square bounded by Jefferson, Huron, Madison and Superior streets. When you complete the job, take your rule and measure the height of your pile. You have as a basis for figuring the fact that at 7 o'clock this morning 20 inches of snow had fallen in Toledo." The mathematical reporter was somewhat staggered, but he set to work cheerfully. He gathered the snow from the 28.6 square miles that are included in the city limits and dumped it into the square as instructed. Before he had got fairly started the small frame houses on Huron street were buried out of sight. Then the Toledo club house, Morton Truck Company's building and Northwestern Natural Gas Company's office and the old residences on Superior Street disappeared from view. Next the reporter was working on a level with the peak of old St. Paul's and soon after he was shoveling snow on the roof of the Secor. He began now to dimly realize the task that had been imposed upon him. As the pile continued to grow, he found himself on a level with the topmost part of the Nasby tower, and a little later was on even terms with the spires of the Cherry street churches. More work, then he made the water works tower appear insignificant. Even then he had made but a small impression on the snow. At noon, a snowball dropped in front of the Blade office and broke, disclosing a note. It was written by the mathematical reporter and contained this interesting information: "I have just finished that assignment, and am so near heaven that I shall remain where I am for an indefinite period. "I made measurements every few feet, and find that I am 10,836 feet above the level of

Superior Street, or over two miles. This block contains 122,880 square feet, being 256 feet on Jefferson and Madison, and 480 feet on Superior and Huron. I am now standing on a mountain that contains 1,331,527,650 cubic feet of snow. How is this for high?"

And the following was said by the oldest inhabitant in Toledo: "For years he has looked with contempt on the younger generation and, when a blizzard or remarkable freak of the weather came, he would remark: "Oh! This is nothing compared to what we had back in the 1860s." Today he is staggered, for he sees his prestige leaving and really puzzles himself to think of a time when it was worse. But he can't. The younger people of today can keep this snow storm in mind and years hence can impose upon their grandchildren in the same way this old-timer did."

LIGHTNING STRIKES AND KILLS BOY IN EARLY 1900

According to an article in the *Sylvania Sentinel* dated 2-9-1939 they mention that lightning struck down in Sylvania and hit the one-room school house known as Ginger Hill. The 1939 article said: "Who remembers way back 35 years ago when lightning struck the Ginger Hill school house and killed Ivan Blalock. Charlie Keeler was a student there at the time and tells us that Ivan had been sent into the entry way for a misdemeanor. During a storm, lightning struck the flag pole, came through the roof and killed the boy as he stood whittling a whistle out of a willow reed. Belle Neidermeyer, another student, was knocked unconscious by the same bolt. Miss Lilly Stone was a teacher there, her brother Jim taught at Centennial and their father Lime Stone was a member of the Board of Education and was also the truant officer. Dr. U.A. Cooke was also a teacher at this school in years gone by."

The Ginger Hill school house did exist, and was located in the Sylvania Township School District No. 6, and was located on the west side of Flanders Road, south of Alexis Road. Using the actual school board minutes of the Sylvania Township School Board of Education it was discovered that the first school that was built on the one acre parcel here in District No. 6 was a brick building in 1883. Then in 1900 that brick schoolhouse was removed and a new wooden school house was built on the same foundation.

At this time I have not been able to verify that the incident really took place. I cannot find a "Blalock" or any variation of that last name who died at that time.

My research findings on this 1939 article included the following:

1. The article was written in 1939 and said that 35 years ago the lightning struck. That means they are saying that it happened in 1904. A review of the minutes of the Sylvania Township Board of Education from 1903 through 1905 mentioned nothing about this incident.
2. I did not find a Blalock family living in Sylvania at the 1900 census, but did find one living in the Village of Sylvania at the 1910 census, taken on 4-26-1910. They are shown renting a home on Monroe Street as follows:

- George Blalock, 45 years old, married 22 years, born in Indiana, employed as a fisherman "on lake."
- Clara Blalock, wife, 43 years, married 22 years, six children born, five children now alive, born in Michigan;
- Hulda Blalock, daughter – 16 years old – not attending school;
- George Blalock, son – 13 years old – attending school;
- Donald Blalock, son – 12 years old – attending school;
- Clara Blalock, daughter – 7 years old – attending school;
- Mary Gillhouse – mother-in-law - 66 years old, widow, six children born, three children now alive, born in Michigan.

3. In the 1939 article it said that Charlie Keeler was a student there at the time. I did find Charley Keeler in the 1900 census living with his parents, Frank and Mary Keeler. He was 9 years old and they were living in the No. 6 school district.

4. It was also mentioned in the 1939 article that Belle Neidermeyer, another student, was knocked unconscious by the same bolt. I did find Isabelle Natemeyer living with her parents, Joseph and Mary Natemeyer in the 1900 census. She was listed as 12 years old and they were also living in the No. 6 school district of Sylvania Township. Records show that she was married in 1914 to Henry Scott and at the 1920 census she was still living in No. 6 school district with her husband and her own three young children.

5. One more clue that the 1939 article gives is the fact that Miss Lilly Stone was a teacher there. But, it did not exactly say that she was the teacher there at the time of the lightning incident. Records do show Lillian Stone hired as a teacher in District No. 6, from the Spring term of the 1901 school year, through the fall term of 1905. Then Florence Cherry was hired for the winter term of 1905 until at the end of 1905, when a petition was filed asking that she be removed as a teacher, and a bitter political feud was happening in the No. 6 school district. Then, as of August of 1906, Katie Coutchure was the teacher in District No. 6. (I did not discover if this big feud had anything to do with the boy being killed by lightning).

6. The 1939 article said that Lilly Stone's "brother Jim taught at Centennial and their father Lime Stone was a member of the Board of Education and was also the truant officer." This information is accurate and can be verified.

7. The article ended by saying: "Dr. U.A. Cooke was also a teacher at this school in years gone by." This cannot be verified and with a complete list of the teachers hired for District No. 6 his name does not appear.

There was one more mention of this lightning strike incident, which appeared in an article written by Kathryn Keller, Sylvania Historian, in the *Sylvania Sentinel* on 5-20-1948. Here's what she said in part of that article regarding this incident: "There was once a brick school on Flanders Road, the Ginger Hill School, which was replaced by a frame structure under rather tragic circumstances. It was spring and a young lad was occupied with a bit of mischief common to boys of that day. He was carving a willow reed whistle. The teacher sent him to the cloakroom for punishment. A storm was brewing and at its height, lightning struck down the flagpole and killed the boy in the cloakroom. From that time there was a crack in the brick wall and it was decided to replace the building with a frame school. This frame school was moved to Alexis Road after it was abandoned and whether it is still in existence we do not know."

I took this 1948 article and researched Mrs. Keller's statements, and found the following:

1. Mrs. Keller is suggesting that the brick school on Flanders Road, known as the Ginger Hill School, was replaced by a frame structure under rather tragic circumstances. So is she saying that the brick schoolhouse was replaced because it was struck by lightning? A review of the minutes of the Sylvania Township Board of Education shows that the brick schoolhouse was replaced in 1900 with a wood frame house. Here are the details:
    *   On 2-19-1900 the school board met to discuss the condition of the school house in District No. 6, because two of the local board members reported that the building was unsafe. A committee of three was appointed to investigate the condition of the schoolhouse and report at the next meeting.
    *   On 2-24-1900 the board met again and the committee submitted their report which said that they examined the building and found the walls in a very bad condition, badly cracked and they believed the walls were not sufficiently tied and in their opinion it was not in a safe condition for school purposes.
    *   On 4-7-1900 the school board held an auction and sold to the highest bidder the old brick school house in District No. 6, except for the foundation. The school building was sold to R.G. Burns for $66.00 and he was given 30 days to remove it from its foundation.
    *   On 4-16-1900 the school board agreed to rent a building from Mr. Charles Gillhouse for school purposes for the spring term of 1900 at $30.00 for three months.
    *   According to the 6-5-1900 minutes of the Sylvania Township Board of Education a new frame school house had to be built in District No. 6 on the present foundation by the end of June 1900. Daniel Coutchure was awarded the bid to build the new wood frame schoolhouse for $899.
2. Going by the above actual records, if what Mrs. Keller said is true, then the lightning struck the schoolhouse before February of 1900, and since she said it was in the spring that the school was struck by lightning then it must have happened in the Spring of 1899 or and Spring before that.

Additional research of this lightning incident included a search of all the local cemeteries looking for Ivan Blalock (or any variation of this name). There were quite a few Blalocks buried in Forest Cemetery in Toledo, Ohio. George and Clara Blalock are on one stone and then their daughter Hazel Irene Blalock is on that same stone who died in 1893. Forest Cemetery records also show a C. Blalock buried here in August of 1893, but it appears that it was Hazel Irene who died in 1893, and the "C" is thought to stand for "child."

I searched Association Cemetery and Ravine Cemetery in Sylvania and found no Blalocks at all. Since any child of Clara Gillhouse Blalock would have been the grandchild of Harvey and Mary Gillhouse, and since they are buried in the VanAuken Cemetery in Whiteford Township, Monroe County, Michigan, I checked that cemetery and did not find a Blalock buried there. I also checked Whiteford Union Cemetery in Lambertville, Monroe County, Michigan and did not find any Blalocks there either, but did find some more Gillhouse family members, who were all related to Clara Gillhouse Blalock, who married George A. Blalock.

There was a William R. and Martha E. Blalock that purchased 20 acres of property in 1886 in Section 12 of Sylvania Township. This property was definitely located in the No. 6 school district. They owned this property until 1896, and at that time moved to Bigelow Street in Toledo. That means that there were Blalocks living in District No. 6 school district from 1886 until 1896. I found a notation in a diary of a Sylvania resident named Aaron B. West. In his diary he made the following note on Wednesday, 2-14-1894: "Sold 250 lbs. of hay to Mr. Blalock of Ginger Hill, to be paid for in a few days." Then he made the following notation on 12-18-1894: "Drove Joe (his horse) to Mr. Blalock's, Ginger Hill, to obtain pay for hay sold him last winter, but found no one at home."

A search on Ancesty.com shows that William R. and Martha E. Robbins Blalock had four children as follows: William O. – born 1861; Ada E. – born 1863; George A. – born 1865; and Etta – born 1872.

In 1886 when William R. Blalock purchased property in Sylvania Township his sons William O. and George A. were still living at home according to the Toledo Directories. The 1887 Toledo Directory shows William R. Blalock still living in Toledo on the northeast corner of Chase and Cincinnati, and this directory no longer lists his sons William O. and George A. living with him. William O. was married in 1885 and George A. was married in 1888.

William O. Blalock married Hattie Lyon in 1885 and they had the following children:

- William Samuel Blalock born in 1886 died 1888
- Roy Percy Blalock born in 1887
- Martha Mabel Blalock born 1888
- Pearl Blalock born 1889 died in 1909
- Myrtle Blalock born 1891
- May Blalock born 1892
- George A. Blalock born 1894
- Charles Robert Blalock born 1896
- Thelma Blalock born 1898

William O. Blalock's wife Hattie died in 1899. William O. Blalock was remarried to a Matilda and he died in 1914. All of William O. Blalock's children lived into adulthood except William Samuel who died when he was two years old.

George Blalock married Clara Gillhouse on 7-28-1888 in Lucas County, Ohio. The recorded birth records show they had the following children:

- Mabel born 1889
- Hazel Irene born 1892
- Hulda born 1894
- George born 1897
- Donald born 1898
- Clara born 1902

All of George A. Blalock's children lived into adulthood except Hazel Irene Blalock who is listed on the headstone of her parents George and Clara Blalock in Forest Cemetery. George A. Blalock is listed living in Toledo until in 1908 when he and Clara purchased property in the Village of Sylvania, and at the 1910 census they were listed living in the Village of Sylvania. The 1910 census shows that Clara Blalock had six children, and by the 1910 census only five were still alive. It was their daughter Hazel Irene Blalock who had already passed away. They had no other children that could have been killed by lightning.

At the 1900 census William R. and Martha Blalock were living in Toledo on Bigelow Avenue. Their son William O. Blalock was found renting a home in Precinct G of Toledo, Ohio at 2633 Maplewood Avenue. He was 39 years old and widowed (his wife Hattie had passed away in 1899). He was employed as a contractor/builder. His children still living at home at this 1900 census included: Roy – 14 years; Martha – 11 years; Pearl – 10 years; Myrtle – 8 years; May – 7 years; George – 5 years; Charles – 4 years; Thelma – 2 years.

William R. and Martha Blalock's son George cannot be located in the 1900 census, but the 1897 through the 1903 Toledo Directories show him as a fisherman living at 3136 Erie Street. The house at 3136 Erie Street is listed as being constructed in 1897 and is believed to have been constructed by George Blalock. He lived here until in 1908 when he and his wife Clara purchased property in the Village of Sylvania.

So, Ivan Blalock, who are you? Were you really killed when you were struck by lightning in the Ginger Hill School? Who were your parents? Why are there no records of your death in any of the school records, or local newspapers?

THE BIG STORM OF THE WINTER OF 1912

This snowstorm started shortly after midnight, and by morning 13 inches of snow fell. Winds blew 48 miles an hour, and then the next day by noon the temperature was 11 degrees. There were drifts 12 feet high in some places. As the day advanced the situation grew worse.

The Toledo & Western Railway that runs through Sylvania called in all workers, as well as any available labor to shovel snow in order to get the car lines running. The newspapers said that the tie ups on the railroad lines handicapped business to a great extent. Delivery and assortment of mail at the local post office was at a standstill. Clerks at the post office had no mail to handle because of the blockade of the trains. It was reported that over 300 men were hired to help shovel the tracks and the winds were so high that as soon as they cleared an area the drifting show blew back.

According to the *Toledo Blade* the first hint of the coming storm was felt about 9 o'clock 2-20-1912, in the form of an occasional gust of wind from the northeast. As the evening advanced the wind steadied and by midnight reached 48 miles an hour. A fine penetrating snow began failing at 10 minutes after midnight and by morning residents found that the fine snow had crept in around their doors, over the window sills and many places thought to be storm-proof. Many residents found the exits of their homes completely blocked by drifts. Telephone service was slow because there weren't enough girls to operate the switchboards, every available man and team were hired to help clear the streets, the interurban railway services were running hours late and the New York Central Railway service were also running hours late.

The *Toledo News Bee* reported on 2-22-1912 that for 30 hours the county shivered in the grasp of the most severe storm in 12 years. The snowfall registered at the weather office was 13 inches, but because of the high winds drifts were brought to a depth of eight or ten feet.

This storm started in central Texas and traveled northeast, reaching the Ohio valley shortly after midnight. In Lucas County they reported a snow fall of a total of 13 inches. Reports said that this storm was the worst since the 2-28-1900 snowstorm when 20 inches of snow fell.

THE SEVERE BLIZZARD OF 1-11-1918

This snowstorm started at about 4 p.m. Friday afternoon, 1-11-1918, and the wind increased and temperature fell rapidly. The reason this was considered one of the severest blizzards was not only the amount of snow that fell, but the temperature. The temperature dropped 39 degrees in 13 hours. On Friday evening, the temperature was 24 above and by Saturday morning at 8 o'clock it was 15 below. The maximum wind velocity was 60 miles per hour and the snowfall by 1-12-1918 was 6.5 inches. In an attempt to clear the snow, deliver the mail and get to work hundreds of citizens were frost bitten. Freight trains and interurban trains were blocked by snow and ice, the coal situation became very serious and the natural gas pressures were low. The deep drifted snow made local delivery practically impossible.

According to local newspapers this blizzard and extreme cold gripped the country from the Rocky Mountains to the Alleghenies and moved on to the Atlantic coast by Sunday, 1-13-1918. Temperatures went down to 20 degrees below zero throughout all of Ohio.

In Toledo and surrounding suburbs the fuel situation rapidly grew serious. Many people were caught unprepared for the severe blizzard and had no coal or only enough to last a day or two. Patrons were told that the streets were so snow blocked that drivers could not get through. People who were dependent on gas for heat found it was so low they were unable to keep warm; some started burning boxes, old furniture and what would they could find. Dealers and industries in the city were not stocked with enough coal to last more than a day or two and the railways reported that they could not move more coal until the storm slowed and the tracks were cleared. They were at an absolute standstill on Saturday, 1-12-1918, and only half the employees were able to report to work.

In Sylvania all schools were closed for the entire week. Buildings were cold and the citizens were notified of this by word of mouth. Every school boy who was large enough was urged to turn out to help dig Sylvania out of its drifts. The downtown Sylvania stores, "particularly those employing girls," all closed.

The Sylvania Township Trustees paid the following individuals in March of 1918 for shoveling snow off the roads during the blizzard:

J.H. Sacker - shoveling snow on road - $6.00
John R. Hattersley - 10 hrs. shoveling snow - $3.00
Earl Box - 10 hrs. shoveling snow on road - $3.00
R. Cory - 10 hrs. shoveling snow on road - $3.00
V.J. Cory - 5 hrs. shoveling snow on road - $1.50
William Cory - 5 hrs. shoveling snow on road - $1.50
William Trettin - 1 hr. shoveling snow - $3.00
David Brown - 10 hrs. shoveling snow on road - $3.00
Walter Brown - 10 hrs. shoveling snow on road - $3.00
I.H. Jacob - 10 hrs. shoveling snow on road - $3.00
John W. Cooper - 10 hrs. team work on roads - $6.00

For many years old-timers of Sylvania told stories about the blizzard of January of 1918. This photo shows the Toledo and Western Railway tracks being cleared of snow, with men standing on the piles of snow along the route, which was as high as the train itself. (Photo owned by the Sylvania Area Historical Society).

TORNADO OF SUNDAY AFTERNOON, 3-28-1920

The 3-29-1920 issue of the *Toledo Blade* reported that a tornado ripped through Sylvania Township on 3-28-1920 (Palm Sunday) and was said to be one of the greatest disasters to hit the Sylvania community. This tornado then continued on a path southwest into Swanton. They said that not a single structure in Swanton, or the territory stretching as far as Delta, six miles away, escaped total destruction. On that same day states as far away as Georgia and Alabama, and as close as Indiana and Illinois, were struck by tornadoes. Lucas County was hit in several areas, but the greatest loss of life and property damage occurred in Raab's Corners and the western portion of Sylvania Township.

It was estimated that 21 people were injured, 50 people were homeless and more than 50 head of cattle were killed from falling debris. Some of the residents of Sylvania Township whose homes and barns were leveled by the tornado included: Daniel Brint, William Brint, D.O. Shull, E.A. Sanderson, Charles Brimacombe, George W. Bamsey, Frank Hahn, Fred Haas, Michael Bowen and Lou Gillett. The Mitchaw church was partly blown down and the Smith Siding general store was totally destroyed. Smith's home and barn were located on Mitchaw Road between Sylvania Avenue and Sylvania-Metamora Road and were also greatly damaged by the tornado. (Michael Smith's barn was reputedly the largest barn in Lucas County at that time. After the tornado, the barn was partially rebuilt to about half the size of the original structure. The Smith house on Mitchaw Road was also rebuilt and is said to still stand today).

The tornado carried homes hundreds of yards, burying people and cattle in debris and removing every fence and telephone pole in the area. Poles and trolley wires fell across the Toledo and Western Railway, putting service at a standstill. Most of the destruction was confined to a one mile-wide swath. Sylvania people and residents of the vicinity spent Sunday evening in relief work, providing food and shelter for the homeless and injured, searching for three reported missing and burying dead cattle. The five doctors of the village of Sylvania were busy all night and until early morning caring for those hurt.

Persons outside at the time that the tornado hit saw what they described as a ball of fire close to the ground, approaching with the roar of a lion.

The *Toledo Blade* referred to the tornado as the severest tornado in northwestern Ohio's history. They said that the death toll in northwestern Ohio was reported to be 19 dead, 100 injured and 50 homeless by the sweeping away of their homes. Telephone and telegraph wires were down in every direction and reports were coming in slowly, but the extent of the damage is shown more severe with every belated message from the affected region extending from Genoa, Ohio to central Illinois. Other areas receiving severe tornado damage on this date included Raab's Corners, Renolett (a small town west of Defiance), Swanton, Bowling Green, Genoa, and Multon.

The tornado was formed in eastern Illinois and zig-zagged a trail of destruction through Indiana. It struck Ohio first at Edgerton, then across Williams, Defiance, Henry, Fulton, Lucas and Ottawa counties. It was reported in the *Toledo Blade* that the gale, which was accompanied by a spectacular electrical storm and rain, completely circled Toledo without striking any part of the city with full force.

In interview notes that were taken by the members of the Sylvania History Buffs during one of their meetings back in the 1970s the following was documented: "In 1920 a different kind of disaster struck Sylvania Township. A tornado! This tornado struck in March, and many houses and barns were destroyed or damaged. Donna Shull Sporleder recalled that day. She lived with her family on Brint Rd. west of Mitchaw Rd. Her grandfather was in the living room and couldn't open any door to get out. Most of the family was downstairs, but she remembers how the calendars were flying around. The upper part of the house was destroyed.

On Mitchaw Rd. between Brint and Sylvania-Metamora Rd., Mike Smith had the biggest barn in Ohio; it was built in 1918. The roof was metal, and when it was shipped to him (at Smith Siding) each piece of metal roofing was marked with his name. When the tornado struck, the roof was partly off and went flying across country, it could be identified by the name on the pieces. The straw mow was above the cows. There were 32 cows at that time and this heavy straw mow and flooring came down on them, killing 20. Later he had a sale to sell the cows, but nobody would bid.

Lester Bittner told of helping to rebuild this barn, (he worked on it for two weeks) but it never was rebuilt as large as it was in the beginning. The frame of the rebuilt barn was made from old 3" x 10" x 8', this material came from old wooden box cars, as it was at the time the railroads were converting to steel cars."

See page 116 of the book titled *Images of America – Sylvania* by Gaye E. Gindy and Trini L. Wenninger published by Arcadia Publishing – 2006, for a few pictures of the local destruction caused by this tornado.

RAIN, SNOW AND SLEET OF MARCH 27, 1934

According to the diary of Hazel Smith, who lived at 8652 Sylvania-Metamora Road, in Sylvania Township, in her diary for 3-27-1934 she wrote: "It rained, snowed and sleeted. The trees are bent down with ice; they sparkled as though covered with diamonds. The electricity was off – all day and tonight. The weight of the ice took down about 28 poles between here and Sylvania."

Then on 3-28-1934 she wrote: "The lights are still off. Ice is still on the trees. The lights didn't come on until 7:30 p.m."

THE DROUGHT OF 1934

It wasn't bad enough that the depression was in full swing in 1934, but between April 17 and June 17 only about one inch of rain fell, and when the rain finally came later that summer, it remained extremely hot. Drought caused heavy damage to crops and schools closed due to the extreme heat. Farmers suffered heavy losses due to this drought. They say that the drought conditions in 1934, and also the excessive heat of 1936, might have been caused in part to the "Dust Bowl" when millions of acres of eroded farmland, along with the dry summers, changed the landscape of North America.

A 2014 study by NASA reported that "using a reconstruction of North American drought history over the last 1,000 years found that the drought of 1934 was the driest and most widespread of the last millennium. Using a tree-ring based drought record from the years 1000 to 2005, and using modern records, scientists from NASA and Lamont-Doherty Earth Observatory found the 1934 drought was 30 percent more severe than the runner-up drought in 1580 and extended across 71.6 percent of western North America."

STORM IN SYLVANIA - JUNE OF 1937

On 6-20-1937 rain, wind and hail hit Sylvania hard. The wind, which at times reached cyclonic velocity, blew down trees, electric light poles and telephone poles. The village of Sylvania was plunged into darkness when the trees, uprooted by the storm, carried light lines to the ground. Damage to poles, and transformers was estimated at nearly $2,000. In Sylvania alone the telephone company had over 50 poles down and three cables were badly damaged. Several large trees were blown down and a portion of the roof on the Whiteford Road Church of Christ was blown off.

The *Toledo News-Bee* called it the worst storms in the history of northwestern Ohio. The storm flooded the area with 2 ½ inches of rain and caused heavy property and crop damage throughout the district. The U.S. Weather Bureau reported that 2.66 inches of rain fell in the 24 hours ending at 7:30 in the morning.

FEBRUARY 1951 SUB-ZERO WEATHER

The *Sylvania Sentinel* of 2-15-1951 said this about the weather: "During the severe weather of the past weeks, Sylvania schools were kept open while those of many adjacent districts closed. We think this all to the good. Children learn little at home now days and most parents find them a source of trouble when inclement weather keeps them indoors. Probably if the schools had closed most of the children would have been out sliding or skating anyway. When the kids are older, they will remember with pleasure the days of sub-zero weather when they bundled up and waited for the bus to take them to school just as our fathers tell us of the times they walked one, two and three miles to school in arctic cold and brag about it."

TORNADOES OF PALM SUNDAY 1965

On Palm Sunday of 1965 a tornado swept a narrow path for ten miles through West and North Toledo leveling scores of residences and business places. By the next day 13 were reported dead, and more than 170 injured, with hundreds of people homeless. This tornado was considered the worst natural disaster in Toledo's history.

The *Toledo Blade* dated 4-12-1965 reported that the major point of destruction was in the vicinity of Suder Avenue and the Detroit-Toledo Expressway, where Fuller's Creekside Addition subdivision was virtually wiped out along with Shoreland, Point Place, and the Lost Peninsula area at the Ohio-Michigan line. Four of the dead were among the 12 passengers on a Short Way Lines bus on the expressway which was literally torn apart as it was picked up and slammed upside down on the roadway by the force of the storm. The storm and devastating winds, hail, and rain, struck suddenly at about 9:30 p.m., first touching down in the vicinity of Sylvania Avenue and Woodley Road. It cut a swath about 200 yards wide easterly along Sylvania Avenue and then swung northeasterly through residential, commercial and industrial sections before it swept out into Lake Erie. A weather bulletin was issued at 9:12 p.m., after the Fort Wayne weather bureau reported that a tornado had been sighted in Van Wert County.

This tornado did not hit Sylvania, but we did get the high winds, rain and hail, and that night we did get the weather warning of the tornado.

SNOW OF DECEMBER 1974

This snow storm started about 2:30 a.m. Sunday morning, 12-2-1974, and before the storm stopped early Monday morning more than 18 inches of snow covered the ground in northwestern Ohio, including the Sylvania area. All major highways in the area were closed to traffic. Many vehicles were abandoned along the streets and that added to the problems faced by emergency vehicles that were attempting to clear the roads.

According to available records emergency housing was set up for snowbound victims in Sylvania at:

- Olivet Lutheran Church at 5840 Monroe Street;
- Sylvania Township Hall, 4927 Holland-Sylvania Road;
- No. 2 Fire Station, 6448 W. Central Avenue;
- Sylvania High School South (today known as Northview), 5403 Silica Drive;
- More than 1,500 travelers spent Sunday night in Sylvania area homes.

Fallen wires caused power outages and by Monday afternoon the area officials could not estimate when the expressway system would be reopened. All City and Township personnel worked from the beginning of the storm on Sunday morning until late Sunday night when the crews started a staggered shift program so that some of the men could get sleep.

Road crews piled snow at the access ramps to the expressway system to prevent motorists from getting onto the roadways until plows could clear and salt the expressway.

On Sunday the southbound traffic on US 23 from the Michigan line was backed up as far as the eye could see and traffic was moving at about 15 mph. Police were requesting that all area residents with four wheel drive vehicles and snowmobiles join in the rescue efforts to aid the thousands caught in the storm.

On 12-2-1974 the *Toledo Blade* said: "Heavy snows, high winds, and freezing temperatures swept across the eastern half of the nation today following a holiday weekend of weather-related accidents. Roads were closed by snow and drifts from the Mississippi River to the Appalachians. Airports at Chicago, Cleveland, and Detroit – already crowded with persons returning home from Thanksgiving vacations – were hampered further by the weather. The hardest hit was northwest Ohio by a record 12 to 18-inch snowfall that blocked several major highways and made countless others treacherous or impassable."

The *Toledo Blade* dated 12-3-1974 said: "The massive snow-removal operation continued in the Toledo area today, with major efforts aimed at unclogging secondary streets. Much of the area is showing signs of recovery from the severe storm that dumped 14 inches of snow here Sunday and crippled most operations for two days."

The *Toledo Blade* dated 12-4-1974 reported that most school systems in the Toledo metropolitan area remained closed for the third day as road crews, most of them working on 12-hour shifts, continued their battle to clear the streets and highways blocked by Sunday's 18-inch snowfall.

The *Toledo Blade* dated 12-6-1974 discussed the fact that a Standard Procedure for Storms should be adopted by the Toledo city administration. The manager said that whatever emergency procedures were established, they would be initiated only during extremely heavy snow storms. It was reported here that the Toledo area had not had a snow storm of this magnitude in 75 years.

The *Toledo Blade* dated 12-9-1974 reported that Toledoans living on residential streets still covered by snow or ice probably will have to wait for warmer weather to take the bumps and skids out of their driving. Two days of temperatures in the 30s and 40s will do far more to clear those streets than city workers now were capable of doing.

THE BLIZZARD OF 1978

On Thursday 1-26-1978 President Jimmy Carter declared Ohio to be in a state of emergency and ordered elements of the 5th Army into the state to help cope with what Governor Rhodes described as "a killer blizzard looking for victims."

Winds gusting as high as 65 mph caused snowdrifts of up to 15 feet deep. Driving was extremely hazardous everywhere and impassible on some roads. Approximately 15 inches of snow was dumped starting Wednesday night through Friday. An estimated 150,000 homes and businesses were without electricity throughout the state by late Thursday night. In Lucas County nearly 30,000 households served by Toledo Edison Company were without power as winds snapped snow laden lines and crews fought to get through to frozen substations. Toledo Edison was advising residents of homes without power to gather with other persons in one place and pool food supplies.

Owners of four-wheel-drive vehicles and snowmobiles answered pleas from law enforcement agencies and political subdivisions to rescue stranded motorists, transport persons needing medical attention and deliver food and supplies to residents otherwise isolated by the heavy snow. Evacuation centers were set up in city buildings and fire halls.

The *Toledo Blade* reported on 1-28-1978, that recovery efforts in Ohio's worst winter storm were underway by Friday 1-27-1978. Federal help was promised—including aid from the Army—but was said to not be enough. The Ohio National Guard was called in to help but federal relief was tied up in U.S. Army bureaucracy, despite President Carter's emergency declaration for the state. Nine rescue helicopters from the 101st Airborne division of the Fifth Army at Fort Campbell, Kentucky, began arriving at Rickenbacker Air Force Base outside Columbus, Ohio late Friday afternoon. The Army had agreed to pay reserves who volunteered for emergency duty, enabling the state to scrap plans to pay U.S. Army personnel with Ohio money through a volunteer militia clause in Ohio law.

Hundreds of Ohio highways remained closed on Friday and prospects were not good for getting any highway systems opened even with 867 workers in the field. Governor Rhodes of Ohio said that without the help of thousands of people in Ohio, we would not be able to cope with this blizzard. He also said that besides the cost in lives and personal hardships, the blizzard was costing Ohioans at least $2.1 million daily in overtime for state workers.

Here in Sylvania the police departments and fire department employees were working for up to three days straight. The State Highway Patrol had set up a satellite office at the No. 2 fire station on Central Avenue, because they could not get to their post. Snowmobiles were obtained from private owners to be used to get to emergencies.

After this event, all the local officials were going to their appointed government officials and requesting the purchase of 4-wheel drive vehicles, and equipment to handle such emergencies in the future, and they were approving these purchases. Problem was, there was not another incident of this magnitude again since.

DROUGHT OF 1988

The drought of 1988 consisted of very little rain and unseasonably high temperatures. May 1ˢᵗ came and from that time on that summer it was hot and humid, and we got no rain. The officials of the City of Sylvania had to impose outdoor water use restrictions. Voluntary compliance went into effect on 6-12-1988, and mandatory restrictions were put in place on 7-7-1988. Restrictions were lifted on September 9 when rainfall and temperatures returned to near normal. Precipitation for the year measured 26.04 inches compared to 38.45 inches in 1987 and 40.55 inches in 1986. During this 1988 drought, 36 percent of the United States experienced these same drought conditions.

Records say that the Maumee River literally dried up and you could see the Glacier-scarred, limestone riverbed. In Sylvania the Ten-Mile Creek, and North Branch of the Ten Mile Creek was dried up and for the first time in many years the riverbed was parched dry. We were able to walk the entire length of the bed of the North Branch to the Michigan line without running into any water.

STORM – INCLUDING TORNADO - END OF JUNE 1998

According to the *Toledo Blade* of 6-28-1998 residents of northwest Ohio were recovering from a tornado and thunderstorms which swept across the region on 6-24-1998, and then additional storms hit on 6-27-1998, fueled by strong winds that downed even more trees and power lines. A lightning bolt struck the roof of the Showcase Cinemas at 3500 Secor Road and loosened its cement-block wall and forced evacuation of the theaters. Dime-sized hail struck in Sylvania and portions of Toledo.

ICE STORM OF JANUARY OF 2002

On 1-31-2002 nearly 90,000 residences and businesses in northern Ohio and southeast Michigan were without power when an ice storm downed power lines, transformers, and substations throughout the region. This power outage lasted for a couple of days for many Sylvania residents. A meteorologist said the ice storm was caused by a weather front that stalled over the region Wednesday night. Cold temperatures and moisture created snow and ice, but a layer of warmer air below thawed it to rain as it fell. On the ground temperatures were freezing so it came down from the sky as rain and froze right onto whatever it touched.

All the trees were covered with a thick layer of ice, which was a beautiful sight, but the weight of the ice brought branches down on power lines and into the streets, causing major damage and problems for the city and township officials. Large bushes and pine trees snapped to the ground from the weight of the ice that formed on their foliage.

FLOODING IN SYLVANIA

In reviewing the records of Sylvania Village and Township as early as 1834 and through 1958, and reviewing all available newspapers published in Sylvania, there was nothing that came to my attention regarding any flooding problems in the area.1958 was the first time I came across a mention of any flooding problems. That doesn't mean it didn't happen, it just means that it wasn't mentioned in any of the thousands of documents that I have reviewed.

According to an article in the *Sylvania Sentinel-Herald* dated 5-7-1958 water stands in the area of the 6000 Block of Glasgow Road most of the year. Charles Gries of 6045 Glasgow said that they called the flooded area "Lake Glasgow." Village officials said that they were hoping that the area may drain better once the U.S. 23 expressway was cut through the eastern edge of the "lake."

In February of 1959 the local newspaper reported a storm that caused some flooding problems in Sylvania. Apparently several days of hard rain caused the Ten Mile Creek by Carroll Motors on South Main Street to flood and the building had two feet of water in the basement. Since the Ten Mile Creek was actually still covered with ice at the time of the rain it was necessary to take a large crane to break several ice jams in the creek so that the water could continue to flow away from the buildings. And Whitt's Inn on North Main Street had two feet of water running in and out the doors. Russell Pierce the owner of the business managed to brew a pot of coffee for his cleanup crew, which included Mr. Pierce, Jessie McClain, Bill DePew and Gene Geer.

On July 4th of 1969 a thunder storm hit Lucas County and flooding could be seen throughout Sylvania also. Cars were halfway under water in some areas. Yards were flooded. Harroun Road along the Ten Mile Creek had standing water on the street. On that day Sylvania residents were holding their STRA All-Star Game at Memorial Field. The game had started and was in the second inning when the storm struck. The 4th of July fireworks were canceled and rescheduled at that point and participants were forced to huddle in their automobiles then attempt the drive home. The *Sylvania Sentinel* reported that the Sylvania street department worked throughout the night, and had all city streets cleared of fallen trees and debris by daybreak. Along Harroun Road near the 10 Mile Creek the water was up past the bridge. I was 10 years old when this storm hit and when it was over our backyard, which today is the gardens of the Sylvania Historical Village at 5723 Main Street, and the entire area was flooded with water up to our knees. You could pick up handfuls of night crawlers just by reaching down into the water.

On 6-16-1970 a series of thundershowers nearly paralyzed the Toledo area, causing flooding, fallen trees, downed electric and telephone lines, power outages and numerous fires caused by lightning. It was reported that roadways still were impassable the next morning. The storm was described as "one of those 50-year storms that occurs every six months." The Toledo Edison Company reported more than 6,500 trouble calls from 3 p.m. to 7 a.m., and many others were not able to put calls through. Wind gusts of up to 74 miles an hour were recorded at the gauge at Edison's Acme power plant in East Toledo.

On 11-4-1971 the Sylvania Township Trustees also received a complaint about County Ditch #19 which runs through a 40 acre farm on the southeast corner of Herr and Sylvania Avenue. The drainage was blocked by silt and sludge, causing damages to crops. The contention was that Medusa Cement was causing such stoppage and should pay for the cost of cleaning it.

The *Toledo Blade* dated 8-26-1972 reported on a group of residents in the area of Nopper Gardens, located in the eastern portion of Sylvania Township, were going to request that City of Toledo officials not allow additional building in that area until adequate sanitary sewers were built. Richard Thome, president of the Nopper Gardens Association, confirmed that the resident group would be requesting a formal commitment. He said that the rapid conversion of former green space into buildings and blacktop along Monroe Street west of Talmadge Road was blamed by residents of the Nopper Gardens area, just south of the Sylvania Township line, for increased flooding and sewer problems. They noted that there was talk of further development, which would make storm and sanitary-sewer conditions even worse. At that time the Ponderosa Steak House had just received approval to build and operate a restaurant on Monroe Street, west of Talmadge Road.

The *Toledo Blade* dated 9-18-1972 reported that a thunderstorm pounded Toledo and the suburbs for most of Sunday night and this morning, causing widespread street and basement flooding, scores of power outages, and a fire in a West Toledo home. The storm was accompanied by lightning and ear-splitting thunder. They reported that the storm dropped 3.61 inches of rain at the Toledo Express Airport between 7 p.m. and 7 a.m., and a half-inch of pea-size hail fell. It was reported that lightning also struck a Toledo Edison feeder line on Erie Street in Sylvania, knocking out power from the Michigan line to Sylvania Avenue and from Talmadge Road to Acres Road at 10:50 p.m. The *Sylvania Sentinel* newspaper dated 9-20-1972 featured a photo of the area of Warner and Goodhue in the Central Avenue and Holland-Sylvania Road area, which was completely flooded to the point you could not see the roads.

In August of 1977 it was necessary for Sylvania City Council to declare a temporary moratorium on certain construction in special flood hazard areas of the city. This temporary moratorium prohibited officials of the city from issuing zoning permits in the flood plain areas. This action was necessary because the city had been notified that its eligibility for participation in the National Flood Insurance Program was going to be suspended if satisfactory flood plain management measures were not enacted. The areas designated as being in the flood hazard area were: the north branch of the Ten Mile Creek, McPeek Drain, Schreiber and Eggeman Ditches and the Ottawa River.

According to the *Toledo Blade* dated 10-4-1986 the Toledo area was deluged by flooded underpasses and basements as more than 2 ½ inches of rain fell in 18 hours. They said it was the fourth consecutive day of rain for the area as far as Bryan, Ohio.

By the early 2000s Sylvania was experiencing more than the usual amount of rain and flooding was becoming a common thing in and around Sylvania, especially in the western portion of the township. For years this area of the township consisted of nothing but farm land that soaked up the rain and kept the Ten Mile Creek flowing at a moderate level. With more and more development, and more and more blacktop covering what used to be farm land, drainage was becoming more and more difficult; besides the fact that for many years cleanout of the ditches and creek were neglected in this area.

From June 21 through 23, 2006 rain hit northwestern Ohio hard. The National Weather Service reported about five inches of rain drenched northwest Ohio between about 7 p.m. and midnight Wednesday. In early July after President Bush visited the area he declared a federal disaster in six flooded and tornado-stricken counties in northern Ohio, including Lucas County.

By 2009 the Sylvania Township Trustees were holding public hearings to discuss the problems of flooding in what was being referred to as the western Lucas County's Ten Mile Creek watershed. It was reported that the problem was not going to go away and frustrated homeowners' needed to protect themselves with flood insurance.

The Lucas County Engineer Keith Earley identified a broad swatch of western Sylvania Township and adjoining townships, west of Centennial Road and centered on Central Avenue, as being in the flood plain of the Ten Mile Creek and its streams and ditches. He warned that parts of the land will soon be declared part of the floodway. He said when this happened new construction or building expansion will not be allowed in these areas. Mr. Early said that in some cases, especially along Herr Road, entire building lots will be affected. Officials were looking into the possibility of creating a drainage utility fund in the county for flood-control projects and the revenue would have to come from special assessments. It was suggested that the area where Prairie Ditch and the Ten Mile Creek come together is only 30 feet wide and it just couldn't handle the water, and it needed to be widened.

The heavy rains of March of 2009 caused severe flooding near the Ten Mile Creek, closing roads, flooding basements and crawl spaces and made large ponds in yards. Residents were wondering why this was happening all of a sudden in the last several years. Some blamed over-development and years of bad planning finally caught up to the area that was once known as the "Black Swamp."

It was also discovered that Fulton County cleared their log jams in the creeks and this may have contributed to the situation and increased the rate of water flow into the township's portion of the Ten Mile Creek. It had been suggested that at least the log jams in the creek through the township be cleared and township officials estimated that to cost between $70,000 and $120,000, which they hoped could be done in the summer of 2009.

The newsletter of Sylvania Township dated July/August/September 2009 said: "The Trustees, working with the Public Works Department, have implemented an aggressive environmental plan to clean ditches throughout the township and remove log jams from twelve points throughout the Ten Mile Creek, significantly improving and minimizing the effects of local flooding in the area. The most dynamic project performed this year is the Ten Mile Creek-jam removal located just south of the Sylvania Avenue and Mitchaw Road intersection. The property owners on each side of the Ten Mile Creek granted right-of-entry onto their private property allowing legal access to the Ten Mile Creek. The worst log jam measured 8' high, 60' long and the entire width of the creek. . ."

An article in the 8-5-2009 *Sylvania Herald* reported that the Sylvania Township Road Department crews removed a very large log-jam from Ten Mile Creek and transitioned the waste product into a valuable mulch commodity for the Olander Park System. They reported that over the past decades, log jams had accumulated at numerous locations along the Ten Mile Creek, and over the last two years the road department improved drainage areas to restore the proper drainage flow and provided relief to flooded areas. After removing the log-jam, the road department contracted a large log grinding machine and turned 25 foot logs into mulch for the Olander Park System landscaping projects.

In October of 2014 the Lucas County Engineer's Office was moving forward on a project to reduce flooding in the westerly areas of Sylvania Township. The project included dredging parts of the Ten Mile Creek and widening the stream. The area was a 1.7 mile section of the creek near Herr Road. The area from Central Avenue and Davidson Drive was also experiencing flooding throughout the year. A study by the Lucas County Engineer's Office was moving forward with a $1.87 million draining project to mitigate flooding of the Ten Mile Creek in the western areas of Sylvania Township. It was reported that in 2006, 2008, 2009, and 2011 flooding shut down Central Avenue and Herr Road for days. The project would widen a section of the creek near Sylvania Avenue to 40 feet

INTERVIEWS AND REMINISCING ABOUT SYLVANIA

SYLVANIA HISTORY TOLD BY LIFE-LONG RESIDENT ALBERT HARRIS RANDALL – 9-8-1932:

This article/interview of Albert Harris Randall appeared in the *Sylvania Sentinel* on 9-8-1932, and is important to Sylvania's history because of the wealth of information that he shared. (The sentences in parenthesis were included by the author Gayleen Gindy):

Mr. A.H. Randall, owner of Randall's Grocery Store, and a life-long resident of the village, has a particularly rich story of memories of early Sylvania which he is sharing with us today.

Mr. Randall was born in the house now occupied by J.C. Goist (at the 1930 census the Goist family lived at 6705 Maplewood Avenue – south side of the street – first house west of the railroad tracks) and was the son of Dallas and Etta Randall, who were early settlers here. Mrs. Etta Randall, who passed away in 1929, is particularly well remembered for her keen interest in the political life of the village. She was one of the only two women ever to serve on the school board here, and she was engaged in compiling a history of the village when she died.

This is Albert H. Randall standing in front of his store that he operated at 5641 Main Street from 1912 until 1935. After that he served several years on the Sylvania Board of Education, several years on Sylvania village council and then was elected Mayor of Sylvania. Mr. Randall was born and raised in Sylvania, and lived out the rest of his life here. His interviews that were published in the local newspapers were so informative that historians today use the information from these interviews to verify much of what we know about very early Sylvania, and the fire of 1887. (Photo from postcard taken in about 1900 and owned by Gayleen Gindy).

The school days of Mr. Randall were spent in the old brick school house on Main Street (5735 Main). The building at the time had only three rooms, basement and both wings having been added since. His first teacher, he recalls, was Miss Fannie Comstock, and the principal there was Aaron B. West. Boys will always be boys, and Mr. Randall recalls how he and his chums would go fishing off the old dam which furnished water power to drive a saw mill located in front of Burnham High School. When no one was near the boys would start this mill, just to see it run. He said that an arsonist struck Sylvania in about 1912. The arsonist worked for the Chandler Cement Block Company, and among other buildings, he burned down Huling's saw mill, which was on the north bank of Ten Mile Creek, across from the Burnham High School. The arsonist was discovered, arrested, jailed, and then eventually escaped to Canada.

Down near the Shell Gas Station was a horse powered cider mill, and after school the youngsters would ride on the sweeps. The baseball ground was the green south of Alberti R. Chandler's store, and Mr. Randall remembers that the baseballs were whittled out of a car rubber. William Fletcher used to turn out ball bats, and quite often it was necessary to pay for windows in the Masonic building. Mr. Randall has seen Sylvania's business district grow from a row of wooden buildings and wooden sidewalks and mud streets to a row of brick buildings, paved streets, cement walks and electric lights.

The following business places were active during Mr. Randall's early years: Harry Bidwell, hotel and livery (5703 Main Street); Washington Leonardson, general merchandise (5693 Main Street); Probert Sisters, millinery (5689 Main); Charles N. Lewis, grocery and bar (5681 Main Street); W.W. Covell, harness shop (5679 Main Street); William B. Warren, Grocery (5675 Main Street); S.M. Judson, grocery (5633 Main Street); S.B. Root, hardware (5627 & 5629 Main Street); Andrew Reger, shoe repair shop (5617 Main Street); Henry Parker, groceries (5609 Main Street); Pop Polley, saloon (5601 Main Street); Warren D. Moore, drugs (5663 Main Street); Isaac Thorp, meats (5661 Main Street); William Bryan, postmaster (5651 & 5655 Main Street); Simeon Parker, saloon (5645 Main Street); Washington H. Huling, general merchandise (5639 & 5641 Main Street).

The old Masonic building (located then at 6521 Monroe Street) housed the Town Hall on the first floor and the jail in the basement. On the east side of Main Street were located James Richie's Wagon Shop, (5648 Main Street); Ben Bellow's Blacksmith Shop and Henry Hubbard's Wagon Shop (5658 Main Street). The only old business building left is the stone part of Bellow's blacksmith shop which is now a part of Clare Cooper's Tire and Battery Shop (5658 Main Street).

The Randall Grocery store was started in October, 1910, where the Toledo Edison is now located (5621 Main), but three years later Mr. Randall removed his stock to his present location (5641 Main Street). He says of this building "My present building has a very dear spot in my heart, as it was here that my great uncle (Washington H. Huling) had his store, and in my boyhood days I used to be in this store a great deal with him. In this way I became familiar with old styles of handling merchandise. In those days sugar, flour, crackers, kerosene and many other commodities were delivered to the grocery in huge hogsheads and had to be weighed out and put in smaller containers. The store now operated by Mr. Randall represents the most modern methods of handling merchandise and serving customers.

Mr. Randall has served two terms on the village council and also two terms on the Board of Education. As a member of council he helped to plan the first sewer system, the first paved streets and the first concrete sidewalks. He was a member of the School Board when Burnham High School was planned.

Notes: While Albert H. Randall operated his store at 5641 Main Street he referred to his store as "The Store with the Orange Front," according to a 1933 advertisement. In a 1934 advertisement he listed Clyde Gault as the manager of the meat department of his store.

SYLVANIA HISTORY TOLD BY LIFE-LONG RESIDENT ALBERT HARRIS RANDALL

NOTE: Facts in parenthesis were added by the author Gayleen Gindy

The following article appeared in the local newspaper, the *SYLVANIA SENTINEL* on 12-24-1936: "LIFELONG RESIDENT RECALLS MAIN STREET OF FIFTY YEARS AGO (BEFORE THE FIRE OF 1887) - Mud Roads, Board Sidewalks, Hitching Rails, Saloons, Harness Shops, Now Only Memories

In a letter received from Mr. A.H. Randall who for many years operated a grocery store on Main Street (5641 Main Street), and who retired a year or so ago, he gives us a mental picture of Main Street as it looked about fifty years ago before the fire starting at Monroe Street and moving north.

My earliest recollection of Sylvania's Main Street, was Pop Polley's saloon (5601 Main Street) situated where the council chambers now stands. Any young man, under 18 years of age, who entered, was quickly thrown out and in no gentle manner.

Coming down the street, the next building was occupied by J.M. Borough's harness shop (5607 Main Street). Next was John H. Parker's grocery store (5609 Main Street) where the first penny candies were sold; a shoe repair shop occupied the rear part of the grocery.

The next building had been occupied as a tailor shop (5615 Main Street) in which a man murdered his wife and burned her body; we boys used to give this a wide berth as we believed her spirit came back and prowled around at night. (See book titled *Murder In Sylvania; As Told In 1857* by Gaye E. Gindy for full details of this horrible murder).

This building was later occupied by Andrew Reger as a shoe repair shop, and he slept in the back room while he was getting started in business.

On the lot next door, the Avery Brothers built a building and started an undertaking shop and furniture store (5621 Main Street). I particularly remember watching the men make coffins and furniture. One of the Avery Brothers had a wooden leg, and the other a glass eye, and we boys were inclined to nickname them (but not so they could hear).

Before the erection of the Avery building a huge tree stood on this lot and to its branches some of the young men about town hung one of the local merchants in effigy. For this they left town, but eventually came back and paid a fine. "The two buildings following were Silas B. Root's hardware and tin shop (5627 & 5629 Main Street), and a stone building occupied by Sylvanus M. Judson (5633 Main Street). When the town burned this was the only building whose walls remained standing. (In 1903 members of the Sylvania Masonic Lodge removed these old brick walls that had survived, and constructed the three story building that we see today).

Then came the Washington H. Huling general store (5639 & 5641 Main Street), Simeon Parker's saloon (5645 Main Street), then the home of William Bryan postmaster and next to that the post office (5651 & 5655 Main Street). Isaac Thorp, whose butcher shop stood next, (5661 Main Street), had the first hand-power sausage machine in Sylvania and an interested audience always was on hand when it was in use.

Next was the Warren D. Moore Drug Store (5663 & 5665 Main Street). Later this was run by Dr. Hanks and his brother Dallas. This store was the first long distance telephone station here, and I remember Dr. Hanks calling my mother into the store to show her the telephone. To prove to her that she could really hear a voice over the wire from Toledo, the doctor called Toledo and got the operator to talk to my mother. Even then she would not believe it, but told him he had someone in the next room doing the talking. She often recalled that experience.

In the vacant lot adjoining a traveling photographer would set up a tent every summer and do a fine business taking tin-type pictures. I still have one of myself, taken by this man.

Next was the William B. Warren store. This building was first occupied by my grandfather as an office and residence, and my mother was born there (5675 Main Street). William Covell's harness shop stood next (5679 Main Street) and then Charlie Lewis' grocery and saloon (5681 Main Street). We boys were always trying to find some excuse to go in there and buy something so we could get a chance to see what men did in a saloon.

The vacant lot next door was kept mowed and flowers were grown next to the street (5687 Main Street owned by the Pease family). Who attended to this, I have not the least idea. On the corner was a double store building occupied on one side by the Probert sisters (5689 Main Street) as a millinery store, and the other side (5693 Main Street) as a dry goods and boot and shoe store. The upstairs was occupied by Taylor Cosgrove as a shop. Later I'll tell you something more of Sylvania's business district in the 1880's."

SYLVANIA HISTORY TOLD BY LIFE-LONG RESIDENT ALBERT HARRIS RANDALL – PART II –

The following appeared in the *SYLVANIA SENTINEL* on 1-7-1937 – Facts in parenthesis were added by the author Gayleen Gindy:

"SYLVANIA OF FIFTY YEARS AGO PICTURED BY OLD RESIDENT

A.H. Randall, Describes Scenes of His Boyhood Days in Sylvania

Mr. A.H. Randall, life-long resident of Sylvania, in an article in a recent issue of the Sentinel, told of his remembrances of Main Street as he knew it as a boy. Mr. Randall's parents were early settlers in the village, and he himself conducted a grocery store here for twenty-five years (5641 Main Street). He is now retired and lives on Maplewood Avenue (6817 Maplewood).

Continuing his reminiscences, he states, "Across Main Street on the northwest corner stood the Bidwell house, owned and operated by Harry Bidwell and known to the boys of the town as "Uncle Harry." This hostelry was operated upon a strictly "temperance" policy. (5703 Main Street).

On the east side of the street were the residences of Dr. Cosgrove (5692/5694 Main Street) and Mrs. Leonardson, (5684 Main Street) followed by Henry Hubbard's wagon shop, Ben Bellows blacksmith shop (5658 Main Street) and Jimmie Richie's wagon and paint shop (5648 Main Street).

From there to the corner (5634 to 5604 Main Street) was a huge vacant lot which was used as a playground for the boys. Exciting games of one-o-cat, two-o-cat, long ball and baseball were staged there.

We did not buy our baseball equipment in those days, but whittled our baseballs out of rubber car springs; our bats were turned of seasoned oak and ash by Uncle Billy Fletcher on an old-fashioned hand lathe for which we boys furnished the power.

Mr. S. Warren lived in a home situated where Howard's Gas Station now stands (In 2018 a small park at the southeast corner of Main and Monroe). The front yard was enclosed by a fence and the roses blooming there were a constant temptation to the small boys of the town. I don't believe Mr. Warren ever had many bouquets from these climbing roses.

Next door stood a stone building owned by the Sylvania Masonic Lodge (6521 Monroe Street). The first floor housed the Village offices, the basement the jail, and the second story the lodge rooms. One look at the jail, and we boys resolved that we would not do anything that could be punished by a jail sentence. This building with the exception of a new front is the same as when I first remember it.

On the southwest corner stood a block of three stores: the first was vacant, (6601 Monroe), the second used as a residence and the third was occupied by George Probert as a shoe repair shop and dwelling. Several thriving businesses were located on the south side. Across the railroad track was a large stave mill and cooper shop, on the bank of the mill pond stood a large grist mill operated by the Chamberlains, a general store was operated by Hiram Hawley and Fenton Clark's grandfather lived in the home which he now occupies. On the corner were a meat market and a saloon.

As a boy, I was raised on Summit Street, and I will try to tell you what it looked like, more than fifty years ago. Beginning at the Michigan line on the east side of the street was the house now occupied by Willard Warren (6056 Summit Street). This house was unoccupied. Its windows broken and doors hanging open. We boys used to visit it with fear as we were told it was occupied by ghosts, but we never saw any.

In the next house (6000 thru 6010 Summit Street) lived Ben Bellows, the village blacksmith, and a friend to all of us. Ben was also the village marshal. The next house was located on the property now owned by Charles Clegg (5902 thru 5930 Summit Street) and was occupied by my parents, and several of my brothers and I myself were born there. The plot of ground on which the Follas and Shull homes (5840 thru 5864 Summit Street) stand was our cow pasture and across the creek back of these properties was a small woods where all the picnics were held. There used to be great squirrel hunting in these woods and they were a favorite playground for the Summit Street boys.

The parents of L.C. Hubbard lived where the David Nhare home now stands (5778 Summit Street) and the next house, where David Buckles lives, was the One Stickney home (One was the given name of Mr. Stickney). Summit Street was quite interesting to me, so I believe I will tell you more about it next week."

See page 53 (the bottom photo) of the book titled *Images of America – Sylvania* by Gaye E. Gindy and Trini L. Wenninger published by Arcadia Publishing – 2006, to see a picture of Albert H. Randall in front of his grocery store located at 5641 Main Street.

ANOTHER FINAL INTERVIEW WITH ALBERT HARRIS RANDALL IN 1959

The *Sylvania Sentinel-Herald* newspaper dated 3-17-1959 reported that they had put a call out to residents asking the question of who had subscribed to their newspaper the longest, and Albert Harris Randall, 88 years old, answered the question by saying that he had subscribed to the Sylvania newspaper since 1892, and therefore they declared that he had received "the newspaper longer than any other living man." As a token reward for his 66-year faith in the newspaper he was granted a free subscription for the rest of his life. They reported that he was born in Sylvania on 10-25-1870 and had lived in Sylvania every year but one ever since. The newspaper then interviewed him and this is what they wrote:

"Mr. Randall, a Main Street grocer for 35 years from 1904 to 1939 well known and respected throughout the township. He is a member of First Congregational Church. It was his store, the A.H. Randall Grocery, he says, which started the Sunday closing of business on Main Street. He took over the general store at one time run by his uncle, Washington Harris Huling, who had brought him up, and sold out on his retirement in 1939 to Burnard and Bissonnette Grocery, now Burnette's in the same building. His uncle also ran a cooper's shop, west of Main Street and north of Ten Mile Creek.

Randall was born in the first house west of the railroad on the south side of Maplewood Ave. The original house has since been remodeled. His mother was Etta Green born in Sylvania in the 1830s and a daughter of Dr. Horace Green one of the original settlers, who died in an early cholera epidemic. His father from New York State was Albert Dallas Randall.

"I went to school in the old Academy, combined grade and high school on the site of Kroger's Main Street store, but had to leave after the fifth grade and help support my family," Randall said. "During the winter, my father could get no other work than cutting wood from the great forests of oak, maple, walnut, hickory and ash on all sides of our little village of about 300. I stacked the wood he cut with his old cross-cut saw. "As a young man," he said, "I took a job as section hand on the old Lake Shore and Michigan Southern Railroad (now the Old Line of the N.Y.C.). After a few years I was made the first station agent, for the Toledo and Western Electric Lines, which had their general office west of Main Street and north of the creek. There I worked from 6 a.m. to 7 p.m. for seven days a week making a grand total of $35 per month."

Randall is the oldest of five brothers, four still living, but retired. Burr, a one-time farmer, lives at Dorr Street and Centennial Road. Archie lives in Toledo, and Horace in Florida. I married a nice little Irish girl in 1892, who lived on a farm a few miles south of Sylvania," he said. "She lived until after we had celebrated our Golden Wedding anniversary, dying in 1942, just 16 years ago. We lived most of our married life at 6817 Maplewood, and successfully brought up two girls and a boy. My son was killed in an airplane accident at Adrian, Mich. One daughter, Mrs. N.C. Hall, lives right next door to me now, and the other, Mrs. O.G. Hoobler in Maumee. I'm a great-grandfather. I've been living by myself, here since 1951," he said, "playing solitaire, reading and sleeping the time away. But my two daughters sure keep an eye on me," he laughed.

"I well remember the big Sylvania fire of 1887 that took all the stores on the west side of Main Street between Monroe and Maplewood. That was the year I was working in Toledo, I was just 17 years old," he reminisced. "By the time I heard about it and arrived home, the whole block of wooden buildings was just smoking ashes. Some of those brick buildings which went up to replace them may look sort of old to you," he smiled. "But it seems like just yesterday that I mixed the mortar which went into them."

Here's the way Mr. Randall remembers the west side of Main before the fire. Starting at the corner of Monroe was Pop's Saloon, then an empty building and continuing north, in order, a boot and shoe repair shop, Root's General Store, Judson's Grocery, Huling's General Store, another saloon, a residence, the Post Office, a meat market, a drug store, a doctor's office, another grocery, a liquor and grocery store, and on the corner of Maplewood a big double building with a ladies' millinery shop on one side and Leonardson's General Dry Goods and Clothier store in the other. Across the street, he said, there was a big wooden wagon shop where Chandler's Hardware now stands. North of that in order were a blacksmith shop, another wagon shop and two big residences. South of Chandler's to Monroe Street was a big open field, our playground where we used to have our scrub ball games." Randall remembers.

"Our baseballs were usually homemade or perhaps we'd take a ball of twine over to the shoemaker and have him sew a leather cover over it for a few pennies. There were no boys' organizations in those days, like the Boy Scouts, but in spite of that, there was never any question of juvenile delinquency or rough gangs, as there is today. One reason was most boys had work to do, or else," he said. "And I guess our parents were a lot more strict than they are now."

"In the spring, Ottawa Creek, that runs behind the present Sentinel office, was a paradise for boys," he reminisced. "White bass, perch, pickerel and suckers came up stream to Ottawa Lake their spawning ground. You could actually catch them by hand. When we could get our fathers' wagons, we used to drive up the bed of the creek to the old stave mill on the flats just north of our office, just to see the fish jump out of the water ahead of us. "But most other times we just walked wherever we wanted to go, which usually wasn't far from home. The horse-and-buggy days were misnamed. Should be 'foot-travel days.' Our lack of transportation, money and many of the other things you have might make you think we had a pretty rough time of it," he said. "But you'd be wrong. We really had fun in the 1870s, 1880s and 1890s, because we had to make it for ourselves. "Today . . ." he hesitated, "Yes I feel sort of sorry for a world which thinks progress means speed. And as for the atom bomb, I don't want to even think about it." (End)

Here I will note that Albert Harris Randall's father, Albert Dallas Randall, kept a diary from March of 1875 until August of 1876 in which he recorded his daily events of working at his uncle's store (Washington Huling) at 5641 Main Street, and taking care of his daily chores at home. This dairy still exists and is now owned by the Sylvania Area Historical Society and is housed in their archives at 5717 N. Main Street.

ROBERT (POP) WYANDT COMMENTS

Mr. Robert "Pop" Wyandt taught school in Sylvania beginning in the 1927-1928 school year at Burnham High School. After he retired he talked about his years in Sylvania and the 9-1-1976 *Sylvania Sentinel* interviewed him saying the following:

"From 1955 on, Sylvania became a 'let's rush and build up' place. Soon everyone began to move into town and before too long there weren't enough schools to house all of the children. The big change came after the 60s, and by then, I was out. I don't know exactly what the change was. First comes change. Only time will tell if that change you call covering all the fields with concrete progress? Or how about automobiles; those machines have killed more people than all our wars put together. Do you call that progress? In the earlier days there was nothing that even looked like drugs. The biggest problem we had as teachers was keeping track of those who sneaked off at lunch to swim in the Ten Mile Creek."

CLARA ADSIT PARKER INTERVIEW

The following interview with Sylvania born Clara Adsit Parker appeared in the *Sylvania Sentinel* newspaper on 12-26-1957. Clara was born in 1880 in Sylvania, the daughter of Orson and Fannie

Adsit. She married Edwin B. Parker in 1909, and they lived in a home that was once located at 6635 Maplewood Avenue, where the Sylvania Police Station is today. She died in 1960. Her father ran a drug store in downtown Sylvania and then her husband took over the business after Mr. Adsit died.

LIFELONG RESIDENT OF SYLVANIA RECALLS CHRISTMAS OF YESTERYEAR - BIG DAY 75 YEARS AGO UNDIMMED BY LOOT, HOOT AND HOLLER – By Wanda Cook

It was a wax doll. Mrs. Parker recalls—a wax doll with a stuffed body. Her name was Susie and she was the most beautiful doll in all Sylvania, in all the world. But Susie had to be kept in an unheated room, and only for minutes at a time was Mrs. Parker allowed to play with her in the warmth of kitchen or parlor. Santa had handed Susie to Clara Adsit Parker at the church Christmas party. There had been a small red rocker another Christmas Eve. And wonder of all wonders, even a bright blue sled with a little painted girl dancing on its top.

That was Christmas as Mrs. Clara Parker of 6635 Maplewood, knew it before the turn of the century. In those days, all celebration took place at the church. Even family gifts were taken to the annual party for distribution Christmas Eve. The huge tree which towered above the tallest father reached clear to the ceiling. It had been cut by members from the nearby woods and hauled by sled to the church.

The tree was laden with tinsel, which was store bought but fringed by hand at home. Chains of cranberries were strung, and youngsters in knit leggings and cloth-topped one-buckle "artics" were sent out across the snowy fields to hunt for wintergreen berries. The most likely berry ground, Mrs. Parker recalls, were the woods by the Lake Shore depot (Convent and Railroad Street). Once at home, however, the armloads of bright berries quickly withered in the steamy kitchen. Frosty fingers had to fly to string them into long loops. Then they were hung in the cold shed or cellar to be taken to the church come Christmas Eve.

The church tree was always adorned with a multitude of tiny red candles. Although a fire hazard was recognized the lighted tree was traditional and perhaps people were unaware of the mass tragedies that occurred in other communities. And so the candle-lit tree was a thing of joy and splendor, until the Christmas fire at the Congregational church in the 1880's. As the volunteer Santa's pillow-stuffed front brushed the tree a lighted candle tipped and fell. In one awful moment the tree in all its magnificence was aflame.

Women screamed; children clutched their new toys and buried themselves in the arms of their grownups. With coats and carriage robes, the men managed to beat back the flames. At last, in a tangle of blackened tinsel, the smoldering tree lay sheared and lifeless. Yet, strangely, the evening's terror did not dim the candlelight of later Christmases. Perhaps the church tree starred in the Christmas role of those years because there was so little other evidence of Christmas. Stores were not festooned with decorations; carols did not blare over loudspeaker, radio or TV. Even the homes had little hint of Christmas other than the tantalizing aromas from kitchen and pantry, the wide eyes of children and the joyful air of expectancy which then as today, touched all hearts with gentleness.

The custom of inviting friends and relatives in for cocktails or eggnog during the holiday season, so popular in America today, dates back to the old English practice of "wassailing" in Elizabethan times, no celebration was complete without the wassail bowl filled to the brim with pungent ale—a cheery invitation to all to come in and help celebrate the Yule. Then, as the guests raised their steaming mugs in a toast to Christmas, the merry cry of "What Hail!" "Wassail!" would ring joyously through the hall."

HORACE G. (CHUB) RANDALL INTERVIEW

Sometime in 1948 an unknown person interviewed a life-long resident of Sylvania by the name of Horace Randall. Mr. Randall was the brother of A.H. Randall who also gave important interviews about Sylvania's history. Horace was born in 1879 and raised in Sylvania, the son of A. Dallas and Mary Etta (Green) Randall. He grew up on Summit Street, and after he was married he lived on Erie Street, and in 1922 constructed a home on the north side of Monroe Street, west of the railroad tracks. He served as Sylvania Postmaster from 1924 until 1933, then served as the marshal of Sylvania and then a police officer.

The interviewee wrote the following (the information in parenthesis is written by Gayleen Gindy to help clarify some of the information):

"One of Sylvania's early post offices was in the Howard Building (6521 Monroe Street) the stone one second east of the corner of Main and Monroe, which was the first Masonic Temple in Sylvania. This building was demolished long before this interview. It was a building on the sloping site near the southeast corner of the intersection.

When William Bryan, crippled by injuries in the Civil War, was the postmaster, he kept an office in a building near Jack Neil's saloon. This building burned when the town burned (This building was located on the west side of Main Street between Maplewood and Monroe Street).

The post office was also at one time in the Knisely Dry Cleaners building, which stood on the southwest corner of Main and Monroe. Mr. Randall thought that Lamont was the postmaster at the time that he also occupied this building as a jeweler. He ended up going to Arizona for his health. The post office was also in the building at 5621 Main Street in the downtown business district. Another post office was located where Don White's barber shop was located (part of the old Farmers and Merchants Bank building, or today the Key Bank building).

Don White, the barber, was one of the avid collectors of fossils from the Silica quarries and had a large display of fossils in his shop. The Sylvania Savings Bank built the building on Maplewood for a post office, which later became the American Legion Hall (Today in 2018 this is the Sylvania Area Credit Union). From here the post office moved to the building on North Main Street (Address 5736 Main Street which today is occupied by attorneys). Mr. Randall said he served as postmaster of Sylvania from 1924 until 1933. There was another post office in Sylvania known as Glanntown, located in what was later known as Silica. Where the new Sylvan Theater is, stood a stone blacksmith and wagoner's shop, and north of that stood Dr. Kennedy's residence and barn. (Sylvan Theater was at 5658 Main Street in downtown Sylvania and Dr. Kennedy's residence was to the north of the theater).

The Washingtonian House was on Summit Street, on the west side just a little north of Monroe Street. The big square house on the northeast corner of Monroe and Summit Street was the Peleg Clark residence. A beautiful stairway in this house was supported by the beams above from the top rather than like traditional stairways. It has been greatly remodeled from the day it was built. Hiram Hubbard lived in this house after Mr. Clark. (This house was moved to the east a little when a gas station was constructed on this corner).

The fare to Smith's Siding on the Toledo & Western Electric Railway was 6 cents. When they played ball games at Smith's Siding the conductor of the train could never carry enough pennies to make change because of the odd amount of the fare.

Huling's Mill was opposite Burnham High School along the creek. It was rebuilt from there to a location near the depot and was then powered by steam rather than by water as at the original location. (The train depot referred to here was located along the railroad tracks just south of Convent Blvd.). When Mr. Randall was a boy the Huling Mill was across the street from where Burnham High School is located (Today in 2018 across from where the new Maplewood School was built) and was vacant. The fences were down. Gypsies frequently camped here and did some horse trading to the financial disadvantage of four or five people in town.

Mr. Horace Green Randall (the man being interviewed here) was a descendent of Dr. Horace Green, one of the early Sylvania doctors. Joel Green studied medicine with his brother Dr. Horace Green. In an early history of Sylvania you will find mention of somebody who got into trouble with other members of his church for washing his buggy in the creek on Sunday (The Sabbath). Mr. Randall thought this member might have been Dr. Joel Green.

The railroad originally had a wooden trestle over the creek in Sylvania. The railroad company filled in this trestle and caused the creek to wash away into an irregular course at this point. Then the creek was straightened out but in a slightly different way from the original bed.

Jim Banks was a great fisherman. He once had a new net and went downhill from the library and scooped up some 700 suckers with one drag of the net. Banks lived on the location of the present Burnham school. Banks Bridge (on Silica Drive) was named for Jim Banks. Across from Bank's place on the northeast corner of Monroe and School Drive was the DeBruine property.

Some of the Toledo and Western employees were: Charlie Engle, a conductor with No. 1 badge, Charlie Kroll No. 3, Tom Engle, a brother of Charlie. Randall was No. 37, but he ended up as No. 13 at the time of the strike. Conductors had uneven numbers and motormen had even numbers. Billy Miller was one of the first motormen. The strike on the Toledo and Western was due to low wages paid during the war time (World War I). All men were getting 48 cents an hour while other places were paying 60 cents and 70 cents. Grievances were put up to the War Labor Board, but they decided they had no authority over the case. So finally the men struck. All men were then guaranteed a nine hour run a day even if the run did not take that time. Some men put in a twelve hour run, but no more than sixteen because of the law. The main T & W office was right here in Sylvania and the car barns too were on the site of the Sautter's Market."

CLYDE GAULT INTERVIEW

TOLEDO BLADE ARTICLE 8-29-1978 "REMEMBERANCES OF A SYLVANIA GROCER – Clyde Gault came to Sylvania in 1929 as the manager of a Kroger store. Four years later he bought the Nationwide Grocery on Main Street, from A.H. Randall. It was the Depression and times were hard.

Many of his customers depended on credit, or on relief. Purchases during the Depression were limited to necessities, like soap, sugar, flour, and a little meat. But the village of about 1,600 residents managed to support four grocery stores, and all were located near the Gault's store. "We all made it," Mr. Gault said. "Customers would come in nearly every day, because there was no refrigeration."

Farmers who made early morning trips to the village would stop at the store, which opened at 6:30 a.m., to buy bacon for breakfast, because meat couldn't be kept overnight, especially during the summer, and it would be the same at noon, people would buy for dinner.

Mr. Gault and his employees, Hi Sharp and Joe Bissonnette, waited on the customers, using a ladder or hooked pole to reach the goods stacked on high shelves. "You could get to be pretty fast with the hook," he said. "Just reach up and catch the items when they fell. You could even stack things with the pole, just throw them up there and push them in place. But you had to watch out for your head if you missed."

The store delivered groceries three times a day, twice in the morning and once in the afternoon. Although operating a grocery store during the Depression wasn't easy, in some ways it was more difficult during World War II.

"Everything was rationed, and you couldn't let the customers buy everything they wanted, so some of them would get pretty mad, "Mr. Gault said. But most of them were cooperative, sharing their extra ration stamps with those who didn't have enough. 'We'd get a delivery of meat early in the morning, and people would line up outside, then rush in and almost fill the store," Mr. Gault said. The Gaults would limit the amount of scarce items customers could purchase, so that everyone could have some.

"One lady ordered six kinds of meat, and I said I could only let her buy two kinds." "Later, I got a call from her husband, saying that he heard we had meat and wouldn't let his wife buy what she wanted. He said he'd like to come down and punch me in the nose, but he never did," Mr. Gault laughed. After his employees enlisted in the services, Mr. and Mrs. Gault worked long hours in the store, sometimes 18 hours a day. They operated the store until 1948. Mr. Gault said

"When we moved to Sylvania in 1929, you could drive down Monroe Street to Secor Road and see nothing but open fields."

JAMES ARMSTRONG TAPE RECORDINGS

In January of 1981 James Armstrong, a life-long resident of Sylvania, was asked to tape record some of his Sylvania history knowledge, experiences and memories. James Armstrong was born in Sylvania in the home located at 6502 Maplewood Avenue in 1913, and he lived at this address his entire life, except when he was forced, because of health reasons, to move to Bryan, Ohio to live with his daughter in about 1978. Jim Armstrong's father was Edwin Armstrong, a doctor in Sylvania from 1903 until he died in 1942. His mother was Myrtle DeMuth Armstrong, who was the long-time music teacher working for the Sylvania school system for over 40 years; riding her horse and buggy from one room schoolhouse to one room schoolhouse teaching music to the children of Sylvania. They were a very well-known family and the entire Armstrong family was known for their love for music. On the first cassette that Mr. Armstrong recorded he started out by saying: "The date is 1-27-1981. This is Jim Armstrong located in Bryan, Ohio, and because yesterday I received a pleasant telephone call from Sister Mary Ann at Lourdes College in Sylvania, Ohio, where I have lived most of my life prior to three years ago. . . ." He said that he had been married to Esther Bostwick from Columbus, Ohio and they had a son Donald Bostwick Armstrong and a daughter Christine Bostwick Armstrong Hoit.

On the first cassette Mr. Armstrong discusses just life in general, the background of the Sylvania History Buffs and discussed the people who were most instrumental in getting the group started. Finally, on side two of the first cassette, he briefly discusses various Sylvania history items. Then he proceeded to record nine tapes. A few of his most important comments are included below:

"The old Wickter barn was one example of what was the livery barn—the place was for travelers who came through Sylvania on dirt roads and trails with Indians still in the locality, stopped here at a hotel that I had a big photograph of, when it was all up in a blaze." (Mr. Armstrong is talking about the old Washingtonian Hotel that was located on the west side of Summit Street north, of Monroe Street). "It was located on what is now directly behind Chandler Hardware, that was the hotel and the barn right behind that, a place to put the horses. To keep them overnight, and when Chandler's bought that land, they bull-dozed the whole barn and put up a storage shed. Well that's just one (to be bull-dozed), and I can recall more, but so many of the landmarks have been obliterated, like one of these fine days, maybe in a few days, the corner where my home is (Maplewood and Summit Street) will be absolutely flat, nothing, trees, gone, my grandfather's trees, my father's trees, my trees, all gone overnight. It'll take just—start at eight o'clock in the morning with a machine and that house will be gone at the end of the day. And the next day, they will bull-doze the whole place, level it all up, and it'll be ready to be resurfaced, as a parking lot."

"Toledo & Western Railroad – Toledo, that was far away. The only way to get to Toledo was to follow the electric railroad down to Trilby—to what is now Sylvania Avenue and then down passed the Overland to Cherry Street and on down Cherry Street to the Central Park to the Toledo

& Western station. That was the principal roadway originally, which originally was an Indian Trail from Toledo to Sylvania, Monroe Street did not exist. Later on in my life, I remember vividly cutting the ribbon, opening the street, the year I do not remember, but I remember the ribbon being cut at a ceremony, on top of the bridge where it crosses the creek in Sylvania on Monroe Street. The T & W and the interurban followed the course that I described in Sylvania to Toledo, and was the principal transportation. The T & W originated in Toledo and went through Sylvania and west to Metamora, Morenci, and Lyons then there was a spur, I think it was called a spur that went up to Adrian and eventually, no—it was a spur at Allen Junction which was to go north into Michigan. But the interurban cars, all electric, would go up to Renci (Morenci) and turn around, and come back to Toledo and they had stations all along the way. I remember Stop No. 15, Allen Junction. I was a young boy when they disbanded the T & W. I suppose I was 15 years old or less and I am prompted to tell you another interesting part of my personal life in Sylvania."

"I loved the atmosphere as a little boy of the ticket house which was located at the foothill of Main Street on the west side, it was a little building 15 x 15, painted a dark brown and I always remember the smell and taste of the items in the vending machine in there, where a penny would get you a little package of rich chocolate and the other machine would give you a package of chewing gum. Also the ticket window, while I'm not sure I remember the individual who sold tickets, he impressed me as a young boy. I remember him by looks at this moment, and my one experience I chose to relate now is a very handsome young man who worked on the T & W for one day. There were two men on each car—the conductor who took care of the people, and the motorman who operated the car in front, and one time as a barefooted boy this man said to me, 'Jimmy, would you like to go for a ride on the T & W tomorrow?' and I said,' SURE!' 'Well you be down here at 6:30 in the morning, with a note from your mother saying that you can spend the day with me, and we'll spend the day on the car. Well, I was there plenty in time the next morning, with a note from my mother. I knew the man at the time. Incidentally 25 or 30 years later, I recalled and tried to find that marvelous man who took me on the day's adventure. I spent a lot of time trying to locate him, not remembering his name only a description, and I was not successful, which was a disappointment to me. I wanted to recall with him, and I wanted to tell him what I got from that day's experience. On this ride that ended at noon at Morenci, I was made commander-in-chief of a car. I got to open the doors, carry on the suitcases of the people that got on, or got off, and I was able to take the tickets, and I want you to know that on the return home, I was permitted to sit on the high stool and push the lever that started the car that made it go faster or slower, and as a little boy—and again, that is something I will never forget. I was in control of that great big car, you wouldn't say rattling down the track, but it was swaying down the track, at what I considered a very fast speed."

"Also, on recalling now about the dam, which is now gone, but was located across the creek about 50 feet upstream from the town bridge on South Main Street. The dam was four or five feet thick and four or five feet high and behind that dam was where we swam, where the older boys swam, and I also did, at a later date, but the time now that I'm thinking of is the time that Bill Denton, a high school boy, and my brother, a high school boy, were swimming there one summer while I was sitting on the bank, and I didn't realize it at that moment, but it was pointed out to me when my brother got home, that my brother was caught underneath a floating raft that they were playing with and had it not been for Bill Denton realizing that my brother was under too long, and if he had not gone under that raft and pulled him out, my brother would have drowned at that time, so when I recall Bill Denton, I recall that incident."

"Next is the gin and sugar church on the north edge property of Sylvania. I know it most on the corner of Summit and Maplewood for that's where I was born in 1913 and spent the next 65 years living there. That property was purchased in 1902 by my father's father for him as a wedding gift when he came to Sylvania as a young medical doctor and his wife, my mother, came from Toledo having been a teacher in the Washington Street Elementary School. The property was purchased for $1,200 from Dr. Taylor Cosgrove; he in turn moved up to Phillips Avenue in Sylvania. Well, in the sales agreement, when purchasing the property, the large barn that stood on this property which is 75 x 75 on the north end of this property stood a large barn and in front of that stood a 55 foot windmill, and those two pieces were not included in the sale and they were moved by the former owner, Dr. Taylor Cosgrove, straight across town where there were a few houses, directly west across town. The windmill was also taken up there and reinstalled and the windmill later was sold to a golf course on Central Avenue when it was a farm owned by a man named Moore. I later visited that farm and was told that the windmill was on the property where I lived. O.K. back to the church, which is now and still is (1981), located on the north edge of this property. It is all my life used as a barn. My father bought the building for $50. In 1903 for $50 the building was moved down Summit Street on skids using a wench and a small pony that turned the wench that wound the rope on the spool which was anchored in the center of Summit Street on the dirt road with large stakes and then when it was wound up the spool with the pony turning—going round and round the spool stepping over the rope hooked on to the building then the spool was unwound and moved down the road 50 feet maybe. Stakes were driven in the ground and the building was pulled another fifty feet. It's hard for me not to go off on a tangent but regarding the moving of this building, it was probably 30 years later that I met by sheer accident an elderly man who was a young boy who drove his pony that wound up the spools that moved the barn and he was hired for 14 cents an hour along with his pony because his pony was a slow pony and because his pony was a slow steady behaved pony. The man remembered as a boy doing that job of helping pull that building down the road. Well, I have spent hundreds and hundreds of hours with many, many experiences from that barn, which I again will not go into detail at this time. It got its name because the people that built the church originally were the Brethren Denomination and they disbanded after so many years. I don't know how many years and the church was vacant for some time and then a Pentecostal rented the church and held their services there. This Pentecostal group is correctly named the 'Holy Rollers.' And when the spirit of God moved them during their service they were known to go through gyrations of spiritual display and to roll in the aisles and under the pews. Well, young people, I assume principally fellows, boys in town, for lack of something to do, it was common for them, to go over and peek in the windows during the service and watch the goings on of this frantically spiritual church group— and so around town it was nicknamed the Gin and Sugar Church based on the interpretation that they sure looked like they were drunk and surely going to heaven. And therefore it was known during its active period as the Gin and Sugar Church. It is now, I think 135 years old, and since I have sold the property by circumstances of duress in my marriage separation. I sold the property to the Reeb Mortuary and they are still using the barn for storage and the upstairs of the barn which was always the hay mar, I have now stored a good many of my family things, as yet, I do not know where to place or dispose of. The upper part of the barn that was so strongly built with great timber crisscrossing, were torn out to the best of my knowledge by my father's father who was a bridge builder throughout Ohio, Indiana and Illinois. Incidentally, was known as the musical bridge builder because wherever he went through these three states to repair or build a bridge or he would stay and board at the nearest convenient place and he always carried music with him—and he either sang in church or started a choir or singing group, or sang with a group. When he left, after repairing or building a bridge, after several weeks or more, he would leave music with a singing group. Well, he helped my father renovate the church by removing the high ceiling—trim work and installing a floor, in other words, lowering the ceiling and using the top half of the barn as a haymow. As a boy jumping from the structure that my grandfather built, in the form of a truss bridge upstairs in that barn, a delight for young people there were two levels of this bridge and any boy who could jump into the hay spread eagle with his hands spread out and above him—with his eyes shut, make a belly whacker in the hay from that high level he was a brave boy—and it was quite an experience, quite a feat to accomplish this. Well without going into more stories of the barn, I will conclude and go on."

"Another memorable institution was in town, Uncle George and Aunt Maggie, and Uncle George was the father of Dr. John Counter, a dentist for many years in Sylvania. It was his father and mother who came from Canada, as middle age people. Dr. Counter's parents—George and Maggie Counter lived in the little house directly at the end of Maplewood, which Dr. Counter bought and remodeled for his parents to live in. Dr. Counter had his dentist office in the next house north—the stucco house, now owned by a bachelor real estate man (1981), and Dr. Counter had as a hobby, a successful business man, a herd of cows across the creek on the other side, and the ravine behind his house—a good sized barn and he owned or rented what is now a good portion of what is the Memorial Park Cemetery as his farm and he built, or a had built, a swinging bridge across that entire ravine which was probably 200 feet long and probably 10 – 12 – 15 feet above the creek bed—it was made of farm fences, one at the bottom and one on each side, with planks on the bottom and cables running clear across that ravine—called the swinging bridge, which was a highlight in my young life going across many times when I was told not to make it swing, and I couldn't go across it without making it swing, but taking rhythmic steps to the middle, the whole long swinging bridge would go up and down and I loved it. Dr. Counter would call "Jim, you stop it. Don't swing that bridge." Well Uncle George took over the milking, and the cooling, and the bottling, and the delivering of the milk around Sylvania for his son, Dr. Counter, for a number of years. And in the basement of the stucco house, he prepared the milk and he had a push cart that he pushed around on the sidewalk in Sylvania, and it was a kind of personalized dairy distribution of milk, delightful, delightful English people with an English accent."

"One time on Maplewood Avenue, on the railroad crossing, there used to be a lumber yard; the Hixon Peterson Lumber yard, which filled up the entire corner where there is an apartment complex now. Because of the people that drove vehicles, and pedestrians that crossed the railroad tracks, and because of trains coming through, several a day at 20 miles an hour, I suppose with their whistle blowing, so many were killed crossing that crossing, I remember as a boy, seeing several terrible mutilated conditions there. It was thought to prompt the people of the dangerous crossing here by placing a cross for each death that had occurred here. A cross about six feet high was stuck in the ground at the right as you cross the tracks and at one time I remember 14 crosses in a group beside the track on Maplewood Avenue showing 14 deaths took place in crossing that track."

"I could say a little more about my pony, I called her "Beauty" and she certainly was a beauty. I have photographs now to prove my point, the most beautiful pony, the most sleek pony I've ever seen. I thought so then and I have photographs to prove it too, that she was a tremendous pony and I could go on with a number of experiences with that pony. One of them was our ride after school. It was common for me to come home, and put on an old pair of pants and go out into the barn and unhook the halter strap and jump on her back, and she would back out of the barn stall and we would ride with no bridle or saddle. I hung on to her main—I could steer her with my knees, hands, and she would behave beautifully, quickly, like a circus trained cattle, and we would ride up Maplewood Avenue to Maplewood school, there we would turn left on School Drive which was then called pig tail alley. Pig Tail Alley was what we now call School Drive, which passes Burnham on the right. When you entered the Pig Tail Alley you saw the lovely big home of Henry Burnham, a Civil War veteran who farmed the land behind Maplewood School, which is now Burnham High School, that was his farm. His wife was the one who gave Burnham Park to Sylvania for recreational purposes for the future. My father took care of him in his old age, and a very quiet little man who was liked by everyone and right behind his house was a large orchard which would now be the playground for Maplewood School, and Pig Tail Alley was a beautiful sandy drive with no rocks…no big weeds, nicely kept, and a winding trail. Well we would gallop through that area and then we would cross going south on Silica Drive, which is what it is called now, cross the Ten Mile Creek and Harms Bridge. It was at this time an old iron bridge and it was called Harms bridge because the farm that is now Northview High School was the location of Mrs. Harms' farm and then we galloped around Silica Drive, bending around the farm which is Northview High School and down at the end I would go into the driveway of what was then Battery F – 135th, which was an artillery company of American Soldiers who were stationed there and the house that is now the property owned by Don Loss, was a motel, and Don's delightful wife, a member of the History Buffs group, Phyllis. The pony and I would ride in through the barn that is still there, and I would stop, and the pony would get a drink out of the watering trough in front of the barn. There would always be men in artillery uniforms working with the horses and the gear, and we would say hello and after the pony had a drink we would gallop around the barn and the corrals and around the parade field and down through the woods and jump over several falling logs which is now Sleepy Hollow and down to the creek where she would stop again in the middle of the creek and get another drink and then we would gallop down out to Erie Street and come back on Erie Street and back to the barn."

"In the portable building of the old Sylvania High School when I first started in the first grade at that time, I had no idea what the word verbose meant, but had to assume that my first grade teacher knew. It is my memory that within the first two days that I entered the school room, she found it was the only recourse to attach in front of my face, and covering all of my mouth and what seemed all of my nose with adhesive tape, as I remember she did a very fine coverage. I felt like I would never speak again, and that my skin was being drawn so far out of shape that it would never go back to shape again, and I can remember without being able to say anything there wasn't much for me to do there and so I left the building at 94 miles an hour and stepped up that pace for two city blocks until I arrived at home, and I can remember my mother removing that tape which I'm sure part of my nose came with it, and I can remember going back to school and sitting very quietly as I watched her hand to see if she had any access to any more tape, because I had enough to last me for at least several days."

"I should like to recount a story of my father when he came to Sylvania in 1902 from Grand Rapids, Ohio, where he practiced his first year of medicine, and enter into the house at Summit Street and Maplewood Avenue, there was at that time a basement only big enough to be a fruit cellar beneath the kitchen. I can vaguely remember two hard coal burners, one in the parlor, one in the dining room, and of course one in the kitchen, and then a few years later he decided to modernize and put in a coal furnace. So he hired men to go down in the fruit cellar of the kitchen and dig by hand a tunnel about 15 feet long, four feet wide, maybe, and six feet tall—underneath the house and then to dig out a room of 10 x 12 and another room 12 x 14 with an outside slanting door. Then it hooked-up into the living room in the form of a box with a metal top, with a grate in front and sides for the heat to come into the house. That was a modern innovation—a great improvement over the coal stoves. In the process of digging underneath the house, the workmen came across a skeleton of what appeared to be a child, small, small child. Well in Sylvania, if you can imagine 500 people in town—arc lights at the street corners, kerosene lamps in the houses, no automobiles, quietness of the dark town, no street lighting, except an arc light on each end of Main Street. If you can picture yourself in that atmosphere, in that small group of community, the workmen assumed that the new doctor had made a mistake in a pregnancy case and had buried the evidence under his house, and rather than embarrass or confront the doctor with the evidence they found they took the skeleton carefully and with great secrecy, the towns principals viewed the remains and word went swiftly through the town that the new doctor was a pretty bad so and so, burying the evidence, hiding it. Well, my dad, who was a great practical joker all his life, heard rumor of the story, but said nothing and with a straight face he continued, except that he would drop a remark around town, something about your doctor, sometimes doctors make mistakes, and doctors are human, and he enjoyed the reaction people knowing what they knew, and who didn't think that he knew the story. Well this went on for quite a while and it got to my mother, and my mother, as a young bride coming from Toledo to the small town of Sylvania, she got rather excited, and when she found out the real story she insisted that my father correct the story and straighten it out. And I understand that my father and mother had a period of dissension because my dad rather enjoyed the notoriety of being a secretive doctor of doing things that were not acceptable—so he let it go until he could hold it no longer, then he passed the word that he understands that the workers found the skeleton of the Cosgrove monkey. The Cosgrove boys, who occupied the house before my dad bought it, were known around town as the 'Cosgrove boys,' and when they found extracurricular activities evident around town, people would say 'I bet it was the Cosgrove boys that did it.' Well the Cosgrove boys had a pet monkey and that pet monkey disappeared—and they never found it until workmen digging under the house found it. So it was straightened out, and my dad was forgiven for malpractice. He asked for the skeleton of the monkey, and said that he had need of it for medical observation purposes and teaching. And so he found on his doorstep a little box, but he did not know who delivered the box, and in the box was the skeleton of this monkey which he carefully wired the bones together, in their normal position, and for a number of years it hung in the back corner of his office, and it was a symbol of fun and conversation, along with possible teaching of the bones of the body for his patients and friends. I as a little boy vaguely remember that skeleton but did not know about the story until some years later in my life."

"I have listed some people in Sylvania that I have known and I would like to mention their names and maybe a word about them"

"A.R. Chandler—one of the principal, if not the principal businessman running the Chandler Hardware Store & Implement Company on Main Street with wide distribution and a large stock availability of farm goods and hardware material. A.R. Chandler lived in the lovely big house, probably the largest home in Sylvania, (5916 N. Main Street) which is now owned, I think by the young man who runs the oil company, Bill Howard, by name. That house was always a little bit, it stood in awe, I stood in awe of it. A.R. Chandler was a businessman to the very end, and from morning to night. He was a quiet spoken businessman. He was hard of hearing all his life and he wore a hearing aid, and I always felt that he had a million dollars in his pockets and lots of change, when he needed it. He was the financial backbone of the Congregational church, since I was a part of it for my first 20 to 25 years of life. A.R. Chandler spent a lot of money on very expensive prized quality flower vaults, and he grew beautiful flowers. He loved the Congregational Church, and it was a big part of his life. He would bring flowers and decorate that church with his growing plants, that were absolutely gorgeous, and then because they couldn't be kept alive any longer he would give them to people to take home. It was a very beautiful expensive expression of beauty that he gave. In business he was out to make every dime that could possibly be made. But his generosity later on—he was most generous in a number of ways."

"I now come to John Iffland—he was very formal, stiff, quiet, perfectly dressed, perfectly mannered, a man quiet spoken and knowledgeable on money matters who was a very integral part of the Farmers and Merchants Bank. A few times the boy I was, I went in and stood there with all the marble and grill work in front of me. But I was afraid if he said anything, for I would have no alternative but to melt. Later on I knew him better in insurance and I found him a lovable person. He died two years ago. He was one I wanted to be interviewed, before he passed on. If you could draw it from him, he was very reserved in manners, but he was one that would have many interesting stories to tell."

"And now Harris Randall, another lovable portly quiet spoken gentlemanly, religious man who with a pencil behind his ear and an apron covering his large stomach would wait on you in his family grocery store along with his tall, quiet reserved wife. Mr. Randall started out in Sylvania in comparative poverty, and told me many wonderful stories of his early life, but I regret terribly that I cannot remember or recall any of them now. For many years he was hired, as a school boy, to get the fire burning in two, and sometimes three churches. He would do this to earn every penny, and worked hard for it. He respected it, and everybody respected him, and he was one of those people in Sylvania that you could trust with your wife, your money, your home, and never have a second thought."

"And almost a double, yet in a little different way was Cliff Hesselbart, a little wiry man, full of action, full of get up and go, talked quickly, who also ran a grocery store along with his very quiet and reserved wife. He is the father of Stanley Hesselbart—now vice president of the Sylvania

Savings Bank. Cliff was a stalwart of the Methodist Church. He was the backbone of the athletic programs of Sylvania, and he was active in community affairs, active in the bank and he was active in merchant groups. He was also active in the church and simply a marvelous fellow. I must deviate for a moment to say how at one time, an interesting incident. My father went into his store to buy something and Cliff was talking terribly and he was so weak, he could hardly move, he was hiccupping all night, and I guess all the day before, and he said, 'Doc I can't do anything. I've got it.' And my dad said, 'You've got a vinegar barrel here, don't you?' He said, 'Yeh.' 'Go get a half glass of vinegar, and drink it down without stopping.' And Cliff hesitated, but went back and he got it. I guess I'm told—he got a half glass of straight vinegar and swigged it down and his hiccups were gone."

"I now speak of Clair Cooper, a tall Abraham Lincoln type of individual somewhat stooped. He must have been six feet five inches tall, and very thin. He ran the Cooper Tire Shop, which was located where the first building north of Chandler Hardware is. It was a little red building, with an awning in front, with tires and belts, and there were batteries in the back that he charged. You could drive in the back and have a tire changed. He later became Mayor of Sylvania, and I was brought before him once for speeding, and I found him, as I remember, very just and very considerate in administering justice to me for whatever it was that I did; some minor infraction regarding traffic. Clair was an outdoor man, a hunter. He had trophies in his store, such as stuffed pheasants and skins of animals. In the latter part of his life, in retirement, he lived in a house, a big house, which is now being bulldozed and is now the parking lot of the bank, on the east side of Summit Street. Whereas, he hunted a great deal, and killed I assume many animals in the latter part of his life, in his back yard, which banked on the creek. He had bushels of grain for the wild birds and pheasants and coons, etc., that would come up there behind his house. He said that it was common, so I went up there a number of times, and I wandered quietly down to see the different animals come from the creek to feed from his feed lock."

"Mr. Beebe, Walter Beebe, later he was the town policeman and his son Kenneth was a good friend of mine, and we played together a good deal in Scout camp, at Camp Miakonda. Well, most tragically–my dad (Dr. Armstrong) called me to hurry up and get the Ford and I ran and got the Ford started and we drove over to the Beebe house and Kenneth had shot himself with his service revolver because of emotional stress regarding a girl. I'll never forget that afternoon. Mr. Beebe, again a very little man. Seemed like I'm mentioning men in Sylvania who were all very small in stature, most of them, many of them, but Walter was a small man who seemed to have all things in charge. Wherever he went he had things well at hand. There was a robbery on Main Street and Walter, in apprehending the thieves was shot by one of the thieves. Walter shot and wounded one and one of the thieves shot him, and the bullet hit him in a large belt buckle that he had on and it saved his life. That's one for the road."

"So I come to Carl Comstock. I guess I could say there were three principal names. He was certainly one of the top successful businessmen of Sylvania. I'm sure there are others. Harold Comstock was his father and again a businessman not morning till night, but all night too, if it was needed. When he went to a farmer, to sell farm products, he might stay for ten minutes to make a sale or ten hours, but when he left he usually made the sale. He was one who was known too—if he came to sell you something, you might as well say, I'll take it, or you will in the end.

Again, I liked him, but I think a good many did not care for him. He was so dogmatic and outspoken, anti-government, anti-business, anti-politician, and he would, if I can say honestly rant and rave on things that were terrible, terrible, and so he wasn't a pleasant person to talk to unless it was business. You'd have to catch him on an off moment, in a friendly few minute conversation with him without getting into the wrong of everything around him."

"Billy Miller, a store of the most intriguing smell of—I'm not sure if it was incense, perfume, or candy or a mixture—and he sold a few groceries, a few novelties, magazines, papers, candy, ice cream, pop, and I'm not sure who frequented his store. Two or three times I went into the store, of all things, I now know—that seems just a couple of days ago—a very, very large engraved smoking pipe. I never smoked it, but I bought it from Billie Miller, and why I bought I don't know, I never used it and I've got it or had it all these years. I was simply attracted to it from its size and looks. He was a roly poly, smiling, nicely spoken man, and once again I have to say his wife was a very tall plain looking, quiet reserved lady who was always quietly in the store overlooking the store, maybe her husband, I don't know for sure."

"The Poulos family were Greeks. Nick and George. George was the oldest—They spoke Greek, they had large noses, they were little men and after they came into Sylvania they set up a delicatessen and a real true ice cream store. They had at that time; I suppose 10 to 12 varieties of ice cream. I don't know if they made their own ice cream or not, but I wouldn't doubt it. The room seemed quite large and it was surrounded by mirrors. Any place in the store you walked, you would see yourself—in mirrors all around the walls, and the whole room was filled with ice cream tables. And they had a peanut machine in there where they roasted peanuts. They fought like cats and dogs, with knives part of the time, and you never knew when you went if they were happy or mad. They'd have their arms around each other in real brotherly love, or they would be chasing each other with knives—you would never know—they were very emotional men, and I liked them both, especially Nick. Nick, I think passed away just a couple of years ago, and it was quite an institution that they had there. I remember very vividly it as an ice cream store."

"Mr. Wilkins, Charles Wilkins, organist, Englishman, quiet spoken, a true English gentleman, who was the organist of the Congregational Church for many years while my mother directed the choir, and I sang in for almost 30 years. He was never a player of piano, just the organ, but he worked and worked and struggled during the week. I realized now how he worked hard in order to play and accompany the choir and the hymns on Sunday morning. The Wilkins family was a very close family, friends of my family. The Wilkins and Armstrongs, and the druggist the Adams', spent Thanksgiving together and Christmas and New Years as a group of three families for I suppose 15 years or more. Mr. Wilkins tuned pianos and lived on North Main Street in a house where I can't tell whether they are living there now, but I remember he had a Model T Ford, 1912—that he kept in absolute perfection condition, and when he put it in the garage after an occasional use he would jack up the wheels to remove the pressure and he covered it with a big black cloth and after he died, that beautiful car, which would be worth a tremendous amount now—or even 20 years ago was worth a great deal—just like new—was sold for $5. A friend of mine purchased that car from the estate. He was a rather rough friend of mine in school, who bought it. The first time he drove it, he ran into a ditch and wrecked it, after the first few miles he drove it. The driver's name was Claude Cherry who lived on Convent Blvd., not far off the Main Street."

"Ray West, with all his manipulation and underhanded dealings of horses, doctoring them, etc. I would guess the greatest tragedy of his entire life was the death of his one offspring, Sarah Belle, probably of high school age. Ray, who was not a cultural man, at any point, you might imagine, in order to pay proper, adequate tribute to his daughter, sent to Rome and had a marble statue of a horse sent to Sylvania, and it is the grave marker for Sarah Belle, which is I assume still standing in Memorial Park Cemetery."

"Ray West Hill – not sure if it is still there, but it is the hill that faces north on which would be accessible from Ravine Drive. We called it Ray West hill because he owned it, and the 20 acres or more that was pasture land. It was on that hill that I remember many experiences. On that hill, I remember vividly even now, after all these years. My brother, five years older, at that time probably a junior in high school, had for several years the fastest sled in town. He was the envy of all the young boys at that time. His flexible flyer, if I remember correctly, my folks paid $12 for it, which at that time was a fabulous amount. It was his prize possession in that period of his life, because he was able to go down Ray West Hill and go farther than any other sled in town. A bit of personal interest it was."

Marshal McCulley – in Sylvania the one police representative in Sylvania was Marshal McCulley. He along with his German police dog checked the business district for robbers from which there was very seldom a need for and he was the Santa Claus type—and always pleasant to ask him about his big gun—which he carried on his holster in his belt, which we knew as a horse pistol. The barrel, I would assume, 12 inches long and a large pistol, at least as a boy, seemed tremendously large, and it was a point of interest regarding Marshal McCulley. Marshal McCulley, during the night while he patrolled the business block in Sylvania, he found it of interest to shoot rats on Main Street. At that time, I have to without remembering exactly, say that Main Street was abandoned and people all had gone home. No cars parked, or horses and buggies and he was a lonesome wanderer during the night."

Jim Armstrong was a very interesting man, as well as very unique. According to the 11-12-1976 *Toledo Blade* he had established the "Gentleman Jim's Escort Service" in an effort to help lonely women. After placing an advertisement in the newspaper he said he received over 300 phone calls from curiosity seekers, kooks, cranks, ladies of the evening, and men who wanted a slice of the pie. In the interview of Mr. Armstrong he said that: "He never got to escort anybody anywhere. Unless he counts the divorcee he took for a spin in his Model-A Ford, the weight-watcher he waltzed around a backyard ice rink, or the tennis player who greeted him at the door undressed." The article described him as a retired school bus driver with a pulpit voice and no-nonsense manner. He was 63-years old and he said that he started the service "Not for profit or personal gain but to attack the terrible disease of loneliness, especially among women." The article also said: "Even though he explained that after his own marriage of 30 years ended in divorce, he learned first-hand that loneliness can be as crippling as paralysis."

MEMORIES FROM HOPE CHANDLER-CLARKE-LAKE

Hope Chandler was born on 12-10-1900, the daughter of Dana G. and Iley Lewis Chandler. When Dana and Iley were first married in 1892 they lived in Riga Township, Lenawee County, Michigan. In about 1901 they moved to a rented home on Main Street in Sylvania and then in 1910 Dana Chandler built a new home at 5848 Summit Street, using the cement blocks that he was manufacturing in Sylvania. In about 1973 Hope Chandler Clarke Lake wrote and told the following story about growing up in Sylvania.

"About my second year in school Papa built a home on Summit Street in Sylvania, Ohio. So I have only a very few memories of much more that happened so will list just a few little things before that time. We didn't have much money but good parents. I don't remember the birth of my younger brother, Glenn Milton, but I do remember one day he was cross and doing a lot of crying and Mamma was rocking him by a window on the front porch and told me to go outside and play peek-a-boo with him. I went and rapped on the window to attract him and my hand broke the little pane of glass and cut a vein in my left wrist. I will carry a bean shape scar always on that wrist.

I can remember how Mamma loved her red and white Dahlias and always had them in our garden. I never liked to pick the flowers because they had spider webs in the bushes. The spiders had small black bodies with yellow, but the legs seemed so long to me. Papa raised rabbits for some of our meat. One night dogs got in the pen and killed a lot. I can still see the pretty little bunnies lying all around.

In this house on Main Street was where Glenn use to have "spasm" and Mamma gave him Fetty water. The Fetty was like a little stone and Mamma told him it was to make the water cool. Oh! How it tasted! Also some nights our supper was what we called "cracker soup." We would put about four crackers, smaller than a soda cracker of today, in a soup plate, spread crackers with butter, salt and pepper. Then put enough hot water on this to soak the crackers. Place a dinner plate over the dish for about three minutes and then eat it. Very good. More so if you are hungry.

One Christmas in this house Glenn and I each got an apple, orange and a beautiful little plate with Santa on them (mine is with Roger Clarke). That was the extent of our gifts but we ate from these plates for years.

We children slept upstairs and the stove pipe from down stairs ran through our room. It was so nice we would warm our pillows around the pipe, then jump into bed, put our feet on the old flat iron Mamma had warmed and wrapped in a flannel cloth and placed at the foot of our bed. On cold winter nights this sure felt good.

When Dad built the house on Summit St. in Sylvania, Ohio in 1906, we had our first bathroom. We didn't use it but only for baths as the water had to be stored in a big tank on the second floor. When it rained all the water from the roof ran into this tank first. When it was full it flowed from the full tank into two cisterns, one in the basement and one just outside. If the rains were not enough then we had to hand pump from the basement back upstairs for pressure. We children had to do this.

We had an outside privy or outhouse. It was a square building, 3-hole affair and Dad had built a block hole about 20 feet down in the side of the hill. This was walled with the blocks and the privy built on top. Lime was put down into this tank affair to help kill flies and sweeten it up. Also lime helped to eat out some of the refuse.

Our streets were all dirt. No pavement then. To cross the street in muddy weather we had to walk across a cement path two feet wide and built up high enough to be above the road and built round on the top. Fine for people but rather bad for horses and wagons to go over the hump.

About 1912 my Dad was one of the first men in Sylvania to own an automobile besides the doctors. It was a Cleveland 90 Touring car, 4-door. My Uncle George Cook, who lived next door, was afraid to ride in it, but one day he did consent if Dad would drive real slow. Dad did and Uncle rode with the door opened so he could jump out. He didn't have to jump. One day my Dad caught my 18 year old brother, Worthy, driving the car too fast, 25 miles per hour, and he was grounded a whole month for speeding. No driving the car and his promise was kept.

We lived next door to my cousin, Wayland Cook (died in 1973) and we use to play together all the time. Our houses were built of cement blocks. They are on Summit St., Sylvania, Ohio. They were high above the Ten Mile Creek. The first time Wayland tried to smoke I was with him on the bank of the creek. We made a beautiful pipe out of a straw (wheat straw) and an acorn for a bowl. Someone had told us grape vine was the best thing to smoke. We broke some up (Green) and Wayland lit it and puffed on it saying it was so good. It did make nice smoke. To my disappointment he said, "Girls don't smoke," so I didn't get to try. I was the lookout for his mother, my Aunt Lottie. He puffed and puffed and all at once his inside got to rolling. He was so sick and started to throw up. I was scared and ran for Auntie who came and put him to bed. I never knew if she knew what was wrong but he never smoked grape vine again. But he did try corn silk.

In September 1906 I was 5 years old. My father had all his teeth pulled and blood poison set in. Being a healthy 5 year old and a tomboy I made it rather rough for him. One of our family friends (Mr. Poling) was superintendent of our one building, two -story, 12 grade school. He told my parents to send me to school as I would be 6 in December and the first and second grade teacher didn't have too many children. So they bought me a 'Big 5' red tablet, a new pencil and a hand me down first grade reader. I didn't care for the reader but that 'Big 5' (5 cent) red tablet was a beautiful thing to me. So I went off to school with my big sister and bigger brother and my big 5 red tablet. The teacher (Miss Nettie Harger) had other ideas and took away my Big 5 red tablet and brand new pencil and told me to go home. I did, crying for my precious gifts. That was my first and last day of school for four months. In those days, if you were six years old by Jan 1st you could start then. I got along with Miss Harger but I never liked her after that and still in 1973 I have a little hurt feeling for her.

In my second year at school, I can remember another little trouble I got into. A little boy who sat across the aisle from me brought in some of the nicest thin paper and we could lay it on a picture and draw the picture on it. I had never seen or heard of such nice paper but the teacher caught us and took all that lovely thin paper away. She said it wasn't nice to draw on toilet paper. What in the world was toilet paper used for? I asked when I got home and was told. It was new to me; we always had a catalogue in our privy. Guess his papa and mamma were rich.

Our school had brick privies with about eight holes in the girl's privy. Each hole had a cover with hinges to put over the hole when you were finished. It had a little window on each end but the boys had broken out the glass with balls and stones. It was awful cold in the winter time. We used these privies all the 12 years I went there to school. It was the old Sylvania High School on Main St.

When I was six years old our church had a Tom Thumb wedding and I was a bridesmaid. John Jones was my partner. My mother made my dress. It was light blue cheese cloth trimmed in wide lace, with a train. Virginia Clarke Buffington has that dress and it is now year 1973, as I write this.

August 1907 I had diphtheria and my great Uncle Taylor Cosgrove was the doctor. They thought I was going to die. Toxins for this had just come in and Uncle was afraid of it but they decided they would rather have me die with them (Uncle and Dad) trying than not so I got his first shot of toxin then. This diphtheria left me with bad eyes and that fall when I went back to school I couldn't see to read. There was a boy my age in our neighborhood and we always played together. In fact I think it was "puppy love." I remember one nice thing this boy (Carson Wood) did for me; I got my spelling words from him. He would spell the word in a whisper until I could spell it and the only word I can remember he taught me was "good." He died a young man.

One year the black walnut tree in our chicken park had a worm nest in it. I felt so badly because they were going to eat my little tree. Dad put a corn cob on a wire, poured coal oil on the cob, lit it and burned the nest out. That tree was still growing in 1972 right where I found it on Summit Street in Sylvania, Ohio.

When I was in school we did not have running water so out in front of the school house was a hand pump on a drilled well. It had three huge brass cups hung by chains on the pump. We all drank out of these. Every once in a while a smart boy would put a dead snake or mouse in one of these to hear us girls scream. Later years the cups were removed and each child had to have a folding cut of his own.

It was my duty to feed the chickens each day. One year Dad took a big turkey in on a debt. It was way before Thanksgiving. He always kept the chickens shut in the coop all winter so Dad put the turkey in with the chickens. He forgot to tell me. When I opened the door out flew the turkey into the top of a tall pine tree. Nothing to do but to call Dad home from work and he shot the old bird out of the tree. We hung it out to freeze until Thanksgiving. At the end of the walk around the back of the house, I always kept an old pair of shoes so when I went to feed the chickens I would slip into these. One day I felt something prick my foot so I used the other foot to step on it and I mashed a large caterpillar in it between my toes. What a mess! I was the one who had to clean the inside of the shoe.

Our father built us a boat to use on the creek. It was made like a mortar box with wood sides and sheet iron bottom so it couldn't tip over. He had damned the creek for us and in summer we used this for a boat. In the winter we used it to coast downhill. It would take about 10 kids to pull it up the hill and only about four could ride down because it would bog down on the hill. Everybody got a ride though, at least once. This hill was very near our home and we called it Hallett's Hill. The best coasting hill in town. Then in summer when the creek was dried up we used this grassy hill and our old boat to coast down on the dry grass. It was almost as good as snow but not so wet. The "hill" got its name from people who lived just beyond. They had a big side porch and in the summer when we were coasting they would hang an old cage with a big green parrot in it. When we children would get noisy the parrot would get noisy, the parrot would swear and yell "shut up." How we laughed and yelled louder than ever.

Fourth of July was a big day in Sylvania. The main street, one block long, was roped off to carriages and horses and etc., streets were hosed and brushed down, booths set up all along the sidewalk. All organizations, churches and merchants had booths. All were decorated with red, white and blue bunting. The bunting was real thin cloth and the stripes went the long way of the cloth. Children saved their pennies for weeks, we never knew about allowances then; we had to work and save. Such fun. My pennies always went for a balloon and some little memento, like a small horse whip or a spindly cane with a flag on it. At 10 o'clock in the morning there was a big parade all through the streets of the town. One main street and the back street, now called Summit St. It was one of the "big days" of our lives. The businessmen bought fireworks. They would fire them at dark; how beautiful they were, though not like today in the '80s.

On our way to school was a vacant apple orchard and there was an old Northern Spy apple tree in it. It had such beautiful apples every year. We children would get apples to eat at recess at school. Nobody seemed to care about these apples or they had enough in their own yards. They were so juicy and I have never been able to find a Northern Spy apple like it in these later years.

Winters were long and white back in early 1900. The creek behind our house always froze over hard. We had ice skates. At night dad would build a big fire from wood, it would light the space where we skated and was a good place to keep warm. Of course every night someone would get a wet foot or fall in, but they always went up to our basement where mother or dad dried their clothes before they let them go home. Also every night dad popped corn for the whole bunch. Always six to thirty kids.

We didn't have any refrigerator then and before ice boxes came in once in a while my parents would buy a block of ice and put it in a wash tub to cool a melon. We had an 'Iceman' who came with a wagon and a horse. The blocks of ice came in 100 lb. blocks and with an ice pick he would chip the block into 50 lbs. or 25 lbs., whichever you wanted. While he was chipping, small chips would fly off and we kids could have them. This was a real treat. So kids always followed the ice wagon.

The family reunions were wonderful. All the Aunts, Uncles and cousins on both sides of our family would be there and everybody brought so much food. Everything was homemade. We didn't know what a box cake was. These reunions were most always at our house because we lived in town.

Every year when we had chicks hatched I would always teach one to eat out of my hand. Every Sunday we had chicken (never in the week) for dinner. Dad always killed one of my chickens. When my pet was of a nice size off would come his head and you can bet that Sunday I didn't eat chicken.

Across the street from us lived two elderly ladies, Mrs. Bennett and her sister Miss Stiles. I just loved these two people and spent a lot of time with them. In the summer it was fun to go there because they had an open well in the kitchen. They would always let me get a cold drink. You let the bucket down on a rope and then turned a big crank rolling the rope on a cylinder to pull up the bucket and water. I can still taste that water; it was always so cold and clear. This was called a 'dug well," and was walled up on the inside.

The only time we had candy was Saturday night. We charged our groceries and every Saturday night Dad paid the bill. The owner would give him a bag of candy. It was divided among us four children. We could eat it when we wanted to but sometimes we made it last almost all week. Christmas we got candy too. But Christmas and birthdays were the only time we ever got toys. We made our own toys and fun.

When I was in high school we got our milk down on Monroe Street where a part of Memorial Park is. Every night either Glenn or I would have to walk down and get it. Each customer had a nail on the wall. We took our bucket of milk and left the empty one on the nail for the next night. In the winter this was a long cold walk.

About 1909; twice a year Mother would take $10 and go into Toledo to buy our clothes, spring and fall. One fall she bought me two new dresses and I was so pleased I had to show the neighbor (Mrs. Brown) across the street. I put on one and strutted over to show her. The cherry trees in her yard were loaded with beautiful ripe red fruit. Mr. Brown had some long stakes standing in the crotch of the tree and when I went to jump down the wind caught the dress and the poles went up under then came out at the waist band tearing the skirt in shreds. I didn't sit for a few days! We never had too many store bought dresses.

When I was of dating age (1917) my boyfriends didn't have autos, they had horses and buggies. We would go for a buggy ride. Sometimes as far as Ottawa Lake, Mich., three miles from home. Sometimes you would see two buggies racing. I never would ride in a race for two reasons: one, my dad didn't let us; and second, I hated to see the horses have to go so fast and the buggy might tip over.

Mother and Dad took dancing lessons in Toledo and one snowy night they went in a bob sled with some other people. Coming home a shaggy dog followed them. Dad and mother were the last to leave the sled and it being such a bad night, dad put the dog in our basement to turn him out in the A.M. It was the first dog I can remember we ever had. He stayed and we called him "shep" and we all loved him very much.

Our fire department was voluntary. In the "council" building doorway was a rope to a big clapper bell in the tower. If there was a fire all businessmen went to help. There wasn't a fire engine but a hose cart which the men pulled to the creek or a cistern or wherever they could get water. This had hand pumps, one on each side. Four or five men on each side pumped it. If there wasn't deep water for this cart they had a bucket brigade. Men would stand in line and pass buckets of water down the lines. A lot of homes were lost but it was the willingness of people to help each other that meant so much.

The milk we used came direct from the cow. It was only run through a cloth then delivered to the houses in tin buckets. At first one of our neighbors had a cow and their children brought our bucket every night, mother put it on the basement floor to keep it cool and sweet. These peoples' name was Leatherman and they had four children.

Then our next milk was delivered by an old man who had a two wheeled cart. Every day he brought our milk to the door. This man's name was Counter. His son was the town dentist. They lived next door to each other. Their houses were on one side of the Ten Mile Creek, the cows and barns were on the East side. To get across they had built a swinging bridge. They stretched fence wire across the wire sides and laid a plank floor. It was high up and the creek ran deep in the spot. Once in a while they would let us children walk across this bridge. It would swing unless you walked very careful and it was a privilege, so we never ran across.

One of the most beautiful sports in my memory is the woods across the creek in back of our house. We had so many wonderful spots. There was a horseshoe shape bowl in one place. We called it, "The old lake bed." Why I do not know, unless sometime someone had told us it use to be a lake bed. This didn't have any trees except a thors apple tree with the biggest and best little red apples. How we would gather them in the fall. They were smaller than a small marble but we thought they were wonderful to eat.

We had one spot where the Black-eyed Susans blossomed so beautiful in late summer. These grew in a meadow and cows were pastured in here, but I can still see their yellow heads with a big brown center. In one part of the woods there was the clearest little stream that ran through it and never dried up. All the trees around this were so big. One place the wild grape vines hung from high up in the trees and we could swing in them. What joys we had. Here we spent hours. We knew just where to look for each little kind of flower and what time of the year they were in blossom. Like the Dutchman's breeches, Adder Tongues, Mayapple, blue, white and yellow violets or Jack-in-the pulpit and it would squeak and we always said, "Jack was preaching."

We learned that the pulp just under the bark of a slippery elm tree was good to chew. That the bark of spice wood shrub tasted good and its root was where sarsaparilla came from. On Sunday afternoons my dad, Dana Chandler, would take all our friends and off to the woods we would go. We would bring home armfuls of flowers and pockets of goodies. We used my mother's fruit jars for vases. She never complained how many we had. Those woods are now part of Memorial Park Cemetery, east of Sylvania, Ohio.

We had bob sleds. They had runners under a large box. These runners were in two sets. One set on the back were stationary while the front one was loose to turn as the horses went. Like a wagon only with runners. They used them on the snow and ice and were drawn by two horses. The young people used these bob sleds for "Bob Sled parties." They filled the box with straw and set it on the floor with lots of warm blankets and away we would go. We also had cutters for the snow. They had one runner on each side and were drawn by one or two horses. They were most always one seated and held two people, although very few had two seats and were drawn by two horses. At Christmas time they put a strap around the horse's bellies. This strap had ball type bells on it and would make a beautiful sound as the horses trotted along. We called them sleigh bells.

My dad and my Uncle George Cook (who lived next door) were two clowns when they were together. They always got along so well. We kids use to suffer by their jokes once in a while. Uncle George had two sons, one about my age and one my eldest brother, Worthy's age. Uncle George always had a big hound dog plus a big dog house. One winter my cousin Wayland and I decided to cut and store ice from the creek. So we worked hard all through Christmas vacation to cut, haul and pack the ice in the hound dog's house. My dad said to pack it in straw and it would keep all summer. We did. The dog slept in the barn in the winter. We filled the house alright. It only kept until the first warm days of spring and Uncle had to clean it out. It was too heavy for us. Next year Uncle told us where to put our ice.

At our house, dad had built a chicken house on the side of the hill to the creek. We had a nice chicken park on the hill with steps of cement blocks down one side (these steps I will talk about again). This chicken house was where Uncle told us to put our ice and when we got it all full of ice we needed to put a lot of rock salt all over the top of the pile. We worked like beavers but didn't fill it, although we did a good job. Then we got pails and pails of salt from Uncle's barn and put it on top like he said. It didn't last too long and Wayland and I had to clean it out ourselves. This wasn't a very nice job because the chickens still roosted in the coop. So dad made us clean that also.

INTERVIEW WITH RICHARD J. DOWNING IN 1989

Richard Downing was the zoning inspector for Sylvania Township at the time that I interviewed him. He came to Sylvania in 1939 as a young boy of eight, with his parents, Hugh and Mary (Stephenson) Downing, older sister Lou Ann and younger sister Jane. His parents were married in 1927 in Peru, Indiana and then they resided in Tipton, Indiana. In 1933 his father started working at Robert's Dairy in Indianapolis, Indiana and he worked there until the industry went on strike. In 1938 his father went to Long Beach, California after hearing that there was work there, but it did not pan out so he returned to Indianapolis where his family was living. These were rough years and his father, as well as thousands of other men were out of work. In January of 1939 the Downing family moved to Sylvania and his father took work at the fertilizer plant on Sylvania Avenue, east of Centennial Road. They first lived on Roosevelt Court in a duplex for three years, and then they moved to the Katie Marsh house on Sylvania Avenue west of King Road. On 6-7-1940 his youngest sister Kay was born in Sylvania.

His father later took a job in the chemical lab at Kaiser Jeep and started night classes at the University of Toledo and they later rented a house on Balfour in Sylvania and lived there 10 years.

Richard graduated from Burnham High School and married his high school sweetheart, Alcy Smith on 6-26-1954 while he was on active duty assignment in Puerto Rico at the Naval facility of the Air Base. Their daughter Lynn was born there on 1-19-1956. After two years of active service they returned to Sylvania where their daughter Cheryl Downing was born on 11-26-1958. Richard worked for the Dana Corporation and then DeVilbiss Company until they closed up. His wife had been working in the administration offices at Sylvania Township for several years and in 1980 the position of zoning inspector was vacant and he filled that position at that time.

His wife continued working in the clerk's office of the township during that same period of time until she was forced to retire in August of 1986. Alcy died of cancer on 8-3-1987. She was only 53 years old. Richard continued as the township zoning inspector until December of 1991, when he retired.

Dick Downing gave me a copy of a tape recorded interview that his mother had recorded about her life. The following is quoted, in part, about her and her family coming to Sylvania looking for work back in 1939: "...Our good friends for many years, Ralph Ellis, came past mother's to tell us he had seen Leon Wright in Tipton. Leon was another Tipton boy whom Hugh had known since grade school. Leon had worked for Martin Marietta Co., fertilizer division in Indianapolis for a few years and had been transferred to Sylvania, Ohio. In fact, at the time they were looking for a location in Sylvania, Hugh had just started his dairy job and we had rented two bedrooms and lived with Lou and their two children, Duane and Patricia, on E. Washington St. in Indianapolis. Some telephone calls were made and Hugh went to work January, 1939 at the fertilizer plant on Sylvania Avenue near Centennial Road in Sylvania. Our first home in Sylvania was on the court in a house near the railroad that had been made into a duplex. We lived in the upper I think three years. Lou Ann, I believe, was in the 4th grade and Dick had half year in Indianapolis and Elizaville. Mr. Courtney, Principal at Maplewood, thought it best to keep him in first. Jane was the only one who went to pre-school. She and Margie McClain, who lived close to us on the court, went to Mrs. Courtney's morning class. I think it was $2.00 a week. Margie's mother and I took turns walking them to the crossing at Main Street and meeting them. Kay was born 6-7-1940, the week school was out. Hugh took the children to mother's while I was in the Toledo Hospital two weeks. Yes, two weeks. When she was three weeks old we went down after them. We then moved to the Katie Marsh house on a few acres on Sylvania Avenue west of King Road, not far from work. There was an orchard on a few acres east of the house and we worked and I do mean we, Hugh & Dick sprayed at least three times and we had lots of beautiful apples and so did everyone else that summer. We would pick them, sort in the barn that we on the hill back of the house and Dick did such a good job of ring packing. We had a sign out and sold as many as we could. We took lots of them to the Catholic orphanage on Central Avenue and the Toledo Zoo free. Also had cider made and sold it by the gallon. No plastic jugs then and if people brought their own containers we knocked off a dime. Oh, yes, I must not forget Chin, the Chow dog. I saw an ad for a Hoover sweeper for sale on Summit St. in Sylvania and Dick went with me to see it. It was in good condition and the price was right - $10.00. These people had a beautiful spade female Chow two years old that fell in love with Dick and Dick with her and as you know, I loved animals, especially dogs. The lady, whose name I can't recall, wanted us to take her home with us and Dick said "Let's do" and I said not until we talk to daddy. It didn't take too much talk and Hugh and Dick went back to Summit to get the dog, feeding dish, water dish and bed. Had a leash on her and took familiar things into the house and got Chin to the door and she turned so quickly she broke the leash and back to the car. It took a lot of coaxing to get her in the house. She was shown every nook and corner. Food and water was put in the kitchen for her as well as her bed (blanket). I don't think the blanket bed was ever used as she slept on the bed or bedroom or wherever she was near one of us. Within a week she had adjusted and was ours. Hugh left the fertilizer plant and started to work in the chemical lab at Kaiser Jeep. He started night classes at U.T. in metallurgy and wouldn't get home til late (10 p.m. or after). I think we would have all been uncomfortable if we hadn't had Chin. One night Dick, Jane and Kay were all in bed and I was doing something in the kitchen and Lou Ann was doing homework at a desk in front of the window facing the porch. Chin had been so restless and kept making little growling noises. I said, "Chin, what's the matter, are you hungry?" About that time Lou Ann came strolling into the kitchen and said in a low voice "there's a window peeper on the porch." I went to the kitchen door with Chin at my heels and said "go get him Chin." She tore out the door and around the house and Lou Ann and I saw from a window a male form running out thru the orchard east of the house. Chin didn't come back until after Hugh got home from night school at U.T. and she was full of burrs. Had a horrible time getting her cleaned up the next day. Thru the grapevine, we contacted a lady, Mrs. Apple, whose mother owned a house on Balfour Rd. Since the mother was no longer able to live alone in a two story house, it would be for rent and the mother was moving in with her daughter. We lived there 10 years. Even approached them about buying. The mother wasn't interested because she had willed it to her only grandchild, Bill Apple. Bill was in the service. All the children got the bus at Alexis Rd. at the south end of our street. Lou Ann worked at the Sylvania Public Library and also at Breldway, a pre-school on Alexis Rd. Leigh Held's mother, Leota Held, and sister Doris Brown owned the school. Leigh and Lou Ann were close friends, and still are. During the summer Kay went with Lou Ann to pre-school. Dick started a Saturday Evening Post route for a short time and went from there to a Blade route, beginning with a few and by the time of his senior year had, I think, over 100 customers. He also, while in high school, ran the movie projector on Main St., swept out Jerry Weintraub's Men's store. Dick went one year to U.T., then three years to Kent State. While in college he was in officers' training and spent a couple summers in Long Beach Navy facility, got an Ensign's rating. He and Alcy, with whom he had dated since juniors in high school were married 6-26-1954. . . ."

I, Gayleen Gindy, the author of this book, worked with both Richard Downing and his wife Alcy Smith Downing at the administration offices of Sylvania Township, through serving as the recording secretary for the two zoning boards, and working at the fire department before that. When Alcy was forced to retire in 1986, I was hired to take her position at the township. Richard and Alcy Downing were well respected people and I always enjoyed working with both of them.

REMINISSING WITH THE SULLINS FAMILY IN THE 1970S

Charles and Carolyn (Daler) Sullins arrived in Sylvania in 1959, purchasing the home at 4802 Brinthaven Road. At that time they already had a daughter, Jill Sullins, who was born in 1958, and a daughter, Gayleen Sullins, who was born in 1959. While living on Brinthaven they had a son, Bart Sullins, born in 1963, and a daughter, Amy Sullins, born in 1965. In 1966 they moved to a home at 5723 Main Street in downtown Sylvania, and then in 1969 Bret Sullins was born. (In 2018 this house is part of the Sylvania Historical Village and is leased to Stellar Blooms flower shop).

The house that we lived in on Main Street was located next to the Sterling Milk Store and Dr. Tallman's offices, where Nancy Fox also had a hair salon in the small one-story portion of this duplex building. This building sat just to the north of our house, but sat back off Main Street; behind and to the right of our house. Across the street was the large old white First Methodist Church and Reeb Funeral Home, where at this time they were also operating an ambulance service.

To the south of our house was the large Cooke/Kuhlman house, which today is the historical museum. We rented our house from Mr. and Mrs. Alfred Kuhlman, who lived in the house next to us. It was one thing to rent a home from someone who lived in the same community, but it was another thing when your landlord lived right next door. There were five kids in our family and Bart was the "middle child," with two older sisters (Jill and Gayleen) and another younger sister (Amy) and younger brother (Bret). Needless to say, with five kids, and all of our friends, there was always something going on in our front, side and back yards, or on our large front porch that wrapped around the entire front and south side of our house.

Mrs. Kuhlman, our landlord, kept a very close watch over us, and her kitchen window overlooked our back porch and backyard. If we were doing something she thought we shouldn't be doing, she would knock on the window and point her finger at us. We would of course pay attention, because she often talked to our mother. We think that Mrs. Kuhlman spent most of her days keeping an eye on us. Also watching over us were all the employees that worked across the street at the Reeb Funeral Home and ambulance business (Jack Watkins, Chris Roby, Mel Wainer, Greg Northrop are the ones I remember). They were often out front, in between calls and funerals, working in the yard, or just talking. We also had the employees working at Dr. Tallman's office watching over us while living here, and then there was Nancy Fox, who parked her car alongside the building where her hair salon was; just to the north of our garage. She was always nice to us kids and all day long we could see women walk in with scarves wrapped around their heads and come out looking beautiful.

The Sullins family lived at 5723 Main Street from 1966 until 1976 and then Jill Sullins-Dallas and her husband Mark continued to live here until 1984. Here's the entire family posing on the back porch of this home in 2009, after they were all grown-up and had children of their own. The five Sullins kids that grew up in this house were: Jill Sullins-Dallas; Gayleen Sullins-Gindy; Bart Sullins; Amy Sullins-Verhelst; and Bret Sullins; all children of Charles Sullins and Carolyn Daler-Sullins-Micham. Gayleen Sullins-Gindy is the author of this series of Sylvania history books. (Photo owned by Amy Sullins-Verhelst).

When I was young, growing up here on Main Street in downtown Sylvania, on any given summer day, in the morning we might have started out pooling our money together and going over to the Sterlings store to purchase the necessary Kool-Aid packets, and then back to our house to set up a Kool-Aid stand in the front of our house; selling a glass for maybe a nickel or a dime. At this time we had lots of people walking passed our house on their way to Sterlings or the Medic Drug store; located in the same building. Some of these people were on their way to the post office, which was right across the street from the Sterling store. Some people would be heading to downtown Sylvania, on their way to the Western Auto Store or Joann's Pet Shop, where J & G's is located today. Or maybe they were on their way to one of the two banks on the east side of Main Street (Toledo Home Federal or Sylvania Savings Bank) or walking down to Chandler Hardware. Some might be walking down to get a hair cut at Don Brown's Barber Shop, or going to McGee's Auto Parts, U-Need-A-Cleaners, Lindau's Drug Store, Seitz Bakery, Jerry's Clothing Store, Peddler Shop Antiques, the Service Barber Shop, Jennings Jewelry or down to the Sylvania Bowling Alley.

Some of the women had just finished getting their hair done at Nancy Fox's salon behind our house, or men, women and children just finished up their doctor's appointment at Dr. Tallman's office. Anyway, we had a lot of foot traffic in front of our house, and most everyone that went by (kids and adults) would buy a glass of our Kool-Aid, including our favorite mailman Pat Reitz. Sometimes, we would have to have one group making more Kool-Aid, while the second group was handling our customers. After we ran out of Kool-Aid, or cups, we would split the money up among all of us and head over to the Sterling store where we could each purchase 10 pieces of candy for a dime. They had every kind of penny candy imaginable: jawbreakers, licorice stick, Jolly Ranchers of every flavor, Bazooka bubble gum, candy cigarettes, Now and Laters, and much, much more. The saleslady, Vivian Russwinkle, had special little brown bags that she would put your candy in so that you each had your own bag as you walked out the door.

Sometimes, instead of spending our money at Sterlings we might take the money next door to Medic, but they didn't have penny candy, you would spend your entire dime on one candy bar instead. Or down to Lindau's Drug Store and get an ice cream cone at their ice cream parlor, which was located on the left hand side of their store as you walked into the front door. Remember? Or, maybe we wanted to stop in a Seitz Bakery and get one of those great glazed donuts. If you had extra money that day you could afford one of their chocolate éclairs, which were kept in a small glass front refrigerator on the back corner wall.

Other times we used the money that we made from collecting glass pop bottles in the woods behind the Sterling store, or in the woods along the railroad tracks; walking along the ditches, going all the way down to where the railroad track bridge goes over the Ten Mile Creek. We would cash these bottles in at Sterlings, and Vivian would pay us the deposit fee of 5 cents per pop bottle and a dime for the actual glass "Sterlings" half gallon milk bottles. I guess this was early recycling. This could be an all day job, and by say four o'clock in the afternoon we might have a couple dollars worth of bottles. Again we would split up the money and buy penny candy, or maybe an ice cream bar, or a "slush" drink at Sterlings. Remember!!

On any given day, while we were holding our Kool-Aid stand, across the street you could have a funeral possession pulling out onto Main Street, several ambulances rushing out on their way to an emergency, or a wedding party exiting the front door of the church with people throwing rice at a happy couple as they rushed to a waiting vehicle parked in the street, right in front of the church, and right in front of our house.

A typical summer day in Sylvania back in 1971, for an eight year old boy growing up in the downtown Sylvania area, as discussed with my younger brother, Bart Sullins: In the summer Bart, Kevin, Rick and Doug built a three-story tree fort in a big tree behind Dr. Tallman's office. (This tree is still there in 2018). In order to get to the higher floors you would climb through a small opening in the floor, and climb up using the strength in your arms. The wood for this tree fort came from all over Sylvania; a piece here and a piece there. The area where the Village Arms apartment complex (Sylvania Gardens) is located today, used to be an old lumber yard, and many pieces of old wood were found lying in the wooded area to the north. They would go down to the Ten Mile Creek behind the Summit Street houses and find wood there also.

This was an entire summer project for this group of boys. Everyone would meet in the morning, and the daily search for more wood would begin. They would purchase their nails down at Chandler Hardware. Everything was within walking distance, and help from parents was not necessary. One time they went over to where they were remodeling the building, where Haymarket Square is today, and the construction workers gave them a bunch of their scraps.

Then, at lunch time they would feast on the wild strawberries that were growing in the field next to the woods behind Sterlings, or from the three wild apple trees that were growing behind our house, on Mrs. Kuhlman's property, or mulberries that were growing on the tree right behind Dr. Tallman's back steps.

One day Bart remembers a man running out of the woods behind Sterlings, and the next thing he knew the police were investigating the crime of a young girl being attacked back in the woods. He remembered the police talking to him, and him giving a description of the man that he saw running out of the woods. This area that we are referring to as "woods," ran from the apartment complex property line, to the railroad tracks, to the rear of the property lines of the Erie Street homes (Where the historical village is located today). Within the woods there was a path that was cut, where people could cut through from Woodrow Drive and Roosevelt Court, by going over the railroad tracks and cutting through to get to the Sterlings and Medic store. Also within the woods was a path cut to the north, and a path to the south, which actually lead to nowhere, but where older kids "hung out."

In the summer, just about every night we had a homemade tent built in our back yard. We would use old blankets, clothes pins, and heavy rocks and build our tents using mom's clothes line. We had blankets on the ground to sit on and played board games in there and played with our Matchbox cars too. Every day and night was an adventure, and the days seemed to last forever. What an awesome place to grown up in downtown Sylvania in the later 1960s and earlier 1970s.

Another memory that I have is my mom's vegetable garden one year. Back before the big apartment complex was built at 6632 Maplewood Avenue (Sylvania Gardens) there was an abandoned lumber yard on this property, and there were cement piers that ran about every few feet where they used to store wood, to keep it off the ground. Well the property was abandoned so we all helped my mom get all the debris out of the space between the first two piers and she tilled it all up and planted her garden between those cement piers. That year we had vegetables all summer long, and lots and lots of cucumbers, which she then made into canned pickles. It was a family project and I remember pulling weeds all summer long out of that garden.

ARTICLES WRITTEN IN 1932 ABOUT EARLY SYLVANIA BUSINESSES AND MEN

Back in 1932 the *Sylvania Sentinel* newspaper started writing weekly articles about some of the men who operated early businesses in Sylvania. These articles were well written and told a great deal of information about early businesses. Remember as you are reading these articles, they were written back in 1932 and 1933, so the landmarks that they are referring to are from that time and not today. I have tried to clarify in most cases by adding notes in parenthesis. Also remember, these articles were not written by me, they were written by the editor of the newspaper at that time. Here are a few of the more important articles that appeared:

Sylvania Sentinel – 9-15-1932 – "**Farmers and Merchants Bank of Sylvania** was organized in the year 1899 as a private bank, and operated as such until December 28th, 1900. It was then incorporated as a State Bank. The incorporators were A.R. Chandler, Thomas Gibbs, J.G. Taylor, W.B. Harris, John Lenardson, L.L. Ford, Arthur Hotchkiss, T.T. Cosgrove, E.F. Rowley and John Bittner. W.B. Harris was elected secretary and cashier at the first meeting and served until 1909. W.E. Irwin became cashier, which position he held until 1917, when John Iffland took over the position and has served ever since.

When first organized the bank used a part of the Chandler Hardware store (5648 Main) as its first banking quarters. The directors meetings were held in the store and it was not unusual to find directors sitting around in wagons and buggies, which were on display in the store. Later, the building now occupied by the Thamletz & Son shoe store (5629 Main Street) was built, and the bank occupied the building until the quarters became too small. In the year 1917 the present building was erected (5604 Main).

At the first meeting of the bank, A.R. Chandler was elected president and is still serving the bank in that capacity, a term of 33 years. The present officers are A.R. Chandler, president; E.G. Howard and V.H. Adams, vice president; J.C. Iffland, secretary and cashier; E.G. Jacobs, assistant cashier; and Lynn Bischoff, bookkeeper and teller. The Board of Directors now serving consists of A.R. Chandler, Fred Clampitt, W.A. Hotchkiss, G.J. Lewis, V.H. Adams, Fred V. Myers, Roy A. Chandler, E.G. Howard and J.C. Iffland. These men are all well-known successful men with varied interests.

Looking back over the records we find that on the day the bank opened, 10-14-1899, the following persons opened savings accounts: W.C. Fletcher, Susie Calkins Langham, S.V. Bell, Charles N. Bellman, Roy Chandler, Claude Webb, George W. Woodward, Kent Eley, Wayne B. Harris, Caroline R. Printup, John Printup, Lansing Potter.

On that same date, the following persons opened checking accounts: A.R. Chandler, George L. Calkins, W.B. Harris, S.G. Whitney, John Samsey, W.A. Cutler, John C. Jones, S.A. Youngs, W.E. Chapple, W.E. Durfee, A.D. Randall, Dan Bay, and George M. Deer."

Sylvania Sentinel – 9-22-1932 – "**George Keene** – who for a dozen years has operated a pool and billiard parlor in Sylvania. Mr. Keene's business life has been a very interesting one. As a young man he made many changes and was always willing to learn something new.

Born in Buffalo, Mr. Keene's parents both died when he was still a young boy. He had often heard them speak of a brother Charlie, who was a captain on a lake freighter, and who had left home when George was just a baby. When he was about 16 years of age he decided to come west and find that brother. Reaching Toledo, the lad had no idea of the method to pursue to locate a sailor, so he went down to the river and sat on a dock near a boat that was discharging a cargo of lumber at the Sprague Lumber Yard. Presently the captain of the boat came to the rail, and stared hard at the young boy, and finally asked him if he was looking for someone. George told him of his search, and the captain proved to be the brother Charlie. He later told George that something just made him speak to the lonesome looking boy on the dock.

Charlie took the newcomer to his boarding house and of course George was soon out looking for a job. His first position in Toledo was as a stage hand at the old Wheeler Opera House in 1885. As the electric light had not yet come into use, it was part of his duties to turn the gas light on and off for lighting effects. Mr. Price, the father-in-law of Mr. E. Acers, and also a Sylvania man, was engineer at the theatre at that time.

After working at the theatre about a year, George was on his way to work one evening when the fire engine came dashing down St. Clair Street. He became so interested in the burning factory that he forgot altogether about the job of turning on the lights. When he finally arrived another man had his job.

Being out of work again, George became interested in watching the farmers at the old Erie Street Market Space. He was finally offered a job by Fowler MacDowell, of Ottawa Lake, for $4 a month. Later he worked for George McCormick and also, for Ebenezer Roberts. At this time, most of the houses and barns were made of logs, and Roberts was still using oxen.

The trip to Toledo with produce and stock was often fought with hardship. The road bed was so soft when it rained that the wheels of the wagon would sink to the hubs not once, but many times on the way.

After a year in Virginia, Mr. Keene worked for the Toledo & Western until the road from Sylvania to Fayette and from Sylvania to Adrian was completed. When laying the rails in the local yards, they were all bent by hand with the aid of a jim-crow.

When this job was over Mr. Keene took over the hotel and saloon, which was located where Fred Myers now has his garage, (5703 Main) with a partner named Louis Burg. Tiring of this he bought the saloon of Mike Ryder, which was located in the store now occupied by Adams Drug store.

After two ventures in the saloon business in Toledo, once in the old Arcade building and once near the Milburn Wagon Works, George again showed his versatility by going into the garage business. He and Oscar Jacobs, also of Sylvania, operated a garage at Ashland and Bancroft avenues, where they transformed touring cars into one ton trucks.

After leaving the garage business, Mr. Keene took up tree surgery and for the next 13 years traveled over many states tending the trees of many wealthy people. While in this business he did work for J.D. Rockefeller at Cleveland; for the Armours and Swifts at Chicago, Lake Forest, Ill.; and Lake Geneva, Wis.; for Patten, the wheat king at Evanston, Ill.; for Marshall Field at Lake Bluff, Ill.; for Wrigley the chewing gum magnate at Lake Geneva, Wis.; and for Mrs. Hetty Green at Wanetka, Ill. In the town of Lake Forest at that time were 44 millionaires, in a population of 5,000.

At the request of Henry Burnham and Haskell Warren and several other Sylvanians, Mr. Keene re-bought the hotel, (5703 Main) which he operated until the country went dry. Since then he has operated a pool room in the Farmers & Merchants Bank building, and in the new building which he built for this purpose several years ago.

Mr. Keene remembers when the site of his present home (5817 Main) was an old orchard, and just beyond was dense forest. On the site now occupied by Dr. Halbert's home, (6606 Erie) was a blacksmith shop operated by Albert Carl. This building was later turned into a cheese factory.

Of the many business enterprises that have occupied Mr. Keene's time, he liked tree surgery the best."

***Sylvania Sentinel* - 9-29-1932 – "Wagonlander Brothers Department Store –** These boys were all born, as one might say, to the business of selling; their parents having owned and operated general merchandise stores in Ottawa Lake and Sylvania from the time the boys were very young indeed.

The father, John Wagonlander, came originally from Findlay, Ohio, and the mother of the boys, Mrs. Mary Wagonlander, was born and raised just a short distance from the Town of Ottawa Lake.

After their marriage, the parents spent five years on a rented farm near Ottawa Lake, where they managed to save $1,000. This capital they invested in the old Dewey Stave factory in 1888. When this business was closed out they entered the general merchandising business with the Jewell Brothers in Ottawa Lake.

When the partnership with the Jewell Brothers came to an end in 1890, the entire stock in the store was divided three ways, and with his share John Wagonlander went into business for himself across the street from the old store building. He did business on sugar and cracker barrels and soap boxes until he could afford shelving and counters. He sold dry goods, hardware, shoes and groceries. Barrel salt was in such demand that it was shipped to the store by car load. Park also recalls that they put in ice for the summer cut from Ottawa Lake, and that he made his spending money by peddling the Chicago Globe, a weekly newspaper. John Wagonlander was also postmaster of Ottawa Lake for 17 years.

The original Wagonlander homestead in Ottawa Lake was burned in 1890 and the parents of the boys built the home now located on the northwest corner of the Ottawa Lake road and the main street of the town. The house, which consists of nine large rooms, was built for $700, including labor and material.

In the year of 1905 Mr. Wagonlander bought out the W.H. Gibbs store in Sylvania (5693 Main), and operated the two stores for about two years. During the many trips between the two stores members of the family drove a horse and buggy. Often the rig would become mired to the hubs, and it was not infrequent for the horse to become frightened at a passing train and run amuck.

After the Gibbs corner (5693 Main) had been sold to Mr. A.C. Dolph for his undertaking parlors, as they were then called, and after Mr. Wagonlander had disposed of his Ottawa Lake store, the concern moved into the building now occupied by the Leader store, then known as the old Edson building (5675 Main). From this location they moved to the store room in the Sylvania Savings Bank (5692 Main – Today J & G Pizza) building where they did business for 17 years.

Jess and Park were made members of the firm in 1908 and in 1919 Morris was also taken into the firm, John Wagonlander passed away in 1920. In 1925, the business was moved to its present location (5679 Main) where the boys carry an attractive stock of dry goods, women's wear, shoes, millinery and a variety line.

When the family first moved to Sylvania in 1907 they occupied what was called the "old Bidwell house," (6527 Monroe) but what is now remodeled into Howard's gas station. Later they built a comfortable home on Maplewood Avenue, which they occupied until they built the bungalow at Main and Maplewood, in which house Mrs. John Wagonlander lived until her death and where Mr. and Mrs. Morris Wagonlander now live.

Among Park Wagonlander's choicest memories of his boyhood, are the picnics on the last day of school in Ottawa Lake, when Jack Bell, who owned a threshing machine, would hitch about a dozen wagons to the engine and pull all the children to Dashner's grove at the head of the lake. He also likes to recall fishing off a certain chicken coop when the lake was very high and bringing home a nice mess of bullheads.

In later days he recalls the activities about the old Victor Burg hotel (5703 Main), with its stone porches facing both Main and Maplewood Avenue. In the rear of the hotel was a great barn, with no interior post, which Park had an idea of turning into a theatre to those early days. He also brought to mind the old hitching rail along the wooden sidewalks of Main Street. The old rail had become sort of sway back from the weight of many and many a lounger.

The three members of the Wagonlander firm have always taken an active part in the affairs of the community. Park served on the Village Council for four years and also as Clerk of the Village for 16 years.

Jess is clerk of the Modern Woodmen, and is engaged in the Fire and Life Insurance business which he conducts from his office in the store. Morris, the youngest member of the firm is now acting as secretary of the Congregational Church and was superintendent of the Sunday school."

Sylvania Sentinel – 10-6-1932 – "Earl C. Orewiler – Our history today concerns Earl C. Orewiler, who has been in the barber business in Sylvania for a good many years. Earl, today does not have many of the ear marks of a husky farmer boy, yet it is true that he was born on a farm near Kunkle, Ohio, and spent his early years tilling the soil, digging potatoes, husking corn, and all the rest of it.

He finally decided to leave the farm and on 6-10-1900, he went to Toledo and started to learn the barber trade. This was the first time he had been in a city of any great size. While learning his trade, he did the porter work in the shop, shined shoes, and slept in the shop, and was paid $1.00 per week in cash.

After he had completed his apprenticeship Earl ventured a little into the restaurant business working in Cable's three cent lunch room in Bowling Green. Here many nourishing dishes were served at three cents per helping. Later he worked in Oblinger's restaurant which stood where Bostwick Braun's hardware store is now located.

On 3-6-1905, Mr. Orewiler bought out the barber shop of Ed Schmaus in Sylvania, and on the 13th moved in and started business. This shop was located on the site where Mr. A.H. Randall is now operating his grocery (5641 Main Street). The same year he moved into the room now occupied by the Little Wonder (5689 Main Street), and in 1908 he moved into his present location (5687 Main Street). .

On June 14th, Earl opened the Crown Theatre in the room occupied now by the Little Wonder (5689 Main Street), which boasted a seating capacity of 123. He retired from the moving picture business after two years. The admission to this theatre was ten cents for adults and five cents for children. The music was furnished by an Edison phonograph. Ralph Dolby operated the projecting machine, and Mrs. Orewiler sold tickets. Earl often found it necessary to open the small window between the theatre and the barber shop and call for quiet from some of the young lads who became over enthusiastic.

During this time he put on several stage shows, including "Night Riders of Tennessee," "Prisoners of Joliet," vaudeville and dog shows. Through this he became adept in the art of make-up upon which subject he still is frequently consulted.

One of Mr. Orewiler's later ventures was a dancing school, which he and Jess Wagonlander organized. Classes were held in Garry's Hall (now P.H.C. hall – 5651/5655 Main) and instruction was given on the waltz, two-step, novelty, lancers and schottische. Some of the boys who took dancing lessons at the Orewiler-Wagonlander school were Frank Reger, Cyril Shull, Ernest Howard, Walter Kuhlman, Fenton Clark, Raymond Shultz, Frank Clampitt, Howard Hine, Ralph West, Walter West, and Leo Reger. The school continued until May, 1919, since which time Mr. Orewiler had devoted his entire time to his barber business.

During his 27 years in business in Sylvania, Mr. Orewiler can recall the following businessmen of the town who have passed away: Will Eley, Will Carl, Barney Clark, Gene Edson, Steven Young, Orson Adsit, Wallace Covell, Victor Burg, Louis Burg, John Werder, H.J. Warren, Clarence Beach, Charles Rockenstyre, Will Hine, John Crandall, Louis Crandall, Owen Clark, John Wagonlander, Thomas Chandler, Bob Leonard, Sam Rothfuss, Roll Rothfuss, Ed Rothfuss, D.O. Washburn, A.C. Dolph, George Lovewell, F.O. Peak, W.B. Harris, Wayne Harris, William Chapple and A.N. Warren."

The *Toledo Blade* dated 3-10-1955 also interviewed Earl C. Orewiler and wrote the following: "Earl C. Orewiler was a barber in Toledo when he purchased a shop on Main Street in Sylvania. It was 3-13-1905 when he opened his barber shop. Sylvania was a town of about 1,000 people and had mud streets. This week Mr. Orewiler is observing his 50th anniversary as a Sylvania barber. He has seen many changes. He used to open his shop at 7:00 a.m., daily and remain open until 9 p.m., on weekdays and until midnight or 1:00 a.m., on Saturdays to accommodate farmers doing their weekly marketing. The pay wasn't great in the earlier days, shaves were 10 cents each and he had to be proficient at trimming Van Dyke beards and in using cigarette papers as wrappers in curling handlebar mustaches. In the old days the barber shop was a popular social center, where townspeople and farmers gathered to gossip and chat. Mr. Orewiler recalls that when he started business, Sylvania had several livery stables, six saloons and no electric lights. The first sewer was installed in 1908 and the waterworks in 1916. The first pavement wasn't until 1910. In addition to barbering, Mr. Orewiler operated a movie theatre in Sylvania for two years (5689 Main) and for seven years he promoted public dances at Garry's Hall (5651/5655 Main). More than 300 persons gathered regularly for the bi-weekly dances. The Toledo & Western ran special cars from Toledo to carry visiting patrons. Mr. Orewiler served one year on village council in the 1920s. Mr. Orewiler had wanted to be a barber since he practiced on his family and chums around the family farm near Pioneer in Williams County, Ohio. He had come to Toledo in 1900 to learn the trade by working in various shops."

In 1937 Don Brown came to Sylvania from Holgate, Ohio, in answer to an advertisement which had been placed by Earl Orewiler. Don worked for Mr. Orewiler for 25 years and in 1962 assumed ownership of the shop." (5687 Main).

Sylvania Sentinel – 10-13-1932 – "**Frank Koepfer** – who founded the Koepfer Hardware Company, nearly 30 years ago, was born in Spencer Township. He was practically brought up in the business world, his father having conducted a general store at Java, Ohio, until his death. At this time the business was taken over by Frank's brother, Julius Koepfer, and which he conducted until his death a few years ago.

It was Frank's delight when a small boy, to get up at midnight and go with his father and drive miles to buy eggs and butter from the farmers in exchange for calico, ginghams, shoes, groceries, etc.

After his father's death, and desiring to carry out his wishes, Frank left the old homestead, went to Toledo and entered Davis' Business College. While a student there he earned his room and board by being a waiter in the dining room of several Toledo hotels.

After finishing his business course, he sought employment at the Dow-Snell Company and was rewarded with a job starting with a salary of forty dollars a month. He stayed with them five years, thence back home to work for his brother Julius, selling implements to the farmers in the Swanton and Metamora territory.

At about this time he had visions of being in business for himself, and Sylvania loomed up as a possible advantageous site. Consequently, in January, 1903, Mr. Koepfer came to Sylvania, rented a building from George Lovewell, where the new Sylvania Post Office now stands (6513 Maplewood). After about a year and four months, Frank rented the large livery barn back of the Victor Hotel (6616 Maplewood).

This occasion was marked by a grand opening which took place on May 14th, 1904. Mr. Koepfer believed in publicity in a big way and on that afternoon and evening, the Sylvania Cornet Band, (which according to the *Sylvania Sun* of that date) "discoursed sweet music." Another big attraction which Mr. Koepfer provided was the "balloon ascension made by the daring and intrepid air navigator, Profession C.R. Clough."

There was also a drawing for which tickets had previously been given out, and the premiums included a hay rake, a plow, a single harness, a three-way wind mill pump, a corn sheller, a roll of wire fence and $15 credit on any purchase. Mr. Koepfer recalls that Will Jeffs won the plow.

The heading on the age-yellowed poster which advertised the Grand Opening indicated that it was Frank's "First Annual" opening. We don't know whether any more celebrations followed, but the first one must have been a lot of fun. When Mr. Koepfer's business outgrew this location he leased the store room in the Masonic building, which he still occupied (5633 Main).

In commenting on the condition of the mud roads surrounding Sylvania in the spring, Mr. Koepfer relates this experience. A carload of farm wagons was shipped to him via the New York Central in March of 1906. He hired Henry Reudy, who operated a dray at that time, to deliver the 20 wagons to his store. Now, beside the mud on "Rockenstyre" hill there was also a quick-sand hole and both of Reudy's horses went down into this hole. One horse was finally extracted, and he was hitched to the one still buried and in this way the unfortunate horse was rescued.

While Frank was still new to this territory, he tried to cross what was known as the old dug way on the Ottawa Lake road. He found one portion completely under water, but decided to try to drive through. Just then his horse fell down and was completely covered with water, the horse fell and struggled to his feet three times, while Frank, although greatly agitated, stayed in the buggy, to keep dry. He was not sure just where the road ended and the lake began. Finally Jack Bischoff unhitched the horse, tied a rope to the rear of the buggy and hitched the horse to the rope. The horse in starting, gave the buggy such a jerk that it turned completely over, and Frank was catapulted over the top and into the water. He then took a different road to the home of George Bischoff where he repaired his binder in wet clothes, but by the time he got home they were dry.

In 1909 Frank began selling Ford automobiles in connection with his hardware and implement line, and in 1914 the business had grown to such proportions that he felt he was unable to care for it alone and Fred Myers was made a partner in the auto business.

With Fred in Metamora and Frank in Sylvania they were conducting the business in both places in 1920, the new building at the corner of Main and Maplewood was erected, the home of the Sylvania Auto Company, when Fred was made a partner of the combined business—hardware, implements and automobiles. After giving up the Ford agency, they took the line of the Willys-Overland products, and that with the Chrysler, gives them a complete price range of automobiles."

An advertisement in the *Sylvania Sun* newspaper in 1904 announced Koepfer's Grand Opening to be held on May 13th and 14th, 1904. Here's what the advertisement reported: "I will hold my first annual opening at my new warehouse, first door west of the hotel, Sylvania, Ohio. I will show as large and as good a line of Surries, Buggies, Wagons, Plows, Binders, Mowers, Windmills, Pumps, Hammock Cultivators, Barb Ware, Sulky Plows, all kinds of Barrows, Planters, Huskers, Farm Trucks and other farm equipment. AND A FULL LINE OF EVERYTHING USED ON THE FARM – I handle only the best and most reliable makes, such as Tiffin Wagons, McCormick Binders, Mowers, Rakes, Tedders, and Huskers; Page Woven Wire Fence; Gale Plows, Sulkies, Gangs, Cultivators, Corn Planters, Discs, Spring and Spike Harrows; Buffalo Pitts Disc, Spring and Spike Harrows; Sterling Hay Loaders and Side Rakes; Clark Buggies and Surries; Ohio Wind Mills, and just such goods as the up-to-date farmer wants. I will show you as fine a line as ever seen in Northwestern Ohio. You will miss a great thing if you don't come. Remember the dates, May 13th and 14th."

Sylvania Sentinel – 10-20-1932 – **"V.H. Adams** – local druggist, spent his early days on a farm one mile west of Sylvania, directly across from the Highland Meadows Golf course, where once was located the old toll-gate house, where fees were collected for the use of the old corduroy road between Toledo and Morenci.

He learned his A B C's from Lottie Scott who was his first school teacher in the old Centennial school (southwest corner of Sylvania-Metamora Road and Centennial) which he attended for eight years, finishing under the able guidance of Nancy Smith, after which he attended the old third grade high school on Main Street (5735 Main).

At that time our school board furnished nothing but shelter for our comfort on which to study and conduct classes. The only playground available was the vacant property or green extending from south of Chandler's store building to Monroe Street. "Old Man" Blanchard owned all the property from the line just back of the Farmers and Merchants Bank building east to Summit Street.

This was excellent garden land, and the "Old Man" always sowed artichokes along the line of the playground much to the dismay of the kids who were bent on foraging his turnip crop.

The only supply of water was furnished by a pump at the corner where the Farmers and Merchants Bank (5604 Main) now stands, and one at the corner of the Sylvania Savings Bank (5694 Main). After William Fletcher's colts ran away, hooked on to the pump, jerking it out and leaving nothing but the bottom of the well, our city councilors, Squire Hopkins, W.H. Huling, Jess Fletcher, Foster Warren, Alonzo Crandall, Jim Young, with a number of their contemporaries, began the agitation for water works, but the old bugaboo "expense" always bobbed up to retard progress, but anyone acquainted with these men will agree that perhaps in these minds was born our present hard water system.

Mr. Adams completed his education in pharmacy at Ada University in the "good old days" when eggs were 9 cents a dozen; butter 10 cents, oatmeal 3 cents, round steak 9 cents, sirloin 11 cents and best cuts of porterhouse 14 cents. Because of these prices one was able to get board and room, with three meals a day, for $2.50 per week.

Even at these low prices a student's money was soon exhausted, and many returned to the farm where the same demoralized prices prevailed, thus lessening a student's chances for further knowledge.

In October, 1902, Mr. Adams opened a drug store in the room now occupied by W.D. Hinckley's paint and wallpaper store (5607 Main Street). After nine years in this location he purchased the building in which he is now located (5645 Main Street), and which was previously known as the Reitter saloon.

Mr. Adams has always been active in civic affairs, having served years as a member of the board of education, two years on the village board of trustees of public affairs, and compiled the rules and regulations under which our present water system is governed."

Sylvania Sentinel – **10-27-1932** – **Yeager's** - "This week we journey to the South Side of town to visit Yeager's Grocery store. Yeager's have conducted this grocery since 1921.

George Yeager was born in Riga, Michigan, where he spent his boyhood on a farm. As he grew into his teens he started to learn the barber trade with George Spencer, who later took the lad in Toledo with him where he completed his apprenticeship.

After George's marriage he lived in Blissfield, but also conducted a barber shop in Riga two nights a week. He and Mrs. Yeager, having no horse and buggy, and the train running at inconvenient hours, would walk from Blissfield to Riga and back again. It was at Blissfield that the two sons, Roy and Clyde, and the daughter Susie Mae, were born and began their education.

After some years of intermittent farming in the Blissfield district and near Remus, in northern Michigan, and railroading, the Yeager's moved to Sylvania. At this time Mr. Yeager worked for the railroad and they soon moved to Stop 15 where they opened a grocery and barber shop combined. Roy and Clyde had meanwhile graduated from Sylvania High School and assisted their parents in this venture.

After Roy's marriage, he and his wife came back to Sylvania and purchased the general store where they are now located from John Redding (corner of Railroad Street and Convent). They were joined later by Mr. and Mrs. George Yeager and Clyde, and the family is still carrying on the business.

Roy Yeager has been president of the Sylvania branch of the Reorganized Church of Jesus of Latter Day Saints, for several years, and served as Elder, as has his father, George Yeager. Clyde is church school director.

The building occupied by the Yeager store was built in 1896 by Bob Leonard, who conducted a general store there for some years. Wages paid on the construction were $1.25 per day, which was considered by the workers to be very fine wages and they worked with great zeal to keep their jobs.

Mr. Leonard sold out to Joe LaPoint, who in turn sold to a man by the name of Richards. After conducting a general merchandising business for several years, Richards sold out to Jennie Hawley. It was from John Redding that George Yeager and sons purchased the store."

Sylvania Sentinel – 11-3-1932 – "**James D. LaPoint** about whose business history we are concerned today, is one of the real "old-timers" in Sylvania's business life. He has been a resident here for the past 36 years, and has been in business for a great share of that time.

Mr. LaPoint was born in Monroe County, Mich., on a farm. He came to Sylvania in 1896, at the age of 21 years. His first venture in business was a grocery and implement store opposite the New York Central depot. Jim made a specialty of selling a fine buggy for $50. He operated this store for about 20 years, or until 1915 when he traded it for a farm.

From 1916 until 1928 several different positions occupied Mr. LaPoint's time. Among these were three years spent as caretaker of the McManus estate, east of Sylvania, and two years as state deputy oil inspector. Jim held this position while James Cox was Governor of Ohio and his duties were to travel over Lucas and Ottawa counties testing carloads of gas and oil.

In 1928 Mr. LaPoint again went into business, establishing the J.D. LaPoint Coal Company of which he is still the proprietor. The yards are located on Convent Boulevard at the N.Y. tracks. Perhaps even more interesting than his business life is the story of Jim's political activities. The fact that he has been committeeman here for about twenty years proves that he is one of the real through and through died-in-the-wool Democrats. He has served as clerk and treasurer of Sylvania Township for nine years, and served in the capacity of assessor for 12 years.

Mr. LaPoint served on the village council for six years, and it was during this time that the brick paving in Main Street was laid. This was the first paving in the village and was put down 29 years ago.

When Jim first came to Sylvania the entire township voted in that council building. There are now eight precincts in the township and at the election Tuesday, booth officials were counting votes until the wee small hours of the morning.

After he had resided here for a couple of years, Mr. LaPoint knew about everyone in the township. At this time there were no banks, and the only transportation service to Toledo, beside the horse and buggy, was the New York Central, which had two trains daily each way, the fare being 35 cents one way.

Mr. LaPoint was one of the crowd that gathered to see the first trolley car pull into Sylvania over the Toledo & Western tracks in 1901. He also recalls that the summer's ice supply was cut in January from the mill pond (Railroad Street and Mill Street) which was drained a few years ago.

We could not close this article without paying tribute to Mr. LaPoint for his service as clerk of the Board of township trustees during the crucial times we are at present enduring. The splendid management of township relief funds by Trustees Michael Bowman, John Cooper and Washington C. Thorp, has kept the township in commendable shape compared to a few of the neighboring townships, as clerk of the board. Mr. LaPoint is striving to fill his post well and to be fair and impartial to all."

NOTE: James D. LaPoint continued to live in Sylvania until his death in March of 1963. His obituary notice said that he lived at 6817 Convent Blvd., that he lived in Sylvania for 67 years, and operated a coal business for many years.

Sylvania Sentinel – 11-17-1932 – "**William Miller**, who has been the proprietor of a confectionary store and news stand (5527 Main) since 1904, was born and raised in Toledo. He has vivid recollections of his birthplace when it was a struggling city of 50,000. His boyhood was spent in the Nebraska avenue district, when that street was one of the best streets of Toledo. His schooling was cut short each year in the early spring when Bill took up the business of herding cattle; his father's and the neighbors. For this he received the magnificent sum of five cents per week. Bill being a thrift lad saved his nickels until he attained the grand total of eighty cents which was borrowed and never returned. Bill then decided it didn't pay to save, so each week he spent his well-earned nickel, thereby reaping the benefit of his toil himself.

At the age of 24 Mr. Miller took a position as a motorman on the Toledo street cars, which he held for two years. In the meantime the Toledo & Western Railway had been completed between Toledo and Sylvania, and when Bill's boss joined up with the new line Bill came along.

It was in March, 1901, that Mr. Miller had the honor of piloting the first regular scheduled passenger car from Sylvania to Toledo. Mr. Miller recalls that this car was well filled and one of its passengers was Mr. F. E. Seagrave, the president of the line. When Charles Engel, the conductor collected the first fare paid, Mr. Seagrave instructed him to keep it. Mr. Engel has the coins to this day.

On its second trip that day this car took down a crowd of theatre goers, being manned by Mr. Hall and John Welch. On the return trip at 11 p.m., all went well until they got to Cherry and Sherman streets, when the front of the car pushed the proper course up Cherry Street, and the rear end of the car turned up Sherman Street. The car was dead-locked there for several hours. Many Sylvanians who were passengers recall this incident vividly.

Mr. Miller worked for the Western for 21 years. He served under the following superintendents: Mart Webb, A.P. Southworth, C.F. Franklin, Wm. Pierce, Mr. Schwartz and Frank Johnson. In April 1922, Mr. Miller left the service and has since devoted all his time to his store.

During his 21 years as Motorman, Bill had no fatal accidents on the line, with the exception of grasshoppers and chickens.

Mr. Miller built his store building in 1904. At this time Sherman Tibbitts also ran a confectionery store where the Bringman Bowling alley (5617 Main Street) is now located. When Mr. Miller came to Sylvania in 1901, he states that he had no idea that he would still be a resident in 1932. But Sylvania is a pretty good place after all, isn't it Bill?"

Sylvania Sentinel – **11-24-1932** – **"Clair Cooper** - proprietor of Cooper's Tire & Battery Shop, was born in Cone, Michigan. When not quite a year old his parents moved to Ohio, and purchased land in Sylvania Township, on Whiteford road. The land was in the woods, and had to be cleared in order to find room to build a home.

Mr. Cooper attended the old Pleasant Point School (Monroe and Corey) and Sylvania High School (5735 Main). Upon leaving school he assisted his parents on the farm.

Clair's next venture was, with the street car company in Toledo, where he worked both as a motorman and conductor. He also ran a car on the Waterville line for several years. After leaving the street railway, Mr. Cooper worked for several years in the sheet metal department of the Overland. Then came a desire to enter the business world, and Clair began to make preparations to go into business for himself.

Forthwith Clair set out for Akron, Ohio, where he worked in the plant of the Goodyear Rubber Co., for six months, without pay, learning vulcanizing and tire repair. When he had attained the necessary proficiency in the work, Clair returned to Sylvania where he opened up a store.

In 1920 Mr. Cooper rented the building now occupied by the Toledo Edison Co., showroom (5621 Main Street), and opened up a tire repair and welding shop. The business prospered and in 1924 Clair found it necessary to find larger quarters.

He then purchased the building on the east side of Main Street known as the old stone blacksmith shop, which is one of the oldest buildings in Sylvania (was at 5658 Main). The walls at the bottom are four feet thick, and Clair tells us that cuts in the stone are marks which surveyors used in making surveys of the village. The walls of this old building withstood the ravages of two fires.

After purchasing this building Clair remodeled it and equipped it with first class machinery for repairing tires, batteries, radios, and also for doing acetylene welding. He also put in a stock of new tires, radios and auto accessories. He opened his new store in March, 1924.

Besides running the store Clair has always been interested in the Sylvania Gun Club, in fact he was one of the organizers of the club. His hobby has brought him many trophies, for Clair is considered one of the crack trap shooters in this part of the country.

In the National tournament held in 1929, Mr. Cooper won second place. In 1928 he was one of a team of five from Ohio that won the International shoot in Tecumseh, Canada. In his shoot Clair's team missed only four shots out of 500. Each state in the Union and each province from the Dominion was represented at this tournament. Mr. Cooper's store has been a mecca for the children of the community as he nearly always has at the store some species of wild life, such as snakes, birds, etc. And knowing Clair as we do, we know that he gets a lot of pleasure out of having the young ones ask questions."

Sylvania Sentinel – **December 1, 1932** – "The subject of our history today is the shoe shop owned and operated by **Gus Thamletz** and his son **Otto** which has been one of the town's substantial business houses for more than fifteen years.

Mr. and Mrs. Gus Thamletz came to Ottawa Lake, Michigan, from the Island of Ruegen, Germany, in 1887. Mr. Thamletz learned the trade of repairing shoes in his native land.

Otto was born in Ottawa Lake and lived there until the age of four years, when his parents moved on a farm near Riga, Michigan. Ernest Thamletz did most of the farm work, as Otto would help only when his father made him. However, when the family moved into the town of Riga in 1912 and Mr. Thamletz build a small shoe shop there; Otto learned the trade with his father.

Otto's next job was taking care of the office at night of Dr. Schneider at Riga and tending his horses. In the fall of 1915 he took a job with the Neil Haas shoe store in Adrian, riding back and forth from his home on the street car manned by Guy Gloyd and Burt Blankley. These men later suggested that Otto might get a job in Sylvania.

Thereupon he came to Sylvania and at the shop of F.J. Reger for work. At this time Frank thought the boy too young to know a great deal about the business, but later did employ him. Otto worked in Reger's shop until Frank came back from the World War.

Then Otto and his father went into business together where the Toledo Edison is now located (5621 Main) and started a modern shoe repair shop. Later Mr. Thamletz purchased the building occupied by the American Restaurant (6601 Monroe Street) where they carried a full line of men's and boys' shoes, besides operating their repair department. In 1920 another change was made when Mr. Thamletz bought the old bank building (5629 Main) next to the Masonic temple and the business was again moved.

Otto says that it is distinctly noticeable that the public is having more repairing done to their footwear since the depression. Fifteen other shoemakers have started business in Sylvania and have left since Otto and his father started in business, according to Otto.

The longest vacation Otto ever enjoyed was a four-day trip to Canada with his wife in 1930, and on another trip he spent three days in northern Michigan with Fred Brint. In 1919 Otto started a taxi service and since then has operated the village's only taxi. Otto's hobby is the raising of game and at the present time he has 65 ring neck pheasants on his place, besides fox, squirrels, raccoons, various breeds of chickens, bird dogs, and pigeons. He is one of the six licensed commercial breeders of game in northwestern Ohio, the other licensed breeders being located at Toledo, Maumee, Waterville and Whitehouse."

MISCELLANEOUS SUBJECTS

BANDS IN SYLVANIA

The first known band in Sylvania was organized by Dr. Edwin Armstrong through the organization called P.H.C. (Protected Home Circle). The 10-23-1902 issue of the *Sylvania Sun* newspaper reported the following regarding the first band: "Tomorrow night the new band will give a pumpkin pie social at Warren's Hall. Supper will be served at 10 cents a plate. The band is a new institution that will do much toward advertising Sylvania, and its low-priced social should receive liberal patronage. The band will play several pieces, their first public appearance. Go and encourage the boys." Another article in this same newspaper says: "The P.H.C. band will give a pumpkin pie social at Warren's Hall tomorrow night. Everybody invited."

Dr. and Mrs. Edwin Armstrong came to Sylvania in 1902. Both of them became accomplished musicians and their home was known for having many musical instruments. Mrs. Armstrong taught music in the Sylvania School System starting in 1905, traveling through the community in her horse and buggy and visiting each of the one-room schoolhouses to teach the pupils music. They loved Mrs. Armstrong and the children often brought hay and grain to school for her horse, named "Cookie."

Dr. and Mrs. Armstrong's son, Jim Armstrong, was tape recorded in January of 1981 saying this about his father, and about the first band in Sylvania: "Next item—is the first Sylvania band. From the photographs there is an old large photograph of the first band in Sylvania. To the best of my knowledge—my dad, who was quite a musical individual, as was his father, had either started or was instrumental in starting the first band in Sylvania. In the picture the spot would be on Monroe Street, south of what is now the parking lot, but was at that time the Sylvania council building, with the picture of the band, imposing 20 to 30 Sylvania people, old and young, and it is of interest to me that when we think of the marvelous expensive uniforms of the bands today in the high schools. The first band in Sylvania—in order to be so called "uniform" had as their uniform, as can be seen in that photograph—black shoes, white socks, black pants, white shirt, a little black bow tie and for head gear they had a cloth Peter's cap, a type that would be given free from painting store companies with their name on it. So that was their uniform. I know nothing of their musical activities, but I do know that my dad (a doctor) at some time was able to buy somewhere, quite a number of light blue woolen, very good quality uniforms with braids, shoulder strapping and a helmet; a German type helmet with a horse hair tail plume on top. They were really decorated uniforms. Sylvania wore those uniforms, but I know that for many years they were stored in a tremendous big trunk, upstairs in the barn where I was born and raised, which is still at the corner of Summit and Maplewood (1981). My mother later, or at that time really, taught music in the school system for 30 years, she used the auditorium above the Farmers and Merchants Bank for putting on school operettas and in this auditorium practiced once a week, I guess. A man from Toledo, Keller, a German fellow with a German moustache, and a German brogue, he came out once a week and practiced over what is now the Sylvania Savings Bank, when the only existing auditorium in town for community affairs was the bank auditorium, that has now all been rebuilt and taken over and made into offices, but I remember the community dance floor or auditorium very, very well. For several years, and this man (Keller) from Toledo, who was hired by the town, came out and directed the band, drank alcohol and chewed tobacco. It was his custom, militaristic type of man, it was his custom (I was not in the band at that time, but my brother was and I remember, my brother talking about it) when he would correct different players in the band, he would grab the instrument from them, and rather roughly take it from them, and he would play their instrument, of which I guess, he could play most of the instruments in the band. He would play the part he wanted to correct and when the owner of the instrument took it back to continue to play, the mouthpiece was so foul with alcohol and tobacco that it was the thing that the whole band rebelled against and it's my memory that Mr. Keller was fired from his job because of this unfortunate habit.

Soon after that Donald Beveridge, who is now retired after working at the Sylvania Savings bank, and as president, I heard took over the direction of the band, and he would be one of the many people that I have on my notes here-would have some interesting things to tell about Sylvania. Not too long after this band with Don Beveridge, Robert Wyandt, a graduate of Bowling Green State University, came to Sylvania to teach music and it was at that period of time that football became prominent, with uniforms in school curriculum used. My mother had started, maintained and directed an orchestra in the town-in the school system, they wanted a band to play at the football games, so Bob Wyandt took over the band and it went from the town band to becoming a school band, and there hasn't been a town band since. That would be about 1930. The band became the school band and then uniforms entered. It has grown until the band is now very spectacular, a big part of the school-of the Sylvania school program.

To continue with the band at a later date there is a picture filed with the history group, a picture that was taken of the town bank—at a later date at which my brother was playing the trumpet and as I gather from the photograph, he was a junior or senior in high school at about 1925, 1926—1925 maybe. That was taken on Main Street in front of what is now the Sylvania Savings Bank. They all dressed in white outfits that would be called sailor outfits with a sailor hat—sailor slip over top—white pants, white shirts." —end of Jim Armstrong interview regarding Sylvania bands–

An old photo of the "Sylvania Band of 1909" appeared in a 1937 *Sylvania Sentinel* newspaper and the caption reads as follows: "Twenty-eight years ago Sylvania did not have a high school band in black and gold uniforms, led by a comely drum major. But a capable appearing group of men furnished the music for various occasions. They are shown above as they led the Fourth of July parade in 1909. How many can you identify? In the first row are Lee Trowbridge, Bill Reger, George Mickens, Jess Peck. Second Row: Darrell Nhare and Robert Cushman. Third Row: – Waffle, Christian Webb, Theodore Gries and Dr. E.E. Armstrong. The rest you will have to guess. (This photo is owned by Mrs. Stella Mickens, of Erie Street, Sylvania)."

After Mrs. Armstrong retired from teaching music in the Sylvania schools, Robert Wyandt had been hired to the Sylvania School System in the middle 1920s, and in 1931 he organized the first high school band in Sylvania. Sylvania has had a school band since that time. For the first ten years that the high school band was organized the players were required to furnish their own instruments, sheet music and uniforms.

According to an article written in 1982 in the *Sylvania Herald* there was a bandstand in Burnham Park and a Sylvania band was formed in the 1920's to play here. Gustav Koehler, of Toledo, and a former member of Sousa's band, came to Sylvania to create a band. Before Sylvania's band was formed, bands from Ottawa Lake or Richfield Center came here to play occasionally. There was always a great deal of negotiating to be done about the bands fees and such fringe benefits as meals at the hotel for the players and feed for their horses.

Later the Sylvania band was known as the Town Band and they were sponsored by the Sylvania merchants. They had white uniforms and they would block off Division Street (Main Street) between Monroe Street and Maplewood on Saturday nights for a band concert. They also played concerts at Burnham Park. The names of some of the band members were: Donald Smith, Curtis Jacobs, Donald Beebe, Kenneth Yeager, Elmer Deer, Arnold Koester, Donald Hughes,? Dauer, Bruce Wagonlander, Bruce Beveridge, Alvin Plikerd, Donald Armstrong, Willard Crockett, Ronald Adams, Jess Reed, Gus Koehler, Donald Beveridge, Ralph Ringenberger, Alfred Carl, Curtis Niles, Cyril McKinney, Lyle E. Koester, Robert Randall, Paul Ringenberger,? Holt, Huber Howard, William Koester, Norman Lochbihler and Park Wagonlander.

An article in the 1-24-1924 issue of the *Sylvania Sentinel* reported that the local band was reorganizing again. The article said: "The first meeting of the reorganized band, under the direction of Donald Beveridge, was held Wednesday night in the W.R.C. hall. A turn-out of 27 pieces, including many of the Medusa bandsmen, certainly put a different aspect on the band situation in Sylvania. Mr. Beveridge wants to make known at this time that anyone wishing to take up an instrument and become a member of the band may report at his home on Monday nights and receive instruction on their instruments. Band practice will be held every Wednesday night in the W.R.C. hall at seven. A cordial invitation to musicians is extended by the director. The enthusiasm of the members of the band is unbounded, and they are preparing to show Sylvania a band in the near future, that will be the equal of any small town band in the state."

Don Beveridge, long-time cashier, vice-president then president of the Sylvania Savings Bank also started a private band in Sylvania starting in the 1940s. The Sylvania Band, under the leadership of Donald Beveridge gave concerts both afternoon and evening on a specially constructed band stand on Main Street in downtown Sylvania.

Donald Beveridge came to Sylvania, Ohio with his parents in 1915 and as reported, went on to become the president of the Sylvania Savings Bank. In a book titled *The Flickertail Tapes; The Life Story of Donald Wayne Beveridge* by Nancy Beveridge, which was recently (2012) donated to the Sylvania Area Historical Society by Nancy. Donald Beveridge was quoted as saying the following about his interest in music and teaching others: "Most of this time I had my own orchestra, too. The orchestra was more of a symphony than a dance orchestra. My mother played the piano. She was a fine musician, and she could play anything. Red Willinger played cello, Charlie Held the clarinet, Dr. Kenneth Cosgrove the French horn, trumpet was Lawrence 'Bill' Cosgrove, trombone was Ronald Adams, and Cy McKinney played the drums. Doc Armstrong played the bass viol. I played the violin and led, and Cliff Peck played the violin also, as did Donald Armstrong. There may have been a few others. We didn't play in the band shell in Burnham Park because there wasn't any band shelf then. We played for all the town gatherings and for the ladies' organizations, such as the Literary Club and the Book Club. Most of these meetings were held in the hall upstairs in the old Farmers and Merchants Bank, which is now Toledo Trust. The hall was mainly used for dances, often big dances. People would come from all over Toledo. Name bands would play. Various groups had parties there, and we always played for those, too. We played some classical pieces, but mainly pops-type stuff."

"I also directed the boy's band for three or four years here in Sylvania. It was a town band, like in the movie '76 Trombones.' We'd play every Wednesday evening out in front of Adams' Drug Store, now Lindau's. The town would set up a platform for us. I would take the chairs out of the upstairs hall over the drug store and put them on the platform. I would solicit the merchants once a week for their dollar contribution. I'd go around and collect the money to support the band and pay me a little something, so I guess I had become a professional musician by then. I had the boy's band at the same time as the orchestra. I played in the Sylvania town band, too, as well as the Medusa band out on Centennial Road. I played tuba and baritone. I never took lessons for these, just taught myself by reading the book and blowing them. I couldn't perform very well, but well enough, I guess. During this same period, before I worked much for the bank, I had as many as twenty-five or twenty-six students on the violin. Lots of kids around Sylvania took violin lessons from me. I gave violin lessons every night and I played solos once in a while, too. This was while I was still in high school. Then my time spent on the violin began to lapse. I didn't do much with it after I became cashier of the bank. I had to decide whether I'd try to be a career musician or a banker. I loved family, and I knew I didn't want to spend my life traveling around here and there in an entertaining capacity. So my violin career began to fade away.

It was around this time that I joined the Methodist choir, soon after I joined the church. I must have been sixteen, or maybe seventeen. Sometime later I became the choir director, around 1925. I led the church choir for seven or eight years. That's probably where I met your mother, Margaret Cribb. All the Cribb girls sang in the choir, Dorothy, Margaret, Elizabeth and Winifred. I taught myself to direct, too. No lessons. My mother and I would go to concerts once in a while, and I would watch what the director did. I learned by trial and error. I'm sure I wasn't very good at first. What seemed to count was what you could convey through your interpretation of the music." (End of quotes from Donald Beveridge).

Other bands in Sylvania were those organized through the public high school. Ben Marsh, a long-time Sylvania resident, said that he remembered marching down Main Street playing the bass drum, with Robert "Pop" Wyandt at the head. Ben Marsh graduated from Burnham High School in 1945.

Robert "Pop" Wyandt, standing in the middle, in the last row, with the bald head, was a teacher at Burnham High School starting in 1927, and was the school's first band leader. This photo was taken in 1936. All bands prior to this Burnham High School band being organized were by private individuals in their spare time. Donald Beveridge seems to get the credit for organizing the first community band. Medusa Cement Company also had an organized band about this same time also. (Photo owned by the Sylvania Area Historical Society).

In a biographical history written about Bruce W. Beveridge, brother of Donald Beveridge, he said: "He was blessed with his mother's talent for music. He played tuba in the Sylvania Village band. Later, he played string bass with Stan Hesselbart's Sylvan Serenaders, a big-band era dance band popular in northwest Ohio, Indiana and Michigan, before World War II. The band regrouped after the war and played for many dances in the area."

The Sandusky Cement Company/Medusa Cement Company was a very community minded company and encouraged their employees to be community minded as well. The employees of the plant formed a band that played at various community events throughout the 1930s and 1940s. They were called the Medusa Concert Band of the Sandusky Cement Company. They often played from the back of a large truck during Fourth of July and Memorial Day celebrations. Their motto:

We **Work** For Medusa on **Work** Days
We **Play** For Medusa On **Holi**days
We **Pull** For Medusa On **All** Days
Medusa Concert Band
The Sandusky Cement Company
Silica Plant.

In September of 1982 our local historian, Kathryn M. Keller wrote: "It's going to be a musical summer, now that we have as brand new bandstand in Burnham Park. This bandstand is not the first in Sylvania's history, but is possibly the fourth. The honor of being first seems to belong to a structure in the depot grove – presently Southbriar at Main Street and Convent Boulevard. I can't date it, but my guess would be about the time of the Civil War. I've never heard a description of the depot grove bandstand. About the only thing I have in a way of facts which I've gleaned from old newspapers, diaries and the minutes of the Grand Army of the Republic (G.A.R.) meetings is that the bandstand became a pulpit for the religious "protracted meetings" as they were called and a podium for orators at patriotic celebrations. Another early bandstand was located at the Sylvania Savings Bank corner, Main and Monroe. Long-time residents of Sylvania describe it as a "flimsy thing there on the commons." Traveling medicine shows generated some entertainment there from time to time – once a tight rope walker – as a way of attracting an audience. There was a bandstand in Burnham Park which many Sylvanians will tell you: "Why it was taken down, no one seems to know." These people, with a note of contempt, say that the city fathers at the time just didn't know what they were doing – that old bandstand was greatly loved and appreciated!"

Once the schools started a band program, that ended the necessity of a town band, and from that time on the school band(s) played for all the town special events.

CLASSIC CARS ARE PRODUCED IN SYLVANIA

The American Custom Industries, Inc., at 5035 Alexis in Sylvania Township produces high-performance sports cars in Sylvania. Robert Schuller, company president, had previously made cars on a production basis, but discontinued for several years during a staggering economy. Then in 1987 he re-entered the market and started producing these cars again at his plant in Sylvania Township.

According to their website they have been serving five generations of Corvette owners since 1968. They manufacture the Corvette fiberglass body components and specialize in the prototyping and manufacturing of both stock and custom items. They also have a complete service department and body and paint shop here on Alexis Road.

Lucas County real estate records show Goldye Schuller purchasing the property at 5029 and 5035 Alexis Road on 3-21-1970. The property was transferred to Robert S. Schuller on 11-4-1974 and stayed in his name until 1-29-1991 when it transferred to Society Bank and Trust, as trustee. Their main business was the manufacture and sale of auto parts and the redesign and restoration of sports cars. They were able to make a car from the floor up. The price of a car to be made in 1987 was $75,000, and the car was fully loaded. The owner said that it was more economical though to begin with the basic structure of an already manufactured car and then give it a new body and a new interior, with a new suspension system, transmission and other mechanical features which are altered as necessary.

According to Sylvania Township zoning records the following additions were added to the building at 5023/5035 Alexis Road:

8-21-1970 – A 41.4 x 61.4 foot addition to the existing commercial building
11-21-1972 – A 44.8 x 61.8 foot addition to the existing commercial building
9-22-1975 – A 64 x 71 foot addition to the existing commercial building
4-11-1977 – A 71 x 170 foot addition to the existing commercial building

In 1976 Robert Schuller had purchased additional property to the east at 5041 Alexis and wanted to expand this business. At the Sylvania Township Trustee meeting held on 4-2-1977 Chief David Drake informed the Trustees that he would not endorse plans for enlarging the American Custom Shop on Alexis Road because the nearest water hydrant was about 1,100 feet from the building. The Trustees met with the owner, Robert Schuller, and Fire Chief David Drake and it was decided that a permit should be issued as long as Mr. Schuller would sign a statement that he would commit to pay a pro rata share based on front footage of the cost of any waterlines extended within 250 feet of his property and agreed to put in a fire and smoke detecting system having a control alarm at the township dispatcher's office.

In May of 1978 Robert Schuller, president of John Greenwood Division of American Custom Shop, Inc., at 5035 Alexis Road filed a $275,000 lawsuit in the Lucas County Common Pleas Court claiming that the trademark or symbol used by Terry Michaelis at the T. Michaelis Corvette Supplies, Inc., that had opened in Maumee was the same version of the car that was designed and built by his firm. Each symbol had a silhouette of a curvaceous car and the new firm was using this in the promotion for the opening of their new Maumee headquarters. This lawsuit was settled between the two without actually going to court and the two were able to work things out.

The *Sylvania Herald* dated 9-5-1979 reported: "American Custom Industries, Inc., world headquarters of the internationally renowned American Special Edition Corvettes is on the move. Robert Schuller, president and chairman of the Board of Directors, began the program 18 months ago to develop the Special Edition Corvettes. Mr. Schuller utilized the expertise in Corvettes gained by his staff combined with his knowledge, creative and engineering abilities and experience as "America's leading Corvette specialist" to produce the ultimate of grand touring motor cars, the American Turbo. In one and a half years American Custom Industries, Inc., had gained international recognition as an innovator in the automotive industry. Mr. Schuller's company produces other Special Edition Corvettes in addition to the American Turbo. Among the selection is the very stylized American Turbo Sportwagon and Convertible, American GT and GT Hatchback, and an American Sportwagon. There is also the convertible and hatchback which is added to the late model stock Corvette body as a conversion job turning point with many new and exciting things that have been planned and programmed to take place during the 1979 years. They represent better service, faster delivery and scores of new and improved products for every Corvette owner and enthusiast from 1963 to the present. With last year's expansion of the Alexis Road facility, the necessary space was developed (over 55,000 square feet) for the only complete Corvette service center. Mr. Schuller prides himself in the fact that he has the finest mechanics, painters and fiberglass craftsmen in the industry. As the only complete Corvette service center, James Avery, vice president of the Coachworks Division, feels that the firm can fulfill the needs of Corvette owners ranging from preventive maintenance to major mechanical and collision repair. Included in the service center is a full mechanical service department complete with a highly sophisticated diagnostic computer, alignment equipment and a 40 ton frame straightener. Included in the Coachworks Division is a full body department and a full paint department. "Not only are we capable of constructing Special Edition motor cars, but we are also capable of rebuilding a totally wrecked Corvette," states Mr. Avery. . . ."

In 1986 Mr. Schuller purchased another parcel to the west of his original property known as 5023 Alexis Road. By this time Mr. Schuller owned the parcels at 5023 Alexis, 5029 Alexis, 5035 Alexis and 5041 Alexis and on 7-10-1986 plans were approved for alterations to the building at 5023 Alexis Road formerly occupied by Quality Tool.

Then in April of 1987 American Custom Industries, Inc. acquired APACS, Inc. a Perrysburg custom fabricator of fiberglass parts. The merger is said to have ended American Custom Industries' dependence on the auto industry and at the same time diversified their product lines. This merger was going to generate more than $2.5 million in sales annually. Mr. Schuller said that his 19-year old firm ran into financial problems in an auto industry slump in the early 1980s, but since then they had built a division capable of supplying custom fiberglass parts of any type, and he was able to start quoting commercial projects too. That's when they started building a specific part that the DeVilbiss Company needed, as well as working to build other parts for other companies.

The 6-2-1987 *Toledo Blade Weekly* featured a picture of a Corvette with the following caption: "Robert Schuller, of Sylvania, displays one of his high-performance sports cars, which are Corvettes that are upgraded by employees." Mike Jones, *Blade* Staff Writer reported that the American Custom Industries, Inc., 5035 Alexis, had gone back into auto production and orders were being received. ". . . Robert Schuller, company president, has made cars on a production basis before, and said it seemed the time was right to re-enter that market. Manufacture of the last group of high-performance cars was halted by a staggering economy, he said. The basic business of the firm is the manufacture and sale of auto parts and the redesign and restoration of sports cars. The production models will be based on Corvettes, which his firm will buy and then build on. "We are able to make a car from the floor up, and currently are building four of them for customers, but we really can't make any money on it. It's more economical to begin with the basic structure of an already manufactured car," Mr. Schuller said. . . "Mr. Schuller reported that the basic business had grown in the last year and that he had 55 employees, compared to 32 at this time last year.

Robert Schuller died in 1988 and on 10-2-1995 all four parcels were sold to Barton E. and Laura J. Lea, and the property remains in that name in 2010, and the name of the business is still American Custom Industries.

The Greenwood Corvettes website at www.greenwoodcorvettes.com said this about Bob Schuller: "Bob Schuller started his Corvette repair business, originally called American Custom Shop, when he had an accident with his 1962 Corvette and couldn't find a satisfactory shop to repair it. During the mid-70s, Schuller joined forces with John Greenwood and the pair developed a series of high performance street machines, including a custom-built turbocharged Corvette. A split followed, but American Custom Industries continued to manufacture and elaborate upon the Greenwood designs. It was also through the Greenwood connection that Schuller developed a relationship with Zora Arkus-Duntov. Late in the '70s Schuller introduced the idea of the Duntov Turbo series. This series evolved over three distinct phases and sold approximately 32 Duntov Torbos – considerably short of the anticipated 200. Additional notable products to come out of the ACI shop included the Spina Bifida Turbo Vette II hatchback and the lightweight Greg Pickett Kevlar-bodied SCCA Trans-Am body. Bob Schuller died in 1988. Now under management by long-time employee Bart Lea, American Custom Industries maintains its position in the Corvette aftermarket and its reputation for quality fiberglass products."

In December of 2002 an 81.6 foot by 34.7 foot addition was added to the building at 5035 Alexis Road.

On 9-22-2004 there was a major fire that destroyed the American Custom Industries building with over $1 million loss. This fire was caused when a worker dropped the gas tank that he was removing from a vehicle and a spark ignited the gasoline.

The building was rebuilt, bigger and better than before, and a zoning permit issued on 11-16-2004 indicated a 7,200 sq. ft. interior renovation plan.

An article in the *Toledo Blade* on 7-18-2005 by Julie M. McKinnon, Blade Business Writer, said: "Sure American Custom Industries does maintenance and repair work on Chevrolet Corvettes, from routine oil changes to complete overhauls. Corvette enthusiasts, who often view their fiber-glass-bodied cars as children, can see such work being done at the company's meticulously clean Sylvania Township building. They can browse through Corvette jackets, T-shirts, and other merchandise there too. But the backbone of the Alexis Road business is done in a building Corvette fans may never notice on the back end of American Custom's property, where more than

750 bumpers and other body parts for models dating back to 1963 are fashioned. Included are bumpers with the word Corvette molded into the fiber glass, for which American Custom is the only manufacturer licensed by General Motors Corp., said Bart Lea, president of the suburban Toledo firm. What we really do to make a living is we manufacture fiber-glass body parts for the Corvette, he said. We ship all over the world. Robert Schuller founded American Custom in 1968 and started the process of making body part molds each time the Corvette was changed, going back to the 1963 model. That gives American Custom an advantage over similar companies that have since cropped up nationwide, said Mr. Lea, who started out as a mechanic at the business in 1977 and bought it from Mr. Schuller in 1994. There's not a body panel on a car from 1963 on that we cannot reproduce, Mr. Lea said. You can give me a frame from a 63 car, and I could build you a car. The bigger challenge for American Custom of late has been its repair and service facility, a major portion of which was damaged during a fire in September, 2004. Damage to the building was estimated at $2 million, and 13 customer cars worth $8,000 to $50,000 were harmed, including nine that were totaled, Mr. Lea said. Still, there was no question the company would rebuild at a cost of more than $1.5 million, Mr. Lea said. American Custom sells body parts through its own catalog, as well as through national outfits such as Corvette America and Eckler's Corvette Parts. Executives for both of those companies praised American Custom's craftsmanship and service. American Custom has been a supplier since the early 1990s to Corvette America, which offers about 90 percent of what American Custom makes, said Dave Hall, vice president of Corvette America. The Pennsylvania firm's primary customer base is 2,000 repair shops worldwide. We have a tremendous relationship with them, Mr. Hall said of American Custom. The relationship has been very strong since the beginning. Toledoan Ruth Frazier has taken her Corvettes to American Custom for service, repairs, parts, paint and accessories for nearly 20 years. When you own a Corvette, you want to have someone who knows what they are doing, said Ms. Frazier, who drives a 2004 Corvette Commemorative Edition. Corvettes are not the only vehicles American Custom works on, although one that Michael Murray raced in the 1970s is what introduced him to the business. Employees take their time and do jobs right on Mr. Murray's exotic vehicles, he said, including some repairs needed on a new Cobra roadster replicated from the 1965 design he recently bought. They are like no others, Mr. Murray of Wauseon said. The customer comes first. American Custom plants to start offering more used parts, such as control arms for 1973 Corvettes. Mr. Lea said it also designs custom fiber-glass parts and their molds for spoilers and other items, he said. Everyone wants to personalize it a little bit, and that's how we make our living, he said."

FIRST MCDONALD'S RESTAURANT IN SYLVANIA

The first McDonald's Restaurant that was built in Sylvania was in the township at 3015 Holland-Sylvania Road, (Holland-Sylvania Road just south of Central Avenue). This McDonald's Restaurant opened for business in 1970. Lucas County Real Estate records show that on 6-26-1970 this property transferred from Walter M. Lehman, Trustee, to Franchise Realty Interstate Corp. This restaurant was rebuilt in 1981 to include a drive-thru window. And now in 2004 it has been rebuilt again, but a little south of the original site. Real Estate records show that on

3-16-2005 McDonalds Real Estate Co. sold their original site at 3015 Holland-Sylvania Road to Jarasgit Nucharee Pipat, Trustee.

The second McDonald's Restaurant in Sylvania opened in 1978 at 5810 Alexis Road on property that was formerly owned by Glenn Knisely. The 11-23-1977 issue of the *Sylvania Sentinel* reported the following: "A McDonald's Restaurant will be erected in the 5800 block of Alexis Road following action by the Sylvania Municipal Planning Commission on Nov. 12. Members of the Commission granted a lot split of 1.43 acres of a total parcel which is owned by Glenn Knisely. The restaurant will be a new concept in this area and similar to the one on Airport Highway. The property is bordered by Acres, Cadet, Elliott and Alexis. Construction is expected to begin in the very near future."

The 12-14-1977 *Sylvania Sentinel* reported: "Ground Broken for New McDonald's On Alexis – A king-size spatula was used to scoop the earth as ground was broken for the 11th McDonald's restaurant in the Toledo area on Dec. 8. The new restaurant is being built at the intersection of Monroe Street and Alexis Road. It is scheduled to open about May 30. The décor of the newest McDonald's will center around the history of Sylvania. Landmarks like Flower Hospital, Olander Park and the Stranahan Mansion will be featured. The landscape and decorative motif will display extensive greenery and offer a rustic atmosphere. The Sylvania McDonald's will have a drive-thru special service window and a computer-like interlock energy conservation system. It will also contain a special Ronald McDonald party room."

6-14-1978 – *Sylvania Sentinel Herald* newspaper: "Sylvania's First McDonald's – The 18th McDonald's Restaurant in the Toledo area opened for business Saturday morning. The restaurant, located at 5810 W. Alexis Road, near Monroe Street, is the first golden arches operation in Sylvania and the world's 4,579[th]. The occasion was celebrated by Council President Richard Hagerty, an ensemble from Sylvania Northview and Southview High School bands and a host of McDonald's officials. John Arnot, director of Public Service, assisted Mr. Haggerty with the ribbon cutting. The grand opening activity included the raising of the American flag, a musical tribute and the cutting of a ribbon strung with 100 $2 bills. The money donated was to the two high school bands. After the ceremony by McDonald's officials, all in attendance were treated to McDonald's world famous cuisine and a tour of the restaurant at the ceremony's close. The Sylvania McDonald's features an apple pie tree which talks at the push of a button, a drive through service window, décor marking famous Sylvania landmarks, extensive trellis work with hanging plants and an energy interlock conservation system. Tom Ringenbach, of Northwood, will manage the restaurant. Chuck Beyer of Point Place is the area supervisor, Robert Card of Sylvania is the operations manager for McDonald's system of northwestern Ohio, which currently operates 16 of the area's 18 McDonalds."

Then in 1994 the third McDonald's Restaurant arrived at 7165 W. Central Avenue (across from Meijer).

FIRST BURGER KING RESTAURANT IN SYLVANIA

The first Burger King Restaurant in Sylvania was constructed at 6307 Monroe Street in 1978 (today in 2018 this building is occupied by Fricker's). The second Burger King Restaurant in Sylvania was at 3128 Holland-Sylvania Road in 1986. The third was at 5871 Monroe Street in 1987 and the fourth was at 7447 Central Avenue in 1997.

FIRST WENDY'S HAMBURGER RESTAURANT IN SYLVANIA

The first Wendy's Hamburger Restaurant in Sylvania was constructed in 1974 at 5802 Monroe Street. Next came a Wendy's Restaurant at 5560 W. Central Avenue in 1975, then in 1994 a new Wendy's at 7251 W. Central Avenue and in 1997 a Wendy's Hamburger was constructed at 5135 Monroe Street.

FROG FARM IN SYLVANIA

The following article appeared in the *Sylvania Sentinel* under the column of "Bits O'Business," in the 7-14-1927 issue: "Residents in the neighborhood of Erie Street between Main and Summit should not become alarmed if they hear a deep croaking at night. For it is rumored a new industry has been or is about to be established in Sylvania—a frog farm. It is alleged that Seley LaDow is president of the new firm which will raise frogs and sell them to the leading hotels of this territory. Some splendid specimens of stock have been imported from the north and it is proposed to run the farm on a purely scientific basis. Great secrecy prevails as to the other members of the concern, but we are informed from fairly reliable sources that Dorr Johnson is to be scientific manager."

GREASERS, JOCKS, SOCIALS, FREAKS AND NERDS

In these days of political correctness this subject may be inappropriate to talk about today, but to me it's part of Sylvania's history, therefore I have interviewed many Sylvania residents, of all ages, in search for answers to when these terms first began. When I attended Sylvania High School (1973-1977), and in talking to people who graduated as early as the late 1960s and through part of the 1980s, there were five categories of students who went to Sylvania High School. They were: The Greasers, the Jocks, the Socials, the Freaks and the Nerds. This is not only written from my own observation and knowledge, but from the observation of people who went to school here between that time period; although I will say that a few that I talked to remember these types of students, but don't remember them having the group names.

The <u>Greasers</u> were the rowdy students; majored in things like auto body repair, print shop, occupational work (O.W.A.), always looking for a fight and always looking for trouble. They had long hair, drank alcohol, smoked cigarettes (with the pack sometimes rolled up in their sleeve) some marijuana, and most lived in the "Little Chicago" or "Dog Patch" areas of Sylvania, but could have included other areas of the city and township. They often wore leather jackets, black boots and were the tough type; driving around in hot rods or supped up fast cars, built or refinished by them. Their girlfriends majored in things like beauty care and wore their hair long and straight. They had no interest in school, school activities or after school activities at all, but instead attended the football games and school dances looking for trouble, looking for a fight. They walked around the football field in gang-type formation just hoping for someone to say something to them, to give them a reason to fight. Most everybody that I interviewed mentioned one name in particular as a well-known greaser, and that name was Doug J. (I would not want to incriminate him). One person that I interviewed that graduated in 1976 said that his senior year, this Doug J. came to the school and completely smashed the display case by the gym.

The <u>Jocks</u> were the athletes, cheerleaders and their fans; always playing some type of sports, wearing athletic gear, "lettered" jackets, getting good grades (sometimes referred to as the "brains"), not causing any trouble; in fact taking part in many school activities and gaining roles of authority during their high school years. They were good looking with shorter styled hair and they always looked clean and clean shaven, known as the "Ken and Barbie" types. Most "jocks" were from the middle to upper-class families.

The <u>Socials</u> were the rich kids; always on their best behavior, always dressing in the most fashionable clothes and walking around like they were better than everyone else, because their parents had money and they lived in the rich expensive homes. They got good grades and loved school. They were often in crowds of their own in school, putting up banners and decorating the hallways, part of the student council and driving around in the brand-new sports cars purchased by their parents, but acting like they were special and above everyone else.

The <u>Freaks</u> (sometimes referred to as "burnouts, "druggies," and "stoners") were usually heavy duty drug users, hippies, off in space, stayed "high" most of the day, or not in class at all, but instead down in the woods skipping class, dealing drugs, smoking pot, popping pills, including "acid." They had long hair that needed to be washed, talked in slow motion and walked with a bob, with their head moving slowly up and down as they walked. They were too "high" to cause any problems, other than giggling a lot. When they did come to class they were often caught by the teacher sleeping at their desks or looking for something to eat. Their eyes were narrow slats of red blood shot features on their face. They did not participate in school activities or extracurricular school activities. Most "freaks" were from the working class parents, although there were a few of the rich kids that were want-to-be "freaks."

The <u>Nerds</u> were the kids that were meek and mild. Never got in to trouble, not athletic, dressed in "nerd" clothes, got ok grades and were usually either painfully thin or painfully overweight. They did not fight and were afraid of the greasers and freaks. Often these nerds were loners or misfits in high school or they hung around with other nerds.

For those students that did not fit into any of the above groups there was no special name that anybody I interviewed could recall. We'll call them the "wild-card" group and there were too few of them to have established a name for them apparently.

I will give an example here of the rivals between the jocks, socials and the greasers. The following is copied from the *Sylvania Sentinel* newspaper dated 9-15-1971:

"A series of fights and confrontations with the police disrupted the annual back to school dance at Sylvania High School on Friday, Sept. 3.

Near the end of the dance a large crowd gathered in the parking lot at the back of the school, due possibly to the heat inside of the gym or a disinterest in the band. The crowd was estimated at 700 by the Sylvania Police department. Around 10:15 p.m., a rash of fights broke out. Many of the participants claimed they were hit for no reason, allegedly by an organized gang.

When the alleged gang left the scene some of the persons hit wanted action taken against the gang by the police. When the officers refused they were spit on, called names, and their cars were rocked by a minority of those present.

The officers ordered the crowd to leave. When they did not leave, the officers called for assistance. City of Sylvania and Sylvania Township police departments and Lucas County Sheriff's deputies responded.

When a small group remained and continued to harass the police, an officer used mace, a safe tear gas used on individuals. Mace was used instead of nightsticks according to Chief Arthur Cole of the City Police department, though the officer was from another department. The majority of the crowd left but a small group went to the Township and made complaints against the officers."

In talking to the next generation of kids at the Sylvania High Schools I am told that today the different groups are called punks, gothics, emos, preppies, band geeks, stoners and even the terms nerds, freaks and jocks are still used, with each still having the same definition as when I was in high school. Also in the same class with the nerds were the dorks and geeks. A 1995 graduate of Sylvania Northview recalled a group known as the "Herds." This was a small group of mix students of all classes.

GYPSIES IN SYLVANIA

The *World Book Encyclopedia* says that "Gypsies, also spelled Gipsies, are a group of wandering people whose ancestors originally lived in India. Today, Gypsies live in almost every part of the world. The best known Gypsy groups in the United States belong to the Rom tribes. The Romani are the largest group of Gypsies."

Some of the colorful images that people see when thinking of the exotic culture of the Gypsies include fortune-tellers, magicians, entertainers, dancers, all in ornate costumes and living a simple nomadic lifestyle. It is said that it is a largely undocumented culture, shrouded in mystery. Most Gypsies changed their old country family names for an Americanized version, which would be a very common surname (i.e.: Davis, Miller, Nichols, Martin, Adams, Lee, Marks, Evans, Smith, etc.).

Legend says that there was a gypsy at the foot of the cross before the crucifixion of Jesus. The gypsy stole one of the four spikes. Christ then blessed the gypsy and gave all gypsies divine approval to steal for all eternity with impunity.

A *Sylvania Weekly Times* newspaper dated 5-4-1899 reported the following: "A couple of gypsy wagons passed through Tuesday."

During World War II the Nazis murdered thousands of European Gypsies by extermination and through deadly medical experiments. Many were forced to undergo sterilization. By the end of the war more than 500,000 Gypsies had been exterminated.

Wikipedia says that "the title "King of the Gypsies" has been claimed or given over the centuries to many different people. It is both culturally and geographically specific. It may be inherited, acquired by acclamation or action, or simply claimed. The extent of the power associated with the title varied; it might be limited to a small group in a specific place, or many people over large areas. In some cases the claim was clearly a public relations exercise.

According to Gypsy custom when a Gypsy king died all close relatives of the deceased "king" went into mourning for a year and during that time they could not sing or attend any form of public entertainment and the women were to wear no cosmetics. However, the mourning could be broken by parties held nine days, six weeks and six months after their death. But, at the funeral of the deceased, it was a three-day wake highlighted by round-the-clock feasting and drinking. Because of this many funeral directors were reluctant to open their parlors to the wakes of the Gypsies because of the inconvenience and loss of business during this three day, non-stop wake. By tradition, members of the family related to the dead king or queen would get practically no sleep until after the funeral.

Sylvania's tie to a Gypsy king was in 1943 when the Gypsy king, George Nichols, died and his funeral was held in the Reeb Funeral Home at 5712 N. Main Street. According to legend, no other funeral home throughout Toledo or Lucas County would allow the dead king's funeral at their establishment because of the three to four day disruption that it was going to cause to their business. The gypsy king's family approached the owners of Reeb Funeral Home in Sylvania and the Gypsies agreed to pay large sums of money if they would allow their king's funeral to be held there. The Reeb family agreed to hold the funeral, and according to legend Reeb Funeral Home made so much money from the funeral that they were able to remodel their existing funeral home. A couple people that I talked to, that remembered this funeral in Sylvania, said that almost all the silverware was missing from all the area restaurants after this event. Residents of Sylvania who witnessed the three day funeral spoke of this event as one of the biggest, and most interesting things to hit the area.

Marjorie Fitkin wrote the following in her article that appeared in *The Herald* on 6-6-1996 titled "A little piece of local Gypsy history": ". . . His funeral took place right here at the Reeb Funeral Home, in the fall of 1943. Paul Reeb, Sr., spoke of it many times before he died with a good bit of nostalgia. One must remember the whole three or four day affair was an event that all of us will forever remember. Jack Watkins, director of the Reeb Funeral Home, spoke at the bonfire held on the property. Ben Marsh, an attorney in Maumee and my resource person, along with four other noted Burnham High School students and Burnham Band members were hired by the Gypsies to play during the funeral. Of course they only knew marching tunes. So, they were seated in the northwest corner of the funeral home where they played as loudly as possible "On Wisconsin" and the Burnham High and Ohio State marching song – over and over and over! And what do you think? They did the same thing at Calvary Cemetery. Ben still remembers the throngs of people at the funeral home, the long lines of Cadillacs (a la 1940) with license plates from many states, and of course, the smell of incense. The frosting on the cake? Each boy was paid $5.00 and that was good money, in 1943. Nostalgia, whether excessively sentimental or a period of great festivity and joy give our lives depth, meaning and also reinforce our own inner strength."

The following article appeared in the *Sylvania Sentinel* on 9-2-1943 regarding the "Gypsy" funeral held at Reeb Funeral Home: "Sylvania Is Scene of Gypsy Funeral – Several hundred gypsies gathered in Sylvania this week to be present at the funeral of their king, George Nichols, 64, who died last Friday in Marshall, Michigan. He had been king of the tribe for 27 years. Sunday, it is reported, the wife of the deceased, will be crowned to reign for the duration. No new king will be chosen until after the war. About 150 of the young men are working in defense plants and several in uniform attended the funeral here. Burial was from Reeb Funeral Home Wednesday at noon, with interment in Calvary Cemetery, Toledo, in a specially constructed mausoleum. George Nichols is survived by his wife, Rosie, four daughters and two sons."

In a written autobiography by Benjamin Marsh who lived in Sylvania Township and graduated from Burnham High School in 1945 he wrote the following about the Gypsy funeral held in Sylvania: "The gypsy funeral. The gypsy king (Miller) died. Reeb Funeral Home in Sylvania had the funeral. 1942? We – 5 from the high school band – were hired to play at Reeb's and at Calvary Cemetery. I, of course, played the bass drum. We weren't very good but we knew at least two pieces: "On Wisconsin" and the "Ohio State Fight Song" (same as the Burnham one) which we played over and over. It must have been extremely loud but the gypsies loved it. We each got paid a pricey sum, $5.00! Big money in those days. Many years later, I represented Paul Reeb, Sr. when he was dying. He would always start a conversation with "Bennie, do you remember the gypsy funeral?"

Other examples of Gypsy king funerals that were held in Toledo was in July of 1951 when the gypsy king Steve Nicholas Davis died at the age of 42 in Battle Creek, Michigan. He had a stroke. On 7-16-1951 automobiles filled with gypsies arrived in Toledo, with the body who was reportedly the king of gypsies in America which numbered approximately 6,000. He was brought to Toledo to be buried in Calvary Cemetery beside his father, George Davis. The *Toledo Blade* dated 7-15-1951 reported: "Most of the gypsies arriving for the funeral were dressed in traditional costumes with gold earrings and other jewelry. Ex-King Eli Miller, 65, abdicated the throne in 1944 because of illness." Steve Nicholas Davis was the son-in-law of Eli Miller, retired leader of a Toledo gypsy tribe that had their headquarters on Summit Street in Toledo. Mr. Miller and several members of his clan journeyed to Battle Creek to accompany the body to Toledo. In 1946 Steve Davis had become gypsy king when his father-in-law died. It was expected that Steve Davis' 16-year old son James would become the new king.

In 1957 the body of the gypsy queen, "Queen" Annie Miller, was in Toledo in the Abele Mortuary. She died in Riverside Hospital, her services were held in Rosary Cathedral and she was buried in Calvary Cemetery. She was the wife of Joe Miller, 727 Summit St, the "king" of Toledo gypsies until 1944, and she was the queen of Ohio's more than 5,000 Brazilian gypsies. When Joe Miller died crowds of gypsy mourners congregated in and around the hospital where he died in Battle Creek and extra police were required to help with traffic. It was reported that the crowd of mourners included some gypsies in expensive limousines. Battle Creek, Michigan was the winter quarters for gypsies who worked in the traveling carnivals.

And one more example of a Gypsy king funeral was mentioned in an article in the *Toledo Blade* dated 11-15-1981 when it was reported that Joe Miller, king of the Toledo gypsy clan was laid to rest in a Calvary Cemetery plot that he personally had picked out two years prior. This article said that Joe Miller had been king of the tribe since 1949. This article also reported that "After the coffin was lowered, the family remained at the cemetery for several more hours, drinking and eating sandwiches, looking not unlike a football tailgate party. Several times, vehicles left for more sustenance. The men stood in large circles, talking, drinking, and smoking; the women stayed apart from the men, collecting refuse in paper bags."

According to an interview of the Langham family of Sylvania, they said: "Gypsies used to camp in Sylvania on the Ray West property on Monroe Street, east of Main Street, on the south side. They camped along the creek behind his house." (Ray West's house was located at 6465 Monroe Street) where today in 2011 the City just finished clearing the land and prepared it for development called SOMO.

Donald Beveridge came to Sylvania in 1915 with his parents and graduated from Sylvania High School in 1921. He later went to work for the Sylvania Savings Bank where he became the president of the bank in 1928. In a book titled *The Flickertail Tapes; The Life Story of Donald Wayne Beveridge* by Nancy Beveridge (2011) this is what Donald Beveridge said about gypsies in Sylvania: "Back then gypsies would come into the bank once in a while. They had dark complexions and they dressed differently. They were Slavic, I think. Years ago they used to camp on the edge of town, where Ray West's barn was. The word 'gypsy' means 'rover.' They never settled down anywhere. I told the bank employees, 'If gypsies come in, don't do anything with them, don't even talk to them.' But one time some of them came in, and they persuaded one of our cashiers to get out some hundred dollar bills. After they had left, we were a hundred dollar bill short when we balanced that night. I think our man was gullible. He was younger then."

HOUSE MOVING IN SYLVANIA

Over the years, studying and researching the history of Sylvania, I would often hear some old-timers saying "Oh, that house used to sit there, but it was moved to here to make room to build a new building" And as I started documenting and reading the old newspapers I did find quite a few house moving events. Apparently the "Long" boys did most of the house moving in Sylvania in the 1920s, 1930s and 1940s.

A 1933 article about the history of the Sylvania Savings Bank said that in 1907 the bank purchased the site at the SE corner of Main and Maplewood from George W. Lovewell. The site had a house on it which was formerly occupied by Dr. Thomas Cosgrove, and in 1907 part of this old Cosgrove house was moved to North Main Street and made part of the house occupied at that time by Mrs. Mary Hicker, and another portion was moved to Erie Street, next to the railroad tracks.

There was a house on the north side of Maplewood Avenue, along the railroad tracks, that survived the hotel and lumber yard fire of 1915, and can be seen in a photo beyond piles of smoldering remains of the lumber yard there. Sometime after that fire the house was moved to 6739 Erie Street and still stands today in 2018.

It was mentioned in the minutes of the Sylvania History Buffs that: "Another house that was moved was the house standing on Main Street (maybe the Green family home or Dr. Kennedy's house). It was split into two parts – one on Maplewood, second from the railroad, the "Dorcas" house and another part taken to N. Main Street next to the Jacob house." (Note by author: I cannot verify which house the Main Street house would have been, but Dr. Kennedy used to live in a home on the east side of Main Street in downtown Sylvania, where today in 2018 is the Edward Jones building at 5678 Main Street, and the Dorcas house is located at 6710 Maplewood Avenue).

A building permit dated 4-16-1926 granted permission to Willie Burnham to move a house basement on the west side of Spring Street between Convent and Mill Street on Lot No. 9 of Clark Addition. Today in 2018 there are two houses on Lot No. 9 of Clarks Addition; one at 5163 Spring Street and one at 5165 Spring Street.

In July of 1926 Keil and Rassel obtained a building permit from the Village of Sylvania to move a house from the east side of Main Street to a new location on the west side of Summit Street between the state line and Erie Street. The permit was signed by Keil & Rassel, by John Keil.

A building permit was requested on 8-6-1926 by Deo D. Shull to move the present house at 5321 S. Main Street, move it north 15 feet, and build a basement under the structure. Then raise the rear to add a two-story addition.

The home of Henry and Celestia Burnham was constructed before 1840 on the property where the old Maplewood School was located at 6769 Maplewood Avenue. In 1928 this house was moved to the northeast corner of Monroe and School Drive by the Sylvania Board of Education so that Maplewood School could be constructed. They then used the old house as a public library until 1957.

In July of 1929 L.H. Coutchure requested a building permit for the owner Mary M. Thamletz to move a frame dwelling and 16 x 22 foot addition to the Roberts property at 5152 S. Main Street.

On 5-2-1930 J.D. LaPoint requested a building permit from the Village of Sylvania asking permission to move a house from the east side of S. Main Street to property owned by J.D. LaPointe on the south side of Convent Blvd, about 150 feet west of the drive to Association cemetery. The permit said that the house was to be placed upon a permanent foundation with a basement. This house still stands today in 2018 at 6817 Convent Blvd.

In 1932 The Sisters of St. Francis had a house on South Main Street moved to their property on Convent Blvd, which still is used today. According to a building permit issued by the Village of Sylvania on 7-25-1932, a mover by the name of C.H. O'Neill was granted permission to move a house on Main Street to the property of the Sisters of St. Francis at 6832 Convent. This permit said that the house was to be placed between the St. Agnes House and their main building.

In April of 1935 F. Morrissee at 5774 Main Street, at the corner of Erie Street, obtained a building permit to move a building to his property and use it as a garage.

In December of 1936 Don Merrick obtained a building permit to move a 16 x 18 foot chicken house at 5740 Main Street to 5953 Monroe Street.

According to the 10-29-1937 Burnham Student Prints newspaper Mr. C. E. Long and Company were moving a house that was located on Main Street, across the street from the old public school grounds. They were moving this house so that a new Sylvania Post Office (5736 N. Main Street) could be constructed. This house was moved to 5742 Woodrow Drive. This required a move through the old school grounds property (the old school had already been removed), over the railroad tracks, and west to the corner of Roosevelt and Woodrow Drive. The Student Prints article by Charles Quinnell, reported: "Don't look now, but there's a house in the middle of Main Street! It was true, Mr. C.E. Long and company were in the midst of moving a house, located directly across from the old school grounds, from Main Street to Roosevelt, via "Cross lots." We asked Mr. Long if this wasn't a large undertaking, realizing that the N.Y.C. railroad tracks where directly in his pathway. "That's apple pie for us," he explained. It does start us to thinking, though, when we have to move a whole city block, as we did on the East side a few years ago. When we set this house down on its new foundation, I'll wager there won't be a thing wrong with it, except possibly a little wallpaper wrinkled around the chimney. When asked how many years he had been in this moving business, he replied, "Well, my Dad told me that if I didn't want to go to school, which I didn't, I would have to go to work. So I followed in Dad's footsteps and have been moving houses for 25 years now." The house, moved by Mr. Long, was one of two that had to be removed from the Main Street site to provide space for the new post office, which will be built there."

In 1938 the Sisters of St. Francis moved the original Catholic Church on S. Main Street and the original Guardian Angel Day School house together to the rear of the property at 5425 Main Street.

In October of 1944 Howard Hine received permission from council to move a garage from the east side of Summit Street to the West side of Summit Street and make repairs.

On 3-5-1946 Sylvania Village Council approved a building permit to allow Ralph H. Sutter to move a dwelling from Summit Street to Glasgow Road, and remodel the dwelling. Estimated cost of $1,500. The facts are that a house that used to sit at 5629 Summit Street was moved to 5675 Glasgow Road and still stands today in 2018. The real estate transfer records for the property at 5675 Glasgow shows that on 11-22-1946 Hildegarde C. Sutter purchased Lot 89 of the Haverford subdivision.

An article in the *Sylvania Sentinel* on 4-8-1948 said: "The large square house recently moved back from the corner of Summit and Monroe to make way for the filling station was built by Peleg Clark. Mr. Clark purchased the land from one of the original proprietors of the village, David White, who built his log cabin in approximately the same location. The Clark home has been remodeled several times. The changed roof line particularly obscures the original lines. Older residents recall the beautiful spiral staircase in this building."

In 1948 J.W. Laux obtained a building permit to move a house from 6518 Monroe Street to 5359 Main Street.

On 7-5-1949 Sylvania Village Council granted a building permit to Raymond Cline to move a commercial building from Stewart Road to the south side of Monroe Street in the village of Sylvania.

On 11-20-1950 Sylvania Village Council granted Robert Fike a building permit to move a private automobile garage from N. Main Street to 5041 S. Main Street.

Sylvania village council minutes dated 3-18-1956 reported that C.J. Myers, contractor, was given approval to move a house from 5532 Acres Road to 5678 Cushman Road.

The *Sylvania Sentine-Herald* dated 10-16-1958 featured a photo of a house being moved. The caption reads: "Houses began mingling with Monroe Street and Alexis Road traffic last week as the right-of-way for relocated US 23 began to be cleared. Brick from this house was removed prior to the haul-away.

In an interview with Lillian Crandell-Ward on 2-11-2003 she said that her and her husband William "Bill" Crandell first lived in a house on Monroe Street where the expressway is today. Mrs. Crandell said that their house was the original clubhouse of the Sylvania Country Club, and when the country club was going to build their current building (5201 Corey Road), Floyd G. Crandell somehow obtained the rights to the building and moved the clubhouse to 5925/5945 Monroe Street. After the house was moved here it sat on a cement slab. At first it was used by the Crandell family as an entertainment building, but her and Bill purchased the property and building in 1954, and owned it until 1958 when the State of Ohio came along and informed them that they needed their property to build the U.S. 23 expressway on and off ramps.

In 1959 and 1960 there was a lot of house moving going on in Sylvania on Monroe Street where the U.S. 23 expressway was being constructed. Some of the houses that were in the way of the proposed expressway were moved to Cushman Road. A few were moved to Balfour Road too.

The minutes of Sylvania Village Council dated 6-2-1958 said that the Drew Cartage Company was moving a house from 5905 Cushman Road to 6129 Glasgow. The minutes of 11-16-1959 said that William H. Fisher was issued a building permit to move a dwelling from Monroe Street to 6052 Glasgow Road.

An article in the 5-26-1960 *Sylvania Sentinel-Herald* said: "This was a familiar scene in Sylvania about two years ago when work on the U.S. 23 interchange at Monroe Street got underway. It's becoming familiar again as the state moves ahead with the extension of the expressway to West Central Avenue. This is the home of Mr. and Mrs. Lester Schofield, 4737 Holland-Sylvania Rd., as it moves south about 1,500 feet to its new lot on the same street. The Schofields elected to move their house rather than have it demolished "since we love the neighborhood and have lived here more than 20 years." The moving took only about five minutes of actual "riding down the road," and hardly affected Holland-Sylvania traffic. The home was right in the path of the proposed expressway, although the Schofields have retained a large portion of the land on which it rested."

There once was a house on the northeast corner of Holland-Sylvania Road and Sylvania Avenue. In 1968 the owner, Sophie Rapp, sold this corner to the Shell Oil Company, but first she had this house at 4008 Holland-Sylvania Road moved to 4315 Holland-Sylvania Road. It stood there at its new location until in about 2000 it was demolished.

When the expressway was extended to Central Avenue, many of the houses along Central Avenue were moved to McCord Road, and then later in the early 1970s when Central Avenue was being widened many houses that were in the right-of-way had to be moved. One house owned by George Whittaker on the south side of Central, west of McCord Road, was moved to 3318 McCord Road by Charles and Ruth Noonan in about 1972. The old Turanski house on Central Avenue was moved to McCord Road. Some of the houses that were on the south side of Central Avenue when the expressway extended were moved to Wilford Drive.

In 1994 when the City officials were making a handicapped access to Harroun Park they purchased the home at 5460 Main Street, which was at that time owned by Ross Deye. Instead of bulldozing the entire house, the front portion of that home was moved to the historical village, where a large two-story commercial/residential home had just been demolished at 5727 Main Street. This front portion of this "catalog" home still stands there in the historical village right next to the public restrooms. In 2018 the building is being rented and they are selling retro candy and fancy chocolates in the old house.

In 1997 Sylvania's train depot, which had been purchased by Gene Paul and Dr. Newton years earlier, and had been used for office space, was donated to the Sylvania Historical Village Commission. At that time they had it moved from 6555 Convent Blvd., to 5735 Main Street. The depot was moved first to the railroad tracks, and then brought down the railroad tracks, heading north, and brought to the property of the historical village. It was then placed on a new foundation along the railroad tracks, with the front of the building facing east.

In 2004, after several years of battling to keep it on its original property, the Lathrop House (5362 S. Main Street) was moved a little to the north and then quite a few yards to the east, on property that could be called 5402 S. Main Street, into Harroun Park. For more information about Sylvania's Lathrop House and the details of the move, read the following book: *The Underground Railroad and Sylvania's Historic Lathrop House* by Gaye E. Gindy.

The old post-Civil War house built by Joseph Printup was located at 8249 Sylvania-Metamora Road/Erie Street (south side of the street just east of Centennial Road). This original farmhouse was built by Joseph Printup when he returned to Sylvania after serving in the Civil War. Then in the 1920s a beautiful gazebo-style porch was added. The Mercereau family lived in this house from 1871 until he died in 1923 and she died in 1931, and then a daughter continued to live here until about 1933. In 1999 this farmhouse was saved from destruction and moved from its original location on the south side of Erie Street just east of Centennial Road to make way for a new gas station/retail complex. The house address today is 8216 Erie Street and it serves as a commercial tea house. (For more information on the history of this house see the article titled "The Sweet Shalom Tea Room."). At this same time a 1970s house that sat next door was also moved behind the tea house.

I am sure there were more structures moved in Sylvania over the years, and these are just the ones that have come to my attention.

MICKEY AND MINNIE MOUSE

If you lived in Sylvania, or traveled through Sylvania's back road in the 1960s and through the 1970s, you remember Mickey and Minnie Mouse. Now, tell me where they were located?

If your answer was at the corner of Maplewood and Summit, you are correct! Everyone has used Summit Street as a cut-through, to avoid going through downtown Sylvania, and some people, especially with children, would go that way just to see Mickey and Minnie Mouse rocking in their rocking chair together at this corner.

These stuffed characters belonged to James Armstrong, who lived on the northwest corner of Maplewood and Summit, and were used to draw attention to his sign advertising his profession of furniture and small maintenance repairs. Another landmark on his property was his old green barn that was decorated on the outside with old artifacts, and a set of stairs leading up to the second floor of the barn. Remember?

The exact time period that Mickey and Minnie Mouse were placed on this corner cannot be determined, but at the 11-4-1957 meeting of Sylvania Village Council, J.H. Armstrong was granted a building permit to construct a sign at 6602 Maplewood Avenue. This sign had Santa Claus rocking in a rocking chair, operated by electric motor. According to an article in the *Sylvania Sentinel-Herald* in 1957, which featured a picture of the sign with Santa in the chair it said: "The chair is a child's cast-off rocker and Santa himself was put together by Mrs. Armstrong. She resurrected the beard from an old false face, sewed him a fine suit of all-weather plastic, and stuffed him with guess what? A bushel of last year's left-over Easter egg grass!"

So apparently after Christmas that year, he changed over to Mickey Mouse in the chair, and then later added Minnie Mouse.

To help explain how Mickey and Minnie came about, and so as not to get the facts wrong I will copy an article that appeared in *The Sentinel* dated 10-15-1969, on page 7, and written by Joan Webb: "Jim Armstrong was doing just what you'd expect a man whose business is furniture and small maintenance repairs to be doing.….painting.

"Does that look more rustic?" he asked as he backed away to survey the unique sign that advertises his occupation.

"Yes, sir," I agreed. "Whatever made you choose Mickey and Minnie Mouse to decorate your sign?" The two four-foot figures sit side by side in a youngster's rocking chair and rock constantly in daylight hours at the corner of Summit and Maplewood in Sylvania, Ohio. Mr. Armstrong cocked his head and grinned. "It all started ten years ago quite by chance when someone gave me an authentic Disney face at a Halloween party. I had been contemplating a new sign and when I saw that mask, I knew it had to be Mickey! I fashioned the body and put the mouse in the rocking chair atop my sign. It's amazing to me the human interest Mickey creates.

"Once a little boy called and in a concerned voice (which Mr. Armstrong imitated) said, "Mickey isn't rocking, is he all right?" I told him Mickey just gets tired rocking all the time, but I keep him rocking now," he confided.

"Another time a little girl called and cried (he mimicked again) 'Mr. Armstrong. Mickey's all alone out in the rain getting soaking wet!" He did look forlorn in bad weather so I built a bigger chair to accommodate two and Minnie came to keep him company, an umbrella was added to shelter them both from the rain and snow and now Mickey doesn't get lonely any longer."

"Have you ever had any trouble with the sign being stolen?" I queried. "Oh, yes," he laughed. "Three or four times Mickey has been appropriated from his chair for kicks. Once he was taken but brought back and placed in his chair a week later. Another time a person in town recognized Mickey "visiting" at someone else's home and took it upon himself to convince the new "owner" that the mouse should be taken home to his own corner. It's unbelievable that people should take such an interest in this creature."

"The last time, about one a.m., two young people who ride my school bus saw two boys confiscating the mouse and immediately gave chase down Maplewood Avenue at a high rate of speed. They caught up with the 'mice nappers' and the chase was reversed. My friends drove to the police station and dashed in screaming their plight. The 'mice nappers' were so excited that they didn't realize where they were and followed right into the parking lot where the police apprehended them.

"Originally I filed charges but after talking with the boys, withdrew them. Unfortunately the judge said that at this point it was out of my hands and booked them. It was on their records but they paid the damages and now we are good friends.

"A few weeks ago I took the sign down because I felt it was too prominent and perhaps I was forcing people to look at it, but there were twenty phone calls protesting, so the mice are back. With this world so filled with suffering and sadness, it's a joy to have created a thing of pleasure for so many people." He related as a school bus rounded the corner and at least thirty smiling kindergarteners waved at him and his mice.

"Figuring two smiles a day for the past ten years, this sign must have given at least 7,300 smiles," estimated Mr. Armstrong conservatively.

He consulted his watch and observed that he had an hour before he must leave for his run. He has driven a school bus to Huntington Farms for over twelve years. One mother exclaimed, "Jim Armstrong has the best behaved bus in the whole school district. The kids love him. They sing and have the best time. I once went on a field trip with my daughter when he drove and the bus ride was more interesting than the place we visited."

He has lived on this same corner all his life. The house of native whitewood is almost a hundred years old and was built by General David White, the founder of Sylvania. "Oh, I remember our old well, the horse and buggy, the old arch lights, the first Model T Fords and the first telephone. Our phone was the second to be installed here, and for years our number was simply 'number 2.' When I was born in 1913, there were only about 200 residents in town."

His workshop is neat as a tack and his home showed evidence of a woman's touch in every corner. About his wife of 26 years, he sentimentally stated, "Esther is the inspiration of my life, and I mean every syllable of that." His love for his son, Don, and daughter was evident too. He showed me a giant Mickey Mouse bank Don gave him for Christmas which was inscribed, "Mickey Mouse Academy Award to James H. Armstrong." "I am richly blessed," he concluded."

In April of 1971 Sylvania's Mickey and Minnie Mouse were vandalized. Jim Armstrong reported to police that he had heard voices, but didn't think too much about it. Upon investigation, however, he found that the figures had been badly torn in an effort to steal them.

Jim Armstrong sold his home to Reeb Funeral Home in 1978, so we know that Mickey and Minnie were gone by then.

If you look real close you can see Mickey and Minnie Mouse sitting in a rocking chair on top of the business sign, which used to sit on the northwest corner of Maplewood Avenue and Summit Street. This was owned by James Armstrong and he ran a repair shop out of his barn, behind his home, so the sign advertised his business. Kids in Sylvania always made their parents drive past this landmark on their way home, even if it did mean going the long way home. (Photo owned by the Sylvania Area Historical Society).

NOTES MADE BY THE SYLVANIA HISTORY BUFFS

The minutes of the Sylvania History Buffs were filled with information about Sylvania history and the people of Sylvania.

The Sylvania History Buffs held their first meeting on 3-22-1974 at the Sylvania Public Library located on the SE corner of Monroe and Silica. At this meeting Jim Armstrong told the group that when he takes youngsters out for a bus tour of historic spots in Sylvania Township he had always pointed out the old stone structure known as "The Cooper House" on Centennial near Brint Road. But one day he raised his finger to point out the house and it wasn't there. That same day Mr. Armstrong went over to the post office and talked to Robert C. Smith about forming a historical society. The next day he placed a news item in the *Sylvania Sentinel* newspaper calling for interested people who thought as he did that the landmarks were disappearing too fast, and something needed to be done about it. He knew that all old structures could not be saved, but saving pictures of landmarks would be possible, and the library officials agreed to house such a collection for historical reference. There were ten people present at the first meeting, they included:

Mrs. Pat Lewis, Branch Head Librarian of the Sylvania Library;
Mrs. Helen Dorothy Wagonlander Gaige;
Mrs. Lillian Carroll;
Mrs. Kathryn Keller;
Mrs. Mary Beth Keller Boyle;
Robert Cass Smith;
Robert Andersen Smith (age 18);
Hazel May Smith;
John H. Chudzinski;
James Armstrong, chairman.

The following important information about Sylvania's history was copied from the various meeting minutes or general notes prepared by Hazel May Smith, as the secretary for the Sylvania History Buffs:

10-29-1974 – Meeting held at the Convent: - "In 1974 farmers in Sylvania Twp. are not able to make a living on 40, 80 or 100 acres as they did 40 years ago. Most farming in this area is done by renting more acreage, as costs are too high, to run a small place as they used to do. Forty, or 50 years ago, the ordinary farmer in this area, raised wheat, oats, corn, hay and usually had a dairy herd. Some years the farmer would raise sugar beets, or tomatoes or potatoes. Now fertilizer cost $175 a ton, an ordinary tractor costs about $10,000, horses are no longer seen on the farms in Sylvania Twp., and it's rare to see a herd of cattle. (There are many people who have riding horses).

The first registered cows in this area were owned by Earl Harroun, on Harroun Road. He was nationally known for his farming practices. He was way ahead of his time and had a special building with a liquid manure system, which is fairly common now.

Chester Beckham of 419 – 13ᵗʰ St. Toledo, who ran a creamery in the early 1900s always said that Harroun's milk was the best he received; but not the richest. Earl Harroun's cows were Holsteins; the kind of cow that gives large amounts of milk, but does not have the highest cream percentage. (Part of this information is from Floyd Cass Smith who knew both men).

There was at one time, about 50 years ago, (1920s) a swinging bridge to cross the Ottawa River, in back of Dr. Counter's house on Summit Street (across from where Maplewood intersects). It was used to get over to the other side where there was a nice grove of trees. It was narrow and had only one hand hold wire on one side, the boys used to get on it and make it swing. Dr. Counter was the town dentist for years.

The steam engine was not commonly used for anything except threshing in Sylvania Twp. Threshing on Sylvania-Metamora Rd. in the early 1900s - The threshing machine was owned by Mike Smith (and family). Ed Smith ran the steam thresher, William Keller was in charge of the separator, and Frank Smith was in charge of the water wagon. There were usually 13 farmers who helped each other at threshing time. (They were Mike Smith, William Keller, Joe Wilson, Sam Decker, Basil Harroun, Floyd C. Smith, Joe Kuhlman, Frank Knapp, Charles Mercereau, David and Harold Anderson, (later they had the Anderson's Elevator at Maumee) Keils and Louis Lathrop).

The wheat (or oats) was cut with a binder (reaper) pulled by horses. One man drove the horses, while another person sat on the side and tripped the bundles of grain off at regular intervals. Others were in the field and would set up the bundles in shocks.

When the time came to thresh, the neighbors gathered with their wagons and horses to help. The farmer furnished the coal that ran the steam engine. The man in charge of the water wagon, had to keep enough water on hand at all times. He sometimes would get it from the creek, or at the quarry, or sometimes from a well, wherever he could get it. Usually threshing started early in the morning. First the big steam engine would come in pulling the separator behind it; this was set in place with the long round metal blower set in place so the straw would be blown in the mow of the barn. Then the engine would back far enough to fit the big, wide, long belt to both the engine and separator.

By the time the first wagons piled high with bundles of wheat were ready to go, men would start pitching the bundles on the separator and it started with a low roar that kept up all day. There were men who were in charge of carrying the separated grain to the granary and emptied into the big bins. Dinner was at 12 o'clock sharp.

While the men were getting their work going the women in the house were busy getting a big dinner. The first thing they did was to set up a wash bench out of doors. On it were a couple of wash basins, some bars of soap, plenty of towels and two big pails of water set in the sun to be warm enough when the men came to wash up. The dinner was put on the table at 12 sharp, and when the men were finished they immediately went back to work. There were from 12 to 18 men usually.

If the next farmer's wife was a good cook, but wasn't generous with her servings, sometimes the men would dawdle to some extent so they could stay and have some more "of that good food for supper," at the same place they had dinner at noon.

One time the neighborhood women decided that serving two big meals was too much and thought it was time to let the men know they all should go home for supper. That was the first "women's liberation" in the area from Smith's Siding to Little Rd. So, all up and down Sylvania-Metamora Rd the women were liberated!

Clyde Comstock had six steam engines. He now lives in Jasper, Mich. and moved his six engines up there in October 1974."

The fifth meeting of the Sylvania History Buffs was held on 7-19-1974 at Jim Armstrong's house (6502 Maplewood). According to the minutes of the meeting "The group divided into two groups to visit the second floor of the old barn on Jim Armstrong's place to see the many antiques he has, too many to tell: two old buggies used by Dr. and Mrs. Armstrong, many pictures, books, old trunks, etc., including the "bear skin" which is so interesting to the school children. The windows have some of the original panes and some of the lath and plaster is still to be seen. The large beams forming the framework of the original steeple are still in place, but the steeple is gone. This barn was once a church and was built between 1845-1850 on the lot just north of the old Congregational church; now Reeb's parking lot on Summit St. First it was a church of the Brethren; they sold it to a Pentecostal group. It was during the Pentecostal Church days that the boys of the town discovered their emotional type of church service and gave it the name of "gin and sugar" church. This church was moved several times before it became Dr. Armstrong's barn. It was on Phillips Ave. then back to Summit St. where a Mr. Potts used it for his barn on the bank of Ottawa River. Then Mr. Potts sold it to Dr. Armstrong for $50. He had it moved to its present location for $50 by putting it on skids and pulling it with a winch. The boy and his pony who worked the winch got 14 cents an hour. Dr. Armstrong had the floor put in to make it two stories and used the upper part for hay."

The following was recorded in the minutes of the 1-21-1975 Sylvania History Buffs: "Jim Armstrong told the story of the small skeleton that was found when the Armstrong basement was being enlarged. As Dr. E.E. Armstrong's home formerly had been the home of Dr. T.T. Cosgrove (6502 Maplewood Avenue), it turned out that the skeleton was that of a pet monkey that belonged to the Cosgrove boys. Dr. Kenneth Cosgrove later put the bones together and for a long time the skeleton was in his office.

Mr. Al Graumlich asked that someone research the "block house" that now stands at the entrance to the DeVilbiss Boy Scout Reservation, on Sylvania Ave. Sylvania, Ohio. This block house was built for Toledo's Centennial celebration in 1933, and was first placed on the corner of Madison Ave. and St. Clair Street in downtown Toledo. Later it was moved to the scout reservation.

In 1916, it was thought that Richfield Center would be the big town, and Sylvania would be by-passed. Sister Mary Augustine tells the story: People thought that the Toledo & Western Interurban car line would be run out on Brint Rd, at the turn of the century (when the official population of Sylvania was 617). Richfield Center had a telephone exchange, and it looked as if it would expand, so, Mike Smith, who owned a large 160 acre farm, built a store on the corner of Brint and Mitchaw Rds. But the T & W came out on what is now Sylvania-Metamora Rd instead. So Mike Smith built another store on the NW corner of Mitchaw and Sylvania-Metamora Rd. He also had a loading dock and a coal yard across the road.

When Mother Adelaide came to Sylvania to locate a suitable tract of ground for the convent, she first looked at a place in Richfield Center. She also looked at the tract of ground which is now the Sylvania Country Club, but because of the nearby transportation decided on the present location on Convent Blvd. (Sylvania became a city, and Richfield Center continues to be a small country community)."

4-18-1975 – from the minutes of the Sylvania History Buffs: "Wayne Farley of Berkey still has the basic wagon that was used for the covered wagon at Sylvania's centennial celebration. He says we should keep the covered wagon in mind for the Bi-centennial. He also says that the covered wagon standing in front of the Cow Palace (Bancroft Road) is authentic.

Fred Folger gave a report on the status of the editors of the *Northwest Ohio Quarterly*. The new editor is Dr. Richard Wright of Bowling Green University. The new editor of *Ohio Cues* is Fred Folger. These booklets go to major college libraries of the whole mid-west, as well as to other libraries.

Marvel Holmes spoke of the Hine family. Howard Hine's father came from England in 1835 and farmed in Sylvania Twp. His farm extended along the Michigan line, from Acres Road east to include what it now Huntington Woods area. Howard Hine, the son, laid out the streets in this farm area, and Don Loss' father developed it. At this time there are only three lots left of the original farm. Mrs. Eva Hine lives in a house on one of those lots on Acres Rd."

The following was recorded by the secretary of the Sylvania History Buffs: "The Bi-Centennial Wagon Train – 5-26-1976: "The Bicentennial wagon train came through Sylvania on 5-26-1976, a beautiful warm Wednesday afternoon. The wagon train pilgrimage was a replay of history in reverse – a train of covered wagons moving west to east to Valley Forge, Pennsylvania "to bring the country back to its birthplace, where Americans will rededicate themselves to the principles upon which our nation was founded. Officially there were several state wagons, and unofficially there were other wagons which temporarily joined the "train." The route through Sylvania was called "The Great Lakes Route." There were four other wagon trains – each converging on Valley Forge. There were 60 state wagons, divided among the five caravans. The state wagons were authentic Pennsylvania Conestoga wagons built at Arkansas Village, Jonesboro, Arkansas to exact official specifications. Each of these caravans converged on Valley Forge on the evening of Saturday 7-3-1976 and will be on display all summer.

These Conestoga wagons were 22 feet long and weigh 1,800 pounds; the horses pulling them were large and sturdy looking. The wheels had hard rubber tires for our modern highways. The color of these wagons is authentic blue-gray. The canvas tops were water proof and fireproofed. There was one man in a wheelchair pulled by a pony. He was said to have come from California and intended going all the way. Sylvania had the honor of having the first encampment in the state of Ohio. The train, and about 100 outriders, cross the Ohio-Michigan State line about 1 p.m. There they were met by the Mayor of Sylvania, Mr. Warren Schuster, the Mayor of Toledo, Mr. Harry Kessler with other officials. Here they had appropriate ceremonies.

The Arizona State wagon was in charge of an Arizona Indian, and when Mr. Don Loss and Mr. "Cap" Averill came riding in with Indian costumes, the real Indian borrowed Don's headdress to have his picture taken. As Mr. Loss and Mr. Averill rode in the parade someone heard this "Yes, they are real Indians from North Dakota." Approximately 70,000 people were reported to be in town to see the parade. People started to come about 9 a.m. Some brought lunches, children sat on the curbs, others brought chairs, some sat on the grass. Everyone was quiet and orderly. It was a once in a lifetime event and people were really interested in this replay of history. It was a chance to be a part of America – a part of America's birthday.

When the "train" finally arrived on Main Street it was escorted by the Sylvania Police motorcycle unit, the Sylvania high school marching band, and the "Union Soldiers Horse Troops." The wagon train went through town and arrived at Olander Park on Sylvania Avenue where they circled their wagons, unhitched the horses and fed them; then the Sylvania Rotary Club served all the wagon personnel a dinner. One said that it was the first time for days that they had green salad for dinner. After the dinner, school buses took the people to McCord Junior High School for showers.

Entertainment was provided for visitors during the evening. Sylvania was so well organized that when Walter Cronkite, a national news commentator, interviewed the wagon master of the train that went through Sylvania, he said on television that the members of his train were treated the best in Sylvania." These minutes were signed by Hazel Smith, Secretary of the History Buffs.

In an interview with Mr. Armstrong, conducted in 1978 by a member of the Sylvania History Buffs, and life-long resident of Sylvania, he listed his occupation as "self-employed – real estate – woodworking – school bus driver." When they asked him who were his childhood playmates he listed the following:

George Hawley – committed suicide – at middle age.
George Bonwell – years in jail for grand theft as young adult.
Dennis Crocket – died as young adult in Army prison.
Kenneth Beebe – killed himself (high school age) with his father's revolver.
Vivian Myers Eichsteadt – now living in Sylvania on Summit Street.
Dorothy Counter – millionaire in real estate and contracting.

OCCUPATIONS OF SYLVANIA RESIDENTS ACCORDING TO CENSUS RECORDS

A federal census count is taken and recorded every ten years and starting with the 1850 census the occupations of our residents were listed. Eighty to 90 percent of the residents living in Sylvania were listed as farmers, or farm laborers starting with that 1850 census through the 1900 census. By the 1910 and 1920 census more and more of our residents were working on the railroads, or on the new electric railway which now had their headquarters in Sylvania, as well as the various Silica plants and stone plants in the western part of the township. By the 1910 and 1920 census about half of our heads of households were working as farmers. Below are some of the other occupations listed, with a list of the residents who were working at these selected occupations from 1850 through 1920:

COOPERS/STAVE MAKERS - (made wooden vessels such as barrels used for storing or carrying merchandise – the 1861 map of Sylvania Township shows that there was a stave factory at the corner of Clark Street (Convent Blvd) and Allen street):

1850 census – William Wiggins, Foster A. Ellis, Peter Disbrow, Samuel Hotchkiss, Dorus Dusenburg, Giles White, Henry Day, Nathan Card, Robert Walker, Samuel Hotchkiss, Edward May, Henry Begus, Joseph Begus, Solomon Roaton, Joseph Roaton, William Phelps, John Laskey, Oscar Ingrham, Henry Gasts, Horace Hollister.

1860 census – George Crandall, George Harman, Nathan Beckwith, John Crivey, Henry J. Parker, John Wiggins, William Gidley, Fredrick Jordon, Warren Polley, William C. Hubbard, Henry Hasson, George R. Hasson, M. Adams, Malcolm Beach, L.S. Thompson, William M. Beach, Marshall Beach, Jason McGlenn, James King, Foster Ellis, Edwin Parkhurst, D.W. Frary.

1870 census – Francis Evison, Benjamin H Whitney, Alex Cherry, Joseph B. Warren, Warren C. Polley, William A. Crandall, Foster A. Ellis, DeWitt C. Dolph, Nathan Heath, William Beach, Henry Packard, Henry H. Babesek, Leonard Bragdon, William C. Adams, Alfred J. Clark, Jason McGlenn, Malcolm Beach, Joseph J. Lloyd, Orren J. Hendrickson, Foster A. Ellis (stave manufacturer), David Baker, Charles O. Dolph, Joseph Nathan, Jr., George Richwin, Theodore Wood, Albert H. Wood.

1880 census – George A. Crandall, Joseph King, Alfred Clark, Steven Cupps, Samuel Cupps, Samuel Wiles, Truman Reed, William Adams, Andrew Cherry, William Cherry, Henry Glaser, Martin Cherry, James Banks, O. Crandall, D. Donovan, W.C. Polley, Foster Ellis, Len Bragdon, Nathan B. Heath.'

1890 census – This census is not available. It was destroyed in a fire.

1900 census – There were no "coopers" or "stave makers" listed at this census

1910 census – Andrew Cherry (cooper – mill).

1920 census – None listed

WAGON MAKERS:

1850 census – Thomas Mortimer, Henry Hubbard, Thomas Jackson.

1860 census – James J. Richie, Henry Hubbard, David Probert.

1870 census – James J. Richie, Russell French, Henry Hubbard.

1880 census – David Swinghammer, H. Hubbard, H. Harroun, James Avery, John Bertholf.

1890 census – These census records are not available because they were destroyed by fire.

1900 census – Henry Dewey.

1910 census – None listed in this census.

1920 census – None listed in this census.

BLACKSMITHS:

1850 census – William Blassdell, C.B. Anderson, Avery Candee.

1860 census – Abram Stevunster, James Lowden, Samuel Pershall, Abram Wintemate, D. O'Connor, Isaac VanWinkle, Abram Stevenson, Timothy Presson, Antone Eahle, David Forbes.

1870 census – Albert D. Blanchard, James Carley, Benjamin Bellows.

1880 census – Fred Hartman, Benjamin Bellows, Alonzo Bellows, John Neil, Thomas Giles, Myron Munn (Gunsmith).

1890 census – This census is not available. It was destroyed by fire.

1900 census – Albert Carl, Frank Emch, Joseph Hittler, Daniel Tracy, Willis R. Eley, William Bush, William W. Carl, Fredrick Hartman.

1910 census – Samuel Reed (railway blacksmith), Hugh McInnis, Charles Rockenstyre, Willis Eley, William Carl, W.F. Moore, Carl Langham (railway blacksmith).

1920 census – Carroll Langham (blacksmith – railroad), Albert Bedard (blacksmith – stone quarry), Joseph Scatkowski, Frank W. Moore.

CARPENTERS/CONSTRUCTION/MASON/PLASTERS (all were listed as carpenters unless otherwise noted):

1850 census – Royal Harwood, Samuel H. Nason, Charles Mortimer, Elijah Green, Washington Collum, Samuel Porter, James P. Warren, Joseph VanHellin (ship construction). 1860 census – Oristin Holloway, David Davis (mason), Harvey Keller, Thomas Lewis, John L. Henderson, William Phelps, Izar Brown, Elijah Green, Thomas R. Smith (mason), William Fletcher, William N. Leonardson (mason), Warren H. Shay.

1870 census – John Laimon, William Fletcher, Oristen Holloway, Orlando Thorp, Homer Sawyer, B.W. Trombley (plasterer), Warren Shay, Charles VanOrman, Frank Boschert, James H. Keller, William F. Drake, Henry Spaulding, Thomas E. Smith, (plaster mason), Elijah Greene, Albert D. Baker (brick and stone mason).

1880 census – Chester Decker (stone mason), Henry Kelb, David Blue, A. Hackman, Spencer Wells, George Combs (stone mason), J. Hendrickson, William Fletcher, John Laimon.

1890 census – Census not available   destroyed by fire.

1900 census – John S. Randall, Samuel Felt, John Sawyer, Chester H. Decker (stone mason), Theodore Hoadley, George Combs (stone mason), William J. Webb, Charles N. Perry (plasterer), William Richardson, William Fletcher, Eugene Pool, George Calkins, Andrew Thorp (brick mason), Henry Frank, Myron Delano (plasterer), Joseph Konz, Jacob Decker (stone mason).

1910 census – Nick Willinger, Ralph Willinger, Henry Willinger, George A. Brown (carpenter for railroad), William Hittler, George L. Calkins, Joseph Counterman (plasterer), William Richardson, Joseph Hittler, Louis Coutchure, Guy Webb, Frank Felt, Thomas Gibbs, Jr., Harry E. Poole, George W. Evans (stone mason), John Symington, Thomas VanPelt, Theodore Hoadley, George Kieffer, George Vaniviere

1920 census - (this census actually listed the type of carpenter for each) – Hugh T. Heaton (carpenter – house), Thomas Pollock (general carpenter), George E. Lee, (carpenter – house), Peter D. Eby (carpenter – house), Samuel H. Felt (carpenter – house), Fay C. Gifford (carpenter – house), Charles J. Ball (carpenter – house), William J. Berger (construction contractor), George C. VanPelt (carpenter – house), Adolph Bieterman (carpenter – house), John A. Champion (carpenter – house), John H. Knepper (carpenter – house), Clinton L. Clark (carpenter – house), Burton F. Clark (carpenter – house), Grove O'Neil (carpenter – house), Maynard Cosgrove (electrical engineer), Daniel G. Hoffman (house builder), Nicholas Willinger (carpenter – house), Charles L. Souder (carpenter – house), Fred A. Keating (carpenter – house), Louis H. Coutchure (carpenter – house), Albert T. Day (carpenter – house), Guy H. Webb (carpenter – house), Henry E. Pool (carpenter – house), Ralph C. Young (general contractor), Arthur E. Weaver (carpenter – house), Mathew J. Donovan (carpenter – house), Joseph Hittler (carpenter – house), Leander T. Sheldon (mason), John H. Heath (carpenter – house), Claude L. Hill (carpenter – house), Martin T. Weaver (carpenter – house). William R. Dowling was listed as the only architect living in Sylvania.

BUTCHERS/MEAT CUTTERS/DEALERS IN CATTLE /FISHERMEN / POULTRY DEALERS:

1850 census – None listed.

1860 census – Thomas Loveby (butcher).

1870 census – Isaac Thorp (butcher), Asa Young (butcher).

1880 census – Isaac Thorp (butcher).

1890 census – This census is not available.

1900 census – John Crandall (butcher), Barney Clark (butcher), Charles Rockenstyre (butcher), Russell Southward (butcher), Howard O. Hine (butcher), Ralph A. Barnes (poultry), Fred O. Peak (stock dealer).

1910 census – Hiram Kiff (butcher – slaughterhouse), George Blalock (fisherman on lake), Barney Clark (butcher).

1920 census – Barney Clark (dealer – cattle), Nace Clark (meat cutter), James P. Clark (meat cutter), Frank G. Crandall (stock dealer), Fenton P. Clark (meat sales), Otto Steinfurth (meat market).

MERCHANTS – GROCERS/HARDWARE/RETAIL STORES:

1850 census – D.B. Stout (merchant), Clark D. Warren (merchant), Haskell D. Warren (merchant), William H. Herden (merchant), Samuel D. Hasty (merchant), Levi W. Bradley (merchant), Foster R. Warren (merchant).

1860 census – Levi Bradley (merchant), Foster R. Warren (merchant), Andrew Wiggins (merchant), Washington H. Huling (merchant), Warren D. Moore (druggist), Washington Lenardson (merchant), Isaac Thorp (merchant), Haskell D. Warren (merchant), Lorenzo Pratt (merchant), P. Valentine Moore (merchant), Garrett VanNess (merchant).

1870 census – Charles N. Lewis (merchant/grocer), Washington Lenardson (merchant), O.C. Wilson (hardware), Washington H. Huling (merchant), Haskell D. Warren (merchant), Sylvanus M. Judson (merchant), Edward W. Beckham (hardware), Peter V. Moore (merchant), Foster R.

Warren (merchant), Hiram Hawley (merchant), Alfred W. Warren (merchant), Charles H. Green (druggist), Warren D. Moore (druggist), Elisha Davis (druggist).

1880 census – Owen Clark, Sylvanus M. Judson, Henry Parker, Silas Root (hardware), L.A. Wright (druggist), William Warren, Charles Lewis, Washington Lenardson, Washington H. Huling.

1890 census – Census records are not available, they were destroyed by a fire.

1900 census – Orson Adsit (druggist), Milton E. Crum, Maynard B. Crum, Albert R. Chandler (hardware), Sylvanus M. Judson, William Bidwell, Milton E. Vesey, Dallas Randall, Barney Garry, James D. LaPoint, Robert J. Leonard.

1910 census – Andrew Reger (shoe shop), Vincent Adams (druggist), Bertha Hittler (milliner store), John Garry (groceries), Alberti R. Chandler (hardware store), Jesse Wagonlander (dry goods store), William C. Mahler (bakery), Orson Adsit (drug store), John Wagonlander (dry goods store), Park Wagonlander (dry goods store), Frank Koepfer (hardware store), William Atkinson (tin shop), Walter Pollock (groceries), John E. Davenport (groceries), James Jefferies (confectionary shop), Gus Jefferies (confectionary shop), James LaPoint (general store), Bert H. Elden (groceries).

1920 census – George H. Keller (groceries), Albert R. Miles (groceries), Albert H. Randall (groceries), Edwin B. Parker (drug store), John Wagonlander (dry goods store), Morris Wagonlander (dry goods store), Frank Koepfer (hardware), Robert A. Shanks (groceries), Charles E. Shanks (groceries), William Atkinson (tin shop), Jess Wagonlander (dry goods store), George J. Poulos (merchant confectionary), Vincent H. Adams (druggist), George C. Mickens (meat store), Howard Hine (meat store), Alberti R. Chandler (hardware store), Clarence A. Bringman (grocery store) Park Wagonlander (dry goods store), Louis H. Richards (groceries), George W. Sly (wholesale dry goods), Orlo Thorpe (groceries), William J. Robbins (ice cream shop), Charles Hansman (tinner shop), David Jennewine (groceries), Minnie Clegg (general store), Frank J. Reger (merchant).

SHOEMAKERS:

1850 census – Adam Gordinier, Elias Leonardson, John Fay, Stephen Porter.

1860 census – Nelson Leonardson, Joseph Kauffman, G.W.L. Probert, Thomas Probert, Joseph Theobold, Arthur Probast.

1870 census – J. Braunschweiger, Christian Braunschweiger, Joseph P. Theobold, Paul Deaublist, Samuel Fox, James J. Theobold, Thomas Probert, George W. Probert.

1880 census – None listed.

1890 census – These census records are not available, they were destroyed by a fire.

1900 census – Andrew Reger, Colon Ostrander.

1910 census – There were no shoemakers listed in this census.

1920 census – Calvin Ostrander (shoe repair).

INNKEEPERS/BAR KEEPERS/HOTEL KEEPERS/RESTAURANTS:

1850 census – Erastus Morse (hotel keeper), M.M. Williams (bar keeper).

1860 census – Lunis Lewis (hotel keeper), A.J. Covell (hotel keeper).

1870 census – Harry Bidwell (hotel operator).

1880 census – Miles Lathrop (hotel keeper).

1890 census – These census records are not available, they were destroyed by fire.

1900 census – Victor Burg (hotel landlord), Dennis Donovan (hotel clerk), John Reiter (saloon keeper), John C. Werder (bartender).

1910 census – Walter Willinger (bartender), Carley Kates (saloon keeper), Jim Kates (bartender), Dallas Kates (bartender), George Keene (hotel keeper), James Strong (bartender), Charles Claussen (restaurant owner), Ralph Stowell (saloon keeper), Louis Burg (saloon keeper), Carl Werder (saloon keeper), William Gise (pool room operator), Chester H. McPherson (boarding house keeper).

1920 census – Nicholas J. Poulos (restaurant), John K. Cooper (restaurant), Jennie Hawley (restaurant).

SAW MILL OPERATORS OR OWNERS/MILLERS/GRIST MILL OPERATORS/ SAWYERS:

1850 census – None listed.

1860 census – John Bertholf (saw mill), Jonathan Sanderson (saw mill).

1870 census – Isaac Shook (saw mill), Leonard Kanavel (employee at saw mill), Henry A. Lucas (miller), William Hubbard, (saw mill at home), Joseph Nathan, Sr. (grist mill), Calvin J. Holman (grist mill owner).

1880 census – Len Kanavel (sawyer), C. Coffin (sawyer), W. Chamberlin (miller), Isaiah Matlock (miller).

1890 census– These census records were destroyed by a fire.

1900 census – George Keene (miller), Uriah A. Pettit (miller).

1910 census – Edward G. Howard (feed mill), S.L. Manz (laborer – heading mill), George E. Brown (laborer – heading mill), Arthur Cherry (teamster – heading mill), Charley Royce (laborer – heading mill), Fred Comstock (foreman – mill).

1920 census – Edwin G. Howard (grain dealer), Edwin C. Howard (miller – grain mill), William B. Haracourt (miller – feed mill).

MISCELLANEOUS OCCUPATIONS OTHER THAN FARMERS:

1850 census – Surveyors – William Butts, Michael Hill; Lawyer – Don A. Pease; Saddler – Samuel G. Warren; Tailors – William Cory, Jane Cory; Gatekeeper – Peter Thorp; Stage Driver – Shelmer Dennis; Clergyman – John Crebbs; Auditor of Lucas County – William F. Dewey; Boatman – Thomas Wiggins, Nelson Lenardson; Laborers – Jesse Davis, George Hubbell, Chester Roberts, George Leflie, Antoni Tulip, John Myers, Arthur Hill, John Showler, John Osborn, George Mortimer, Rufus Squire, Elisha Kimball, Isaac Thorp, William Nottage, Richard Kimball, John Peters, Hiram Hollister, Chester Nottage, Abram VanAlstine, Edward Mulooney, William Mulooney, Sylvester Riggs, Gilbert Blaine, Patrick Fanigan Thomas Bennig, Nelson Adams, James T. Johnson, John Endicott, Hiram VanAtta, Zerah Daniels, Daniel B. Curtis, Charles Walker, Harley Johnson; Plank Road – Lucian B. Lathrop; Dangerean Artist – Dilatus Learey; Clerks – Augustus Milliard, Warren Moore, Theodore Jewell, Zurill Cook; Machinist – Jedediah Jessup. (All railroad employees are listed in volume two of this book under "Railroads.")

1860 census - Surveyors – William M. White; Postmaster – Andrew Printup; Store Clerks – Luther H. Cook, Joseph Warren; Furnace man – Ira Blanchard; Teamster – George W. Hamilton; Lucas County Clerk – Peleg T. Clark; Tailor – Joena Harwood, David Gistwite; Painter – John Pascal,

Jeremiah E. Day, Alex Cherry; .Sailor – John Spike; Artist – Emerson H. Eaton; Speculator – A.L. DeWolf; Milliner – Catherine H. Green; Engineer – Burnet Lewis; Gentleman – William F. Dewey, Shadrach W. Allen; Stove manufacturer – James Mann; Mechanic – Ithamar P. Smith. (All railroad employees are listed in volume two of this book under "Railroads.").

1870 census - Cheesemaker – W.D. Mercereau; Mechanic – Caleb Blanchard; Hostler – Samuel Mellon; Jewelry- Henry Lyon; Tinner – Silas Root; Driving Team – George A. Crandall; Huskster – King Cline; Basketmaker – August VanDorp; Harness maker – Smith G. Warren, Wallace W. Covell; Agent for Patent Rights – Henry Parker; Clerk in store – A. Dallas Randall; Door Keeper Washington D.C. – Samuel H. Decker; Justice of the Peace – William Bryan; Barber – William H. Garrison; Tailor – Reuben Sawyer; Jeweler – Henry Lyon; Tinner – Silas Root; Postmaster – William F. Dewey; Tailoress – Amanda Bridham, Jane Turner; Commercial laborer – Tim Breseham, Anderson Harper; Dress maker – Hannah White. (All railroad employees are listed in volume two of this book under "Railroads.").

1880 census - Patternmaker – Lewis Garris; Basketmaker – John Beringer; Gunsmith – Myron Munn; Machinist – William Garris, F. Chamberlin; Peddler – Benjamin Rhodes; Canvasser – William Smith; Gas fitter – George Briggs; Traveling salesman – D. Randall, Foster Warren; Deputy Sheriff – Nathaniel S. Cooper; Dentist – George Hill; Painter – George Rex, Hiram Wellman, Jesse Fletcher; Gardener – George Hattersley; Traveling salesman – Marvin Draper; Watch cleaner – Henry Baker; Undertaker – William Avery; Tailor – R. Sawyer, Jacob Linbiz; Tinner – Thomas Shea; Postmaster – William Bryan; Hotel landlord – Henry Bidwell; Minister – Joseph Cater, Martin Adsit, J.C. Thompson; Harness maker – Wallace Covell. (All railroad employees are listed in volume two of this book under "Railroads.").

1890 census – This census is not available it was destroyed by fire

1900 census - Harness maker – Wallace W. Covell; Milkman – Thomas Everett; Preacher – Amos Thorp; Paper hanger – Enoch Eley, Albert Wood; Millwright – David Blue; Soldier U.S.A. – Vernie Seager; Machinist – James Donovan; Salesman – Lewis M. Woodruff; Barber – John E. Hewitt, Sherman M. Tibbetts; Lumber man – Romes Burns; Livery man – Lansing F. Potter; Editor – John Sampsey; Undertaker – Abda Dolph; Dressmaker – Anna Probert; Milliner – Elida Probert; Capitalist – Henry Burnham, Nathaniel S. Cooper, Orville Hine, Thomas Gibbs, Foster Warren, George Lovewell; House painter – Samuel Mellon, William E. Bryan, S. Bennett, George H,. Tibbetts William Cochran, Preston Randall; Tinner – William Atkinson; Carpet weaver – Julia Heath; Preacher Earl Keller, Joseph Torrence, Nelson Bellman; Picture dealer – Thomas Allen; Real estate sales – Haskell Warren; Optician – Frank Lamont; Postmaster – William Chapple; Florist – Ernest Cushman; Artist – Ella Torrence; Attorney – John C. Jones; Salesmen – Claude E. Webb, Alfred Warren, Joseph E. Torrence; Day laborers: Arthur Lavoy, Homer Lavoy, Daniel Wolf, August Goldwisch, Irving H. Stow, John H. Forbes, William Conn, Frederick Breckenridge, Arthur Wood, Lester Cartwright, Harry W. Cartwright, John W. Cooper, Frank Southward, George W. Kiser, Charles Gillhouse, Ernest Sawyer, Thomas Kennedy, Monte C. Roberts, Oscar Bernholtz, Byron Cunningham, Harry Reed, Valentine G. Cooper, Cletus Lewis, Frank Doremus, Peter Kay, Alexander Kay, Peter Langenderfer, Nicholas Cooke, Charles A. Fox, Foster W. Comstock, Ara C. Comstock, Charles Comstock, Robert Bertch, Frank Burnham,

Oscar A. Crandall, Clarence A. Crandall, Sidney E. Crandall, Charles Probert, George Clark, Theodore H. Hallett, Amos Barber, George Barber, Robert Yates, Clarke Whitney, Conrad Wepler, Fredrick Gee, Richard Gee, Wilbur Lewis, Charles McGlenn, William Driscoll, Charles Freeman, Miles E. Roberts, Mark W. DeBruine, Albert H. Randall, Fredrick S. Webb, Arthur Vesey, John B. Webb, William Beebe, Leo Gloyd, Hiram Kiff, Claude Carl, James Young, Clarke Dings, Hiram Wellman, James McDowell, George Derusha, Burr Randall, Charles Burns, Carl Werder, Daniel Donovan, Mathew Donovan, Patrick Hogan, Owen Clark, James P. Clark, Fredrick Doherty, Christopher Doherty, Owen Doherty, John C. Garry, Guy Bell, William Kimber, Eddie Kimber, William Crandall, James Ostrander, George A. Crandall, Hugh Clarke, Herman Stytle, Levi Davis, Arthur Comstock, George Brown, John VanHouten, Charles Eley, Munson Hawley, Frank Burnham, Fredrick Hartman, Chester Roberts. (All railroad employees are listed in volume two of this book under "Railroads.")

1910 census – Harness maker – Patrick Dolan; Barbers – Frank Green, Earl Orewiler, Orville Hine; Bank Employees – Leo Reger, William Irwin, Herman Rothfuss; Cement factory owner: Dana G. Chandler; Livery men – James French, John A. Crandall, Ray West; Dentist – John A. Counter. (Railroad and Electric railway employees are all listed separately in volume two under "Railroads" and Doctors are listed separately in volume two under the medical section).

1920 census – Junk collector – William Fowler; Greens keeper – golf course – Caleb G. Barton; Scout reservation caretaker – H. William Wagonhauser; Trucking – Douglas Wood, Clayton L. Young; Veterinary – George Lovewell; Baker – Earl Blanchard, Jack H. Blanchard, Enoch Eley; Coal yard – Myron D. Drwier, George T. Cook, Burt H. Elden; Barber – Earl C. Orewiler, Glenn Green, Frank J. Green; Shoe maker – Gustave Thamletz, Otto Thamletz; Horse dealer – Ray J. West. (Railroad and Electric railway employees are listed separately in book volume two in the section under "Railroads," and Doctors are listed separately in book volume two under the medical section).

OIL AND GAS WELLS IN SYLVANIA

The *Sylvania Sentinel* dated 7-29-1920 said: "Oil Well No. 1 now down over 1,500 feet and several feet into Trenton rock. Tuesday morning the drill rope broke near the top of the well leaving the drill and about 1,200 feet of rope in the hole. Work is delayed until this can be fished out."

Kathryn Keller, Sylvania Historian, said the following in her 3-22-1978 Sylvania Sentinel - Sylvania Chronicle series of articles about the history of Sylvania: "Oh, we had our hopes and our oil excitement too! There was a company formed to do some exploratory drilling at one if not two sites. They found no oil. One site was the Parker farm, now Highland Meadows Golf Course. Another was "near the bridge on Sylvania Avenue." But we don't know which Sylvania Avenue creek bridge – the one near Mitchaw or the one at the Boy Scout Reservation."

In an interview of long-time resident of Sylvania, Worthy Chandler, he said: "Oil wells were a big fad about 1924 to 1926. Stock was sold in the projects. Ed Parker shot one on Sylvania Avenue near the creek. On Central Avenue there was a well, gas burned off of it. Gordon Hathaway was interested in the projects."

The April-May-June 2005 Sylvania Area Historical Society Newsletter and reads as follows: "SYLVANIA'S OTTAWA RIVER OIL AND GAS COMPANY – About 1927 or 28 a fellow came to Sylvania and sold people in Sylvania on the idea of drilling for oil. Stock in this company was sold and many Sylvanians purchased shares. One of the wells was on the site of France Stone Company. Another was drilled across from Burnham High School in the creek bottom, both of these turned out to be dry. No oil was ever found, the contract between the oil company and Sylvania ran for twenty years. Those who put up the money for the venture lost it all."

The minutes of Sylvania Village Council dated 10-7-1932 said: "Mr. Pember, an individual was present and stated he was going to drill for gas near Sylvania, that he was now leasing land for that purpose and hoped to be able to supply our village. He presented his plans to council and asked that they lend their support and give their cooperation. More definite plans were to be presented at the next meeting." The minutes of council dated 10-21-1932 said: "A communication was received and read from Nelson H. Pember giving the names of nearby Ohio towns having municipally owned gas plants."

12-2-1932 – The minutes of Sylvania Village Council reported: "Mayor reports having been advised that Mr. Pember had preparations made so that drilling will be started on the gas well shortly after the first of the year."

8-18-1933 – The minutes of council said: "Mayor reported on Highland Meadows well pumping crude oil and that well had been abandoned for the present. Dr. DeVore, County Health Commissioner took samples for examination."

9-15-1933 – Council minutes said: "A letter from the State Department of Health was read showing trouble in Highland Meadow's well. Samples examined show 1.4 parts per million. The Letter also suggested an effort to case off the oil vein should be made or abandon the well as the amount of oil would not injure users but would prove unsatisfactory for home use."

10-6-1933 – Council minutes said: "The oil in Highland Meadows well was next discussed with Mr. LaDow present representing the Golf Club and Mr. Trowbridge present for the Board of Trustees of Public Affairs. Mayor Quinnell appointed Councilman Russell to represent the Village to make a thorough check of the well together with representatives of the Water Board and Golf Club."

11-3-1933 – Village councilman Russell reported taking samples from the oil at Highland Meadows well to a chemist at the Gulf Oil in Toledo for examination. He stated that the sample was not a sufficient quantity to make a test. It was decided to have Arthur Bernholtz pump the well and see if the oil would return so that a sample could be taken for a test.

12-1-1933 – The Mayor reported that an investigation had been made on the Highland Meadows Golf Club well by officials of the Club and that the oil was being forced from the old oil well.

Councilman Russell reported that the sample of water drawn from the village lines up at Metzinger's had been analyzed by the chemist at the laboratory in Wayne, Michigan and showed 1,300 bacteria per 100 C.C. The Mayor said that the County Health Department had since then taken samples for examination.

The 9-3-1936 issue of the *Sylvania Sentinel* said this about drilling for oil: "WILL DRILL FOR OIL AND GAS AT SILICA – Michigan Operators Will Start Drilling Operations On France Stone Co. Property Next Week – That the rock formation in the vicinity of Sylvania indicates the presence of oil and gas in paying quantities, was reiterated today by Elmer A. Roth, A Michigan oil and gas operator. In fact Mr. Roth was so impressed with his inspection of the rock strata that several tracts of land were leased and arrangements for drilling were made. The first of a series of four wells, which will be drilled into the Trenton formation, will be located on the property of the France Stone Company on Silica Road. Mr. Roth has released drilling contracts to Mr. C.O. Moore, of Mt. Vernon, Ohio, who is now rigging up, and actual drilling should commence by the first of the week. The drilling has been financed by Mr. Roth and Detroit associates, and there is no stock being offered to the general public. According to geological and geophysical information, the location selected is very favorable, and much is expected from this first well. Should gas be found in these test wells, the nearby towns, including Sylvania, may be fortunate enough to have natural gas in the near future. Mr. Roth announces that this well will not be treated as a mystery well, but that weekly reports of drilling progress will be given and published in the *Sentinel*."

Another item regarding an oil well was in the 5-13-1937 issue of the *Sylvania Sentinel*: "The oil well at Silica, which has been the in process of drilling for the past several months, was shot at 7:30 on Wednesday evening. According to Elmer Roth, who has been in charge of operations, results will not be definitely known for several days since the well must now be cleaned out. After the time bomb was placed in the well, 150 feet of sand was packed onto it to hold the explosion, and a minor detonation was heard at 7:30 when this time bomb exploded. However, about 8:15 the well "let loose" and shot oil and gas 100 feet over the derrick three different times. Two hundred feet of oil showed in the hole on Thursday morning and Wednesday night Mr. Roth estimated between five hundred thousand to one million cubic feet of gas pressure."

The third item regarding drilling for oil in Sylvania was a notation made by Sylvania Historian Kathryn M. Keller in an article she wrote that appeared in the *Sylvania Herald* on 9-6-1978. In this article she was writing about the Highland Meadows golf course, which was originally the farmland and home of Hiram Parker. She said: "Somewhere, supposedly in the creek flats, on the Parker farm, a company once set about drilling for oil but with no success."

REMEMBER?

Who remembers the curve on North Main Street being called Sylvania's "death curve?" In 1947 they were calling it that because of the frequent accidents that occurred here with cars coming into Sylvania from Michigan, and heading south. There were numerous accidents here, and several of the vehicles ended up, at different occasions, through the front porch of the old Wellman home, later owned for many years by the First Church of Christ Scientists, and then starting in 1999, Keith's Hair Design, at 5768 Main Street. (See the *Sylvania Sentinel* newspapers dated 10-17-1934; 5-13-1937; and 8-7-1947 for reports of vehicles going off the road and hitting the front of this structure).

Who remembers when the Christian Science Church was located at 5768 N. Main Street (1942 to 1999)? Who remembers that starting in 1951 they hung a sign in their front yard in the shape, or replica, of their church structure here? (A building permit was issued by the Village of Sylvania on 2-25-1951 for this sign).

Who remembers MacDonald grocery store and antique shop in the 5500 block of Whiteford Road where "Minnie the cigar store" pewter Indian stood on the porch? According to the owners (Mr. and Mrs. William MacDonald) Minnie had been sitting on the porch of this store for ten years, as of April of 1956. According to the 4-12-1956 *Sentinel-Herald* "Mr. and Mrs. William MacDonald who own Minnie had long wanted a cigar store Indian. Although they had collected and bought and sold antiques for years they never could find one that was for sale. Cigar store Indians have become a rare commodity. Yet oddly enough, from the 1840s to the beginning of this century wooden Indians were everywhere."

Who remembers in the 1950s when George and Anna Nolasses operated a vegetable stand at the corner of Flanders and Monroe Street?

Who remembers Fun City U.S.A. toys? They used the address of 5890 Monroe Street, but actually faced Alexis Road (1970s). Later the Pharm and now in 2018 Rite Aid.

Who remembers Marguerite Asman working at the "Coast to Coast" peanut stand at Central Avenue and Holland-Sylvania Road after school and on weekend in 1938?

Who remembers George Ballas Buick on South Main Street, at the bottom of the hill in the old Carroll Motors/Fenstemacher building? Records show that his first customer here was David Pearlman, who purchased a 1970 Buick LeSabre. (While the 1971 models were scheduled to be out, a strike against General Motors delayed production that year).

Who remembers Stroh's Ice Cream Parlor in Southbriar complex (1970s) where Dr. Read Backus later had his dentist office and now Trusted Dental?

Who remembers "Honest Joe" at 7131 Sylvania Avenue selling beans, beets, cabbage, tomatoes, squash, onions, dill and cucumbers, today where Boulevard Church of God is located? He advertised in the *Sylvania Sentinel* in 1969, but continued selling his vegetables through the 1980s.

Who remembers W.H. Carpenter of 6626 Blossman Road selling produce from his home from 1960 through 1977?

Who remembers Van's Place, a combination butcher shop and tavern on Central Avenue at Centennial Road, operated by Floyd VanSickle in the late 1930 and early 1940s. He and his wife Ceilia then later owned and operated Van's Colonial House steak restaurant?

Who remembers Charles Reiter who owned 2 ½ acres of land on Holland-Sylvania near Central Avenue in 1936 where LA Fitness is located today?

Who remembers the Hing Mee Chinese-American Restaurant at 6256 W. Central Avenue, just east of I-475 and US 23 overpass?

Who remembers the skating pond with heated rest cabin in the woods on the south side of Monroe Street (5635 Monroe) where the neighborhood children skated and played ice hockey? This was the woods owned by the Phillipps and Foths and was just east of where the Versailles in the Woods apartments were built in 1975.

Who remembers Poor John's Pizza – first, in the rear of 5629 Main (at the rear of today's (2018 Executive Diner), and then moving to the Southbriar Shopping Complex? Good pizza – Remember?!!!

Who remembers kid's Saturday afternoon movies in the auditorium at Burnham Auditorium? (Early 1970s).

Who remembers Someplace Else Restaurant – one of the first places in Sylvania to offer a Sunday brunch buffet?

Who remembers Leo Wittscheck being the Deputy Chief of the Sylvania Township Volunteer Fire Department No. 2 on Central Avenue? He had joined the force in 1950 and achieved the rank of Deputy Chief in 1963, after serving as Captain and Assistant Chief. He retired in 1971.

Who remembers 1960 when Rita McCormick worked at Jerry's Clothing store? John K. Dawley worked at Schmidt's and Dawley Sohio service station? Mary Ann Warren worked at Lindau Drugs? Don LaPoint worked at Chandler Ace Hardware? George A. Wilson worked at Carroll Motor Sales? Mary Sharp worked at Kroger's located at 5735 Main Street where the Element 112 Restaurant is located today in 2018? Sophia Romaker worked at Chandler's Hardware? Margie Brenner worked at Lindau's? and Violet Gaige worked at Holliday's?

Who remembers the large green flag at the front entrance of Olander Park to indicate that it was safe to ice skate on the lake?

Who remembers Tex Fondren delivering driveway stone, top soil and fill sand from his property at 4713 King Road? (1960s, 1970s).

Remember ice skating in Memorial Field, developed by the city's Recreation Department? (1971).

Remember Felix Trettin being the longtime owner of a Sylvania Township greenhouse and truck farm on the southwest corner of Sylvania Avenue and Corey Road? The business was called Trettin Greenhouse and he had two greenhouses, his home, several outbuildings and a soil preparation area on the property. Before the I-475 expressway went in he also used that land behind his greenhouses for planting. He was a truck farmer also and grew watercress, tomatoes, beans, cabbage and cauliflower on the property before the expressway. According to his obituary notice he and his sister-in-law, Dora Trettin, seeded pansies and other plants. He had one leg and wore a prosthesis, but into his 80s he still cut an acre of lawn with a push mower. Mr. Trettin was born on this property on 1-18-1906 and attended a one-room schoolhouse and the former Sylvania High School. He died at the age of 93 years in 1999.

Remember getting your dog license at Howard's Hardware on W. Central Avenue? And getting your vehicle license plates there too? Remember the long lines? (1970s).

Remember loose garbage lining the streets of Sylvania before Sylvania Council directed the city police to begin rigid enforcement of the anti-litter ordinance. (1971).

Who remembers Kroger on North Main Street (1950 to 1966) – 5735 Main, where Sterlings, Marino's, Bumble and now where Element 112 Restaurant is located?

Remember when Emery Graham fixed lawnmowers in his garage on Holland-Sylvania Road, just south of the Sylvania Township building? (1970s thru 1995).

Remember when the Sylvania Missionary Baptist Church members began to construct a church on the west side of Holland-Sylvania, just north of where Harroun Road intersects? 18 members became an independent church on 9-20-1951 and started meeting at the V.F.W. Hall near the site of their new church. . Brother Merritt Hamilton was obtained as their pastor. According to the 9-4-1952 *Sentinel-Herald* in April of 1952 members began to construct a church on a lot on Holland-Sylvania Road, just south of the Sylvania Township Equipment building. The first services were held in this new church on 9-7-1952.

Remember when the Elmer Hartman family lived in an old two-story home on Holland-Sylvania Road where the Swiss-Aire Apartments are today? (1906 to 1960s).

Remember when the expressway was being extended to Central Avenue and Mr. and Mrs. Lester Schofield moved their house from 4737 Holland-Sylvania, south about 1,500 feet rather than have it demolished? (1960)

Remember when Chief Happy Dear of Sylvania opened the programs at Camp Miakonda with the fire lighting ceremony of the American Indian? (1940s).

Did you know that in 1923 Sylvania had a Dewey Light Company? R.E. Dewey, President; Miles H. Cartwright, Vice President; Franklin H. Carpenter, Secretary Treasurer; Gladys Dewey, Assistant Secretary and Treasurer.

Did you know that in 1928 The Logcabin Inn Barbecue – with "real Spanish barbecue sandwiches" was located on Monroe Street at Whiteford Road in a real log cabin? E.N. Heckman was the proprietor. The 1928 advertisement reads: "Everybody Eats Them, Everybody Says, "MY, HOW GOOD!" – Cigars, Cigarettes, Candies, Soft Drinks, Purity Ice Cream – STOP TO EAT— YOU'LL FIND IT A TREAT" By 1931 it was called Ernie's Place.

Did you know that in 1928 there was a Sylvania Auto Laundry located in the Dolph-Reeb building (SW corner of Main and Maplewood)? They washed and polished cars. George L. Rader was the manager.

Did you know that in 1929 the Fuhrer Gardens Sandwich Shoppe was located at Monroe and Summit Street? "Real Barbecues and all varieties of Sandwiches. . . Hot or Cold Meals and Lunches at all hours – Hear and Enjoy the Electramuse – Open Day and Night – Monroe at Summit – Sylvania, Ohio."

Did you know that in 1931 Richmond's Inn was at the corner of Alexis and Whiteford – including "Short Way" Bus Stop and Ticket Office? Lunches, Candies, Cigars, Cigarettes, Ice Cream and Soft Drinks.

Did you know that in 1931 there was the Monroe Street Barber Shop, operated by Don H. White in a building that once sat on the SW corner of Main and Monroe? His advertisement said: "Special attention given to ladies' and children."

Who remembers Bob Wilcox Motor Sales located at 6423 Monroe Street? In December of 1948 they were giving "Free Rides" in the new Kaiser-Frazer automobiles?

Who remembers Bob Mey's articles in the *Sylvania Sentinel* titled: "Bottom Drawer"? He often wrote about incidents involving his wife who he fondly referred to as the "Old Girl" or "O.G." Great stories! (1970s).

Who remembers The Stork's Nest, way out on Bancroft where later it was the Cow Palace, and now Ventura's Mexican Restaurant today in 2018? Fred Stork started the business, and then later Harold J. Miller was the proprietor. Miller then made it by hosting weddings, banquets and receptions, according to an advertisement in the 1950 Burnham Wyandotte Yearbook.

Who remembers the Chile Pot Restaurant? Central and Holland-Sylvania – Sandwiches, Fountain Service, Steaks and Chops – Open 24 hours – Merl & Charlotte.- From the 1950 Burnham High school Wyandotte Yearbook.

Who remembers The Posy Shop operated by Mrs. J.L. Cook, 5425 Monroe Street, near Whiteford Road? – 1940s. The shop was also operated for a period of time by Richard and Gladys Scheureman. She was killed in an auto accident in September of 1952.

Who remembers the Happy Hollow Riding Academy at the corner of Central and Millicent Avenues? A 1941 advertisement said: "Horses 75 cents per hour – half hour – 50 cents – Pony Rides – 6 for 25 cents. Day Camp Cross-country Rides on Ponies or Horses - $1.25 – 9:00 to 11:30 a.m. – Free Picnic Grounds – Children's Parties a Specialty."

Who remembers John C. Iffland sold "Strong-Reliable-Old Line" insurance out of his home at 6526 Erie Street, with an office in the basement? (1940s, 1950s, 1960s, 1970s). They called him "Iffy."

Who remembers Robert F. Adams Grocery – northwest corner of Central and Holland-Sylvania? (1940s, 1950s, 1960s)? His father, Charles Adams, operated a store here starting in 1925, and then in 1939 he purchased this property and built a "super gas station" here, and converted an existing building into a grocery store. Charles retired in 1946 and turned the business over to his son Robert. In 1960 Bob Adams started selling the Red and White brand groceries after purchasing the contents of the store that had been operated by Cliff Hesselbart, in downtown Sylvania, who had just retired. In 1966 S.S. Kresge Company purchased the property and constructed their first Ohio K-Mart store here. This store operated here until 2008. In 1966 they called their new 110,000 square foot department store and grocery store the new "one-stop shopping center."

Who remembers in the 1930s then the Sylvania Township Trustees had a voting booth constructed near the northwest corner of Central and Holland-Sylvania, and they used to hold their public meetings in this voting booth?

Who remembers Rock's Ice Cream – South side of Monroe St. east of Whiteford Road? This was owned by Frank Rock. They sold wholesale and retail ice cream here on Monroe Street through the 1940s and part of the 1950s. He retired in 1953 according to his obituary notice.

Who remembers Neff's Place – Groceries – Meats – Ice Cream and Mobil Gas and Oil – Central Ave., and King Road – Across the street from Central Elementary School?

Who remembers the good food at Michael Angelo's Restaurant at 6008 W. Central Avenue (corner of Central and Warner)?

Do you remember Tom Swinghammer operating the Scottdale Market starting in December of 1938 on the north side of Monroe Street, just east of Laskey Road in Sylvania Township, and then in November of 1946 Guy Luse left Hesselbart's to operate in partnership with Tom Swinghammer? Tom Swinghammer and Guy Luse then later went on to operate the Bellevue Market in Toledo at Monroe Street and Bellevue Road. According to Thomas E. Swinghammer's obituary notice in the *Toledo Blade* on 5-28-1972, in 1948 he joined with five other grocers to share advertising costs under the Food Town banner. When he retired he was vice president of Seaway Food Town, Inc., and was one of the firm's founders.

Do you remember in December of 1959 they were selling Christmas trees at 6121 W. Central Avenue, across from the Melody Inn?

Who remembers C & L Automotive located in the Laux building on the south side of Monroe Street, just east of Main Street? Chuck Tipping is the owner. From 1980 until 1984 he moved to the Howard's building on the southeast corner of Main and Monroe; from 1984 to 1995 he operated on Alger Drive and now since 1995 to current (2018) located at 5519 Alexis Road. (He and his employees are the only ones allowed to touch the Gindy cars).

WHO REMEMBERS THESE ADVERTISEMENTS?:

1948 – Schmidt Sohio Service – Complete Lubrication Service – Central Ave & Holland-Sylvania.

1949 – Laughlin Bros. Central and Centennial – Texaco Gas & Oil.

1949 – J. Billings and Sons Sohio – Super Service – We Never Close – Central Ave. at Centennial Road.

1949 – Cooper Appliance – Philco and Norge – Monroe and Whiteford.

1949 – The Kozy Korner – Sandwiches – Light Lunches – Ice Cream – Holland-Sylvania Road corner of Sylvania Avenue.

1949 – Fender's Friendly Market – Full line of Groceries & Meats – Free Deliver – 5450 Monroe Street.

1949 – Crawford Appliance – 5365 Monroe Street – Television Service & Sales – Stromberg – Carlson.

1949 – Chili Pot – Central Ave at Holland-Sylvania – Sandwiches, Fountain Service – Steaks, Chops & Special Sunday Dinner – Open 24 hrs. Noble & Sis. Proprietor.

1949 – Nick's Sunoco Service – 6515 Monroe – A to Z Lubrication – Washing – Flats Fixed – Tire & Battery Service.

1949 – Reed's Grocery – Meats – Groceries – Holland-Sylvania Road.

1949 – Elden-Bischoff General Store – "Always a Friendly Welcome" – 5270 Alexis – Sylvania, Ohio

1949 – Rock's Ice Cream – 5441 Monroe Street – Sundaes – Sodas – Cones – Carry out Pints and Quarts.

1949 – Nichols Red & White Store – Groceries – Meats – Silica, Ohio.

1949 – Bob's Market – South side of Sylvania Avenue, just east of McCord Road.

1950 - Bob's Country Market – Home Cured Hams and Bacon – Country Meats – Work Clothes – School supplies – Central Avenue at Centennial Road.

1950 – The Pin Cushion – Men's, Women's and Children's Accessories – Notions and Dry Goods – 5442 Monroe Street.

1950 – Schmidt Sohio Service – Complete Lubrication Service – Central Avenue & Holland-Sylvania.

1950 – Daisy Belle Beauty Shop – 5709 Webster Road – Sylvania, Ohio.

1992 – Video Adventures operated by John Crowner – 6423 Monroe Street - Renting and selling video movies and games. (We miss you John!). Aaron Wizgen opened up Video Entertainment in 1981 and in 1988 John Crowner took over the business and changed the name to Video Adventures. By 2001 the Challenge Bike Shop occupied the west side of the building, while since 1989 Apex Printing Center operated in the east portion of the building.

RINGING OF THE CHURCH BELLS IN SYLVANIA

According to an article in the *Sylvania Sentinel* on 1-14-1937, a number of people had complained to the mayor of the village of Sylvania about the ringing of the bell of St. Joseph's Church, and asked why the bell was rung three times each day. And the answer to this question was answered in this way: "Three times a day the bell sounds from the belfry of the Catholic Church, and the faithful are reminded of the mystery of the Incarnation and of the Redemption of mankind. The prayer said during the ringing of the bell given to this action its name. The opening words in Latin are "Angelus Domini." In English we have "the angel of the Lord." This devotion dates from the fourteenth century. It is one that should be emphasized today. The Bishops at that time urged their people to say this prayer that peace might reign among the nations. For that reason it was long known as the peace bell. When the whole world appears to be walking in the shadow of war, we need a renewed dedication to peace. The world needs to think of peace if we are to have peace. Catholics can assist this noble cause by faithfulness to the recitation of the Angelus. Let them pause during the ringing of the peace bell and pray to the Prince of Peace that He may give peace to His principality on earth."

According to long-time residents of Sylvania, the whole town, in the early years, lived by the bells. The large old brick school on Main Street (today in 2018 where the historical village is located) had a bell that during the week rang to regulate the starting and ending of school. Then the bell of St. Joseph's Church rang three times each day, including one at 6 p.m., which told the kids of Sylvania to head home for dinner. And on Sunday mornings the three church bells of the Congregational (Summit Street), the Methodist (North Main Street) and the Catholic (South Main Street), called their members to worship, each bell with its own distinctive ring.

ST. JOSEPH ANTIQUE ANNEX

This was a business that was operated by volunteers of the St. Joseph Church, in an old two-story house on the east side of Main Street (5402 Main Street), which the church had purchased on 5-8-1967 from Fred L. & Rita M. Peterson. The shop was a money making project of the ladies of the parish. They began sponsoring an antique show annually beginning in 1968. Father George Schmit, who had become pastor in June of 1967, helped make it a reality.

This shop operated until 1977, and after 10 years had a great story to tell. Sue Christmyer of the *Sylvania Sentinel* wrote the following article about the annex:

"'Running an antique shop surely beats bingo,' Rev. George Schmitt said as he supervised the closing of St. Joseph's Antique Annex, located on South Main Street. After 10 years, the store has closed as Father Schmitt plans to retire next June. Profits realized from the sale of antiques have been used for upkeep of the parish and the parishioners didn't have to conduct games to raise funds.

It all started 12 years ago when three women were discussing how to raise funds for the church. When questioned as to how she would raise money, Cleo Smilo replied, "Well, I certainly wouldn't sell bingo tickets, I'd sell antiques." For two years the women sold antiques at the festival, which was held yearly by the church. When Father Schmitt, was appointed pastor of St. Joseph's Church, he originated the idea of using a parish-owned house across Main Street for selling the antiques.

Cleo Smilo, Dorothy Newton, Betty Coughtries, Harriett Miller, Irene Lajiness, Fran Geary and Monica Ott all had a hand in voluntarily maintaining the store and keeping it stocked with antiques. The women received no compensation other than knowing that the work they were doing was for the church and their pleasure in handling the antiques.

The entire stock was either purchased at other sales or was on consignment. "We really didn't think it would be here this long" one woman commented. Another volunteer was Howard Schlagheck. He assisted where and when needed. He is now in Zambia, Africa, where he is still helping. His son is a missionary priest there.

Patrons of the store were "from the area and from California to New York." Through Father Schmitt, whose avocation is the theater, said stars that appeared at the Masonic Temple and the Westgate Dinner Theater patronized the store. Furniture from the store was loaned for theatrical productions and the stars would visit the Annex on Saturdays and Sundays (which required more volunteer work). But, as one of the woman said "We loved every minute of it." Some of the stars that visited the store were Tony Sandler, Ralph Young, Burt Reynolds, Karen Valentine, Vickie Lawrence, Leonard Nimoy, Hans Conreid, Norm Crosby, Lyle Waggoner and Mrs. Harvey Korman.

Recently an autograph book was kept in the store. The volunteers wish that they had started it earlier because they missed getting so many important signatures. Those who have been here and signed the book recently are: Lois Nettleton, Eloise O'Brien (Mrs. Pat), Sue Ann Langdon, Ricardo Montalban, Sergio Franchi, and Sandler and Young (they visited the store four times). Totie Fields wrote in the book "from a Good Jew to Father George and the Ladies." Totie signed it on 7-31-1975, just prior to her surgery. Kaye Ballard, on 8-8-1975, wrote "To St. Joseph Antiques - My Love, My Friendship! Something Old, Something New, That's why I love you. God Bless."

When Burt Reynolds was in a play at the Masonic, the Annex loaned an antique chair, Burt sat down in it so hard it collapsed. The ladies at the Annex had it repaired and for a while had a sign on it, "This is the chair that Burt Reynolds broke." Eventually it was purchased by a woman, probably because Burt broke it rather than the fact that it was an antique. It was through the ladies at the Annex that a Rolls Royce, which was locally owned, was sold to Sergio Franchi. The women told Sergio about the car, he saw it, he liked it, and he purchased it.

Bob Bodie and Ken Gambolis, who helped out at the Annex, drove the car to Las Vegas where they had a night on the town, courtesy of Sergio. As one of the women summed it up, "If it hadn't been for Cleo's knowledge about antiques and Father's contacts, I don't think we could have made it the big success that it was."

Cleo, by the way, is not a member of St. Joseph's officially, that is, but I am sure that the volunteers, Father Schmitt, and all who know her, consider her to be a member."

SISTERS OF ST. FRANCIS

Because of the amount of space that would be needed to write about the religious orders and organizations of Sylvania, I have not included those subjects in these volumes. But, the Sisters of St. Francis, and the Sylvania convent, are a huge part of Sylvania's overall history, and therefore I will discuss when and how they first made Sylvania their home. Some of the information provided was obtained from the following sources: a book titled *Our Mother* published in 1959 by the Sisters of St. Francis of Sylvania, Ohio; a document titled: Sisters of St. Francis, Sylvania, Ohio – Our Buildings 1916-1972; and from actual property deed documents on file in the Lucas County Auditor's office; Sylvania Village Council minutes; Federal U.S. Census records; and the numerous newspaper articles that appeared in the Sylvania newspapers over the years. Other sources are documented throughout this history as well.

Starting first with the property today known as 6832 Convent Blvd., this property was purchased on 5-14-1915 by Joseph Hittler, Jr. and consisted of 85 acres. He purchased this property from Albert "Bert" R. Miles. Mr. Hittler and Mr. Miles were neighbors for many years, living across the street from each other in the 5700 blk. of North Main Street. That year Mr. Hittler, who was a master carpenter by trade, built a home on this 85 acre parcel.

In November of 1916 the senior Sisters stationed at Holy Cross Mission and at St. Philip Mission in Minneapolis, Minnesota were summoned to Rochester, Minnesota where it was announced that a new Province was to be established in Toledo, Ohio, to teach the Polish immigrants in the diocese, and asked the Sisters who they recommended to head the project. They all responded that Sister Mary Adelaide Sandusky would be their recommendation. Sister Adelaide was loved by all and was known for her efficient leadership as the Director of St. Teresa's College in Winona, Minnesota. The Rochester Franciscans sent 23 teachers to staff three area schools.

Two Sisters (Sister Adelaide and Sister Antoinette) arrived in Toledo to assume their new position. The congregation was officially established on 12-8-1916, and Sister Adelaide was officially installed as the first Provincial Superior. A temporary habitat was established in an old vacated church on Dexter Street in Toledo, Ohio.

So it was that Sister Adelaide, Sisters from the St. Hedwig Mission and Sisters from Rochester, Minnesota came together; with Sister Adelaide and Sister Antoinette appointed Mistress of

Novices. These Sisters came to Toledo at the request of Bishop Joseph Schrembs to help with the critical need for teachers among the Polish immigrants in the diocese.

In the spring of 1917 Bishop Schrembs, Mother Adelaide and Sister Antoinette went out in search of a site in which to build a "city of God." As they drove down what would later become known as Convent Blvd, their Ford got stuck in front of the Hittler residence and they went to get help. At that time they found out that the Hittler farm was for sale. "As she looked down the almost impassable country dirt road that wound its way into the farmlands, she whispered audibly, "Yes, this will be our Convent Boulevard." Twenty years later, not only was the road named "Convent Boulevard," but the entire area was transformed into a beautiful park whose virginal woods are today recognized by the Ohio State Forestry as a 'Class A Conservation Reserve.' "What Mother Adelaide saw in this property at that time was the fact that it was near the railroad station, near town, close to the church and also near the interurban railway depot as well."

The following property was purchased by the Sisters throughout 1917:

- 8-3-1917 – Joseph Hittler, Jr. sold to the Sisters of Immaculate Conception: Range 6 Town 9 Section 9 – SE ¼, North ½, except the West 16 acres and Range 6 Town 9 Section 10 – SW ¼ - That part SW of railroad and North of Clark Subdivision. This was the parcel that had the residential home on it that had just been constructed by Joseph Hittler, Jr., as well as two old barns.
- 8-3-1917 – Joseph Hitter, Jr. sold to the Sisters of the Immaculate Conception – Range 6 Town 9 Section 10 – SW ¼ - Part of the W ½ SW of Maumee Road, excluding Clarks Subdivision, that part SW of railroad and North of Clarks Plat.
- 8-6-1917 – Fred O. Peak sold to the Sisters of Immaculate Conception: Range 6 Town 9 Section 9 – NE ¼ West 12.06 acres that part South of Toledo & Western Railroad & SE of the road. Consisting of 12.06 acres.
- 9-24-1917 – Moses Bittner sold to the Sisters of Immaculate Conception: Range 6 Town 9 Section 9 NE ¼ All of lots 165 to 182 Block 20 vacated in the Village of Sylvania.
- 9-24-1917 – Emory & Edit Holt sold to the Sisters of Immaculate Conception: Range 6 Town 9 Section 10 in the SW ¼ - That part NW ¼ between the railroad tracks and Maumee Road. The South .40 acres of the N 1.78 acres. This was property along S. Main Street where there was a home. It later served as St. Cecilia Conservatory of Music and in 1934 it was moved over the railroad tracks and onto the property of the Sisters of St. Francis. Then it became a residence hall for the Postulants and became known as Carmel Hall

Before Mother Adelaide, foundress of the Sylvania Franciscans, passed away in 1964, and before she died she was tape recorded recalling the stories of their first years in Sylvania. One of the most interesting of these stories was her memorable trip by rail to attempt to get some barracks lumber in Grand Rapids, Michigan in order to build the first convent buildings. Shortly after arriving in Sylvania, Mother Adelaide had been advised to take the Chicago train from Toledo leaving at 6:40 a.m. She left Sylvania the day before to stay in Toledo for the night so she could get to the depot in time. The train pulled out and before long the train stopped at a little town. Mother

Adelaide said she looked closely at where they had stopped and saw the newly purchased Hittler farm and realized she was in Sylvania, right back where she started the day before.

Money was scarce and Mother Adelaide persuaded Mr. Hittler to wait for part of the payment on the house and property until the end of the year. She then set out to operate a farm. They sold produce, melons, berries, etc., to earn money, but were unable to make enough to support the expenses so … she abandoned farming to commerce her dream of beautifying the grounds into a park. In August, 1919, the parent community in Rochester, Minnesota paid for the land in Sylvania.

The house that they purchased from Joseph Hittler served as the official residence of the General Superior and was first known as the Loretto House, and one of the horse barns on the property continued to be used as a barn until it became a temporary laundry area too, and then later converted the horse barn into St. Agnes Hall. It appears that the only thing that remained of the original horse barn was the basement level.

Joseph Hittler, Jr., who owned this property and home at the time that the Sisters purchased it, was born in 1865 in Ohio. His parents were Joseph and Theresa Bodenmiller Hittler. His father was born in Alsace, France and his mother was born in Rhineland, Baden, Germany. His mother died in 1910 and his father died in 1914, both while living in Sylvania. They had eight children with only four of them living to adulthood. The four of their children who lived to adulthood were: Lucy born 1862 died 1916; Joseph, Jr. born 1865 died 1945; Theresa born unknown died unknown; and William born 1880 died 1940.

Joseph Hittler, Sr. and his wife came to the United States in 1865. They are first listed in our 1870 census living in Whiteford Township, Monroe County, Michigan. The first piece of property that Joseph Hittler, Sr. purchased in Sylvania was in 1891, and was located in downtown Sylvania where he opened up a blacksmith shop, which he ran here until he sold in 1906 to Frank Moore. He was elected to serve on Sylvania Village Council in the years 1893, 1894, 1903, 1904 and 1905.

So by 1917 the Sisters owned a residential home on S. Main Street, which they used as the residence of the administration, and they owned the large parcel off what at that time was being called Clark Street, but later became Convent Blvd., which had a new residential home on it that had been built by Joseph Hittler, Jr. in 1915. They also had two large barns on that property which were both already there when Hittler purchased it; one for horses, the other for cows. There was also a hen house on the property. The Hittler house became the second official residence and was the administration office until 1923. In 1923 the first resident chaplain, Father William Carroll, was appointed, and this house was called Loretto House, and was the chaplain's residence, until 1967. Then they made it the Bishop's residence when Bishop George Rehring lived here after he retired from active duty in the Diocese of Toledo.

The barn near the main building went from a regular barn, to a temporary laundry area, then a store room, garage and finally a trunk room, before it was finally razed in 1961.

Regarding the largest parcel of property that the Sisters purchased from Joseph Hittler, Jr. that property was originally owned as follows before the Sisters purchased it:

3-18-1848 – Shadrach W. Allen
5-21-1862 – Joshua W. Allen
5-21-1862 – Peleg T. Clark
1887 – Transferred to Fanny Clark (widow of Peleg T. Clark)
3-16-1892 – George P. Dolph
9-20-1897 – Albert K. Miles (87 acres)
12-14-1897 – Albert R. & Maude L. Miles
5-11-1915 – Albert R. Miles
5-11-1915 – Lucy M. Hawley (sole heir of Albert & Maude Miles)
5-14-1915 – Joseph Hittler, Jr.
8-3-1917 – Sisters of the Immaculate Conception

In 1917 construction started on additional buildings and this was during the First World War, when building materials were very difficult to obtain. These temporary buildings were constructed to house their growing community, and St. Francis Hall was built, which was used as a dormitory and a Chapel. It had two wings. After the chapel was built, and this was no longer used for services, this became a temporary auditorium known as St. Therese Hall. Then it was remodeled as a study and community room for the novices. Then it returned to a residence for professed Sisters. Finally in 1973 the structures had extensive remodeling and became known as the Early Childhood Development Center for preschoolers.

A 1917 map of the campus of the Sisters of St. Francis shows the following buildings on the property: the Hittler farm house, a large barn behind it, chicken coop, a dairy barn and St. Francis Chapel/St. Teresa Dormitory. Other items noted on this map include "berry runs" on the western portion of the property, a pasture just to the north of the berry runs and an orchard on the north portion of the property. Over on the east portion of the property is shown a "tree nursery."

Also in 1917 formal education was started and four candidates were enrolled that first year. Sister Stanislas was appointed the first principal, and in the fall of 1918 they started conducting Provincialate High School. This was later to be known as St. Clare Academy, which was relocated from St. Hedwig in Toledo to the Sylvania property.

In 1918 a flu epidemic broke out throughout the United States and the Sisters were asked to help. That's when they began their expansion into health care.

In 1918 a man by the name of William Cherry, who had been working for the Sisters of St. Francis as their superintendent, was murdered by a highly intoxicated man that he did not know, while driving down Convent Blvd. The murderer was Steve Traskawitz, about 28 years old, and the newspapers of that time described him as a Hungarian. According to Sylvania's Marshal Wood, Traskawitz had been removed from a New York Central passenger train a few hours before because he was intoxicated and had kicked another passenger in the face. At the time he was removed from the train, the agent instructed Mr. Beebe to call an officer and have the suspect taken care of. Mr. Cherry, who worked as the superintendent of the convent farm for the Sisters of St. Francis, was driving down Convent Blvd. on his horse and buggy when Traskawitz jumped in front of Cherry's team of horses causing Mr. Cherry to stop. The stranger then climbed into the wagon and refused to get out. Cherry took him as far as his farm and let the man off, and to get away from the house started to walk with him to the depot. While walking Traskawitz evidently, without any warning, struck Mr. Cherry in the side of the neck, severing the large veins which caused death immediately. Shortly after, Mr. Cherry was found dead, a description of Traskawitz had been obtained by a man who was at the station at the time he was thrown off. Cliff and Jess Peck, brothers, located the man and turned him over to Marshal Wood who immediately took him to prison in Toledo, fearing he would be lynched by the irate citizens. The murderer was brought before Judge Chandler and plead guilty. We never did find additional documentation to indicate what the county courts sentenced him with.

An advertisement in the *Sylvania Sentinel* dated 6-22-1918 reads: "Announcement – Instructions will be given in Piano, Voice, Violin, Harmony, Theory of Music at the Convent of the Immaculate Conception – Sylvania, Ohio."

By 1919 St. Anthony Hall was built on the Convent grounds. This building originally served as their kitchen, dining rooms, laundry, dormitory, bedrooms, offices, reception rooms, classrooms, chapel, library, community room and infirmary. In 1962 it became a novitiate and then in 1969 changed to the House of Prayer.

Father Bernard Crane of St. Joseph Church conducted their Chapel services for them from the beginning until 1923, and on Sundays and special occasions Jesuit Fathers from Toledo conducted services.

At the 1920 census the following women were listed living at the "Convent of Immaculate Conception" on Clark Street (Convent Blvd.) – (these names are spelled as well as can be determined. The handwriting is very hard to read):

1. Mother Adelaide – owned home – free of mortgage – 45 years old – born in Ohio;
2. Sister Antoinette – 53 years old – Born in Poland;
3. Sister Elizabeth – 42 years – Born in Minnesota – housekeeper;
4. Sister Judith – 23 years – Born in Minnesota – teacher;
5. Sister Francis Regis – 17 years – Born in Pennsylvania – student;
6. Sister Bernadine – 17 years – Born in Minnesota – student;
7. Sister Benvenita – 17 years – Born in Minnesota – student;
8. Sister Gonzaza – 17 years – Born in Michigan – student;
9. Sister Clarilla – 17 years – Born in Poland – student;
10. Sister Agnes Marie – 18 years – Born in Minnesota – student;
11. Sister Seraphia – 27 years – Born in Minnesota – teacher;
12. Sister Rita – 28 years – Born in Poland – housekeeper;
13. Sister Apolloina – 29 years – Born in Poland – housekeeper;
14. Sister Martha – 34 years – Born in Poland – housekeeper;
15. Sister Genevieve – 24 years – Born in Poland – housekeeper;

16. Angela Czyszczon – 24 years – Born in Poland – housekeeper;
17. Alma Kakal – 17 years – Born in Minnesota – student;
18. Sophia Gacck – 15 years – Born in Minnesota – student;
19. Louise Kapinos – 16 years – Born in Minnesota – student;
20. Amea Mecek – 16 years – Born in Minnesota – student;
21. Mary Mroz – 15 years – Born in Poland – student;
22. Helen Fudali – 15 years – Born in Minnesota – student;
23. Clara Gruba – 18 years – Born in South Dakota – student;
24. Mary Matz – 16 years – Born in Minnesota – student;
25. Rose Matz – 18 years – Born in Minnesota – student;
26. Hedwig Maloch – 17 years – born in Minnesota – student;
27. Louise Koscielniak – 17 years – Born in Minnesota – student;
28. Stella Wojciak – 16 years – Born in Minnesota – student;
29. Sophia Dombek – 17 years – Born in Minnesota – student;
30. Henrica Jarosz – 17 years – born in Minnesota – student;
31. Julia Dombek – 16 years – Born in Minnesota – student;
32. Genevieve Wojciak – 16 years – Born in Minnesota – student;
33. Regina Mihalska – 20 years – Born in Minnesota – student;
34. Sister Henry – 32 years – Born in Minnesota – teacher;
35. Sister Laurenitia – 26 years – Born in Ohio – teacher;
36. Sister Camillus – 22 years – Born in Minnesota – teacher.

In a letter that Rev. B.P. Crane wrote to Mr. Park Wagonlander, Clerk of the Village of Sylvania, dated 12-12-1925, Father Crane wrote: "I ask your kind office in securing approval of Village Council to have a private cemetery for the sisters on their grounds. The sketch of their architect reveals that it will be located better than seven hundred feet off Convent Blvd. Will kindest regards be you and to all members of village council, I remain yours sincerely, B.P. Crane."

The following letter was returned to Rev. B.P. Crane by the Clerk of the Village of Sylvania: "Dear Sir: Your letter under date of Dec. 12th, 1925 and map showing the location of private a cemetery for the Sisters on their grounds was presented to council last evening at our regular session and I have been instructed to inform you that it is not necessary to pass any legislation on same as long as Council accepts same. Therefore please accept this letter as an acceptance and approval of same. Very Truly Yours, Clerk of Council."

The 8-11-1927 issue of the *Sylvania Sentinel* reported the following: "FRANCISCAN SISTER DIES AFTER LONG ILLNESS – Sister Mary Margaret, Franciscan Sister, whose residence was at the Convent of the Franciscan Sisters of the Immaculate Conception in Sylvania, passed away Friday at Providence Hospital, Sandusky after a long illness. Funeral services were held Tuesday in the Convent Chapel, Sylvania, followed by interment in Calvary Cemetery, Toledo."

The first permanent building was built on the Convent property by the Franciscan Sisters was started in 1929 and called St. Clare Academy Hall. This building provided high school classrooms, a library, science laboratories, music rooms, art rooms and offices, and had dormitories on the second floor. The cornerstone was laid by Samuel Cardinal Stritch, then Bishop of Toledo, on 12-8-1929, and the building was ready for occupancy in 1930. According to a list of buildings prepared by the Sisters of St. Francis it was stated that the St. Clare Academy was needed because they were seeking North Central accreditation. In 1950 a separate wing was built on the west, housing Duns Scotus Library and a wing for the administration areas called Lourdes Hall, with the second floor used as living quarters.

With the construction of St. Clare Academy Hall in 1930 they also added a boiler room as a separate unit, which was built some distance from the new Hall. The boiler room included what they called an "unsightly smoke-stake" on its side. Records say that the smoke-stake was removed as soon as other fuel arrangements were made. Attached to the boiler room was a new laundry area, which was used for that purpose until 1955 when separate facilities better equipped were erected.

Also in 1930 St. Agnes House was reconstructed from the original cow barn that was on the property and made into a dormitory by adding a second floor and complete laundry services in the basement. They added the entrance and front wings. According to documents the common room of this building still has the old barn beams.

At the 1930 census there were 65 females and two males living at the Convent. All were listed as single/not married. The list indicated that all were "members in training for religious community." The following individuals were listed (the handwriting is very difficult to read, so I have duplicated the names as best I could read):

1. Anna Sandusky – 55 years old – born in Ohio – executive;
2. Mary Tlochynska - 63 years old – born in Poland – no occupation;
3. Augusta Kosmider – 65 years old – born in Ohio – teacher;
4. Pauline Miholai – 59 years old – born in Silicia – supervisor – farm;
5. Frances Pinska – 40 years – born in Poland – no occupation listed;
6. Mary Jazewska – 46 years old – born in Minnesota – teacher;
7. Sophia Waty – 35 years old – born in Minnesota – teacher;
8. Helen Warpeha – 31 years old – born in Minnesota – teacher;
9. Eva Kitz – 38 years old – born in Ohio – teacher;
10. Anna Zajner – 24 years old – born in Minnesota – teacher;
11. Albina Sterz – 22 years old – born in Minnesota – teacher;
12. Elizabeth Kusek – 33 years old – born in Poland – occupation – none;
13. Luella Stashon – 36 years old – born in Poland – occupation – none;
14. Emilia G-?- - 24 years old – born in Minnesota – occupation – none;
15. Eleanor Okanstar – 24 years old – born in Ohio – occupation – none;
16. Victoria Leiska – 25 years old – born in Nebraska-occupation none;
17. Celilia May – 25 years old – born in Ohio – occupation – none;
18. Elizabeth Rybicka – 22 years old – born in Minnesota – occ. – none;
19. Frances Kotowska – 27 years old – born in Ohio – occ – Novice;
20. Julia Pendsimas – 21 years old – born in Minnesota – occ – Novice;
21. Helen Follas – 19 years old – born in Ohio – occ – Novice;
22. Anna Sembs – 19 years old – born in Minnesota – occ. – Novice;

23. Lillian Mikalay – 19 years old – born in Pennsylvania – occ-Novice;
24. Mary Tomseh – 19 years old – born in Minnesota – occ-Novice;
25. Anna Libeckoske – 21 years old – born in Minnesota – occ. – Novice;
26. Stella Lapata – 17 years old – born in Minnesota – occ. – Novice;
27. Bernice Restuh – 18 years old – born in Minnesota – occ. – Novice;
28. Lercadia Kesinska – 18 years old – born in Minnesota – occ-Novice;
29. Mary Sterz – 19 years old – born in Minnesota – occ – Novice;
30. Thereses Drewnish – 16 years old – born in Minnesota-occ.-Novice;
31. Bernice Sabesha – 16 years old – born in Pennsylvania-occ-Novice;
32. Matilda Disezynska – 17 years old – born in Ohio-occ-Novice;
33. Anna Konzolhn – 17 years old – born in Minnesota –occ- Novice;
34. Sophia Nowakoska – 17 years old – born in Michigan-occ.-Novice;
35. Jeanette Cieplas – 16 years old – born in Ohio – occupation-Novice;
36. Lottie Pimonska – 16 years old – born in Michigan – occ – Novice;
37. Stella Kosh – 17 years old – born in Minnesota – occ-Novice;
38. Irene Surminska – 17 years old – born in Ohio – occ-Novice;
39. Catherine Bartko – 16 years old – born in Pennsylvania – Novice;
40. Rose Senko – 18 years old – born in Minnesota – Novice;
41. Anna - -?- - 16 years old – born in Minnesota – Postulate;
42. Ajolouis Laskoska – 16 years old – born in Minnesota – Postulate;
43. Adeline Kubih – 16 years old – born in New York – Postulate;
44. Agnes Kuduh - 16 years old – born in Minnesota – Postulate;
45. Josephine Mushols – 15 years old – born in Minnesota – Postulate;
46. Mary Danjewis – 16 years old – born in Minnesota – Postulate;
47. Lena Sathewick – 16 years old – born in Michigan – Postulate;
48. Theodoria Miazga – 15 years old – born in Minnesota – Postulate;
49. Sophia Stenoska – 15 years old – born in Minnesota – Postulate;
50. Emily Gesioska – 14 years old – born in Ohio – Postulate;
51. Florence Zolska – 15 years old – born in Minnesota – Postulate;
52. Mary Jasos – 14 years old – born in Wisconsin – Postulate;
53. Mary Bicenit – 15 years old – born in Minnesota – Postulate;
54. Helen Kasper – 16 years old – born in Ohio – Postulate;
55. Rose Bacesko – 18 years old – born in Michigan – Postulate;
56. Martha Kostua – 17 years old – born in Michigan – Postulate;
57. Helen Chimura – 16 years old – born in Ohio – Postulate;
58. Veronica Fralhosha – 14 years old – born in Michigan – Postulate;
59. Genevieve Mikolay – 15 years old – born in Ohio – Postulate;
60. Veronica Swaja – 15 years old – born in Minnesota – Postulate;
61. Delphine Kejnas – 15 years old – born in Ohio – Postulate;
62. Salome Bah – 15 years old – born in Ohio – Postulate;
63. Rose Cerel – 21 years old – born in Ohio – Postulate;
64. Helen Preis – 15 years old – born in Michigan – Postulate;
65. Charlotte Bersnska – 15 years old – born in Michigan – Postulate;
66. Norbert M. Shumaker – Boarder – male – 34 years old – single – clergyman – Catholic School.

67. Raymond G. Kirsch – Boarder – 35 years old – single – clergyman – Catholic School.

It was reported in the histories of the Sisters of St. Francis that as time went on Mother Adelaide purchased thousands of seedling evergreens from the government and planted them throughout the woods, and later she transplanted them where needed for landscaping.

The 1-21-1932 issue of the *Toledo News-Bee* newspaper reported the following: "50 GIRLS, NUNS FLEE EARLY MORNING FIRE – Blaze Sweeps One End of Convent Dormitory at Sylvania – Fifty girl students and nuns were forced to flee early Thursday when fire swept one end of the dormitory of the Franciscan convent at Sylvania. Damage amounted to $500. The blaze was discovered in the furnace room at 5:40 a.m. and the fact that it is the custom of those at the convent to rise at 5 a.m. probably averted a panic. Nuns in the convent were attracted by the flames and went to the aid of those in the burning building while members of the Sylvania township volunteer fire department fought the blaze. The firemen under the leadership of Chief "Dutch" Williams fought for more than half an hour before the blaze was under control. The fire destroyed the heating plant of the dormitory and parts of the building that were not damaged by fire were drenched with water."

Among the old records that still exist in scrapbooks that belong to the Sylvania Township Fire Department the following letter was saved in one of the earliest scrapbooks. The letter was received from Mother Adelaide, General Superior, Sisters of St. Francis of 6832 Convent Blvd. dated 1-23-1932: "My dear Mr. Williams and the Sylvania Volunteer Fire Department: This is to express to you our deep and sincere thanks. The help in distress which you volunteer to perform you performed so fully in serving us last Thursday morning that the entire household of eighty persons rings with praise and appreciation of your efforts. The enclosed check is but a small token of our expression of gratitude. The public expression of the feeling that as citizens of the town of Sylvania our lives are secure because of your prompt service is a priceless token. This token we owe you and the town of Sylvania. Sylvania may well be proud of its Volunteer Fire Department and its Chief. Once more let us repeat, our lives and our property are secure in the thought of being taken care of by the Sylvania Volunteer Fire Department under Chief Darrell Williams. We are, Very gratefully yours, Mother Adelaide, General Superior."

In 1932 the house that the Sisters owned on South Main Street, near St. Joseph Church, which served as the residence for their administration and then as St. Cecilia Conservatory of Music, was moved to the Convent property on the other side of the railroad tracks to serve as a residence hall for the Postulants, which was named Carmel Hall. This building was expanded over the years. A building permit was granted by the Village of Sylvania on 8-15-1932 to move the residence to 6832 Convent Blvd. between St. Agnes House and the main building on their parcel containing 89 acres. The house mover listed on the permit was C.H. O'Neill of Toledo, Ohio. Mother Adelaide signed the permit.

12-2-1932 – The minutes of Sylvania Village Council said: "Bernard Webb was present representing the Sisters of St. Francis requesting that they be permitted to make a change in the driveway at Convent. They agreed to furnish the materials and labor necessary to raise the level of the manhole in order to make the improvement. Moved by Councilman Hinckley, seconded by Councilman

Park that the Sisters of St. Francis be authorized to make the improvements as requested. All expenses to be paid by them and all work to be completed under the supervision of Mr. Bernholtz. Motion carried all voting yes." (Mr. Bernholtz was Arthur Bernholtz who was serving as the street superintendent for the Village of Sylvania at that time).

On 12-22-1936 Sylvania Village Council held a special meeting in order to approve a building permit for the Sisters of St. Francis. The permit granted them permission to add on to the north side of the boiler room, where they did the laundry. According to this permit the builder was listed as their "employees." The addition was estimated to cost $2,000.

A map of the "Campus of the Sisters of St. Francis" dated 1938 shows the following buildings: St. Francis/St. Theresa Dormitory, St. Agnes Hall, Carmel Hall, Loretto House with large barn behind, St. Anthony Hall, Portiuncula, St. Clare Hall, a power house and a St. Joseph Workshop. The map also shows an orchard, lily pond and a cemetery.

9-16-1938 – Sylvania Village Council approved a building permit to relocate a building that was to be used as a school owned by the Franciscan Sisters. The permit said that a frame school house at 5373 Main would be enlarged. The builder was listed as Henry J. Spieker Company of Toledo, Ohio and the Architect was listed as Willfred D. Holtzman of Toledo, Ohio. The estimated cost of this work was listed as $3,500.

4-1-1940 – A building permit was requested by the Sisters of St. Francis to construct an $8,400 dormitory on their property on the north side of Convent Blvd. The permit was granted by Sylvania Village Council. A set of blueprints dated 6-4-1940 prepared by Willfred D. Holigman, Jr. Architect, of Toledo, Ohio is listed as the "Dormitory Building for Sisters of St. Francis."

On 5-27-1940 the 1940 census was taken on Convent Blvd., in Sylvania, Lucas County, Ohio, at the Sisters of St. Francis Convent. The census taker, Grace M. Beebe, recorded the following living at the convent (the 1940 census also asked the question "highest grade of school completed" which has also been included here):

1. Anna Sandusky – 65 years – Mother Superior – Convent – highest grade C-6;
2. Mary Janniah – 63 years – assistant Superior – Convent – highest grade C-2;
3. Sophia Hatty – 45 years – Secretary – Convent – highest grade C-7;
4. Eva Kitz – 48 years – Treasurer – Convent – highest grade C-4;
5. Mary Koczynsks – 70 years – teacher – college highest grade C-4;
6. Mary Kendora – 65 years – Sister – Convent – highest grade C-2;
7. Sophia Tryban – 70 years – Sister – Convent – highest grade H-4;
8. Mary Pelvach – 53 years – seamstress – Convent – highest grade C-1
9. Peloyia Czubek – 50 years – Student Sister – College – highest grade;
10. Frances Glinez – 65 years – Sister – Convent – highest grade H-3;
11. Stella Baretiniak – 52 years – Teacher – Convent – highest grade C-4;
12. Mary Jozewski – 56 years – Teacher – Convent – highest grade C-3;
13. Frances Pinaha – 50 years – Music teacher – Convent – highest grade C-3;
14. Augusta Koswider – 74 years – Sister – Convent – highest grade C-2;

15. Helen Warperba – 41 years – Teacher – Convent – highest grade C-8;
16. Julia Bielen – 37 years – student Sister – Convent – highest grade C-3;
17. Agnes Postrona – 33 years – teacher – Convent – highest grade C-4;
18. Palagia Kindchen – 33 years – teacher – Convent – highest grade C-4;
19. Mildred Butler – 30 years – teacher – Convent – highest grade C-4;
20. Elizabeth Kazah – 42 years – housekeeper – highest grade 6th grade;
21. Mary Jebn – 47 years – housekeeper – highest grade – 6th grade;
22. Stella Fisher – 27 years – student – sister – highest grade C-3;
23. Albina Steck – 32 years – student – sister – highest grade C-3;
24. Bernice Resteck – 27 years – teacher – highest grade C-4;
25. Cecilia May – 34 years – housekeeper – highest grade 8th grade;
26. Louise Kostick – 36 years – student sister – highest grade C-5;
27. Bernadette Zomeek – 20 years – student – sister – highest grade C-2;
28. Pauline Makow – 41 years – housekeeper – highest grade 8th;
29. Henrietta Ganzel – 21 years – student – sister – highest grade C-2;
30. Lillian Feldman – 32 years – student – sister – highest grade C-4;
31. Anne Watty – 37 years – student – sister – highest grade C-4;
32. Helen Lesiah – 25 years – teacher – highest grade C-3;
33. Martha Adams – 25 years – student – sister – highest grade C-4;
34. Lillian Czaeski – 30 years – housekeeper – highest grade H-1;
35. Mary Teart – 33 years – student – sister – highest grade C-2;
36. Frances Crawford – 45 years – student – sister – highest grade C-7
37. Susanne Symie – 31 years – student – sister – highest grade C-4;
38. Magalen Pelc – 49 years – housekeeper – highest grade 6th;
39. Stephanie Jay – 21 years – student – sister – highest grade C-1;
40. Eleanor Jabwski – 19 years – highest grade C-1;
41. Renina Noys – 18 years – Novice - highest grade C-1;
42. Gales Wanda – 19 years – student – sister – highest grade C-1;
43. Lottie Olkowski – 18 years – student – sister – highest grade C-1;
44. Adeline Naroz – 18 years – Novice – highest grade C-1;
45. Josephine Kiella – 18 years – Novice – highest grade C-1;
46. Angeline Tobaka – 18 years – Novice – highest grade C-1;
47. Joan Petra – 18 years – Novice – highest grade C-1
48. Helen Shelmack – 20 years – Novice – highest grade C-1;
49. Lucy Galon – 19 years – Novice – highest grade C-1;
50. Mary Senho – 18 years – Novice – highest grade C-1;
51. Angela Maslow – 18 years – Novice – highest grade C-1;
52. Genevieve Jacek – 18 years – Novice – highest grade C-1;
53. Genevieve Sopezyk – 24 years – Novice – highest grade C-1;
54. Josephine Dupla – 18 years – Novice – highest grade C-1;
55. Mabel Shaska – 22 years – Novice – highest grade C-1;
56. Jane Serena – 18 years – student – highest grade H-4;
57. Veronica Katt – 18 years – student – highest grade H-4;
58. Anna Konazka – 18 years – student – highest grade H-4;
59. Bernice Ostroski – 18 years – student – highest grade H-4;

60. Susanne Kramer – 18 years – student – highest grade H-3;
61. Mary Sobozak – 17 years – student – highest grade H-3;
62. Lenore Daniels – 17 years – student – highest grade H-2;
63. Pauline Poplar – 17 years – student – highest grade H-2;
64. Michelline Poplar – 17 years – student – highest grade H-2;
65. Gladys Czayowski – 17 years – student – highest grade H-4;
66. Sophia Wilt – 16 years – student – highest grade H-2;
67. Miles Reynolda – 16 years – student – highest grade H-2;
68. Eleanor Gay – 16 years – student – highest grade H-2;
69. Harriet Wazah – 24 years – student – highest grade H-1;
70. Mary Zaremb – 15 years – student – highest grade H-1;
71. Paulette Gozda – 15 years – student – highest grade H-1;
72. Dorothy Harempa – 14 years – student – highest grade H-1;
73. Helen Stobeck – 20 years – student – highest grade C-1;
74. Veronica Janonsia – 20 years – student – highest grade C-1;
75. Cecilia Muskola -15 years – student – highest grade H-3;
76. Stephenia Niedbala – 18 years – student – highest grade H-4;
77. Rose Truos – 18 years – student – highest grade H-4;
78. Caroline Wilk – 21 years – student – highest grade C-1;
79. Edward M O'Hare – 63 years – chaplain – highest grade C-6;
80. Maurice C. Herman – 32 years – assistant chaplain – highest grade C-6;

The *Sylvania Sentinel* dated 1-15-1942 reported: "The Sisters of St. Francis are commemorating the 25th anniversary of their foundation in Sylvania. They established the convent here in December 1916."

The following article appeared in the *Sylvania Sentinel* on 9-24-1942: "Sister Antoinette of the Franciscan Convent is one of the most ardent gardeners in this community. Having been retired from teaching service at the Convent she gives her entire time to her flowers. She has two small greenhouses besides her outdoor flower beds, and she knows and loves every plant. Sister Antoinette and Sister Stanislas have been located at the Convent in Sylvania for 26 years."

On 12-17-1942 the *Sylvania Sentinel* reported that an overheated furnace caused only minor damage of the St. Francis Convent, Monday noon. They reported that the Sylvania Fire Department answered the call.

A May 1943 Sylvania Telephone Directory listed the following: "Rev. E.M. O'Hare – 6834 Convent Blvd. – Phone 68." And listed the following: "Sisters of St. Francis – 6832 Convent Blvd. – Phone 101."

In 1944 John Chudzinski was hired by the Sisters of St. Francis as their engineer for St. Francis Assisi, which later became Lourdes College.

According to the Sylvania Sentinel dated 10-24-1946: "Sister M. Isadore, 70, of the Sisters of St. Francis, Sylvania, died Sunday in Providence Hospital, Sandusky, Ohio. As a member the

Franciscan order nearly 50 years Sister Isadore was engaged in teaching in her earlier years, and in hospital work since 1922. One of her first appointments was teaching at St. Helwig School, Toledo. She was assigned duty in hospitals of the order in Sandusky, Texas and North Platte, Neb. Surviving are a nephew, Father Isadore of the Franciscan Fathers, Toledo; niece, Sister M. Julia, and cousin, Sister M. Isabelle, both of the Sisters of St. Francis, Sylvania, and other relatives in Cleveland. Services were held in the Convent Chapel. Tuesday at 9:30 a.m., Burial was in Porta Coeli cemetery, Sylvania."

9-7-1948 – Sylvania Village Council approved a building permit for the Sisters of St. Francis for the construction of an administration building at an estimated cost of $76,000.

6-6-1949 – According to the minutes of Sylvania Village Council, the Sisters of St. Francis were approved for a building permit to construct a library building at an estimated cost of $100,000.

On 3-6-1951 Sylvania Village Council granted the Sisters of St. Francis a building permit to construct a school building on Convent Blvd., for an estimated cost of $70,000.

In 1954 Eugene "Tex" Fondren was hired to work for the Sisters of St. Francis. According to the obituary notice in the *Toledo Blade* on 12-29-2011 for Eugene "Tex" Fondren: ". . . Then Tex worked for the Sisters of St. Francis Convent in Sylvania, OH from 1954 to 1977. He felt he wanted to repay a debt he owed the Catholic Nuns who had raised him at the orphanage. He loved and admired the Franciscan Nuns so much that they became part of his family, including the novices whom he referred to as "the kids" in perpetuity."

In an interview with Willard Edson on 9-23-1974, who grew up in Sylvania in the house at 5365 S. Main Street, which later became the rectory for St. Joseph Church, and then later was demolished and the current St. Joseph Church was constructed on this property, he said this: "The Sisters of St. Francis had a big white dog, Plato. Their place was very still at night. They had no telephone until they were finally hooked up with the Richfield Center exchange. The first call they received the day before Thanksgiving was someone inquiring if this was the jail. This was the time when the K.K.K. was very active and Mother Adelaide's first reaction was to think persecution was beginning, but the call turned out to be from Mrs. Clark who was bringing over a fresh pie for the sisters. Every morning at seven o'clock when the church bell was ringing for mass a baggage car and one coach would come into the Sylvania train station and wait for a long time. The conductor called to see if there were passengers or parcels to be picked up, then the train would back up if there was."

An article written by Kathryn Keller in the *Sylvania Sentinel* dated 7-3-1974 says: "The Sylvania convent is an outgrowth of the Franciscan motherhouse in Rochester, Minn., which had staffed several parochial schools in northwestern Ohio for many years. Shortly after the Diocese of Toledo was established in 1910, Bishop Schrembs asked for more sisters to teach in his diocese. In answer, Mother Adelaide came to Toledo with 23 sisters and $50 to live initially on Dexter St. Within a few years the sisters began looking for a tract of land on which to start a new motherhouse. One day they were riding out the unpaved road that is now Convent Blvd., and their car got stuck in front of the house shown in this picture. In getting help to extricate themselves, they learned that Joe Hittler who lived here was planning to sell his farm of 89 acres together with the house and farm buildings. Mother Adelaide sized up the location. It was close to the New York Central Station, and it was within walking distance of the Toledo and Western Electric Interurban line. Convenient and reliable transportation was a must for her sisters who went out to their teaching posts each September and returned in June for summer study and activities. With this and other considerations, the Hittler farm seemed ideal and the sisters bought it. It was the time of World War I. Building material was scarce. Mother Adelaide, ever resourceful, found some barracks lumber for sale in Adrian, and with it, she directed the building of the one story structure along Convent Blvd., with have since been brick veneered and are still in use. These buildings were the original living quarters and the chapel, while the Hittler house served as the administration building. In 1923, it became the home of the first resident chaplain, Father William Carroll. There have been several additions and remodeling of the house through the years. As Mr. Hittler (a master carpenter himself) built his home. . .”

The following article appeared in the *Sentinel-Herald* dated 4-12-1956: “The Sisters of Saint Francis bid farewell to a retiring caretaker at a testimonial dinner served to employees last week. The dinner was served, said the Sisters, ‘to honor and respect Mr. John Yeager as a just man.’ Mr. Yeager retired after ten years of service at the convent. ‘We wish him many blessings and many happy days,’ said the Sisters.”

Lourdes Junior College was established in 1957 and was authorized by the State of Ohio in January of 1958, and granted membership in the North Central Association of Colleges and Secondary Schools in March of 1964. Mother Justinian Warpeha was its first president. It became a four-year institution in 1982. When Lourdes was first opened in 1958, it served primarily the Sisters of St. Francis and it wasn’t until 10 years later that Lourdes welcomed lay women to their campus.

On 6-2-1958 Sylvania Village Council approved a building permit for the Sisters of St. Francis to construct an administration building on their property at 6832 Convent at an estimated cost of $275,000.

In early 1960 work started on a large chapel on the Convent property. On 1-21-1960 the *Sentinel-Herald* featured a photo of the steel lacework of the chapel that was being constructed, the following caption was written under a photo: “Another impressive structure being added to the Village of Sylvania skyline is the new chapel of the Convent of the Sisters of St. Francis. When the building permit for this structure was issued last summer, it was for $1 million, not counting the furnishings. Henry J. Spieker has the general contract. The church is located at the north end of the convent area and can be seen easily from Silica Drive.”

The following was written by Kate Rogers in the 2-11-1960 issue of the *Sentinel-Herald* newspaper: “Last Thursday, we went over to the Convent of the Sisters of Saint Francis to watch the removal of a smoke-stack. This one was 102 feet high and 4 feet in diameter. It was taken down by use of a crane and was removed in one piece. . . . It was put up in 1930 when a new wing was added to the Convent. Now, the heating plant has been converted to a gas-oil arrangement. There never was any smoke from the stack to speak of so it created no nuisance but more automatic methods are now being used and at least one Sister is glad to see the stack gone. She is Sister Mary Asenia, official photographer for the Convent. Every time she wanted to take a particular view of the yard and buildings, there in all its glory stood the smoke-stack. A few of the Sisters say they will miss it. It had staunchly withstood all the rigors of thirty years winds, storms and anything else the weather cared to hand out."

According to the *Sylvania Sentinel* dated 4-23-1964: "Lourdes Junior College, Sylvania, has been accepted for membership in and accredited as a Junior College by the North Central Association of Colleges and Secondary Schools at its annual meeting April 7th. The College, operated by the Sisters of St. Francis, at their convent in Sylvania, admits as students, only those who are prospective members of the congregation. They have received the certificate of Authorization from the Board of Education of the State of Ohio on January 13, 1958. Sister M. Agnes, Dean, and Sister M. Constantia, Guidance Service Director, represented the college at the committee by type of the Commission on Colleges and Universities. Sister M. Constantia was a member of the Receiving Committee."

On 7-4-1964 Mother Adelaide passed away. Her funeral memorial card reads: "In Memory of Our Beloved Venerable Mother M. Adelaide – Born in Cincinnati, Ohio 10-10-1874 – Entered the Sisters of St. Francis, Rochester, Minnesota 6-6-1893 – Appointed to establish a new Foundation of Sisters of St. Francis in Sylvania, Ohio 12-8-1916 – Died in Sylvania, Ohio 7-4-1964 – Grant, O Lord, eternal joy to our beloved Foundress Venerable Mother M. Adelaide – Sisters of St. Francis – Sylvania, Ohio.'"

Mother Mary Adelaide's obituary notice appeared in the *Toledo Blade* dated 7-5-1964 and reads as follows: "Mother Mary Adelaide, OSF founder and head of the Sisters of St. Francis Community with its Motherhouse at 6832 Convent Blvd., Sylvania, died yesterday in Mercy Hospital after a brief illness. She was 89. Until entering the hospital two days before her death Mother Adelaide directed the widespread activities of the community which she founded in 1916. On June 10, she was presented the Stella Maris (Star of the Sea) award by Mary Manse College. The annual award is given by the college to an outstanding Catholic woman. Mother Adelaide was sent here 50 years ago to establish an extension of the order in Toledo. The former Anne Sandusky and a native of Cincinnati, she entered the Sisters of St. Francis order in St. Paul. She was active in the organization of the College of St. Theresa at Winona, Minn., and was director of the college when she was named by the then Bishop Joseph Schrembs of Toledo to organize a province in Toledo. Arrangements were made to purchase 89 acres of farm land a year after Mother Adelaide arrived in Toledo. St. Clare Academy and Lourdes Junior College have since been established at the site. The building program started in the 1920s has been carried on continuously with the latest expansion Padua Hall, a science building, nearing completion. Under her direction, the Motherhouse has grown to more than 500 Sisters. They are engaged in the operation of 11 hospitals in five states, including Providence Hospital, Sandusky, and St. Francis and Holy Cross hospitals, Detroit. Sisters of the Community also provide teachers for elementary and high schools in Toledo and other cities in Ohio, Michigan, Texas, Minnesota, and California. Mother Adelaide received a Master of Arts degree from Columbia University and studied at the Minneapolis School of Fine Arts, the University of Minnesota, and Harvard University. A sister, Mrs. Mary Schultz of St. Paul, survives. Services will be at 10:30 a.m. Wednesday in Our Lady of Peace Chapel at the Motherhouse. Burial will be at Porta Coeli Cemetery."

A map dated 1966 of the campus of the Sisters of St. Francis shows the following buildings on their property: St. Francis Dormitory, Padua House, St. Anthony Hall, St Agnes Hall, Assisi Hall, Serra Hall, Carmel Hall, Portiuncula, Duns Scotus Library, St. Clare Hall, Lourdes Hall, Mother Adelaide Hall, St. Joseph Workshop, garages, laundry building, power house, auditorium, St. Joseph Cafeteria, Regina Hall, Maria Hall, Chaplain's Residence, Queen of Peace Chapel, Umbria Hall, Madonna Hall and a gardening building.

In 1967 Bishop George Rehring came to Sylvania when he retired from active duty in the Diocese of Toledo. He made his home in the old Hittler house that was on the property of the Sisters of St. Francis. When Bishop Rehring died in 1976 his estate was left to the Sisters of St. Francis of Sylvania.

Sister Ann Francis Klimkowski taught for 21-years as an elementary teacher, high school teacher and principal before joining the faculty at Lourdes College where she taught and was a dean before becoming president for 17 years. She joined the Sisters of St Francis in 1953 and recalled that when she first arrived here she remembers "People in the area were very curious about the campus and often would conjecture about all the activity there. Sisters were open to becoming better known and made a concerted effort to be good neighbors, a philosophy that continues today."

7-2-1970 - According to the minutes of the Sylvania Township Trustees the trustees authorized the Sisters of St. Francis to draw up to 25 gallons of gasoline from the township pump for their leased automobile to help with the operation of the "Tot Lot". The gasoline was to be charged against the recreation appropriation.

7-1-1971 - The Sylvania Township Trustees authorized $3,000 to be allocated from the parks and recreation appropriation to be spent by the Sisters of St. Francis in 1971 in providing a program at the Huntington Farms Tot Lot. This amount was to include gasoline for their leased auto.

In the early 1970s an agreement was signed with St. Vincent's School of Nursing and that led to males attending classes on the Lourdes campus.

5-24-1973 - The Sylvania Township Trustees authorized expending up to $200 for the Huntington Farms summer program, supervised by the Sisters of St. Francis, plus gasoline expenses necessary for the program.

In 1974, during a flash thunderstorm, Sister Jeremias Stinson said that she took cover from the rain in the small chapel on the property of the Sisters of St. Francis. By this time it was in disarray and in desperate need of repairs. That was when she put together a plan, and started working on the inside and outside of the chapel. The official name of the chapel is Our Lady of Angels, but Sister Jeremias said that it was best known as "Portiuncula" meaning "little portion" in Italian. Construction on this chapel started in 1930 and was finished in 1936. The history on the chapel is that it was during the Great Depression years that they wanted to build the chapel, and the sisters had to take out a loan, with the agreement that it would be built within six years. They said that when the note was due, the sisters prayed all night about the banker who would determine whether they could keep their property. Obviously the banker heard their prayers, and by 1945 an addition was added, because of a leak in the south side wall.

7-3-1974 - In response to a letter received by the trustees from Huntington Farms of Sylvania, Inc., the Sylvania Township Trustees approved that the Sisters of St. Francis be permitted to spend a maximum of $200 in township funds for gas and materials to operate a recreational program.

From 1974 through 1986 Sister Mary Ann, M.A. and M.S. in L.S. historian and librarian, and Sister Mary Augustine, PhD, Archivist, both Sisters with the Sisters of St. Francis of Sylvania, became members of the Sylvania History Buffs. They gave hundreds and hundreds of hours to keeping this group going throughout these years, using room 208 in the old Burnham High School Building at 6850 Monroe Street as their headquarters. Between these two Sisters and numerous other volunteers the Sylvania History Buffs recorded and documented many of Sylvania's old-time stories through interviews with residents and through their minutes and letters written. These stories would be lost to history if not for these historical society members. Sister Mary Ann recorded pages and pages of letters that she wrote in an effort to find a permanent storage and a meeting place for the group, always discussing ways to interest new members. Her letters fill an entire notebook.

At the 10-29-1974 meeting of the Sylvania History Buffs Sister Mary Augustine gave a talk about the early history of the Sylvania convent, beginning in 1916. She said: "The place consisted of several different pieces of ground owned by several different owners. The farm fronting on what is now Convent Blvd. was the part with the buildings on it, and was sold to them by Joe Hittler. The area on the southeast was an apple orchard. There were all kinds of apples, and the Sisters used to make cider and dried apples for winter. Now 58 years later there is one of the original apple trees still standing and giving fruit. It is a winter apple, a Russet apple tree. At the north side, nearest the Ten Mile Creek, there was a peach orchard. The ground on which the Convent cemetery is laid out, was a wheat field. In between, the Sisters raised pumpkins, watermelons, all kinds of garden vegetables and potatoes. There were raspberry patches, currants, two beds of strawberries; and berries were taken to Toledo to market. The Sisters raised pigs, and took care of the cows. Then came the time when the Sisters stopped farming and went to school. It became too expensive to grow their own food, and was cheaper to buy it. In 1931 they hired two men to run the farm, and take care of the grounds. As the farm was sandy, Mother Adelaide wrote to the U.S. Dept. of Agriculture to find out how to keep the soil from blowing away. So, according to their information, she bought tiny evergreen trees for 2 cents apiece and had them planted through their farm area, which accounts for the many large fir trees on the grounds now."

5-1-1975 - In response to a letter from Huntington Farms of Sylvania the Sylvania Township Trustees approved $200 to be allocated to the arts and crafts summer program sponsored by the Sisters of St. Francis.

On 2-29-1976 Bishop George J. Rehring, former Bishop of Toledo, died. His will requested that his entire estate be left to the Sisters of St. Francis of Sylvania, and he named the sisters as executors of the estate. The estate consisted of a modest checking account and personal effects, including books, clothing and Episcopal insignia.

4-22-1976 - The Sylvania Township Trustees received a request from Huntington Farms of Sylvania, Inc. for $300 for the Summer Arts and Crafts Program conducted by the Sisters of St. Francis. The trustees approved $200 for this program.

3-31-1977 - The Sylvania Township Trustees authorized $300 to Kathy Brenner, Director of Huntington Farms of Sylvania, Inc., for the arts and crafts program sponsored by the Sisters of St. Francis.

In early April of 1977 John M. Dasher was named the new director of admissions at Lourdes College by Sister M. Rosaria Petra, President of the college, which at this time was an accredited junior college administered by the Sisters of St. Francis of Sylvania. Mr. Dasher is said to have degrees from Amherst College and from the University of Missouri-Kansas City. At the time that he was hired he was a Ph.D. student at the University of Toledo.

4-20-1978 - The Sylvania Township Trustees authorized the expenditure of up to $400 for summer arts and crafts program supervised by the Sisters of St. Francis.

In the late 1970s the Sisters of St. Francis leadership authorized a feasibility study to determine if there was support for a four-year Catholic college. Sister Ann Francis Klimkowski became president of the college and her and her team worked to develop programs to attract students.

In 1979 John Chudzinski retired after 35 years working as an engineer for the Sisters of St. Francis at the St. Francis Assisi (Lourdes College). He had started in 1944.

5-31-1979 - According to the minutes of the Sylvania Township Trustees they allocated $400 to the annual Sylvania Township summer recreation program for children supervised by the Sisters of St. Francis in the area of Huntington Farms.

8-21-1978 - The following Sisters of St. Francis were appointed to serve at St. Joseph School during the 1978-1979 school year: Sister Maria Goretti, principal, Sister M. Faith, Sister M. Gervase, Sister M. Josina and Sister Rachel Marie.

According to the *Sylvania Herald* dated 1-8-1980 the Franciscan Sisters of Sylvania were inviting high school girls interested in their order to join them the weekend of Jan. 19 and 20 at the convent at Lourdes College. They said that the purpose of the "live-in" was to provide a chance for reflection and interaction with the sisters. They would have the opportunity to meet sisters involved in various stages of sisterhood, tour the grounds of the convent, and participate in various recreational activities.

The Blade of Toledo dated 5-6-1982 reported that: "Lourdes College in Sylvania has come a long way since 1916 when its founder, Mother Mary Adelaide, transformed the former Hittler farm into a training site for the Sisters of St. Francis. It was established as a private institution 25 years ago, in 1957, and chartered as a two-year liberal arts college the next year. Lourdes believed that a two-year program would encourage aspirants for the Franciscan sisterhood to obtain additional education elsewhere. The college admitted lay students on a full-time basis a decade later in 1969 and men in 1975. In the fall, Lourdes will offer its first, independent four-year programs, which were recently approved by their Ohio Board of Regents. Sienna Heights faculty members have been commuting from Adrian, Mich., to Lourdes for a joint, four-year business administration program. "We're extending all of the areas we have right now," Sister Marie Andree, acting president, said. The college will add 376 courses over the next four years in conjunction with its two new programs—the bachelor of individualized studies and the Bachelor of Arts in religious studies."

In September of 1982 the Franciscan Life Center on the Lourdes College campus was completed and employees of the Rudolph/Libbe Inc., and their families toured newly finished project. The building was constructed as a multi-purpose facility for the college as well as for the Sisters of St. Francis and general community events. The building contained more than 100 arches and was adorned with a number of dramatic ceramic mosaic murals that were created by three members of the Sisters of St. Francis community and were installed by masons from Rudolph/Libbe.

In July of 1983 Sister Ann Francis Klimkowski was named the president of Lourdes College. The Sisters of St. Francis reported that she carried on the visionary spirit of the foundress of Lourdes College, Mother Mary Adelaide Sandusky. Sister Ann Francis held a Master's Degree in business education from Bowling Green State University and received her Ph.D. in higher education from The University of Toledo in 1983. She had served Lourdes College as foundress and first director of the Life Long Learning Center that later became the Department of Continuing Education. In 1981 she became acting academic dean and in 1983 the president of Lourdes College.

From 1987 until 1995 enrollment at Lourdes College increased from 785 to 1,601 and they offered degrees in both Bachelor of Arts and Sciences. They developed programs that included a state approved teacher education degree and a basic nursing program. The Lourdes College graduating class of 1995 included students from 38 other cities, and under the leadership of Sister Ann Francis Klimkowski, they said that the college was expanding to meet the needs of the community, true to the Franciscan commitments and mission.

In 2000 The Sylvania Franciscans reported that their property on Convent Blvd. was in an area that had been devastated by the Emerald Ash Borer. They said that they had over 1,800 Ash trees on their property that were affected by the Ash Borer. Sister M. Jeremias Stinson was their expert and she created an Eight Step Pilot Program, which included research, identification, selected removal, treatment, and replacement. They were offering help to private landowners as well in order to conserve, maintain and improve the natural resources and environment through education and demonstration. They were requesting donations from area residents to help give them the resources to treat the Ash trees.

On 3-3-2001 the Inauguration of Dr. George C. Matthews, the sixth President of Lourdes College, was held on the Lourdes College campus.

Sister M. David Narog of the Sisters of St. Francis wrote the following in 2003 which is in the files of the Sylvania Historical Society: "Coming from Minneapolis, Minnesota to Sylvania, Ohio in 1932 a first impression was: "What a quaint, clean, story-book town. How reserved and quiet the people were. Walking down Main Street there was just a nod and a smile from them prompting the thought Sylvania must be a settlement of people from England. There was a brook flowing through the town, a town of about one long shopping block and another shorter one. Turning the corner at Convent Blvd., there was a Franciscan Convent. How different – all those trees. Where did they come from? Someone must have planted them – they're different. A few residential buildings stood along the street and about a block into the property was a Spanish – type building called St. Clare Academy. Upon inquiring, the convent had 89 acres. Now, that was a strong reminder of the more expansive Middle West. Yet, how Sylvania grew over the years! Businesses were established, homes, churches, and schools, both public and private were built. Parks and recreational centers sprang up. Quite Sylvania expanded on all sides and the new homes were filled with children of the future."

On 2-29-2004 the Board of Trustees, faculty staff, students and alumni of Lourdes College held the Inauguration of Robert C. Helmer, Ph.D. as the seventh President of Lourdes College at the Queen of Peace Chapel at Lourdes College. A reception followed at Franciscan Center Commons.

In December of 2006 the Sisters of Saint Francis celebrated their 90th Anniversary. In a letter that they sent to Sylvania area residents it reads: "celebrate with us by hanging this ornament on your tree, we, in turn, will hang the returned ornament on our tree. It will no longer be just an ornament but a pledge of prayers for you and your intentions. The ornament celebrates every season. Once the Christmas tree is taken down, the ornament continues in prayer. Each ornament is placed in a container near Rosary Care Chapel and remains there all year. Every time a Sister enters the Chapel she takes an ornament and prays for your intention(s). Celebrate our 90th Anniversary with us! As you think about a gift for your loved ones, please think of us. Supporting our diverse ministries including education and all levels of social work, human services, health care, counseling, religious education, parish and retreat ministry, food pantries, a foster home and a mission in Haiti. Together, we accomplish what neither of us could do alone. Blessings, Sister Carol Ann Grace, O.S.F., Development Director."

By 2009 the Sylvania Franciscan Sisters are a congregation of over 200 religious women serving in education, health and human services, parish work, social work, communications, the arts, administration, legal services and prison ministry. They serve principally in Northwest Ohio, Central Texas and Minnesota. The Sylvania Franciscans also sponsor Convent Park Apartments, adjacent to their Campus, and the Sylvania Franciscan Academy for pre-school to eighth grade students on Silica Road, the Franciscan Care Center on Holland-Sylvania Road and the Bethany House in Toledo as a long-term shelter for battered women and their children.

In December of 2009 the Sisters of St. Francis of Sylvania celebrated their 93rd anniversary as a women's religious community, and the founding of their Congregation. An anniversary celebration was held in which it was reported that in 1916 the Rochester Franciscans sent 23 teachers to staff three area schools, at the request of Toledo Bishop Joseph Schrembs. A year later the Sisters purchased 89 acres in Sylvania, where they established their Motherhouse. In honor of the occasion, the Sisters gathered in their dining room to celebrate and then attended mass in Our Lady Queen of Peace Chapel to give thanks for the past and reflect on the future. Sister Mary Jon Wagner, Assistant Congregational Minister, spoke to the gathering and invoked a favorite prayer of Mother Adelaide Sandusky, foundress of the Congregation.

In 2009 Lourdes was asked to take over operation of the Franciscan Academy from the Sisters of St. Francis who had opened the school in 1973. By the end of the school year of 2014, Lourdes University announced their plans to close the Franciscan Academy. This affected 172 students in grades kindergarten through eighth grade, as well as 23 full-time and 14 part-time staff.

In December of 2010 the Sylvania Franciscans celebrated 94 years, and in honor of this occasion more than 100 Sisters from this area gathered in the Rosary Care Center dining room on the Motherhouse grounds in Sylvania in celebration, and then attended Mass in Our Lady Queen of Peace Chapel to give thanks.

President Robert Helmer and the Sisters of St. Francis announced in August of 2011 that Lourdes College was now Lourdes University.

In April of 2012 the Rosary Care Center, a long-term care nursing facility for the Sisters of St. Francis of Sylvania, was ranked fifth out of more than 950 skilled nursing facilities in resident satisfaction by the Ohio Department on Aging. Cheryl King was the administrator of the Rosary Care Center. The center was built in 1975 and is a four-story, 76-bed, long term nursing facility for the older members of the Sisters of St. Francis, men and women from the Diocese of Toledo and in the fall of 2011 started allowing relatives of those in religious orders in the Toledo area.

In early March of 2013 David J. Livingston, PhD, was appointed the ninth President of Lourdes University. He was selected from 65 candidates and brought years of experience in Catholic Higher Education, a background both in science and Theology and a vision for Lourdes University and the Sylvania Franciscan Village. Dr. Livingston replaced the interim president, Dr. Janet Robinson.

The Sisters of St. Francis celebrated the 96th anniversary of the founding of their Congregation on Dec. 8, 2013. In honor of the occasion more than 100 Sisters from the area attended Mass in Our Lady Queen of Peace Chapel to give thanks for the past and reflect on the future.

In August 2013 the Sisters of St. Francis of Sylvania celebrated the Jubilees of 19 Sisters, Sister Julianna Sienko, celebrated 80 years as a Sylvania Franciscan. Sister M. David Narog, 75 years, Sister Julie Myers, 25 years. Those celebrating 60 years were Sister Jeanette Zielinski, Sister M. Austin Onisko, Sister Joan Jurski, Sister Eleanor Furman and Sister M. Gervase Lochotzki. Those celebrating 50 years were: Sister M. Jeremias Stinson, Sister Mary Thill, Sister Carol Ann Grace, Sister Patricia Zielinski, Sister Brenda Rose Szegedy, Sister Josina Antolak, Sister Dorothy Mrock, Sister Josephine Dybza, Sister Geraldine Nowak, Sister Carol Hoffman and Sister Janet Snyder.

In early August of 2013 Lourdes President David Livingston, Ph.D., appointed Geoffrey J. Grubb, Ph.D., as provost. The Interim Provost Keith Schlender, Ph.D., had retired in July of 2013. Dr. Grubbs started as a member of the Lourdes community 28 years ago. During his time at Lourdes he served from professor and chairperson of Religious Studies to Interim Vice President for Academic Affairs to most recently Dean of the College of Arts & Science.

In early April of 2014 work was completed on the $6.5 million expansion of Franciscan Care Center. The 25,000 square foot addition increases the total number of beds from 99 to 109, with 25 private suites reserved exclusively for short term rehabilitation residents. It was sponsored by the Sisters of St Francis.

On 5-30-2014 the Sylvania Chamber of Commerce sponsored a gala honoring Sister Jane Mary, who was inducted in the Distinguished Artists' Hall of Fame. This event was held in the train barn of the historical village.

On 5-30-2104 a friend of Sylvania history and a friend of the Sylvania Area Historical Society passed away. Sister M. Rosamond Jasinski was involved with the historical society for many years and was always interested in documenting our history and the history of the Sisters of St. Francis. According to her obituary notice, she passed away one month before she would have celebrated her 60th Jubilee as a Sister of St. Francis. She was born in Toledo, Ohio 3-22-1933 and her parents were Rose Staskiewicz and Wallace Jasinski. She entered the Sylvania Franciscan Order in June of 1951, after graduating from Central Catholic High School in Toledo and receiving the Bishop's Cross for excellence in religious studies and community service. She professed her first vows in August, 1954, and her final vows in August, 1957. Her obituary notice also said that she received her B.A. and M.A. degrees in Education and History from the University of Detroit after preliminary studies at Teresa's Extension College in Sylvania, and then she updated her theology at Lourdes College in Sylvania. After 35 years of teaching Sister Rosamond "was asked to establish the Development Office for the Sisters. She attended workshops provided by the National Catholic Development Conference in Chicago, St. Louis and Toronto, and then organized the Development Office for the Sisters and became a trained grant writer at which she was quite successful. She continued to research and write grants until a few months before her death. Sister Rosamond also organized and directed the Wholistic Resource Center for the Sisters."

In June of 2014 unknown vandals caused about $20,000 damage to the shrine and dozens of trees on the property of the Sisters of St. Francis. Also, someone randomly cut off tree limbs and spray-painted trunks and limbs of about 40 trees throughout the campus woodlands, trails and prayer garden area. They also damaged the baby Jesus statue in the nativity shrine, cutting the feet and part of a hand. It was reported that about 10 to 15 of the damaged trees were "reduced to sticks" and had to be cut down. The vandalized trees had been purchased through federal grants and private donations and the trees were difficult to replace. They said that nothing like this had happened on their property since in the early 1970s when someone pushed down 14 pillars from the fence line along Silica Drive and Convent Blvd.

The Blade of Toledo dated 7-18-2014 printed an article titled "St. Francis sisters lead tours of art" The article was written by Natalie Trusso Cafarello, Blade Staff Writer, and reported on the following: Sister Joan Jurski took a group of eight for a tour around the Motherhouse Grounds at 6832 Convent Blvd., next to Lourdes University buildings. It was reported that since the sisters settled in Sylvania in 1916 they had created a tapestry of art around the campus that reflected the spiritual roots of St. Francis. The group walked to the chapel of Our Lady Queen of Peace where at the foot of the door there was a blue-tiled bath with a serene water fall, representing the sacrament of baptism. She said that about 10,000 blue tiles cover the high-ceilinged chapel forming circular and square motifs, and patterned with symobils of the Virgin Mary. Before the altar there was a colorful San Damiano Cross, which was a replica of the crucifix to which St. Francis prayed. (The original relic was in the Basilica of Saint Clare in Assisi, Italy). The chapel had stained-glass windows with images of saints. There was a 35-foot wooden cross outside carved completely of black locust taken from the campus, and the only metal were the nails hammered into Jesus' hands and feet.

Sister Jane Mary Sorosiak was the resident ceramic mural artist whose works were nationally recognized. She shared her "Alverno Studio" with the art students until 2014 when she expanded her working space after some of the art rooms were moved to the old Franciscan Academy at 5335 Silica Drive.

The Blade of Toledo dated 7-19-2014 reported that: "The Sisters of St. Francis have announced the site of a Catholic elementary school that closed at the end of the school year will become home to Lourdes University programs and a Franciscan Health counseling center. Franciscan Academy is the former K-8 school operated by Lourdes University on property owned by the Sisters of St. Francis. Franciscan sisters founded the school in 1973, and the university took over operations in 2009. Sister Mary Jon Wagner, congregational minister, said the 36,600-square-foot building at 5335 Silica Dr. will be used for Lourdes University's fine arts program, admissions office, and some graduate classes. The university's graduate admissions office is currently in a trailer. In addition, the former school will house some services of Sophia Center, also located on the Sisters' Motherhouse Grounds. The counseling center is a part of Sylvania Franciscan Health, sponsored by the sisters."

In March of 2015 Sister Gretchen Faerber, 77, was holding her Easter bake sale at Lourdes University for the 25th year. Her bake sales over the years raised funds for the many ministries that the Sisters of St. Francis supported. She said that it all started with a Christmas bake sale that was hosted in November of 1990.

Sylvania Franciscan Sister Rosine Sobczak was honored for her 25 years of partnering with environmentally friendly people to draw attention to the need to be more aware of our environment. In 1990 she co-founded a group called SAVE (Science Alliance for Valuing the Environment) to help educate people to what we are doing to the world we live in. Each year they hold an award ceremony to thank individuals for what they are doing to improve the environment.

Sister Jane Mary Sorosiak received the 2015 Franciscan Federation award for "Reflecting the beauty and goodness of God" through her artistic expression as a ceramic mural artist. Sister Jane Mary entered the Sylvania Franciscans in 1955. She taught for two years and then was the first art teacher at Cardinal Stritch High School, and taught there for 14 years, before joining the staff of Lourdes College, as an assistant professor of art, and taught an additional 27 years. She began making ceramic murals and today she had more than 100 pieces hanging in places such as the lobby of St. Joseph Hospital in Bryan Texas, and St. Raphael Church in Garden City, Michigan, the Knights of Columbus Hall in Fishkill, N.Y. and St. Andrew Russian Greek Church in Segundo, California.

The First August 2015 issue of the *Sylvania Advantage* reported the following: "Lourdes University President David J. Livingston, Ph.D., and Board of Trustees Chair, Ernest C. Enrique, announced the ground breaking ceremony of the Russell J. Ebeid Recreation Center, which encompasses the second phase of its Mid-Campus Expansion project. The groundbreaking ceremony will begin at 2 p.m. on Sept. 2, 2015 at the Convent Blvd. entrance of the mid-campus in Sylvania, Ohio. Light refreshments will be served. The Russell J. Ebeid Recreation Center will feature indoor competition-level basketball and volleyball courts, home and visiting locker rooms, training rooms, Gray Wolves suite, ticket office, concession area, two-story atrium with mezzanine level, spirit wall, and offices for coaches. Fitness components include cardio, yoga, free weight, aerobics and spinning rooms; and classrooms. The facility will open in fall 2016. The nearly 49,000 square foot facility was designed by Stough & Stough Architects with an eye toward possible future expansion. Seating capacity for games is projected at 1,000." Another report after the groundbreaking was held said that the goal of the Mid-Campus Expansion was to connect the university's academic and campus life facilities. The first phase established a lighted pathway and landscaped grounds, lacrosse and soccer practice fields, green space, a fire pit and spirit rock.

In 2016 a second retail business was opened, which they called All Good Things II, in the Rosary Care Center on the grounds of the Sisters of St. Francis. The original store was opened in 2009 in the Madonna Hall where a couple of Sisters made and sold greeting cards and artwork. Over time additional items were added for sale and they started selling additional artworks made by the Sisters, to include prayer pillows, paintings, handcrafted jewelry, clay-fired tiles, scented lotions and soaps, and hand-painted scarves.

In March of 2016 Mayor Craig Stough and Sylvania City Council of the City of Sylvania presented the Sisters of St. Francis a proclamation to commemorate their 100th anniversary year. Those present from the leadership team of the Sisters of St. Francis of Sylvania, at the public meeting, where the award was presented included: Sister Rachel Nijakowski, Councilor; Sister Theresa Darga, assistant congregational minister; Sister Pat Gardner, congregational treasurer/councilor; and Sister Mary Jon Wagner, congregational minister.

In June of 2016 Lourdes University named Mary Ann Gawelek their 10th president effective 7-1-2016. She replaced David Livingston, who was leaving as of 6-30-2016, to become president of Lewis University, in a suburb of Chicago. Ms. Gawelek had served for 20 years at Seton Hill University in Greensburg, Pennsylvania, where she was most recently their provost. She had also served as their dean of faculty, and was a professor of psychology.

The newly built Russell J. Ebeid athletic facility opened their doors in September of 2016. Part of this facility was built on property that used to be the site of the old Sylvania school bus garages and office of transportation off Brint Road, and extending north to Convent Blvd. Russell J. Ebeid was the retired president of Guardian Glass Group. Stough & Stough Architects designed the building, Kurt Miller and David Spalding were the project supervisors and Lisa Babich was the project manager working for Miller Diversified, the general contractor.

In September 2016 a Sylvania Franciscan Centennial Gala banquet was held in honor of the 100th anniversary of the Sisters of St. Francis in Sylvania. Three people were granted Franciscan awards at this event. The event started with a Mass in Our Lady Queen of Peace Chapel and the gala followed at the Franciscan Center. Tickets were sold for $100 each.

In December of 2016 the Sylvania Franciscans (Sisters of St. Francis of the Congregation of Our Lady of Lourdes) held a special mass at the Queen of Peace Chapel on the motherhouse grounds where sisters from Northwest Ohio and the nation gathered to celebrate the 100th anniversary of their religious order. Their day consisted of the Mass, presided at the Mass was the Most Rev. Daniel Thomas, Bishop of the Diocese of Toledo, then a luncheon and dinner event. The invited guests and a program hosted by retired Ohio Supreme Court Justice Judy Ann Lanzinger, who had a special connection to the sisters. Although she did not take final vows, she was part of the St. Francis community in her youth. A couple of days later the sisters had a luncheon scheduled at the Rosary Care Center for the sisters there. The centennial year started with a Mass on Dec. 8, 2015, then celebrations on Feb. 11, the feast day of Our Lady of Lourdes; July 16, the anniversary of their founder Mother Adelaide's first vows; Aug. 11, the feast day of St. Clare; and Oct. 4, the feast day of St. Francis.

The assistant congregation minister for the Sisters of St. Francis, Theresa Darga, was in her 49th year with the Sisters and Sister Shannon Schrein, a councilor on the sisters' five-person leadership team, came in 1965 when she was 15 years old. The following year, in 1966, they celebrated the 50th anniversary of the congregation.

Two longtime members of the Sisters of St. Francis of Sylvania community were honored during the 100 year anniversary for their significant contributions to the Sisters of St. Francis community and what is now known as Lourdes University. Sister Marie Andree Chorzempa and Sister Ann Francis Klimkowski were the two that were honored. Sister Marie Andree took on the beginning process of growing Lourdes College from a two-year institution to a four-year college during her tenure as president, and Sister Ann Francis took over the office of president in 1983 and implemented the move to four-year status during her two years as president.

In June of 2017 Sister M. Dominica Niedbala and Sister M. Rose deLima Kott celebrated 75 years as a Sister of St. Francis. Sisters Adrienne Urban, Kathleen Ottrock, Patricia Simpson, and Ruth Margaret Peterson celebrated 60 years. Sisters M. Jordan Schaefer, Mary Ann Szydlowski, Nancy Ferguson, M. St. Anthony Chrzanak, and Theresa Darga celebrated 50 years.

The Blade, Toledo, Ohio, dated Saturday, 4-21-2018 featured an article in the Religion section of their newspaper titled: "Stretching to the heaven" by Nicki Gorny, Blade Staff Writer. This article praised the work of Sister M. Jeremias Stinson, superintendent of the environmental stewardship, gardens, shrines, and woodland management for the grounds of the Sisters of St. Francis on Convent Blvd. Sister Jeremias was reported as the 74-year-old nun who zipped around the grounds on a John Deere Gater. She gave the reporter a sampling of the more than 5,000 mature trees that shaded the grounds, which included oaks, firs, and pines, with 250 native species in all, which she had mapped and documented. Sister Jeremias said that the motherhouse property holds the distinction of having the most diverse number of plant specimens in the region. The grounds were also recognized as a conservation sanctuary, as approved in 1930 by the Lucas County Conservation District and Ohio Forestry Division. This article said that Sister Jeremias had overseen the grounds since 1974, when she submitted a proposal to leave her position as a local school teacher and work full time at keeping the grounds, developing the shrines, paths and other landscape elements of the campus. Sister Jeremias said that Mother Adelaide led the original sisters who established this convent in Sylvania in 1916, and she said that when the 89 acres was purchased much of it was farmland and the rest was natively wooded. Mother Adelaide took it upon herself to obtain and plant trees on the campus to stabilize sandy hills, create windbreaks and fulfill other practical functions. In 2006 the emerald ash borer killed off 1,841 trees on the campus and she replanted an area that she called the "new woods" on the grounds near Ten Mile Creek. The article ended by Sister Jeremias saying: "I followed her footprint," she said of Mother Adelaide."

STRAWBERRY PICKING IN SYLVANIA

Strawberries in Sylvania go back many years because of the many areas with sandy soil, which drains well. In the early days, just about every farm in Sylvania had their patches of strawberries, and within the village just about everyone had at least a row of berries along their rear property line.

Myself, growing up on Main Street in downtown Sylvania in the 1960s and 1970s, we could walk behind the Sterling's store (today where the historical village is located) where there was a big open field, and we could pick strawberries that were growing wild there. To this day I've never tasted any strawberries as good as those. They were small, but so good.

Some of the farmers in Sylvania grew strawberries for a living. A couple of the names of residents in Sylvania that had many acres of strawberries included: George Deer, who lived at 5071 S. Main Street, but owned farmland along Harroun Road at Holland-Sylvania Road where he grew strawberries; Matthew Fuhrer, whose farm was near the northeast corner of Central and Centennial (now the mobile home park, Centennial Manor); Burt Fuhrer, whose farm was along Holland-Sylvania Road; Romain and Harold Creque, whose farm was (is) on Central Avenue at the western border of the township; Albert and Anna Reed on Brint Road. I'm sure there were more, but these were the well-known ones.

Mr. Fuhrer hauled his berries into Toledo to sell. Family records say that he had to get up at midnight, hitch his horses up to the loaded wagons and travel the old country roads down Monroe Street in order to get to the market in downtown Toledo in time for the market to open. Mr. Fuhrer brought so many strawberries, for so many years, that at the market he became known as the "Strawberry King."

Both Mr. Deer and Mr. Fuhrer were the early strawberry growers in this area and would hire local young boys and girls in the summertime to help with the picking, and they would pay them a fee for each quart they picked.

Mr. and Mrs. Burt Fuhrer were good employers according to the *Sylvania Sentinel* dated 7-17-1919, which said: "STRAWBERRY PICKERS PICNIC – Thursday, July 10th Mr. and Mrs. Burt Fuhrer took a truck load of jolly strawberry pickers to Toledo Beach. They were the pickers who stayed by them during the season and picked when strawberries were scarce as well as when the vines were loaded with fruit. Burt spared no pains or expense to see that they had a good time while there."

Back in the 1930s and 1940s Albert and Anna Reed had a large field of strawberries behind their house in the 7000 block of Brint Road (south side). According to an article in the *Bend of the River* magazine, in the April 2002 issue, Rachel Stanton, the granddaughter of Albert and Anna Reed wrote the following about picking strawberries for her grandmother in Sylvania: "As soon as school was out for the summer we knew strawberry picking would come in a week or two. It made a short vacation but it was the only way we teenagers had to earn money. Grandma Reed hired everyone and there would be ten to twenty picking strawberries for her. I don't remember exactly how much of her garden farm was planted to berries, but I know we picked every day until sometime in July. Two persons worked a row with one picking on each side. Many times kids would work ahead of their partner and found it impossible to resist reaching across a row to select larger berries—they filled the basket faster! We were each given a wooden carrier that held eight empty quart baskets. As a quart was filled it was set under a strawberry bush. At the end of a row, or when our eight baskets were filled we took them to the makeshift tent set up for that purpose. Salaries were meager by today's wage scale. We were paid from three cents to ten cents a quart and at the peak of the season could pick about 100 quarts a day. The competition was evident with adults trying to exceed the kid's efforts. To avoid mosquitoes, or any other insects I wore my dad's coveralls with a rubber band around my ankles and wrists to keep the bugs out. Of course we all wore straw hats. After picking a row in the hot Northwestern Ohio sun we were anxious to take the full baskets to grandma's tent. She wrote the number of quarts picked on a pay card and at the end of the day we were paid for what we had picked. The tent was usually found under a tree and cold drinking water refreshed our thirst before returning to the patch. Near the end of the season, when days were especially hot and humid, we worked in the mornings. . . .My brother and I accompanied grandad to Toledo's city market to sell the crates of fresh strawberries. This meant we were up at 5 a.m. and at the downtown Toledo market for the 6 a.m. opening. Hucksters and grocery men inspected the berries and bargained with grandad on his price. At the height of the season we would be offered $5 a crate or maybe $3, if the weather was hot and humid so that the berries were spoiling, or they could sell for as much as $10 a crate at the end of the season when only a few gardeners were at the market. Many times we were at market for a short time. Once the bell rang to open the gates to start selling and buying a load could be sold in minutes"

Harold and Romain Creque, brothers, are the more recent farmers in Sylvania known for their strawberries. They grew their grain and tomatoes, but they are most popular for their strawberry patch and stand. They started this in the late 1950s and within a few years they were selling berries from a stand on Central Avenue and later on Sylvania Avenue. They also had a pick-your-own strawberry patch and many area residents would come out every year for that until that business slowly died, because the people of today just don't have the time to do that anymore. But the family continues on with the business and you can still purchase their strawberries at their roadside store.

The *Sylvania Advantage* newspaper for July of 2012 featured a picture of Creque's strawberry fields and reads: "It's Strawberry Picking Time at Creque's – L-R: Cousins Sally Micsko, Teddy, Charlie, Henry and Louie Walker spent their first day of summer vacation picking strawberries at Creque's. Later, they made strawberry jam for their families and to use as gifts."

Wilma J. Creque passed away on 12-10-2013 and according to her obituary notice that appeared in *The Blade* of Toledo she assisted with work on the family farm for years and enjoyed talking to the many customers that came to purchase strawberries. Her husband was Romain Creque who passed away in 2009.

SYLVAN SERENADERS

This was a group of guys from Sylvania who organized a band and played at various events, as hired. According to an article in the *Sylvania Sentinel* this group organized in 1935.

An article in the *Sylvania Sentinel* on 1-21-1937 said that the Sylvan Serenaders were planning a gala event for the Fourth Annual President's Ball. The ball was being held at the Burnham High School Auditorium. The article said: "Stan Hesselbart and his Sylvan Serenaders, who have charge of the affair this year, will provide the music and entertainment for the evening. . . " The article went on to explain that these annual community gatherings were held throughout the nation to provide funds to carry on the work of the Warm Springs Foundation in Georgia, and also to provide funds to aid in work among local victims of infantile paralysis, as 70% of the receipts stay in the communities.

The 12-12-1940 *Sylvania Sentinel* reported: "Stanley Hesselbart and his orchestra, who recently opened the Band Box Ballroom, are announcing an "Early Bird" admission price of 25 cents between 8:30 and 9:00 p.m. After that time the admission is 35 cents."

An advertisement appeared in the 1941 Burnham High School Yearbook that reads: "Stan Hesselbart his Sylvan Serenaders and the Band Box Ballroom." It was in November of 1941 that the group first started the Band Box Ballroom.

Soon after the group started playing on the second floor of the Sylvania Savings Bank (5604 Main) Joseph Bissonnette started playing with the group and according to an article written about Mr. Bissonnette "He is noted for his scat singing with the Sylvan Serenaders, the local dance orchestra in which he plays the saxophone."

The 11-10-1941 *Sylvania Sentinel* reported the following: "Stan Hesselbart and his orchestra are announcing the opening of the Band Box Ballroom Saturday, November 15. The hall, located above the Sylvania Savings Bank, has been undergoing redecorating and painting and an attractive sign has been posted on the outside. Admission will be 35 cents and dancing will be from 9 to 1 o'clock. Members of the orchestra are Stan Hesselbart, Bruce Beveridge, Bill Burnes, Charles Quinnell, Mel Snyder, Joe Follas, Larry Miller and Betty Souder, vocalist."

A family history written about Bruce W. Beveridge said that: "He played tuba in the Sylvania Village Band. Later he played string bass with Stan Hesselbart's Sylvan Serenaders, a big-band era dance band popular in northwest Ohio, Indiana and Michigan before World War II. The band regrouped after the war and played for many dances in the area."

Within seven months of starting the Band Box Ballroom events, the head of the group, Stanley Hesselbart was inducted into the Army. The following article appeared in the *Sylvania Sentinel* on 7-23-1942: "The address of Stanley Hesselbart, who was inducted into the Army recently, is: Flight B, 357th T.S.S. (Spe) Army Air Corps, Jefferson Barracks, Mo." Stan writes that he considers himself lucky to get into the air corps, that the food is fine and the weather extremely warm."

In August of 1942 Stanley Hesselbart wrote a letter to Mr. and Mrs. Quinnell who published it in their *Sylvania Sentinel* newspaper under the column titled "The Mail Bag." In the letter Stanley wrote, in part: ".....I Miss the band very much, but then I guess you can't expect to get over things like that overnight." Under that same column titled "The Mail Bag," Stanley wrote often with a new address for his friends to keep in touch with him while away.

The 1-28-1943 *Sylvania Sentinel* reported the following: "Sgt. Stanley Hesselbart was the guest of honor at a party Saturday evening in the home of Mr. and Mrs. Charles Quinnell. The event brought together a group who had played together as an orchestra for seven years, until some of the boys had been called in to service. Those enjoying the evening of entertainment were Mr. and Mrs. Joe Follas, Mr. and Mrs. Harold Snyder, Malcolm Snyder, Toledo, Maurice Barden, Lyons, the guest of honor and Mr. and Mrs. Quinnell."

Finally the 10-18-1945 issue of the *Sylvania Sentinel* reported the following: "STANLEY HESSELBART NOW DISCHARGED – T/Sgt. Stanley R. Hesselbart, son of Mr. and Mrs. Clifton Hesselbart, 6768 Erie Street, arrived home last Sunday morning with his discharge from the Army. Stan, who worked in the Sylvania Savings Bank before his induction into the Army, spent three years and four months in service, and arrived overseas on 3-22-1944. The Bronze Star was awarded to Stanley for his excellent work as assistant to the Base Administrative Inspector. His efficient assistance to the administration and supply clerks of the various squadrons in the group formed a distinct contribution to the success of the Ninth Air Force tactical air power. He was attached to the 397th B-26 Marauder Bombardment Group, famed as the "Bridge Busters." His group, commanded by Lieutenant Colonel Jimmie W. Britt, earned the name of Bridge Busters by knocking out 9 of the 14 bridges destroyed behind the invasion coast of France in the single week before D-Day. They established a medium bombardment record for the European theater of Operations by flying 100 missions in 119 days. The group was awarded six bronze battle stars for participation in major ETO campaigns"

The following appeared in the *Sylvania Sentinel* in the 11-8-1945 issue: "Stanley Hesselbart who spent 19 months overseas with the 599th Bombing Squadron is back at his old job now in the Sylvania Savings Bank. No doubt he is glad to be back and we know that the bank is glad to have him back."

TELEPHONES IN SYLVANIA

They say that the telephone system replaced the gossip you heard around the pot-bellied stove at the rear of our town stores.

The earliest mention of telephone service in Sylvania was in the minute book of Sylvania Village Council on 5-15-1885. On that date council granted a right-of-way to the Michigan Bell Telephone Company to set up telephone poles and string lines "from the Sylvania Corporation limits on Adrian Road (North Main Street) to Erie Street; on Erie Street to Summit Street; along Summit Street to Ottawa (Monroe Street) and then east to the corporation limits."

Alexander Graham Bell, from Scotland, came to the United States in 1871 and by 1874 had developed the idea of the telephone. He was a teacher of the deaf in Boston and at night he experimented with a harmonic telegraph, a device for sending several telegraph messages at one time over one wire. On 6-2-1875, one of the metal reeds of the harmonic telegraph stuck. Bell's assistant, Thomas A. Watson, plucked the sound in his receiver. He realized that the vibrations of the reed had caused variations of electric current. On 3-10-1876, Bell finally succeeded in speaking words over the telephone. He was about to test a new transmitter. In another room, Watson waited for the test message. When suddenly, Bell spilled some acid from a battery on his clothes. He cried out: "Mr. Watson, come here. I want you!" Watson heard every word clearly and rushed into the room. Bell had invented the first successful telephone. In June of 1876, Bell exhibited his telephone at the Centennial Exposition in Philadelphia. Scientists praised his work, but the public showed little interest until early in 1877, when Bell gave many telephone demonstrations.

Alexander Graham Bell, Thomas A. Watson, Gardiner G. Hubbard and Thomas Sanders formed the Bell Telephone Company in 1877. Hubbard was Bell's father-in-law, and Sanders was the father of one of Bell's pupils. They had helped pay for Bell's experiments. In 1878, the first telephone exchange opened in New Haven, Conn., it had 21 customers. Soon exchanges opened throughout the United States.

In 1878, two companies were formed as successors to the Bell Telephone Company: The New England Telephone Company and a new Bell Telephone Company. The New England Telephone Company licensed in telephone service in New England, and the Bell Telephone Company licensed phone service in the rest of the United States.

So, on 5-15-1883 the Michigan Bell Telephone Company was granted the right of way to set up poles and string lines in the Sylvania corporation limits. Then on 5-4-1901 William E. Chapple was granted another telephone right-of-way.

At first, telephone operators switched telephone calls manually by plugging electric cords into a switchboard. The first telephone exchange or telephone switchboard office was located in the back of William E. Chapple's store which was also the post office and his newsstand. Mr. Chapple's newsstand was located in downtown Sylvania in the building we know as 5621 Main Street. Mr. Chapple operated his newsstand at this location from 1887 until 1909. Between the years 1901 and 1909 Mr. Chapple also served as postmaster of Sylvania. It is unknown exactly what years the switchboard was located at this location, and originally there were two telephone companies in Sylvania. In 1914 the two companies merged into one to be known as Sylvania Home Telephone Company. Other locations of the telephone switchboard offices in Sylvania include:

5633 Main Street in the Masonic Temple Building on the second floor, in the front;

5693 Main Street – The building on the southwest corner of Main and Maplewood, on the second floor;

5689 Main Street – when the telephone switchboard was located here it was the Sylvania Savings Bank;

5694 Main Street – after 1907 – building on the southeast corner of Main and Maplewood, on the second floor where the bay window is located

5645 Main Street – PHC Hall – according to a 1921 newspaper article;

6511 Maplewood Avenue from 1914 to 1947;

6627 Maplewood Avenue from 1947 to current – Ohio Associated Telephone Company, General Telephone Co. of Ohio and then Verizon.

In an article that appeared in the *Sylvania Sentinel* on 12-24-1936, written by Albert H. Randall, he wrote a letter giving a mental picture of Main Street as it looked about fifty years earlier. He described the west side of Main Street before it was destroyed by the fire of 1887. Mr. Randall begins by describing the buildings beginning with Pop Polley's Saloon at the NW corner of Main and Monroe Streets and heading north. In one part of the article he says: "Next was the W.D. Moore Drug Store. Later this was run by Dr. Hanks and his brother Dallas. This store was the first long distance telephone station in Sylvania, and I remember Dr. Hanks calling my mother into the store to show her the telephone. To prove to her that she could really hear a voice over the wire from Toledo, the doctor called Toledo and got the operator to talk to my mother. Even then she would not believe it, but told him he had someone in the next room doing the talking. She often recalled that experience."

In an article written by Kathryn Keller in the *Sylvania Sentinel* on 1-29-1975 titled: "When Telephones came to the Sylvania Area." She begins: "There's an old story that tells of the time a beloved and highly respected lady in the community came into a Sylvania store where the proprietor was talking on his newly installed telephone, one of the first in town. He asked the lady if she too would like to talk to Toledo. She put the receiver to her ear and she heard a voice. "But you can't make me believe I'm talking to Toledo. It's somebody in your back room who's talking." In another part of this same article she said: "To get some perspective, time-wise, the incident of the lady talking to Toledo supposedly took place in Dr. Hanks' Drug Store. Dr. Hank died in 1895."

The following information was reported in the minutes of the Sylvania History Buffs on 4-18-1975: "There were many of the Sylvania girls who were telephone operators, among them were Lucella Randall Hall, Margaret Calkins, Marguerite Griest, Elsie Comstock Hine, Jane Eley and her assistant Barbara Farley. Maynard Cosgrove was once a telephone operator. The first telephone was installed in A.R. Chandler's Hardware store on Main St. It was a wall telephone that had to be cranked to get the attention of the operator. His phone number, of course, was #1. Dr. E.E. Armstrong's telephone number was #2. Mrs. Mayme Donald was the telephone operator at the time the Marshal Walter Beebe was shot in the belt buckle by a burglar in the Myers building. He shot one of them, who was found three hours later dead on Wagonlander's lawn, two doors west of Dr. Armstrong's place on Maplewood Ave. The other burglar got away. They were from Detroit."

Now back to the minute book of Sylvania Village Council. On 3-4-1901 village council granted William E. Chapple a telephone right-of-way and he operated a switchboard in the back of his post office. In reviewing the Sylvania Township Trustee minute books from 1880 to 1928, the first time the Trustees paid for phone services was in May of 1903; to Home Telephone Company. They paid $1.40 per month at first and then they continued to pay Home Phone Company approximately $1.00 per month for many years. Most of the time the checks were made payable to the Home Phone Company, but occasionally they were be made payable to Sylvania Phone Company. Beginning in 1917, all checks were issued to the Sylvania Home Telephone Company through 1928.

On 9-26-1906 Sylvania Village Council granted a right-of-way to Whiteford Telephone Company. Within ten years after the second telephone company was organized the two companies merged and became Sylvania Home Telephone Company.

Mathias Lochbihler was the President of the Sylvania Home Telephone Company and founded the company. He was also affiliated with the Sylvania Savings Bank. Dwight O. Washburn was the Secretary/Treasurer of the Sylvania Home Telephone Company, and he was also affiliated with the Sylvania Savings Bank. When Mr. Lochbihler first began operating a telephone switchboard in the building at 5689 Main Street, in downtown Sylvania, that building was owned by Sylvania Savings Bank.

In 1907 the Sylvania Savings Bank constructed a new bank building across the street on the southeast corner of Main and Maplewood and then the telephone company's switchboard was located on the second floor of that building for a period of time. The bay window on the second floor, on the south side of the building, was where the telephone switchboard was located.

An article in the *Sylvania Sentinel* on 2-11-1910 says: "BOOST IT ALONG – Manufacturing Company Wants to Locate Here: A representative of the Dayton Telephone Lockout Manufacturing Co., of Dayton, Ohio will be in Sylvania next Wednesday evening to confer with the citizens of this place regarding the building of a plant here. While there are several systems of a like nature on the market, this system is the only one operating without a ground. Mr. Charles Gries, the local manager of the Home Telephone Co., says he has two lines equipped with their system and during the four months they have been in use they have given entire satisfaction. So far the work of the company has been largely experimental and they had the apparatus manufactured for them by large electrical concerns. However, the experimental stage has been passed and the device has proven a genuine success. The company now wishes to reap the profits that are bound to accrue through the sales of this device and wish to manufacture it themselves, having refused numberless offers for the purchase of the invention. The company became interested in placing the plant in Sylvania through Mr. Charles Gries and when the time arrived for their taking over the complete manufacture they decided to come here and see if the people of Sylvania wanted such an industry. This system makes it possible for two persons on a party line to converse without others on the same line being able to hear. The business is in its infancy and is bound to bring great returns. Investors all over the world have worked for years to perfect such a device. Such a manufacturing concern would advertise Sylvania throughout the world and be the means of bringing other industries to this place. They will employ from 25 to 30 people, mostly skilled labor. The company is not looking for a donation. They wish to incorporate under the laws of the state and wish to sell enough of their stock to local investors to insure its location here. Come to the Exhibition Company's hall next Wednesday evening, see the system demonstrated and hear the plan explained."

At the 1910 census of Sylvania township and village indicates that the following individuals were listed working as telephone employees:

Edgar Bell – 32 years – manager – telephone employee – dwelling #111
Jesse Peck – 28 years – lineman – telephone – dwelling # 47.
William Barton – 46 years – laborer – telephone employee – dwelling #38.
Charles Gries – 29 years - manager – telephone company – dwelling #140.
Bessie Jones – 18 years - operator – telephone company – dwelling #143.

An article in the *Sylvania Sentinel* on 11-14-1912 reads: "The Sylvania Home Telephone Company is enjoying a healthy growth. During the past month twenty new phones were added to the local exchange."

The following news article appeared in the *Sylvania Herald* on 12-5-1912 as follows: "Changed at Local Telephone Office - Miss Gladys Vesey, who for some time has been in charge of the local telephone exchange, has resigned her position, taking effect Monday of this week. Her place is filled by Miss Bessie Jones, who needs no introduction to Sylvania phone users. Miss Vesey and her brother Stanley expect to leave Saturday for Phoenix, Arizona where they are suited with the country they will make their home. They will be accompanied on the trip by Gordon Pelton, whose brother Floyd is in Arizona."

According to the minutes of the Sylvania Masonic Lodge, a telephone company in Sylvania by the name of Central Union Telephone Company occupied the front three office rooms in the Masonic Temple Building (5633 Main Street). In January of 1907, John C. Jones, Attorney at Law, began leasing the three front office rooms on the second floor of the Masonic Lodge Building. In July 1907 John C. Jones surrendered his lease for the three office rooms and made arrangements for the Central Union Telephone Company to take over the lease and in fact, Central Union Telephone Company signed up for a ten year lease at $100 per year, payable monthly in advance and a free telephone would be placed anywhere the Masonic lodge members directed. The lease began 8-1-1907.

In reviewing the minutes of the Sylvania Masonic Lodge, the next time this telephone company is mentioned is in their minutes on 3-14-1908 when their records show receiving $8.35 from Citizens Telephone for lease payment for February of 1908.

There is no mention of the telephone company again until the minutes of 6-25-1910 when a motion was made and seconded, that "the Secretary be instructed to inform Mr. Ford, President of People's Home Telephone Company, occupying the front rooms of the hall to vacate at once." The motion carried. It is not known why they were being asked to vacate the building. There is no mention in the minutes after that date as to whether they did vacate.

A notice in the *Sylvania Sentinel* on 12-19-1912 reported: "The local telephone office will be closed on Christmas Day from twelve until two p.m., in order to give the force a little time to enjoy the holiday."

On 3-3-1913, but not officially recorded with the Lucas County Auditor's office until 1-14-1914, Lavern Moore sold the Sylvania Home Telephone Company the west 48 feet of Lot 45 in the Whiteford Division in the village of Sylvania. They then constructed the building at 6611 Maplewood Avenue on that parcel. On 7-7-1930 this property transferred into the name of Ohio Associated Phone Company.

According to the obituary notice of Mathias Lochbihler in the *Toledo Blade* on 5-27-1939: "Mr. Lochbihler was active in the telephone business in Richfield Center and Sylvania for 25 years before selling out his interests to the Ohio Bell Telephone Company 15 years ago. Mr. Lochbihler founded the Sylvania Telephone Company."

According to old-timers of Sylvania Charley Gries was the telephone company back in the early days. They said: "He was one of those all-around mechanical marvels, before our age of specialization, who could do anything and everything. He set poles, strung lines, installed service, repaired instruments and knew the switchboard like the back of his hand."

The *Sylvania Sentinel* listed the following classified ad in their newspaper on 2-26-1914: "WANTED – a telephone operator, from 4 until 8 p.m. Call Sylvania Home Telephone Co."

The following sentence appeared in the *Sylvania Sentinel* in March of 1916 under the "News Items of Local Interest" column: "Mrs. Tuttle, chief operator at the telephone office is quite seriously ill with pneumonia."

At the 1920 census taken in the village and township of Sylvania the following individuals were listed as working for the telephone company under the column of "occupation":

<u>Charles Gries</u> – 38 years – lineman for telephone company.

<u>Carlie M. Follas</u> – daughter (of James B. Follas) – 18 years – telephone operator.

<u>Mary A. Donald</u> – 42 years – widow – chief operator.

<u>Mildred L. Williams</u> – 17 years – step-daughter (of Leander Sheldon) – telephone operator.

<u>Beulah M. Beebe</u> – 16 years – daughter (of Otto Beebe) – operator.

<u>Dolores J. LaVigne</u> – 15 years – daughter (of Jerry B. LaVigne) – operator

<u>Pearl D. Cooper</u> – 20 years – married (to Harry Cooper) – telephone operator.

<u>Lucille L. Ferguson</u> – 18 years – single – telephone operator.

<u>Flora A. Rush</u> – 23 years – daughter (of Benham Rush) – telephone operator.

In the 11-11-1920 issue of the *Sylvania Sentinel* the following was reported: "The telephone office will be closed on Thanksgiving day from 12 until 2 in the afternoon, so that the operators may have dinner."

In 1921 Mayme Donald, night telephone operator, saw a suspicious looking stranger in town and alerted Marshal Walter Beebe. A shoot out on Main Street followed.

The clerk of the Village of Sylvania sent a letter to the Sylvania Home Telephone Company of Sylvania, Ohio dated 1-19-1924 which said: "You are hereby requested by village council to remove a telephone pole located in front of the driveway of Heber Howard's property on Monroe Street at your earliest convenience."

On 11-7-1925 the clerk of the Village of Sylvania sent a letter to the Public Utilities Commission of Ohio in Columbus, Ohio stating that regarding the joint application of the Sylvania Home Telephone Company and the Sylvania Telephone Company No. 3870, the village officials had no objections.

The *Toledo News Bee* newspaper – 10-28-1926: "SYLVANIA PHONE POLES REMOVED – Underground Conduit System Completed – Telephone poles along Main St. were cut down and carted away Wednesday under the direction of Max Lochbihler, manager of the Sylvania Telephone Co. This marked the completion of the underground conduit system which has been installed during the summer. Most of the lines have already been cut over, and within a few days the new system will be in use. Organized in 1901, this exchange has progressed, with several changes of ownership, to its present capacity, with 450 subscribers. The new fireproof building has been occupied a year. The old type of telephone which necessitated ringing as a signal to the operator, is being eliminated from all private lines. More than 16,000 feet of cable have been laid to conduct the lines underground."

On 12-31-1926 the Sylvania Home Telephone Company changed ownership to the Sylvania Telephone Company.

The following article appeared in the *Sylvania Sentinel* on 2-17-1927: "PHONE OFFICIALS ARE ENTERTAINED - Inspect New Local Exchange of Sylvania Company - Members of the Northwestern Ohio Telephone Association composed of officials and representatives of the telephone companies in Lucas and Williams counties and southern Michigan were entertained at the new plant of the Sylvania Telephone Co., on Tuesday. After an inspection of the exchange a luncheon was served by the local operators in the P.H.C. Hall. A business meeting was held in the hall. Among those who attended the meeting were: F.J. Spencer, president, Wauseon; A.B. Lathrop, treasurer, Swanton; Mr. and Mrs. C.E. Smith, secretary, Morenci; Mr. Gross of the Nagel Electric Co.; Messrs. Sullivan and Souppe of the Gratbar Electric Co.; Mr. Farnsworth, Waterville; Mr. Feller of the Ohio Bell Co."

In January of 1981 James Armstrong, a life-long resident of Sylvania, was asked to tape record some of his Sylvania history knowledge, experiences and memories. James Armstrong was born in Sylvania in the home at 6502 Maplewood Avenue in 1913. He lived at this address his entire life, except when he was forced, because of health reasons, to move to Bryan, Ohio to live with his daughter. Jim Armstrong's father was Edwin Armstrong, a doctor in Sylvania from 1903 until he died in 1942. His mother was Myrtle DeMuth Armstrong, who was the long-time music teacher working for the Sylvania school system for over 30 years; riding her horse and buggy from one room schoolhouse to one room schoolhouse teaching music to the children of Sylvania. They were a very well-known family and the entire Armstrong family was known for their love for music. Mr. Armstrong made a total of nine "cassette" tape recordings of himself and the following was one of the items that he discussed: "Another person in Sylvania that I remember very vividly, and I consider him an institution, was Charlie Gries, and I called him Mr. Telephone. When Charlie took over the telephone business, this one man, a wiry man, who spoke out of the side of his mouth and he didn't use his lips very much, he kind of spoke in satirical terms, but very likeable underneath, quick in his action, quick movements, and not very sociable, but Charlie worked out of a small barn located where the City of Sylvania has their big implements stored just north of that storage building which is located on Summit Street, south of Maplewood, but in that barn he kept all the telephone poles, piled up in front. As I remember he had a Model T. Ford, he drove and pulled those poles to their place and he alone, and I mean all by himself, he would set the poles in the ground and then run the wires on it, and connect to the junction box for the operator to be connected at the telephone office, and he would install your phone and he would repair and check your telephone in those early days. The lady I can see and that I first remember so vivacious in her job as phone operator, Sara someone Carroll or Von. Phones were given numbers, but you did not need to know the number, just simply lift the receiver and ask for some person, and if the operator usually knew who—she would listen in on your conversation, not in a 'caddy' way, but in a helpful way. Many times she would cut into your conversation and give you information that she knew about—that was helpful. And my dad had what I always thought was the second phone installed in Sylvania, and our phone number was the number 2, and all my life Doc Armstrong had telephone number 2. Charlie later retired and he lived in a house, the first house west of mine on Maplewood Avenue. At one time he had a 6 foot solid plank fence around the entire back yard and raised skunks. I as a little boy used to climb up and peek over, and I was told never, never to do that. I never knew why, until later, that the skunks would get excited if somebody new entered their territory, but I used to carefully peek over and I used to think that someone would jump at me or bite me or something, and there were all those pretty little skunks with their burrows, and I always wanted to go over and play with them, but I never dared because Charlie said, 'Don't you dare.' Charlie said, 'All little kids follow his direction.'"

The following article appeared in the *Sylvania Sentinel* on 3-10-1927 under the column "Bits O'Business": "Permission was granted the Sylvania Home Telephone Co., to sell all of its property to the Sylvania Telephone Co., by the Public Utilities Commission."

In the 4-14-1927 issue of the *Sylvania Sentinel* the Sylvania Telephone Company, By M. Lochbihler, a "Notice of Increase Rates" appeared. This notice reported: "Public notice is hereby given that the Sylvania Telephone Company has filed with the Public Utilities Commission of Ohio its Schedule No. 7, specifying increased rates for telephone service at Sylvania, Ohio to become effective May 1st, 1927, such increased rates being as follows:

Individual Lines – Business $4.25; Residential $3.90.
Two Party Lines - $3.50.
Four Party Lines – Residential $2.50
Extensions – Business $1.00; Residential .75 cents."

Originally most homes had what they called party lines. As you can see from the above advertisement you could have a "two-party line" or a "four-party line." What this meant is you shared a line with other nearby residents. If they were on the phone you waited until they were done, and vise versa. You didn't know any better, therefore it worked out fine. In today's world of cell phones, this would never work out.

The following advertisement appeared in the *Sylvania Sentinel* on 7-21-1927 in a full page ad titled: "SYLVANIA NEEDS TOWN FELLOWSHIP – THE COOPERATION OF ALL CITIZENS OF SYLVANIA IS OUR GREATEST ASSET". The advertisement reads:

"We sell Sylvania to the Rest of the Nation – SYLVANIA TELEPHONE CO. – M.J. Lochbihler, Manager."

The following article appeared in the *Sylvania Sentinel* on 9-1-1927 under the column titled BITS O'BUSINESS: "Charles Gries of the Sylvania Telephone Co., returned last Friday from a two weeks stay at Elk Rapids, Michigan, where he enjoyed trout fishing. We have no reason to doubt the veracity of Charles when he tells of the velocity of the big ones there. However, he admits that he has not had his fill of fish yet."

The following article appeared in the *Sylvania Sentinel* on 9 15 1927: "SYLVANIA PHONE BOOST APPROVED BY STATE - The public utilities commission of Ohio has authorized the increase in rates asked for by the Sylvania Telephone Co. of Sylvania. The increase applies to both business and residential telephones. When the application for an increase was filed by the company several months ago a suspension of 120 days was ordered by the commission and the rates were collected under bond, to be refunded to subscribers if the commission found they were not justified."

The following article appeared in the *Sylvania Sentinel* on 10-6-1927 under the column titled BIT O'BUSINESS: "The Sylvania Telephone Company is busy preparing the new telephone directory and asks that all firms wishing to place an ad in the new book get in touch with the bookkeeper at the telephone office at once."

The following article appeared in the *Sylvania Sentinel* on 11-3-1927 under the column titled BITS O'BUSINESS: "Earl Mattimore, bus driver, is recovering nicely from an operation for appendicitis in Toledo hospital, and expects to return home Tuesday. Mrs. Mattimore is night operator at the Sylvania Telephone Co."

On 7-7-1930 the building at 6511 Maplewood, which had been owned and occupied by the Sylvania Home Telephone Company since 1-14-1914, was sold to Ohio Associated Telephone Company. Ohio Associated owned this building until 3-28-1949 when sold to Edward W. & Fern I. Darowski. In 1930 when the Sylvania Telephone Company sold all of its property, assets, franchise and rights to Ohio Associated Company the equipment that was being used was still the type where you cranked the phone to summons the operator and then they had to ask what number you wanted, and then plug the caller's line into the line they were calling. After the Ohio Associated Telephone Company took over, the magneto system continued until 1937, and then the common battery service started. In 1937 there were 375 telephones in the village and township, and then by the end of 1947 there were 1,180 subscribers. By the end of 1957 - 4,969 phones; then in 1967 there were 12,845 telephones; and in 1974 there were 22,227 telephones handled by the Sylvania system.

The *Sylvania Sentinel* in their 4-23-1931 issue informed the public of the following: "The Sylvania Telephone Exchange will not give out information regarding fires after April 25th. In a letter to the Mayor the company explains their stand on the question. The letter quoted in part, follows: In connection with fires in Sylvania, in the past, as you know, the practice has been, that after a fire is reported to the telephone office the operators take care of blowing the whistle and calling the fire department. What probably has not been brought to your attention is that as soon as the whistle blows everybody within hearing distance of the whistle dashes to the telephone and asks "Where is the fire?" This information has always been given, with the result that for fifteen to twenty minutes after the whistle blows our operators do nothing but answer fire calls. If an emergency call for a doctor, or ambulance, or another fire call should come in during this period it would be unavoidably delayed, and the operators severely and unduly criticized for it. In addition to this, everybody who has means of conveyance dashes madly to the fire, with the result that the fire truck is hampered in getting to the fire, and the firemen hindered in their work at the fire."

The following advertisement appeared in the *Sylvania Sentinel* on 6-16-1932: "AN UNUSUALLY SOUND LOCAL INVESTMENT NOW AVAILABLE TO LOCAL PEOPLE - Do you seek a regular income—a safe place for your reserve funds—a sound investment? Such an opportunity is now available to all residents of this community through the 6% Preferred Shares now being offered by the employees of this company. Price $90.00 per share yielding 6.66%. If you prefer to purchase from income, investigate our Monthly Investment Plan. OHIO ASSOCIATED TELEPHONE CO. – Offered by Employees June 20 to July 2."

The following article appeared in the *Sylvania Sentinel* on 12-10-1936: "TELEPHONE COMPANY MAKING IMPROVEMENTS – The Ohio Associated Telephone Company is making many improvements in their Sylvania equipment. They are now engaged in installing over 350 new telephones in the district served by the Sylvania exchange. In the office all equipment will require the preliminary cranking to call the operator. Telephones can be had either in the cradles, desk or wall styles. All of the outside lines will be re-built and many new poles will be erected. The new switchboard will be cut into service about March 22nd, and Mr. Harmon Shively, local plant superintendent, states that the service by the local office will be greatly improved."

The 5-13-1937 issue of the *Sylvania Sentinel* reported the following: "On Thursday the Ohio Associated Telephone Company cut over to the new switchboard which has recently been installed in the local office. All day Thursday the operators were in more or less confusion, attempting to learn the new board, the new numbers, answer the complaints, make satisfactory explanations to irate subscribers and to carry forward "business as usual." The old telephones may now be set aside, and users may avail themselves of the new instruments to the "cut over." These new phones eliminate the old-fashioned box with its well-known crank, and we can now face our city cousins without apologizing for our antique telephone equipment. The girls in the telephone office ask your indulgence for a day or two, for the installation crew is still making adjustments, and many distressing situations are entirely beyond their control. They are a pretty smart set of young women and they'll give you tip-top service just as soon as it is humanly possible."

In the *Toledo Blade,* on 5-27-1939, is the obituary notice of Mathias Lochbihler. He was the president of the Sylvania Telephone Company for 25 years owning the business from 1900 to 1925: "SYLVANIA BANK PRESIDENT DIES – Mathias Lochbihler, 75, ill 2 weeks; Rites to Be Monday – Mathias Lochbihler, 75, president of the Sylvania Savings Bank Co., for seven years, died in his home yesterday after an illness of two weeks.

Born in Detroit, Mr. Lochbihler moved to Richfield Center, Ohio, when four years old and had lived in Richfield Center and Sylvania ever since. Mr. Lochbihler was active in the telephone business in Richfield Center and Sylvania for 25 years before selling out his interests to the Ohio Bell Telephone Co., 15 years ago. Mr. Lochbihler founded the Sylvania Telephone Co.

Mr. Lochbihler had resided in Sylvania for the last 20 years. He had been president of the bank since Jan. 11, 1932. He was a member of the Knights of Columbus in Toledo, the Catholic Knights of Ohio in Richfield Center and the Toledo Chamber of Commerce.

Mr. Lochbihler apparently was in good health when he returned from vacation in Florida five weeks ago, members of his family said, but was stricken with a heart ailment two weeks ago.

He was last of a family of seven boys. With his wife, Elizabeth, he celebrated his 49th wedding anniversary April 14. He also leaves a foster son, Charles Edward Gries. Services will be in his home at 5645 Summit Street, Sylvania, at 8:30 a.m., Monday and in St. Joseph's Church, Sylvania at 9 a.m. Burial will be in Calvary Cemetery. Members of the Knights of Columbus will recite the rosary in the Lochbihler name tomorrow at 8:30 a.m."

The following advertisement appeared in the *Sylvania Sentinel* on 12-21-1939: "HOLIDAY CHEER – EMPLOYEES OF OHIO ASSOCIATED TELEPHONE CO."

On 8-14-1941 the following article appeared in the *Sylvania Sentinel*: "TELEPHONE COMPANY TO INSTALL NEW CABLE - At the meeting of the Village Council on Monday evening, a representative of the Ohio Associated Telephone Company was present and discussed plans for laying an underground cable on the west side of Main Street, and making a step up to the sidewalk. This would be an advantage because of the high curb line on the west side of the street. After some discussion a motion was made by Councilman J. Homer Moscoe and seconded by Councilman Lochbihler that the underground cable be layed on the west side of Main Street and on the west side of the curb between Maplewood Avenue and the south line of Monroe Street. The Village to remove and replace white way lights on bases constructed by the telephone company. That the company stands all expense for material and labor except that for removing and replacing white way lights. The motion was carried, all councilmen voting yes, except C.V. Courtney."

On 9-15-1941 Sylvania Village Council approved a building permit for the Ohio Associated Telephone Co., for an addition to their building at an estimated cost of $6,000. Their building was located at this time at 6511 Maplewood Avenue. (Today known as 6611 Maplewood).

The *Sylvania Sentinel* of 5-3-1945 reported the following: "We have heard considerable favorable comment relative to the proposed action by the Boosters Club about the telephone situation in Sylvania. This interest, as manifested by comments, in itself will accomplish nothing, but without it little could be done. We are convinced that if the great majority of the citizens of the community are dissatisfied with conditions as they are, something can and will be done to remedy them."

Sylvania Sentinel of 5-17-1945: "BOOSTERS HEAR REPORT REGARDING TELEPHONES – "To make any progress in this matter of getting Toledo service for our telephones, we must have united action by the members of Boosters Club," stated Ben Schlatter, chairman of the committee to investigate ways and means to effect the change. This statement was part of the report, as prepared by the committee of the Boosters Club, at the meeting last Monday night in Burnham cafeteria. A showing of hands of those members of the club who favored the change revealed unanimous approval which insured a united agreement by the seventy-odd members of the club. Mr. Schlatter also pointed out that the change would raise the cost of the monthly rates of all phones slightly, but for those who have many toll calls (which include all calls to Toledo) the raise would be infinitesimal or even would result in lower costs to many. It was brought out in the discussion that followed the report of the many ways that the elimination of the toll would be of great benefit to business in Sylvania. The question was also raised as to how many more phones would be in demand if Toledo service could be had without toll charge. The committee was instructed to carry on and to take any necessary steps to further this project. The Ohio Associated Telephone Company will be informed of the desire for the change as will the Public Utilities Commission in Columbus. Further reports of this committee will be awaited by the membership of the club with great interest."

The *Sylvania Sentinel* of 5-17-1945 reported: "The opinion of the members of the Boosters Club seemed to be unanimous that Sylvania has a great handicap in the toll charge in the phone service. A count of the subscribers in the new telephone book of the local telephone company reveals that there are 792 phones listed. Possibly there are many of those subscribers who are entirely satisfied with the present service, but we can't help but wonder how many people are potential subscribers if they could have Toledo service without toll charge. We must remember that many of the people who live in Sylvania Township have little interest in this locality, other than to sleep here. Their work is in Toledo.

Most of the business men with whom we have talked are greatly interested in having Toledo service without toll. It is not only that the call to Toledo costs extra, but that toll charge is enough to prevent many possible customers in the Toledo exchange to call here for business.

Of course, the fact that communities to the east, south and southwest have the Toledo service, while we do not makes us feel that there is discrimination being shown. This is a mere coincidence and not intentional, but the result is just the same.

This change in service will have to come some time and the sooner the better for the whole township. It just is not in the cards for this one community to be set aside while our neighbors get the benefits of progress."

The following article appeared in the *Sylvania Sentinel* on 7-26-1945: "TELEPHONE SUBSCRIBERS BEING ASKED TO VOTE – All present subscribers to the Ohio Associated Telephone Company are being asked to express their desire as to having Toledo telephone service with Toledo rates. This is being done by workers who volunteered Monday night at the meeting of the Boosters Club in Burnham High School.

The special meeting was called so that the telephone committee, headed by Mr. Ben Schlatter, could report on the negotiations with the Ohio Associated Telephone Company to date.

Mr. Schlatter reported in full as to the meeting which had been held by his committee with the officials of the company. The report was substantially as follows:

The Ohio Associated Telephone Company offers Sylvania Township, Toledo telephone service with Toledo rates as soon as it can possibly be done, provided that at least 75 percent of the present subscribers wish it; that negotiations with the Ohio Bell Company in Toledo can be worked out; that the Public Utilities Commission in Columbus will approve it. The company officials also pointed out the present difficulties of manpower, manufacture of necessary equipment, etc. However with these difficulties overcome they promise dial service with no toll charge to Toledo and Holland. Under the present arrangement Perrysburg cannot call Holland without a toll as it is not contiguous, and in our case, Maumee and Perrysburg would also be considered in the same way. The company assured the committee however that if this arrangement in Toledo is changed, our rates would be made the same.

The estimate of the crowd present at the meeting Monday was about 115 and not one word of opposition was voiced to the proposed change. This agrees well for the proposal and the number of enthusiastic volunteers who took cards which will be used for the signature of the subscriber, also assures the quick completion of this phase of the project. The cards were prepared by the company and are a complete file of all the present subscribers with the present type of service and rate, and also the new Toledo rate for the same type of service. Thus each subscriber will know just what the change would mean to him in rate cost.

Mr. Schlatter and the committee estimated the large percentage of subscribers would come under the rural rate, which is now $2.25 per month and would be $2.50 or the village rate for four party lines of $2.75.

Those present at the meeting were also told that the minimum time which the change could be made was estimated at three years and it might be five years. Considerable engineering is involved, a new and large building required, and from four to six times the number of trunk lines will be required to Toledo to handle the expected increase in calls. Fourteen captains have been appointed to which the 870 subscriber cards have been given. Each captain has workers assigned to him which will mean that actually only about six or seven subscribers will have to be seen by each worker. The names of the captains are: Jesse Crandall, Roy Dague, William Wright, Roy Chandler, Ray Corbin, Winona Bowman, Harry Pownell, R.C. Minogue, Clarence Meinen, Murrell Smith, Ira Baumgartner, Darrell Williams, Homer Moscoe, and John Harroun."

The following article appeared in the *Sylvania Sentinel* on 8-16-1945: "SYLVANIA TELEPHONE USERS SUBSCRIBE - It has probably been a long time in this community since a committee of residents worked together with as much enthusiasm as they did on the recent telephone campaign sponsored by the Sylvania Boosters Club, as part of their program for civic improvements, and the entire group of workers are to be congratulated on their splendid effort. The campaign headed by Ben Schlatter, who acted as chairman, aided by an able group of team captains, was conducted in record time. Every telephone user in this community was contacted with 704 out of 750 cards signed requesting Toledo service at Toledo rates making a total of 86% of the residents in favor of the change.

The first meeting of this committee with the team captains was held July 23, and completed August 13, with only 10 cards unsigned because of inability to contact three parties. They will be given an opportunity to sign later. Team Captains assisting the committee were as follows: Roy Chandler, Roy Dague, Murrell Smith, Bill Wright, Ray Corbin, Clarence Meinen, Jesse Crandall, "Pete" Minogue, Harry Pownell, Homer Moscoe, John Harroun, Darrell Williams, Ira Baumgartner and Winona Bowman.

The Boosters Club Committee who made the investigations, directed the canvass and will carry on until the job is finished, consists of: Ben Schlatter, Chairman, assisted by Roy Chandler, Roy Dague, Jesse Crandall, Clarence Meinen and Ira Baumgartner, Secretary."

The local telephone office on Christmas Day 1945 reported the highest number of incoming and outgoing calls in the history. There were 430 calls to Toledo alone plus 89 recorded long distance calls beyond Toledo, plus at least 3,000 local calls. All of these calls were handled by three "girls" for most of the day

On 1-18-1946 the Ohio Associated Telephone Company purchased the property at 6627 Maplewood Avenue in Sylvania from Ethel Cooke and in 1952 the property records indicate that the name changed to General Telephone Company of Ohio. In 1947 the telephone company built a building on this land which still stands today in 2018, with some additions added over the years.

The *Sylvania Sentinel* reported the following in their 1-24-1946 issue: "TELEPHONE COMPANY BUYS NEW LOCATION - Mr. T.G. Reger, local realtor, announced Monday that the Ohio Associated Telephone Company had purchased a new site for the location of the new building which will be required to give the service promised the company's subscribers last summer. The new building is the first step in the expansion necessary to give service to Toledo without toll charge. The new site is located on Maplewood just west of the alley. The sale included 134 feet frontage on Maplewood St., of which the 50 feet adjoining the alley was sold to Dr. W.L. Lathrop. This 50 feet runs back 125 feet and leaves the west 84 feet frontage for the telephone company and gives them a depth of 165 feet with access to the alley of 40 feet."

An article in the *Sylvania Sentinel* on 9-5-1946 reported that the Ohio Associated Telephone Company's local telephone station was handling an average of 2,700 calls per day with the busy hours running as high as 202 on the average. The outward tolls ran an average of 450 calls per day with an average of 40 during the busy hour. The average of incoming toll calls were 950 per day with the average during the busy hour being 81, or in other words, more than twice as many incoming toll calls as outgoing are serviced. The superintendent of the Ohio Associated Telephone Company reported that with the present equipment only five operators could be used at a time, and these five operators were on duty from 9 a.m., to 6 p.m., except from 12 noon to 1 p.m., and from 4 to 6 p.m., when four operators were on duty."

Apparently the complaint of the residents of Sylvania was that many subscribers were unable to get the local operator many times. The superintendent explained that each operator had ten lines to operate and during busy hours all fifty of the lines are in use and with the removal of the receiver of some subscribers, no light is flashed on the board of the operators, thus they are unaware that someone is trying to get central. So, he said that if the operator does not answer, it means that all the lines are busy. From the report, little could be done to improve the telephone service until the new system of dial and free Toledo service was installed."

On 1-15-1948 the Ohio Associated Telephone Company informed the residents of Sylvania that the construction work and installation of equipment in the new telephone building on Maplewood Avenue in Sylvania was progressing and that the new automatic equipment was rapidly being installed and when complete Sylvania would have one of the most modern telephone exchanges in the country.

After the conversion to the dial type system, free toll in Toledo took place, there would be 43 circuits to Toledo for calls going from Sylvania to Toledo, and 35 circuits from Toledo to Sylvania. This would eliminate any conflict between outgoing and incoming calls. In addition there would be six circuits from Sylvania to Holland and six from Holland to Sylvania, toll free. Then there would be additional circuits for toll calls only. This program was promised to be a great improvement to Sylvania's telephone service.

The 2-19-1948 issue of the *Sylvania Sentinel* reported the following: "DIAL TELEPHONE SERVICE AT MIDNIGHT FEB. 28 - It is expected that the present telephone service will be cut over to dial service at midnight, Saturday, Feb. 28. That is, the Ohio Associated Telephone Company has all plans made for the changeover to take place at that time unless some unforeseen incident occurs which would prevent it. Mr. Tennant, Supervisor of the company, stated Wednesday noon that 1,200 present subscribers would enjoy the dial service, of which some 200 have been added in the past three months. An additional 300 more subscribers will have telephone service within a day or two after the conversion. These additional subscribers already have phones installed, but are without service. This will culminate almost three years of intensive engineering and study looking toward this step in improved telephone service for the Sylvania area. A crew of 12 men have been brought into Sylvania to interview all subscribers and obtain their acceptance of the new rates applied for by the Bell Telephone Company. That company has recently applied to the Public Utilities Commission for a raise in rates which it considers justifiable under present conditions. The increase as applied for would mean an additional 50 cents per month to all business phone users; 10 cents per month to all resident private lines; and five cents to all two party lines. The four party line subscribers would have no increase in rate."

The 3-4-1948 issue of the *Sylvania Sentinel* reported that the business men along Main Street had been practically tearing their hair out and bemoaning the big deals which have been lost because of their failure to reach their customers or be reached by them. The fact of the matter was reported by company officials that every subscriber wanted to use the phone at the same time and this is just not possible. Too many calls are going out to see if the dial system works. Also too many calls were made with incorrect dialing. And too many receivers are left off the phone (usually in disgust) which reduces the number of lines available for other parties. The reporter said that it would be well to remember the following simple directions for phone use: To dial a local number: lift the receiver, listen first for the dial tone, then dial the number which will always be prefixed by the numeral 2 (example 2-2222).

To dial a Toledo number: lift the receiver, listen for the dial tone, then dial the number which will always be prefixed by the numeral 9, (example 9-Jo-2222). To dial a Holland number, follow the same procedure as for Toledo except using the numeral 7 instead of 9."

The dial system and toll free to Toledo began in 1948 and this ended the career of the telephone operator. She had been known as "Central" and knew all the town happenings.

According to the deed records of the telephone company's property at 6619 Maplewood Avenue, in 1952 the ownership was changed from Ohio Associated Telephone Company to General Telephone Company of Ohio.

The following article appeared in the *Toledo Blade* on 8-2-1956: "PHONE CO. OFFICES GO TO BANK BUILDING – TO USE COMPANY BUILDING FOR MORE EQUIPMENT - The Telephone business office now located at 6627 Maplewood Avenue will be moved to Suite Number 4 on the second floor of the Sylvania Savings Bank Building at 5604 Main Street on Monday 8-16-1956.

E.C. Kimball, Western Division Manager of the General Telephone Company of Ohio said the move was being made in order that the Maplewood Avenue location could be modified and expanded for the installation of extensive amounts of central office equipment. Mr. Kimball said that arrangements had been made with the Sylvania Savings Bank to accept payment of telephone bills as a matter of convenience for the Sylvania subscribers.

Telephone bills may now be paid at the Sylvania Savings Bank; Howards Hardware Store located on West Central Avenue or the Telephone Business Office. All other transactions involving service changes or account inquiries will be handled by company representatives in the business office. The building work at the exchange office on Maplewood would involve two major steps. A part of the equipment will be moved into the present business office quarters and the wall separating the wire center office in the rear of the building will be removed to gain floor space for the installation of 500 subscriber lines. Mr. Kimball said that this installation is scheduled for late this year and will provide central office line relief required to handle the many requests for individual line services."

In May of 1957 General Telephone reported that they were adding 600 new lines which would increase the line capacity in Sylvania by 32 percent. The total number of lines that were already in service at this time was 2,500. A building addition was currently under construction at their building at 6619 Maplewood Avenue, in the rear, would provide space for the installation of more than 6,000 subscriber lines in the building.

On 8-10-1961 it was reported that telephone users in the Sylvania area would have the nation and parts of Canada at their fingertips. That's when General Telephone Co., would introduce Direct Distance Dialing (DDD)—a service that lets customers dial their own station-to-station long distance calls. Final preparations for DDD were being made in the company's central office at 6627 Maplewood Avenue. Robert Mooney, local manager, said a new phone directory and a personal blue book would be sent to customers. Instructions for using DDD were in these books. The key to DDD would be the number "1". To dial any number in northwestern Ohio, except in the local calling area, phone users would dial "1" ahead of the desired number. Mooney said a three-figure area code must be dialed to reach phones outside this area code before dialing the regular phone number. After Aug. 20, the code for calling nearby Holland numbers would change from 1 to 8 since 1 will be the DDD code number. To make a call to Holland, Sylvanians will dial 9 and the regular number."

The *Sylvania Sentinel* dated 8-17-1961 said: "1961-62 telephone directories are being distributed this week by the General Telephone Company throughout the Sylvania exchange. Robert Mooney, local manager, said deliveries should be completed at the end of this week. The new book will have complete instructions on Direct Distance Dialing, which will go into effect Sunday, August 20 in Sylvania and Toledo."

The *Sylvania Herald* reported on 2-15-1962 that General Telephone had just installed their 7,000[th] Sylvania phone in a new home, honoring Sylvania as one of the Company's fastest growing exchanges. Informal ceremonies were held in the home of Mr. and Mrs. John Evers at 4732 McCord Road, the recipients of the 7,000[th] telephone in Sylvania.

The 5-10-1962 issue of the *Sylvania Herald* announced that the General Telephone Company of Ohio planned to erect a telephone sub-office on three lots on McCord Road just north of Central Avenue. The total estimated cost of the new sub-office was $515,000, including equipment. The purpose of the new sub-office was to serve the southern section of the Sylvania exchange area. The new office was scheduled to go into service on 9-15-1963.

On 8-2-1962 the *Sylvania Herald* reported the following: "SYLVANIA PHONE NOS. TO CHANGE AUGUST 18 – MARKS DATE OF 7 – DIGITS - Numbers of some 500 telephones here will be changed to the 7-digit ANC (all number calling) system on August 18, General Telephone Co. of Ohio announced today. Robert Mooney of Sylvania, local commercial manager, said the changes will appear in the 1962 Sylvania phone directory. The rest of Sylvania's numbers will switch to ANC in September 1963, when the company's new sub-station on McCord Road is completed. Numbers being changed this month will use all-numeral prefixes of 882 or 888— instead of TU 2 or TU 8. The last four digits of the 500 new numbers also are being changed, Mooney noted.

These changes are necessitated by rearrangements of phone switching equipment in process in the main central office here, he said. Customers to be served by the McCord sub-office will retain the TU 2 prefix until the 1963 directory is issued. At that time they will be assigned ANC numbers prefixed by 841.

In addition, many of the TU 2 and TU 8 numbers are not being changed this month. When switched to ANC in 1963, only the prefix will change to all numerals—882 or 888—but the last four digits will remain the same. - All-number calling, Mooney added, increases by almost 50 percent the amount of phone numbers possible with seven turns of the dial. The letter-numeral prefix system is limited because suitable prefix names cannot be derived from certain letter combinations on the dial. Phone users to be served by the McCord Road sub-station will have numbers prefixed by 841."

By April of 1967 Sylvania's office of the General Telephone Company announced that 2,200 additional lines were being installed in the two Sylvania offices of the company in an effort to provide better and more complete service to local customers. Mr. Robert Mooney, Manager of the Sylvania exchange, said that 1,400 new telephone lines were being placed in the Sylvania office. This would allow the company to offer 1,400 new private lines, or 2,800 two party lines, or 5,600 four-party lines. In addition, 800 new lines were being installed in the McCord office.

4-4-1968 – At the meeting of the Sylvania Township Trustees there was discussion regarding forming a committee known as "Citizens for Better Phone Service" regarding service provided by General Telephone.

6-5-1969 - According to the minutes of the Sylvania Township Trustees there was an article in the Wall Street Journal concerning problems with General Telephone Company of Ohio in Medina, Ohio. They related a problem of a Corey Meadows resident on a four party line and a private line would not be available until next January. The clerk was directed to contact Jack Roberts, general manager of the local telephone office, to improve service.

According to the 8-20-1969 issue of the *Sylvania Sentinel* General Telephone Co. of Ohio had just completed a major $180,500 addition to their call-switching families and presented a progress report on the preparations for Toledo metropolitan toll-free calling. Jack R. Roberts, Sylvania district commercial manager, said the equipment project added facilities for 1,400 new customer lines and terminal connections for 1,300 new phone numbers. They also boosted Sylvania-Holland toll-free trunks. All facilities were to be completed for final testing in September of 1969. An Oct. 5 start date had been agreed upon by General Telephone of Ohio and the Ohio Bell Telephone Co., for metropolitan calling. The two companies were making extensive equipment and trunk additions to handle the toll-free calls. Once in service the metropolitan calling would add Whitehouse, Perrysburg and Maumee to Sylvania's local calling area. The charges that were being assessed for calls between Sylvania and the three exchanges would be dropped. It was also noted that a 400-line, 500-terminal equipment addition was under way at General's sub-office on McCord Road in Sylvania Township. It was scheduled for completion in November of 1969. They would be reducing party lines and increasing Sylvania exchange to 10,960 lines. They service 14,900 telephones (including extensions) in a 26.7 square-mile area. At year-end 1959 Sylvania had slightly more than 6,000 telephones and the company had put almost $4-million into capital additions in Sylvania the last 10 years.

7-16-1970 - The clerk of Sylvania Township was asked to write a letter to the P.U.C.O., regarding GTE and their possible rate increases, requesting a hearing to be held locally regarding the proposed rate increase so that local residents could be heard.

In January of 1973 General Telephone Co. of Ohio reported that they budgeted $1 million for expansion of telecommunication facilities in the Sylvania exchange. It was then announced that the General Telephone Co. of Ohio, which served about 30 percent of Ohio's land area, filed a request for a $13.5 million annual rate increase with the Public Utilities Commission of Ohio. It would amount to an average boost of almost 8 cents a day in basic service rates for residential customers.

A two-page advertisement in 1973 for the General Telephone Company features photos of the facilities in Sylvania that this telephone company operated at this time. The four photos that were featured were: The Southbriar Business Office at 5129 S. Main Street; Maplewood Central Office – 6627 Maplewood Avenue; McCord Central Office at the corner of McCord at Central; and the Future King Road facility known as the Plant Reporting Center at 4420 King Road.

In July of 1973 the General Telephone of Ohio employees were out on strike as a result of failure to reach an agreement on their contract negotiations. The strike started on 7-16-1973 and picket lines were set up at the General Telephone facilities throughout the state. By early August the company reported more than $675,000 in vandalism to the utility's equipment. One employee, who was a Sylvania resident, was arrested by police for cutting a General Telephone Company cable at McCord and Coppersmith.

On 1-28-1976 General Telephone announced plans to put $6 million into expansion and modernization of communications facilities here the next five years. The customer service man was Kenneth J. Wallery, and he said that the major highlight was the electronic switching in

Sylvania by 1980. The new electronic system was scheduled to replace the existing electro-mechanical facility in the main office at Maplewood Avenue just west of Commerce Street (the alley). Construction of a new building to house the electronic switching unit was scheduled for completion in 1978 and a new structure would be constructed next to the current building on Maplewood. At this time Toledo provided operator and switching for Sylvania's long distance calls. The Sylvania exchange covered almost all of Sylvania and Sylvania Township, but also extended into Michigan. Sylvania's exchanges were 882, 885, 841 and 888. They covered an area of 29.2 square miles with a total number of customers of 12,604. 81.4 percent of Sylvania's residential customers had one-party service. At this time in 1976 they had 80 employees working in the exchange.

12-2-1976 - The Sylvania Township Trustees discussed the services of United Telephone, which serves a large area of the township west of Centennial Road. It was noted that residents in that area must call long distance in order to call the emergency numbers. They suggested setting up a foreign exchange number for emergency calls at a cost to the township of $82 per month, which was the current rate.

12-16-1976 - The Sylvania Township Trustees were advised that it would cost $83.25 per month for a TX line from Richfield Center to Sylvania to handle emergency calls on a direct, instead of long distance, basis. It was felt that this cost was excessive for the benefits to be derived.

Starting 6-1-1977 telephones with push buttons instead of a dial were available to phone users through the Sylvania General Telephone Co. of Ohio. The new optional service was known as "Touch calling" and it was faster than the old fashioned dial type because there was no waiting for the dial to return after each digit. The additional cost to customers was $2 extra per month for residential phone users and $2.50 for businesses. A one-time conversion charge of $7.50 was also added.

In January of 1982 consumers started being able to purchase phones outright, and telephone companies lost the ability to charge customers for leasing their telephone equipment. At that point they had to start competing with other manufacturers for phone sales. General Telephone at that time offered its customers the chance to rent or buy new telephones from them when telephone charges were deregulated.

An article in the *Toledo Blade* dated 11-10-1988 said that GTE Corp. would cut nearly 7,000 middle management and hourly employee jobs over the next four years as a result of a restructuring of its telephone operations. The company said that a fair portion of the cuts would come from employees opting for early retirement.

In June of 1990 GTE in Sylvania had 40 employees and 21,000 customers in the Sylvania district, according to Dan Hipp, Sylvania local manager for GTE. He said that in 1990 GTE Telephone operations would invest more than $310,000 in expansion and service improvement to their facilities in Sylvania.

By January of 1994 GTE announced that they would cut 17,000 jobs in their telephone operations over the next three years, including management, cable workers, installers and service representatives. GTE also announced that they were reducing the number of its customer contact centers that handled calls from customers and some of its billing centers. They also said that 19 regional centers that monitored and managed GTE's national network would be reduced to one center.

In February of 1996 President Clinton signed a bill into law that opened all telecommunications markets to competition by removing regulatory barriers. The law encouraged competition among local providers, long distance services and cable telephone companies.

On 6-30-2000 Bell Atlantic merged with GTE and named the new entity Verizon Communications, and then on 7-1-2010 Verizon sold many of its former GTE properties to Frontier Communications. Sylvania's local telephone properties are still under the name of General Telephone Company.

In 2001 it became necessary to dial the area code and then the 7-digit number, even on local calls, when dialing a phone number. This was necessary because of the use of cell phones. By this time just about every person had a cell phone and they were running out of phone numbers within each area code. Today, with cell phones, many of GTE's original customers are eliminating their land-line home telephones and relying entirely on their cell phones.

TREE CITY U.S.A.

Naturally with a community named Sylvania, we would have to be part of the Tree City U.S.A. program, especially when the name Sylvania comes from the word "Sylvan" which is the Latin word for "woods or trees." By 2009 the City of Sylvania had been named a Tree City U.S.A. community for the 27th consecutive year by the Arbor Day Foundation in cooperation with the National Association of State Foresters and the USDA Forest Service, to honor its commitment to community forestry. Since 1983 Sylvania had met the four standards in order to become a Tree City U.S.A. community, which includes having: a tree board or department; a tree care ordinance; a comprehensive community forestry program; and an Arbor Day observance and proclamation. Sylvania has over 7,000 trees, including the largest tree, a bur oak on the front lawn of the administration building at 6730 Monroe Street.

An invoice dated 4-17-1914 was found among some of the old documents that once belonged to the clerk of the Village of Sylvania. There was an invoice from Spielman Bros. Nurserymen and Small Fruit Growers and they purchased 200 ornamental trees at $57.00. The breakdown was 120 Norway Maples; 60 Car. Poplar; and 20 American Elm.

The most recent tree planting project in Sylvania started in October of 1971 when city councilman C. Justus Brown presented the city's proposed program for tree plantings along the public right-of-ways. The program was analyzed and prepared by Arthur Landseadel, on a four-year plan and funds had been budgeted. The plan called for one thousand trees in the initial planting slated to begin soon. 50 percent of those would be on main traffic arteries. The plan called for Blue Ash, Flowering Crab, Linden, Plane and Maple trees.

In 1972 the tree-planting program continued in Sylvania. According to an article in the *Toledo Blade* dated 7-19-1972 landscapers completed the initial step in Sylvania's first municipal tree-planting program with the placement of 1,076 trees along city streets. Sylvania City Council had authorized payment of $18,005 to Creque Bros. Landscape Co., who handled the tree planting project. More than a dozen varieties of trees were used along the rights of way for the esthetic value, to provide shade, and to improve the ecology. Flowering crab and ash predominate, but other varieties were used so some provide early summer blossoms and others offer autumn colors. The first year's plantings represented about 20 percent of the city's needs as recommended in a tree survey made for the city about a year ago. The tree survey indicated that large segments along major roadways and residential streets in the city were bare.

An article in the *Sylvania Sentinel*'s 1973 Progress Report said that: "Sylvania utilizes a 5c per front foot assessment for the planting and maintenance of street trees. In each of the first two years, 5000 to 6000 trees have been or are to be planted. In addition to the planting and maintenance, these funds are used for removal of diseased or dead trees as the fund allows.

In 1978 the City of Sylvania hosted the Tree City USA awards program put on by the National Arbor Day Foundation and the Ohio Department of Natural Resources, Division of Forestry.

In August of 1979 members of the Parks and Recreation Committees of city council were to meet with Councilman C. Justus Brown and City Forest Ranger Arthur Landseadel to plan a program to study and recommend additional tree plantings in the city.

In September of 1979 the proposal of Arthur W. Landseadel to update the street tree survey for $1,900 was approved with the passage of an ordinance. It was reported that a street tree survey was completed earlier but new developments and annexation had added additional streets to the City's street system. The estimated cost of $150 per mile for new streets added since 3-1-1971, and $400 for compilation of reports. The new survey was expected to be completed by November of 1979. The Director of Public Service, John P. Arnot requested that council take formal action to authorize the installation of 53 trees in the Wildwood Forest Preserve in the Grove Bel area, two streets adjacent to Northview High School and seven along U.S. 23 utilizing street tree funds and the city contractor.

In 1982 the City Parks and Forestry Division planted 286 new trees along 12 city streets and council passed legislation as to the type of trees that could be planted in public right-of-ways, spelled out regulations on topping, pruning and placement of those trees and appointed a street tree committee.

The 5-18-1983 *Sylvania Herald* featured a picture of Sylvania's Mayor Seney receiving the plaque. The caption of the picture reads: "On April 29, Arbor Day, the City of Sylvania became one of 10 in Ohio to receive the first-time designation as Tree City USA from the National Arbor Day Foundation. Lieutenant Governor Myrl H. Shoemaker, right, presented the award to Mayor James

E. Seney, center and City Forester Art Landseadel at ceremonies in Columbus." Then the 6-1-1983 *Sylvania Herald* reported that city officials were planting a red maple tree to commemorate the state designation of Sylvania as Tree City USA in the triangle at Alexis, Monroe and Acres.

The 10-9-1984 *Sylvania Herald* featured a photo of Jeff Howard assisting Joe Laing lift one of the trees that was to be planted along downtown Main Street in part of the city's downtown revitalization project. In addition to the trees, other improvements were to include brick sidewalks and new street lamps.

In February of 1985 Mayor James E. Seney announced that the City of Sylvania had been named a Tree City U.S.A. for the third time. A flag with the program's logo and a walnut-mounted plaque was to be received. On Arbor Day, 4-30-1985, the city received the flag and other recognition in a public ceremony. The following is quoted from the letter that the city received: "A community's tree planting program is a living memorial to the citizens' concern for the quality of life. The beauty of the trees and their practical benefits, will last for years to come. The Tree City U.S.A. Award is an excellent indication that tree-care responsibilities are being taken seriously."

The 1985 annual report for the City of Sylvania reported that over 175 trees were planted through the Forestry Division's Street Tree Maintenance and Planting Program in 1985, and for the fourth consecutive year, the City of Sylvania received the national Tree City, U.S.A. Award in 1986.

The Arbor Day celebration for 1988 included the installation of the "Triad of Trees" statue in the triangle formed by Monroe-Alexis-Acres. Also in celebration, Mr. Landseadel, city forester, announced that two trees in Sylvania that were older than the city itself would receive a sprucing up free of charge by L.E. Savory Tree Service, Inc., which had "adopted" them to give them new life. The two white oaks were on a tree island at Monroe Street and Corey Road and Mr. Landseadel referred to them as Sylvania's "heritage trees." One of the trees was estimated to be 245 years old, and the other between 185 and 210 years old. The *Sylvania Herald* on 6-1-1988 reported that following a year and a half of meetings, consultations with the artist, a fund raising campaign, etc., the dedication of the Triad of Trees took place before an assemblage of city officials and residents of the area.

In April of 1991 Sylvania was named Tree City USA by the National Arbor Day Foundation for the ninth year.

On 6-8-1999 Sylvania City Council passed an Ordinance #70-99 to create a Sylvania Tree Commission to promote the acquisition of, to encourage the donation of funds for, to advise on the care of, to provide ongoing inspection, care, advice and services for, to provide advice, opinions, and counsel with respect to all matters concerning City trees and care thereof. The Commission was to consist of nine persons.

In April of 2000 the City of Sylvania hosted the 25th Northwest Ohio Tree City USA Awards Program. The event featured a trolley bus tour of the city street trees and the compost facility. At this event 52 communities in northwest Ohio (including Sylvania) were presented with Tree City USA designations. This was the 18th year that Sylvania was named a Tree City USA.

In 2001 Sylvania had been the recipient of the National Tree City U.S.A. award for 19 consecutive years. According to an article in 2001 it was reported that the city was still populated with approximately 30,000 trees within 5.9 square miles, equating to 5,840 trees per square mile. The Acer rubrum, or fall red maple was the predominate native species. At this time the value of street trees in the city was estimated at $1,638,000.

In April of 2007 the City of Sylvania was honored with the award of Tree City USA for the 25th year. At this time Art Landseadel, the city forester, said that since 1975 the city's parks and forestry division had planted about 7,400 street trees. Homeowners were paying a tree assessment of 30 cents per front foot, or between $12 to $15 for the average homeowner, and the city had budgeted $203,440 to cover the expense of planting, maintaining, and trimming shade trees in 2007 in city parks, public lands and along street right-of-ways. During the Arbor Day event this year potted Colorado blue spruce trees were given to schoolchildren and the public to be planted by them.

In 2011 the City is again named a Tree City U.S.A. community for the 29th consecutive year. Since 1975, over 7,700 street trees had been planted by the city of Sylvania Parks and Forestry Division. In 2011 there were plans to plant 500 trees in Harroun Park to replace trees lost to emerald ash borer damage. The forestry programs of the city also prune and take care of the trees in the parks, street right-of-ways and public lands.

For Arbor Day on 4-27-2012 the city was celebrating their 30th consecutive year of being named Tree City U.S.A. by the National Arbor Day Foundation. A sugar maple tree was being donated by the Sylvania Rotary Club to be planted in the Sylvania Historical Village. The ceremony was conducted by Mayor Craig Sough and City Forester Art Landseadel.

In March of 2013 the City of Sylvania was named a Tree City USA community for the 30th consecutive year. Sylvania's Art Landseadel, who was 91-years old, and still serving as the city forester, said that he recalled the city did not have many street trees in the 1940s when he began working on the project. He was asked to develop a park system, green space and a tree planting program.

In January of 2017 Pat O'Brien, supervisor of the city of Sylvania's Parks & Forestry Division, hosted a group of 22 municipal forestry administrators and volunteer tree commissioners, including: Toni Andres, Judi Young, Cheryl Rice, Sandi Sarakonda and Rick Barricklow, members of the Sylvania Tree Commission, for a two-day workshop. The program was offered by Stephanie Miller of the Ohio Department of Natural Resources. This program helped the volunteer commission members learn how to do their jobs for efficiently and educated people about trees.

UNDERGROUND RAILROAD AND ANTI-SLAVERY MEETINGS IN SYLVANIA

A history of Sylvania would hardly be complete without some reference to the Underground Railroad. Research experts over the years documented Sylvania, prior to the Civil War, as a stop on this Underground Railroad. This Underground Railroad had no tracks and no trains, and it was not underground at all. It was a network of people from the Mason-Dixon Line to Canada, who harbored fugitive slaves escaping from the South, and passed them along to the next stop until they arrived in Canada where they would be free from slavery. A few of the many escape routes from the South to Canada led through Sylvania, and according to the Harroun family's well-documented oral family histories, the Harroun family and the Lathrop family of Sylvania became involved in helping these fugitive slaves escape to freedom. Sylvania resident David Harroun brought the fugitives from Maumee to Sylvania in an old lumber wagon drawn by horses. The slaves were hidden either at the Harroun house, in their attic, or in the hayloft of their barn, or at the Lathrop House directly west and across the fields from the Harroun house. The Lathrop family had a special room in the basement of their home that was concealed and hidden behind a set of double ovens. From Sylvania the slaves were taken to Bedford Township, Michigan, and Hall Deland, known as the "Night Hawk," who then escorted the fugitives to French settlers on the Detroit River, where they were ferried across to Canada and freedom. At times they may have been taken to Petersburg or Monroe, Michigan when it was not safe to go to Bedford.

Most of the residents in Sylvania were also known to be very much against slavery prior to the Civil War. The headlines of the *Toledo Blade* of 11-22-1850 read: "Great Excitement at Sylvania, 150 Men, 50 Boys, and 4 Woman in Council. Charley Miller among the People." This article reported that ". . . One of the largest and most enthusiastic meetings that has been held here in these diggings, came off at this place last evening. . . " It was also reported that several days' notice was given by the circulation of handbills, "calling upon the people to assemble, without distinction of party, for the purpose of discussing the Fugitive Slave Law. . . " It was agreed "that there was a strong opposition to the late law in this vicinity among all parties and classes. . ."

According to the *Toledo Blade*, residents of Sylvania met on 6-14-1856. They resolved to seek the impeachment of the President of the United States, Franklin Pierce, because of the "tyrannical enactments having been forced upon the Free Settlers of Kansas and the cold blooded murder of their brethren in Kansas by Government officials." The residents of Sylvania hoped that "slavery had reached its zenith of power." The article starts by saying: "The Friends of Freedom of Sylvania and the surrounding country met at that place, on the 14th, to express their views in relation to existing matters to our Union. Names mentioned from Sylvania included: Joel Green, Esq., Don A. Pease, Rev N. Shapley, Rev. C. Stoddard and D.B. Stout, C. Candee, W.M. White and J.O. White, J.G. Klinck, Esq., P.T. Clark, S. Pershall, J.U. Pease, E. Gardanier.

The *Daily Toledo Blade* dated 9-1-1856 printed a "Letter to the Editor" from E. Gordanier, of Sylvania, Ohio, Chairman in support of the Republican candidate for President, John C. Fremont of California. He reported that: "The inhabitants of School District No. 3, Sylvania Township, convened at the Schoolhouse, on the evening of Friday, 29th, to consider the interests of Freedom and Fremont. By motion, E. Gordanier took the Chair, and O. Lenardson, acted as Secretary. We had a glorious gathering. . . The meeting was addressed by the Rev. Mr. Thopley, Pastor of the Congregational Church of our village, and Messrs. Wm. White and Don A. Pease, all of whom were listened to with attention. They vividly pictured the evils of oppression in all its forms; the necessity of striving to bring about the election of the candidates in favor of freedom and free soil whose minds can never be pliant to the will of southern demagogues; also, the evils that would necessarily follow in case of Freemont's non-election. . . " Rev. Mr. Crane was also present.

Honorable George Crane – I mention him because he was one of David White's (one of Sylvania's founding men) "most trusty friends" according to David White's Last Will and Testament.

George Crane lived in Toledo, Ohio and in Adrian, Lenawee County, Michigan. He lived in the same community that David White lived in before they both came to this area (Palmyra now Macedon, Wayne County, New York). Both George Crane and David White came here in 1831. According to George Crane's biographical write-up in the Lenawee County, Michigan history, it says: "Mr. Crane was an earnest member of the Society of Friends, and when the Friends' meeting house was projected, he gave three acres of land upon which to erect the building and for a burial ground, and assisted otherwise more than any other person towards the construction of the church. He was a Quaker, and his ancestors came from England." All Quakers, with very few exceptions, were known to help the fugitive slave in any way possible. David White and his sons William, James and David were said to have helped the fugitive slaves also.

For a complete record of the Underground Railroad in Sylvania please read: *The Underground Railroad and Sylvania's Historic Lathrop House*, By Gaye E. Gindy – 2008.

MURDERS IN SYLVANIA

LIST OF KNOWN MURDERS IN SYLVANIA

Sylvania has always been a very safe community, and the murder rate is very, very low, therefore I am able to list, in a small amount of space, the murders that have occurred in the Sylvania community (township and village/city) since the beginning through 2010. The list includes only those murders that occurred within the boundaries of Sylvania. (The list does not include Sylvania residents who were murdered outside of the city or township):

- **2-4-1857 – Olive Bickford-Davis-Ward** was murdered by her husband Return Jonathan Meigs Ward in a home that was once located on the west side of Main Street, just a little north of Monroe Street (where the bowling alley/Rite Aid/Ace Hardware building is today). The murder weapon was a smoothing iron and the cause was the fact that she had informed him that she was leaving him in the morning. In an attempt to hide the fact that he murdered his wife, Mr. Ward cut up her body, and little by little burned, what he thought was all the evidence, and then burned up her body in a heating/cooking stove in their small home. The residents of Sylvania became suspicious when they found that Mrs. Ward was no where to be found, and evidence started indicating that Mr. Ward had killed her. They found enough evidence within the ashes of the stove that he was charged. A trial was held and Return Ward was indicted by the Grand Jury of Lucas County for the crime of murder in the first degree. He was sentenced to die on 6-12-1857, and on that date he was executed. (For a complete detailed report on this murder read the book: *Murder in Sylvania, Ohio; As Told In 1857* – By Gaye (Gayleen) Gindy - 2007.

- **5-13-1865 – Mr. Buchanan** - The *Daily Toledo Blade* reported on 5-15-1865 that men by the name of Baker and Richards were in Ottawa Lake, Michigan and then came to Sylvania and stopped at our local hotel (at this time we had three hotels, all located in the downtown district, within one block of each other). As they were sitting in the "barroom" a man by the last name of Buchanan was with others that he knew and they were talking about a Baker girl from Ottawa Lake and were using "language unbecoming gentlemen." Mr. Baker told the men that the girl they were talking about was his girl. Buchanan continued talking in a very insulting manner. In an effort to avoid trouble Baker and Richards got up and left. They drove back to Ottawa Lake and Buchanan followed, and when Baker arrived at his home Buchanan started pounding on the door and threatening to whip Baker. Baker then ran back to the buggy, where Richards was waiting, and they started heading toward Sylvania again, with Buchanan still threatening him the entire way. Baker and Richards arrived at Sylvania just ahead of Buchanan, and Baker decided to go back into the hotel. At that point Baker decided he would no longer run. He went into the bar room and ordered a "glass of ale" and at that point Buchanan stepped up behind Baker, and hit him in the neck. He then cornered Baker and while Buchanan was hitting him in the face Baker stabbed Buchanan in his side, cutting him four or five times which was fatal. After an examination by the Justice of the Peace Baker was acquitted of the murder and released, calling it self-defense.

- **10-10-1918 – William Cherry** was murdered by a highly intoxicated man that he did not know, while driving down Convent Blvd. The murderer was Steve Traskawitz, about 28 years old, and described as a Hungarian. According to Marshal Wood, Traskawitz had been removed from a New York Central passenger train a few hours before because he was intoxicated and had kicked another passenger in the face. At the time he was removed from the train, the agent instructed Mr. Beebe to call an officer and have the suspect taken care of. Mr. Cherry, who worked as the superintendent of the convent farm for the Sisters of St. Francis, was driving down Convent Blvd. in his horse and buggy when Traskawitz jumped in front of Cherry's team of horses causing Mr. Cherry to stop, and then the stranger climbed into the wagon and refused to get out. Cherry took him as far as his farm and let the man off, and to get away from the house started to walk with him to the depot. While walking Traskawitz evidently, without any warning, struck Mr. Cherry in the side of the neck, severing the large veins which caused death immediately. Shortly after Mr. Cherry was found dead, a description of Traskawitz had been obtained by a man who was at the station at the time he was thrown off. Cliff and Jess Peck, brothers, located the man and turned him over to Marshal Wood who immediately took him to prison in Toledo, fearing he would be lynched by the irate citizens. The murderer was brought before Judge Chandler and plead guilty. I never did find additional documentation to indicate what the county courts sentenced him with.
- **7-28-1931 – Thomas Stevenson** was killed by Troy Clarkson, step-son, 27 years old, of Huntington Road during a family quarrel. Troy Clarkson admitted to striking the blow but insisted that he struck to defend his mother and other members of the family when Stephenson came home very intoxicated.
- **11-25-1931 – Ed Mason** was killed by Elijah Latham in the community known as Silica located in Sylvania Township. This occurred during an argument over a game of cards. No other details could be found.
- **9-12-1933 – John L. Parker** was murdered by Floyd (Sailor) Baldwin on the property of the Sylvania Country Club in Sylvania on the 15th tee. Mr. Parker was with a group of gentlemen who were playing golf. Mr. Baldwin and others drove up on to the golf course in a vehicle, with handkerchiefs hiding their faces, and commanded "Stick em up fellows, it's a hold up." The gunman walked to where Mr. Parker was standing and started thrusting his hand into his trouser pocket and pulled out a package of cigarettes. Mr. Parker grabbed the bandit and began to struggle with him. A shot was fired and both men fell to the ground. The robber dropped his weapon and as they scrambled to their feet the bandit recovered the gun and fired again, but missed. Another shot was then fired

and struck Mr. Parker in the left eye. When the gunman reached down to pick up some object, one of the golfers said that the handkerchief slipped from the murderers face giving him an opportunity to identify him. Both the bandits ran to their automobile and drove swiftly down the dirt road toward Holland-Sylvania Road. Soon after, Harry Patterson, 35 years old, was determined to be the driver of the getaway vehicle. After several weeks of searching for the murderer, Floyd (Sailor) Baldwin, 25 years old, was positively identified, in a photo, by one of the other golfers that was present at the time of the murder. On 9-16-1933 the *Toledo Blade* announced that warrants charging Floyd (Sailor) Baldwin, former pugilist, and Harry A. Patterson, painter, who lived on Dorr Street near Reynolds Road, with first degree murder, were obtained by Jay Gilday, deputy sheriff at the office of the City Prosecutor Steve Fazekas. The warrants accused the men of slaying J.L. Parker, insurance agent, during a hold up of six golfers at the Sylvania Country Club in Sylvania, Ohio at the 15th tee on 9-12-1933. By 9-18-1933 the *Toledo Blade* reported that Harry Patterson was arrested and he named Floyd "Sailor" Baldwin as the murderer in the murder, and on 9-19-1933 the police reported that they were hunting for Baldwin. On 10-10-1933 Deputy Sheriff Leo Flanagan, 38, was shot and fatally wounded at 1:30 a.m., in a gun battle with Floyd (Sailor) Baldwin who had been sought since Sept 12 for the murder of John L. Parker. Baldwin was wounded in the right leg but escaped after a shoot-out which occurred on Wamba Drive near Nebraska Avenue, one block west of Westwood Avenue. By 10-11-1933 Lucas County Sheriff David Krieger was announcing that Deputy Sheriff Ernest Cooley was on indefinite suspension following the startling revelation that Leo Flanagen, deputy sheriff, was accidentally shot and killed by Deputy Cooley during the shoot-out with Floyd (Sailor) Baldwin on Wamba Drive in Toledo. Baldwin was finally captured and convicted of this murder.

- **6-1-1935 – Alta Miller**, a 42 year old widowed mother of 10 children, was brutally murdered by an unknown suspect while walking home after working at the Little Wonder Restaurant in downtown Sylvania (5689 Main Street). It was believed that Mrs. Miller was struck from behind as she walked down the street, at night, on her way home. The exact location of her murder was never determined, but it was somewhere between downtown Sylvania and her home which was located near the corner of Sylvania and Silica Road in Sylvania Township. It was determined that after she was murdered the murderer drove her dead body to Sylvania Avenue and dumped it by a ditch near her home. A three-foot wooden cudgel with an iron bolt on one end was found in a nearby field, and across the street a hammer was discovered. A man's tan colored cap with grease-stains was found 25 feet from where Mrs. Miller was lying, there were fresh imprints of a man's shoes leading across a newly mowed field, and a part of a letter, or note, torn into pieces was found nearby also. A part of the note said "show this to no one. . . " Mrs. Miller was last seen by Horace G. Randall, the Marshal at Sylvania, shortly after she left the restaurant, and she had told him that she had arranged with a friend to be driven home. She was known in the neighborhood as a highly respected woman, so much so that she declined rides with her neighbors unless they were accompanied by their wives or children. One suspect was brought in and questioned, and according to the newspapers he was 35 years old and had lived a short distance down the street from the Miller residence for about 15 years. He had known Alta Miller and her family for many years but had not seen her for about four weeks. When questioned about his whereabouts on the night of the murder, the man stated that he did not remember everything because he had been drinking heavily. At about 11:00 p.m., he drove to a store in Sylvania and bought a couple bottles of wine and returned home; at that time he was already heavily intoxicated according to witnesses. From that time on, this man did not know what he had done, because he had been too drunk to remember, but neighbors reported that he was roaming the neighborhood with a shotgun demanding whiskey, and already in a complete state of intoxication. One neighbor even said that he was wearing a hat similar to the one found near the body, and by the time he went to another house he did not have the hat. As detectives interviewed people after the funeral they realized that this man was the only neighbor who did not attend the funeral. Detective Frazier Reams obtained an arrest warrant and investigators went to his home. They took him into custody and searched his house. The detectives were looking for a murder weapon and the clothes he was wearing on the night of the murder. They found a hammer in his car with blood and human hair on it, and a stain on the front seat of his car. Investigators were unable to find his overalls, but they did find a burn pile out in his back yard which contained a button from a pair of overalls. A $5,000 bond was set for him, and Detective Reams questioned him again. The prosecutor told the suspect that he believed that he had murdered Alta Miller and should confess. The suspect was very nervous, but denied he had anything to do with her death. They placed the cap, found at the scene, on the suspects head and it fit. The grease on the hat was similar to the kind of grease that they used where he worked. The investigator told the suspect that he knew that he killed her and showed him photos of Alta during the autopsy. The suspect shook his head and restated that he had not killed her. The investigator then described how he thought the murder happened. He said that he had stopped and offered Alta a ride home. When she refused because he was drunk and alone, he had tried to force her into his car. A struggle occurred and he killed her with the hammer that was found in his vehicle. The well-known male suspect still continued to deny murdering her. They questioned the stains on the front seat of his car and he said that they had been there for a long time. They had to release him because of lack of evidence. The investigation continued off and on for 11 years, but this murder was never solved.

- **8-12-1954, Mary Jolene Friess**, 17 years old, was brutally murdered by Bernard Schriber in a wooded area east of Irwin Road and north of Bancroft in Sylvania Township. The 8-13-1954 *Toledo Blade* article said the following: "A 17-year-old Sylvania Township girl was raped and slain yesterday by a killer who left her mutilated body in a patch of woods, off Irwin Rd. With two stab wounds in the chest, the body of Mary Jolene Friess, 5034 Courville Rd., was found shortly after 4:30 p.m., a short distance north of West Bancroft St." Most of her clothing had been torn off by her assailant. Dr. Paul Hohly, coroner, said that her death was caused by a knife wound which had pierced her heart. There was evidence that the girl had been struck on the head, beaten and strangled. Dr. Hohly estimated the time of her death at about 11 a.m. In addition to the knife wounds, there was a gash along the left side of the girl's head, her right eye was blackened and her left arm bruised. Blood on both her hands was believed by police to be that of the killer. Dr. Hohly and Detective Capt. Alfred Bartkowiak said the girl obviously put up a desperate struggle for her life. No murder weapon was found. The girl's sun glasses were discovered lying on Irwin Rd. near the point where she apparently had fled into the woods with the killer in pursuit." As this murder was being investigated a telephone call was received from an anonymous woman who told the Lucas County Sheriff that Bernard Schriber had told his mother the day of the murder that he had killed the girl. On 8-21-1954 Bernard Schriber confessed to the rape/murder of Mary Jolene Friess and reported that he had used a hunting knife with a 6-inch blade to kill her. On 3-15-1956 Bernard Schreiber was put to death in the Ohio Penitentiary's electric chair."

- **4-6-1972 Frank Welzbacher**, 36 years old, of 4556 Brookhurst Road in Sylvania Township was abducted from a Monroe Street carry-out at 5412 Monroe Street, by two men after they robbed the store of $80. The proprietor, August Durban, of 4622 Willys Pkwy., told police he was alone when two men came into his store. One man carrying what was described as a big revolver threatened Mr. Durban then opened a cash register and took the entire tray of cash. The other man remained near the door. The men asked Mr. Durban if he had a gun. When he replied in the negative, one told him, "You're coming with us," and pushed him to the front door. As they were going through the door, Mr. Welzbacher was approaching. Mr. Durban said he broke away from the men and shouted to Mr. Welzbacher run, it's a holdup." They took Mr. Welzbacher with them at this time. A search was conducted which included Sylvania Township Police and the FBI. On 4-9-1972 Mr. Welzbacher's dead body was found just over the state line, and two escapees from the Marion, Ohio Correctional Institute were charged by the FBI with kidnapping and murder. Lawrence F. Lamont, 27, of Toledo and James Allen Patterson, 40, of Lima, were charged with the murder. Both received life sentences, on top of the time they were already serving for prior crimes. The *Bedford Now* newspaper dated 10-6-2012 reported that 40 years after the brutal, execution-style killings were committed, authorities have issued a multiple-count murder warrant against a former Monroe County man who remains in an Ohio prison on forgery charges. The Monroe County Prosecutor's Office issued a six-count warrant against 68-year old who had been incarcerated since the 1972 crime spree. He had been convicted of kidnapping, and there was a chance that he could be released from jail. Due to the pressure from the victims' families they were going to try him for the murder to make sure he stays in jail for the rest of his life. The other accomplice in this case had already died in prison.

- **7-5-1972 – Richard E. Fox**, 39 years old, of 4800 Box Lane in Sylvania Township. He was shot twice in the head and once in the chest in his home. A first degree murder warrant was issued for William S. Vargas, 24, a parolee. He was also charged with assault for shooting Sharon Fox three times in the head and once in the neck and jaw when she was attempting to escape. (Mrs. Fox survived this shooting). On 7-10-1972 William Vargas was arrested in Laredo, Texas. Mrs. Fox told police that Vargas, a friend of the family, had come to their house, shot her husband in a hallway, and then shot her four times in the head. While Vargas was in the Lucas County Jail awaiting his trial, on 5-25-1973, Mr. Vargas attempted to escape from the county jail. But that charge was dismissed after prosecution witnesses refused to testify. According to the 11-2-1973 *Toledo Blade*: "William S. Vargas testified at his trial Friday that he did not shoot and kill Richard E. Fox, but conceded that he might have told a detective that he shot the victim's wife in self-defense. Vargas is on trial charged with the first-degree murder of Mr. Fox. He told the jury that he stopped at the Fox home at 4800 Box Lane, Sylvania Township, on 7-5-1972, after 2:30 a.m. to tell Mr. Fox that he had information that might lead to the recovery of a stereo set that had been stolen from his home. He said that while he was at the Fox home he heard the couple quarrel in the bedroom, and that Mr. Fox emerged pointing a gun at him and demanding names of men who allegedly were dating Mrs. Fox. Vargas said he told Mr. Fox he knew of no such men. He said Mr. Fox then demanded that he write down the name of the person who stole the stereo set. Vargas said he wrote the name "Jake" and a telephone number, at which point Mrs. Fox entered the kitchen-hallway area, "shouting something like 'No, no, Richard,' and the couple then struggled. "A bullet went out." Vargas testified, "I saw Richard's head bob up." Then, according to Vargas, Mr. Fox stepped back with Mrs. Fox in possession of the gun." Mrs. Fox bit his lip as they struggled, and he took the gun from her and began telephoning the police, Vargas said. Mrs. Fox ran into the bedroom and he discontinued the call and followed her, he testified. Vargas told the jury that he was "dazed, in a state of shock." He said he asked Mrs. Fox "why she did it" Mrs. Fox "mumbled something about 50 or 60 thousand dollars insurance," he said. . . "Mr. Vargas said he was on parole, and because of the fear of being jailed he did not call for medical attention for Mr. Fox. He admitted that the revolver was his, but he said that he had given the gun to Mrs. Fox because she was scared of her husband. Vargas said he threw the gun away along a roadway in Texas and that he was captured in Mexico and arrested in Laredo, Texas. During his trip back to Lucas County Vargas made an admission about the shooting to Sylvania Township detective Donald Wood, and Detective Wood testified that Vargas admitted shooting both Mr. and Mrs. Fox. Vargas was found guilty of murder in the first-degree by a jury of six men and six women in a week-long trial and they reached the verdict on 11-6-1973. He was sentenced to life in prison, although Vargas continued to testify that Mrs. Fox shot her husband to collect $50,000 in insurance money and that she was shot during a struggle with Vargas for the gun.

- **6-12-1973 – Unknown victim** - The skeletal remains of an unidentified man in his mid 20's were found in an isolated wooded area off Silica Road in western Sylvania Township. The body was fully clothed, but there was no identification. No weapons were found. It was discovered by a bulldozer operator working in the area. One wound was at the left side of the head, the other at the back. The *Toledo Blade* dated 8-13-1973 reported the following: "Two months after being discovered in an isolated wooded area in western Lucas County, the skeletal remains of a man in his mid-20s remain unidentified. Lt. Robert C. Achtermann, of the Sylvania Township police, said that there was nothing new in the case at all." The body was found fully clothed, but there was no identification. The man had been shot twice in the head with a large-caliber weapon and had been dead about 60 days before being discovered off Silica Road, according to Dr. Harry Mignerey, Lucas County coroner. He ruled the death a homicide. Township policemen continue checking telephone tips from persons who say they know the identity of the Negro man, but it has been about three weeks since the last missing person's report. As it turned out, that man reported as missing had joined the army and was stationed in Louisiana, Lieutenant Achtermann said." As far as I can determine this murder was never solved, and the identity of the man was never determined.

- **12-8-1973 - Standley Brandum,** 25, of 4615 Holland-Sylvania Rd., Apt. 61 was strangled and then stabbed 11 times. The death was ruled a homicide. There was no sign of a struggle. His hands and feet had been bound behind his back with clothesline and the stab wounds were in his back. Chief Boehme said the apartment was not ransacked and apparently nothing was taken. No weapon was found, and the number of assailants was unknown. Mrs. Bette Brandum, 22, found her husband on the floor of the living room when she returned home from a music festival. According to the 12-18-1973 *Toledo Blade*: ". . . The chief said police continue to work on the theory that the killing was drug-related, a viewpoint Mr. Brandum's family and friends reject. The choking, stabbing, and "hog-tieing"—as police refer to the method in which Mr. Brandum was bound—are all indicative of drug world murder methods, Chief Boehme said, and a small quantity of marijuana was found in the apartment." It appears that this murder was never solved.

- **11-24-1979 – Sharon V. Parker**, 27, of Macomber Street in Toledo was found shot to death and was found in a ditch along Crissey Road north of Bancroft Street in Sylvania Township. Sylvania Township police chief, Robert Boehme, said that a relative of Mrs. Parker made the identification and that the investigation was continuing. Her death was ruled a homicide caused by two gunshot wounds to the head. According to the minutes of the Sylvania Township Trustees of 11-29-1979 the Sylvania Township Police were still working on this homicide case. In May of 1981 Bernard Foster was arrested on a charge of aggravated murder in the 1979 shooting death of Sharon V. Parker. According to the *Toledo Blade* dated 1-14-1982 Bernard Foster was charged with aggravated murder in Lucas County Common Pleas Court. His trial started on 1-14-1982. Mr. Foster was 25 years old and lived at 1246 Hamilton St., in Toledo. During the first day of the trial Sharon Parker's mother, Rosie Davis, screamed and cursed at the defendant for killing her daughter, and was removed from the courtroom. At this time Foster was also being tried on an attempted murder charge of a man on 1-15-1981 who was wounded from a gunshot wound. Mr. Foster denied any involvement in the crimes, but his former girlfriend testified that Foster made statements to her admitting that he killed Mrs. Parker. He said that witnesses were testifying against him to get even with him for other unrelated disputes. At this time I am unable to locate any additional information as to whether Mr. Foster was found guilty of the Parker murder.

- **1-2-1985 – Patricia Stichler**. At about 1:50 a.m., Patricia Stichler, 30, was stabbed to death in her home on Brinthaven Road in the city of Sylvania. She was stabbed approximately 30 times in the chest, abdomen and face, including two fatal slashes to her throat. An autopsy showed she sustained 51 other minor cuts. The intruder apparently entered the home through an unlocked bathroom window and struggled with Ms. Stichler in the bedroom where her body was found. The attacker then apparently fled the home through the bathroom window. Ms. Stichler had hosted a New Year's Eve party at her house for about 15 people, and within 24 hours later she was found murdered. The attack occurred just a few feet away from where her three daughters had been sleeping. This murder was never solved. In May of 1985 a personality assessment profile had been developed by the Federal Bureau of Investigation's Behavioral Sciences Unit regarding the killer. A nylon knife sheath was sent in for laser analysis in an effort to obtain fingerprints. The profile included such information as the race, sex, age range, physical build, marital status, educational background, general employment and degree of sexual maturity of the killer. In 1998 the case was reopened and the Sylvania Police Department re-interviewed everyone involved in the case. They took available DNA samples that had come from the scene and entered it into the national database, but the murder still remained unsolved. Today in 2018 this murder has still not been solved. The *Toledo Blade* dated 9-28-2012 said that the unsolved stabbing death of Patricia Stichler was one of the first cases featured on the Ohio Attorney General's website in a program to solicit more tips to close murder cases.

- **10-25-1986 – Irvin Smith**, 62, of 6234 Bonsels Pkwy., was found dead about 8:30 a.m., in his living room. Neighbors had become concerned about his safety because they had not seen him since 10-24-1986. Mr. Smith had a large head wound. There were no signs of a struggle and no weapon was found. The *Toledo Blade* dated 12-6-1986 reported that a Sylvania Township man was indicted by the Lucas County grand jury on charges of aggravated murder and forgery in connection with the bludgeoning death of the man's neighbor. David A. Taulker, 33, of 6249 Bonsels Pkwy., was charged with killing Irvin L. Smith during a robbery in which a $50 money order allegedly was stolen.

- **9-22-1993 – Christopher Hammer**, 22 years old, was beat up, tied and buried alive by Archie Dixon, 20 years old, and Timothy Hoffner, 21 years old, in a shallow grave in the woods at the end of Friedly Drive and Rega Drive in Sylvania Township. The suspects made plans to steal and sell Christopher Hammer's 1987 Dodge Daytona car for $2,800 at a used car dealership. Mr. Hammer had been living with Dixon and Hoffner for about two weeks before they planned the murder. Police said the homicide investigation was triggered after the victim's car was sold to a used car dealership on West Central Avenue. A friend of Christopher Hammer saw the vehicle at the used car sales lot and reported it to police. Through intensive interviews the police found the buried body and obtained full confessions. It was Mr. Hoffner who led detectives to the burial site. It was also determined that Kirsten Wilkerson, 29 years old, drove the vehicle to the murder site. She ended up telling the court that the two men started hitting Mr. Hammer with fists, and Mr. Dixon broke a wine bottle against his head. She said that Archie told her to clean up the puddles of blood in the living room. They took Chris into the bedroom and tied him up, they then started talking about going out and digging a hole and they left. They came back and led Mr. Hammer into the car and told her to drive to the burial location. Ms. Wilkerson was being charged with murder, but a plea agreement was allowed to plead guilty to kidnapping in return for her testimony against Hoffner and Dixon. It took the jury eight hours of deliberation over two days to find Archie Dixon guilty of three counts of aggravated murder by prior calculation and design, in the commission of an aggravated robbery, and in the commission of a kidnapping, and also guilty of aggravated robbery, kidnapping, and three counts of forgery. Timothy Hoffner was found guilty of eight felonies, three counts of aggravated murder, aggravated robbery, kidnapping, and three counts of forgery in connection with the death of Christopher Hammer. The jury in the case recommended the death penalty. Archie J. Dixon also received the death penalty for his part in the murder. Kristen Wilkerson was sentenced to six to 25 years in prison for her role in the murder, but served two years in the penitentiary at Marysville, Ohio, and in 1998 was granted shock probation and released with five years of probation. Today in 2010 Dixon and Hoffner both are on death row at Mansfield Correctional Institution. In December of 2010 a federal court overturned the conviction and death sentence of Archie Dixon and gave prosecutors six months to retry him or set him free. The U.S. Circuit Court of Appeals found that police waited until after Dixon confessed before informing him of his Miranda rights and offering him a deal that never materialized. Apparently when police started questioning Dixon they were questioning him on forgery charges, not the murder. They later got a confession at the Toledo police station when the focus shifted to murder, and then they advised him of his rights before recording that confession. Christopher Hammer was 22 years old when his life was taken from him. *The Blade* of Toledo dated 6-9-2015 reported that Archie J. Dixon, 42, and Timothy Hoffner, 43, were both on death row at Chillicothe Correctional Institution. Both Dixon and Hoffner were parties to a challenge to Ohio's death-penalty process that was pending before a U.S. District Judge.

- **1-12-1994 – Bibi Englund** – 28 years old – was murdered by 19 year old Nathaniel Beauregard. Ms. Englund was the co-manager of the Wendy's Old Fashioned Hamburger restaurant at 5560 W. Central Avenue. She arrived at work to open for the day at about 6 a.m., and soon after Mr. Beauregard broke out the glass in the door on the west side of the building and at gunpoint forced Ms. Englund to open the safe and give him the money. He then forced her into the back cooler and told her to stay there. When Ms. Englund soon came out of the cooler he shot her in the face. Witnesses observed a black male running down Republic Blvd., carrying a dark-colored athletic bag with a horizontal stripe on the front. Surveillance cameras at nearby businesses were viewed and additional investigation by the Sylvania Township Police revealed who the killer was. The case was presented to the Lucas County Grand Jury and by December of 1994 the case was completed. Mr. Beauregard was found guilty of aggravated murder, but was spared from the death penalty. Two judges said that they spared the life of killer Nathaniel Beauregard because the shooting was "spontaneous" and an act of "panic." A third judge pointed out the advance planning that went into the robbery; Beauregard's knowledge that someone would be at the restaurant early in the morning to open the safe, and that he loaded six shells into his 357-magnum before he entered the store. Beauregard had attended Sylvania Southview High School and admitted to stealing $800 in the robbery which he said he spent on a computer game and a telephone pager for a friend. "The evidence most telling of the cold-blooded and calculated nature of this aggravated murder came straight from the defendant's own mouth," the judge wrote. Beauregard told police he shot Mrs. Englund in the face at point-blank range after she emerged crying from the food cooler he had ordered her into. Mr. Beauregard was sentenced to life in prison, with eligibility for parole in 33 years.

- **4-8-1996 – Rhonda Wheeler**, 30 years old, was in critical condition in Medical College Hospital, in Toledo, Ohio, after her car exploded and burst into flames as she was getting ready to leave work. Mrs. Wheeler, the mother of two young boys, was leaving work at Austin Associates, Inc., 7205 West Central Ave., Sylvania Township, when the car exploded about 4:45 p.m. and burst into flames. Mrs. Wheeler was pulled from the car by two of her co-workers at the financial consulting firm. Police were investigating the incident and were waiting to talk to Rhonda Wheeler in the hospital. At first Robert Wheeler, her husband, was suggesting that a bookie that he owed money to might have placed the bomb in his wife's car. Then he claimed that he only meant to destroy the auto in order to get insurance money to pay off gambling debts, and that he did not intend for his wife to be harmed. He said that a faulty timing device caused the explosion to occur when his wife got into her car. Rhonda Wheeler died on 4-17-1996 from injuries sustained from this explosion, and police were never able to talk to her. Robert Wheeler, days later, after they had searched his home, admitted to building the eight-inch, galvanized device.

He admitted placing it under the driver's seat of his wife's 1994 Grand Prix, and he admitted that the 30-year-old mother of two boys died because of his actions. But both his defense attorney and his father said the real killer was something much less tangible than wires, metal fragments, and timing devices. It was a gambling addiction that drove the Chrysler Corp. engineer to blow up the car for the insurance money in hopes of paying off nearly $20,000 in gambling debts. Wheeler pleaded guilty in U.S. District Court in Toledo to a six-count indictment and his attorney asked for the lower end of the sentencing scale on the argument that Wheeler's addiction to gambling was beyond his control. He was sentenced to six life terms in federal prison by U.S. District Judge John Potter. When Mr. Wheeler was inducted, prosecutors noted the following: Mrs. Wheeler's life insurance policy was for at least $100,000, that Wheeler had previously shot someone with a pellet gun and that a former wife had once found a bomb in her car. Rhonda Romancik-Wheeler, 30 years old, was a native of Brook Park, Ohio.

- **12-15-2004 – John Riebe**, 39 years old, was murdered by Eric Babos, 42 years old. Mr. Riebe was a self-employed air conditioning and heating repairman, and Eric Babos did work for him. At 3:20 p.m. Riebe's two daughters returned home from school and found their father dead in the home at 5129 Talmadge Road, in Sylvania Township. Mr. Riebe was shot seven times with a 28-caliber handgun in the living room of his home while he was playing his guitar. In November of 2005 a jury found Mr. Babos guilty, and he received a life term for murder. He was eligible for parole in 18 years. In March of 2006 Babos' attorney filed a motion in Lucas County Common Pleas Court asking for a new trial, claiming that police withheld information that could have helped his client in his trial. The attorney said that a drug dealer who the victim owed money admitted to a witness that he shot Mr. Riebe, and that the township police knew of this confession, but did nothing. The motion said that the witness told police and police told the witness that he was a liar and that they already had their guy. The judge denied the motion, ruling that the jury would have reached the same verdict had the evidence been available to the defendant.

- **10-25-2005 – Rhonda Anaya** - At 3:06 a.m., Sylvania Police responded to a 9-1-1 call from a female who reported that her father was hurting her mother. Upon arrival at 8034 Littlefield Court, Danny Anaya, 54 year old engineer employed at GM Powertrain in Michigan, answered the door and police subsequently found Rhonda Anaya, 42 years old, lying on the kitchen floor dead; there were signs of a struggle. Danny Anaya was arrested for the murder of his wife Rhonda Anaya and bond was set at $5 million. An autopsy revealed that Mrs. Anaya was stabbed multiple times in the neck and chest. The murder weapon was a large kitchen knife, which it was suspected that Mr. Anaya had placed in the victim's left hand before police arrived, because Mrs. Anaya was right-handed. The 2-22-2006 *Toledo Blade* said that Mr. Anaya had plead not guilty by reason of insanity to one count of aggravated murder. He was ordered by Judge McDonald to undergo psychiatric evaluation. One year after the murder, in October of 2006, the trial finally started after four continuations. According to the *Toledo Blade* dated 10-13-2006, Mr. Anaya testified that he killed his wife during a heated argument in self-defense. Then a 15 year old son, a 16 year old daughter and a 17 year old daughter testified that they were all home at the time of the murder, but had been sleeping, and woke up to screaming. One daughter testified that she saw her father wearing rubber gloves and had a large kitchen knife tucked in his trousers, and moments later she saw her mother being stabbed three times in the chest. The younger brother said that he woke up to screaming and other noises in the house. He got up and his father met him on the stairs and told him to go back to bed. The boy said he saw rubber gloves in his father's back pocket. And the other daughter testified that she heard her mother tell her father that she was sleeping, and that he was choking her. Mrs. Anaya had filed for divorce from her husband in July 2005, and there were allegations of abuse by Mr. Anaya against the children too. Sylvania police had been called to the house five times between May 13 and Aug. 1ˢᵗ for various reasons. During the trial, testimony was given that investigators found the bloody clothing that Mr. Anaya allegedly wore; he had dressed in five layers of pants and had on at least two shirts. Four containers of carpet cleaner were also found that had been purchased a couple days before, as well as a package of rubber gloves and empty mulch bags were used to line the trunk of his company car.

The jury heard testimony for three days, and deliberated about nine hours over two days. Jurors were presented with overwhelming evidence supporting the state's contention that Anaya had planned the homicide in advance, and that it was a clear case of aggravated murder. But, the jury came in with a lesser verdict of murder, which means that the murder was not premeditated. Mr. Anaya had testified that he killed his wife in self-defense, stating that Mrs. Anaya attacked him in the kitchen with the knife after a heated argument. Mr. Anaya was sentenced to a mandatory life sentence, and was eligible to ask the parole board to be released from the sentence in 14 years. Rhonda Lynn (Hatcher) Anaya was buried in Ravine Cemetery in Sylvania, Ohio. Her obituary ends by saying: "No amount of adversity could prevent Rhonda from loving and protecting her children, she was a true "port in the storm."

MAN FOUND DEAD IN SYLVANIA TOWNSHIP

The *Sylvania Sentinel* dated Thursday 11-20-1947 said that the body of a man was found hanging from a limb of a tree on Flanders Road, north of Alexis Road last Saturday by hunters. Efforts to identify the man were being made by fingerprints which were still unsuccessful. The body had been hanging for several days and its condition as a result made positive identification difficult. He was at Reeb Funeral Home. I never located any other information. I am not sure if this was a murder or a suicide; most would have assumed that if it was a murder there would have been additional information in subsequent newspapers, but nothing was found. Does anyone know any more on this story?

REFERENCES USED FOR ALL VOLUMES

LOCAL, COUNTY, STATE AND UNITED STATES RECORDS

Lucas County, Ohio Auditor's Office – Property deed and transfer records.

Lucas County, Ohio Probate Court – Wills and estate records.

Lucas County, Ohio Recorder's Office – Property deed and transfer records.

Sylvania, Ohio Village Council minute books.

Sylvania Township, Ohio Trustee minute books.

Sylvania Township, Ohio Association Cemetery records and deeds.

Sylvania Township and Sylvania Village Poll records from 1835 to 1890.

Sylvania Township and Sylvania Village school enumeration records.

Sylvania (Ohio) Lodge of Free & Accepted Masons No. 287 minute books from 1856 to 2007.

United States Federal Census Records – 1820 to 1930.

NEWSPAPERS

Daily Toledo Blade – Toledo, Ohio.

Sentinel-Herald – Sylvania, Ohio.

Sylvania Herald -Sylvania, Ohio published by Herald Newspapers.

Sylvania Sentinel - Sylvania, Ohio

Sylvania Sun – Sylvania, Ohio

Sylvania Weekly Times – Sylvania, Ohio

Toledo Blade – Toledo, Ohio.

Toledo City Paper – Toledo, Ohio

Toledo Commercial – Toledo, Ohio.

Toledo Daily Herald and Times – Toledo, Ohio.

Toledo News-Bee – Toledo, Ohio

Toledo Times – Toledo, Ohio

BOOKS

Beveridge, Nancy, *The Flickertail Tapes; The Life Story of Donald Wayne Beveridge*, 2011.

Comstock, Ernest B. *The History of the Harroun Family in America – Seven generations; descendents of Alexander Harroun of Colerain, Mass. 1691-1784.* Dallas, Texas: Comstock, 1940.

Cosgrove, Maynard G. *A History of Sylvania for the First Hundred Years.* Sylvania Sentinel Publishing, 1933.

Cosgrove, Maynard G. *A History of the First Congregational Church, Sylvania, Ohio – 1834 – 1934 - For the First Hundred Years.* Sentinel Publishing Co. 1934.

Downs, Randolph C. *The Conquest Volume 1 and Canal Days Volume II* – Maumee Valley Historical Society – Lucas County Historical Series – 1968.

Fetzer, Madeline Logan – *Voices of Whiteford - Whiteford Township, Michigan.* Whiteford Township Bicentennial Committee, 1976.

Galbreath, Charles B. *History of Ohio* –– Volume II, Chicago, New York, The American Historical Society, Inc., 1925.

Gindy, Gaye E. *Murder In Sylvania, Ohio – As Told In 1857.* AuthorHouse – 2007.

Gindy, Gaye E. *Next Stop Sylvania, Ohio: A History of the First Train Line West of the Alleghany Mountains, and its Journey Through Sylvania.* Sylvania Historical Village Commission, 1998.

Gindy, Gaye E. *The Underground Railroad and Sylvania's Historic Lathrop House.* AuthorHouse – 2008.

Illman, Harry – *Unholy Toledo*, Polemic Press, 1985

Killits, John M. *Toledo and Lucas County, Ohio 1623-1923.* Chicago, Ill, S.J. Clarke Publishing Co., 1922 (Three-volume set).

Matthews, Alfred. *Ohio and Her Western Reserve.* New York, D. Appleton and Company, 1902.

McAlester, Virginia & Lee. *A Field Guide To American Houses.* Alfred A. Knopf, Inc., New York, 1984.

Polk, R.L. & Company. *Polk's Toledo city Directory.* Publisher: The Toledo Directory Company. 1858 to 2001.

Scott. *Scott's Toledo city directory.* Publisher: The Toledo Directory Company. – 1866-67, 1868/1869 – 1876/1877.

Scribner, Harvey, Editor-In-Chief. *Memoirs of Lucas County and City of Toledo.* Madison, Wisconsin, Western Historical Association 1910.

Sylvania History Buff Members. *Sylvania Yesterday and Today* – 1976.

Waggoner, Clark. *History of Toledo and Lucas County.* New York; Toledo: Munsell & Co., 1888.

Wendler, Marilyn VanVoorhis. *Foot of the Rapids – The Biography of a River Town Maumee, Ohio 1838-1988.* Canton, Ohio: Daring Books, 1988.

Williams. *Williams' Toledo city directory,* - Publisher: The Toledo Directory Co.., - 1850s and 1860s.

Winter, Nevin O. *History of Northwest Ohio.* Chicago and New York, The Lewis Publishing Co., 1917, Volume 1-3.

Wyant, Robert "Pop." *2,000 and 1 Facts, Figures and People of Sylvania 1867 – 1967.* Lithographed by Mohawk Specialties and Printing Co., Sylvania, Ohio, 1971.

MISCELLANEOUS SOURCES

Armstrong, James – Member of the Sylvania History Buffs – multiple tape recordings of him talking about growing up and living in Sylvania.

Crandall, Lou R. collection, and records prepared by John & Margaret (Wenzel) Crandall of South Carolina – housed at the Sylvania Heritage Center – 5717 N. Main Street, Sylvania, Ohio.

Gindy, Gaye E. - Interviews with various residents over a 30 year period of time as noted.

Keller, Kathryn. Letters between Kathryn Keller, Sylvania Historian and Maynard Cosgrove, Sylvania Historian – Sylvania, Ohio, 1974-1975.

Keller, Kathryn. Articles in the Sylvania local newspapers between 1948 and 1986.

Smith, Ara. Member of the Sylvania History Buffs - Interview notes taken in the 1970s and 1980s.

Smith, Hazel. Secretary to the Sylvania History Buffs – meeting minutes and notes.

Sylvania Masonic Lodge Members. *Sylvania Masonic Lodge No. 287 Centennial Program* – 10-6-1956.

Sylvania Congregational Church – Early minute books.

NOTE: All other sources and references are documented within the text of this book.

ABOUT THE AUTHOR

GAYLEEN E. GINDY is a free-lance writer and author from Sylvania, Ohio, and for many years has also been known as Gaye E. Gindy. She has been researching the history of the Sylvania community for over 30 years. She was employed for 33 years with the public entities of Sylvania Township and the City of Sylvania, working in the services of the Sylvania Township Fire Department, Administration offices of Sylvania Township and the City of Sylvania Police Division.

She also wrote a weekly history column for the local newspaper, the *Sylvania Herald*, for five years titled "Sylvania As It Was," and has had history articles appear in:

The Bend of the River, Lee Raizk, Publisher, The magazine of the historic Maumee Valley;
Fort Industry Reflections, published by the Lucas County Chapter OGS;
Sylvania AdVantage, publisher Sharon Lange;
Sylvania Herald published by Herald Newspapers.
Vintage Sylvania, Vintage Aerial, LLC and Toledo-Lucas County Public Library
Toledo History Museum – Quarterly – Toledo History Museum, Inc. March/June 2011
Hook & Letter – Toledo Firefighers Museum, Inc. newsletter.

Mrs. Gindy has been a member of the Sylvania Area Historical Society since it was formed in 1991, and has served as a board member/secretary-treasurer, on the Sylvania Historical Village Commission from 1995 to 2007.

Gayleen and husband, Sam, have been married 40 years. They have a son, Allan; daughter, Samantha; daughter-in-law Audrey; and two granddaughters: Sophia and Ella.

This is her twelfth book. Other books include:

- *Next Stop Sylvania, Ohio:* A History of the First Train Line West of the Allegheny Mountains, and its Journey Through Sylvania – Published by Sylvania Historical Village Commission - 1998;
- *Bridging Time:* A History Of Sylvania – Published by Herald Newspapers - 1999;
- *Sylvania, Ohio – Images of America,* Published by Arcadia Publishing, co-authored by Gaye E. Gindy and Trini L. Wenninger – 2006;

- *Murder In Sylvania, Ohio – As Told In 1857* – Published by Gaye E. Gindy - AuthorHouse – 2007.
- *The Underground Railroad and Sylvania's Historic Lathrop House* – Published by Gaye E. Gindy – AuthorHouse – 2008.
- *Sylvania, Lucas County, Ohio; From Footpaths to Expressways and Beyond* – Volume One – Published by Gayleen Gindy – AuthorHouse – 2012.
- *Sylvania, Lucas County, Ohio; From Footpaths to Expressways and Beyond* – Volume Two – Published by Gayleen Gindy – AuthorHouse – 2012.
- *Sylvania, Lucas County, Ohio; From Footpaths to Expressways and Beyond* – Volume Three – Published by Gayleen Gindy – AuthorHouse – 2013.
- *Sylvania, Lucas County, Ohio; From Footpaths to Expressways and Beyond* – Volume Four – Published by Gayleen Gindy – AuthorHouse – 2014.
- *Sylvania, Lucas County, Ohio; From Footpaths to Expressways and Beyond* – Volume Five – Published by Gayleen Gindy – AuthorHouse – 2015.
- *Sylvania, Lucas County, Ohio; From Footpaths to Expressways and Beyond* – Volume Six – Published by Gayleen Gindy – AuthorHouse – 2017.

Printed in the United States
By Bookmasters